Second Edition

CRISIS ASSESSMENT, INTERVENTION, AND PREVENTION

Lisa R. Jackson-Cherry
Marymount University

Bradley T. Erford
Loyola University Maryland

PEARSON

Boston   Columbus   Indianapolis   New York   San Francisco   Upper Saddle River
Amsterdam   Cape Town   Dubai   London   Madrid   Milan   Munich   Paris   Montreal   Toronto
Delhi   Mexico City   São Paulo   Sydney   Hong Kong   Seoul   Singapore   Taipei   Tokyo

Vice President and Editorial Director: Jeffery W. Johnston
Senior Acquisitions Editor: Meredith Fossel
Editorial Assistant: Krista Slavicek
Vice President and Director of Marketing Margaret Waples
Senior Marketing Manager: Christopher Barry
Senior Managing Editor: Pamela D. Bennett
Production Manager: Maggie Brobeck
Manager, Central Design: Jayne Conte
Cover Designer: Karen Salzbach
Cover Photo: © Sternstunden/Fotolia
Full-Service Project Management and Composition: Niraj Bhatt, Aptara® Inc.
Printer/Binder: Courier/Westford
Cover Printer: Courier/Westford
Text Font: 10/12 Palatino

Credits and acknowledgments for material borrowed from other sources and reproduced, with permission, in this textbook appear on the appropriate page within the text.

Every effort has been made to provide accurate and current Internet information in this book. However, because the Internet and the information posted on it are constantly changing, it is inevitable that some of the Internet addresses included in this textbook will change.

The first edition of this text was published under that title *Crisis Intervention and Prevention*.

Library of Congress Cataloging-in-Publication Data

Jackson-Cherry, Lisa R.
  Crisis assessment, intervention, and prevention/Lisa R. Jackson-Cherry
  Marymount University, Bradley T. Erford, Loyola University Maryland.—Second edition.
    pages cm
  ISBN-13: 978-0-13-294696-4
  ISBN-10: 0-13-294696-3
  1. Crisis intervention (Mental health services) I. Title.
  RC480.6.E74 2014
  362.2–dc23   2012037260

10 9 8 7 6 5 4 3 2 1

ISBN 10:   0-13-294696-3
ISBN 13: 978-0-13-294696-4

PREFACE

The purpose for writing this text was to convey the practical implications of and applications for dealing with crisis situations. Prior to September 11, 2001, crisis counselors' and university faculty members' conceptualization of crisis was generally limited to individual clients, primarily addressing suicidal client needs. But recent events (e.g., terrorism, school shootings, natural disasters), coupled with renewed societal concerns over continuing violence (e.g., homicide, intimate partner violence, rape, sexual abuse), have expanded our conceptualization of crisis and the needs of the new generation of counselors. This text addresses this expanded concept of crisis in today's world and includes the practical applications that will help crisis counselors to be able to serve diverse clients immediately in a changing world.

Preservice students and mental health professionals in the field need all the crisis management help they can get in order to hit the ground running. This short text provides vital information on assessing and reacting to various crises involving suicide, homicide, intimate partner violence, sexual assault/abuse, bereavement/grief, substance abuse, natural disasters, war, and terrorism. The text provides practical applications for various crisis situations experienced by crisis workers. The text allows students to become familiar with various crisis issues and situations and to practice necessary skills before encountering the problem for the first time in the field. The text features numerous crisis situations not found in other crisis texts and is of benefit to various counseling specialties (e.g., school, mental health, pastoral). Students see the process as a whole and are exposed to crucial information, clinical considerations, and practical experiences on every crisis topic.

NEW TO THIS EDITION

The second edition of *Crisis Assessment, Intervention, and Prevention* has been purposefully revised with new and expanded content to address the needs of a diverse group of counselors in the field and counselors in training. The following features are new to this edition:

- *Voices from the Field* in each chapter provide on-the-ground perspectives written by practicing counselors and counselors in training.
- A new chapter addresses military deployment and reintegration issues.
- New and expanded chapters address crisis counseling in the community and schools and providing effective death notifications.
- A totally revised suicide risk assessment and intervention chapter is new to this edition.
- A totally revised chapter on understanding and treating substance use disorders with clients in crisis is included.
- An entire chapter is dedicated to ethical and legal considerations in crisis counseling.
- An entire chapter is dedicated to counselor safety and self-care in crisis situations.

ORGANIZATION OF THIS TEXT

The text is divided into two parts. Part I: *Elements of Crisis Intervention*, which includes Chapters 1 through 5, reviews the fundamental information related to crises and crisis intervention. In Chapter 1: *Overview of Crisis Intervention*, by Stephanie Puleo and Jason McGlothlin, the authors acknowledge that crises occur in a variety of settings for a variety of reasons. Responses to crises are equally variable.

Chapter 1 also provides basic frameworks for assessing and conceptualizing crises, along with a discussion of how crisis intervention may differ from traditional counseling.

Chapter 2: *Safety and Self-Care in Crisis Situations* was written by Charlotte Daughhetee. When responding to a crisis, counselors need to be able to act promptly, meaning that crisis preparedness is essential to best practice during emergency situations. A brief overview of crisis planning guidelines, crisis counselor safety procedures, and counselor self-care concerns are presented.

In Chapter 3: *Ethical and Legal Considerations in Crisis Counseling*, Paul F. Hard, Laura L. Talbott-Forbes, and Mary L. Bartlett propose that crisis counselors well versed in crisis procedures and processes will be able to provide ethical, skilled help in all types of crisis conditions. The goal of this chapter is to provide information of ethical and legal considerations related to preventive measures, federal legislations, sentinel court findings, and relevant application of best practices regarding privacy matters in crisis counseling.

Chapter 4: *Essential Crisis Intervention Skills*, by Joseph Cooper, provides an overview of the fundamental skills needed to engage in effective crisis intervention work. The skills covered in this chapter focus on Ivey and Ivey's (2007) microskills hierarchy. At the heart of this hierarchy is the basic listening sequence, an interrelated set of skills that will not only foster the development of rapport with clients, but also aid in the identification of interventions to help achieve a successful resolution to the client's crisis state. Examples of the skills in use, as well as practice exercises to foster individual skill development, are provided.

Part I concludes with Chapter 5: *Risk Assessment and Intervention: Suicide and Homicide*, by Judith Harrington and Charlotte Daughhetee. This chapter recognizes that suicide and homicide continue to play increasingly important roles in American society and on the world stage and that they affect us personally as we, family members, friends, and those in extended social networks struggle with the ever-increasing challenges of modern life. As personal liberty has increased, the chance for violent responses to stressful situations has increased. The effectiveness of the care given by professional emergency first responders, as well as the effectiveness of ordinary people in responding to their own crises and the crises of those about whom they care, is improved by background knowledge involving current trends in and treatments for suicide and homicide impulses.

Part II: *Special Issues in Crisis Intervention* comprises the remaining chapters of the text. Chapter 6: *Understanding and Treating Substance Use Disorders with Clients in Crisis*, by William B. Sterner, reviews substance use disorders and the disease of addiction, including causes, manifestations, and treatment. There are numerous models and theories about the causes of alcoholism and drug addiction, and this chapter introduces the medical and moral/legal models as well as important genetic, sociocultural, and psychological theories.

In Chapter 7: *Intimate Partner Violence*, by Amy L. McLeod, John Muldoon, and Danica G. Hays, intimate partner violence (IPV) is defined as the infliction of physical, sexual, and/or emotional harm to a person by a current or former partner or spouse with the intent of establishing power and control over the abused partner. IPV is a major public health concern, and it is imperative that crisis counselors be able to recognize and respond to IPV survivors competently. This chapter provides an overview of the facts and figures associated with IPV, discusses the cycle of violence commonly experienced in abusive relationships, and explores various perspectives on survivors who stay in relationships with abusive partners. Common crisis issues experienced by IPV survivors, including dealing with physical injury, establishing immediate safety, and reporting IPV to the police are also highlighted. In addition, this chapter explores special considerations regarding IPV in lesbian, gay, bisexual, and transgender (LGBT) relationships, relationships characterized by female-to-male violence, abusive relationships in racial and ethnic minority populations, and abusive dating relationships among adolescents and young adults. Guidelines for crisis counselors who are conducting IPV assessment, responding to IPV disclosure, planning for client safety, and addressing the emotional impact of IPV are provided. Finally, the goals, theories, and challenges associated with IPV offender intervention are discussed.

Chapter 8: *Sexual Assault*, by Robin Lee and Jennifer Jordan, reveals that sexual assault is one of the most underreported crimes, with survivors facing a number of potential physical, psychological, cognitive, behavioral, and emotional consequences. Crisis counselors who work with survivors of sexual assault need to be aware of the multitude of challenges these individuals face, best practices for treatment, and support services available in the local community.

In Chapter 9: *Sexual Abuse*, by Carrie Wachter Morris and Elizabeth Graves, child sexual abuse is defined, signs and symptoms described, treatment interventions discussed, and guidelines for working with law enforcement and child protective services personnel provided. In addition, this chapter addresses sexual offenders, their patterns of behavior, and common treatment options.

In Chapter 10: *Emergency Preparedness and Response in the Community and Workplace*, by Jason McGlothlin, the information and interventions from the preceding chapters are integrated into an overview of the various disasters and crises that crisis counselors may need to address. Crisis intervention models and clinical implications for disasters and hostage situations are explored.

In Chapter 11: *Emergency Preparedness and Response in Schools and Universities*, by Michele Garofalo and Bradley T. Erford, crisis management in the school is explored, including the components of a crisis plan and the role of school counselors and other school officials. Mitigation and prevention strategies are emphasized as critical elements in the school environment. Crisis preparedness, response, recovery, and debriefing procedures are applied to school and university settings. Special emphasis is given to strategies for how to help students and parents during and after a crisis event. Like Chapter 10, the content of this chapter infuses information found in previous chapters to allow readers to synthesize what they have previously read.

Chapter 12: *Grief and Loss*, by Lourie W. Reichenberg, covers approaches to crisis counseling with mourners, theories of grieving, and the variables that affect how a bereaved person mourns. The chapter also addresses how timing, cause of death, and the role the relationship played in a person's life all mediate the mourning process, followed by an attempt to distinguish between "normal" grief and complicated mourning.

Chapter 13: *Military Deployment and Reintegration Issues*, by Seth C. W. Hayden, acknowledges that serving the needs of military personnel and families presents unique challenges for counselors working in a variety of settings. Military families are a significant part of our communities, with more than two thirds residing in the larger civilian community and the remainder on military bases. While this population has long benefitted from the work of skilled counselors, the current and anticipated needs of military and their family members requires an understanding of military culture in addition to effective methods to support this population. This chapter provides an in-depth discussion of the military experience and offers various approaches to assist military service members and their families.

Chapter 14: *Death Notifications*, by Lisa R. Jackson-Cherry, concludes Part II with an outline of the components that should be implemented when preparing for and providing effective death notifications. A death notification given with empathy, calmness, and accuracy of information can assist the person with a sense of control. The information in this chapter has been included to assist crisis counselors to be prepared and equipped when called upon to either give or assist with a death notification. Effective death notifications decrease the need for intense debriefings and a complicated grief process, reduce counselor burnout, and may open the door for individuals to seek counseling when they are ready.

ACKNOWLEDGMENTS

We thank all of the contributing authors for lending their expertise in the various topical areas. As always, Meredith Fossel, our editor at Pearson, has been wonderfully responsive and supportive. Special thanks go to the outside reviewers whose comments helped to provide substantive improvement to the original manuscript: Al Carlozzi, Oklahoma State University; George K. Hong, California State University, Los Angeles; Nicholas Mazza, Florida State University; Eric Ornstein, University of Illinois at Chicago; Toni R. Tollerud, Northern Illinois University; and Barbara F. Turnage, Arkansas State University. We would also like to thank the reviewers whose feedback and suggestions helped shape this revision: Leah Clarke, Messiah College; Todd R. Gomez, Northeastern State University; Tara M. Hill, Old Dominion University; and Cheryl Sawyer, University of Houston.

BRIEF CONTENTS

Part I   **Elements of Crisis Intervention**

Chapter 1   Overview of Crisis Intervention   1
     Stephanie Puleo and Jason McGlothlin

Chapter 2   Safety and Self-Care in Crisis Situations   27
     Charlotte Daughhetee

Chapter 3   Ethical and Legal Considerations in Crisis Counseling   47
     Paul F. Hard, Laura L. Talbott-Forbes, and Mary L. Bartlett

Chapter 4   Essential Crisis Intervention Skills   67
     Joseph Cooper

Chapter 5   Risk Assessment and Intervention: Suicide and Homicide   85
     Judith Harrington and Charlotte Daughhetee

Part II   **Special Issues in Crisis Intervention**

Chapter 6   Understanding and Treating Substance Use Disorders with Clients in Crisis   127
     William R. Sterner

Chapter 7   Intimate Partner Violence   157
     Amy L. McLeod, John Muldoon, and Danica G. Hays

Chapter 8   Sexual Assault   193
     Robin Lee and Jennifer Jordan

Chapter 9   Child Sexual Abuse   219
     Carrie Wachter Morris and Elizabeth Graves

Chapter 10   Emergency Preparedness and Response in the Community and Workplace   245
     Jason McGlothlin

Chapter 11   Emergency Preparedness and Response in Schools and Universities   267
     Michele Garofalo and Bradley T. Erford

Chapter 12   Grief and Loss   293
     Lourie W. Reichenberg·

Chapter 13   Military Deployment and Reintegration Issues   327
     Seth C. W. Hayden

Chapter 14   Death Notifications   343
     Lisa R. Jackson-Cherry

CONTENTS

About the Editors   xviii
About the Contributing Authors   xx

Part I   Elements of Crisis Intervention

Chapter 1   Overview of Crisis Intervention   1
Stephanie Puleo and Jason McGlothlin
Preview   1
A Brief Introduction to Crisis Intervention   1
Crisis Intervention Theory   3
   The ABC–X and Double ABC–X Models of Crisis   5
   Elements of Stress and Crisis Theory   7
   Ecological and Contextual Considerations   10
Key Concepts Related to Crisis   12
   Stress   12
   Trauma   13
   Responses to Trauma   14
   Coping   14
   Adaptation   15
   Resilience   16
Crisis Intervention as a Unique Form of Counseling   18
Roles of and Collaboration Between Mental Health Workers During Crisis   19
   Professional Counselors   19
   Psychiatrists   20
   Psychologists   21
   Social Workers   21
   Paraprofessionals   21
   Hotline Workers   22
Fundamentals of Working with Clients in Crisis   23
Complications of Individuals Responding to Crisis   25
    Summary   25

Chapter 2   Safety and Self-Care in Crisis Situations   27
Charlotte Daughhetee
Preview   27
Safety Concerns and Precautions   27
   Proactive Approaches   28
   Safety Issues   28

Professional Self-Assessment   36
   Self-Assessment of the Counselor During Crises   38
   Countertransference   38
   Burnout and Compassion Fatigue   39
   Vicarious Trauma   40
   Vicarious Resiliency   41
   Self-Care   42
      Summary   46

Chapter 3   Ethical and Legal Considerations in Crisis Counseling   47
Paul F. Hard, Laura L. Talbott-Forbes, and Mary L. Bartlett
Preview   47
Preventive Considerations   48
Health Insurance Portability and Accountability Act   49
Family Educational Rights and Privacy Act   52
The *Tarasoff v. Regents* Decision   56
Negligence and Malpractice   60
Documentation and Record Keeping   60
Confidentiality   61
Informed Consent   62
Termination in Crisis Intervention   63
Spiritual and Multicultural Considerations   65
   Summary   66

Chapter 4   Essential Crisis Intervention Skills   67
Joseph Cooper
Preview   67
Essential Crisis Intervention Microskills   67
Attending Skills   68
   Eye Contact   68
   Body Position   70
   Vocal Tone   70
   Silence   71
The Basic Listening Sequence   72
   Asking Open and Closed Questions   72
   Reflecting Skills   76
      Summary   83

Chapter 5   Risk Assessment and Intervention: Suicide and Homicide   85
Judith Harrington and Charlotte Daughhetee
Preview   85

Suicide Intervention   86

   The Scope of the Problem   86

   Prevention, Intervention, and Postvention   88

   Prevention: Public Education, Competency, and Attitudes   89

   Training   91

   Postvention   106

Homicide   110

   Assessment of Homicide: Homicide Risk Factors   112

   School Homicide and Violence   113

   Workplace Homicide   115

   Threat Level Assessment   116

   Referral   119

   Treatment Options   119

   Homicide Survivor Needs   122

     Summary   125

Part II   Special Issues in Crisis Intervention

Chapter 6   Understanding and Treating Substance Use Disorders with Clients in Crisis   127

William R. Sterner

Preview   127

Substance Use and Society   127

   Classification of Drugs and Terminology   128

   Current Research on Substance Use, Crisis, and Society   129

Etiology and Risk Factors of Substance Abuse and Dependence   130

   Disease (Medical) Model   130

   Moral Model   131

   Genetic and Biological Models   131

   Social Learning Model   132

   Psychological Model   132

   Multicausal Model   133

   Factors that Increase Risk for Substance Abuse and Dependence   133

Screening, Assessment, and Diagnosis of Substance Use Disorders   134

   Screening   134

   Assessment   136

   Diagnosis   137

   Commonly Used Screening and Assessment Instruments   138

Assessing a Client's Readiness to Change   139

Treatment Admission and Placement   141

Substance Abuse Treatment and Crisis   142

Relapse and Crisis   149

Harm Reduction   150

Support Groups   151

Co-occurring Disorders and Crisis   152

Multicultural Perspectives, Substance Abuse, and Crisis   153

Summary   156

Chapter 7   Intimate Partner Violence   157

Amy L. McLeod, John Muldoon, and Danica G. Hays

Preview   157

Overview of Intimate Partner Violence   157

Cycle of Violence Theory   159

Phase 1: The Tension-Building Phase   160

Phase 2: The Acute Battering Incident   160

Phase 3: The Honeymoon Phase   160

The Duluth Model   161

Learned Helplessness Theory   161

Alternatives to Learned Helplessness Theory   161

Common Crisis Issues   162

Attending to Physical Injury   163

Establishing Immediate Safety   163

Reporting IPV to the Police   163

IPV in Special Populations   165

Race and Ethnicity   165

Female-to-Male Violence   170

LGBT Violence   171

Disability Status   172

Elder Abuse   173

Dating Violence Among Adolescents and Young Adults   173

The Crisis Counselor's Response to IPV   174

Screening for IPV   174

Response to IPV Disclosure   177

Safety and Harm Reduction Planning   178

Intimate Partner Violence Shelters: Opportunities and Challenges   179

Addressing the Emotional Impact of IPV   180

Batterer Intervention   182
  Safety   183
  Cessation of Violence   183
  Accountability   183
Theories/Approaches to Batterer Treatment   184
  Power and Control Theory   184
  Moral Development Theory   185
  Attachment Theory   186
  Feminist-Informed Cognitive-Behavioral Theory   187
Challenges in Batterer Intervention   187
  Underreporting of IPV Incidents   187
  IPV and Anger Management   188
  Financial Resources   188
  Completion Rates   189
    Summary   191

Chapter 8   Sexual Assault   193
Robin Lee and Jennifer Jordan
Preview   193
Sexual Assault   193
Prevalence of Sexual Assault   194
Definitions and Terms Related to Sexual Assault   195
  Definitions and Types of Rape   196
  Rape Myths   201
Effects of Sexual Assault   201
  Physical Effects of Sexual Assault   202
  Emotional/Psychological Effects of Sexual Assault   202
  Cognitive/Behavioral Effects of Sexual Assault   203
Interventions with Survivors of Sexual Assault   203
Treatment of Survivors of Sexual Assault   205
  Short-term/Immediate Interventions   205
  Long-term Interventions   206
  Cognitive-Behavioral Approaches   206
Ethical and Legal Issues Regarding Sexual Assault   209
  Spirituality and Religious Issues Related to Sexual Assault   210
  Multicultural Issues and Victims with Special Needs   212
Perpetrators of Sexual Assault   213
  Prevalence and Characteristics of Sexual Assault Perpetrators   213

Treatment of Sex Offenders   214
Summary   217

Chapter 9   Child Sexual Abuse   219
Carrie Wachter Morris and Elizabeth Graves
Preview   219
Child Sexual Abuse   219
Prevention of Child Sexual Abuse   220
Prevalence of CSA by Gender, Age, Race, and Ability   221
Definition of CSA and Related Terms   222
Definition of Child Sexual Abuse   222
Statutory Rape   223
Cycle of Child Sexual Abuse   223
Signs and Symptoms of Child Sexual Abuse   224
Intervention Strategies for Victims of CSA   224
Initial Disclosure and Interviewing for CSA   226
Reporting CSA   231
Reporting Past Incidents of CSA   233
Treatment of Survivors of CSA   233
Coping Strategy Considerations and Their Impact Upon
Treatment Planning   236
Perpetrators of Sexual Assault and Child Sexual Abuse   238
The Prevalence and Characteristics of Child Sexual Abuse Perpetrators   238
Treatment of Sex Offenders   241
Summary   243

**Chapter 10   Emergency Preparedness and Response in the
Community and Workplace   245**
Jason McGlothlin
Preview   245
Standards for Crisis Counseling Preparation   245
Leadership Roles in a Multidisciplinary Crisis Response Team   247
Characteristics of and Responses to Disasters, Terrorism,
and Hostage Situations   248
Interventions After a Disaster or Act of Terrorism   252
Psychological First Aid   253
Critical Incident Stress Management   254
Crisis Counseling Program   255
Natural Disasters   256
Winter Storms   256

Earthquakes   256

Floods   257

Heat Waves   258

Hurricanes   258

Tornados   258

Wildfires   259

Hostage Situations   261

   Summary   265

**Chapter 11   Emergency Preparedness and Response in Schools
   and Universities   267**

Michele Garofalo and Bradley T. Erford

Preview   267

Characteristics of and Responses to School Crises   267

   Mitigation and Prevention   268

   Preparedness and Advanced Planning   270

   Response   276

   Recovery   279

   Debriefing   280

   Helping Students During and After School Crises   280

   Helping Parents/Guardians During and After a School Crisis   281

   Notifying Students of a Death, Accident, or Event   283

School Responses to National Crises   284

Responding to Crises in Higher Education Settings   289

   Summary   291

Chapter 12   Grief and Loss   293

Lourie W. Reichenberg

Preview   293

Historical Perspectives and Models of Grief Work   293

   Lindemann's Approach   295

   The Death Awareness Movement: Kübler-Ross   295

   Worden's Task Model of Grieving   298

   Attachment and Loss   299

Understanding Grief   301

   Cultural Similarities in Grieving   302

   Ambiguous Loss and Disenfranchised Grief   303

Mediators of the Mourning Process   305

   Relationship: The Role of the Person Who Died   306

Cause of Death   309

Normal Versus Complicated Bereavement   310

Interventions for Grief and Loss   312

Restoring Life's Meaning   313

Interventions   318

Group Support   319

Working With Children   320

Family Interventions   321

Difficulties in Grief Counseling   321

Withdrawal   321

Counseling the Crisis Counselor   323

Summary   326

Chapter 13   Military Deployment and Reintegration Issues   327

Seth C. W. Hayden

Preview   327

Relevance of Military Personnel and Families to Counselors   327

Relevance of the Military Population to Counselors   328

Military Culture   328

Mental Health and Military Stigmatization   329

The Cycle of Deployment   330

Issues for Military Personnel as It Relates to Deployment   331

Issues for Military Families Related to Deployment   332

Familial Stress Associated with Deployment   332

Reunification   333

Military Families and Traumatic Brain Injury   334

Counselor Intervention with Military Service Members   334

Interventions for Post-traumatic Stress Disorder   335

Family Involvement in the Treatment of PTSD   336

Traumatic Brain Injury   337

Risk Assessment   338

Supporting Military Families   338

Adaptation within Military Families   339

Spirituality and Religious Needs of Deployed Military Service Members   340

Summary   342

Chapter 14   Death Notifications   343

Lisa R. Jackson-Cherry

Preview   343

Effective Death Notifications   344

   In Person and in Pairs   346

   In Time and with Accurate Information   346

   In Plain Language   348

   With Compassion   349

   Follow-up   350

   Debriefing with Team Members   350

      Summary   351

References   353

Index   377

ABOUT THE EDITORS

Lisa R. Jackson-Cherry, PhD, LCPC, NCC, ACS, NCSC, PCE, is a professor and chair of the Department of Counseling at Marymount University. She coordinates the clinical mental health counseling, pastoral counseling, and Ed.D. in Counselor Education and Supervision programs. She received her Ph.D. in Counselor Education and Supervision, an Ed.S. in Counseling, and a Masters of Criminal Justice from the University of South Carolina (and her B.A. from the University of Notre Dame of Maryland). She is the recipient of the American Counseling Association's Carl Perkins Government Relations Award for her initiatives in psychological testing; the recipient of the Outstanding Service Award, Leadership Award, and Meritorious Service Award given by the Association for Spiritual, Ethical, and Religious Values in Counseling (ASERVIC); and Outstanding Service and Leadership Award from the Licensed Clinical Professional Counselors of Maryland. Dr. Jackson-Cherry is a Licensed Clinical Professional Counselor in Maryland, National Certified Counselor, Approved Clinical Supervisor, and National Certified School Counselor. She is approved as a Pastoral Counselor Educator by the American Association of Pastoral Counselors and is certified as a Disaster Mental Health Counselor by the American Red Cross. She served on the Executive Board of the American Association of State Counseling Boards and is past-president of ASERVIC. She is the past membership Co-Chair and Southern Regional Representative for the Counseling Association for Humanistic Education and Development and has served as past Secretary and Legislative Representative for the Licensed Clinical Professional Counselors of Maryland. She is a current member of the Board of Professional Counselors and Therapists in Maryland, serving as past board chair and past chair of the Ethics Committee and Legislative/Regulations Committee. She is a current ASERVIC representative to the American Counseling Association Governing Council. Her research focuses mainly on the areas of ethical and legal issues in counseling and supervision, military deployment and reintegration issues, risk assessment, and religious and spiritual integration. She teaches courses primarily in the areas of crisis assessment and intervention, pastoral counseling integration, clinical internship experiences for clinical mental health counseling, and supervision. She is currently in private practice in Maryland, where she works with children and couples. She serves as a lead counselor with COPS Kids (Concerns of Police Survivors) during National Law Enforcement Officers Week, providing group counseling to children who lost a law enforcement officer-parent in the line of duty. Prior to her faculty appointment in 2000, her previous clinical experiences consisted of clinical director for mobile crisis team, behavioral specialist (grades K–5), conflict resolution coordinator/counselor (grades 9–12), group cofacilitator for a women's maximum security correctional facility, dual diagnosed population, police department youth counseling services division, and crisis intervention training facilitator for law enforcement basic trainees and hostage negotiators. She has written numerous articles and book reviews and participated extensively at state, national, and international conferences over the past 20 years.

 Bradley T. Erford, PhD, LCPC, NCC, LPC, LP, LSP, is the 2012–2013 President of the American Counseling Association (ACA) and a professor in the school counseling program of the Education Specialties Department in the School of Education at Loyola University Maryland. He is the recipient of the American Counseling Association (ACA) Research Award, ACA Extended Research Award, ACA Arthur A. Hitchcock Distinguished Professional Service Award, ACA Professional Development Award, and ACA Carl D. Perkins Government Relations Award. He was also inducted as an ACA Fellow. In addition, he has received the Association for Assessment in Counseling and Education (AACE) AACE/MECD Research Award; AACE Exemplary Practices Award;

AACE President's Merit Award; the Association for Counselor Education and Supervision (ACES) Robert O. Stripling Award for Excellence in Standards; Maryland Association for Counseling and Development (MACD) Counselor of the Year; MACD Counselor Advocacy Award; MACD Professional Development Award; and MACD Counselor Visibility Award. He is the editor/co-editor of numerous texts, including *Orientation to the Counseling Profession* (Pearson Merrill, 2010, 2014), *Group Work in the Schools* (Pearson Merrill, 2010), *Transforming the School Counseling Profession* (Pearson Merrill, 2003, 2007, and 2011), *Group Work: Processes and Applications* (Pearson Merrill, 2010), *Developing Multicultural Counseling Competence* (Pearson Merrill, 2010, 2014), *Crisis Assessment, Intervention and Prevention* (Pearson Merrill, 2010, 2014), *Professional School Counseling: A Handbook of Principles, Programs and Practices* (pro-ed, 2004, 2010), *Assessment for Counselors* (Cengage, 2007, 2013), *Research and Evaluation in Counseling* (Cengage, 2008), and *The Counselor's Guide to Clinical, Personality and Behavioral Assessment* (Cengage, 2006). He is also a coauthor of three more books: *Thirty-Five Techniques Every Counselor Should Know* (Merrill/Prentice-Hall, 2010); *Educational Applications of the WISC-IV* (2006, Western Psychological Services); and *Group Activities: Firing Up for Performance* (2007, Pearson/Merrill/Prentice-Hall). He is the general editor of *The American Counseling Association Encyclopedia of Counseling* (ACA, 2009). His research specialization falls primarily in development and technical analysis of psychoeducational tests and has resulted in the publication of more than 50 refereed journal articles, 100 book chapters, and a dozen published tests. He was a member of the ACA Governing Council and the 20/20 Committee: A Vision for the Future of Counseling. He is past president of AACE, past chair and parliamentarian of the American Counseling Association–Southern (US) Region; past-chair of ACA's Task Force on High Stakes Testing; past chair of ACA's Standards for Test Users Task Force; past chair of ACA's Interprofessional Committee; past chair of the ACA Public Awareness and Support Committee (co-chair of the National Awards Sub-committee); chair of the Convention and past-chair of the Screening Assessment Instruments Committees for AACE; past president of the Maryland Association for Counseling and Development (MACD); past-president of Maryland Association for Measurement and Evaluation (MAME); past-president of the Maryland Association for Counselor Education and Supervision (MACES); and past-president of the Maryland Association for Mental Health Counselors (MAMHC). He was also an associate editor and board member of the *Journal of Counseling and Development*. Dr. Erford has been a faculty member at Loyola since 1993 and is a Licensed Clinical Professional Counselor, Licensed Professional Counselor, Nationally Certified Counselor, Licensed Psychologist and Licensed School Psychologist. Prior to arriving at Loyola, Dr. Erford was a school psychologist/counselor in the Chesterfield County (VA) Public Schools. He maintains a private practice specializing in assessment and treatment of children and adolescents. A graduate of the University of Virginia (PhD), Bucknell University (MA), and Grove City College (BS), he has taught courses in testing and measurement, psychoeducational assessment, lifespan development, research and evaluation in counseling, school counseling, counseling techniques, practicum and internship student supervision, and stress management (not that he needs it, of course).

ABOUT THE CONTRIBUTING AUTHORS

Mary L. Bartlett, PhD, LPC-CS, NCC, CFLE, earned her doctorate in counselor education from Auburn University. She presently holds the position of Vice President of Behavioral Sciences for a national consulting firm, and she serves as an independent consultant, suicidologist, and international speaker. With 15 years clinical and teaching experience, she is an authorized trainer for the Suicide Prevention Resource Center and the American Association of Suicidology, and is a qualified master resilience trainer. In addition, Dr. Bartlett assists leadership of the U.S. Department of Defense on the prevention of suicide and other mental health related topics.

Joseph B. Cooper, PhD, LPC, NCC, is an associate professor in the department of counseling at Marymount University . He received his doctorate in counselor education from the University of North Carolina at Charlotte. Dr. Cooper has over 16 years of experience providing individual, family, and group substance abuse and mental health counseling services in the agency, school, and private practice settings. His current research interests include attachment theory, intensive short-term dynamic psychotherapy, and neurophysiology. He maintains a private practice in Washington, DC, and is a guest faculty member for the intensive short-term dynamic psychotherapy program at the Washington School of Psychiatry.

Charlotte L. Daughhetee, NCC, LPC, LMFT, is a professor in the graduate program in counseling at the University of Montevallo, with, counseling experience in K–12, university, and private practice settings. She earned her MEd in school counseling in 1988 and her PhD in counselor education in 1992 from the University of South Carolina. She has experience in crisis intervention in school and university settings and has presented and published on crisis intervention. She is the program coordinator for the University of Montevallo Counseling Program and she coordinates the school counseling track.

Michele Garofalo, EdD, LPC, NCC, is the assistant chair in the Department of Counseling and School Counseling Program Director at Marymount University. She has worked as a school counselor at the elementary and middle school levels in both independent and public schools. She consults with area schools on a variety of school-related topics and mental health issues. Dr. Garofalo has maintained a private practice where she works with adolescents and families. She teaches school counseling courses and provides supervision for school counseling practicum and internship students. Her research interests include bullying, character education, adolescent stress, counselor training and supervision, and ethical and legal issues.

Elizabeth G. Graves is an assistant professor in the Department of Human Development and Psychological Services at Appalachian State University. She has worked extensively with children and adolescents in public school, community mental health, and inpatient psychiatric care settings. Her research interests include child sexual abuse and trauma in children and adolescents.

Paul F. Hard, PhD, LPC-S, NCC, is an associate professor of counselor education at Auburn University at Montgomery. He has provided individual and group counseling in both private practice and community agency settings, focusing on addictions, relationship counseling, sexual minorities, and trauma. His research interests have been in the areas of ethics, counselor/professional impairment and wellness, complicated grieving in prenatal and postnatal loss, professional credentialing and advocacy, sexual minority issues in counseling, and ministerial termination.

Judith Harrington, PhD, LPC, LMFT, in private practice in Birmingham, Alabama, is an approved trainer for the assessing and managing suicidal risk curriculum for mental health professionals on behalf of the Suicide Prevention Resource Center at SAMHSA and the American Association of Suicidology. Since 2008, she has instructed the graduate counselor education curriculum on suicide for the University of Alabama at Birmingham and the University of Montevallo. In addition, she currently serves on the Standards, Training, and Practices Committee for the National Suicide Prevention Lifeline at SAMHSA. She has served the suicidally bereaved community by facilitating the SOS Bereavement Group for the last 12 years, and was the first- and twice-elected president of the nonprofit Alabama Suicide Prevention and Resources Coalition (ASPARC).

Seth C. W. Hayden, PhD, NCC, is the program director of Career Advising, Counseling, and Programming in the Florida State University Career Center. He has conducted career, couples, individual, and group counseling in community mental health, hospital, secondary school, and university settings. His research interests include career development and theory, clinical supervision, co-occurring mental health and career issues, military personnel and families, and spirituality in counseling and counselor preparation.

Danica G. Hays, PhD, LPC, NCC, is an associate professor and chair in the Department of Educational Leadership and Counseling at Old Dominion University. She has conducted individual and group counseling in community mental health, university, and hospital settings. Her research interests include qualitative methodology, assessment and diagnosis, domestic violence intervention, and multicultural and social justice issues in counselor preparation and community mental health.

Jennifer Jordan, PhD, LPCS, NCC, is an associate professor in the counseling and development program at Winthrop University. She is past president of the Southern Association of Counselor Education and Supervision (2011–2012). She specializes in group counseling and working with children and adolescents.

Robin Lee, PhD, LPC, NCC, is an associate professor in the professional counseling program at Middle Tennessee State University. She received her doctoral degree in counselor education and supervision from Mississippi State University. Her interests include counselor training issues, ethical and legal issues, counseling supervision, women's issues, and generational characteristics.

Jason McGlothlin, PhD, PCC-S, is an associate professor in the counseling and human development services program at Kent State University (KSU). He also serves as the coordinator of the community counseling and school counseling programs at KSU. He earned his doctorate in counselor education from Ohio University and is currently a Professional Clinical Counselor with Supervisory endorsement (PCC-S) in Ohio. Prior to joining the KSU faculty, he practiced in community mental health, private practice, and suicide prevention/hostage negotiation facilities. Dr. McGlothlin has had a variety of local, state, and national leadership positions in the counseling profession. His current areas of teaching, publication, and research include the assessment, prevention, and treatment of suicide and counselor education accreditation. He is the author of *Developing Clinical Skills in Suicide Assessment, Prevention and Treatment* (American Counseling Association, 2008).

Amy L. McLeod, PhD, is an assistant professor at Argosy University in Atlanta, Georgia. Her research interests include women's issues, crisis counseling, assessment and diagnosis, and multicultural issues in counselor education and supervision. Her clinical experience includes work in a private practice and at Ridgeview Institute, a mental health and substance abuse hospital.

John Muldoon, PhD, LPC, CAAP, is an assistant professor at Kean University in Union, New Jersey. Formerly, he worked for the behavioral services unit for a regional hospital system, facilitating intensive outpatient and outpatient recovery groups, as well as maintaining an individual caseload, where the majority of his clients were dually diagnosed. His most significant experience was as the director of Alternatives to Violence, a program for domestic violence offenders, for seven years.

Stephanie Puleo, PhD, LMFT, LPC, NCC, is a professor in the Department of Counseling, Leadership, and Foundations at the University of Montevallo in Montevallo, Alabama. She is certified by the American Red Cross in disaster mental health. Dr. Puleo earned her doctorate in counselor education at the University of Alabama as well as master's degrees in community counseling and in school psychology. In addition to coordinating the marriage and family counseling program track at the University of Montevallo, she provides counseling and psychometric services to individuals, couples, and families in the Birmingham and central Alabama area.

Lourie W. Reichenberg, MA, LPC, NCC, received her undergraduate degree in psychology from Michigan State University and her master's degree in counseling psychology from Marymount University, where as an adjunct faculty member she teaches counseling theories, abnormal psychology, and crisis management. Her specific interest areas include loss and life transitions, crisis management, and suicide prevention and postvention. She is coauthor of two books and editor of more than 20 books, has published numerous articles, and has conducted more than 50 presentations on various topics. She is a Licensed Professional Counselor in several states and has a private practice in Falls Church, Virginia.

William R. Sterner, PhD, LPC, NCC, is an assistant professor in the Department of Counseling at Marymount University. He worked for a number of years as a clinical mental health counselor and drug and alcohol counselor in various community counseling settings. He also has experience conducting drug and alcohol assessments, case management, and treatment placement with clients in the criminal justice system. His research interests include supervision, quantitative methodology, spirituality issues in counseling, substance abuse, incivility issues in higher education, and counselor competencies in assessing and managing suicidality.

Laura L. Talbott, PhD, MCHES, is an associate professor in the Department of Human Studies at the University of Alabama at Birmingham. She has served as a prevention specialist with general college student health issues and director of substance abuse prevention programs at a large university. Her research interests include the prevention of substance abuse, education and early intervention with potentially suicidal persons, and other public health issues that impact young adult health.

Carrie Wachter Morris, PhD, NCC, ACS, is an associate professor in and codirector of the school counseling program at Purdue University. She received her doctoral degree in counseling and counselor education from the University of North Carolina at Greensboro. Her clinical experience includes work in schools and at an inpatient behavioral health center for children, adolescents, and adults. Her research interests include crisis prevention and intervention in the schools and pedagogy in counselor education.

Overview of Crisis Intervention

Stephanie Puleo and Jason McGlothlin

PREVIEW

Crises occur in a variety of settings for a variety of reasons. Responses to crises can come in various forms and can include multiple levels of complexities. In this chapter, basic frameworks for assessing and conceptualizing crises are presented, along with a discussion of how crisis intervention may differ from traditional counseling.

A BRIEF INTRODUCTION TO CRISIS INTERVENTION

If asked to think about a crisis, what comes to mind? Natural disasters? School shootings? Suicide? Domestic violence? How do some people survive such traumatic events adaptively and with resilience, while others endure mental health issues for months or years afterward?

To begin, situations such as tornadoes, earthquakes, acts of terror, and suicide, although sharing traumatic characteristics, do not in and of themselves constitute crises. These are, instead, events that trigger crises. Typically, a crisis is described using a trilogy definition; that is, there are three essential elements that must be present for a situation to be considered a crisis: (1) a precipitating event, (2) a perception of the event that leads to subjective distress, and (3) diminished functioning when the distress is not alleviated by customary coping resources.

When terrorists bombed the World Trade Center in New York City in 1993, crises ensued for many individuals and families. Six families lost loved ones, approximately 1,000 individuals were injured, and the jobs, careers, and work of countless people were interrupted. Using the trilogy definition, it is obvious that all of those who experienced diminished functioning following the event were in crisis. People throughout the rest of the world, however horrified, continued to function as normal and therefore were not in crisis.

CASE STUDY 1.1

The Nguyens

Vin and Li Nguyen are recent immigrants to the United States. They reside in a small town along the Gulf Coast of Mississippi, where a number of other Vietnamese immigrants have settled. Like many members of the community, the Nguyens are learning to speak, read, and write English and are hoping to become naturalized citizens of the United States some day. After arriving in the United States, the Nguyens invested all of their money in an old shrimp boat in order to support themselves by selling their daily catch to local seafood processing facilities.

In 2005, the shrimp boat was heavily damaged, and the seafood processing facilities were destroyed by Hurricane Katrina. Subsequently, the Nguyens had no income for quite awhile. With limited income and no health insurance, they relied on the county department of public health for prenatal care when Li became pregnant. Li's pregnancy progressed normally; however, her daughter was born with spina bifida. As you read this chapter, try to conceptualize the Nguyens' situation according to the crisis models presented.

Discussion Questions

1. What incidents have occurred in the Nguyens' lives that could be considered provoking stressor events?
2. Beyond the provoking stressor events, are there additional stressors that the Nguyens must address?
3. What resources are the Nguyens using?
4. What additional information do you need to determine if the Nguyens are in crisis?
5. What factors will predict the outcome for this family?

The trilogy definition is reflected in the work of several notable contributors to the crisis intervention literature and applies to individuals and groups as well as to families (Boss, 2002; McKenry & Price, 2005). Recently, James (2008) reviewed a number of definitions that exist in the literature and summarized crisis as "a perception or experiencing of an event or situation as an intolerable difficulty that exceeds the person's current resources and coping mechanisms" (p. 3). As a first exposure to the potential characteristics of crisis, read Case Study 1.1 and answer the discussion questions that follow.

According to Slaikeu (1990), a crisis is "a temporary state of upset and disorganization, characterized chiefly by an individual's inability to cope with a particular situation using customary methods of problem-solving, and by the potential for a radically positive or negative outcome" (p. 15). While it is always hoped that a positive outcome would occur, there are occasions when a radically negative outcome such as suicide happens, thereby precipitating further upset.

VOICES FROM THE FIELD 1.1
My First Day

Beth Graney

I spent the summer planning all the classroom lessons and groups I would offer students in my first position as the only school counselor in a K–12 system in a rural Iowa school. After the principal shared with me that the previous counselor never really connected with many of the kids, I knew I needed to be especially creative to win their trust. The principal told me the town had a saying, "If you aren't born here, you are not from here!" How would a big city girl from Chicago ever fit in?

All of these thoughts raced through my head, drowning out the din of my radio as I drove the 20 miles to school. The newscaster's report that a couple had been killed in a motorcycle accident the previous night barely registered. When I arrived early that morning the principal greeted me at the door and pulled me into her office. The parents of two of our students had been killed the night before and the other students had already arrived at school crying. "You have to do something," she blurted as she hurried off to take care of notifying the rest of the staff. My mouth went dry and my thoughts started to race. What should I say? What should I do? What strategies would be most effective? More importantly, I thought I don't know a single student in this building!

As I entered the room, I realized that it was more like 20 kids ranging in age from early elementary to high school. As I put down my bag on the desk, I looked at all the crying kids and pulled up a chair in the large classroom that was now my office and said, "Who wants to start"? At first it was, "They

are my friends, my neighbor, and our classmate!" I listened. Soon someone said, "My grandma is sick," and then another, "My dad lost his job," and "My parents are getting divorced." I listened. As the morning progressed, some kids went on to class, others went home, and more came from class or home to share their grief and fears with the group. I listened some more. When the long day finally ended, I didn't know everyone's name that I had written on the sign-in sheet, but I had a growing sense of the community.

Two days later, after listening to many students and teachers explain how this tragedy affected them, the principal told me the funeral service would be held in the gym because the gathering would be so large. She thought it would be important for me to be there to support the kids in case anyone needed immediate assistance. I listened as the minister and other family members eulogized the parents. After the service, I met many of the parents and community members, and again I listened to their grief and pain. When a person dies, the family and friends grieve. But in a small town, when someone dies the whole town grieves.

As I drove home that day, I felt drained and wondered if I was helpful because I had no great insights or strategies to offer the student or parents as to why something so difficult and tragic had happened. All I really did was listen. It was then that it struck me that it was the first skill ever taught in graduate school: Listen! And so began one of my most memorable years in counseling. My phone didn't stop and my sign-up sheet was never empty. I made the transition from city girl to rural school counselor. I listened.

CRISIS INTERVENTION THEORY

The study of crisis intervention began in earnest during the 1940s in response to several stressor events. During World War II, numerous families experienced disorganization and changes in functioning after individual family members left home to participate in the war effort. In most cases, disorganization was only temporary and families found ways to adjust. Families that had the most difficulty reorganizing and adapting to the absence of their loved ones seemed to experience the greatest degree of distress (Hill, 1949). Studies of families in crisis following war separation led Reuben Hill to propose a model through which family stress and crisis could be conceptualized by taking into account the family's resources, perception, and previous experience with crises. Additional research on families and crisis events was launched following a more acute stressor event, the Cocoanut Grove nightclub fire that claimed nearly 500 lives in Boston, Massachusetts. Studies of the responses of the survivors of the fire, family members of those who died, and the community illuminated some common reactions to such a traumatic event and led Gerald Caplan and Erich Lindemann to propose recommendations for responding to community crises. In the decades following the 1940s, the original models proposed by Hill, Caplan, and Lindemann were expanded, with more attention to contextual variables and outcomes.

Gerald Caplan and Erich Lindemann are often credited as pioneers in the field of crisis intervention. Their work began after the tragic Cocoanut Grove nightclub fire, in which so many people died in Boston in 1942. Lindemann, a professor of psychiatry at Harvard Medical School and Massachusetts General Hospital, worked with patients dealing with grief following traumatic loss. Although many people died as a result of the fire, hundreds who were at the nightclub on that fateful night survived. The survivors and the grieving relatives of those who perished provided Lindemann with an opportunity to study psychological and emotional reactions to disaster. Based on his interviews with those who survived the fire as well as relatives of the deceased, Lindemann (1944) outlined a number of common clinical features, including somatic distress, feelings of guilt, hostility, disorganization, behavioral changes, and preoccupation with images of the deceased. Lindemann referred to these symptoms as "acute grief," which was not a psychiatric diagnosis but was a call for intervention nonetheless. Today, many of the symptoms of acute stress disorder identified in the *Diagnostic and Statistical Manual of Mental Disorders* (DSM-5; American Psychiatric Association [APA], 2013) seem to parallel Lindemann's description of acute grief.

In addition to describing clinical features of acute grief, Lindemann outlined intervention strategies for dealing with it. Because acute grief was not considered a psychiatric diagnosis per se, Lindemann suggested that helpers other than psychiatrists could be of assistance. This idea was further fueled by the large number of people in need of intervention following the Cocoanut Grove fire, and became a cornerstone in the conceptualization of community mental health.

In response to the needs of the number of people experiencing acute grief following the nightclub fire, Lindemann worked with his colleague Gerald Caplan to establish a communitywide mental health program in Cambridge, Massachusetts, known as the Wellesley Project. By studying and working with individuals who had experienced loss through the fire or similar traumatic events, Caplan developed the concept of "preventive psychiatry" (Caplan, 1964), which proposed that early intervention following a disaster or traumatic event can promote positive growth and well-being.

Building on Caplan's model, Beverley Raphael (2000) coined the term "psychological first aid." Following a train accident in Australia in 1977 in which a many people died, Raphael worked with bereaved families and injured survivors of the train disaster. She advocated for attention that included comfort and consolation, immediate physical assistance, reunification with loved ones, an opportunity to express feelings, and support during the initial period of time following a traumatic event. In particular, she described the need to consider Maslow's hierarchy of needs, and the importance of attending first to basic survival needs before attempting more traditional forms of counseling (James, 2008; Raphael, 2000). In describing crisis reactions, Raphael noted that the full impact of trauma frequently is felt a considerable time after the initial crisis event, often during a period of "disillusionment." Much of her work subsequent to the 1977 train accident focused on the prevention of post-traumatic stress disorder.

Caplan (1961) offered this explanation:

> People are in a state of crisis when they face an obstacle to important life goals—an obstacle that is, for a time, insurmountable by the use of customary methods of problem-solving. A period of disorganization ensues, a period of upset, during which many abortive attempts at solution are made. (p. 18)

What is important to note in Caplan's description is that the concept of crisis refers to an outcome of a precipitating event, not to the precipitating event itself. Similar to more recent definitions of crisis, Caplan described the outcome, or the crisis, as the state of disequilibrium that is experienced.

There are several schools of thought pertaining to crisis theory, and the concept of disequilibrium following a stressful event seems to be common to all of them. Some theories focus on the disequilibrium experiences of individuals, while others take a more contextual, systemic stance. Many researchers and theorists take the point of view that the disequilibrium that constitutes crisis can be understood by examining an individual's past experiences, cognitive structures, behaviors, and competencies. For example, Freud concluded from his studies on hysteria that many of the neurotic symptoms that contributed to his clients' states of disequilibrium were expressions of repressed memories of past traumatic events. Their disequilibrium was sustained by destructive defense mechanisms.

Other theorists who focused on individuals contend that the disequilibrium of crisis is the result of ineffective psychological tools, such as negative or faulty thinking, weak self-esteem, and maladaptive behavior. According to "adaptational" theory (James, 2008), individuals who become incapacitated or dysfunctional following stressful events are those who first perceive and interpret stressful events negatively. Negative thoughts, irrational beliefs, and defeating self-talk lead to paralyzing rather than helpful behaviors. From a cognitive-behavioral perspective, crises may be ameliorated when individuals replace their faulty thinking and ineffective behaviors with more positive thoughts and adaptive behaviors. From an interpersonal perspective, self-confidence and self-esteem also counter the disequilibrium of crises as individuals become more focused and reliant on their own abilities (James, 2008).

Systemic and ecosystemic theories of crises take into account the context and environment in which crises occur. From a systemic point of view, all parts of a system are interrelated, and any change in one element (e.g., person, issue, event) leads to change in the whole system. Crises may be seen as a convergence of factors that are interrelated. No one single factor causes a crisis. When crises occur, they typically do not involve only one person. Depending on the type of crisis, one individual may be at the epicenter of the crisis, but the crisis likely will be the culmination of a variety of variables and will affect that individual's family and community as well.

The ABC-X and Double ABC-X Models of Crisis

The ABC-X and Double ABC-X models of crises were developed through research with families, but the concepts outlined in the models may be generalized to individuals

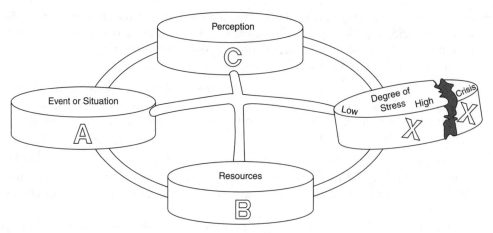

FIGURE 1.1   The ABC–X model of family crisis.

or to larger groups or communities. From his studies of families experiencing separation and reunion as a result of World War II, Reuben Hill (1949, 1958) postulated the ABC–X model of family crisis (Figure 1.1). According to this theory, there is an interaction among a provoking stressor event (A), the family's resources (B), and the meaning that the family attaches to the stressor event (C). The crisis (X), a state of acute disequilibrium and immobilization of the family system, is an outcome of this interaction.

Hill's original ABC–X model continues to provide a framework for much research in the area of stress and crisis; however, a few scholars (Boss, 2002; McCubbin & Patterson, 1982) have expanded the model. Among the better-known variations of Hill's work is the double ABC–X model of crisis proposed by McCubbin and Patterson (1982). Writing from a systems orientation, which assumes that systems naturally evolve and become more complex over time, McCubbin and Patterson considered recovery and growth following crisis. The concept of adaptation was introduced to describe lasting functional changes that occur in order to meet the demands of a crisis or stressful event. According to these scholars, Hill's original model was somewhat incomplete in that it outlined only those factors that contributed to a crisis or breakdown in functioning. Following a state of disequilibrium or incapacitation, additional stressors may accrue, and additional resources may be identified and acquired. Subsequently, new perceptions that take into account the original event and related hardships or stressors are formulated, along with the application of resources and coping strategies to meet the needs of those stressors.

According to McCubbin and Patterson (1982), there is a "double A" factor that includes Hill's original concept of a provoking stressor plus the buildup of further stressors that must be addressed. These stressors may include unresolved issues related to the crisis-provoking event, changes that occur unrelated to the event, and any consequences of attempts to cope (McKenry & Price, 2005). The "double B" factor refers to resources available at the time of the provoking stressor, as noted by Hill, along with tangible and intangible resources that have been acquired or strengthened. Fortified coping resources would be included in this concept. The "double C" factor refers not only to perceptions and meanings assigned to the original provoking stressor but also to accumulated stressors, resources, coping, and the entire situation. Perceptions are influenced by religious beliefs, family and cultural values, and how the situation may have been reframed. In the model proposed by McCubbin and Patterson, the original crisis (Hill's X factor) constitutes a beginning point, while adaptation ("double X") occurs later in time. Adaptation is an outcome variable involving changes in functioning and perception. More than the simple reduction of stress, adaptation is the degree to which long-term change has occurred in response to the demands of stressor and crisis events.

McCubbin and Patterson (1982) referred to positive long-term changes that occur in response to crises as bonadaptation. It was their contention that following crises, some individuals and families do not merely return to their previous states of equilibrium, instead, they are better able to function and handle stress and crisis events. While McCubbin and Patterson referred to positive adaptation as bonadaptation, others have labeled this concept stress-related growth (Park, Cohen, & Murch, 1996) or posttraumatic growth (Tedeschi & Calhoun, 2004)

Elements of Stress and Crisis Theory

PROVOKING STRESSOR EVENTS   Stressor events are those occurrences that provoke change in the functioning of an individual or system. Such events may be positive or negative, and while some are normal and predictable, others are unforeseen. In general, stressor events may be categorized as either normative (developmental) stressor events (i.e., those stressors that occur at points of normal developmental transitions) or nonnormative (situational) stressor events (i.e., products of distinctive, unexpected, catastrophic situations). Many families anticipate normative/developmental stressor events such as children graduating from high school and beginning college, while few anticipate nonnormative stressor events such as the school shootings at Virginia Tech in 2007 and at Chardon High School in northeastern Ohio in 2012. Existential crisis—a crisis that results in a perceived conflict with meaning, purpose, or values (and may or may not be related to one's religious or spiritual views)—can be experienced as the primary crisis event or be a result from the primary crisis.

Boss (1988) categorized stressor events and situations by source, type, and severity. Sources are either internal (i.e., originating within the family) or external (i.e., attributable to someone or something outside the family). Examples of internal stressors include partner violence and chemical dependency. These stressors begin within the family and are accompanied by changes in the way the family functions. Partners and family members often adopt various roles, behaviors, and communication styles in attempts to cope with and survive the actions of the abusive or addicted person. As familiar coping strategies become increasingly inadequate, families cease to function effectively and healthily. "Crises" in these families are rarely a one-time occurrence.

Another example of an internal stressor is infertility. Within the context of the family life cycle, most couples expect to be able to conceive and carry a pregnancy to term. Infertility is considered an internal stressor because the inability to achieve a successful pregnancy originates with one (sometimes both) of the partners as opposed to something outside of the family. It can become a crisis situation because the partners face psychological and relationship changes that affect the way they function. Each menses is encountered as a crisis situation. In response to this crisis situation, many couples are able to redefine their relationships and reframe their meanings of pregnancy and parenting; unfortunately, however, many couples do not respond well and ultimately separate.

External stressors originate outside the family but affect functioning nonetheless. Examples of external stressors include natural disasters, terrorism, financial decline due to the stock market, and the rising cost of oil. Some external stressors are attributable to forces of nature (e.g., hurricanes, tornadoes, earthquakes), some to humans (e.g., violent crimes, job termination), and some to a combination of the two. Individuals and families typically have less control over external stressors than they do over internal stressors. For example, families have little control over the stock market. However, the ramifications of a declining stock market could have a substantial influence on a family's future.

As with internal stressors, however, the degree to which crises caused by external stressors are experienced is contingent on available resources and the meaning attached to the stressor event. In the United States, the spring 2011 tornado outbreak (an external stressor) interrupted normal functioning and triggered crises for hundreds of families in Alabama, Missouri, and 13 other states. Families who seemed to be the most resilient and to have the least difficulty recovering from this crisis were those with available resources such as social support, housing, and financial assets.

Many stressors are normal, predictable, and developmental in nature. Stressor events of this type generally are an expected part of everyday life and of the family life cycle. Typical normative stressor events include "birth, puberty, adolescence, marriage, aging, menopause, retirement, and death" (Boss, 2002, p. 51). Although these events are expected, they have the potential to disturb the equilibrium of an individual or family and result in crisis.

The type of crisis-inducing stressor that initially comes to mind for many people is the catastrophic, situational, unexpected event. Such stressors tend to be unique, are not predicted, and are not likely to be repeated. Examples of catastrophic stressors include those that may be attributable to human behavior, such as the bombing of the Alfred P. Murrah Federal Building in Oklahoma City in 1995, or to natural disasters, such as the 2011 earthquake and tsunami in Japan. Other nonnormative stressors may not be catastrophic at all and may actually be positive, but they nonetheless may still have the potential to disrupt equilibrium. Examples include winning the lottery or locating a lost child or relative. Unexpected stressor events such as these may also be categorized as nonvolitional stressors. Volitional stressors, on the other hand, are recognized by the amount of choice and control the individual or family has over them. Examples include wanted changes in jobs or residences and planned pregnancies. Although volitional stressors are wanted, initiated, pursued, or orchestrated by the individual or family, they still have the potential to trigger a crisis if resources and meaning do not match needs and requirements. Changing jobs for the sake of career advancement, for instance, may require a move to a geographic location where housing is unavailable or unaffordable. A planned pregnancy, even if everything goes according to plan (i.e., no medical complications, a single birth, and a healthy baby), may mean that financial and social support may be inadequate.

Beyond classifying stressors by their source and type, Boss (2002) described stressor situations according to their duration and severity. Some stressors are onetime events, happen suddenly, and resolve quickly; these are considered acute stressors.

An automobile accident, for example, might disrupt a family's equilibrium as broken bones heal and alternate transportation is used, but ultimately, the family's balance is restored. Other stressors, such as lifelong illnesses, infertility, and poverty, persist over long periods of time and are considered chronic. Families caring for aging family members may experience chronic stress and may face disequilibrium and crisis each time the elderly family member's health takes a turn for the worse. The crisis is triggered by changes in health but is the result of additional demands for financial, social, and other resources as well as the perception and meaning the family attaches to the elderly person's decline. Finally, it is important to consider whether a stressor situation is an isolated event or part of an accumulation of stressor events. It is often the case that any one stressor event may not be enough to trigger a crisis, but the cumulative effect of the pileup of stressors taxes resources, disrupts equilibrium and functioning, and results in crisis.

RESOURCES Resources may be defined as traits, characteristics, or abilities that can be used to meet the demands of a stressor event (McCubbin & Patterson, 1982) and that can be available at the individual, family, or community level (McKenry & Price, 2005). They may be tangible (e.g., food, clothing, shelter) or intangible (e.g., social support, self-esteem). When resources are adequate to meet the demands created by a stressor situation, the situation is less likely to be perceived as problematic—and less likely to lead to crisis. Two types of resources are important: those that are available and used to mediate the initial stressor and those that are acquired, developed, or strengthened subsequent to a crisis situation (McCubbin & Patterson, 1982). Individual resources may include finances, education, health, and psychological qualities, whereas family resources include the internal, systemic attributes of cohesion and adaptability, along with resources such as financial management, communication skills, compatibility, and shared interests. Community resources include external supports, such as social networks, on which the individual or family can draw.

MEANING OR PERCEPTION Whether a stressor event results in crisis depends not only on available resources but also on the meaning attached to the event. Many theorists, researchers, and clinicians believe one's meaning and perception of the event is the main determination of whether an event becomes a crisis. The meaning attributed to a stressor event is subjective and comes from the way it is appraised through both cognitive and affective processes. Factors contributing to this qualitative variable include the ambiguity associated with the stressor situation, denial, and the belief and value orientation of the individual or family. Ambiguity occurs when facts cannot be obtained. It is often the case that specific information about the onset, development, duration, and conclusion of an unpredictable stressor event is unavailable. When information is unavailable, individuals may be uncertain in their perception of who is included in their families or social support systems. With limited understanding about who is in and who is out, it becomes difficult to ascertain how various roles, rules, and functions will be carried out. Whereas sometimes stressors themselves are ambiguous because data are not available, at other times facts are available but are ignored or distorted. The resulting denial may be a useful coping strategy in the short term but may be damaging if it prevents further action during a crisis situation (Boss, 2002; McKenry & Price, 2005).

COPING   In his original ABC–X model, Hill (1949, 1958) considered coping behaviors as part of the family's resources (represented by "B") to be used in response to demands of a stressor event ("A"). While many researchers agree that coping behaviors are a subset of available resources, coping itself is a separate construct, often interacting with both resources ("B") and perception ("C"). According to Pearlin and Schooler (1978), any effort taken to deal with stress may be considered coping. Thus, coping is a process that requires cognitive as well as behavioral activities (McKenry & Price, 2005). Cognitively, people experiencing stressor events must appraise what is happening and assess any potential for harm. They must also evaluate the consequences of possible response actions. According to Lazarus (1976), these appraisals occur before any coping mechanisms are employed. Following appraisal, there are three types of coping responses that may be used: direct actions, intrapsychic mechanisms, and efforts to manage emotions.

Direct actions are those behaviors that typically are thought of as "fight or flight" responses. Examples include acquiring resources, asking for help, and learning new skills (McKenry & Price, 2005). These actions are used in relation to the environment in order to master stressors and are thought of as problem-focused coping strategies. Emotion-focused coping strategies, conversely, involve mechanisms used to change feelings or perceptions when there is little that can be done to change a stressor. Intrapsychic responses are those responses that are often thought of as defense mechanisms (e.g., denial, detachment) and allow people to alter their interpretations of the stress-provoking situation (Boss, 2002; McKenry & Price, 2005). Additional emotion-focused strategies are used to manage emotions generated by the stressor. Examples include the use of resources such as social support or of alcohol and drugs. Obviously, specific coping responses are neither adaptive nor maladaptive; they are simply efforts to manage.

Ecological and Contextual Considerations

Boss (2002) and Collins and Collins (2005) suggested that stress and crisis are affected by contextual factors. Collins and Collins advocated a "developmental-ecological" perspective to conceptualizing crises. Some crises are triggered by stressor events that are developmental in nature; that is, these developmental crises are expected events in the life span of the individual or family. However, regardless of whether the stressor event is developmental or situational, life span variables must be considered to determine their meaning and impact on the stress or crisis situation. In addition to considering developmental factors, Collins and Collins maintained that the context provided by environmental factors such as interpersonal relationships, community resources, and society at large must be recognized. This approach suggests that each crisis is unique, since the ecological determinants for each person will be unique. Therefore, crisis counselors need to be aware that even though many of the clinical considerations and approaches may be similar for a specific crisis and for many individuals experiencing that crisis (e.g., sexual assault), the person in crisis will experience the crisis differently than someone else due to the unique and personal ecological determinants. In essence, do not simply generalize and implement a generic approach to a particular crisis without first assessing the client's unique ecological factors.

Boss (2002) proposed a similar contextual approach to the study of stress and crisis, stating that "factors in addition to the stressful event influence family vulnerability or breakdown" (p. 28). According to Boss, stress is mediated by contextual dimensions, which may be either internal or external. The internal context includes three dimensions that may be controlled or changed: the structure of the family, psychological elements such as perception and assessment, and philosophical elements such as values and beliefs. The external context is composed of environmental or ecosystemic dimensions over which there is no control. External influences on stress and crisis include historical, economic, developmental, hereditary, and cultural contexts.

CASE STUDY 1.1 (continued)

The Nguyens

Stressor events are those occurrences—positive or negative, predictable or unforeseen—that provoke change in the functioning of a system. They may be categorized as normative or nonnormative. The Nguyen family has experienced a number of provoking stressors, some of which they chose, others that they did not.

Stressors may be categorized by source, type, and severity, and they should be considered within the external context. This includes variables such as culture, history, education, and heredity over which the Nguyen family has no control. Crisis counselors who work with the Nguyens need to explore the family's Vietnamese culture as well as possible additional cultural issues related to being part of an immigrant community along the Gulf Coast of the United States. Imbedded in these considerations is the fact that the Nguyens chose to leave Vietnam for the United States some 30 years after the Vietnam War. What kinds of social prejudices and biases does this couple face simply by being Vietnamese? Are there additional biases that they endure by virtue of being immigrants in a post-9/11 U.S. society?

The Nguyens' situation is complicated by their economic status, another component of their external context. Prior to Hurricane Katrina, they were making a living in the shrimp industry. They had few bills and no debt; however, they had no medical insurance. On those rare occasions when they required medical attention, they were able to use community public health resources. In the aftermath of Hurricane Katrina and the tough economic times that followed, numerous public, nonprofit health agencies were forced to close their doors, making it difficult for the Nguyens to access prenatal care. When their daughter was born with a birth defect, they found it necessary to travel to a larger city to receive care for her needs. Thus, they incurred transportation and lodging expenses, further affecting their delicate economic status.

Having lost their livelihood as shrimpers to Hurricane Katrina, the Nguyens were forced to look for work elsewhere. They were fortunate to have a rather large social support network as well as acquaintances who helped them find employment once retail outlets began to reopen in the months after the hurricane. Unfortunately, the retail jobs they found paid little more than minimum wages and did not include medical insurance. The Nguyens' educational background and minimal fluency in English made it difficult for them to pursue higher-paying jobs.

The Nguyens were also influenced by internal contextual factors—those factors that originate within the family and are accompanied by changes in the way the family functions. When they chose to leave their family and friends in Vietnam in order to move to the United States, the structure and definition of their family became less clear, particularly given the limited opportunities they had to return for visits. They also were forced to wrestle with issues related to caring for their aging parents. Once the Nguyens were living in the United States, their family structure changed further when they became parents themselves.

For the Nguyens, a relatively young couple, becoming parents could be considered a "normative" stressor—something normal, predictable, and developmental in nature. The stressor of becoming parents could also be considered volitional, as a degree of choice was involved. Conversely, nonnormative stressors are those that are unexpected. A catastrophic event such as Hurricane Katrina and all of its ramifications should certainly be classified as nonnormative. For the Nguyens, having a child with spina bifida is also a nonnormative and nonvolitional stressor, and its lasting implications make its presence chronic.

To ameliorate their situation, the Nguyens have several resources, derived from both internal and external contexts, on which they may rely. Although they left friends and family behind in order to move to the United States, they are members of a fairly large immigrant community in Mississippi. From this community, they receive a tremendous amount of social support. In addition, the Nguyens were able to use public community resources for health care and for other basic survival needs in the weeks and months after Hurricane Katrina. The Nguyens possess strengths such as initiative, resourcefulness, and a strong work ethic that have helped them to be resilient in the face of their stressors.

KEY CONCEPTS RELATED TO CRISIS

To help plan effective crisis response strategies, it is important to keep a number of key concepts in mind but to be aware that many of the terms used in the stress and crisis literature are used inconsistently, interchangeably, or without specificity (Boss, 2002). For example, in Western culture, the word *stress* is widely used to describe emotional phenomena ranging from feeling mild irritation and frustration to being frozen with fear. As the word relates to crises, however, it applies more to the ability to function than it does to affect. While the definitions of many terms seem intuitively obvious, some have unique connotations within the context of crisis intervention. In this section, key phrases and concepts used to describe crisis intervention theories and models are defined.

Stress

The term *stress* was introduced into medical literature by Han Selye (1956), to describe nonspecific responses of the human body to demands that are placed on it. Stress activates what Selye called the "general adaptation syndrome," which is associated with biological responses. Changes in hormonal patterns, such as increased production of adrenaline and cortisol, over time, may deplete the body's energy resources, impair the immune system, and lead to illness. Selye distinguished between two types of stress: (a) distress (i.e., changes that are perceived negatively) and (b) eustress (i.e., changes that are perceived positively). He noted that distress tends to cause more biological damage than eustress, the latter seeming to contribute to well-being. Thus, how stress is perceived has an effect on adaptation.

The terms *stress* and *crisis* often have been used interchangeably in the literature, thus creating a bit of confusion. Boss (2002), has attempted to distinguish between the two concepts, stating that stress is a continuous variable (i.e., stress may be measured by degree), whereas crisis is a dichotomous variable (i.e., there either is or is not a crisis). Stress may be thought of as a process that exists over time, such as the stress of having a loved one serving in the military in a hostile environment. In contrast, crisis may be thought of as a temporary period of time during which typical coping ceases and there is intense disorganization and disequilibrium. A family accustomed to coping with the stress of having a loved one serving in the military overseas may experience crisis when that individual returns home. The family's boundaries, structure, and coping mechanisms may have changed during the loved one's absence, leaving the family inadequately equipped to function with that loved one's homecoming.

Stress is defined as pressure or tension on an individual or family system. It is a response to demands brought about by a stressor event and represents a change in the equilibrium or steady state of an individual or family system (Boss, 2002; McKenry & Price, 2005; Selye, 1956). The degree of stress experienced hinges on perceptions of, and meanings attributed to, the stressor event. While anything with the potential to change some aspect of the individual or family (e.g., boundaries, roles, beliefs) might produce stress, increased stress levels do not necessarily always lead to crises. Often, stress can be managed, and the family or individual can arrive at a new steady state.

Trauma

Stressor events that involve trauma are powerful and overwhelming, and they threaten perceptions of safety and security. Some may be single incidents of relatively short-term duration, whereas others may occur over longer periods of time, resulting in prolonged exposure to the threatening stressor (Collins & Collins, 2005). According to the DSM–5 (American Psychiatric Association, 2013), a traumatic event involves threatened or actual death or serious injury, or a threat to the well-being of oneself or to another person. Traumatic events may be human-caused accidents or catastrophes, such as the 2003 ferry disaster in New York City. The ferry reportedly had not been running a straight course and struck a concrete pier while attempting to dock at the Staten Island end of its run. The crash killed 11 people and injured dozens of others. Other traumatic events include acts of deliberate cruelty. The multiple terrorist attacks on September 11, 2001; the bombing of the Alfred P. Murrah Federal Building in Oklahoma City in 1995; and school shootings such as those at Westside Middle School in Jonesboro, Arkansas; Columbine High School in Littleton, Colorado; Virginia Tech in Blacksburg, Virginia; and Chardon High School in Chardon, Ohio, all are examples of acts of deliberate human cruelty, as are the numerous homicides and sexual assaults that occur in the United States each year. Additional traumatic events include natural disasters—events such as Hurricane Floyd, which struck the Carolina coast in 1999 and resulted in 56 deaths; the F-5 tornado that left a trail of death and destruction in Oak Grove, Alabama, in 1998; the flood that occurred in Cedar Rapids, Iowa, in 2008; and the earthquake that resulted in tens of thousands of deaths in China in 2008.

Responses to Trauma

In general, people experiencing traumatic events respond with intense feelings of fear and helplessness (American Psychiatric Association, 2013). Most people respond to trauma within a normal range of reactions to abnormal events, whereby the individual's baseline is not disrupted to the point that causes impairment or dysfunction. Others become significantly distressed and impaired, and a few develop illnesses such as acute stress disorder (ASD) and post-traumatic stress disorder (PTSD). The risk for psychological disturbance tends to increase with the magnitude or intensity of the traumatic stressor and with the degree to which the event was human caused and intended to harm.

Following the Cocoanut Grove fire in 1942, practitioners began to become aware of "common reactions to abnormal events" that do not necessarily constitute psychiatric illnesses. Reactions to traumatic events typically include physical, behavioral, cognitive, emotional, and spiritual responses, which tend to occur in stages, but ultimately are temporary. These transient reactions are often referred to as reactions to post-traumatic stress. Physical responses involve the autonomic nervous system as the person prepares to "fight or flee" and may be experienced through symptoms such as palpitations, shortness of breath, nausea, muscle tension, headaches, and fatigue. Behaviorally, individuals may experience sleep and dietary changes, social withdrawal, purposeful avoidance of or attention to reminders of the trauma, changes in relationships, and increased use of alcohol or other mood-altering substances. Cognitive responses include rumination, preoccupation, forgetfulness, and difficulty concentrating. Emotional responses include distress, anxiety, impatience, irritability, anger, and symptoms of depression. Finally, spiritual responses are centered on existential questions and attempts to find meaning in the traumatic event. These reactions may transpire over a period as long as two years, but they are not considered pathological.

While most people return to a level of equilibrium and healthy functioning following a reaction to traumatic stress, some may experience consequences that impair their ability to function. Many of these individuals experience two of the traumatic stress-related anxiety disorders described in the DSM-5 (American Psychiatric Association, 2013): acute stress disorder (ASD) and post-traumatic stress disorder (PTSD). These two disorders are similar in their symptomology and differ mainly in their temporal association with exposure to the traumatic event. According to the DSM-5, the diagnostic criteria for ASD and PTSD include hyperarousal (hypervigilance, difficulty concentrating, exaggerated startle responses, sleep disturbance), reexperiencing (flashbacks, nightmares, intrusive thoughts), and avoidance (attempts to avoid reminders of the traumatic event, inability to recall components of the event, detachment, dissociation, restricted affect)—symptoms that lead to distress and impairment in key areas of functioning such as work and interpersonal relationships. If these symptoms appear within one month of exposure to the trauma, ASD is diagnosed. If exposure to the traumatic event occurred more than a month prior to the development of these symptoms, PTSD is diagnosed. If symptoms persist for more than three months, PTSD is considered chronic.

Coping

Since crisis is defined as what happens when usual coping strategies fail, it is important to examine the term *coping*, which may be defined as any behavioral or cognitive action that is taken in an effort to manage stress. In general, coping is considered a process

(Lazarus, 1993). The process begins with an appraisal of a stressor and its potential for harm. If the situation is perceived as challenging or threatening (as opposed to irrelevant), further assessment takes place to determine what responses are possible and what their potential outcomes might be. Responses to stress fall into three broad categories: problem-focused coping, emotion-focused coping, and avoidant coping (Lazarus, 1993; Linley & Joseph, 2004).

Problem-focused coping involves taking direct behavioral actions to change or modify aspects of the environment that are thought to be the causes of stress. When this type of coping strategy is employed, efforts are made to define the problem, generate possible solutions, weigh alternatives in terms of their costs and benefits, choose an alternative plan, and act. Emotion-focused coping, on the other hand, is more likely to be used in situations deemed unlikely to change. The aim of such coping is to reduce affective arousal so that the stressful situation may be tolerated, and it generally involves cognitive processes that change the meaning of a stressor or create emotional distance from it. Avoidance-focused coping, the third type of response to stress, may be viewed as a subset of emotion-focused coping, in which responses such as distraction or diversion are employed to avoid the stressor and the emotions that would be associated with it.

Coping may lead to successful or unsuccessful, adaptive or maladaptive outcomes. Following the experience of a traumatic stress event, for example, some individuals may choose to increase their alcohol consumption. While this behavior does little to address the needs brought about by the stressor, it may be an effective (albeit unhealthy) way to keep unwanted emotions at bay (McKenry & Price, 2005). Whether coping averts crisis and leads to adaptation depends on the particular person who is experiencing stress, the specific type of stress being encountered, and the features of the stressful encounter that the person attempts to manage (Lazarus, 1993). Although problem-focused, emotion-focused, and avoidance-focused coping have all been linked to adaptation or post-traumatic growth (Linley & Joseph, 2004), none of these approaches to coping guarantees a positive outcome. Problem-focused coping seems to be most valued in Western culture (Lazarus, 1993) yet it can be counterproductive if the situation that is causing stress is unalterable. If the stressor is unalterable, problem-focused efforts fail and distress is likely to persist. In such times, emotion-focused coping might be the better option. Avoidance-focused coping is least likely to result in adaptation or growth and most likely to lead to impaired well-being (Linley & Joseph, 2004).

Adaptation

Adaptation—an outcome of stress or crisis—is the degree to which functioning has changed over an extended period of time and may be measured by the fit between the individual or family system and the environment. Some individuals and families benefit from the challenges of adversity (Linley & Joseph, 2004). Successfully dealing with adversity often results in an outcome that is better than one that might have been reached without the adversity. Many individuals and families change to the point where they have the resources to meet the demands of stressors while continuing to grow. Some researchers have referred to this positive outcome as stress-related growth (Park, Cohen, & Murch, 1996) or post-traumatic growth (Tedeschi & Calhoun, 2004). Quite often, changes have occurred in functional behaviors such as rules, roles, boundaries, and interpersonal communication patterns, resulting in families being better equipped to meet the challenges of future stressors. Conversely, for some individuals and families, an imbalance continues between stress demands and the capability to meet those demands. Many families may adopt unhealthy and unproductive responses to stress. Unhealthy coping behaviors, such as addictions or domestic violence, result in additional stress. Furthermore, it is often the case that coping behaviors that appear to be healthy contribute to stress. A parent, for example, might take a second job in order to increase the family's financial resources. Working extra hours, however, removes that parent from the home and may contribute to strained family relationships and a decrease in other nontangible resources.

Resilience

Individuals or families that bounce back from adversity are considered to have resilience. There are three distinct types of phenomena that are included in discussions of resilience: better than expected outcomes in high-risk groups of people, effective functioning that is sustained even under highly adverse conditions, and effective functioning that is regained or recovered after trauma (Masten & Obradovic, 2008). Numerous studies have attempted to identify factors that determine these outcomes. Although there has been some confusion in the literature about whether to conceptualize resilience as a personal trait or as a dynamic process (Luthar, Cicchetti, & Becker, 2000), the prevailing viewpoint favors process. Thus, resilience may be defined as the dynamics that contribute to positive adaptation following exposure to experiences that have the potential to disrupt functioning (Luthar, Cicchetti, & Becker, 2000; Masten & Obradovic, 2008)

Early studies of resilience focused on individuals with schizophrenia and factors that would predict the course of the illness for them, but most research through which the concept has been studied and developed has focused on children experiencing adversity. Among the multiple adverse conditions studied have been parental mental illness, chronic illness, poverty, community violence, abuse, and catastrophic events (Luthar et al., 2000). Through these studies, a variety of concepts have been identified as protective factors that operate to ensure resilience. For the most part, these factors involve relationships (Luthar, 2006).

Masten and Obradovic (2008) summarized several fundamental adaptive systems that seem to make a difference in human resilience. Beginning in early childhood, adaptation and the likelihood of resilience seems to depend on the quality of relationships with attachment figures. Attachments that are described as "secure" seem to moderate anxiety by allowing children to feel confident, connected, and reassured. As secure, confident children mature, they develop competence, self-efficacy, and mastery. Mastery develops as individuals learn they can interact successfully with their environments. In times of adversity, those with mastery motivation are likely to persist in their efforts to manage the environment.

Related to mastery is the ability to apply cognitive skills to solving problems. People who are resilient seem to be better at applying cognitive skills during times of adversity than those who are less well adapted. During times of high stress or threat of harm, it is important to be able to continue to think and plan effective responses. Thinking and problem solving during stressful situations are enhanced when emotions, arousal, and attention are self-regulated (Masten & Obradovic, 2008).

Being a part of larger social systems also seems to play a role in resilience. Social groups and networks provide resources such as information and support that are important in dealing with adversity. For children, attending school provides opportunities to acquire knowledge, develop social skills, and pratice self-regulation, all resources that might be called for in times of stress. For older children, adolescents, and adults, being part of friendship networks, clubs, work groups, or civic organizations also has the potential to contribute to resilience. Among the larger systems most studied are religion and spirituality. Religious and spirtual connections provide attachment-like relationships and social support, as well as opportunities to practice self-regulation through prayer and meditation (Masten & Obradovic, 2008). In addition, religious and spiritual beliefs influence the way people attribute meaning to stressful situations and events and contribute to post-traumatic growth (Gerber, Boals, & Schuettler, 2011).

Whether individuals experiencing adverse conditions demonstrate resilience depends on the operation of protective systems that have evolved through biology and culture (Masten & Obradovic, 2008). If the systems are operating normally, the capacity for resilience is optimal; if they are damaged, the potential for resilience is compromised.

VOICES FROM THE FIELD 1.2
Human Resiliency in the Aftermath of Katrina

Beth Graney

Landing in the New Orleans airport six weeks after Hurricane Katrina devastated the coastal areas was the first of many eerie and unsettling sites we were to experience over the next two weeks. Six school counselors from our county were given permission to volunteer with the Red Cross Disaster effort to provide counseling to victims of the hurricane. Our mission, or so we thought, was to offer assistance to school-aged children. However, upon arriving we quickly found that the Red Cross had different ideas. Due to the devastation caused by the hurricane, most children were still with parents in shelters throughout Louisiana and other states.

As a Licensed Professional Counselor (LPC), I was able to function as a counselor/therapist; however, "my office" was outside, at a drive-through Red Cross site handing out food and cleaning supplies to folks who had lost their homes or were beginning the clean-up process. As cars came through we offered people advice on safety issues for cleaning up mold, pamphlets on medical concerns typical after a devastating event, and warning signs of depression and other mental health concerns. The days were long and hot with a steady stream of cars from 7 a.m. to 6 p.m. or later. From the beginning I enjoyed talking

to people, listening to their experiences, sharing their pain, but at first I wasn't clear about how I was offering counseling or mental health assistance.

Yet as the days passed I noticed that many of the people came again and again and each time I heard a little more of their story. Some days a person seemed pretty upbeat only to come back later in the day with tears, anger, or frustration at the bureaucracy involved in getting anything meaningful accomplished. I heard stories of amazing escapes from the hurricane or the flooding from the levees bursting. People told me how they witnessed great acts of selflessness and heroism—stories that never made the papers. Others talked of all they lost: "I don't even have one picture of my three kids," "I not only lost my house, my possessions, my car, but my job too," "All of my important medical papers are gone as well as all of my insurance information." Most heartbreaking were the loss of friends and relatives: "I still can't reach my daughter," "My mother died because she wouldn't leave her house." One woman was trying to find a place to continue her chemotherapy treatment from breast cancer while another talked about leaving with her son who was a quadriplegic and trying to replace important medical equipment she could not bring when she left.

(Continued)

Yet, each day, there was laughter and happiness in spite of the hurricane, because people had survived and so they could begin again. At times, people pulled their car out of the line so we could talk in-depth about their situation—not for answers necessarily, just for a few brief moments to allow themselves to grieve before they got back in line to pick up yet another bottle of bleach and a new mop to continue their clean-up.

I learned many things about people and how they come to terms with hardship, loss and devastation. First hand, I learned that Maslow was right: people's primary needs such as food, clothing, shelter and safety must first be met before they can deal with higher level emotional needs. I learned that people can and do survive against overwhelming odds and the most difficult of circumstances. Often they do so with great resolve, courage and even optimism. Quickly I noted that most people were able to deal with the loss of their possessions because they realized they could have lost the important people in their lives. Humor along with revisiting past success was the most commonly used strategies to deal with the hardship people were experiencing. I learned that normalizing sadness, fear, grief, and many other emotions comforted people more than I would have expected and that even in the most difficult times, most people see humor and joy in life.

On the trip home, my colleagues and I, after lots tears and discussion, individually and collectively came to the conclusion that people really are resilient and go on to become stronger through difficult times. As for me, I learned that I can sleep on a cot with 80 other people snoring and coughing in the same room. I can go a day without a shower; I can eat a meal from the ERVE (Red Cross Emergency Response Vehicle); and I can stand on my feet for 12 hours a day in hot weather! I learned that, just like the people who survived the storm, you bond with those who have responded to the same disaster because no one else fully understands what you have experienced. Most of all, I learned that I am more resilient than I knew and sometimes the best, most helpful counseling does not take place in a nice quiet office!

CRISIS INTERVENTION AS A UNIQUE FORM OF COUNSELING

Crisis intervention is a unique form of counseling, distinguished from other forms of counseling by its purpose, setting, time, and intervention plan. The American Counseling Association (2011) defines counseling as a professional relationship that empowers diverse individuals, families, and groups to accomplish mental health, wellness, education, and career goals. While crisis intervention does not stray from this definition, the ways in which relationships are formed, clients are empowered, or goals are accomplished often seem divergent from other forms of counseling. It is sometimes the case that crisis intervention occurs within counseling relationships that are ongoing. For example, a client who already has an established relationship with a counselor in a school or agency may reveal suicidal ideation, making it necessary for the counselor to adjust to a crisis intervention strategy. At other times, crisis intervention occurs between counselors and clients who do not already know each other. Disaster mental health counselors respond by going to sites where catastrophes have occurred and meeting new clients in these environments. Typically, there is only one meeting, which may be as brief as a few minutes and will likely occur in a chaotic setting with minimal privacy. Whether working in an office or in the field, within established counseling relationships or new ones, the crisis counselor's goal is the safety and stability of clients—that is, working toward restoring equilibrium. Once the client is safe and stable, other forms of counseling may be initiated or resumed. Consider, as an analogy, a car accident in which an individual may have experienced a severe medical trauma. It is essential for the EMT to stabilize the patient to prevent further injuries prior to transferring (referring) the patient to a surgeon at the hospital.

Traditional counseling is typically a scheduled event that lasts for a specific period of time (e.g., a 45- to 50-minute session), and it is expected to consist of more than one such session over a period of time. Traditional counseling sessions take place in mental health agencies, private practices, hospitals, correctional facilities, residential facilities, and other locations related to mental health services (Gladding, 2010).

Because crisis is not a scheduled event, crisis intervention thus happens at the spur of the moment. While crisis intervention can take place in nearly any counseling setting, it has much broader borders—taking place in one's home (e.g., after a child is reported missing), a makeshift shelter (e.g., after a hurricane), an emergency room (e.g., after a rape), or any one of numerous other contexts.

ROLES OF AND COLLABORATION BETWEEN MENTAL HEALTH WORKERS DURING CRISIS

Most individuals who work in mental health professions are familiar with basic counseling skills that can help clients adapt during crises or stressful situations. The brief descriptions that follow here illustrate how different mental health professionals—including professional counselors, psychiatrists, psychologists, social workers, paraprofessionals, and hotline workers—can be helpful in crisis situations.

Professional Counselors

In practice, professional counselors differ from psychiatrists and psychologists in that they work from a prevention point of view. Such counselors often work through advocacy and collaboration and play a vital role in a comprehensive crisis leadership team (Kerr, 2009). Professional counselors can provide short-term or long-term therapy and may work with individuals or groups. Similar to psychologists, many professional counselors may diagnose and treat mental and emotional disorders. Overall, this group of mental health professionals will need a minimum of a master's degree to become licensed to practice (Gladding & Newsome, 2010). Professional counselors can assist individuals in crisis situations by

- Helping them to gain insight into the ways crisis affects their lives in a cognitive, behavioral, and emotional manner over a lengthy period of time.
- Providing specific treatment goals and objectives related to crisis.
- Monitoring and assessing the magnitude of severity of a crisis situation.
- Providing insight into co-occurring mental and emotional disorders and crisis (e.g., showing a client diagnosed with bipolar disorder how to cope with and monitor crisis).
- Providing specific crisis intervention strategies during a crisis and over a period of time.
- Providing clients in crisis with resources and preventative measures.
- Assisting in alleviating symptoms associated with the crisis.
- Preparing clients to handle future crises.

Some professional counselors bring various types of expertise in crisis intervention to their work, as these examples illustrate:

- Marriage and family counselors work from a systemic perspective. They provide support for couples and families and may involve the family in the resolution of the crisis on a short- and long-term basis.

- Pastoral counselors provide religious or spiritual integration in times of a crisis. Often, a crisis involves a spiritual or religious disconnect or dimension that must be explored. It is also important to understand any religious or spiritual coping mechanisms that were effective in the past that could be applied to the present crisis. Certainly the notion of incorporating spirituality into crisis intervention has an abundance of benefits and is not the sole property of pastoral counselors. All counselors would want to explore how one's religious and spiritual beliefs can provide solace in times of crises.
- Chemical dependency counselors specifically address the use of drugs and alcohol as a coping mechanism during crisis.
- Professional counselors who specialize in treating children, adolescents, adults, or geriatric populations bring a developmental perspective to the conceptualization and treatment of crisis.
- School counselors work to maximize student achievement and to "promote equity and access to opportunities and rigorous educational experiences for all students" as well as helping to facilitate "a safe learning environment and work[ing] to safeguard the human rights of all members of the school community" (American School Counselor Association, 2008, p. 2). School counselors can be helpful in school crisis situations by using individual counseling, group counseling, and classroom guidance activities and by collaborating with key stakeholders. Individual counseling can be helpful to those who are directly affected by crisis (e.g., by working with a student on expressing feelings after his or her house caught on fire). Providing group counseling to those who have been exposed to crisis (e.g., by establishing a support group for students who have divorced parents) could ease the pain of the initial impact of the crisis and create a support network among the group members. School counselors may provide primary or secondary preventative programs via classroom guidance activities on crisis, suicide, handling stress, self-regulation, and communication skills. Lastly, school counselors may collaborate with school system personnel as well as with parents, families, and members of the community on preventing and responding to crisis (e.g., by providing school staff with materials and training on recognizing suicidal behavior).

Psychiatrists

As noted earlier in this chapter, much of the early work in the field of crisis intervention was done by two psychiatrists working in the Boston area in the 1940s. According to the American Psychiatric Association (2008), psychiatrists are physicians who have obtained specific training and experience in treating mental and emotional disorders. The key difference between the scope of practice of psychiatrists and that of other mental health practitioners is that psychiatrists can prescribe medication to clients.

> Psychiatrists are especially suited to triaging direct and indirect victims in various settings, such as on consultation in hospitals' emergency rooms, intensive care and burn units, general medical floors or inpatient psychiatry units. Or psychiatrists may volunteer for agencies such as the American Red Cross, where they may be part of a mental health team providing grief support, notification of death to family members, or crisis intervention. (American Psychiatric Association, 2004, p. 21)

Psychologists

Clinical and counseling psychologists are mental health practitioners who engage in the assessment, diagnosis, and treatment of mental and emotional disorders. To be licensed to practice, state licensure boards require completion of the doctoral degree. In a few areas of the United States, including New Mexico and Louisiana, and in the Indian Health Service and the military, where access to psychiatrists is often limited, psychologists with specific training may prescribe medication. With regard to their participation in crisis intervention, much of their work is identical to that of professional counselors.

Social Workers

Social workers engaged in crisis intervention also function in a manner similar to professional counselors. Depending on the scope and focus of their of practice, some social workers may be employed after earning a bachelor's degree, while other, more specialized clinical practice settings may require a master's degree. Although performing many of the same duties as counselors, social workers are well equipped to concentrate on the resource needs of their clients.

Paraprofessionals

Some individuals within the mental health community have limited formal education and training, in the professional mental health field but they perform essential tasks (e.g., case management duties, residential care) for individuals in crisis. Paraprofessionals can

- Manage resources that help facilitate stabilization (e.g., make sure clients keep all medical, financial, emotional, environmental, and social service appointments).
- Ensure clients are aware of appropriate resources that could be seen as preventative actions to crisis (e.g., make sure that a client has appropriate resources to pay a natural gas bill to have heat in the winter).
- Provide an outlet for clients to decrease isolation and talk to others (e.g., talk with individuals in crisis and provide assurance that someone cares for them and their situation).
- Participate in executing the modality and frequency aspects of the treatment plan—in other words, make the connections set out in the treatment plan. For example, the professional counselor may develop a treatment plan for someone in a residential program that involves attending Alcoholics Anonymous groups daily, attending a group on a specified psychosocial issue three times per week, and addressing a medical issue. The paraprofessional case worker may be responsible for following through with the treatment plan by assisting the client in making the appointments and setting up transportation to the appointments or groups.

To be effective, a crisis worker, whether a professional or a paraprofessional, must be able to (a) rely on life experiences and emotional maturity to remain stable and consistent, (b) remain calm and poised in order to de-escalate the situation, (c) use creativity and flexibility to adapt to rapidly changing situations, (d) maintain energy and resilience to keep up with the rigor of working in a crisis situation, and (e) use effective clinical skills in a timely fashion in order to create a trusting and safe environment and suspend one's values just for the crisis time in order to stabilize the client and refer him

ACTIVITY 1.1
Who Does What and Why?

In the crisis situations that follow, what might be some activities, interventions, responsibilities, and considerations for each of the mental health professionals discussed earlier?

Crisis Situation 1

Alan and Mary have been married for 3 years. Alan has been cheating on Mary for the past 6 months, and Mary has been cheating on Alan for the past year. Each is unaware of the other's infidelity, but the stress in their house is severe. They yell constantly, and Mary throws objects during arguments. In the past month, Alan has begun to slap Mary during these arguments. Last night Alan hit her so hard that he knocked her unconscious. Mary is now in the hospital talking to a social worker: "I'm afraid of my husband," Mary says, "but I don't have anywhere else to go. I feel so alone."

Crisis Situation 2

John F. Kennedy High School, located in a primarily low- to middle-class rural community, comprises approximately 1,000 students, most of whom know one another. Within the past 4 months, the school has been evacuated five times as a result of a call

indicating that there is a bomb in the building and that "everyone should get out." As a result of these threats and evacuations, students are scared, parents do not want to send their children to school, and teachers and other school personnel are frightened to go to work. Students also have begun to accuse each other of calling in the bomb threats, and several students have been ostracized and bullied. The Parent Teacher Organization has called a meeting tonight to address this issue.

Crisis Situation 3

Walter Taylor is a 74-year-old African American male who has worked all of his life as a plumber. He has been married to his wife, Martha, for 52 years and has four children and six grandchildren. Due to intense flash floods within the past week from melting snow, the Taylor household is 7 feet under water. When the water came, Walter, his 40-year-old daughter June, and his 13-year-old granddaughter Beverly had to be rescued from their house by boat. Walter's house is destroyed, Beverly is having nightmares and does not want to leave her family, and June is recovering from a head trauma caused while being evacuated.

or her on to another professional (James, 2008). Keep these characteristics in mind as you complete Activity 1.1.

Hotline Workers

Hotline workers are often the first point of contact for many individuals experiencing a crisis and may handle any number of crises resulting from suicidal and homicidal ideation, domestic violence, substance abuse, and sexual assault. There are hotlines that specialize in specific crisis situations such as those mentioned previously. There are even crisis hotlines for specific age groups (e.g., a hotline dedicated to teen callers). Typically, hotline workers are not mental health professionals but volunteers who have undergone specific training in responding to crises. No matter what their focus, crisis hotlines play a vital role in assessing, intervening in, and preventing the occurrence of crises. Crisis hotline workers perform essential tasks during a crisis situation:

- They assess the severity of the crisis situation and the lethality of the caller.
- They provide immediate crisis intervention to the caller in an attempt to de-escalate the crisis. This is critical in a crisis situation because the caller does not have to

TABLE 1.1 Toll-Free Hotlines

General Crisis Intervention Hotlines for Youth (dealing with conflicts, family stressors, suicide, runaway youth, drugs and alcohol, homelessness, and so on)

- Boys Town Suicide and Crisis Line: 800-448-3000 (voice) / 800-448-1833 (TDD)
- Covenant House Hotline: 800-999-9999
- National Youth Crisis Hotline: 800-442-HOPE

Child Abuse Hotlines

- ChildHelp USA National Child Abuse Hotline: 800-4-A-CHILD (voice) / 800-2-A-CHILD (TDD)
- National Child Abuse Hotline: 800-25-ABUSE

Domestic Violence Hotlines

- National Domestic Violence/Child Abuse/Sexual Abuse Hotline: 800-799-SAFE (voice) / 800-787-3224 (TDD) / 800-942-6908 (Spanish speaking)
- Domestic Violence Hotline: 800-829-1122

Substance Abuse/Alcoholism Hotlines

- Alateen: 800-352-9996
- National Cocaine Hotline: 800-COCAINE
- National Drug Information Treatment and Referral Hotline: 800-662-HELP

Poison Control Hotline

- Poison Control: 800-362-9922

Rape Hotline

- National Rape Crisis Hotline: 800-656-4673

Suicide Prevention Hotlines

- National Suicide Hotline: 800-SUICIDE (voice) / 800-799-4TTY (TDD)
- National Suicide Prevention Lifeline: 800-273-TALK / 888-628-9454 (Spanish speaking)

make an appointment with a professional or wait to get help. Most hotlines are 24-hour services open 365 days a year.
- They provide resources to the caller that may help resolve the crisis. Table 1.1 presents a selection of toll-free hotlines that serve those in crisis.

FUNDAMENTALS OF WORKING WITH CLIENTS IN CRISIS

The procedures for working with clients in crisis begin with determining, based on assessment efforts, how best to approach such individuals to de-escalate the crisis. In other words, there is a need to assess whether the situation calls for counselors to be directive, nondirective, or collaborative.

Directive approaches call for counselors to "direct" or lead the person in crisis in a specific direction. Clients in crisis are typically scattered and unable to plan beyond their current situation. Therefore, providing some form of direction may help. For example, if someone is highly uncertain, spontaneous, or ambiguous and, at the same time, unable to get out of a crisis state, providing direction could provide immediate, though temporary, relief to feelings surrounding the crisis situation.

Nondirective approaches allow the person in crisis to come up with the directives while the crisis counselor facilitates that process. If the client can make rational decisions, even though a state of crisis exists, a nondirective approach may empower the client to make progress toward de-escalation. For example, asking clients who are recent flood victims "What might be of most help to you now?" allows them to respond with specifics, rather than having the counselor guess what is needed. The thought process and response of such clients may also empower them and allow them to feel they are regaining some control over their own lives.

A collaborative approach focuses on showing the person in crisis that the counselor is a participant in the journey toward stabilization and normalcy, and that others can provide help, decrease isolation, and increase resource allocation. Collaborative approaches are considered a blending of directive and nondirective approaches—but with a flavor of togetherness. In other words, a collaborative approach provides support and a sense of working together toward a common goal.

Now complete Activity 1.2 to gain practice identifying these various approaches.

ACTIVITY 1.2

Examples of directive, nondirective, and collaborative approaches in crisis situations follow. Discuss how each could be an appropriate statement in specific circumstances.

Example 1

- Please put the gun down. (*directive*)
- Why don't you want to put the gun down? (*nondirective*)
- I want to help, but knowing you have that gun in your hand scares me. Can you put the gun down for me so I can help you more? (*collaborative*)

Example 2

- Try to calm down. (*directive*)
- What's the best way for you to calm down? (*nondirective*)
- Boy, I'm really upset. Let's try and calm down for a bit. (*collaborative*)

Example 3

- I'm going to call the police. (*directive*)
- Do you think calling the police will help? (*nondirective*)
- If I bring you the phone, would you call the police? (*collaborative*)

VOICES FROM THE FIELD 1.3
Chardon High School

Jason McGlothlin
The day after the shooting at Chardon High School in February 2012, I volunteered to work with the students who witnessed the shooting and their families. I met with two students for about an hour and a half each

and a family for about two hours. I listened to their graphic and detailed reports of what happened and saw the tears they shed. I heard the worries they had about returning to the school and the condolences for their classmates who were injured and dead. I heard the

(Continued)

countless statements of reaching out to others and of "I hope _____ is okay" and "I need to call _____'s family." I share this story not to discuss what I did but the effect it had on me. Listening and seeing such tragedy, such raw emotion and devastation, had a great impact on me not only as a professional but personally as well. I remember coming home that day and giving my 6-year-old an extra long hug and listening to him explain the shooting because his teachers talked about it at his school.

However, seeing these students reach out to others and care for their community instilled in me a sense of hope. The notion of self-care, burnout prevention, and taking care of self is critical. However, crisis intervention is a rollercoaster of emotions for counselors. Counselors quickly become immersed in the emotional state of the crisis, and then leave. We all need to find the unique way we can take care of ourselves.

COMPLICATIONS OF COUNSELORS RESPONDING TO CRISIS

There is an old saying that exists in the field of counseling: "If you haven't had a client in crisis, then you haven't worked with clients long." Complications of working in crisis situations and with clients in crisis can take a physical, emotional, and professional toll on crisis counselors. It is important when reading the remainder of this text to consider the various options of self-care while helping others manage a crisis—proactive ways to avoid burnout, to manage personal emotions during highly emotional crisis situations (e.g., when working with suicidal clients), and to ensure optimal physical, cognitive, and psychological presence for working with clients in crisis. Working with others in a state of crisis is not easy. Crisis counselors need to stay abreast of their own well-being in order to help others.

Summary

A crisis is a situation with a precipitating stressor event, a perception of that event that leads to distress, and diminished functioning when the distress is not relieved by familiar coping resources. Many individuals and families are resilient and benefit from having met the challenges of a crisis situation. How well an individual or family adapts following a crisis is often determined not only by the nature of the stressor event itself but also by the presence or absence of other stressors, the availability of tangible and intangible resources, and how the entire situation is perceived. Crises may be provoked by predictable events that occur during normal, developmental transitions during the lives of individuals and families or by situational events that often are sudden and unexpected.

Crisis intervention begins with an assessment of the provoking event, reactions and responses to the provoking event, and other contextual variables that influence the situation. While there are times when a crisis counselor's response to a crisis appears indistinguishable from traditional counseling, crisis intervention generally is thought to be quite different from traditional counseling. Paraprofessionals and professionals from a variety of helping disciplines provide crisis intervention services, often working in teams where each helper may focus on a particular area of expertise. Working with clients in crisis places helpers at risk for vicarious trauma and burnout. The work is difficult, but the rewards are immeasurable.

Safety and Self-Care in Crisis Situations

Charlotte Daughhetee

PREVIEW

When responding to a crisis, counselors need to be able to act promptly; thus, crisis preparedness is essential to best practice during emergency situations. A vital part of crisis preparedness is attention to counselor safety and security. This chapter presents an overview of safety and security procedures along with a discussion of burnout, compassion fatigue, vicarious trauma, resiliency, and counselor self-care concerns. A major component of best practice for counselors is attention to their own safety and well-being. This is especially true during the stress of crisis.

SAFETY CONCERNS AND PRECAUTIONS

In addition to its emotional and psychological toll, a crisis event produces many safety and security concerns. Crisis planning and preparedness can facilitate a coordinated response among various crisis response units to mitigate further suffering for crisis survivors and to generate a safe environment for crisis workers. Basic safety precautions on the part of the crisis counselor when working with high-risk or dangerous clients can reduce the chances of harm to the counselor, client, crisis workers, and others. The ultimate success of crisis intervention, whether it involves responding to one suicidal client or to thousands of hurricane survivors, depends on planning and on the training and preparedness of team members.

Proactive Approaches

Although some people are naturally inclined toward preparedness and plan for every reasonable contingency, most people might intend to get around to emergency planning but never seem to follow through with the preparations. Schools, institutions, and communities do not have the luxury of putting off the development of a crisis plan. When a crisis event occurs, particularly a large-scale disaster that affects many people, crisis teams must be ready, with roles defined and each person trained in his or her role. McConnell and Drennan (2006) state that "we need to give serious consideration to strong, well-resourced and forward thinking contingency planning if we want to tame and gain control over a crisis when it hits" (p. 59). However, while crises have huge impacts on systems and communities, they are usually low-priority items with respect to planning and resources. The Federal Emergency Management Agency (FEMA) stresses that crisis planning is an ongoing cycle of planning, organizing, training, evaluating, and improving. An effective crisis team is one that coordinates and collaborates throughout both planning and crisis response. FEMA provides helpful information about crisis planning on their website http://www.fema.gov/, and Chapters 10 and 11 of this text have additional information on emergency preparedness and response.

Safety Issues

As part of a crisis team, counselors contribute to the success of crisis intervention through collaboration with other crisis workers. Ultimately, this collaborative spirit enhances public safety. Even as they are working to achieve public safety, crisis counselors must also be aware of their own safety and take proactive steps to ensure a secure counseling environment.

INTERACTION WITH LOCAL AUTHORITIES   A crisis team comprises workers from across the community who come together in response to a crisis event. Mental health providers are an essential component of any crisis team, and all members of a crisis response team should work together toward the same goal, which is to advance the recovery process following a disaster. Survivors of crises need access to medical care, food and water, shelter, mental health services, basic safety, and sometimes religious/spiritual connections; the realization of recovery is possible only when there is interagency cooperation. It is important to remember that each crisis worker has a unique role. In the event of large-scale property damage, the safety and security of the area will be maintained by law enforcement, in some cases with the assistance of National Guard troops. Firefighters and medical personnel provide rescue and first aid assistance and

---

ACTIVITY 2.1

In small groups, discuss the following questions. If a natural disaster such as a tornado or earthquake hits your area today, would you be prepared? Would you have enough food and water for at least three days, a battery-operated radio, flashlights, candles, extra batteries, and so on? Do you have cash and gas in the car in case you must evacuate? Are you prepared? Why or why not? What other aspects need to be taken into account in preparing for this type of disaster? In general, do you think the citizens in your community are prepared for such a disaster? How does the level of community preparedness affect crisis intervention?

VOICES FROM THE FIELD 2.1

Managing Reactions to Clients' Traumatic Experiences

Victoria E. Kress

One Friday afternoon during rush hour, I was stopped at a red light when I noticed a young man sitting in the car next to me. He appeared to be very happy; he was singing along to the radio and playing air drums on his dashboard. I thought to myself, "Why is he so happy? He's sitting there in that Toyota Camry, maybe headed to happy hour, and seemingly oblivious to what is going on in the world all around him. If he understood what was really going on in this world, he would back off the air drums."

By nature, I am an optimistic, positive person. How, why, and from where had these thoughts emerged? Three months earlier I had started a new job as a counselor at a residential intensive treatment center for adolescents and children. All of my clients had experienced multiple instances of sexual, physical, and verbal abuse, and neglect by their families. Nothing could have prepared me for the horror stories to which I was exposed. For example, earlier that week, one of my client's trauma narratives was particularly difficult to listen to as it involved sexual abuse by seven different people, including her mother who would hold her down as she was raped. All of this occurred before the age of six years. Also, earlier that day, I found out that the father of my client made a plea deal with the court and would only have to serve three years in prison despite having sexually abused my client since the age of four years. As the counselor, I had to convey this information to my client on Monday morning. How do you explain to a child that a lifetime of humiliation and pain translated into a mere three years in prison in the eyes of the criminal justice system?

The frustration I felt with the perpetrators and the systems that were supposed to keep children safe was, at that point, palpable. My schemas or views on the world, and my assumptions about justice and fairness had been shaken. At this point, I had an important task to tackle: I had to integrate the cold realities of the world (e.g., how humans are capable of behaving, the public justice system's limitations) into my personal belief system so I could be most helpful to my clients. To help my clients, I had to be hopeful and optimistic, yet appropriately realistic. I needed to value the guy in the car next to me playing the air drums.

Many years later, I specialize in—and love—counseling trauma survivors. For me personally, I have found that the following three strategies help me to stay balanced in doing this work. First, behaviorally in my day-to-day life, I make sure I have regular experiences with those who are healthy and well, and in adaptive situations to remind myself that most people are good and that change is always around the corner. I also try to do at least one thing each day that is relaxing, fun, or creative. Second, cognitively, I stay connected with the experiences of people who have endured traumatic experiences and are thriving and doing well. And I hold to a belief that people are resilient and that most people who endure traumatic experiences do not develop long-term affects; rather they will move ahead and thrive. And third, spiritually, I stay anchored by believing that all negative experiences help us to grow and become stronger. They build character and help us clarify our values. They impart or help us create meaning in our lives. They deepen our ability to connect with others and with all of humanity. And ultimately they help us better understand our fragility, and thus accept what we can and cannot control.

collaborate with crisis counselors by referring clients in need of mental health evaluation services. It is important for crisis counselors to understand that during the initial impact of a crisis, the most critical needs correspond to the physiological and safety needs in Maslow's hierarchy of needs—shelter, food, water, and safety as well as the need to be connected with family. Mental health providers are used at this time to assess clients in order to prevent further personal crises stemming from the disaster, but specific clients often do not need the services of these mental health professionals until weeks or even a longer period after the onset of the crisis.

It is essential that counselors be culturally sensitive and demonstrate cultural awareness, knowledge, and skills. Different cultures may react to crisis situations in different ways behaviorally, psychologically, and emotionally. Some cultural groups may distrust government agencies, which can complicate rapport building. Cultural stigmas may cause some clients to be reluctant to seek mental health care when they are in crisis. In addition, socioeconomic status has a profound effect on crisis survivors, with low-income clients often having few or no resources beyond immediate disaster aid. In order for effective crisis intervention to take place, multicultural factors must be considered in the triage and treatment of clients in crisis.

Dykeman (2005) notes that culture affects both counselor and client responses to crisis. It is important for counselors to be aware of their own culture and worldview and to confront their cultural assumptions and biases. To be effective, they must build rapport and communicate understanding. Multiculturally competent counselors are able to appreciate differences and to work with clients and client communities to identify resources. Crisis affects entire communities, and counselors should enter affected communities with a spirit of collaboration while seeking to form respectful cooperative partnerships with community leaders. In this way, counselors can better understand the unique needs of the community (West-Olatunji & Goodman, 2011).

CASE STUDY 2.1

Crisis Counseling in a Rural Community

Bill is a counselor newly trained in disaster mental health. He has been living and working in a large city, and so far his experience in crisis intervention has been based in an urban area, where he has provided crisis intervention after an apartment fire and at a school following the death of a teacher. Recently, after horrific tornados tore through a rural community in another part of the state, Bill was dispatched to a small town, which for generations had served as the gathering place and community focal point for the surrounding farm families. The town has sustained extensive damage. About half of the buildings were wiped out, and every building left standing has been significantly damaged. The two churches and the local elementary school are gone. There was extensive loss of life (20% of the local population) including many children who were in the school when the tornado hit. Farms near the town experienced loss of livestock, barns, and crops. The small town/rural culture of this area sustained a severe blow. Also, because everyone knows everyone else in a small rural town, , all survivors have been affected by the grief and trauma of loss. While traveling to the site, Bill reflects upon the fact that he knows nothing about farming or rural life. He has never been on a farm, and he has never spent any time in a small town.

Discussion Questions

1. How can Bill better understand the culture of the population he is now encountering?
2. How might this culture be different from the urban culture Bill is used to?
3. What cultural assumptions or biases might Bill have about this culture?
4. What steps should he take to connect with the community?

SAFETY CONCERNS IN CRISIS COUNSELING   When clients are a danger to themselves and others, crisis counselors work in partnership with local authorities to ensure everyone's safety. Law enforcement is usually involved when a client presents a threat to public safety, as with high-threat homicidal and violent clients. Clients who pose a danger to themselves and others may need to be hospitalized (see Chapter 5 for information on voluntary and involuntary hospitalization). Counselors should not transport such clients to the hospital, and should instead enlist the client's family or friends if the client is low or moderate risk and is voluntarily entering an inpatient unit. A high-risk client who is being hospitalized involuntarily will likely need to be transported to the hospital by ambulance or by police. If a high-risk client suddenly leaves a counselor's office, the counselor should not attempt to physically stop the client and should notify law enforcement for assistance. Because counselors work closely with hospitals and medical personnel during intervention and treatment of suicidal and homicidal clients, a strong working relationship between mental health providers and local authorities is essential to effective crisis intervention. It is the policy of most police departments, during a transport of clients who are at risk, to restrain the person they are transporting for the safety of the client and the public as well as the police officer. Police officers are not counselors; their role is to protect the public. Chapter 5 of this text provides information regarding assessment of suicidal and homicidal ideation.

PHYSICAL SAFETY   Given the likelihood that crisis counseling often takes place in the field, counselors are likely to find themselves in hazardous surroundings and therefore must be aware of safety procedures for their own security and the well-being of their clients. According to FEMA, first responders (firefighters, police, paramedics) are on the front lines of disaster and face danger from numerous threats, including damaged infrastructure, secondary collapse, unfamiliar surroundings, unstable structures, falling or tripping hazards, falling material or flying objects, exposure to hazardous materials, decontamination, exposure to smoke, dust, fire, noise, electrical hazards, contaminated air and water, and dangerous equipment (FEMA, 2006). Crisis counselors are not likely to be on the front lines of disaster initially, but they will still be in areas with some of the dangers listed above and should be aware of potential hazards in the environment. After the primary response, counselors may be out in the field and should be careful around damaged structures and other hazards. It is imperative that mental health field workers obey all field safety guidelines established by the emergency management team.

All counselors must be knowledgeable about basic safety precautions before entering disaster areas. Because survivors are sometimes reluctant to leave their property and may put their own lives at risk, counselors can offer them information about disaster relief services and basic safety concerns and can encourage them to seek help. Counselors must be aware of their surroundings and the context of their interactions with survivors. It is easy for them to become complacent with misguided ideas such as "I'm a helping professional—who would hurt a person trying to help someone else?" The reality is that individuals who perceive they or someone they care for is being threatened (physically, mentally, spiritually) may go into "fight or flight" mode, thereby creating a precarious situation for counselors and other crisis workers.

Individual clients in crisis can present an increased risk for the counselor, particularly the sole practitioner in private practice. One of the most dangerous settings for a counselor is an isolated private practice. Despenser (2005, 2007) notes that sole private practitioners are vulnerable because their practices are secluded from others and there may not be an adequate prescreening process to identify clients with borderline or psychotic disorders. Despenser stresses that the most dangerous setting is a counselor practicing alone in his or her home due to the isolation from others. Even counselors who have solo practices in multipurpose buildings with other people nearby are at risk, as the other occupants in the building may not be aware of calls for help. Counselors working in an agency or organization might also be at risk if the company denies or downplays the potential of risk from dangerous clients.

Although private practitioners rely upon referrals for much of their livelihood, it is prudent for them to consider where the referral is coming from and to obtain as much information as possible from professional referral sources. New clients should be screened carefully. Despenser (2007) identifies three referral mechanisms: (1) referrals from other professionals; (2) nonprofessional referrals (former clients or friends); and (3) self-referred clients who find the counselor's name listed online, for instance. When another mental health professional, a doctor, or a lawyer makes a referral, it is vital that the counselor discuss with the referral source the reasons for the referral and other pertinent information. Generally, with nonprofessional referrals, the counselor will not be able to learn much about the client. While a counselor may have some sense of security in these cases, depending upon the nature of the counselor's relationship with the nonprofessional referral source, it is still essential that the client be screened via phone before the counselor agrees to provide services. Self-referred clients should always be screened. It is very common today for counselors to have their own websites and to list themselves on online professional resource sites. These online resources provide potential clients with comprehensive information regarding the counselor and serve as excellent marketing tools. However, although the potential client can screen the counselor through an effective system, the counselor has no information about the self-referred clients and should screen potential clients through phone calls. Screening phone calls are critical to counselor safety, particularly with clients referred by nonprofessionals or with self-referred clients. During screening calls, it is crucial that counselors pay attention to their intuition and not ignore subtle warning signs. Despenser (2007) stated that ignoring red flags and gut feelings may be due to a need to be needed, not wanting to appear unhelpful, or countertransference issues. Your intuition is an indispensable screening tool. Listen to it.

During a screening phone call, ask the client for medical and psychological history including medications (Despenser, 2007), and legal history. Ask why the client is seeking counseling now to determine if there is a recent crisis event in the client's life. Be alert for information regarding past incidents of self-harm or violence. Pay attention to the client's tone of voice and any verbal cues that the potential client might express, such as "You must get lonely by yourself in that office." Safety procedures for new clients could include having another person present in the office area for the first session with a new client. For sole practitioners who work in office buildings, the building security personnel could be asked to stay close by when a counselor is meeting with a new client. Again, it is vital that sole practitioners listen to their own gut feelings when screening a new client. A counselor who experiences fear during a screening call should decline to treat that client. For the sole practitioner looking to build a practice, it is tempting to take any and all referrals; however, safety considerations should be at the forefront of the decision-making process.

How do counselors recognize dangerous clients? Unfortunately, initially it may not be evident, but there are some factors that can indicate a greater risk for dangerous behavior. Signs for concern in a client include a history of violent behavior, a psychiatric or forensic history, intoxication, erratic speech and behavior, and sexual posturing

CASE STUDY 2.2

Safety Precautions for Counselors

Cathy Jones is a part-time sole practitioner, a professional counselor who sees clients in the evenings from 5:00 p.m. until 9:00 p.m. at an office building. On most nights, she is the only person in the building. She is trying to build her practice and has been networking and promoting her practice any way she can. She receives a voice mail from someone named Mr. Smith, who explains that he is looking for a counselor. She returns his call, and the following conversation takes place.

CATHY:	Hello, is this Mr. Smith?
MR. SMITH:	Yes, that's me.
CATHY:	This is Cathy Jones. I'm returning your call.
MR. SMITH:	Oh yeah, the counselor.
CATHY:	You left a message saying you want to set up a counseling appointment? I'm calling to see if we might be able to decide if I'm the appropriate counselor for you.
MR. SMITH:	Great, yes, I found your name and picture on that site about counselors and I thought you looked like a nice lady. So I decided to call you.
CATHY:	Can you give me an idea of why you're interested in counseling?
MR. SMITH:	Well, my girlfriend just broke up with me and I'm pretty upset about that. I can't believe she would do this to me after all we've been through. I guess I shouldn't be surprised, women always let me down. I've been in counseling before and I know how it works. I've got plenty of money, so you don't have to worry about me being able to pay your fees.
CATHY:	So, you're grieving the loss of this relationship.
MR. SMITH:	Yeah, I know I've got to get a handle on this before I spiral out of control. My last girlfriend called the cops on me when I confronted her new boyfriend, and I don't want that to happen again. I really want to handle things differently this time. I know I have to change how I react to things like this.

Discussion Questions

1. Should Cathy Jones take on Mr. Smith as a client?
2. Why or why not?

and insinuation (Twemlow, 2001). Additionally, Despenser (2007) identifies warning signs such as a history of self-harm and abuse, vengeful or paranoid statements, and recent changes in the client's situation or support system. Whenever possible, counselors should get a thorough history, preferably from the referral source, before seeing a client. Once again, the dangers of self-referred clients and those referred by nonprofessionals is evident in that it is not possible to get such a history.

Twemlow (2001) also emphasizes the perils of an isolated practice and suggests that counselors should have an escape route that cannot be blocked by chairs or coffee tables, install panic alarms, and even consider carrying pepper spray. If a client becomes threatening, Twemlow emphasizes the need for the counselor to remain calm and attempt to redirect the client, thereby defusing the threatening situation.

Violent clients pose a real threat to counselors, and some form of aggressive client behavior is likely to occur in every mental health provider's career (Tishler, Gordon, & Landry-Meyer, 2000). In a study of Georgia mental health providers, Arthur, Brende, and Quiroz (2003) found that 29% of the practitioners surveyed had feared for their lives at some point during their careers and that 61% had suffered some type of physical or psychological assault during their careers. Arthur et al. suggest that mental health professionals working with clients at a high risk for violence (e.g., those working on inpatient forensic units) exercise the following safety preparations: "securing wall frames, pictures, and diplomas on walls; identifying dangerous items that could easily be thrown; wearing proper clothing that cannot be grabbed by clients (e.g., ties, scarves); and installing a safety warning alarm" (pp. 40–41). Furthermore, Arthur et al. also suggest that private practitioners and agency employees institute safety policies that include "office or body alarms and clue names or words that others would recognize when assistance is needed" (p. 40).

Thienhaus and Piasecki (1998) identified risk factors for client violence, concluding that past violence is the number one predictor of potential future violence. Counselors should also take note of any loss of reality testing, such as delusional thinking or hallucinations. Impulse control issues (e.g., mania, intoxication) are also risk factors for violence. Every counselor, regardless of setting, should institute safety rules and abide by them. To assume that violent client behavior "couldn't happen here" is to put oneself in peril.

Another danger faced by mental health providers is the threat of being stalked by a client. Purcell, Powell, and Mullen (2005) did a random survey of 1,750 psychologists and found that 19.5% had experienced stalking. The majority of stalking incidents involved male outpatient clients, and the majority of stalked psychologists were female. Most of the stalkers had a diagnosis of a personality disorder or psychotic disorder; however, some of the stalkers were diagnosed with substance abuse, major depression, or anxiety or had no previous clinical diagnosis. Purcell et al. found that clients who stalk were motivated by a need for intimacy, infatuation, resentment or revenge, or a misinterpretation of the therapeutic relationship as a friendship or romance. They stress that mental health providers must be very clear about the nature of the therapeutic relationship and set firm boundaries, preferably in writing. Setting boundaries should include not allowing contact between sessions, not extending session length, keeping personal information private (the counselor's home address and phone should be unlisted), and not placing personal objects such as family photographs in the office, which may give the client too much personal information or may create an atmosphere of familiarity. When clients cannot respect the nature of the therapeutic relationship and continually violate boundaries, the counseling relationship should be terminated and the client referred for a psychiatric evaluation. In extreme cases, the counselor may have to obtain a restraining order for self-protection. As always, counselors should seek supervision and consultation and should clearly document all events, actions, and decisions.

Some agencies offer in-home counseling, especially to low-income clients who may have difficulty finding transportation to counseling centers. In-home counseling is a highly effective service delivery method, but it brings with it increased safety concerns. In-home services should never be conducted alone; counselors should be accompanied by co-counselors or behavioral aides. In-home counseling agencies should make it a practice for counselors to check in by phone prior to each session and after leaving the client's home. Spencer and Munch (2003) emphasize that when conducting in-home counseling, counselors should familiarize themselves with the community and the environment. Where are the building exits? Is there adequate lighting? Also, they should be aware of other people who may be present at the home. If the counselor feels uneasy about the environment, he or she should leave the premises.

Many agencies do not allow counselors to provide transportation to clients. If an agency does allow client transportation, the counselor should obtain liability coverage from the agency for client transportation. The car should not contain weapons or loose objects that could be used as weapons, and car keys should remain in the possession of the counselor at all times (Spencer & Munch, 2003). Clients should be seated where the counselor can see them. When personal safety is in doubt, it is best to arrange for alternative transportation.

Mental health providers working in forensic inpatient units have an increased risk of harm from violent clients. Such clients may be put in restraints, and staff at inpatient units must be trained in proper restraint methods. Sullivan et al. (2005) stress that staff training should focus on using therapeutic methods to deescalate a violent client and on empowering the client to take ownership of his or her treatment so that the need for restraint can be reduced. Inpatient mental health workers should be cognizant of the fact that federal policy requires that alternatives be attempted before restraints are used and that restraints be used only when absolutely necessary. In addition, there must be a defined amount of time that a client will remain in restraints, and a restrained client must be assessed in a timely manner. Flannery and Stone (2001) suggest that inpatient facility staff be trained in early warning signs of violence and in the identification of high-risk clients. After violent incidents, staff should be debriefed and provided with support and training.

Remember, violence can occur in any and all counseling settings. Examine the safety of your setting, and consider these questions: Do you screen clients? Do you have a mechanism to call for help? Is your office set up with an escape route in the event of client violence? Do you have safety rules, and if so, do you abide by them? Crisis preparedness and adherence to basic safety precautions are essential factors for successful crisis intervention in immediate crisis situations and in transcrisis—a crisis that has not been completely resolved and may always be present and may reemerge when triggered by any stressor.

CASE STUDY 2.3

Counselor Safety

Carol works as a college counselor at a small university counseling center that has one other counselor on staff. The counseling center is located in the basement of a campus office building that is vacant each day by 6:00 p.m. Carol and her colleague have an unwritten safety rule that they will not schedule appointments later than 4:30 p.m. Carol occasionally breaks this rule when she knows the client well. One day a married female student named Victoria calls to inquire about marriage counseling; she states that she and her husband, Robert, are disagreeing about many issues and they want couples therapy to improve communication. Carol suggests several possible appointment times, but Victoria works and cannot possibly come in until 6:30 or 7:00 p.m. Since the case seems straightforward, Carol agrees to meet the couple at 7:00 p.m. for an initial session.

When Carol unlocks the counseling center door and admits the couple, she immediately feels anxious. The husband's appearance seems unkempt, and he does not make eye contact with Carol. Carol and the couple proceed to her office, fill out intake forms, and go over informed consent. Although Robert is quiet, he appears to be amenable to treatment, signing all documentation. Carol feels increasingly uneasy, and for the first time, she realizes that her office is arranged with the clients between her and the only door. Robert stares at the floor while Victoria explains to Carol that she and her husband have been disagreeing because he has a diagnosis of paranoid schizophrenia and he refuses to take his medication. Victoria hopes that through couples counseling, Robert will become more compliant with his medication and they can learn to communicate and interact more positively. Carol maintains an appearance of calm and listens to the Victoria while Robert remains silent.

When Carol finds out from Victoria that the Robert is under the care of a psychiatrist, she explains to the couple that before any relationship work can be effective, it is necessary that all medical issues be addressed. She further explains that it would be inappropriate for her to work with the couple unless she was working collaboratively with the psychiatrist. The couple agrees to make an appointment with the psychiatrist the next day, and Carol has them both sign releases in case the psychiatrist wishes to speak with her. Carol escorts the couple from the counseling center and breathes a sigh of relief as she locks the door behind them.

Discussion Questions

1. What was Carol's initial mistake?
2. How could she have handled the situation differently?
3. What factors might have caused Carol's complacency with regard to safety?
4. What safety plan changes should Carol and her colleague institute?

PROFESSIONAL SELF-ASSESSMENT

A major component of ethical practice is the ability of the counselor to monitor his or her own mental health and engage in self-care. Welfel (2013) points out that counselors face emotional challenges both in the workplace and home. Counselors have lives,

VOICES FROM THE FIELD 2.2
Dealing with an Aggressive, Hostile Woman in a Prison Setting

Matthew J. Paylo

As the mental health director at a female maximum-security prison, I was familiar with managing aggressive behaviors. It seemed like a daily occurrence that my staff was asked by prison personnel to aid in the de-escalation of an individual who was managing a specific stressor or rebelling against the restrictiveness of the prison setting in general. As a director, I often used professional development trainings to aid new mental health staff in dealing with various crisis situations specific to the prison setting. Later, I would realize I still had a few things to learn about managing crises.

One Saturday in November, I found myself trying to get ahead on evaluations and paperwork, and I was the only mental health staff member in the prison. A correctional officer contacted me regarding Delia, a woman who initiated a dispute with another woman on her wing. The correctional officer had managed to lead Delia off the wing and into a holding cell. He reported that she was screaming and clearly agitated by the situation. Delia had been involved in our anger management program, and I recalled that she had recently head-butted a sergeant. The staff had limited tolerance for her actions and behaviors.

As I got to the scene, I evaluated the environment and deemed it was safe to enter and engage the woman. Another correctional staff member asked if I wanted to enter the cell; having worked with the prisoner for over six months, I did not hesitate. Assessing on the continuum of escalation, I had surmised that she was not just anxious or defensive but was acting out and using intimidation and posturing to relay her level of frustration. I spoke her name softly, and respectfully inquired about the precipitating event. Using my already existent relationship with her, I transitioned her to focus on communicating verbally instead of acting out physically. Trying not to overreact to her language and threats, I attempted to show her empathy on how difficult this situation must have been for her. Avoiding a power struggle with her was another aim of mine and she seemed to be slowly de-escalating (i.e., she was no longer pacing in the cell and her fists were no longer clenched).

Yet on reflection, I remembered that I was standing not off to the side but directly in front of Delia. This face-to-face posture was an obvious point that I had missed at that moment. Her eyes gazed at the floor and when she raised them toward me she reacted to my stance in a less than positive way. She immediately stated, "Who the f*** do you think you are trying to control me? You can't stop me from leaving. I'll take you out." At that moment I realized my posture was intimidating, and I moved two quick steps to my left. Delia immediately threw a right-handed hook as I moved just out of her reach. The correctional staff flooded the cell.

The point of this story—the same point I have relayed to my staff and students— is that even if you are saying all the right things in the right way, nonverbal communication (posture, positioning, affect, facial reactions, etc.) is often more important and can set the tone for the entire interaction.

---

family responsibilities, community obligations, and crises that affect their personal lives. In addition, they are not exempt from mental disorders and substance abuse. In order to provide ethical best practice, counselors must nurture self-awareness and actively engage in self-care. This is particularly important for a counselor working in crisis situations. Self-assessment is the process whereby counselors self-monitor and maintain self-awareness of their reactions, behaviors, feelings, and thoughts, thereby recognizing how these internal processes affect their sense of self and their functioning as helping professionals. Self-assessment is crucial to effective crisis intervention. A counselor who is unable to attend to his or her internal state is unlikely to be of much help to others. Self-awareness and self-care are fundamentally important to best practice.

Self-Assessment of the Counselor During Crises

Self-assessment and intentional self-care, while important for all counselors, are of particular importance to counselors who work with traumatized clients. Crises take an emotional, cognitive, and even physical toll, and counselors should debrief with colleagues or supervisors and periodically do self check-ins to monitor for indications of reduced functioning. Since a lack of resiliency and health on the part of the counselor can hardly foster wellness in a client, counselors have a responsibility to monitor their own mental health and seek supervision and counseling when needed. Failure to attend to self-assessment and restoration can lead to burnout, compassion fatigue, and vicarious trauma—and ultimately to counselor impairment. This is especially critical during crisis intervention circumstances when emotions are running high, the environment is charged with anxiety, and clients are suffering and in distress. Basically, commitment to assessment and maintenance of a healthy mind, body, and spirit is essential in the preservation of wellness and best practice. In our culturally diverse society, it is important to remember that self-assessment also includes regular evaluation of counselor values, which affect the care counselors give. Counselors are obligated to learn and consistently assess how their own cultural, ethnic, and racial identities affect their values and beliefs about the work they do. The way in which counselors perceive themselves and their own cultural context, as well as the cultural context of the clients they serve, can also affect their maintenance of a healthy mind and spirit.

Welfel (2013) highlights some specific recommendations regarding self-awareness for best practice. Counselors should be mindful of the risks associated with practice and also celebrate the rewards associated with helping others; should set clear limits and not overextend themselves; should engage in self-care; should recognize when they are emotionally exhausted and seek support, including counseling; and should avoid emotional isolation. It is the ethical obligation of all counselors to be mindful of their own health and well-being and to engage in restorative practices.

Countertransference

Countertransference occurs when counselors ascribe characteristics of significant people and events in their past to their clients. Client emotions, behaviors, and issues may stir up unresolved or buried emotions within a counselor, who might then identify too closely with the client and use the counseling relationship to fulfill unmet needs. Dealing with one's own "stuff" is a vital aspect of good practice and healthy self-assessment. Exploring personal issues and increasing self-awareness underpin healthy practice and should be an ongoing part of counselor self-care and work. It is important for counselors to examine their internal reactions to clients. In cases that evoke unresolved issues, counselors should seek consultation, supervision, and personal counseling. A self-aware counselor will be cognizant of times when a client's issues strike close to home and interfere with the counselor's ability to be objective. Welfel (2013) recommends that counselors check in with their professional support system to examine each counselor's interpretations of a case and to determine when a case that strongly trigger a counselor's issues should be referred. In cases of referrals, counselors should seek supervision and possibly personal counseling.

Burnout and Compassion Fatigue

Skovholt (2001) describes burnout as "a profound weariness and hemorrhaging of the self" (p. 107). Burnout occurs when counselors exhaust themselves both physically and emotionally through overwork and a lack of self-care. Burnout can result in a sense of emotional numbness and detachment from clients. Obviously, counselors experiencing burnout face lowered job satisfaction and increased absenteeism. Health problems can develop, thus complicating the possibility for a return to functioning. Counselors and other mental health professionals are at risk for burnout due to the emotionally intense nature of their jobs. Burnout is a cumulative process; over time, emotional exhaustion builds and may result in a sense of detachment and cynicism that leads to a diminished capacity to provide best practice (Newell & MacNeil, 2010).

Empathy, the quality that lies at the core of counselor efficacy, can also be the very factor that leads to counselor burnout (Lambie, 2006). Through empathy, a counselor comprehends a client's circumstances and emotional responses. Empathic counselors communicate understanding and create a therapeutic environment for client healing. Most counselors enter the profession because they naturally possess empathic qualities and care about others; however, daily exposure to client trauma and pain can overwhelm a counselor and lead to burnout. Sadly, burnout ultimately damages a counselor's capacity to experience empathy and function as a helper.

Lee, Cho, Kissinger, and Ogle (2010) used the Counselor Burnout Inventory (CBI) to examine counselor burnout. The CBI scales are Exhaustion, Incompetence, Negative Work Environment, Devaluing Client, and Deterioration in Personal Life. The study identified three types of counselors facing burnout: (1) well-adjusted counselors, who indicated the highest levels of job satisfaction and positive self-esteem; (2) persevering counselors, who while having burnout symptoms such as exhaustion were able

CASE STUDY 2.4

A Counselor's Countertransference Experience

Rachel is an LPC in private practice. She went through a messy divorce three years ago and feels she has healed from that experience. Today she has a new couple coming in to see her. They are seeking counseling and state that they want to try to save their marriage. During the intake session, Rachel is struck by how similar the husband is to her former husband. His angry tone of voice and some of the emotionally charged statements he makes to his wife remind Rachel of difficult encounters in her own marriage. Rachel feels herself wanting to protect the wife. She thoroughly dislikes the husband.

Discussion Questions

1. Should Rachel continue to see the couple? Why or why not?
2. If she decides to continue, what can she do to ensure best practice?
3. If she doesn't decide to continue, what should she do regarding her own self-care?

to respond appropriately to client needs and had positive self-esteem; and (3) disconnected counselors, who had high levels of client devaluation, which can be connected to compassion fatigue, and also had low self-esteem. The study also found that persevering counselors had higher incomes than well-adjusted counselors, with disconnected counselors having the lowest income. Job satisfaction and self-esteem seemed to be the differentiating elements between the burnout types. The use of burnout assessments such as the CBI could foster more targeted intervention and support, thereby addressing burnout more effectively.

Counselor exposure to client pain and suffering can lead to a sense of being overwhelmed by client stories; this goes beyond burnout to a condition called compassion fatigue. Figley (2002) notes that compassion fatigue differs from burnout in that burnout is a state of exhaustion caused by the emotional nature of the counseling profession and overwork, whereas compassion fatigue is preoccupation with traumatic client cases and personal identification with this trauma. This overidentification with trauma creates symptoms within the counselor that are comparable to the symptoms of posttraumatic stress disorder. Fortunately, self-care can be used to combat the exhaustion of mental and physical resources, the generalized stress of burnout, and the emotional exhaustion of compassion fatigue. Conversely, the concept of compassion satisfaction describes the satisfaction of helping others and being an effectual mental health professional (Lawson & Myers, 2011). Wellness and self-care are factors in fostering compassion satisfaction for counselors.

Related to compassion fatigue is the concept of secondary traumatic stress. Although these terms are often used interchangeably (Newell & MacNeil, 2010), secondary traumatic stress refers specifically to behaviors and emotions resulting from exposure to traumatic stories. Essentially, the empathic exposure to another person's trauma experience affects a counselor's behavior and reactions. For example, a counselor experiencing secondary traumatic stress might become more irritable or hypervigilant.

Vicarious Trauma

Counselors who work with traumatized clients may experience vicarious trauma, which differs from burnout, compassion fatigue, and secondary traumatic stress. While all are similar constructs and all generate secondary trauma reactions, vicarious trauma additionally affects a counselor's worldview and sense of self (Trippany, White Kress, & Wilcoxon, 2004). Counselors who work with trauma clients are at a higher risk of vicarious trauma than are counselors working in other settings.

While burnout is a response to occupational stress, vicarious trauma involves a personal cognitive reaction within the counselor to a client's experience (Dunkley & Whelan, 2006). Essentially, exposure to the trauma stories of the client can trigger pervasive alterations in a counselor's cognitive schema; specifically, there are disruptions to the counselor's sense of safety, trust, esteem, control, and intimacy. In effect, the boundary between the client's trauma experience and the counselor's worldview is blurred, as the counselor's beliefs and thinking begin to shift in response to exposure to client trauma (Newell & MacNeil, 2010). Trippany et al. (2004) developed the following guidelines for vicarious trauma prevention: (1) case management specifically limiting the number of trauma clients per week as much as possible; (2) peer supervision, which provides an avenue for debriefing and consultation; (3) agencies assuming responsibility to provide supervision, consultation, staffing, continuing education, and employee benefits, including personal counseling; (4) training and education on trauma work; (5) personal coping mechanisms, which include leisure activities and creative endeavors; and (6) spirituality to facilitate connection and meaning. While all counselors must be alert to signs of vicarious trauma, it is particularly important for counselors working with trauma clients to be intentional about self-care and self-awareness in their professional and personal lives.

Vicarious Resiliency

An emerging concept in mental health is *vicarious resiliency* (Hernandez, Gangsei, & Engstrom, 2007). While counselors can be affected adversely by trauma work, they can also experience affirmative thoughts, feelings and beliefs through hearing their clients' stories of resiliency—adaptation to difficulties in a positive and empowered manner. According to Hernandez et al., "therapists may find their ability to reframe negative events and coping skills enhanced through work with trauma survivors" (240). The capability of clients to deal with trauma and restore their lives was found to be empowering to therapists. Vicarious resiliency can lead to increased hope in one's ability to cope with problems as well as an increased belief in human empowerment. Hernandez et al. also noted that it is possible for vicarious trauma and vicarious resiliency to co-occur; however, the effect of vicarious resiliency as a mitigating factor for vicarious trauma is unknown at this time.

CASE STUDY 2.5

Jennifer

Two years ago Jennifer and her husband, Ryan, lost their house in a fire. They were able to escape with their two children, and the family dog without harm, but the family lost everything in the fire. Jennifer worked through this crisis with Ann, her counselor until six months ago, when she moved into a new home in another city. She has come back in to see Ann for a follow-up appointment.

ANN:	It's so good to see you, Jennifer. I appreciated you emailing me the pictures of your lovely new house. It's been a long journey.
JENNIFER:	Yes, I appreciate you being there for me through this. So much of what we worked on has helped me cope. I see things differently now.
ANN:	How so?
JENNIFER:	Well…life, life is what really matters. I mean, at first I was in shock and I couldn't believe it. I questioned God, I had so many mixed up emotions.

ANN: Yes, I remember how difficult it was for you to accept and cope with this tragedy at first. But I also remember your courage in seeing through, not only the nuts and bolts details of insurance and moving, but also your resolve to face feelings and place this event into your life story as a challenge met and an opportunity to learn and grow.

JENNIFER: I guess that's what I want to focus on today with you. I'm different because of the fire. Of course, I wish it hadn't happened, but I believe I'm a better person because of it and I wouldn't want to trade that growth and knowledge about what I can accomplish and also about what really matters.

ANN: The fire helped you discover the resiliency you had within you all along.

JENNIFER: Yes, I appreciate my husband and children more. I know that life, relationships, and loved ones are what really matter. I don't care about material things anymore. I no longer mourn the possessions I lost in the fire because I know the emotions connected to them were because of the people they reminded me of. A fire can never take away my memories of my grandmother and mother. The memories are real, the antiques were things that can be replaced but I haven't lost my memories. I feel very free and joyful. I appreciate every day and every person in my life.

ANN: You're living life with more awareness of love and relationships. How wonderful to fully realize the depth and importance of the people in your life.

JENNIFER: I think back to how I was before the fire, I was so distracted and busy and I often took my family for granted. Now I'm thankful every day for life and the people I love.

Discussion Questions

1. What has Jennifer learned through her crisis event?
2. What might the counselor learn from Jennifer's story?
3. How do stories like Jennifer's foster vicarious resiliency

Self-Care

It is imperative for mental health professionals to engage in restorative activities in order to regroup, revitalize, and avoid the effects of burnout, compassion fatigue, and vicarious trauma. Counselor well-being is dependent on intentional choices to manage time, nurture personal and professional relationships, and grow as a professional (Meyer & Ponton, 2006). Grafanki et al. (2005) found that leisure activities, social

VOICES FROM THE FIELD 2.3
A Personal Reflection on Self-Care

Charlotte Daughhetee

Since I have been writing about self-care, I decided to do a completely unscientific survey. I asked my friends how they relax and rejuvenate. Here are some of the answers I got: riding a bike 100 miles, reading a book, fishing, gardening, yoga, attending NASCAR races, lying in a hammock taking a nap, having a beer with friends, cooking, watching NCAA basketball, walking the dog, quilting, fencing, and playing a harp.

As you can see, relaxation comes in many forms. A meaningful authentic self-care plan should be tailor-made for each individual. All mental health professionals need to be intentional about integrating personalized enjoyable activities into unique self-care plans that come from personal experiences. Ask yourself, "when did I feel relaxed and renewed, and what was I doing?" Take what you were doing and do more of it! Follow a solution-focused approach to self-care.

Clients can also benefit from exploring their own distinctive methods of revitalization and restoration. Instead of recommending standard stress relief activities, encourage clients to create their own program, something that truly reflects the activities they love, by having them explore the life-enhancing activities that have worked for them in the past. Once clients have identified their self-care activities, have them plan those activities into their week.

So, as I head into a new week, what activities are included in my self-care plan? Walking, lunch with friends, a movie with my husband, reading a new book about Tudor England, and bird-watching in the state park. How about you? What will you do this week to refresh yourself and enhance your wellness?

---

support through connection with friends and family, spirituality, and time in nature were important elements that served to counterbalance the effects of burnout in the mental health field.

Another key component of self-care is seeking support, supervision, and consultation. This is particularly important for practitioners who may practice in isolation. Savic-Jabrow (2010) found that sole practitioners identified supervision as their primary form of support and self-care. Trainees and beginning counselors are supervised as part of their professional evolution, but it is important for counselors to seek out peer support through supervision and consultation throughout their careers. This type of ongoing support is an essential part of continuing competency and best practice (Daughhetee, Puleo, & Thrower, 2010).

It is clear that counselors have a personal and professional responsibility to engage in self-care. Newell and MacNeil (2010) stress the need for self-care as a best practice and stress the need for burnout assessment, peer support, continuing education and training on early warning signs, and self-care practices. Monitoring one's own mental, physical, and spiritual health; managing time; nurturing relationships; and fostering professional growth are vital elements of self-care and best practice.

Resolve to make self-care a priority and start designing your self-care plan today. An excellent resource for wellness and self-care information is the American Counseling Association's Task Force on Counseling Wellness and Impairment, which was established in 2003. For information on the task force and wellness resources, visit the ACA website at http://www.counseling.org/wellness_taskforce/index.htm

VOICES FROM THE FIELD 2.4
Taking Care of Myself

Hayden Belisle

I vividly remember my professors and internship supervisors explaining the importance of self-care and the value of supervision throughout graduate school. I also recall thinking that I would get around to that "one day." On particularly difficult days, during my internship and during the first couple of years that I was practicing as a school counselor, I sought solace in "retail therapy." I could be overwhelmed by a very troubling case, and it was amazing how much better I would feel after a good trip to the mall. Well, as you might imagine, the relief from the stress was fleeting… and not covered by insurance! I share that, not to make light of a very important issue, but to be honest about the fact that I didn't take caring for myself as seriously as I should have at the very beginning of my career.

By my second or third year as a school counselor, I was beginning to feel somewhat burned out. I questioned whether or not I had made the right career choice. I know that feeling burned out when your career has barely even started seems crazy, but it happens. I had extremely challenging cases and many students and situations that absolutely broke my heart. This was very difficult for me to deal with, and although I have an incredible support system outside of work, I was not participating in peer consultation or supervision of any type.

Believing that my call in life is to be a counselor, I knew that I had to make some changes, not only for myself but for the children and families I was working with. I began seeking opportunities to consult with other counselors and I tried to be intentional about taking better care of myself. This helped tremendously. Knowing that I had a network of colleagues who were just a phone call away if I needed help on a case or simply someone to listen to and support me was a great relief. After putting it off for several years, I finally began the process to become a licensed professional counselor last year. This may sound dramatic, but after my first session of supervision, it felt as though a huge boulder had been lifted from my shoulders. Having the opportunity to discuss cases and get feedback from someone that I highly respect and trust as a professional has been invaluable. I have found that it has greatly enhanced my confidence as a professional and it has challenged me to continue growing and improving. I can honestly say that I have felt far less overwhelmed and emotionally drained since I started meeting with my supervisor. My only regret is that I did not start sooner!

I would encourage anyone who is entering the counseling profession to develop a strong support system that includes other counselors and a plan for self-care. It is extremely easy to get burned out when you are not intentional about taking good care of yourself. When we don't care for ourselves, we cannot give our clients the care that they deserve.

CASE STUDY 2.6
Supervision in Crisis Counseling

Kurt, a recent graduate of a counseling program, has a job in an agency that provides services to low income individuals, couples, and families. State budget cuts and an economic downturn have increased the client load beyond capacity. Kurt is pursuing his LPC and receives supervision from an approved counselor outside of his agency. This has proved to be a good thing because the director of the agency is too stressed and overwhelmed to provide supervision. Everyone at the agency is overwhelmed.

Although Kurt is thankful for all the client contact hours he is receiving, he is beginning to wonder how he will maintain his current pace. He keeps up with all of his case notes but has noticed that some of the other counselors put off doing case notes and paperwork and that they seem cynical about their clients. He feels like he is barely keeping his head above water and the job is very hard on him. His LPC supervisor has expressed concern about his caseload and the effect it might have on him and on his ability to provide appropriate care, but Kurt has assured her that he's doing fine.

A major stressor at the agency has been the behavior of the director. While at times the director is jovial and supportive, he sometimes flies off the handle for no reason and becomes enraged. Kurt has not been on the receiving end of these rages yet, but everyone on the staff seems to walk on eggshells and dreads that they will be the next target. They are all thankful for those days when the director is in a good mood, but as time passes the staff is beginning to sense that the director is becoming increasingly stressed and they dread the inevitable outbursts of rage.

Kurt has not addressed the director's behavior with his LPC supervisor. He doesn't want her to think poorly of the director, and he also wonders if maybe it's not as bad as it seems. One day the director is in a particularly bad mood, and the staff is tense and nervous. Kurt hears the director screaming at the receptionist and calling her names in front of a waiting room full of clients. That evening, Kurt comes clean with his supervisor about how bad things are at the agency. His supervisor says, "What you're describing is the cycle of abuse." Kurt is stunned and realizes that the entire staff at the agency has been caught up in an abuse cycle.

Discussion Questions

1. Why do you think Kurt has avoided telling his supervisor the truth about his workplace?
2. Do you believe the director is impaired? Is client care at risk?
3. What effect does the director's behavior have on staff? On clients?
4. What, if anything, should the supervisor do with this information?
5. What should Kurt do?

VOICES FROM THE FIELD 2.5
Figuring Out What Works for You

Maegan Vick

Worn out? Tired? Typing papers while attempting to watch your favorite show? Working late to help clients who have long left your office? These are all the signs of an overworked individual. They are also signs of a passionate and dedicated counselor. It is hard sometimes to put that book down, turn off the computer, or even allow your mind to temporarily forget one of the many clients and coworkers you are dedicated to helping. But you have to draw that line somewhere. Otherwise you face counselor burnout and a decline of your own happiness and effectiveness. Self-care has to be placed at the forefront for counselors. If you are not good to yourself, you cannot possibly be any good to others. It took some tears, sleepless nights, and pure fatigue for me to understand this point clearly.

Everyone has to figure out what works for them. What works for me includes truly looking at the children I work with and stopping for a few moments to enjoy them, rather than worrying over how to fix their situations. It is me driving to that old barn and watching the horses graze in the sunset. It is me pulling off the side of the road to buy some pumpkins from children selling them for Halloween and me picking wildflowers in a nearby field. It is me spending time with my family and friends. It is also me saying "no" to people, and knowing that doesn't mean I don't care to help them. It simply means I care enough to take care of me. It is also scheduling that appointment with my counselor when I see the need. It is me listening to my body, soul, and mind and knowing when boundaries need to be set, knowing when I need "me time." In

(Continued)

the world of counseling, it is very easy to get stuck in that rut of giving away your time to everyone else and leaving none for yourself. New and veteran counselors, a word to the wise: Do not get stuck in that rut. Ongoing supervision and implementing effective self-care strategies are important for crisis counselors. It is essential for counselors to include self-reflection as part of self-care questions such as the following:

1. Do you listen to yourself and realize you need to set boundaries and schedule some "me time"? What signs tell you that you are in need of self-care?
2. What activities, people, etc., in your life help you refuel? How could you integrate these into your life more consistently?

VOICES FROM THE FIELD 2.6
Self-Care and Working with Suicidal Clients

Rachel M. Hoffman

I remember my first experience working with a suicidal client quite well. I was working in an inpatient setting, and although I had expected to encounter suicidal clients I wasn't quite prepared to encounter suicidal clients who did not appear, at least initially, to want to change. Working with someone with a complete disregard for his or her own life challenged my personal belief system and, although I had been prepared as a counselor, I still found myself wanting to fall back on convincing the client of reasons to live. Thankfully, I had the support of a strong clinical supervisor and, through his guidance, I was able to bracket my own feelings related to death in order to be helpful to the client.

It is important to have realistic expectations for change and to recognize that the process of suicidality is not one that is quickly resolved. Understanding the function of assessment, intervention, and follow-up is an important consideration for working successfully with suicidal clients. I believe that it is important for counselors to understand that part of being helpful with suicidal clients is understanding that change may be a slow process. However, it is necessary for counselors to remember that clients are not only capable of change but also possess the skills to make those changes.

I believe that self-care is of the utmost importance when working in crisis situations, especially those dealing with suicidal clients. Debriefing with a supervisor or peer can be helpful in the immediate aftermath of a suicidal crisis. Making time daily to engage in self-care is an essential consideration for counselors who work in stressful situations. Personally, I've found that taking a "5-minute mindfulness break" each day can help me reconnect and regroup in a healthy way.

Summary

Crisis counselors must be cognizant of their own personal safety and well-being, particularly in crisis situations. Disaster sites are dangerous, and counselors should pay close attention to their surroundings and obey the rules and safety guidelines of the crisis team. Basic proactive safety precautions are a necessary aspect of good practice. Counselors practicing in isolation are particularly vulnerable; they should have clear safety plans that are followed and they should carefully screen potential clients. Counselors who work with high-risk clients or in high-risk settings must be aware of safety rules and remain alert to their environments.

A critical aspect of crisis counseling is the need for crisis counselor self-assessment and self-care. Crisis and trauma clients can take a toll on crisis counselors, who may experience countertransference, burnout, compassion fatigue, and vicarious trauma. Counselors should also be aware of concepts such as vicarious resiliency and compassion satisfaction, which describe the positive aspects of working with crisis and trauma clients. Crisis counselor self-care practices are a necessary component of effective crisis intervention and include wellness activities and support through consultation and supervision.

3

Ethical and Legal Considerations in Crisis Counseling

Paul F. Hard, Laura L. Talbott-Forbes, and Mary L. Bartlett

PREVIEW

While crisis planning can never be perfect, it does provide a framework for appropriate response and decision making in urgent situations. Prepared crisis counselors well versed in crisis procedures and processes will be able to provide ethical, skilled help in all types of crisis conditions. This chapter will examine the ethical and legal considerations related to preventive measures, federal legislations, sentinel court findings, and relevant applications of best practice regarding privacy matters in crisis counseling. Crisis counselors need to be particularly aware of state and federal laws and professional ethics that govern and advise practice. The discussion will focus on prevention considerations, the Health Insurance Portability and Accountability Act (HIPAA), the Family Educational Rights and Privacy Act (FERPA), also known as the Buckley Amendment, the *Tarasoff* decision, confidentiality, and termination issues. Throughout sections of this chapter, legal and ethical information related to crisis and disaster response and malpractice issues related to normal developmental life crises are presented in the context of standard clinical practice. Consideration should be given to counselor care in disaster circumstances when care is limited to psychological first aid and suspension of some standard practice considerations. In such circumstances the need for ongoing counseling, psychotherapy, and formal assessment will normally be referred to case management or other area providers (American Red Cross, 2005), a topic that will be discussed here.

PREVENTIVE CONSIDERATIONS

It has often been observed that it is far more effective and economical to prevent a problem rather than to correct it. Primary prevention of ethical and legal issues in counseling is a far more effective strategy than the costly and distressing efforts to address an ethical or legal lapse after it has occurred. Counselors can focus on three areas to foster core prevention: (1) wellness, (2) continuing education, and (3) peer supervision and consultation. While there is no panacea to prevent ethical or legal violations, when these three areas are synthesized into the counselor's professional worldview, best practices are embedded that act as a shield for both client and counselor. Wellness strategies, continuing education, supervision, and peer consultation are among the more common prevention recommendations in this regard.

WELLNESS The American Counseling Association (ACA) 2003 Task Force on Impaired Counselors (Lawson & Venart, 2005) observed that counselors working in disaster or crisis circumstances are particularly vulnerable to secondary trauma, vicarious trauma, or compassion fatigue. Because such a compromised condition may leave the counselor vulnerable to ethical or legal lapses, attention to the well-being of the counselor is therefore vital as a preventive measure. Pearlman and MacIan (1995) noted 10 helpful strategies for crisis counselors to use to promote and maintain wellness: (1) discussing cases with colleagues, (2) attending workshops, (3) spending time with family or friends, (4) travel, vacations, hobbies, and movies, (5) talking with colleagues between sessions, (6) socializing, (7) exercising, (8) limiting caseload, (9) developing one's spiritual life, and (10) receiving supervision. Not only are these important to maintain ethical practice, Lawson and Venart (2005) noted that wellness and self-care are vital to counselors since the care that they provide to others is only as effective as that the care they give themselves.

CONTINUING EDUCATION Continuing education is required by certifying and licensing bodies as a means of ensuring that a counselor's practice remains both competent and current. Many such entities also require that a portion of the continuing education be related to ethics in order to ensure that counselors continue to be versed in current ethical issues as well as current ethical decision-making models. Mascari and Webber (2006) strongly encourage counselors to participate in continuing education to effectively compare their professional behavior with the standard of care. They also highly recommend making routine review of the professional codes of ethics a part of their ongoing personal education.

SUPERVISION AND PEER CONSULTATION As stated long ago in the Bible (Proverbs 11:14) 'in the multitude of counselors there is safety'. This is particularly true in the case of ethical practice. Many sources urge the use of peer consultation and supervision as a means of ethical instruction and practice (Dansby-Giles, Giles, Frazier, Crockett, & Clark, 2006; Mascari & Webber, 2006; Wozny, 2007). Dansby-Giles et al. (2006) recommend the use of ethics circles (or group round-table discussions) to engage counselors in healthy debate regarding how to handle various ethical dilemmas. Engaging in peer consultation when confronted with ethical problems exposes those concerns to colleague input and enhances protection for both the counselor and client. It is commonly understood that avoiding conversations related to ethical dilemmas out of shame or fear often results in negative outcomes; whereas pursuing open and honest dialogue about client challenges reduces the likelihood of negative outcomes that may occur in isolation.

HEALTH INSURANCE PORTABILITY AND ACCOUNTABILITY ACT

The Health Insurance Portability and Accountability Act (HIPAA) of 1996 is legislation implemented to address a number of perceived shortcomings in the management of information in the health care industry. Conceived in early 1990, the present legislation covers a wide range of areas that impact both the health care industry and patients (HIPAA, 2011).

WHAT IS HIPAA?   In the 1970s and 1980s, the American public perceived that health care information was not controlled and protected by the health care industry to the degree that it should be, in view of the increasing ability during those years for data to be compiled, manipulated, and used to negatively affect individuals and families. As a result of several high-profile cases and the resulting pressure on Congress, the legislative branch created health care information handling and protection standards of their own and communicated to the health care industry that these rather restrictive standards would be implemented if the health care industry did not solve the problem on its own.

The health care industry subsequently promulgated standards for information handling, management, and control that met congressional approval, and Congress enacted these standards in HIPAA (Public Law 104-191). HIPAA went into effect on August 21, 1996, and included four areas of legislation: (1) privacy requirements, (2) electronic transactions, (3) security requirements, and (4) national identifier requirements (Corey, Corey, & Callahan, 2007; Jensen, 2003; Remley & Herlihy, 2010; U.S. Department of Health and Human Services, 2002). However, the version of HIPAA that became law in 1996 did not include privacy rules, and Congress instructed the U.S. Department of Health and Human Services (DHHS) to dictate privacy rules for the health care industry if Congress did not pass such rules within three years. The three-year period was provided in order to give the health care industry a chance to develop privacy rules, submit them to Congress, and get them passed. This did not occur, and in the absence of such legislation, DHHS followed the requirement of the 1996 act and implemented standards for privacy of individually identifiable health information, referred to as the Privacy Rule, which became effective in 2003. The Privacy Rule is still in effect and can be located at the HIPAA website of the DHHS Office for Civil Rights (Corey et al., 2007; Jensen, 2003; Remley & Herlihy, 2010; U.S. Department of Health and Human Services, 2002).

The Privacy Rule seeks to balance the concept of individual privacy against the need for medical professionals to have access to information in order to best do their jobs. It establishes that the right to privacy with regard to medical information is not absolute and therefore puts the onus on designated health care providers to protect the information they collect, use, and transmit. The Privacy Rule and other aspects of HIPAA govern information that contains personal identification categorized as protected health information (PHI). The PHI must be treated according to the procedures established by HIPAA whenever it is created, transmitted, or received in any form whatsoever: electronic, paper-based, or by means of oral transmission. In short, if information contains individually identifiable material, it is considered PHI and is fully impacted by HIPAA (Horner & Wheeler, 2005; Remley & Herlihy, 2010).

Those who collect, use, or transmit PHI and who are covered under the requirements of HIPAA are referred to as covered entities. Terms such as *health care provider* and *health care* are sometimes used to refer to covered entities. The HIPAA legislation defines covered entities as those employed by a health plan, a health clearinghouse, or a health care provider. Health care provider is further defined as "a person or organization who furnishes health care as a normal part of their business; who bills for health care, or who is paid by a third party to provide health care" (Horner & Wheeler, 2005, p. 10). In this way, HIPAA defines terms relating to the players in the health care arena and establishes standards through the Privacy Rule that define how these individuals or organizations are to collect, use, transmit, and handle information that contains individually identifiable material relating to health care.

THE IMPACT OF HIPPA   Over the intervening years, the health care industry sought to ensure that HIPAA-compliant operations were in place across the entire spectrum of health care providers, with various degrees of success. Part of the difficulty that has been experienced with HIPAA implementation is a result of the complexity of the regulations, combined with the various electronic information-handling systems that exist, the lack of standardization between them, and the continuing transition period between paper-based record keeping and the full electronic record-keeping goal of HIPAA. As systems become more standardized, dramatic cost savings will be achieved when the transition to electronic records is completed. However, there is resistance, both on the individual provider level and institutionally, to many of the goals of the HIPAA legislation (Uses and Disclosures of Protected Health Information: General Rules, 45 C.F.R. § 164.502, 2002). As a result, many health care providers are reluctant to share information fearing they will violate the standards and suffer penalties, which can range from fines to imprisonment, to sanctions by licensing boards depending on the violation.

At the clinic level, one of the most dramatic effects of HIPAA has been the requirement to perform and document a range of nonclinical, procedural actions to establish that the client has been informed of, understands, and agrees with a variety of requirements, rights, and privileges that HIPAA dictates. Since HIPAA puts the onus on the organization to show that it has complied with the requirements, counselors provide their clients with a written declaration of their rights under the HIPAA legislation, including the procedural practices regarding the clinic's collection, use, transmission, and handling of HIPAA-defined PHI. These procedural practices include, but are not limited to, what information clients can access, how they can access it, to whom their information is distributed, and how they can voice concerns regarding access to or dissemination of their private information; as a result, clinics require their clients to sign a statement indicating they have received and understand such information. Covered entities must also appoint a privacy officer who is responsible for ensuring that all staff handling PHI are trained and compliant with HIPAA (Remley & Herlihy, 2010).

HIPAA has also affected clinic operations through the establishment of the minimum necessary standard, which relates to the amount of information that can be released about a patient. Federal regulations establish that communications about a patient that involve PHI should consist only of that which is minimally necessary to achieve the purpose of the communication (Privacy Rule 45 C.F.R. § 164.502[b][1]2003). Interestingly, the minimum necessary standard does not apply to PHI when it is used for or disclosed in the process of medical treatment or payment for medical treatment or in the conduct of health care operations, when it is used by or disclosed to DHHS, or when it is used by or disclosed to the patient himself or herself (Horner & Wheeler, 2005).

HIPAA requirements have adversely affected research as a result of reliance on complicated consent forms and privacy protection materials that, while not specifically made necessary by HIPAA regulation, were felt by the organizations and institutions participating in the research to be a necessary protection against accusations of failure to implement the requirements of HIPAA. The requirements made organizations less willing to host research projects, while the forms that were felt necessary by the organizations to document their compliance with HIPAA were seen to decrease the number of people willing to participate in the research (Shen et al., 2006). Some organizations were hesitant to fully implement the electronic data interchange requirement of HIPAA for fear that such entirely electronic record-keeping methods might have a greater potential for unauthorized access, theft, or abuse than paper-based records, which were thought to be easier to segregate and control than electronic records would be (Chung, Chung, & Joo, 2006). HIPAA had less of an adverse impact on public health reporting, since it does not restrict the transmission and use of PHI when such transmission and use are made to public health agencies and as long as the source of the information complied with HIPAA requirements when it collected the information (Campos-Outcalt, 2004).

HOW HIPAA AFFECTS CRISIS COUNSELING   Crisis counseling differs from the kinds of services that are typically provided by health care workers. Crises such as hurricanes, tornadoes, and homicides typically occur quickly and often in unanticipated ways, so crisis counselors must respond quickly to stabilize and provide a way for people to move forward. There may be limited time to obtain HIPAA-required releases when critical care is needed, or it may be impossible to obtain such releases as a result of severe injury, unavailability of family members, or other unforeseen consequences of the disaster. According to the U.S. Department of Health and Human Services (2005a), HIPAA is not intended to interfere with the provision of emergency medical care associated with declared emergencies such as hurricanes, and covered health care providers may exercise their professional judgment and act as long as such actions are in the best interests of the patient.

Actions permitted by health care workers may include disclosure of individually identifiable medical information to government officials at the local, state, or federal level; police; first responders; public health officials; or anyone whom the health care providers deem necessary to best serve the patient. In any case, the federal government has the authority to waive sanctions and penalties associated with violations of

VOICES FROM THE FIELD 3.1
HIPAA and Social Media

Gina Palmer
HIPAA and social media do not mix. With the popularity and pervasiveness of social media in our everyday lives, it is easy to see how patient privacy can be breached without even realizing it. My rule is to never post messages or comment about work in any way; never post pictures from work and never "friend" any current or past patients via social networking sites. The rest is common sense.

the Privacy Rule, even in cases where a public health emergency is not declared (U.S. Department of Health and Human Services, n.d.).

For work with clients who are a serious threat to safety, the HIPAA Privacy Rule allows disclosure of PHI under the "Serious Threat to Health or Safety" provision. Release of information to anyone whom the health care provider reasonably believes may lessen the threat to health or safety (including the target of the threat) is allowed; however, in the case of a threat to health and safety, release of PHI to law enforcement is allowed only when the information is needed to identify or apprehend an escapee or a violent criminal (U.S. Department of Health and Human Services, 2006).

In cases where a crime has occurred or where law enforcement officials are investigating a suspected crime, disclosure of PHI is allowed under the "Law Enforcement Purposes" provision, which sets out various situations relating to law enforcement in which disclosure of protected information may—and, in fact, must—be made (U.S. Department of Health and Human Services, 2005b).

FAMILY EDUCATION RIGHTS AND PRIVACY ACT

In 1974, Congress passed the Family Educational Rights and Privacy Act (FERPA), also known as the Buckley Amendment, prompted by concerns about privacy violations and the inclusion in educational records of immaterial comments and personal opinions (Weeks, 2001). Confusion regarding HIPAA and FERPA continues to be of concern as institutions of higher education and governmental partners struggle to strike a

CASE STUDY 3.1

Protection of Privacy

Rose is a transitioning male to female transgender person who is living in a shelter after having lost her home in coastal flooding near San Francisco following the tsunami in Japan in 2011. Formerly known as Robert, Rose disclosed her transgender status to the shelter counselor and requested special accommodations for privacy. The counselor left Rose's documentation visible on his desk while tending to other client needs. A shelter worker inadvertently saw the note, and attempting to be of help to the counselor (and to Rose), mentioned the special needs request to other shelter workers. Rose's circumstances subsequently became known to other shelter residents resulting in objections from the community and embarrassment to Rose.

Discussion Questions

1. How are privacy regulations for client privacy to be observed in disaster shelter circumstances?
2. What minimum expectations for privacy should a client expect in a shelter?
3. In circumstances of a breach of information, what steps should be taken to sanction these actions?
4. Who should be sanctioned and how?
5. What can be done to minimize the damage of a breach of privacy?

balance. This is of particular concern for counselors who work in an educational environment and are providing direct mental health services. Counselors working in this environment should remain current in their understanding of federal privacy regulations, the content to be disclosed in the educational record, and the need to document student mental needs (Barboza, Epps, Byington, & Keene, 2010; U.S. Department of Education, 2008; U.S. Department of Health and Human Services, 2008).

WHAT IS FERPA?   Essentially, FERPA (20 U.S.C. § 1232g; 34 CFR Part 99) gives parents certain rights to their child's educational record until the child is 18 years of age (an "eligible student"). After this point the right to privacy regarding the contents of the educational record is provided to the eligible student, thus denying parental access without consent (U.S. Department of Education, 2008). All schools, public or private, that receive federal funding must follow FERPA or face the loss of federal funds (Remley & Herlihy, 2010). According to the U.S. Department of Education (2008), a parent or an eligible student has the right to inspect and review the student's educational records. Additionally, the parent or eligible student who believes an educational record to be inaccurate may ask to amend the record. If a school refuses to amend an educational record, the parent or eligible student can request a formal hearing and may place in the record a statement about the information being contested.

Schools must obtain written permission to release information; however, FERPA allows the release of information in certain situations—for example, when a student transfers to another school and there is a legitimate educational interest; or when financial aid is being requested, a judicial order has been issued, or there is an emergency. Parents are to be notified when records are transferred to other schools and may receive copies of said records upon request (Remley & Herlihy, 2010). Under FERPA, colleges may release educational records, such as grades and financial records, to parents of college students claimed as dependents on parental tax forms. The release of student records to parents occurs either when the parent shows tax record proof that the student is a dependent or when the student signs a waiver allowing the release of records to parents (Weeks, 2001).

IMPACT OF FERPA   FERPA has had a major impact on the practice of record keeping in schools. With the advent of parental and student access to school records, school personnel had to be certain student records contained only essential and accurate information. Prior to FERPA, records might contain information about minor disciplinary actions and personal opinions, including derogatory remarks that could be damaging to students. Essex (2004) states that to abide by FERPA "school personnel must be certain that all information recorded in the student's educational file is accurate, necessary and based on reasonable grounds" (p. 111). FERPA ended the practice of untrained individuals entering psychological diagnoses into student records and also ended the inclusion of unsuitable negative remarks.

Before FERPA, educational institutions could be quite lax about how they communicated student information. In fact, Senator James L. Buckley of New York was motivated, in part, to introduce this legislation due to such abuses of confidential material (Weeks, 2001). Schools were known to reveal contents of student records to parties who had no educational interest or need to know. FERPA has served to advance professionalism in educational institutions, while at the same time securing students' rights to privacy and confidentiality.

VOICES FROM THE FIELD 3.2
Protecting Confidentiality During a Crisis

Cindy Wiley

Your first priority as a counselor is to protect your client—in this case a school-aged student's life. Julie has come to you in crisis, trusting in you to alleviate pain while guarding and maintaining confidence. When a student presents in such a state, it is hard to remind that student, and yourself, that while what you talk about is confidential, there are exceptions to that confidentiality. I think most counselors are afraid that the counselor-student relationship, which is paramount, will be ruined even if confidence is appropriately breached for the safety of the student. If worded in a manner that adequately portrays your concern and need to involve other resources, most students will understand. What students will ultimately remember is that you genuinely care for them and their well-being. In a state of crisis, most students are truly asking for help. Your job is to make sure that you "circle the wagons" to support them.

FERPA contains a provision that exempts certain personal records. Records that are in the "sole possession of the maker" and are not revealed to others are excluded from FERPA (Russo & Mawdsley, 2004, p. 81). This includes records made by school personnel such as crisis counselors who keep such records in their "sole possession." Due to this exemption, counseling case notes are not considered part of the educational record and do not have to be revealed (Remley & Herlihy, 2010).

HOW FERPA AFFECTS CRISIS COUNSELING   According to the U.S. Department of Education (2007), an emergency situation creates an exception, and schools may release information from records in order to protect the health and safety of others. It is important to note that this exception is only for the time of the emergency and is not blanket consent to release student information. The information may be released to appropriate individuals who are tasked with protecting health and safety such as law enforcement officials, medical personnel, and public officials. Law enforcement officials hired by schools are considered school officials and therefore have an "educational interest" and are permitted to view records. Threatening remarks made by a student and overheard by school personnel can be reported to appropriate officials because such remarks are not considered part of the educational record.

The aforementioned policies apply to higher education settings as well, with the following additions. Regarding disciplinary actions and rule violations, the final results of a disciplinary proceeding may be released to an alleged victim even if the perpetrator has not been found guilty of violating rules or policies (U.S. Department of Education, 2007). If a perpetrator has been found guilty of violating rules or policies, the institution may disclose the final results of a disciplinary hearing to anyone. Most colleges and universities have their own campus police; investigative records of campus law enforcement are not subject to FERPA and may be released to outside law enforcement without student consent.

In situations concerning health and safety, higher education institutions may disclose educational records to a parent if the student is involved in a health or safety issue or is under 21 years of age and has violated the school's drug and alcohol policies. Also, according to the U.S. Department of Education (2008), "a school official may generally share information with parents that is based on that official's personal knowledge or observation of the student." Therefore, in situations where a student's behavior involves the health and safety of self and others, school officials can communicate with parents. In fact, a school official may report concerns about student behavior to anyone, though

---

VOICES FROM THE FIELD 3.3

Covering All of the Bases After a Crisis

═══

Susan Hart

It's always heartbreaking when a student dies by suicide. Because all eyes are on the counseling center to effectively intervene, I must consider a vast spectrum of scenarios when such a tragedy happens. First, I ponder about the student and what could have happened to generate such utter hopelessness and despair. I also consider the family. What a shock and excruciating loss they must be experiencing. Next, I look at the campus community that will be affected. We know that those close to a person who dies by suicide are at particular risk of suicide themselves. Then, I examine the social implications. When this information becomes public, what impact will this suicide have on the university image? Finally, I consider possible legal ramifications. Was the student a client? If so, what was the content of the counseling sessions? Did the counselor document well and refer appropriately? There are many issues to consider in this moment of crisis. Nothing about it is simple. In order to design an effective university-based intervention strategy, it's essential to think through these situations from a diverse perspective.

---

it is wise to make such reports only to campus personnel, such as administrators, counselors, or campus police, who can intervene appropriately with the student (Tribbensee & McDonald, 2007).

The interaction between HIPAA and FERPA can be very confusing and frustrating to parents, staff, and faculty members (Shuchman, 2007). Rowe (2005) explains that HIPAA contains a FERPA exemption that excludes FERPA-covered records from HIPAA regulations; however, it must be remembered that treatment records such as counseling case files are exempt from FERPA but may be covered by HIPAA. The interplay between HIPAA and FERPA has yet to be fully understood, and currently higher education institutions are interpreting HIPAA and FERPA in various ways. FERPA was never intended to block the information flow between institutions and others concerned about student health and safety; therefore, faculty, staff, and administrators who are troubled about the welfare of a student may contact the student's family or other entities and express general observations about health and psychological concerns, while protecting the privacy of medical or mental health records (Shuchman, 2007).

It is not uncommon for school counselors to make contact with a parent once it is determined that a child is a potential threat to himself or herself. Consider the following example:

COUNSELOR (C):   Hello, Mrs. Smith. This is Ms. Collins. I'm your daughter Jill's school counselor. Today your daughter's teacher, Mrs. Potter, found a note Jill had written that suggested she is feeling suicidal and may have a plan to kill herself. I met with Jill and believe she is having passing thoughts of suicide but do not believe she has a current plan. It is school policy for me to contact a parent to pick up the child and make a referral for further assessment.

PARENT (P):   I can't come right now. I'm in the middle of a meeting. Jill has been talking about suicide for several weeks since her father left us. I think she is just seeking attention.

C: Yes, Jill mentioned she is feeling very sad about her father leaving, and this is why she is considering suicide as an option. We take all reports of potential suicide seriously to ensure student safety, and require the student be seen for follow-up before returning to school. I realize this is inconvenient, but I truly believe your daughter is in emotional distress.

P: Thanks for your concern, but I really don't think it's that serious and I simply can't leave work right now, especially since my husband left. I can't risk losing my job.

THE *TARASOFF V. REGENTS* DECISION

In the American Counseling Association (ACA) *Code of Ethics* (2005), counselors are charged with recognizing trust as an important component of the counseling relationship, and they are obligated to facilitate a trusting relationship through the maintenance of client confidentiality. However, disclosure is required "to protect clients or identified others from serious and foreseeable harm or when legal requirements demand confidential information must be revealed" (Standard B.2.a, p. 7). This standard was adopted as part of the counseling practice after the landmark California Supreme Court case of *Tarasoff v. Regents of the University of California* (1976).

In 1969, Prosenjit Poddar was seen by a psychologist on a voluntary outpatient basis at the University of California, Berkeley. Poddar confided his intent to kill a woman he claimed to be his girlfriend, a woman the psychologist surmised to be Tatiana Tarasoff, when she returned from Brazil. The psychologist, alarmed by the disclosure, contacted the campus police and then began proceedings to have Poddar committed for a psychiatric evaluation. In the interim, police picked Poddar up and questioned him. The police found Poddar to be rational. He promised not to have contact with Tarasoff, so the police released him. The psychologist followed up on his concerns with a letter to the campus police chief in which he again expressed his concern; however, the supervisor of the psychologist requested that the letter be returned, ordered all case notes destroyed, and ordered that no further action be taken. Poddar did not return to see the psychologist nor was he committed or evaluated by any additional mental health professionals. Furthermore, no one contacted Tarasoff or her family to alert them that a threat had been made. Two months later Tarasoff was stabbed to death by Poddar, and her parents brought suit against the University of California Board of Regents (Cavaiola & Colford, 2006; Corey et al., 2007; Remley & Herlihy, 2010). Initially, a trial court ruled that the university was not liable because Tarasoff was not the patient in this case, and therefore it had no duty of care toward her. Upon appeal, however, the California Supreme Court ruled there are some circumstances in which a therapist should break confidentiality, specifically when such a disclosure is necessary to avert danger to the client or others. This act of breaking confidentiality when disclosure is necessary to avert danger is known as the duty to warn (Melby, 2004).

WHAT WAS THE EFFECT OF *TARASOFF V. REGENTS*?   Part of what makes this case and the duty to warn/protect complicated is that there have been many interpretations of this case ruling. Melby (2004) points out that just how and when a counselor should break confidentiality differs depending on circumstances; and since many states depend on court rulings rather than statutes to guide the actions of a counselor, this issue is not black and white. Melby also indicates that many legal experts are "unable to offer specific advice about when therapists should alert the police or potential victim about a threat to human life" (p. 4). While some courts have limited the application of the duty to warn to situations in which victims are identifiable, subsequent decisions have indicated that the duty to warn extends to unknown victims, which further complicates the matter. Another confusing part of this ruling are the terms *duty to warn* and *duty to protect*, which are often used interchangeably by professionals.

Legal definitions of the terms *duty to warn* and *duty to protect* are established by state legislation and state court rulings, so these definitions will vary from state to state. Counselors must be aware of the laws applicable to the states in which they are licensed and in which they intend to practice. Generally speaking, the duty to warn and the duty to protect represent degrees of what is essentially the same duty: first, the duty to inform someone of a danger or hazard with the idea that he or she will take action to protect himself or herself (this is the duty to warn); second, the duty to protect someone by taking an action that reduces the danger or hazard to that person directly (this is the duty to protect). For example, when a counselor makes a telephone call to a family member whom a client has threatened, the counselor does so under the concept of duty to warn. If, on the other hand, the counselor arranges to have a client hospitalized who has threatened to harm himself, that action is taken under the concept of duty to protect, since it consists of a direct action (hospitalization) that makes it less likely that the client will execute the threat. In the *Tarasoff* case, the victim was not protected, and the appellate court ruled that the health care provider should have taken steps to protect the victim. In addition, in *Gross v. Allen*, a 1994 California appellate court case, the court ruled that the *Tarasoff* concept applied not only to cases in which clients threaten homicide but also to cases in which clients threaten suicide, so reasonable measures are expected to be taken in cases of threatened suicide (Nugent & Jones, 2009; Simon, 2004).

The *Tarasoff* ruling, in fact, establishes a duty to protect and not just a duty to warn. The ruling and interpretation of the *Tarasoff* principle for counseling professionals involves the awareness of the protective measure as a legal obligation to warn an intended victim of potential harm. For example, case outcomes have indicated that the duty to warn is extended to those who are foreseeably endangered by a client's conduct, including people who are unintentionally injured by the client, whole classes of students that have been threatened by the client, bystanders who may be injured by the client's act, and individuals whose property is threatened by the client (Corey et al., 2007; McClarren, 1987; Melby, 2004; Remley & Herlihy, 2010). Furthermore, in *Ewing v. Goldstein* (2004) the court ruled that in California a therapist could be held liable for failure to warn when the information regarding the client's potential to harm another person is obtained from family members who may be participating in counseling with the client. Additionally, Remley and Herlihy (2010) point out that the *Tarasoff* doctrine is not applied in every jurisdiction of the United States; specifically, Texas has rejected this doctrine.

When a decision is made that a client is a danger to another person or persons, the crisis counselor must then determine what the necessary steps are to prevent the harm from occurring. After notifying the potential victim and/or contacting appropriate authorities as needed to ensure the intended victim's safety, the counselor must take other steps to prevent harm, which can include continuing to work with the client on an outpatient basis. This uses the less restrictive action, whereas pursuing involuntary commitment would be considered a very restrictive option. These decisions are challenging for most counselors. Therefore, it is highly recommended that counselors seek supervision and consultation on a regular basis—but particularly whenever the issue of breaking confidentiality becomes a factor in practice. This is also known as the *duty to consult principle* and can assist crisis counselors in decreasing liability issues in similar cases. Counselors should not practice in isolation, should practice following reasonable standards, and should maintain accurate documentation to fall back on in order to verify when and why decisions regarding breaking confidentiality were made, particularly as they relate to the duty to warn (Knapp & VandeCreek, 1982).

Another consideration regarding confidentiality and the issue of duty to warn is how multicultural factors come into play. Perhaps the best way to preserve the counseling relationship, should the need arise to break confidentiality or to follow through on the duty to warn arise, is to assess how clients' cultural needs may influence your practice. This assessment should occur not only at the onset of the counseling relationship but also, as indicated in Sections B.1 and B.2 of the *ACA Code of Ethics* (2005), periodically throughout your work together. This is essential regardless of cultural context.

HOW TARASOFF V. REGENTS AFFECTS CRISIS COUNSELING   Collins and Collins (2005) identify three goals for a crisis worker dealing with a potentially violent individual: (1) ensure that the client remains safe, reduce lethality, and stabilize the environment; (2) help the client to regain short-term control; and (3) connect the client with appropriate resources. The course of accomplishing these three goals, however, is balanced against the counselor's decision that a duty to warn exists and confidentiality must be broken in part to accomplish those very goals. Counselors working with people in crisis often encounter unique circumstances when a duty to warn or protect prevails; one particularly challenging circumstance is dealing with clients who are HIV and AIDS positive.

The *Tarasoff* case and deliberations surrounding a counselor's duty to warn have become a routine aspect of counselor education and are an expected consideration in the standard of care. Counselors, however, should be cautious when broadly applying duty to warn since various states may apply this principle differently and others have enacted no law similar to the *Tarasoff* decision. Herbert and Young (2002) report that, while 27 states have an actual duty to warn, 10 states give permission to warn, 14 states have no such law, and one state has enacted legislation rejecting *Tarasoff*. For example, a study queried psychologists representing four states regarding their knowledge of legal and ethical obligations to clients in imminent danger, resulting in alarming findings: (1) the majority were incorrectly informed about their state's law and believed that they had a legal duty to warn when they did not, or (2) they assumed that warning was the only available legal option and when there were other options available that did not impede on client privacy (Pabian, Welfel, & Beebe, 2009). While the principles of duty to warn and duty to protect are useful, counselors should not assume that *Tarasoff* applies without explicitly researching their state law. Counselors should be aware of the changing nature of legislation and of the pertinent regulations for their own state.

Interestingly, even though in Texas counselors may not break confidentiality to warn or protect a person whose life has been threatened by another, they are mandated to report suspected child abuse and have the option of reporting positive HIV results to various entities (Barbee, Ekleberry, & Villalobos, 2007). Likewise, the *ACA Code of Ethics* (2005) indicates that counselors are "justified in disclosing information to identifiable third parties, if they are known to be at demonstrable and high risk of contracting the disease" (Standard B.2.b). The *ACA Code of Ethics* further stipulates, however, that counselors must confirm the diagnosis and assess the client's intent to inform the third party about his or her disease or to participate in any behavior that may be harmful to an identifiable third party. The word *justified,* as compared to *required,* warrants consideration; in addition, counselors are encouraged to evaluate their own thoughts about whether or not they will agree to work with, and how they will effectively work with, clients who are HIV positive. It is also important to keep in mind that not every exposure to HIV results in harm, thus making the process of determining how to proceed a gray area that a crisis counselor must navigate carefully. When dealing with this and other precarious issues of this sort, crisis counselors are wise to stay informed about specific statutes in their jurisdiction that have been passed regarding the duty to warn and third-party conversations and, of course, to review the guidelines of confidentiality periodically with clients, as well as seeking supervision and consultation as needed (Corey et al., 2007; Huprich, Fuller, & Schneider, 2003; Remley & Herlihy, 2010).

CASE STUDY 3.2

Assessing When to Implement a Duty to Warn

Stan, an employee at a hunting equipment retailer, escaped harm from a building during an active shooter incident involving two Middle Eastern perpetrators. A few months later, Stan began experiencing symptoms of post-traumatic stress disorder and was sent to counseling through his Employee Assistance Program (EAP) when his supervisor noticed an increase of conflicts with coworkers. In the most recent session, Stan became agitated and shouted to the counselor, "I hate those people. I'm going to kill them all," after which he abruptly left the session.

Discussion Questions

1. Does this incident indicate a duty to warn?
2. What *Tarasoff* criteria are met or not met?
3. How should the counselor proceed?

NEGLIGENCE AND MALPRACTICE

Once a counselor and a client have entered into a professional relationship, the counselor has assumed a duty of care toward the client. A breach of duty owed to another is considered negligence; negligence that occurs in a professional setting is malpractice, also referred to as professional negligence. Malpractice is established "if the court finds that this duty was breached, through an act of omission or commission relative to the standard of care" (Berman, 2006, p. 171). The standard of care is care that does not depart from what "reasonable and prudent" counselors with similar training and in similar situations would carry out. To prove malpractice, four factors—the "4Ds"—must be present: "a dereliction (breach) of a duty (of care) that directly (proximately causes) damages (a compensable injury)" (Berman, 2006, p. 172). In the event of a lawsuit, a counselor's only defense is documentation in the case file that proves that the counselor conformed to the standard of care.

DOCUMENTATION AND RECORD KEEPING

There is a useful old saying in the helping professions: "If it's not written down, it didn't happen." A counselor may have done everything right with a client, but failure to document means that no evidence exists of the counselor's actions and decisions. Documentation is an essential part of standard care and best practice. Appropriate professional documentation and record keeping display diligence and also reflect the promotion of client welfare (Cohen & Cohen, 1999). While client welfare is a counselor's main purpose, there is no denying that documentation can either help or hurt a counselor in legal cases. Mitchell (2001) asserts, "In a courtroom, your counseling records can be manipulated in ways you cannot imagine" (p. 7). This is particularly crucial in crisis situations such as suicide, homicide, or disaster relief where the risk of litigation increases.

Moline, Williams, and Austin (1998) state that records should at a minimum include "identifying data, background/historical data, diagnosis and prognosis, treatment plans, informed consent, progress notes, and termination summary (includes evaluation of all services client related)" (pp. 32–33). It is crucial that a risk assessment be conducted on every client. If the assessment produces any degree of lethality (either stated or observed), it is equally important to justify the actions taken and to follow up in subsequent case notes on the status of the risk. In addition, they note that certain material should not be included in records. Inappropriate information is anything that is not treatment-related and that could be problematic if viewed by others. Such information includes "personal opinions, discussion of a third party, sensitive information, [and] past criminal behavior" (p. 32). In cases of threats to self or others, documentation of follow-up assessments should also be included in the client's notes.

Crisis counselors must keep documentation of their interventions with clients. Admittedly, crisis conditions (e.g., a disaster site) are not always conducive to writing case notes, but crisis counselors need to clearly document exact dates, pertinent details, assessments, and treatment decisions. It is important to remember that although case notes must be succinct, they should never be vague. Case notes must be specific enough to demonstrate that the treatment reflected prevailing standards of care. The documentation must clearly illustrate the session with details that capture the essence of what occurred and validate treatment decisions. The need for client files to be in a locked and

CASE STUDY 3.3

Privacy Rights Records

When Jeff was 16 years old, he saw a counselor for conduct issues. During one of the adolescent sessions, Jeff volunteered that he had tried on his sister's undergarments. Ten years later Jeff is experiencing a life crisis: His estranged wife is suing for custody of their children, and Jeff is concerned that his childhood counseling record may be discoverable by the court.

Discussion Questions

1. If you were Jeff's adolescent counselor, how might you have best documented the issue he described?
2. What information should and should not be entered into the clinical record?
3. Can you offer any reassurances regarding the retention and availability of his older record?
4. If you were his current counselor, how would you record this disclosure about his previous therapy?
5. What information should Jeff's attorney be aware of regarding his rights of confidentiality?

secured location applies during crisis events, and providing for confidential file storage in crisis situations must be addressed in crisis planning.

CONFIDENTIALITY

Gladding (2006) defines confidentiality as "[t]he professional, ethical, and legal obligation of counselors that they not disclose client information revealed during counseling without the client's written consent" (p. 34). The *ACA Code of Ethics* (American Counseling Association, 2005) states "counselors do not share confidential information without client consent or without sound legal and ethical justification" (Standard B.1.c). In situations where a client is a danger to self or others or where the professional counselor is mandated by law to report abuse or is required by a court of law to disclose information, confidentiality can be legally breached. In situations other than these, a client must give consent for the release of information. Client records are confidential, and they must be kept in a secure and locked location for a specified time in accordance with professional

ACTIVITY 3.2

Examine the following case note entries. Rewrite these entries to improve them.

1. Client says she is doing better today.
2. Client's appearance is good.
3. Client went to doctor as requested.
4. Client began new medication last week.

ACTIVITY 3.3

You have just determined that your client is a potential suicide threat, and you must therefore break confidentiality and notify someone to discuss a plan of safety. Decide whom you will contact and exactly what you will discuss. Write a narrative of the conversation you will have with both the client and the person(s) to whom you will be disclosing. Consider how much you may disclose, what guidelines you are given by the *ACA Code of Ethics* to handle this scenario, and to what other sources you might look in determining how to guide your conversations.

ethical standards and the legal requirements of the state and HIPAA regulations. In crisis and disaster circumstances, provisions for confidentiality are certainly more challenging; however, the ethical standards and requirements of the profession still apply. Counselors should be aware of the latitude that may be allowed for confidentiality in difficult circumstances, yet strive to ensure the protection of client information.

INFORMED CONSENT

Clients enter counseling without much information about what will take place. They may in fact often have many misconceptions about the process of counseling and the nature of the counseling relationship. Clients must enter counseling freely and be fully informed of what is to be expected in the counseling relationship. Informed consent occurs when clients understand all the possible risks, benefits, and potential outcomes of counseling (Moline et al., 1998). The *ACA Code of Ethics* (2005) states that "counselors have an obligation to review in writing and verbally with clients the rights and responsibilities of both the counselor and the client" (Standard A.2.a). The *ACA Code* further specifies that the counselor must explain to the client "the purposes, goals, techniques, procedures, limitations, potential risks, and benefits of services; the counselor's qualifications, credentials, and relevant experience; continuation of services upon incapacitation or death of a counselor; and other pertinent information" (Standard A.2.b). Informed consent forms should also include an explanation of office policies, fees, billing arrangements, record keeping, the right to refuse treatment, and the potential effect of refusal. Both client and counselor must sign the informed consent form in order for it to become part of the counseling record.

In circumstances of crisis or large scale disaster, obtaining informed consent will rarely involve papers and a clipboard. Documented consent in such circumstances may be impossible, impractical or delayed, at a minimum. For example, a counselor may be called upon to provide support to someone wrapped in a thermal blanket at the scene of a disaster standing in front of the ruins of their home. Counselors should introduce themselves, explain their role, describe the general limitations of confidentiality, and ask permission to speak with them. The counselor may ask a few practical questions:

"What are you not comfortable with me disclosing when I contact those you have asked me to?"

"How do you want me to identify myself and my association with you when I call?"

"If I contact a person, and he or she is not there, may I leave a message and identify myself?"

If a crisis victim refuses intervention, the counselor should withdraw, offering to be available in the event that future service is wanted. If the client agrees to speak with the counselor, consent needs to be reassessed throughout the exchange and may be withdrawn at any point should the survivor elect to discontinue (American Red Cross, 2005; Gamino & Ritter, 2009). The privacy of the client should be protected as much as the circumstances of the disaster allows. Protecting privacy may involve moving the survivor from more trafficked areas or moderating one's voice to minimize the likelihood of being overheard. Often the counselor may be asked to contact others on the survivor's behalf such as community resources or loved ones. The counselor should clarify with the survivor, that they give consent for the contact, who they wish to have contacted and what specific information to share, being mindful to share only the minimal amount necessary. Linkage such as this may often be deferred to disaster case managers if necessary.

TERMINATION IN CRISIS INTERVENTION

Because crisis intervention is generally brief and focused on immediate needs, crisis counselors must use appropriate termination skills with clients. Appropriate termination should not only bring closure for the crisis counseling relationship but also bolster the goals and plans laid out in the crisis counseling process. A distinction should be made between termination and abandonment.

Termination occurs when a counselor or a client decides to end the counseling relationship. According to Standard A.11.c of the *ACA Code of Ethics* (2005), professional counselors terminate cases when the treatment goals have been reached and the client no longer needs counseling, when the client isn't being helped by further counseling or might be harmed by further counseling, when the client or someone associated with the client poses harm to the counselor, or when the client does not pay counseling fees. In those circumstances where clients need further counseling services after termination, the counselor provides the client with referral information for other appropriate mental health providers. Unfortunately, lack of attention to termination documentation can lead to lawsuits based on abandonment (Mitchell, 2001). A final termination summary should be added to the client file. Mitchell (2001) recommends that this summary include (1) the reason for termination, (2) a summary of progress, (3) the final diagnostic impression, (4) a follow-up plan, and (5) other pertinent information.

When clients are neglected, deserted, or negligently terminated, the counselor has committed abandonment of the client. The *ACA Code of Ethics* (2005) prohibits

---

VOICES FROM THE FIELD 3.4
Confidentiality During Chaotic Circumstances in the Field

Erin Martz

When providing counseling services in a disaster mental health capacity, you may find yourself facing a variety of ethical challenges. One issue to consider is the feasibility of ensuring confidentiality in potentially chaotic situations. Bear in mind that many first responders with whom you will be working may request access to information to maintain the welfare of those being helped collaboratively. Approach these requests from a treatment team perspective to ensure clients feel informed and empowered in a potentially disempowering and confusing time in their lives.

abandonment; Standard A.11.a states, "Counselors do not abandon or neglect clients in counseling. Counselors assist in making appropriate arrangements for the continuation of treatment, when necessary, during interruptions such as vacations, illness and following termination."

Mitchell (2001) highlights circumstances that increase a counselor's risk of malpractice due to abandonment:

- A client comes to treatment erratically.
- Records do not verify outreach efforts to a client who breaks/misses appointments.
- High-risk clients drop out of treatment.
- A client is "fired" or refused treatment.
- A professional therapist and client have not discussed/agreed on closure.
- A client is not notified in writing that a case is being closed.
- The record indicates a failure to review/consult/refer.
- Staff notes do not verify that a plan is being followed. (p. 71)

Mitchell recommends that clients be given written information about the closure plan, including contact information for other counselors or resources. In the event that a client misses appointments and stops coming to counseling, the counselor should send a follow-up letter expressing interest in the client's welfare and asking the client to contact the counselor within a set period of time if the client wants to resume counseling. If a termination letter is to be sent to the home of the client, written consent to send any information to that address should have been obtained during the informed consent process. Similarly, written consent to leave any information on a client's phone should have been obtained during intake. The written consent should state the specific address or phone number for which the client has granted permission. The counselor should document all attempts to contact a client.

CASE STUDY 3.4

Termination Considerations

Sarah lost her home and two family members in a series of tornadoes that swept across her state recently. She began to experience symptoms of acute trauma and approached you for care as a disaster relief counselor. You began seeing Sarah regularly since arriving at the disaster site. Sarah engaged well therapeutically, and appeared to be making progress. You were notified by the Red Cross that your term of service will be up in a week and need to terminate with each of your assigned cases at the location. When you mention discontinuing services with Sarah, she becomes distressed.

Discussion Questions

1. What obligations do you owe Sarah?
2. How will you ensure her continued recovery?
3. To what resources can you refer her?
4. Which ACA ethical code is applicable in this case?

As mentioned previously, termination in a mass crisis or disaster circumstance should be understood from a special perspective. Formal assessment, admission, and ongoing counseling normally are not possible under such circumstances. According to the American Red Cross (2005), ongoing care and provision of counseling services should be referred to local counseling services, case managers, and area providers in order to avoid therapeutic abandonment. An example of how such a conversation would occur follows:

COUNSELOR (C):   I'm glad we had the chance to work together these past few weeks since your home was destroyed. I understand this has been a very surreal and overwhelming time for you.

CLIENT (CL):   I don't know what I would have done without you.

C: Well, actually you did a lot of the work to move forward under difficult circumstances and have a lot to feel proud of. You have devised a plan of recovery for yourself, are in the process of securing more permanent housing, and have been able to return to work with transportation assistance. All of this means our work together has reached the right conclusion. At this time, I'd like to suggest community resources you may access for longer-term recovery support.

The severity of responses to mass crisis may have long-lasting effects for some. Psychological distress may remain high long after crisis counseling support services have been provided to those affected. This begs the question, what ethical responsibility do counselors have to ensure a healthy transition from crisis counseling to appropriate community-based treatment services once the additional support has been removed? There is some uncertainty about this limit of responsibility; therefore, many counseling training programs include crisis intervention course work. For those who are already in practice, it is recommended they seek some training in crisis response counseling to explore whether they want to work with crisis populations, or how they will if a person who has survived a mass disaster is referred to them for support (Norris & Rosen, 2009).

SPIRITUAL AND MULTICULTURAL CONSIDERATIONS

To dismiss discussions surrounding a client's religious or spiritual views related to a crisis is to devalue the client's worldview and not treat the entire person. Often, clients may entertain ideas that tragedy has come about as a result of God's wrath or disfavor. Counselors should be prepared to safely explore these concerns. This requires that counselors examine their own religious or spiritual biases and that they understand that many survivors have endorsed symptoms of secondary trauma of a spiritual nature (Zalaquett, Carrion, & Exum, 2009). Disaster workers might hear clients question whether their sin had brought the disaster upon them. Another aspect to consider may be prompted when the disaster occurs in a school system where the common separation of church and state is stressed. However, keep in mind that according to the Supreme Court, the First Amendment as applied to public schools, was intended for public schools to not offer sanctions or support a specific religion or faith over others. Counselors must find a balance between honoring guidelines of state, yet recognizing (and honoring) the needs of clients regardless where the tragedy took place (Remley & Herlihy, 2010).

In the case of a counselor responding to a person's life crisis, perhaps related to suicide, an examination of personal religious beliefs is essential to ensure maintaining a value neutral assessment. Failure to take a nonjudgmental stance may result in further risk to the client; by assuming the client has the same moral or religious beliefs counselors may foster shame and anger within the client who then may withhold pertinent information needed to assess level of lethality (Granello & Granello, 2007). Even secular counselors should exercise sufficient latitude to explore these questions with clients; doing less results in a failure to meet the needs of the client.

Research has indicated that marginalized populations may find predisaster norms set the tone for the postdisaster reality. Therefore, contrary to popular belief, disaster is not a social leveler, and minorities may find that their circumstances have declined (Enarson, Fothergill, & Peek, 2006). Counselors should therefore be versed in multicultural sensitivity and make efforts to indicate their sensitivity to multicultural issues. For example, Asian Americans are primarily focused on time orientation that is either past or present. In contrast, Native Americans tend to be present-oriented when exposed to traumatic circumstances. These variances require that counselors be aware how time orientation, and similar factors, influence crisis response of clients in order to accurately assess current mental status and needs (Remley & Herlihy, 2010). At the same time, it is important to not place all persons from a perceived culture into the same template but to assess individuals in their unique cultural perception. Having an understanding of differences is important, but making decision based on assumptions may not be helpful.

In addition, some cultures are more socially focused rather than individually focused. Responses from people of these cultures will be directed toward what is most beneficial to the community's best interest. People from different cultures will vary in terms of eye contact, body language, affect, and willingness to discuss personal matters and in their response to authority figures. Ethical practice requires the development of multicultural competence among counselors; therefore counselors are responsible for being well versed in multicultural competencies when serving others (American Counseling Association, 2005; Remley & Herlihy, 2010).

Summary

It is imperative that crisis counselors be well acquainted with legal and ethical obligations. Privacy laws such as HIPAA and FERPA have provisions for crisis situations, but confidentiality is still central to ethical practice, even during times of crisis. Crisis counselors must be familiar with the particulars of HIPAA and FERPA and other legal requirements in their state. Furthermore, counselors should consult with an attorney to remain current on the legal aspects of care in crisis as well as standard practice circumstances. Ethical obligations, including prevention strategies, duty to warn, documentation, informed consent, referral, and termination, must be attended to whether the crisis counselor is working one-on-one with a client in life-crisis or intervening with clients in a large-scale disaster. Crisis counselors should also be careful to include multicultural and spiritual considerations in predisaster training. Planning, preparedness, and a commitment to ethical practice in all situations will ensure that crisis counselors maintain standards of care whatever the situation.

4

Essential Crisis Intervention Skills

Joseph Cooper

PREVIEW

This chapter provides an overview of the fundamental skills for the provision of effective crisis intervention work. The skills discussed here will focus on Ivey and Ivey's (2007) mircoskills hierarchy. At the heart of this hierarchy is the basic listening sequence, an interrelated set of skills that will not only foster the development of rapport with clients but also aid in the identification of interventions to help achieve a successful resolution to the client's crisis state. Examples of the skills in use as well as practice exercises to foster individual skill development are provided.

ESSENTIAL CRISIS INTERVENTION MICROSKILLS

The essential foundational skills necessary for effective crisis intervention work are indeed the basic tools on which the success of interventions may depend. It is important to stress that these skills will help to create the counselor-client relational conditions necessary for positive change. However, we also need to stress that the skills covered in this chapter are *basic* counseling microskills applied to crisis situations. These basic skills form the foundation for the use of more advanced counseling skills.

These microskills will provide the client with alliance-building constructs such as empathic understanding, genuineness, and acceptance, and they will greatly facilitate the development of a safe therapeutic environment (Rogers, 1951). These skills will also aid in establishing rapport with the client. Rapport can be understood as a harmonious or sympathetic relationship. In crisis intervention work, the development of rapport starts with the initial contact and continues throughout the process. The crisis counselor's primary concern should be fostering this rapport in order to develop a cohesive and supportive relationship with the client. How the crisis counselor conducts himself or herself is crucial, as this may be the client's first encounter with a counselor and this interaction may either encourage or discourage the client from seeking counseling in the future or from following up when a proposed crisis plan is developed.

The skills covered in this chapter focus on Ivey and Ivey's (2007) mircoskills hierarchy—a set of verbal and behavioral responses that facilitate the process of counseling and alliance formation regardless of the crisis counselor's theoretical orientation. For some, this chapter may be a review of the basic skills taught in a previous skills course, while for others it may be the first consideration of these skills. Either way, it is always important to continuously be aware of and practice effective skills, since this is the hallmark of effective crisis counseling. Ivey and Ivey present these skills as a hierarchy that is organized within a systematic framework. At the bottom of the hierarchy are the basic attending skills, such as patterns of eye contact, body position, vocal tone, and silence. A bit farther up the skills hierarchy is the basic listening sequence, which includes asking open and closed questions, reflecting skills, and summarizing. In this chapter, each of these basic skills is reviewed, along with practical examples of the skills in use.

ATTENDING SKILLS

Good communication involves more than just verbal content, for crisis counselors communicate with more than just words. Much of their communication takes place nonverbally. The next time you are engaged in conversation with someone, take a moment to pay attention to all of the nonverbal cues your partner is giving you. What does his facial expression say to you? What is conveyed by the look in his eyes? Does he have a closed or open body stance? Although important in social relationships, these attending skills are even more important in the counseling relationship. Bedi (2006) surveyed clients who had received counseling and asked them to identify the specific counselor behaviors that most helped to form a working alliance. Following validation and education, clients ranked nonverbal gestures and presentation and body language as the most important alliance-building factors. These nonverbal attending behaviors communicate a counselor's interest, warmth, and understanding to the client and include behaviors such as eye contact, body position, and tone of voice.

Eye Contact

Maintaining good eye contact is how a crisis counselor conveys interest, confidence, and involvement in the client's story (Egan, 2002). Through eye contact, clients know a counselor is focusing on them and fully committed to the helping process. Moreover, for those clients who have difficulty with closeness, making eye contact can be an important vehicle of change (Vaillant, 1997). However, good eye contact is not the same as staring your client down. There should be natural breaks in eye contact; eye contact should be more of an "ebb and flow" as you collect your thoughts and listen to the client's story. Also, it is essential to be sensitive to differences in how eye contact is expressed across cultures. For example, whereas direct eye contact is usually interpreted as a sign of interest in the European-American culture, some Asian and Native American groups believe direct eye contact is a sign of disrespect (Ivey & Ivey, 2007).

ACTIVITY 4.1

Form dyads where one person takes the role of listener while the other takes the role of a speaker who talks about anything of interest for about 5 minutes. During this time, each listener should maintain the eye contact as he or she would normally do so in everyday conversation. After 5 minutes, participants should take some time to process the experience. What feedback does the speaker have regarding the listener's level of eye contact? Was it too much? Darting? Too little? Empathic? What was most comfortable? Based on the feedback, do the exercise again, but this time have the listener try to incorporate some of the feedback received about his or her level of eye contact. Process the activity again, and then switch roles.

Some African Americans may maintain greater eye contact when talking and less eye contact when listening, and many African American men will not look directly into the eyes of an authority figure because in the Black cultural context avoiding eye contact shows recognition of the authority-subordinate relationship (Johnson, 2004). Also, for clients who are overly fragile or under much stress and pressure, direct eye contact may increase their level of anxiety. For example, let's say you are seeing a client in crisis, a 20-year-old female college student who states she was raped last night. As she tells you what happened, you notice she stares down at the floor and often avoids your eye contact. Should you confront her on her lack of eye contact and ask her to look at you directly when she speaks? Of course not. Her lack of eye contact is probably due to her feelings of shame and anxiety and is serving as an emotion-regulating function. In a crisis situation, especially if a client is feeling overwhelmed or ashamed or is experiencing paranoia, be aware that a client who avoids your eyes is probably doing so as a protective mechanism.

So how do you determine how much eye contact to maintain with a client? Unfortunately, there is no universal rule or criterion for what is considered either appropriate or inappropriate eye contact; as already noted, this varies among cultures as well as the nature of the emotions involved in the crisis situation. A good rule of thumb to follow is to maintain a moderate amount of eye contact while monitoring your client's level of comfort and to adjust your eye contact accordingly (Young, 2008). Also, it is helpful for you to become aware of your own attending behavior so you can understand how this behavior may affect the counseling relationship. Activities 4.1 and 4.2 will help you gain a deeper understanding of your own attending behaviors.

ACTIVITY 4.2

This exercise will help you become aware of how your clients might perceive your overall pattern of nonverbal communications. Begin by breaking up into pairs, where one person will be the communicator and will face the other person, who will serve as the mirror. For the next 5 minutes, the communicator can talk about anything he or she wants, and throughout this time, the mirror is to nonverbally mirror each gesture, facial expression, eye contact, and movement of the communicator. It is important that the mirror not attempt to "interpret" the message that is being sent by the communicator but just to mirror the perceived nonverbals. At the end of 5 minutes, process this experience with each other. What was it like to see your nonverbals mirrored back to you? Did you learn anything about how you come across to others? Is there anything you would want to change or to do more of?

Body Position

As with eye contact, your body position should convey to the client your interest and involvement. Face the client and adopt an open, relaxed, and attentive body posture, as this will assist in putting your client at ease. Counselors should not cross arms and legs and should not sit behind a desk or other barrier. In addition, Egan (2002) recommends that the counselor lean slightly toward the client, as this communicates that the counselor is listening to the client and interested in what the client has to say. Slouching in a chair or leaning away from the client may be perceived by the client as lack of interest or boredom. The physical distance between counselor and client should also be taken into consideration; getting too close can be overwhelming and uncomfortable, whereas too great a distance can make the counselor appear aloof and may be awkward for the client. Although in Western cultures the average physical distance for conversation is typically 2 to 4 feet, this "comfort zone" will vary from client to client (Young, 2008). When in doubt, one idea is to let the client arrange the chairs at a distance that meets his or her individual comfort level. However there are exceptions to this. For example, in a crisis setting, you may be faced with a client who is paranoid, or experiencing homicidal or suicidal ideation. Would you want to be within hitting or kicking distance from this client? Also, it would not be a good idea to have this client sitting between you and the door. Use your best judgment. By taking into account body position, you can create a safe environment for both you and your client. Your safety should always be a priority. You should never do anything that makes you feel uncomfortable or jeopardizes your physical safety.

Vocal Tone

Have you ever had the experience where you are engaged in conversation with someone and you find yourself becoming increasingly anxious and tense regardless of the topic? The next time this happens pay attention to your partner's tone of voice, for you may be unconsciously responding to the emotional tone conveyed in your partner's voice. Emotions are frequently conveyed via tone of voice. The pitch, pacing, and volume can all have an effect on how a client responds emotionally to a crisis counselor. There is much to be said for a calm and soothing voice in times of distress, especially when the client is in a crisis situation. Do not underestimate the power of this attribute; your control and calmness may be among the greatest benefits to your client in crisis. Your voice can do much to help create a soothing and anxiety-regulating atmosphere for the client. Learn to use your voice as a therapeutic tool. For instance, if your client is overly agitated, it is often helpful to speak more slowly and in a soothing tone, as this will help your client to slow things down and begin to focus.

In relation to this, be aware of your own internal process and how your tone of voice is conveying your *own* emotional state when working with a client in crisis. It is not uncommon for your own rate of speech to increase when you hear something that causes you to feel anxious, such as a client who discloses homicidal ideation to you. If your client is agitated and using pressured speech, and your speech is also beginning to race as well, then this could exacerbate your client's state. It can also be helpful to convey a sense of empathic understanding by giving emphasis to the specific words used by your client. This technique of giving increased vocal emphasis to certain words or short phrases is called *verbal underlining* (Ivey & Ivey, 2007). For example, consider the difference between "You were very hurt by your husband's actions" and "You were

ACTIVITY 4.3

In small groups, assign one person to be the speaker. Instruct the speaker to talk in a normal tone of voice for a few minutes about anything of interest. Have the other group members close their eyes as they listen to the speaker, paying close attention to the tone of voice, pacing, volume, and so on. After 2 or 3 minutes, stop and have the listeners give the speaker feedback on his or her voice. What was their reaction to the tone, volume, accent, rate of speech, and other characteristics? After this processing, repeat the exercise, but this time have the speaker make changes in voice tone, volume, or pacing to deliberately create different reactions. How do the listeners respond to the changes in vocal qualities? What were the listeners emotional responses that corresponded with the various vocal qualities? Finally, have the listeners imagine themselves as a client in crisis. What types of vocal qualities would they prefer to hear?

very hurt by your husband's actions." In the latter comment, the counselor places the emphasis on the word *very* to help reflect the intensity of the client's experience. Activity 4.3 will facilitate a greater awareness of the vocal subtleties in the spoken word.

Silence

Beginning crisis workers often have difficulty using silence with their clients. They want to keep talking to fill in any lapses or void in the session, usually as a way to mollify their own anxiety and discomfort with a client in crisis. Or worse, they will engage in a monologue or resort to lecturing or teaching the client. However, constantly intervening or throwing a barrage of questions to a client in crisis can feel overwhelming and intrusive to the client who is already feeling overwhelmed. Clients in crisis need space to think, to sort out their thoughts, and to process what is happening. The crisis worker needs that time as well. Many beginning counselors are afraid to use silence, because they believe the silence conveys their incompetence as a counselor. However, it is quite the opposite. Silence, if used appropriately and at the right time, can convey acceptance and empathic understanding. In essence, the message is that "I am here for you if you need me, yet I respect your need to take your time with this." Consider the following interchange between Carol and her counselor.

CAROL: I just had another miscarriage, my third one, and I'm almost certain I'll never have children. On top of that, my husband is

VOICES FROM THE FIELD 4.1

Reflective and Active Interventions

Crisis intervention requires us to be both reflective *and* active in our interventions, and it is important to know when to use each. Here is an example of the need to be active: I once had a client in crisis who set her shirt on fire while sitting in the waiting room as I was getting her file and preparing for the session. This was not a time to reflect and listen! We put out the fire; made sure she was not injured, and then actively assessed suicidal/homicidal intent, safety issues, and developed a plan of action, which called for her to be hospitalized. I had to take an active and directive role in ensuring her safety. Crisis counseling often requires us to be quick on our feet and to have the ability to explore alternatives and to actively assist our clients in dealing with their problems.

growing more distant too, and I worry he might leave me for someone who he can have a family with.

COUNSELOR (C):   So you're also feeling worried about how this is going to impact your marriage, and whether or not your husband will want to be with you.

CAROL: (*Silence for 30 seconds as she looks down and to the right.*) Yes, but I realize that if he truly cared for me, that he wouldn't leave, and I think he is just as hurt and in as much pain as I am. It's my own insecurities really. And if he did want to leave, then he is not the right person for me to be with. I deserve better than that.

C: (*Silence for 20 seconds as the counselor gathers her thoughts.*) So there are a couple of things at work here. First, your husband's behavior could represent how he is grieving, and your insecurities were distorting how you have been making sense of his behavior. And second, you realize that what is important for you is to be with someone who truly and genuinely cares for you and is committed to the marriage.

THE BASIC LISTENING SEQUENCE

The basic listening sequence represents a set of interrelated skills used to achieve three overarching goals: (1) to obtain an overall summary and understanding of the client's presenting issue, (2) to identify the key facts of the client's situation, and (3) to identify the core emotions and feelings the client is experiencing (Ivey & Ivey, 2007). In short, these skills allow you to understand the structure of your client's story. Through the use of these skills, not only will you convey empathy, respect, warmth, and congruence to your client, but also you will be laying the foundation for your understanding of the client's issues and the development of subsequent interventions to help achieve a successful resolution to his or her crisis state. The basic listening sequence involves the ability to ask open and closed questions as well as the reflecting skills—paraphrasing, reflecting feelings, and summarizing. An explanation and overview of these skills, examples of each skill in use, and some brief exercises to help you practice these basic listening skills follow.

Asking Open and Closed Questions

Questioning is a primary skill that allows crisis counselors to gather important and specific information about clients. Questions allow counselors to make an accurate assessment of their clients' issues and to guide and focus clients so they can make the most effective use of the counseling session. However, the use of questioning can be a double-edged sword. Used inappropriately, questioning can impede communication and block client disclosure. Drilling clients with questions can give too much control to the crisis counselor. Moreover, bombarding clients with questions could confuse and frustrate them as well as increase their level of anxiety. Crisis counselors definitely do not want counseling sessions to sound like an interrogation, although many of the initial intake questions are used to gather information and therefore necessary in crisis intervention. Counselors must be careful to appropriately pace the questions to guard against increasing clients' stress levels. Thus, crisis counselors need to be aware of how to use questions appropriately and pay close attention to the types of questions used to gather information. The two types of questions, open and closed questions, are examined next.

OPEN QUESTIONS   Open questions usually elicit fuller and more meaningful responses by encouraging the client to talk at greater length. Open questions typically begin with *what, how, could, would,* or *why* and are useful to help begin an interview, to help elaborate the client's story, and to help bring out specific details (Ivey & Ivey, 2007). With open questions, the client can choose the content and direction of the session and take more control. The following guidelines illustrate the use of open questions for crisis workers:

1. *To begin the interview:* "What would you like to talk about today?" "How can I be of help to you today?" "Tell me why you've come in today."
2. *To elicit details:* "Give me an example." "What do you mean by 'just give up'?" "What do you usually do when you're feeling down?"
3. *To enrich and deepen:* "Tell me more." "What were your feelings when that happened?" "What else is important for me to know?" "In what ways does that help?"
4. *Focus on plans:* "What are some things you can do to stay safe?" "Who are some people you can call when you feel this way again?" "How will you make that happen?"

Finally, be careful when using *why* questions and questions that are leading in nature. Questions that begin with "Why" often cause the client to intellectualize and can lead to a discussion of reasons. In addition, *why* questions can cause the client to become defensive or criticized, to feel "put on the spot." When this happens, it is not uncommon for the client to become more guarded and to shut down. For example, think back to a time when you were younger and your parents asked the question "Why did you do that?" How did you feel and what was your reaction? Take a moment to consider the following: "Why do you hate yourself?" versus "You say you hate yourself. Help me understand that." Which of these approaches would you prefer your counselor to use? In addition to making clients become more defensive, *why* questions can also lead clients to feel more hopeless and despondent, as in this example:

COUNSELOR: Why do you continue to go back to a man who abuses you?

SUSAN: I know, I know. It sounds pathetic.

Another roadblock to the use of effective questions involves questions that are leading in nature. Leading questions often contain a hidden agenda because the answer or expectation is already imbedded within the question. Although well intentioned, these types of questions place too much power in the hands of the crisis counselor and tend to push the client in a preconceived direction. Here are a couple of examples of leading questions: "You didn't really want to kill yourself, did you?" or "Don't you think you will feel better if you stop drinking?" Try to guard against the use of these types of questions. Crisis counselors want to hear a client's story as he or she understands and experiences it. Open questions allow the counselor the opportunity to achieve this end without imposing values and expectations on the client.

CLOSED QUESTIONS   Closed questions can be used when crisis counselors need to obtain very specific, concrete information and get all the facts straight. Such questions typically either elicit a "yes/no" response or provide specific factual information, such as the number of drinks a client consumes in a week or the age at which he or she began experiencing symptoms. In contrast to longer-term counseling, where information is gathered more slowly and the treatment plan develops over many weeks, crisis counseling often requires quick and focused responses. Thus, closed questions are very useful and in fact necessary in crisis counseling because the counselor must gather specific information to aid in the prompt assessment of the problem and development of a plan of action (James, 2008). Here are some examples of closed questions:

"Are you thinking of killing yourself?"

"When did these symptoms begin?"

"Do you have a family member or friend to call on when you are feeling overwhelmed?"

"How old were you when your parents divorced?"

As can be seen from the above examples, closed questions are good for obtaining the necessary details to aid in assessment and intervention when a client is in crisis. However, you must guard against the overuse of closed questions, which can cause clients to shut down and become passive because you are training them to simply sit back and wait for the next question to answer. A good rule of thumb to follow is to move from the general to the specific in your assessment. In other words, begin with open (i.e., general) questions, and as you gather information and hear the client's story, move to more closed (i.e., specific) questions to obtain the details important for the assessment and subsequent development of an intervention plan.

There is a category of closed questions that is similar in nature to leading questions and should not be used. Referred to as *negative-interrogatives* (James, 2008), they are closed questions that are used in a subtle way to coerce the client into agreeing with you. Questions that begin with *don't, doesn't, isn't, shouldn't, aren't,* and *wouldn't* often suggest a command for the client to do something. For example, "Shouldn't you stay away from her?" or "Isn't it a good idea to stop drinking?" imply the client should agree with the crisis counselor and do something different. For counselors who want to work collaboratively with clients, a better way to ask this question would be: "You stated earlier that one of the problems that brought you in today is your drinking. Would you like some information on how I can be of help to you with that?" The following dialogue provides a brief example of how the crisis counselor uses a blend of open and closed questions to obtain important information about Susan, who recently discovered her husband is having an affair and is planning on leaving her.

SUSAN: I've gotten to where I can't even sleep at night. My mind just races, and I can't stop thinking about everything.

COUNSELOR (C):   Tell me more about some of the thoughts you have been having as you lay in bed unable to sleep. (*Open question to facilitate exploration and information gathering.*)

SUSAN: That I will never be in a happy relationship again. That my husband never really cared about me and just used me. That this pain will never stop. I wonder how I can get my life back together without him.

C: You wonder if you will find peace again without him and want so much for this pain to go away. (*Empathic paraphrase.*) What are some of the feelings you have been experiencing? (*Open question.*)

SUSAN: Mainly down—angry and depressed. I feel this tremendous pain inside my chest, very hurt and sad I guess. I feel like he never really cared about me. He is so selfish.

C: You're feeling very hurt and betrayed. Susan, tell me when you began experiencing these symptoms? (*Closed question to identify timeline of symptoms.*)

SUSAN: I would say about three months ago, when I found out about his affair, but they have gotten much worse over the last month.

C: You say they have gotten worse over the last month. What do you make of that? (*Open question to identify client's understanding of her progressing symptoms.*)

SUSAN: Well, when I first found out about the affair, I would talk a lot with my friends and family, but I felt like they were getting sick of hearing me complain all the time. So lately I have just been trying to tough it out and deal with it on my own.

C: And is this the first time you've sought counseling for this?

SUSAN: Yes.

As this example demonstrates, the crisis counselor began with open questions to encourage exploration and to help identify the client's thoughts (e.g., "I will never be in a happy relationship again") and feelings (e.g., anger, grief, and hurt) associated with the breakup of her marriage. The crisis worker then moved to closed questions to obtain more specific information regarding the duration of her symptoms and her experience in counseling.

OPEN VERSUS CLOSED QUESTIONS   As mentioned earlier, in crisis intervention work, crisis counselors often need to use closed questions to quickly identify and bring out specific details in order to seek the resolution of the crisis state. However, you can often obtain the same information by asking open questions, so try to refrain from moving too quickly into a closed questioning approach unless you are unable to obtain the information otherwise. Consider these examples of closed questions and their open question counterparts:

Closed	Open
Were you afraid?	What feelings did you experience?
Are you concerned about what you'll do if your husband returns?	How do you think you may react if your husband returns?
Do you see your drinking as a problem?	What concerns do you have about your drinking?

Notice in these examples that you can probably get all you need to know, and much more, by a subtle change in the wording of your questions to make them more open in nature. Now get some additional practice by completing Activity 4.4.

Reflecting Skills

Reflecting skills are a set of interventions used to help stimulate clients' exploration of their thoughts and feelings related to the presenting problems. Such skills serve a number of important purposes. At the most basic level, reflecting skills are a form of active listening that convey to the client your interest in and understanding of what the client may be struggling with. Thus, reflecting skills allow you to convey empathy, genuineness, and acceptance to the client, and this in turn will facilitate the creation of a sense of safety. Moreover, reflecting skills will stimulate a deeper exploration and understanding of the problem so that the client can examine the issues more objectively. The reflecting skills covered here are paraphrasing, reflecting feelings, and summarizing.

PARAPHRASING   A paraphrase is how a counselor feeds back to the client the essence of what has just been spoken. By paraphrasing, the counselor reflects the content and thoughts of the client's message. In other words, the crisis counselor is mirroring back to the client, in a nonjudgmental way, an accurate understanding of the client's communication and the implied meaning of that communication. Thus, paraphrasing is a reflecting skill used to convey empathic understanding and to facilitate the exploration and clarification of the client's problems (Ivey & Ivey, 2007). It is important for counselors to be sure the paraphrased information is accurate by checking with the client. Some clients in crisis may not feel they can refute what is being said, or their crisis state may impede their ability to completely follow the session; however, paraphrasing gives these clients permission to approve or disapprove of the accuracy of the paraphrase and its implied meaning, thereby increasing their control. When the counselor paraphrases the client's information inaccurately and does not seek affirmation by the client, the

---

ACTIVITY 4.4

Take a moment to practice changing these questions from closed to open questions.

1. Why did you quit your job?
2. Do you think you should stop using drugs?
3. Do you get eight hours of sleep a night?
4. Did you feel angry with him?
5. Don't you think there are other ways for you to cope with your anger?

counselor may then define the actual primary presenting problem inaccurately, which in turn may change the direction of the session and/or interfere with the development of the most appropriate treatment plan for the client. This is compounded when the client needs the counselor to use a more directive approach due to the severity of the crisis. Young (2008) proposed that reflecting skills are important because they provide the counselor with a way to do the following:

1. Communicate empathy.
2. Give feedback that enables the client to confirm or reject the impression he or she has been giving.
3. Stimulate further exploration of what the client has been experiencing.
4. Capture important aspects of the client's story that may have been overlooked or covert. (pp. 123–124)

As can be seen, paraphrasing, if used appropriately, is a powerful therapeutic tool. Appropriate use means crisis counselors must develop the ability to take the essence of the client's statement and reflect back those thoughts and facts in *their own words*. When the counselor uses paraphrasing accurately, the client will continue to explore and elaborate. On the other hand, the counselor should not "parrot" back to the client what has been said. Parroting back would be a simple word-for-word restatement, not a paraphrase. Consider this example:

SUSAN: I feel so put down and disrespected by my husband. He is just like my father in a lot of ways. He was verbally abusive and full of anger. I never really felt important to him. Why do I let men treat me this way?

C: You feel put down and disrespected by him.

As you can see from the above paraphrase, the crisis worker simply parrots back what the client has said, which adds little and keeps the focus superficial. A better response might be:

C: Although you're trying to understand this pattern of hurt and disappointment that you've experienced from the important men in your life, it sounds like you're blaming yourself for this.

To develop your paraphrasing skill, you may find it helpful to first identify the key words or content that captures the essence of your client's concern. Once you have the key content in mind, try to translate this into your own words. Following are some examples of a client's statements, the possible key themes or words, and the resulting paraphrase.

EXAMPLE 1

Client: I'm so fed up with my marriage. I try and try to get through to him, and he just shuts me out.

Possible key themes or words: *fed up, being shut out, failed efforts to connect.*

Paraphrase: You're at your wit's end with this. In spite of your efforts to connect, you come up against a closed door. Is that correct?

ACTIVITY 4.5

Think about the following client statements and try to identify the key themes or words. Then, based on these key themes or words, develop a paraphrase of your client's statement.

1. "I don't know what to do with my life. I hate my job and everything seems so meaningless. I can barely muster the energy to get out of bed in the morning. Sometimes I just want to sleep for days."

2. "I'm still in shock that my husband is having an affair. I really can't believe it. I thought we had the perfect marriage. How could I have been so stupid to not see this was happening? I feel like such a fool."

3. "I can't tell if I am coming or going. I can't sleep, I have nightmares, and I feel like a zombie throughout the day. I am so tense my body aches. No matter what I do, it just keeps getting worse."

EXAMPLE 2

Client: Exactly, and that's why I've been thinking about leaving him. I know I deserve much better, but I just keep going back to him. I can't seem to make that first move.

Possible key themes or words: *leaving her husband, being stuck, hesitation, self-worth.*

Paraphrase: Although a part of you knows this is not the way you want to live your life, it's still difficult to break out of this cycle. Is that right?

As you can see from these examples, identifying the key words or themes can really aid in your ability to develop accurate paraphrases that convey the essence of your client's meaning without coming across as superficial. Use Activity 4.5 to practice your paraphrasing skills.

REFLECTING FEELINGS   A wealth of research attests to the usefulness of accessing and working with feelings and emotions in counseling (Greenberg & Pascual-Leone, 2006). Naming and identifying a client's feelings can serve a number of important functions (Young, 2008). By reflecting feelings, a crisis counselor can help the client to become aware of the emotions experienced in relation to the issue at hand. This awareness can then increase the client's overall level of self-awareness and deepen his or her

VOICES FROM THE FIELD 4.2
Reflecting Your Way Through a Crisis

Clients often come to counseling in crisis. They may be feeling overwhelmed, confused, think they are going "crazy," or in more serious cases, feeling suicidal or homicidal. In these situations our own anxiety might lead us to become overly directive, give unwanted advice, or drill clients with questions. However, I have found doing the opposite is the key. In other words,

using reflecting skills in these situations can go a long way to help a client become more emotionally regulated with you. Simple paraphrases, reflecting feelings, and even silence can help the client to feel understood, accepted, and safe. And I have found that clients are more likely to take the risk of changing and developing a healthy plan of action when they feel safe with you.

self-disclosure. In addition, reflecting feelings can have a positive impact on the thera-peutic relationship, and a convincing amount of research has shown the quality of the therapeutic relationship to be one of the strongest predictors of counseling outcomes (Horvath & Bedi, 2002). Moreover, it is not necessarily the specific theoretical approach of the helper but the strength of the therapeutic relationship that is associated with the successful achievement of a client's counseling goals (Nuttall, 2002). The therapeutic relationship should be characterized by an experience of mutual liking, trust, and re-spect between the client and the helper. In addition, helper qualities such as accurate empathy, unconditional positive regard, and genuineness greatly contribute to the de-velopment of the helping relationship (Rogers, 1951). Thus, the reflecting skills play an important role in the development of this vital working alliance by conveying these "relationship enhancers" to a client (Young, 2008). As with paraphrasing, reflecting feelings can promote the development of accurate empathy and help to create a safe environment for the client.

To reflect feelings, a crisis counselor must be able to recognize and put words to those feeling states observed in the client. And what is the best way to practice this? One way is to work on becoming more aware of your own feelings and being able to accu-rately name these feelings. This in turn will help you to accurately recognize and name the feelings clients may be experiencing. For example, in my counseling skills class, I will walk around the class and ask each student to tell me how he or she is feeling *right now*. The most common responses I receive are "fine," "good," and "ok." Notice, however, that these are not feelings and do not provide me with any understanding of what my students may be really feeling. I then explain the importance of being able not only to correctly identify and name the core feelings we all experience as humans (e.g., anger, sadness, fear, surprise, joy, love, disgust) but also to accurately recognize and name our moment-to-moment feeling states that represent the finer shadings of those core emotions. For example, some of the finer shadings of the word *anger* are *irritated*, *bitter*, *enraged*, *frustrated*, and *sore*. By increasing your feelings awareness and feelings word vocabulary, you will be able to more easily and correctly identify and respond to a client's feelings.

How does a counselor identify the feelings in clients, especially if these feelings are not explicitly stated? When clients do not state their feelings directly, counselors may still be able to infer these feelings either from the context of a client's communica-tion or from the client's nonverbal behaviors (e.g., facial expression, posture). Thus, it is important to attend not only to what is being said but also to how it is being commu-nicated. The following practical tips will aid you in reflecting a client's feelings (Evans, Hearn, Uhlemann, & Ivey, 2008; Ivey & Ivey, 2007):

1. To aid in identifying a client's feelings:
   a. Pay attention to the affective component of the client's communication.
   b. Pay attention to the client's behavior (e.g., posture, tone of voice, facial expression).
   c. Use a broad range of words to correctly identify the client's emotions.
   d. Silently name the client's feeling(s) to yourself.
2. To aid in reflecting feelings to a client:
   a. Use an appropriate introductory phrase (*Sounds like. … Looks like. … You feel. … It seems. …*).

b. Add a feeling word or emotional label to the stem (*Sounds like you're angry*).
c. Add a context or brief paraphrase to help anchor or broaden the reflection. This context should add the link or meaning for the perceived feeling (*Sounds like you're angry at your father's refusal to put you in his will*).
d. Pay attention to the tense. Present tense reflections can often be more powerful than past tense reflections (you *feel* angry versus you *felt* angry).
e. Do not repeat the client's exact words (parroting).
f. Reflect mixed emotions (*You're feeling both angry and hurt about your father's behavior toward you*).
g. Check out the accuracy of the reflection of feeling with the client (*Am I hearing you correctly? Is that close? Have I got that right?*).

Consider the following example:

SUSAN:	I just sit around the house wondering what to do. We used to spend time with my husband's friends, but they know that we're no longer together. So there is no one for me to really spend time with. I really miss them, and my own friends seem so busy. I would hate to burden them with all of my problems.
C:	You're feeling both sad and lonely right now, and you're concerned you may be just another burden on your own friends. Is that about right? (*Reflection of feeling with check for accuracy.*)
SUSAN:	Yes, I don't want to bring everyone down with all my problems.

When reflecting feelings, a useful way to help defuse a client in an emotional crisis state is to also reflect the client's stated, or unstated, need or goal that is implied within the context of their narrative. The formula for this would be: "You feel _____ because _____ and you want (or need) _____." For example:

MIKE:	Every time I do something for her, it's not good enough and she puts me down. (*Yelling.*) It's all I can do to keep from hitting her.
C:	You're *feeling* so angry and hurt right now *because* she puts you down, and you really *want* to be more respected and valued in your relationship.

Here is another example:

SUSAN:	I can't seem to take it anymore. After my husband and daughter were killed in the car accident, everything just fell apart for me. I just think maybe I should be dead too.
C:	You're *feeling* so much pain and grief *because* of the loss of your family, and you want so much to find you own *peace* now.

In a crisis situation, the above interventions can go a long way to help your client feel safe with you, to diffuse overwhelming emotions, and to set the groundwork to begin working on a plan of action.

ACTIVITY 4.6

Take a moment to read each vignette and to identify the feelings embedded within the client's communications. Once you have identified the feelings, come up with your own reflection of feelings.

1. "I don't know what to do. My husband keeps working late into the night, and I feel like I never get to see him. When we do get some time together, he is moody and reserved. To make matters worse, I saw a charge on our credit card statement to a local hotel. I think he might be having an affair."

2. "Ever since I was mugged I've been having a hard time. Because of the nightmares, I can't sleep at night, and I'm exhausted all during the day. On top of that, I'm panicky and nervous all the time. I worry I might be losing my mind."

3. "I can't believe what my father did. He stole all the money from the trust fund grandmother had willed to my brother and me. I've been calling him day and night, and he won't return my calls. I might have to get a lawyer, but I don't know how I'm going to afford it. Why would he do this to us?"

There is one last point to consider when reflecting feelings. Whereas in traditional psychotherapy the focus is often on uncovering feeling after feeling by attempting to unearth the "core" issue, in crisis intervention work the task is quite different. Thus, guard against going too far with uncovering feelings, as this could exacerbate the clients' crisis state by overwhelming them with emotion. Strive for a balance of skills to build rapport, and when you do reflect feelings, be sure to keep the focus directly related to the client's presenting concerns (James, 2008). Activity 4.6 will give you an opportunity to practice identifying feelings so you can develop accurate reflections of feelings.

SUMMARIZING   The final skill in the basic listening sequence is summarizing, a process through which a crisis counselor can begin to put together the key themes, feelings, and issues that the client has presented. By distilling the key issues and themes and reflecting this back to the client, counselors can begin to help clients make sense of what may have originally seemed to be an overwhelming and confusing experience. In addition, when clients are feeling overwhelmed and are flooded with anxiety, they will often go on tangents in many directions, making it difficult for the crisis counselor to keep up. When this occurs, brief summaries are often a useful tool to help refocus the client and reintroduce some structure into the session, which will help to modulate the client's (and the counselor's) anxiety. Thus, a summary not only is used to end a session or to begin a new session by recapping the previous session but also can be used periodically throughout the session, helping to keep a focus and putting together the pertinent issues at hand for the client.

So when should a crisis counselor summarize? Although much will depend on the client and the content being discussed, Evans et al. (2008) offered a number of useful suggestions to help determine when a summary is in order: (1) when your client is rambling, confused, or overly lengthy in his or her comments; (2) when your client presents a number of unrelated ideas; (3) when you need to provide direction to the interview; (4) when you are ready to move the client from one phase of the interview to the next; (5) when you want to end the interview; and (6) when a summary of the prior interview will provide you an opening to the current interview.

When summarizing, you do not have to report back to the client every single detail he or she has disclosed. This would, of course, require a prodigious memory. The key is to capture the important elements, content, feelings, and issues and to reflect these back to the client in a concise manner. The following three types of summaries are particularly relevant to crisis intervention counseling:

1. *Focusing summaries:* These summaries are often used at the beginning of the session to pull together prior information the client has given and to provide a focus to the session. "Last time we met you were having trouble sleeping, and you were having nightmares and feeling panicky throughout the day. We identified some coping skills and relaxation exercises for you to use. Tell me how these have worked out for you so far."

2. *Signal summaries:* These summaries are used to "signal" to the client that you have captured the essence of his or her topic and that the session can move on to the next area of concern. Signal summaries help to provide both structure and direction to the session. "So before we move on, let me make sure I understand things correctly. You discovered your husband is having an affair. ..."

3. *Planning summaries:* These summaries help to provide closure and are used to recap the progress, plans, and any recommendations/agreements made. Such summaries are good for ending the session on a positive note and for providing a sense of direction for the client. "Let's take a look at what we've covered today. Ever since you were mugged, you've been having panic attacks and nightmares. We covered some coping techniques and relaxation exercises for you to practice between now and the next time we meet. ..." (Young, 2008, pp. 161–163).

So, to put it all together, here is one more example of a summary statement: "Let me see if I understand you correctly. Yesterday you found out your son has been using cocaine for the last six months and has stolen money from you on a number of occasions. You're experiencing a mixture of feelings, especially shock and anger, and you're worried he might turn out to be an addict like your father was. However, you're determined to do all you can to not let that happen to him. How about discussing some possible directions we can go in from here." Note that this summary captures the key issues and feelings without being too wordy and offers a transition for the counselor and client to begin identifying some action steps to take. The following dialogue between Susan and her crisis counselor demonstrates the skills of paraphrasing, reflecting feelings, and summarizing:

SUSAN:	I really thought things were going well with my husband, so this came as a complete shock when I found out about the affair.
C:	You were really blindsided by this. (*Paraphrase*)
SUSAN:	Exactly! And I've been trying to push away the pain, but I can't seem to stop thinking about it. I just want to strangle him for putting me through this.
C:	Even though you want so much for the pain to go away, it's still there, especially your hurt and anger toward him. (*Paraphrase with a reflection of feeling*)

SUSAN:	Yes, and sometimes I can't tell which is worse, my anger or just the hurt I'm going through. I sometimes lie in bed at night and wish something terrible would happen to him. I'm not saying I want to kill him or anything, but I just want him to suffer like I'm suffering.
C:	And this reflects the intensity of your grief right now, wanting to see him suffer, too. (*Reflection of feeling*)
SUSAN:	Very true.
C:	So, in essence, you never expected something like this to happen to you, and it has been difficult for you to tough it out and to push away the pain, grief, and anger that you've been feeling. Is that about right? (*Summary with check for accuracy*)

Summary

In this chapter, the basic counseling skills used in crisis intervention work were reviewed. The use of these skills will aid in the development of the counseling relationship with the client and will greatly facilitate the creation of a safe therapeutic environment. The nonverbal attending behaviors such as eye contact, body position, and tone of voice communicate interest, warmth, and understanding to the client. Be sure to face the client and adopt an open, relaxed, and attentive body posture, while maintaining culturally appropriate eye contact with the client. Tone of voice should be steady and clear and should be used to convey a sense of safety, warmth, and security for the client.

The skills covered in the basic listening sequence include asking open and closed questions, paraphrasing, reflecting feelings, and summarizing. The basic listening sequence allows the gathering of important information about the client's issues and the development of trust and rapport. Finally, the basic listening sequence allows the crisis counselor to pull together the key issues to begin the collaborative process of determining a plan of action for the client. Open and closed questions are used to gather information, to aid in assessment, and to provide focus and direction to the session. Paraphrasing is a reflective skill used to mirror back to the client, in a nonjudgmental way and in one's own words, an accurate understanding of the client's communication and the implied meaning of that communication. Like paraphrasing, reflecting feelings is a reflective skill used to convey to the client an understanding of the client's emotional experience. Through this awareness, the client can reach a higher level of overall self-awareness and deepen self-disclosure. Summarizing puts together the pieces, helping the client make sense of what may have originally seemed to be an overwhelming and confusing experience. Summarizing can also be used to keep the session focused, to provide direction to the interview, and to provide closure to the session by reviewing the progress, plans, and any recommendations/agreements made. By using these skills appropriately, you create the necessary conditions for positive change.

Risk Assessment and Intervention: Suicide and Homicide*

Judith Harrington and Charlotte Daughhetee

PREVIEW

Suicide and homicide are viewed as preventable public health problems in both the United States and throughout the world. Death rates caused by suicide and homicide are no longer viewed as atypical. Rather suicides and homicides have the capability to affect us personally as family members, friends, coworkers, neighbors, members of extended social networks, and even the professional community struggle with the implications of these preventable deaths. Whether intervening before suicide or homicide occurs, as it is occurring, or after it has occurred, mental health counselors play a vital role in society's response to helping those in need with violence-free coping strategies, intervention based on sound practices, or if necessary the best and most productive short-term and long-term response to those left in the aftermath of suicide or homicide. While few expect suicide or homicide to happen to someone they care about, the chance of being closely and personally affected by a suicide or homicide over one's lifetime is no longer distant, if it ever was. The effectiveness of the care given by professional emergency first responders and crisis counselors, as well as the effectiveness of ordinary people responding to their own crises and the crises of those about whom they care, is improved by background knowledge involving current trends in and treatments for suicidal and homicidal impulses and the aftermath if it occurs. This chapter is explicitly for crisis counselors who wish to learn how to be effective in responding to members of their communities touched by suicide and homicide.

*The authors and editors thank Dr. Mary Bartlett for her outstanding contributions to this chapter during the first edition of this book.

SUICIDE INTERVENTION

The Scope of the Problem

Suicide is a public health problem that all crisis counselors, regardless of setting, must learn to assess and treat because of its prevalence in society. In 2009, the United States lost 36,909 citizens to suicide, a higher rate of deaths (12.0 per 100,000) than at any time during the last 15 years. Suicide in the total U.S. population (encompassing all age brackets) moved from the 11th most common cause of death to the 10th leading cause of death. Suicide as a cause of death is alarmingly high for many age groups. For children between the ages of 10 and 14 years, it is the fourth leading cause of death; for youth aged 15–24 years, it is the third leading cause of death; for young adults between ages 25 and 34 years, it is ranks as the second leading cause of death; and for 45–54-year-olds, and 55–64-year-olds, respectively, suicide is the fifth and eighth leading cause of death (Centers for Disease Control and Prevention, 2012; American Foundation for Suicide Prevention [AFSP], 2012).

Only for youth aged 10–24 years does homicide as a cause of death rank higher than suicide, with it being the third leading cause of death within groups of 10–14-year-olds and the second leading cause of death for 15–24-year-old youth. In all other age groups 25 years and older, there are more suicides than homicides, with only two age brackets in which homicide registers as a top 10 leading cause of death nationwide (Centers for Disease Control and Prevention, 2012). In fact, over the past 60 years, suicide rates have quadrupled for males in the 15–24-year-old age category, and they have doubled for females overall. It is estimated that each day there are approximately 12 youth suicides, and for every completed suicide there are between 100 and 200 attempts made. This suggests that at its lowest rate 1,200 young people attempt suicide each day (American Association of Suicidology, 2006b; Centers for Disease Control and Prevention, 2007).

From a statistical standpoint, counselors should know what the terms *incidence*, *rate*, and *cause of death ranking* mean. *Incidence* is a nominal figure that states literally how many lives were lost to suicide (or any other type of malady). For example, the incidence in County XYZ in 2009 may have been that 75 persons died from suicide. *Rate* is a figure explaining data that has been interpreted by leveling a playing field statistically; in other words, if all members of a population were divided up into groups of 100,000 people (or some similar round number), the rate would mean that X number of people died per 100,000. For example, County XYZ, a very urban and populated county, lost 75 persons to suicide, but its rate of suicide was 11.9 per 100,000, or 11.9. By contrast, County RST, a small, rural, unpopulated county, lost 16 citizens to suicide (incidence), but its rate of suicide was 34.7 per 100,000, or 34.7.

Epidemiologists study the causes of death, in part, to understand why, for example, the incidence is lower in a rural county, while the rate is considerably higher. Another example to illustrate this point is that the suicide rate for the elderly, age 65 years and older, is approximately 18 in 100,000, but the incidence is lower here than in other groups because the population number of elderly persons is lower. A high rate of 18 in 100,000 though is considered alarming and professionals want to learn why higher risk groups are more prone to die by suicide than lower risk groups. Youth has a lower rate of death than the elderly; however, suicide is ranked as the third leading cause of death among youth, which is also alarming.

Cause of death ranking is often illustrated in chart form listing the 10 highest incidences of deaths per cause (e.g., heart disease, malignancies, respiratory disease, liver disease, unintentional injury). There are many special at-risk groups (e.g., military personnel, Native Americans, the elderly, persons with life-threatening depression and/or bipolar disorder, victims of bullying, youth, GLBTQ youth), for whom suicide death rates are higher than the average population, or for whom the cause of death ranking is higher than for most. However, individuals in any demographic group are susceptible to a suicidal psychiatric emergency when certain co-occurring and multiple factors generate risk for vulnerable persons. In other words, no matter what demographic or risk group a client may inhabit, anyone can become suicidal, and when in the counselor's office, that client is a one-person sample. Further, while there were over 36,000 suicides in 2009, there were more than 1 million suicide attempts in the same year, sometimes resulting in permanent injury or disabling conditions, and sometimes imperiling a concerned person who tried to prevent the suicide from happening (AFSP, 2012).

The suicide rate is at an all-time high both within the United States and throughout the world. According to the World Health Organization (2007), over the past 45 years completed suicides have increased by 60%, with suicide attempts occurring more than 20 times more frequently than completed suicides among the general population. Worldwide, the prevention of suicide has not been adequately addressed and remains a taboo topic in many areas. Only a few countries have included prevention of suicide among their priorities, and inaccurate and insufficient reporting remains a problem worldwide. Effective suicide prevention requires input from multiple systems and increased government involvement.

The primary victims are the deceased; the secondary victims are the survivors of loss. Survivors, not to be confused with attempters, are individuals affiliated with the suicide attempter who survived a suicide attempt. When examining the vast effects of suicidal fatalities, mental health professionals must be prepared to serve the high numbers of secondary victims, those who survive the loss. Conservative estimates are that an average of 1 in 6 persons are directly affected by this traumatic form of death, and according to a study by Bland (1994), mental health service providers in the United States could potentially serve between 221,000 and 1,033,000 newly identified survivors each year. Secondary victims can develop an elevated risk for suicide, more protracted depression, anxiety, and trauma reactions, longer and more complicated grief and bereavement, more demands on medical and mental health services, and a greater potential for lost time at work and school.

Mental health professionals continue to be undertrained in suicide intervention (Farrow, 2002; Granello & Granello, 2007; Range et al., 2002). Clinicians experience the assessment and treatment of suicidal clients as one of the most common and most challenging of clinical emergencies regardless of setting. It is consistently rated by counselors as a highly stressful experience, has a significant emotional impact on the treating clinician, and has become a frequent basis for malpractice suits against counselors over the past 15 years. It is imperative for crisis counselors to strengthen their competency prior to serving suicidal clients, since, due to the high incidence of suicide and suicide attempts, there is little way of avoiding this clinical crisis over the course of one's career (Granello & Granello, 2007).

ACTIVITY 5.1

Form a group in which participants stand in two lines facing each other. At the direction of a leader, the participants in line 1 ask their partners in line 2, "Are you feeling suicidal?" The members of line 1 should then move to the right (or circle to the other end of the line if they are at the far-right end of the line), and ask the next partner the same question. Continue doing this until all line 1 members have asked everyone in line 2 the same question. Then repeat the activity, but this time, every member of line 2 now asks members in line 1, "Are you feeling suicidal?" After the exercise, discuss together as a group these questions:

• Which role did you prefer: being the person asked or being the person doing the asking? Explain.

• Why do you think it is important to practice asking the question, "Are you feeling suicidal?"
• How do you feel about using the word *suicide*, or about looking someone in the eye and asking him or her directly about suicide?
• What are some other equally direct and nonjudgmental ways that you could ask about someone's intention to self-harm?
• What has been your experience with suicide, both personally and professionally? Consider what you do and do not know about working with a client in a suicidal crisis or emergency. What more do you need to know before you work with a client who is suicidal?

Prevention, Intervention, and Postvention

Mental health professionals, as a part of providing effective intervention, also invariably grapple with prevention, intervention, and postvention—the three intertwined parts of the mental health profession's responsibility to safeguard clients from unnecessary risk for death from suicide and its protracted aftermath. From a systemic perspective, prevention influences intervention, intervention influences postvention, and postvention influences prevention at both the microlevel (i.e., the individual and direct care levels) and the macrolevel (i.e., the knowledge, research, best practices, and multiple system collaboration levels).

Prevention involves suicide-proofing communities, raising the level of public education and appropriate responding, and collaborating with and equipping other stakeholders such as government leaders, educational institutions, community agencies, faith-based organizations, and groups that serve at-risk populations. Prevention also influences counselors to be proactive and to set up early detection procedures for suicide risk. Intervention involves direct service to individuals or families with acute or chronic risk (e.g., low, moderate, or high risk clients) with a strong emphasis on assessment and reassessment, treatment planning, safety planning, means restriction, transition management, and follow-up.

Postvention was once thought to mean exclusively ministering to the needs of those immediately bereaved and traumatized by suicide. In current professional discourse, postvention is undergoing revision in its meaning and is thought to encompass a wide range of postventive responses to not only those who are bereaved due to suicide loss but also to those who have attempted (but not completed) suicide. Postvention also aims to strengthen the collaborative meta-planning of crisis centers, practitioners, and hospital emergency departments and the clinical networks that safeguard those who have entered and traverse the mental health system at various points (Cerel & Campbell, 2008; Murphy, 2010). Postvention initiatives also include the voices of survivors of loss who speak on behalf of their deceased loved ones. These personal stories are powerful aids in mental health advocacy efforts, including local, regional, national, and international initiatives with suicide prevention allies and organizations as well as legislators and politicians (Andriessen, 2009).

Prevention: Public Education, Competency, and Attitudes

PUBLIC EDUCATION   Public and mental health experts believe that the burden for protecting the public is shared by everyone. Many public awareness and mental health programs have been started by citizens who have been impacted by a personal crisis and had a desire to make a difference for others. This belief has been at the core of many successful health initiatives, such as widespread training among citizens for cardiopulmonary resuscitation (CPR), Mothers Against Drunk Driving (MADD), Smile-Talk-Reach (STR) for detection of possible stroke symptoms, and public education campaigns promoting hand-washing during flu epidemics, to name but a few. Gatekeeper suicide prevention training is considered one of the top three preventative initiatives related to suicide prevention (Mann et al., 2005). The gatekeeper strategy includes the widespread training of family members, friends, neighbors, teachers, coaches, coworkers, and all concerned persons to recognize and assist when suicide warning signs are exhibited. Mental health professionals and crisis prevention counselors play an essential role in gatekeeper training as change agents, trainers, and message bearers to the public that suicide is preventable. The strategy aims to enhance an enlightened awareness of risk factors, warning signs, and appropriate response, much like CPR training has saved lives through the help of many "ordinary citizens." Functions of crisis counselors in the prevention arena may include mental health advocacy, social justice advocacy, public awareness campaigns through community events, professional service on suicide prevention boards and foundations, and direct clinical and early-detection care with individuals who present with risk.

Counselors have access to a plethora of resources in the field of suicidology and through best- and evidence-based practices, can consult with and influence employers, agencies, and school administrators in their prevention planning and community response to suicide. The Question-Persuade-Refer (QPR) gatekeeper training curriculum under the direction of Paul Quinnett (2012) and the QPR Institute is a training program that lends itself well to training large groups either in class or online. Another reputable gatekeeper training program, Applied Suicide Intervention Skills Training (ASIST), is available through the Living Works organization that can be accessed through their website at http://www.livingworks.net/page/Applied%20Suicide%20 Intervention%20Skills%20Training%20(ASIST).

Gould (2010) evaluated and summarized school-based prevention programs, citing four types of evidence-based curricula: (1) awareness/education programs, (2) screening programs, (3) gatekeeper training programs, and (4) peer gatekeeper training programs. For more specific tools on planning prevention strategies within schools, a valuable resource for school counselors and administrators is provided by the University of South Florida (http://theguide.fmhi.usf.edu/). Visitors to this site will find a wide range of school-based suicide prevention recommendations and program designs useful to both counselors and administrators for effective response with prevention, intervention, and postvention. These guidelines may be adapted by counselors in other agency and clinical settings as well.

One often untapped resource for prevention outreach is faith-based organizations. Experts assert that a person's connection to a faith-based community and spiritual convictions are protective factors, but it is unclear if appropriate prevention, intervention, and postvention sensitivities are happening from within church cultures. For hundreds of years, suicide has been linked to religious beliefs (Campbell, 2005; Granello & Granello, 2007), both as a response to religious persecution, but more often in negative, stigmatizing, and attributive ways, with church leaders and followers communicating that suicide is a sin, that completers will go to hell, that the suicidal person isn't or wasn't "right with God." Bearers of these types of messages are unenlightened regarding the epidemiology and causative factors of suicide. While religious or faith group community members are more often a part of the protective response to persons at risk for suicide, perhaps unwittingly, some contribute to risk factors or create obstacles that impede at-risk persons from obtaining qualified help. It is always important to assess a person's faith or spirituality base in the context of protective or risk factors.

COMPETENCY AND ATTITUDES   One of the most important preventive measures that a crisis counselor can take is to become adequately trained in effective assessment and risk management of suicide (Suicide Prevention Resource Center [SPRC], 2012; American Association of Suicidology [AAS], 2006a). The SPRC and AAS developed a thorough and expert-designed best-practices curriculum for professionals in clinical, college, and employee assistance program settings. As a part of this curriculum, counselors are oriented to definitive core competencies. Of the 24 criteria, the SPRC and AAS place strong emphasis on proficiencies related to professionals' attitudes and approach; knowledge about suicide; assessment and formulation of risk; documentation; formulation of treatment plans; management of care; and legal and regulatory issues related to suicide (SPRC, 2012).

The SPRC/AAS Core Competencies related to attitudes and approach urge mental health professionals to monitor their own reactions to suicide, resolve the tension between the counselor's goal to prevent suicide and the client's goal to end psychological pain, and maintain a cooperative and collaborative working alliance, among other recommendations. All too often, counselors are distracted by their own anxiety, beliefs, attitudes, and myths associated with having a suicidal client before them, and for various reasons they are unable or unwilling to conduct a comprehensive assessment that best protects the client. Harrington (2007) and Simon (2004) identified obstacles that may interfere with objective and professional care management, including counselor fear or anger, counselor/client dynamics, problems integrating modern knowledge about suicide (contrasted with being influenced by personal attitudes or beliefs), lack of resources, inadequate assessment, poor treatment planning, inappropriate management of care, and failure to document—all conditions that may impede a clinician's effective performance.

When counselors do not complete periodic self-examinations of their own response to suicide, it is not uncommon for them to negatively attribute the expressed thoughts and behaviors of their suicidal clients as attention-seeking rather than as help-seeking. Table 5.1, summarized from the research of Campbell (2005), reviews the risks when mental health professionals fail to accurately recognize suicidal intent. Outcomes can result in death even when the client did not intend seriously to make a lethal attempt. This is especially true with parasuicidal individuals, who may not intend to die but who exhibit risky behaviors, self-injury, and a preoccupation with death. Often,

TABLE 5.1 Risk Based on Intent to Die and Survival

	Survival: Client Dies	Survival: Client Lives
Intent: Client Wants to Die	**Suicide** Died by suicide. Possibly a previous or multiple attempter. Likely chose more lethal means.	**Suicide Attempt** Intervention is successful. Ambivalence is present and helping works.
Intent: Client Wants to Live	**Accidental Suicide** An attempt gone awry. Client did not mean to die, but rescue or intervention eludes the victim.	**Parasuicide** So-called attention-seeking, or a drama queen or king, or a cry for help. Forty times more likely to die by suicide due to warning signs being ignored or minimized.

Source: From F. Campbell, *Intention style and survival outcome*. Baton Rouge, LA: ASIST Trainers.

parasuicidal clients are labeled as attention-seekers or drama queens or kings, and their risks go untreated, resulting in being 40 times more likely to become a suicide attempter whose suicidal "gestures" may result in death or permanent injury.

Maris, Berman, and Silverman (2000) itemized ten errors that interventionists may make when treating persons at-risk for suicide: (1) superficial reassurance, (2) avoidance of strong feelings, (3) [over-]professionalism, (4) inadequate assessment of suicidal intent, (5) failure to identify the precipitating event, (6) passivity, (7) insufficient directiveness, (8) advice-giving, (9) stereotypical responses, and (10) defensiveness. It is clear that when counselors have done the work necessary to understand and manage their own reactions to the suicidal crisis, they are better prepared to respond with empathy, genuine concern, and positive regard and to use a best-practices and competency-grounded approach to comprehensively assess, intervene, manage, and if necessary, refer (Sethi & Uppal, 2006). It is well understood that the client-counselor therapeutic alliance is a protective factor in the ongoing assessment and care management of a suicidal client's safety; a well-established relationship increases the counselor's ability to obtain information from the client in order to increase treatment options as well as to assist the client through a painful period when other sources of emotional support are limited. As part of its checklist when formulating level of suicide risk, the SPRC (2006) *Assessing and Managing Suicidal Risk* includes specific items related to quality of the therapeutic alliance and any transitions with providers during care management. Finally, counselors are directed to the National Registry of Evidence-based Programs and Practices (Substance Abuse and Mental Health Services Administration [SAMHSA], 2012; SPRC, 2012) and resources from the National Suicide Prevention Lifeline Standards, Training, and Practices Committee for existing and emerging authenticated practices in the field.

Training

The window of intervention with an actively suicidal person brings many, even seasoned mental health professionals to the question, "Ok, now what do I do?" and "Did I do enough?" There are resources available that offer step-by-step guidelines and well-researched rationale for these responses. Books by Rudd, Joiner, and Rajab (2004), Jobes (2006), and Chiles and Strosahl (1995) are but three guides counselors can use for in-depth study. *The Harvard Medical School Guide to Suicide Assessment and Intervention*

(Jacobs, 1999) and the *Comprehensive Textbook of Suicidology* (Maris, Berman, & Silverman, 2000) also provide comprehensive information. SAMHSA regularly produces resources for mental health professionals, including free and downloadable products from its Center for Substance Abuse Treatment.

Frequently, "refresher" and special topic courses and webinars are available through continuing education production companies, and through host suicide prevention organizations online. The emphasis on intervening with suicidal and homicidal clients in the remaining sections of this chapter will assist readers in answering the question, "What do I do now?"

ASSESSMENT   Intervention begins and continues with effective assessment of suicidal risk. Granello and Granello (2007) asserted that treatment planning includes assessment and reassessment. The AAS core competencies document (American Association of Suicidology, 2005) makes the following recommendations to clinicians:

- Weave risk assessment into sessions on an ongoing basis.
- Discover risk factors and protective factors.
- Identify if the client exhibits suicide ideation, behavior, or plans for self-harm.
- Assess for any warning signs of imminent risk.
- Confer with other collateral persons as needed.
- Formulate a definitive profile of the level of risk.

Formulation of risk (SPRC/AAS, 2006) involves forming an appropriate clinical judgment that a client may attempt or complete suicide imminently or later. The clinician should be able to determine acute or chronic suicidal risk and prioritize and integrate these impressions into a treatment or care management plan, while factoring in important developmental, cultural, and gender-related data relevant to the client.

There are two important objectives in assessing for suicidal risk. The profession's standards (SPRC/AAS, 2006; National Suicide Prevention Lifeline [NSPL], 2006) assert that the clinician or interventionist assess for the presence of acute versus chronic risk, and determine if the risk is considered low, moderate, or high with respect to immediate risk for death or injury, based on the specificity of lethality and availability of intended means, presence of intoxication, chance of intervention, degree of ambivalence, and so forth. The NSPL (2006), in its policy and assessment protocol position statement, recommends that crisis counselors, as a part of its suicide risk assessment policy and standards for network crisis centers, assess for the presence of desire to attempt suicide, capability to attempt, and intent to die. Acute and chronic risk, level of risk, the desire/capability/intent model, and methods for assessing are presented in the sections that follow.

A preamble for conceptualizing acute and chronic risk, alongside level of risk (i.e., low, moderate, or high) is to visualize risk on a continuum (see Table 5.2). The highest risk is considered as emergent (or emergency), imminent, or acute, and it is possible that an individual's risk has arisen swiftly, perhaps as a result of a recent event, setback or anticipated disappointment, or perceived failure. The acutely at-risk individual exhibits behavioral warning signs (enactments of suicidal behaviors) and demonstrates little (or less ambivalence about dying [wants to die to end the pain] than someone with chronic risk), has specificity of plan, method, timeline, and chooses more lethal means. The chronically at-risk individual may be considered to be in crisis or heading to crisis state, may have struggled with risk factors for a long time, may be ambivalent about

TABLE 5.2 Schematic Continuum for Conceptualizing Chronic and Acute Risk		
Low or No Risk	**Moderate Risk**	**Highest Risk**
"Normal" functioning: no acute or chronic risk present; normal reactions to life's stressors, ups and downs; no plan, no prior history of attempts, exposure to suicide, etc. **Protective factors:** effective care for mental, physical, substance abuse disorders; access to interventions; support for help-seeking; limited access to highly lethal means; strong connections to family; community support; support through ongoing medical and counseling relationships; problem solving skills, conflict resolution skills; cultural or religious beliefs that support self-preservation.	**Crisis state or headed to crisis:** chronic risk; perhaps ambivalent about living/dying; has a less specific plan. **Risk factors (or markers) as part of profile:** in a risk group (age, gender, ethnicity); prior attempt(s); family history of attempts or completions; substance abuse; mental illness, physical illness; survivor of abuse; family problems; relationship problems, disruption, loss; absence of support; death trend, accumulated losses.	**Emergency:** acute risk; imminent risk; not very ambivalent; more specific plan, more defined and lethal methods; has a timeline. **Demonstrates Behavioral Warning Signs:** • Feelings, such as hopelessness, helplesssness, anxiety, shame, self-hatred, pervasive sadness. • Acts or events, such as loss, defeat, betrayal, humiliation; giving away cherished possessions, settling affairs, paperwork; rehearsing use of intended method; substance abuse, saying goodbye. • Changes, such as uncharacteristic or reckless behavior, agitation, personality changes, mood changes, changes in sleep, eating, activities of daily living, loss of interest; makes threats, gestures or attempts, statements of death or "I won't be needing this."

dying and living, may have risk factors in his or her profile but not yet have a specific plan, method, or timeline to launch an attempt.

To summarize, counselors must remember that there is no one differentiated profile of a typical at-risk individual. Warning signs differentiate a client who may likely be in acute risk, and risk factors may be "markers" for chronic risk with the potential for acute risk later if warning signs are exhibited. Protective factors are mediating conditions which reduce the impact of risk factors. Table 5.2 provides a schematic continuum to assist assessors in mapping generalities of risk; there is no one type of suicidal client, or a simple checklist. Clinical judgment based on a variety of assessment tools is always recommended.

ACUTE VERSUS CHRONIC RISK   If the crisis counselor begins to suspect that risk factors are present, it is important to learn quickly about how acute or chronic the risk may be. Acute risk means that the individual evidences that he or she may hurt himself or herself in 24 hours or less, stating specificity about a plan, intent, means, and method (Kleespies, 1998). In practice, many clinicians allow for a larger window of time for imminent risk than 24 hours based on the client's stated plans. For example, if a client says "Next Saturday is my 40th birthday, and I'm going end it all on Friday night . . ." which is four days from now, then it would be appropriate to consider this as acute risk and to take appropriate measures.

Jobes (2008) concluded that a strong relationship existed for acute risk among situations, events, personal defeats, embarrassments, and humiliations that may swiftly tip the scale into emergency, imminent risk, or acute mode. Examples of these events might include the breakup of a relationship, getting fired from a job, discovering a betrayal, learning of a foreclosure or a decision to declare bankruptcy, or perceiving one of these setbacks as a huge disappointment or burden to one's family. These events can quickly trigger an acute internal response in someone with suicidal risk factors, so counselors with an acutely at-risk client must be prepared to be more decisive, more directive, and armed with appropriate treatment responses. In summary, acute risk suggests the presence of immediate, imminent, or emergency risk indicated by the intent to die (i.e., to end psychological pain) or to attempt suicide. Acute risk is associated with more formulated specificity about how the client intends to carry out an attempt and generally involves more lethal means.

Jobes (2008) also found that chronic risk is more likely associated with long-term patterns of relationship difficulties. Risk for suicide with the chronically-at-risk may reveal feelings of suicidality with less specificity, less lethal intent, and greater ambivalence about dying, but instead with more long-running, passive suicidal feelings reflected in statements such as "What's the point?", "I wish I could make all this go away, it will never get better!", and "If something happened to me, I wouldn't mind." Individuals with chronic risk can be described as having "markers" of potential suicide risk that is not currently imminent. In other words, individuals may present with some identifiers of persons who could become acutely suicidal but are not currently in imminent danger. Just as with other medical diagnoses, the client in your office with a family history of cancer (a risk factor) may or may not ever be stricken with cancer. A person who is chronically at risk may thus have "markers" for potential suicide, but must be watched closely for the possible emergence of active or acute risk. A few of these chronic "markers" might include a client

- whose demographic status is in line with certain known risk groups,
- who has a diagnoses including but not limited to mood disorders, anxiety, eating disorder, thought disorder, substance abuse/dependency, or some personality disorders;
- who has a history of trauma, violence, self-injury, previous hospitalizations, low self-esteem, high self-hate, tolerance and acceptance toward suicide, oppression related to sexual orientation, perfectionism, and other factors.

It is important to note that someone with chronic risk can become acutely suicidal, and acutely suicidal persons could potentially ease into long-term chronic risk status. But Jobes (2008) found that acutely risk-prone persons responded better to intervention, problem-solving skills, and effective techniques for resolution of suicide risk with the prospect of long term successful risk reduction than did chronically at-risk persons. An excellent resource itemizing acute versus chronic risk factors can be found at the AAS website, www.suicidology.org. Counselors are urged to download these comprehensive checklists and use them in direct assessment for the formulation of risk process.

In summary, chronic risk suggests the presence of longer term potential of suicidality, but with less specificity of intent or plans (e.g., means, methods) to carry out an attempt. The counselor has more time to help the client resolve his or her psychological

VOICES FROM THE FIELD 5.1
Lessons Learned with a Suicidal Client

Gerald Juhnke

Early in my career, and before the advent of cell phones, I worked as a counselor at a large community mental health agency. That is how I met Emily, a 22-year-old, single female who had a history of severe depression, hallucinations, and two critical parasuicides. Her latest parasuicide resulted in a three-week psychiatric hospitalization. Upon her hospital release, Emily was assigned to my client caseload.

During my first meeting with Emily, her case manager, and her psychiatrist, I was struck by the severity of her continued depression. The psychiatrist assured Emily that once her medications achieved a greater therapeutic threshold she would be feeling better. Together the case manager, psychiatrist, and I helped Emily create a thorough safety plan. She agreed to contact the 24-hour crisis number or page me if she experienced suicidal ideation or her auditory or visual hallucinations returned.

Although I voiced concerns to the psychiatrist and hospital supervisor regarding Emily's release, I was assured Emily was not deemed an imminent threat to herself and reminded of the hospital's "least restrictive environment" policy. Upon returning to my home agency, I informed my direct supervisor, a man of great compassion and significant clinical experience, of my concerns. Despite existing agency policy that inhibited clients from counseling more than one time per week, he encouraged me to schedule daily sessions with Emily until I felt she was safe. Some 20 years later, I know his decision saved Emily's life.

Our first two sessions were unremarkable. Emily reported that she preferred being home rather than in the hospital, and she denied suicidal ideation or hallucinations. However, during our third session, it was evident Emily had further decompensated. When pressed, Emily reluctantly discussed the inner voices that ceaselessly called her name and demanded she kill others and herself. When I asked a scaling question regarding suicidal intent, Emily quickly stood, opened the counseling room door, and ran out of the building.

When I exited the building, Emily was about a half block ahead of me. I immediately ran after her. When I finally got relatively close, she ran into oncoming traffic. The cars slammed their brakes and tires squealed as they averted hitting her. She turned and ran down an alley into a neighborhood. As we ran past a man on the front porch of a home, Emily pointed at me and screamed,

"Help me! He's trying to kill me." The man yelled back, "Stop chasing her or I'll call the police!" I turned and cried, "Call the police. I need help!" The man grabbed a rake and pursued me. However, he quickly became winded and stopped chasing me. A few minutes later Emily ran inside an old house. I heard her scream, "Daddy! A man's trying to kill me!" I stood in the driveway of the house near the sidewalk, fearing that Emily's family members would come out with shotguns and shoot me. I panicked when the door to the house flung open and a woman came running out. The woman looked at me and said, "Some crazy person just broke into my house!"

Minutes later, I heard a police car siren. I stepped onto the street and frantically waved my arms hoping the officer would stop. The police officer saw me and immediately slammed on the car's brakes. I knew the crisis was over. The police could pull my client from the house and restrain her until we could talk to my clinical supervisor and determine what to do.

The next thing I knew, the patrol officer tackled me and handcuffed my hands behind my back. As I attempted to explain the situation, he jammed me in the back seat of the patrol car. He then spoke to the woman who had been standing next to me, and he disappeared into the house. When he emerged, he had Emily. She resisted arrest and immediately was handcuffed. He then opened the police car's rear door and shoved her into the seat next to me. Once things were sorted out, he drove both Emily and me back to the agency, where she was reevaluated and rehospitalized.

As an inexperienced counselor, I learned much from these events. First, I learned to pay closer attention to my gut feelings and never simply accept the dismissive decisions of mental health professionals. Now when I believe a client should remain hospitalized, I strongly advocate on his or her behalf. Second, I learned the importance of being a compassionate supervisor who truly listens to supervisees. Despite the many cases my supervisor had, he made time to listen. He heard my concerns and responded accordingly. Had he not broken agency policy and insured Emily receive daily counseling sessions, Emily likely would have committed suicide before our next weekly session. Finally, I learned never to chase a client. I potentially placed my client, others, and myself in danger by chasing her. Instead, I contact police and allow them to use their training and experience.

pain (and his or her need to end the pain), can be less directive, and may not resort to immediate protection such as hospitalization as a treatment strategy, The counselor will instead reassess suicidality regularly, manage safety, and attempt to stabilize long-term risk with effective counseling.

LEVEL OF RISK: LOW, MODERATE OR HIGH   Table 5.3 presents a sample risk assessment guide from the Crisis Center, an AAS-accredited crisis center that has been serving clients for more than 40 years. the guide reflects the telephone counseling tools used by many crisis centers to assess the level of suicidal risk of suicidal callers. Variations of this checklist are also used by law enforcement "hostage negotiators" or crisis response teams (Texas Association of Hostage Negotiators, 2003).

TABLE 5.3 A Suicide Risk Assessment Guide

Variable	"Low" Risk	"Moderate" Risk	"High" Risk
Plan			
Method	Pills, slash wrists	Drugs, alcohol, car wreck	Gun, hanging, jumping
Specificity	Vague, no plan	Some specifics	Very specific—knows how, when, where
Availability of means	Not available—will have to obtain	Available—has means close by	Has in hand or in progress
When attempt is planned	48 hours or more	24–48 hours	Presently or in the next 24 hours
Chance of intervention	Others are present	Others are available or expected	No one nearby, alone, isolated
Intoxication	Has not been drinking	Limited use of alcohol (1–2 drinks)	Heavy drinking, combining with drugs, and/or evidence of intoxication
Degree of ambivalence	Readily acknowledges desire to live	Aware of some desire to live	Does not consciously acknowledge any ambivalence. Decision is made.
Acute versus chronic	Problems are chronic/chronic suicidal ideation	May have current ideation, gestures, or behaviors	Sudden loss or traumatic precipitating event (Loss or trauma is defined by the client.)

Warning: This risk assessment alone is not enough to formulate a clinical impression. Practitioners are advised to study all warning signs and predictors in context with patients and clients. This is designed to assist in the process of a complete and thorough assessment. You must assess for lethality, prior history of suicidality, recency of suicidality, current functioning, changes in behavior and mood, etc. In addition, there are more formal validated suicide assessment protocols available from publishers, and you might seriously consider psychiatric evaluation from a qualified psychiatrist skilled in suicide risk assessment. Counselors are encouraged to compare risk assessments with more than one versus only one measure, such as in-session interview, paper and pencil assessment with a validated instrument, interrater reliability with a second clinician (supervisor, psychiatrist, suicide risk consultant, etc.), collateral interview with family, previous therapists, etc. Remember, *lethality* is not the same as *intent to die* but is related to *reversibility*. A person may ingest chemicals or suffocate with a sock, and yet take a long time to die, but irreversible damage may be done, thus rendering "life" and survival highly compromised or could result in death.

Source: Permission granted by The Crisis Center, Birmingham, Alabama.

In addition, the National Suicide Prevention Lifeline (2006) recommends following a rubric of assessing risk based on the individual's desire, capability to attempt, and intent to die or attempt suicide. Desire, as it related to suicidality, is indicated by desire to harm self or others; psychological pain such as hopelessness, helplessness, or feeling trapped; and perceiving oneself to be a burden on others. Suicidal capability is evidenced by

- a past history of suicide attempts, exposure to someone else's death by suicide,
- a history of or even current violent behaviors toward oneself or others,
- having the means to hurt oneself or others,
- current intoxication or substance abuse,
- recent dramatic mood changes or loss of orientation to reality, and
- extreme agitation, rage, increased anxiety, decreased sleep, and recent acts or threats of aggression.

Suicidal intent is reflected by

- an attempt in progress,
- a plan with a known method to hurt oneself or other,
- preparatory behaviors (for example, giving away possessions, finalizing one's business affairs, saying goodbye [perhaps cryptically], counting pills, reading up on how to use the method, loading and reloading the gun, rehearsing the method), and stated intent to die.

The concept of desire to die by suicide is grounded in the original works of Beck, Joiner, and numerous experts (NSPL, 2006) with influences such as no reasons for living, wishing to die, and passive suicidality (not caring if death occurred). It is important to credit leading researchers, such as Joiner (2005) and Rudd (2006) whose work figured significantly in the NSPL recommendations for suicide risk assessment (NSPL, 2006).

Suicide desire alone does not fully explain an individual's risk level; the counselor must further examine the client's evidence of "capability" and intent to attempt suicide. Capability, in suicidological terms, is characterized by a sense of fearlessness to attempt, a sense of "competence" or capacity to attempt, and having specificity and means available by which to launch the plan to die or to attempt suicide. Joiner (2005) and Rudd et al. (2004) cited major factors that are contributory or definitive of suicide capability: history of attempt(s) and/or of violence, exposure to a suicidal death, availability of means, current intoxication or tendency toward frequent intoxication, acute or severe symptoms of mental illness (e.g., psychological pain, agitation, insomnia, loss of reality), recent and significant mood changes, extreme rage or increased agitation, and sleep deprivation. Joiner found that both suicidal desire and suicidal capability are of concern, but that suicidal capability is of greater concern.

Within this risk assessment model using the desire, capability, and intent constructs, suicidal intent is considered the most important because those with suicidal intent often engage in suicidal, behavior. Neither desire nor capability predicted active behaviors toward seeking death as strongly as intent, as demonstrated through research with actual suicidal callers to crisis centers (Kalafat, Gould, & Munfakh, 2005). Strong intent to die indicates low ambivalence about dying; for example, a high wish for death leads to low reasons for living, which leads to a more lethal method selected.

Alternatively, intent to die coupled with higher levels of ambivalence may allow for the exploration of reasons for living, and the client may present with attempt plans or means that are less lethal. The recommendations issued by the National Suicide Prevention Lifeline (2006) include the concept of *buffers*, which are similar to protective factors that may modulate risk. These may include (1) immediate supports, (2) social supports, (3) plans for the future, (4) engagement (or therapeutic alliance) with the helper, (5) ambivalence for living (partly wanting to live and partly wanting to die or end the pain of living), (6) core values and beliefs, and (7) a sense of purpose. Counselors who explore indicators of suicidal risk with a client may form clinical impressions based on the NSPL risk assessment recommendations, which urge clinicians to ask, during one session, three questions in this way:

1. Are you thinking of suicide?
2. Have you thought about suicide in the last two months? (This question further explores recent ideation even if current ideation [today] is not present.)
3. Have you ever attempted to kill yourself? (Prior attempts are considered very high as a risk factor.)

VOICES FROM THE FIELD 5.2
Treating Nonsuicidal Self-Injury

Amanda C. La Guardia

After completing my bachelor's degree, I started working in the mental health field as a case manager assigned to a small number of children and adolescents who had been identified as "at risk" for being removed from their homes and placed into foster care or long-term inpatient facilities. My job was to help ensure these youngsters stayed with their families. I was with each family for up to 12 hours per week, which was more than their licensed counselors. Needless to say, I frequently felt that I did not have the training necessary to help in the way that was needed (which is why I decided to pursue my master's in counseling). One of the biggest challenges I faced with many of my clients was treating nonsuicidal self-injurious behavior. I worked with several adolescent females who used self-injury as a way of coping with either the psychological impact of the trauma they had experienced or their emotional turmoil. I also encountered elementary school-aged boys who engaged in self-injurious behaviors for similar reasons. Rather than perceiving this as a coping strategy, many of the counselors I worked with judged these behaviors to be the result of mental illness. For example, borderline behavior was a fairly consistent assessment for the females and impulsivity as a result of hyperactivity was a common assessment for the boys. Thus, I noticed clinicians often did not focus on nonsuicidal self-injury as an important treatment concern. I knew better, but I needed training.

In many cases, the clients that engaged in the most frequent self-injurious behaviors were also contemplating suicide. They would injure themselves in order to deal with their overwhelming emotions (or lack of emotional connection) and to prevent acting out on their suicidal thoughts. This combination was tricky. I knew they needed a better way of coping, but I didn't want to take away the method that they felt kept them from walking down a more dangerous path. Formal and informal ways of assessing their suicidal ideations as well as their need for self-injury became equally necessary. Self-injury and suicidal ideation are separate issues, but they are often interconnected.

Together with my clients, we discussed what situations (external and internal) tended to lead to self-injurious behaviors and worked on developing new ways of coping. I didn't ask them to stop, but I did ask them to take care of themselves and encouraged them to find new ways of dealing with their pain because they deserved happiness however they defined it; they were worth it. I let them know I would be with them as they struggled and then I made sure that I was.

METHOD OF ASSESSMENT: INTERVIEW, WRITTEN INSTRUMENTS AND MULTIPLE TYPES   In suicide risk assessment, as with concepts related to the assessment of almost any phenomenon, it is wise to draw data from a variety of methods and sources. There is not one prototypical suicidal person, and there is not one cookie cutter risk assessment protocol. Suicide risk assessment relies heavily on clinical judgment and interpretation of available facts, indicators, evidence of past behaviors, rating of current mood and symptoms, and consideration of all these data against the backdrop of the field's knowledge of risk factors, protective factors, epidemiology, and causative factors that are known to increase the risk of suicidal death. It is advisable to be prepared with quality in-session (whether in person or by phone) interview techniques, and also with suicide risk assessment instruments that yield reliable and valid results.

Suicide risk assessment should always begin at the first session in traditional counseling, and it should be the main assessment goal in any crisis situation, including putting one or two specific questions on intake forms completed by the client or the client's caregiver, such as "Are you feeling suicidal or having thoughts of suicide?"; "Have you ever attempted suicide?"; and "Have you ever lost a loved one to suicide?" If a client indicates *yes* to any of these questions, the assessment should begin immediately. If the client or caretaker does not indicate *yes* to any of these questions on the intake forms, then the clinician should still be poised to listen and look for general indicators. These would include in-session affect, self-report, responses to direct questioning as well as several potential suicide risk factors: (1) current depression or a history of depression; (2) alcohol or drug abuse; (3) suicide ideation, talk, planning; (4) prior attempt(s); (5) a plan with a lethal method; (6) social isolation and limited support; (7) hopelessness or cognitive rigidity; (8), being an older, white male; (9) a history of suicide in the family; (10) unemployment, and/or vocational problems; (11) relationship and/or sexual problems, or family dysfunction; (12) stress and negative life events; (13) impulsivity, agitation, aggression; (14) physical illness; and (15) evidence of more than one of these 14 factors and comorbidity (Maris, 1992).

The field has produced a variety of mnemonic devices to help counselors remember risk factors and warning signs to assess for suicide in session or on the phone. The most comprehensive of these was generated by experts associated with the AAS who in 2006 introduced the **IS PATH WARM** acronym, which visually summarizes the key warning signs to check with a client during a session: Ideation; Substances; Purpose; Anxiety; Trapped; Hopelessness; Withdrawal; Anger; Reckless; and Mood.

Granello and Granello (2007) review several other mnemonic tools:

- *NO HOPE:* No meaning; Overt change in clinical presentation; Hostile environment; Out of hospital recently; Predisposing personality factors; Excuses for dying.
- *PLAID:* Prior attempts; Lethality; Access to means; Intent; Drugs/alcohol.
- *MAP:* Mental state (thinking); Affective state (emotions); Psychological state (circumstances).
- *SLAP:* Specificity; Lethality; Availability; Proximity of help.
- *PIMP:* Plan; Intent; Means; Prior attempts.

Crisis counselors can use these acronyms to form checklists that can be used when risk factors become apparent.

Shea (2002), a former emergency room doctor, developed and researched the Chronological Assessment of Suicide Events (CASE) method. With one of the highest risk windows for at-risk persons being the hours, days, and weeks just following a hospitalization for suicidal status, he was concerned with how emergency room personnel adequately and accurately identified level of risk. The CASE method pays particular attention to the immediate features of the patient's or client's suicidal risk, the conditions just prior to the psychiatric emergency (i.e., a 6–8 week build-up or a pile-up of distress), the influences prior to 6–8 weeks of build-up (e.g., long ago exposure to suicide, family history of suicide, traumatic events), and concludes with questions about the "now" of suicidal feelings and impending days ahead. His approach emphasizes five skill sets of question-asking:

1. Shame attenuation (normalizing feelings).
2. Behavioral incident specificity, (e.g., "Where is the gun?"; "Where are the bullets?"; "And then what did you do?"; "And after that, what did you do?"; "How many pills do you have?"; "Who knows about your plans?").
3. Gentle assumption (e.g., a presupposition such as "What ways have you thought of killing yourself?" as contrasted with "Have you ever thought about killing yourself?").
4. Symptom amplification (e.g., "How much time do you spend thinking about suicide . . . in a 24-hour period?" to which the client may respond, "No, just when my children are at their father's house on the weekends.").
5. Denial of the specific. This technique often shocks counselors in suicide intervention training, as it requires clinicians to ask clients if they have considered many different methods, which is counterintuitive to the myth that if we talk about suicide, we will give clients the idea for how to do it.

Jobes (2006) developed an assessment method that merges the interview with the written instrument tool. Known as the Collaborative Assessment for Managing Suicide (CAMS), his product is evidence-based and theory-based, and it also includes close collaboration with the client in session to understand the details about their suicidal risk. Jobes's assessment findings are then closely wed to safety planning and treatment planning.

Several published self-report instruments are available for purchase. The Positive and Negative Suicide Ideation Inventory (PANSI) is a 20-item self-report measure of positive and negative thoughts related to suicide. Items include statements such as "I am in control of my life" and "I think about killing myself," to which clients respond on a 1–5 point Likert-type scale. This instrument is intended for use with adults and has been used as an informal screening device for high school students. The instrument is a simple and relatively easy assessment for crisis counselors to use.

The Beck Scale for Suicide Ideation is a self-report instrument requiring 10 minutes to administer that evaluates a client's thoughts, plans, and intentions to commit suicide. It is a 19-item interviewer-administered rating scale that includes items such as "I have made plans to commit suicide" and "I have access to lethal means." This instrument is unique in that it asks the client to recall the time when he or she felt most suicidal and answer the questions from that perspective. It includes items such as "I was ____% decided to commit suicide" and "I have only felt that suicidal ____ (number of) times."

In exploring assessment tools used within the United States, none has been identified that empirically assessed cultural appropriateness for use with various multicultural populations. Effective assessment procedures, regardless of culture, appear to include the following elements:

- Phrasing questions effectively to elicit the most information about suicidal thoughts
- Specifically sequencing or structuring questions about suicide
- Sequencing questions about specific aspects of suicidal thoughts, plans, and behaviors
- Collecting information from collateral sources to best determine how to proceed

In addition, how a counselor phrases and sequences assessment questions should be considered in the context of specific cultures (American Psychiatric Association, 2003; International Association for Suicide Prevention, 2000; Shea, 2002).

There are a plethora of authenticated written suicide assessment instruments available without charge in the public domain or for purchase. We are aware of over 70 products that are tailored to measure suicidality, depressive suicidality, and parasuicidality; suicidality with the elderly, adults, youth, and children; suicidality with youth in the judicial system; suicidality organized around reasons for living, and more. Because there is no one sourcebook to learn about all of these instruments, counselors may want to search the catalogs or websites of specific publication companies, PsychAbstracts library holding services, and the *Mental Measurements Yearbook*. They may also follow a cyber-referencing route and navigate the Internet to find myriad products, original citations, and reviews.

Counselors making decisions about what products to invest in on behalf of their agency or client populations will want to compare goodness of fit based on several variables such as cost to purchase and resupply, ease in scoring, test-retest properties, administration time for clients, administration time for staff, in-session versus out-of-session assessment possibilities, thoroughness of the information yielded, seamlessness of fit with documentation strategies, and youth and/or adult version availability, reliability, validity. Results from written assessments should become permanent artifacts in client file documentation and subsequently compared to determine the improvement or worsening of the condition. Some of the websites (among many) to search for instruments include the following:

- www.healthline.com/galecontent/
- www.testagency.com/?test/show/168; www.tjta.com/products/TST_007.htm
- www.minddisorders.com/Br-Del/
- www.psychassessments.com.au/Category.aspx?grpld=all&cID=172
- www.encyclopedia.com/doc/1G2-3405700081.html
- www.neurotransmitter.net/suicidescales.html

MULTIPLE TYPES OF ASSESSMENT   It is advisable that crisis counselors assess clients more than once, and preferably more frequently with clients who are clearly at risk of suicide. This would mean both across multiple sessions in a counseling or treatment episode, and also even within the same session by asking about intent in different ways. In addition, it is good practice to use more than one means of assessing, including interview-style assessments or formal written and published assessment as mentioned above. Other means of gathering and confirming data may be in the form of interrater reliability (e.g., when you collaborate with a colleague or supervisor to verify findings), in-session conjoint assessment with another care team member, consulting with a psychiatrist or other expert, or use of a suicide risk assessment consultant. Finally, collateral information from family members or friends is important if the at-risk individual has been open with them about feelings or behaviors that are suicidal in nature.

TREATMENT PLANNING AND CARE MANAGEMENT WITH A SUICIDAL CLIENT   After having assessed for a client's acute or chronic risk as well as having determined what level of risk, many mental health professionals might again ask, "Now what do I do?" Assessment is only part of the intervention process. Again, the Rudd et al. (2004), Jobes (2006), and Chiles and Strosahl (1995) resources, among others, provide qualified step-by-step recommendations for appropriate treatment planning and responding. Just as all treatment plans for clients seeking counseling for any condition are customized to meet their needs, the same is true for clients at risk for suicide. The assessment process yields valuable information to assist with the design of appropriate treatment interventions. This section will review several ideas for counselors to consider, beginning perhaps with the most important intervention of all, the development of a customized safety plan.

Developing a safety plan with the client is an industry standard and expectation, but many mental health professionals were trained to write a "no-harm contract." Based on research, best-practice thinking, examination of the potential for false security regarding liability, and more evolved legal, ethical, and clinical reasoning about how much a suicidal client might be able to "agree" to such a "contract," the no-harm contract has been replaced with professional and empirical preference for the safety plan. Many, if not most, acutely at-risk suicidal clients are not in a psychiatrically oriented or lucid condition to shoulder the burden for knowing enough about suicide or safety planning.

While some authors have referred to safety plans by varying nomenclature (such as crisis response plan and self-care plan), the National Suicide Prevention Lifeline (NSPL) Standards, Training, and Practices Committee recommends the term *safety plan*.

> "We would always use the term 'safety plan'. . . other terms [crisis response plan or self-care plan] are too vague and do not explicitly reference the fact that keeping the individual safe is the primary goal in developing a plan—vagueness is not good. In addition, we would never reference a 'safety plan' without explicitly stating the avoidance of anything that resembles a 'no harm contract'—so would attempt to eliminate any confusion at the outset"
>
> (personal communication with G. Murphy, September 22, 2010).

Stanley and Brown (2008) have written extensively about the components of a safety plan and recommend that clients ask the following questions:

1. When should I use the plan?
2. What I can do to calm/comfort myself if I am feeling suicidal?
3. What are my reasons for living?
4. Who can I talk to?
5. Who can I talk to if I need professional assistance?
6. How can I make my environment safe?
7. What should I do if I'm still not feeling safe?

Stanley and Brown addressed not only what should be included in safety planning but also how to talk through its use with clients.

A comprehensive safety plan addresses specific behavioral actions, determined in concert with the client, and would include several key focal points including means restriction, self-soothing options, self-care options, family involvement options, resource development, and crisis response options (personal communication, M. Gould and D. Jobes, November 10, 2010), in addition to the recommendations that Stanley suggests as well. One essential component of safety planning is to address means restriction (Coombs, Harrington, & Talbott, 2010; Mann et al., 2005) since firearms are the most frequently used method to complete suicide in the United States—and the most lethal.

An example of a safety plan is presented in Table 5.4, written with specific behavioral actions.

A well-done assessment will facilitate a client's ability to trust the clinician, provide more information, and allow the counselor to understand when, how, and under what conditions the client becomes vulnerable to suicide. For example, if a client has revealed that she wants to elude life, particularly when her husband and she experience conflict, her treatment plan might recommend couples counseling and conflict resolution skill building. If an 80-year-old widower reports being desperately vulnerable between the hours of 5 and 8 p.m. each day as he imagines everyone having dinner with

TABLE 5.4 An Example of a Safety Plan

I will . . . *(List specific behaviors such as the examples listed below)* **Customize the plan with your client.**	**Related to Means Restriction**	**Related to Soothing Feelings**	**Related to Self-care**	**Related to Family Support**	**Related to Using Resources**	**Related to Crisis or Emergency Support**
Remove gun and ammunition from house, car, truck, cabin, barn.	✓					
Fill doctor's prescriptions weekly (not a month at a time).	✓					
Take my dog to play in the park.		✓				
Call a friend.		✓				
Eat three meals a day.			✓			
Drink nonalcoholic or noncaffeinated beverages.			✓			
Avoid lonely times by going to my sister's.				✓		
Spend the night at my cousin's house.				✓		
Go to bipolar support group.					✓	
Call my sponsor, or go to a meeting.					✓	
Call the NSPL 800-273-TALK.						✓
Go to my primary care physician psychiatrist, ER.						✓

their loved ones, a treatment plan for him should increase social support during the 5–8 p.m. period of vulnerability. Safety plans should always involve resources, actions, and coping mechanisms that the client is able and willing to put into place, and they should be unique to his or her situation. Written contracts that are signed by the client are a best practice.

OUTPATIENT MANAGEMENT   Earley (2006) lamented how difficult it was to secure appropriate durations for in-patient treatment because of insurance payment restrictions. He investigated the trend for transinstitutionalization, wherein clients who may be dangerous to themselves or others have difficulty obtaining appropriate medical care except when identified by law enforcement when troubles arise. In addition, Granello and Granello (2007) described the potential for counselors to generate "false positives" when assessing for risk; that is, determining that suicidal risk was high for clients when it was low, thus unnecessarily referring clients to inpatient hospitalization for suicidal risk. In contrast, a false negative evaluation might occur when the clinician fails to accurately assess the presence of suicidal risk when there is risk. It is not uncommon in almost any community for there to be limited mental health care in hospitals due to the unavailability of beds, limited insurance coverage for adequate lengths of stay, and other factors. These conditions have increased the demands on counselors in outpatient settings to treat and manage the care of low or moderately at risk clients without the benefit of the security that inpatient hospitalization can provide.

As a result, mental health counselors are expected to manage outpatient care more vigilantly with greater provisions for access to care. Recommendations include increasing the frequency of sessions—for example, from one to two sessions per week—or increasing the length of the sessions, perhaps from 50 minutes to 90 minutes. Provisions might also be made for the client to call in for safety checks in between sessions at designated times (Newman, 2012). In addition, clinicians should consider inviting trusted family members or supports to a session to be sure that family members are sufficiently aware of suicidal risk and are involved in safety planning provisions. Counselors should also have collaborative relationships established with psychiatrists in their community as referral options. For clients without insurance, it is especially important to know which community agencies, public mental health resources, and mental health initiatives in a community are set up to provide psychiatric care and potentially distribute needed medications for the uninsured. Primary care doctors (internists and general family medicine physicians) are also options when psychiatrists have long waiting lists.

No one person or clinician can be solely responsible for the inpatient or outpatient care of someone who is suicidal. Mental health counselors are advised to think of care management as a team approach. For more acutely suicidal clients, extra vigilance may be necessary to be sure that they are not left alone (24/7) or at vulnerable times. Family members may be the most centrally responsible person to be sure, for example, that means restriction (e.g., removal of guns, ammunition, pills) is conducted. Other team members may include facilitators of community support groups that are well matched to the client's needs. For example, communities often have support groups for divorce recovery, job hunters, persons with bipolar disorder, Alcoholics Anonymous 12-step groups, veterans, bankruptcy, bereavement, etc. Depending on the circumstances of the suicidal client, accessing group support for specific needs or even individual services at these relevant agencies can become a part of the "syllabus" for care. Crisis center phone numbers should be given to the client for between-session support. If the community does not have a nearby crisis center, the phone number for the National Suicide Prevention Lifeline—1-800-273-TALK (8255)—is the best number to provide. Helpers at the NSPL will assist callers in accessing the nearest resources.

A "syllabus" for care might be a step-by-step time management plan the client can develop with the counselor for use when particularly vulnerable, alone, or between sessions. Specific times set in writing for when the client might do activities such as exercise, sleep, eat meals, attend support group meetings, go to the bookstore, and run errands can assist clients who are disoriented with depression, or not functioning well. An adage in suicide intervention is that the clients are encouraged to be able to participate in their own rescue to the degree that they are capable. It is often the case and recommended that the clinician, crisis center counselor, or helping professional may become considerably more directive during times the at-risk individual is hindered from functioning normally. As the client resumes functional ability, the client would be entrusted to direct personal choices. This should be a consideration for as long as the client is struggling to perform activities of daily living.

Transitions are a particularly vulnerable time for persons at-risk of suicide, and counselors who work with clients via inpatient, outpatient, or partial hospitalization should anticipate and plan for transitions. These transitions might include a change in level of care (from more restrictive to less restrictive, or vice versa), provider, circumstances (e.g., a parent who has come to the client's city to assist during the crisis plans to return home to a remote location), medication, or relationship (e.g., a recent breakup). Extra safeguards may be built into the care management plan (e.g., more frequent short-term phone contacts between sessions or updated safety planning).

If a clinician believes that a client should be hospitalized, both clinician and client should collaborate in such a way that the client will voluntarily elect to seek admission. When there is some client resistance to hospitalization, the involvement of a trusted family member is recommended to facilitate the decision to go voluntarily. Sometimes a primary care physician or psychiatrist can be influential in securing admission to a hospital. As a last resort, a client may need to be involuntarily hospitalized. States differ as to the process, and it is essential that clinicians understand the laws and practices in the state in which they are practicing before they ever see clients. It is better to know what to do prior to a crisis for both the clinician and the client. Some states require courts to mandate the "commitment" of an individual; others allow licensed professionals to initiate an emergency petition for involuntary hospitalization with law enforcement transportation; some states integrate mobile crisis teams, while others rely on a community service board that would make the final assessment and determination based on the clinicians' observations. The crisis counselors should also establish professional relationships with community service officers in their jurisdiction and become familiar with protocols.

The follow-up with a client who is at-risk for suicide is critical practice (Murphy, 2010). The CDC reported that over one million persons attempted suicide in 2009, and prior attempts constitute a very high risk factor for future attempts. Follow-up as a clinical standard is a form of active postvention that is both preventive and interventive. Follow-ups may include regularly scheduled phone calls, letters, or notes, and even texting or e-mailing, or they may include systemic agreements with provider organizations (e.g., between agencies or practices and hospital emergency room departments). Data about follow-up assessments with crisis center callers is very encouraging in that callers who sought out suicide intervention assistance from centers are very positive and motivated to reduce ambivalence about wanting to die. Clinicians may direct family care team members to obtain helpful booklets from agencies such as the Feeling Blue Suicide Prevention Council (www.feelingbluespc@aol.com) to assist family members of an attempter following a suicide attempt SAMHSA also has several "after an attempt" resource booklets for medical providers, attempters, and family members of attempters that can be obtained at http://store.samhsa.gov/shin/content/SMA08-4359/SMA08-4359.pdf.

Finally, a word is warranted about theoretical orientation and responsiveness to suicidal clients. Many experts prefer to recommend cognitive behavioral therapy or dialectical behavioral therapy. When individuals are acutely suicidal, it is as if they have a "brain condition" with cognitive distortion and perception and proportion difficulties. Much has been written about theoretical application, but ultimately, the intrapsychic themes, psychodynamic themes, self-actualization, and other constructs are better explored after the acute risk has been managed and reduced. CBT may not be the most effective approach with a high lethality case during the crisis period.

Postvention

Each year, a conservative estimate of persons who become newly bereaved due to the loss of a loved one by suicide numbers over 220,000. In a decade span of time, that number would be well over 2 million persons. The job of bereavement counselors is an important one, due both to the large number of survivors of suicide loss in the population and also to the misperceptions and myths about suicide both before and after death. Survivors of suicide loss often report feeling misunderstood, stigmatized, and marginalized (Montgomery County Emergency Service, Inc., 2006). They are prone to bereavement and sorrow, complicated mourning, and post-traumatic symptoms (Harrington, 2011). Their bereavement may be punctuated by the complexities of believing that their loved one "chose" death, as contrasted with viewing suicide as a multifactorial process of debilitation and vulnerability (Survivors of Loved Ones' Suicides [SOLOS], 2006). They may have lost a child, a sibling, or a partner with a cloud of unknown circumstances, such as a bad business deal, a negative performance evaluation at work, or an unspoken act of infidelity that they could not work through, to name a few. All people have bad days and bad events, and make bad choices, yet they do not become suicidal. And so it is important to remember the multiple risk factors that individuals who attempt suicide confront.

The circumstances surrounding the immediate scene of a suicide may include the involvement of law enforcement, investigators treating the scene as a murder, potential arrest warrants being issued, limited or gruff communication with personnel such as coroners or first responders, all punctuated with a yellow crime tape around the scene. Of course, many survivors report exemplary conduct on the part of these professionals, and so it is not a universal problem. Adults and children alike are often witnesses to the actual suicide, may discover the body, or have to be involved in cleanup. Many family and religious complications can ensue, with conflicts possible between stepfamily members, family-of-origin, or in-law family members who may disagree about stating the cause of death openly to the community. Sometimes the suicide may be like a domino in a row of dominoes that continue to fall. For example, consider the scenario in which a middle-aged man dies from suicide, leaving financial problems that result in foreclosure or bankruptcy for the surviving family members, leaving college-aged children unable to continue their schooling and a partner/mother who must reenter the workforce. The suicide can become one crisis of many in a sequence of events, not unlike the Hill ABCX or Double ABCX model of crisis in McCubbin and Figley (1983).

Counselors providing postvention grief services to survivors of loss will want to become familiar with complicated bereavement and mourning, to learn about counseling techniques and countenance directly related to working with suicide loss, and especially to be aware of the feelings of helplessness, sense of responsibility, and internalized guilt that the bereaved feel after a suicide. Many family members have knowledge of their loved one's struggles and may have assisted in ways that prolonged the life of their loved one. Yet, the traumatic circumstances, the stigma or belief that it was a rational choice, or the complicated mourning leave survivors clinging to a sense of guilt-framed attribution of responsibility. Even love, appropriate attention, and excellent clinical care cannot fully immunize someone against suicidal thoughts and behaviors (Blauner, 2002).

Crisis counselors should become familiar with how to find suicide bereavement groups that exist in many localities around the country by visiting either the AFSP or the AAS websites for comprehensive listings. While survivors of suicide loss often report that they speak the same language, a language that other bereft persons do not fully understand, not all survivors will think that a group is the best option for them. Jordan (2006) offered suggestions for other therapeutic responses that counselors can recommend, such as bibliotherapy and Internet resources, psycho-education, family guidance, survivor outreach, cyber groups, survivor conferences, and activism, with activism marking a full circle from postvention to prevention.

Finally, some counselors become crisis advisors to employers, agencies, schools, faith-based groups, and communities. These professionals should be familiar with the national resources available for responsible communication with the media following a suicidal death. All of the prominent national associations have such resources available on their websites for distribution to decision-makers, spokespersons, and even media representatives in order to use the public news forum responsibly, to prevent suicide contagion, and to avoid glorifying or misrepresenting knowledge about suicide.

CASE STUDY 5.1

After reading the following brief cases describing potentially suicidal cases, indicate whether you believe the suicidal risk is low, moderate, or high, and whether it is an acute or a chronic risk.

Case A

Kelson is a 22-year-old white male infantryman who has just spent 27 months in Iraq. He is headed home for an extended furlough, and he does not understand why he is fidgety and agitated on the 18-hour plane trip home. When he arrives home, he learns that his girlfriend from before he went on active duty is now involved with one of his high school buddies, which he found out about from another friend while running an errand. In addition, his dad has remarried a woman whom Kelson has not met before. The marriage occurred nearly two years ago when he had been deployed for just four months. His new stepmother has moved into the house where Kelson used to live before deployment. His younger brother, in the meantime, graduated from high school and is now in college two states away from home. Kelson goes on a drinking binge the first night he is home and gets into a scuffle at the bar. As a soldier, he knows how to use firearms.

❏ Acute risk *or* ❏ Chronic risk

❏ Low risk ❏ Moderate risk ❏ High risk

Risk factors:_____

Warning signs:_____

Protective factors:_____

Demographically relevant information:_____

Case B

Devon is an African American college student who has learned to cope by "doing more." If having one part-time job is good, then two part-time jobs are better. She is prone to getting overinvolved in extracurricular activities, as she thinks that by really overachieving she will be selected for her preferred sorority in college. She has been seeing a counselor because she just can't seem to focus in class and her grades are not quite good enough to meet the requirements of her sorority. Her counselor has asked her if perhaps she is depressed. She was bullied as a teenager by others regarding her appearance and being overweight, and she states that her father also treated her gruffly her entire life. She is bright, attractive, and likeable, but she does not view herself that way. She cannot explain why she is crying all the time, as she believes that she is working as hard as anyone can to "keep it together." She feels that she has put a big strain on her mother and her friends for not "having it together." She has daydreamed about taking a bunch of pills.

❏ Acute risk *or* ❏ Chronic risk

❏ Low risk ❏ Moderate risk ❏ High risk

Risk factors:_____

Warning signs:_____

Protective factors:_____

Demographically relevant information:_____

Case C

Charles is a white male, aged 77 years. During his retirement, he has played a lot of tennis and spent time at his hunting cabin with friends. One of his long-time tennis buddies of over 30 years died suddenly from a heart attack on the tennis court only minutes after Charles had left the club. In addition, Charles's wife has been diagnosed with lymphoma and is undergoing treatments. While she is doing well in spite of the fatigue of the treatments, Charles is very worried about the possibility of her imminent death (before his own), and since his adult children have busy lives and reside in another region, he is primarily the sole caregiver for his wife. Together, they have made a decision to not get out and socialize as much as they had formerly, and they seem to be more socially isolated, except for his occasional tennis matches. On a recent visit to his physician, the doctor became worried and asked him if he was thinking of suicide.

❑ Acute risk *or* ❑ Chronic risk

❑ Low risk ❑ Moderate risk ❑ High risk

Risk factors:_____

Warning signs:_____

Protective factors:_____

Demographically relevant information:_____

Case D

Dakota is a Native American, aged 34 years, who has struggled with substance abuse for many years. Because he feels that his drinking is a loyal gesture to his friends, he has had difficulty in abstaining or understanding the risks of chemical dependence. His father committed suicide when Dakota was 16 years old, and as the oldest son, he was urged to become the head of the family, take care of things, and not repeat the mistakes of his father. Last night, Dakota got a second drunk driving charge. He is in a panic about the shame and embarrassment that this will bring on his family. He has told a friend that he is going to the cliffs to fly with the eagles.

❑ Acute risk *or* ❑ Chronic risk

❑ Low risk ❑ Moderate risk ❑ High risk

Risk factors:_____

Warning signs:_____

Protective factors:_____

Demographically relevant information:_____

Case E

Sandra is a white female, aged 47 years. She has just finalized a divorce from her third husband. For most of her life, she has placed a high premium on having a relationship with a partner, yet her commitments and marriages have seemed rushed and not very thought out, according to some friends and relatives. She is devastated when things don't go well, and her pattern of relationships has been somewhat chaotic and often conflicted. Similarly, she has seen a number of counselors over the years. Sandra's current counselor, in talking to her most recent prior counselor, learned that she has never attempted suicide actively but has often talked about wanting to die "if it happened." She is not sure how she would do it because she is afraid. Sandra is an adult survivor of childhood sexual abuse. She has a church within which she is active, and doesn't think it would be "ok" to actually attempt suicide.

❑ Acute risk *or* ❑ Chronic risk

❑ Low risk ❑ Moderate risk ❑ High risk

Risk factors:_____

Warning signs:_____

Protective factors:_____

Demographically relevant information:_____

VOICES FROM THE FIELD 5.3

A Special Plea for Special Needs: Crisis Intervention with Low Cognitive Functioning Clients

Amanda Evans

A common theme that I noticed when working at the in-patient psychiatric unit as a graduate student was helping professionals struggling to assist patients in crisis who were lower cognitive functioning. I can specifically remember several clients who were misunderstood by the hospital staff due to their level of cognitive functioning and were subsequently provided more restrictive care. I think it is very important as a counselor to be mindful that just because a client is an adult does not mean that the client can manage the responsibilities or cognitive complexity of adulthood. A patient who appears to be a 50-year-old male may in fact function cognitively as an adolescent, or as a child. This can be challenging in a hospital setting when clients in crisis require immediate, effective, and appropriate medical attention.

Oftentimes, patients who were lower functioning were expected to cope and manage the unit in the same way as their higher-functioning peers. This included maintaining personal hygiene, medication compliance, following the unit's rules, and establishing appropriate boundaries with their peers. In addition,

I noted counselors who provided treatment to these clients struggled with gathering intake information and establishing aftercare goals. This difficulty in serving lower functioning patients was most evident in the staff's attempt to de-escalate crisis situations. In my opinion, clients who are lower functioning are commonly misinterpreted by helping professionals leading to unnecessary rapid escalation in crisis situations, physical restraints, and possibly medical restraints.

Based on my personal experiences, I want to encourage counselors-in-training to consider alternative methods to communicate with clients in crisis. When low cognitive functioning patients are in crisis, expecting mature, rationale decision-making may be an unrealistic expectation; however, helping clients to express themselves, calm down, or self-soothe is ideal. In addition to talking through a crisis, working with individuals through the use of pictures, schedules, sign language, silence, or techniques specific to the client's needs can be very helpful in de-escalating a crisis situation. At times, competent care requires stepping outside of the box and using alternative interventions to best assist clients.

HOMICIDE

While most counselors are aware that they are likely to encounter suicidal clients in their counseling practice (Laux, 2002), they may underestimate the need for expertise in assessment and intervention skills with homicidal clients. There is a general assumption that clients with homicidal ideation are found primarily within the domain of forensic mental health and therefore are not a concern for most counselors. Obviously, clients with a history of mental disorders and violent offenses do present an elevated risk to the public, and mental health professionals working with violent offenders endeavor to balance public safety and client rights (Carroll, Lyall, & Forrester, 2004). But violent client behavior is documented in both inpatient and outpatient treatment facilities and therefore ought to be of concern for all mental health practitioners (Tishler et al., 2000). Ongoing reports from today's media reveal that the potential for violence and homicide exists in families, schools, colleges, the workplace, and across all communities. Accordingly, it is essential that counselors in all practice settings be equipped to assess the lethality of clients with homicidal ideation and be capable of making decisions regarding the referral and treatment of dangerous clients. In addition, counselors in all settings may be called on to provide services to homicide survivors. A homicidal crisis is intense and has long-lasting repercussions for individuals and communities who are left struggling to make sense of their traumatic loss and complicated grief (Currier, Holland, & Neimeyer, 2006). Furthermore, counselors working with clients who experience homicidal ideation find the experience very disturbing (Walfish, Barnett, Marlyere, & Zielke, 2010).

Homicide can be defined as the willful killing of one person by another person. The FBI reported that in 2010 there were 12,996 homicides, which is a decrease from the previous year, and preliminary studies of the 2011 crime statistics indicate another decrease in homicides. Currently, the homicide rate is at its lowest point since 1964. The FBI reported homicide incidents of 13,636 for 2009, 14,180 for 2008, 14,831 for 2007, 14,990 for 2006, and 16,692 for 2005, indicating a trend of falling homicides each of the past six years. While these trends are encouraging, the trauma of homicide is all too real for many people, and knowledge about crisis response related to homicide is essential for counselors.

According to the Bureau of Justice Statistics (2010), general trends in homicide over the years are as follows: homicide rates doubled in the mid-1960s to the late 1970s, peaking in 1980 at 10.2 per 100,000 citizens: there was another peak in 1991 at 9.2 per 100,000 and the rate has dropped since 2000 to the lowest levels since the mid-1960s. According to the FBI (2010), the homicide rate in 2010 was at 4.8 per 100,000. Why has there been a steady decline in homicide? Oppel (2011) noted that the decline in all violent crimes has baffled the experts. There are many theories, including demographic changes, more people in prison, and an increase in the number of police, but criminologists have been unable to pinpoint the true cause for the decrease.

Even though there has been a decrease in homicide, the reality is that homicide has a huge impact on our society and on the families and communities touched by homicide. On average, 77% of homicide victims and 90% of homicide offenders are male. Of women victims, 38% were murdered by husbands or boyfriends. Thus, although females do commit homicide, males are the primary risk population. Diem and Pizarro (2010) note that in intimate partner homicide, male offenders are most often motivated by jealousy or dominance issues while female offenders are usually motivated by fear for their own safety. African Americans are disproportionately represented among both victims and offenders as are young people. Approximately one third of victims and one half of all offenders are in the 18–24 year age range.

"I could just kill him!" That is not an uncommon declaration from a client venting anger at a difficult partner, peer, or work colleague, and counselors must be able to ascertain frustration from true risk of violence (Welfel, 2013). Such threats of harm toward another usually transpire when a client is experiencing extreme psychological suffering and is attempting to resolve feelings of distress (James, 2008). The counselor is then tasked with determining whether such pronouncements are simply common idiomatic expressions of anger or are legitimate lethal threats. Fortunately, in most instances, clients are merely indulging in hyperbole to give voice to intense anger or frustration; however, counselors must be prepared to recognize and assess potential lethality in cases where resentment and infuriation have escalated into homicidal ideation and possible violent actions.

Working with potentially violent clients presents a challenge to crisis counselors as they attempt to provide treatment, assess possible violent behavior, and protect would-be victims (Collins & Collins, 2005). When counseling a violent client, the protection of the public is always on the table. The noteworthy case of *Tarasoff v. Board of Regents of the University of California* clarified that the duty under California law to warn individuals who are in peril is of greater importance than the preservation of client confidentiality (Cohen & Cohen, 1999). Thus, counselors must assess the threat of lethality toward others and warn possible victims of harm. While all other states mandate the duty to warn, it is a good idea for crisis counselors to become familiar with the particular details of their own state laws regarding the duty to warn, as these issues are constantly being addressed by legislators at the state and national levels. Welfel (2013) noted that while codes of ethics allow breach of confidentiality regarding dangerous clients, there are state laws that require client protection to take place through hospitalization of the threatening individual (Ohio) or contacting police rather than directly contacting the intended victim (Texas) and breaching confidentiality. Furthermore, Welfel points out that some states clarify that the harm must be imminent before confidentiality can be breached; consultation with other mental health professionals, as well as legal consultation, is strongly urged before confidentiality is breached. In addition, crisis counselors should be cognizant of their own safety and implement appropriate precautions, as discussed in Chapter 2.

Assessment of Homicide: Homicide Risk Factors

There are some basic indicators and risk factors that tend to be associated with homicide and violence. However, a word of caution: While these risk factors may assist crisis counselors in assessment, it is important to remember that the existence of risk factors does not mean the client will become violent, and conversely, the absence of risk factors does not indicate a lack of homicidal intention. Remember, each case must be evaluated on its own terms.

In many instances, homicide appears to be fueled by interpersonal discord. According to the FBI (2010), in 2010 approximately 42% of victims were killed by someone known to them, such as a family member, a friend, or an acquaintance, and 38% of women victims were killed by their husbands or boyfriends. Most often, homicide motives were relational and included romantic triangles, disputes over money or property, and arguments fueled by substance abuse. The majority of murders were perpetrated by men, and firearms were the most common killing method; 67.5% of 2010 homicides were carried out using a gun. Obviously, heightened emotions, substance-induced impulsivity, and easy access to firearms cultivate a context for rash, violent actions, sometimes resulting in death.

Klott and Jongsma (2004) note that, among other behaviors, homicidal males tend to exhibit impulsivity and have a history of mental illness, family violence, job instability, and overall insecurity. They usually have a need to control intimate relationships and may exhibit possessiveness and rage. The need to control others is most clearly demonstrated in domestic violence cases where batterers control their partners through threats, physical violence, isolation from friends and family, and limited access to money (Collins & Collins, 2005).

Darby, Allan, Kashani, Hartke, and Reid (1998) found that male adolescent offenders are likely to have the following characteristics: a history of academic difficulties, substance abuse problems, and involvement with the juvenile justice system. Family of origin disruption and violence, parental endorsement of violent and abusive conduct, and the availability of guns were also found to be significant influences on male adolescent homicidal behavior. Loeber et al. (2005) studied risk factors in youth homicide and identified long-term risk factors, including a childhood diagnosis of conduct disorder and family poverty as well as contextual factors such as peer delinquency, drug abuse, and access to weapons. According to Roe-Sepowitz (2007), female adolescent murderers tended to have a history of substance abuse, prior involvement with the juvenile justice system, and very little parental supervision. Peers exert a powerful influence on adolescents, and the peers of female adolescent homicide offenders were prone to abuse substances and also to have had previous involvement with the juvenile justice system. In addition, adolescent female offenders had indications of mood disorders and exhibited difficulty with anger management. These risk factors speak to the need for early intervention with children and adolescents at-risk, as well as their families, through the school and the juvenile justice systems.

School Homicide and Violence

Columbine High School; Oklahoma Junior High School; Perry Hall High School, Maryland; Pearl High School, Mississippi; Delaware State University: Virginia Tech University (2007 and 2011); Northern Illinois University—these are are just a few of the names that remind us that K–12 schools and higher education settings are vulnerable to heinous acts of violence. As with violent incidents in other settings, school shootings are precipitated by a complex interplay of personal issues and environmental circumstances. Again, it is important to note that the presence of certain traits cannot predict actual violent acts, but since most violent students communicate their intentions, ongoing threat assessment can help school officials prevent violence and provide intervention to troubled students (Cornell, 2007). O'Toole (2000) recommends that evaluation of a potential school shooter's level of threat be approached with a four-pronged assessment model that includes investigation of several factors: (1) the student's personality, behavior, and traits; (2) family dynamics, family violence, and family attitude toward violence; (3) school dynamics, culture, and climate; and (4) social dynamics, peer network, and community culture. The more areas in which a student has difficulty, the more the student's threat should be taken seriously. Serious threats will necessitate the notification of school officials and possibly law enforcement.

Leary, Kowalski, Smith, and Phillips (2003) examined 15 K–12 school shooting incidents that occurred between 1995 and 2001. The shooters ranged from 11 to 18 years of age. In all but two of the events, the primary motivation was interpersonal rejection—mainly bullying, teasing, and ostracism—and in half of the events, the perpetrators had experienced a specific rejection, such as a romantic breakup. Erford, Lee, Newsome and Rock (2011) note that revenge for bullying or social rejection is a specific motivation for many school shootings. Bullying prevention must be considered an important facet of any school violence prevention program. According to the *Virginia Youth Violence Project*, a safety study conducted in 2007 indicated that schools that had both a structured and supportive environment had lower levels of bullying. Creating a school climate that lessens bullying incidents and provides appropriate help for bullying victims may avert violent incidents. Schools must address environmental factors to improve safety and reduce school violence threats. The *Virginia Youth Violence Project* is an excellent resource for both K–12 and college settings. More information can be found at http://youthviolence.edschool.virginia.edu/

The U.S. Secret Service (2010) offered this analysis:

> School-based attacks are rarely impulsive acts. Rather, they are typically thought out and planned in advance. Almost every attacker had engaged in behavior before the shooting that seriously concerned at least one adult—and for many had concerned

three or more adults. In addition, prior to most of the incidents, other students knew the attack was to occur but did not alert an adult.

Violence in school is usually planned, and school staff and faculty need to be attentive to signs and symptoms of violence as well as being alert to school environmental factors that give rise to bullying, rejection, and the promotion of violence (Miller et al., 2000). Kanan (2010, p. 32) highlights the following 10 findings regarding threats of violence in schools :

1. Incidents of violence are rarely impulsive acts.
2. Prior to most incidents, other people knew about the attackers ideas or plans.
3. Most attackers did not threaten their targets directly prior to advancing the attack.
4. There is no active or useful profile of students who engage in targeted school violence.
5. Prior to the attack, most attackers engaged in some behavior that caused concern or indicated a need for help.
6. Most attackers were known to have difficulty coping with significant losses or personal failures.
7. Many attackers felt bullied, persecuted, or injured by others prior to the attack.
8. Most attackers had access to and had used weapons prior to the attack.
9. In many cases, other students were involved in some capacity.
10. Despite prompt law enforcement responses, most shooting incidents were stopped by means other than law enforcement interventions.

A key point to consider in school shootings is the fact that attackers usually indicated to someone their intentions. Most of the time, other students had some hints that a fellow student was ready to lash out. Part of the difficulty that schools face is the fact that students are reluctant to tell an adult their suspicions. Payne and Delbert (2011) noted that the use of an anonymous hotline for students to report threats, mistreatment, or bullying can be an effective deterrent to school violence events.

In general, college campuses are safe environments, and there is a lower rate of crime on college campuses than off campus (Carr, 2005; Cornell, 2007). Horrific shootings on college campuses are more reflective of problems with mental health access and compliance than of problems with campus safety (Cornell, 2007). Colleges and universities should combat violent incidents through training for faculty, staff, and even students. The implementation of threat assessment and prevention programs on campus and campus-wide warning systems could provide the means to thwart future acts of violence and protect student lives. Cornell (2007) presents four steps that can be used by threat assessment teams in school settings:

1. *Identify a threat:* This occurs either through someone communicating a threat or behaving in a threatening manner.
2. *Evaluate seriousness:* Information is gathered and the threat is either determined to be transitory (and thus resolved) or is determined to be substantive and the next step is engaged.
3. *Intervene*: Actions are taken that may include law enforcement involvement, notification of potential victims, and mental health assessment;
4. *Monitor safety plan*: Documentation and follow-up must occur.

Cornell also stresses that for campus threat assessment teams to be effective there must be administrative support, education across campus, and cross-disciplinary teamwork.

CASE STUDY 5.2

Risk Asessment in Schools

Mark is a 10th grade student who is very withdrawn and has few friends. Janice, the school counselor, is concerned about Mark. Last year there was a case where some of the other boys were bullying Mark, and he displayed suicidal ideation. Mark has been seeing a counselor for the past year and the bullies were punished; however, Janice has a gut feeling that the bullying continues "under the radar" of school officials. Mark's English teacher recently stopped by to show Janice Mark's test. Mark did not answer a single question, but instead, drew pictures of guns all over the test.

Discussion Questions

1. What should Janice do?
2. What questions should she ask?
3. What process should she follow?
4. Are there any special considerations since they are in a school setting?

Workplace Homicide

According to the Bureau of Justice Statistics (2010), workplace homicides decreased from a high of 1069 homicides in 1993 to 521 homicides in 2011. Most workplace homicides involve robberies, and individuals who work in retail and hospitality establishments are at greater risk, as are customers and bystanders in these settings. Workplace shootings have decreased slightly from 2010. According to the Bureau of Justice Statistics (2012), workplace homicides accounted for 458 deaths and 242 suicides.

According to the Centers for Disease Control and Prevention (2011), the most dangerous workplace risk factors involve the following:

- Contact with the public
- Exchange of money
- Delivery of passengers, goods, or services
- Having a mobile workplace such as a taxicab or a police cruiser
- Working with unstable or volatile persons in health care, social service, or criminal justice settings
- Working alone or in small numbers
- Working late at night or during early morning hours
- Working in high crime areas
- Guarding valuable property or possessions
- Working in community-based settings

The FBI's National Center for the Analysis of Violent Crime (NCAVC; 2001) explains workplace violence in terms of these categories: (1) violence from criminals who have entered the workplace to commit a crime, (2) violence from customers, clients, patients, and the like, directed toward workers who are providing services, (3) violence against supervisors or coworkers from current or former employees, and (4) violence from an outside person who has a personal relationship with an employee. Prevention of violence from an outside person is nearly impossible, though safety measures can be established to improve workplace security. Violent acts on the part of employees cannot be specifically predicted, but the following indicators can be used for threat assessment in the workplace: personality conflicts on the job; mishandled termination or disciplinary action; family or relationship problems; legal or financial problems; emotional disturbance; increasing belligerence; ominous increasing threats; heightened sensitivity to criticism; acquisition of and fascination with weapons; obsession with supervisor, co-worker, or employee grievance; preoccupation with violent themes; interest in recent publicized violent events; outbursts of anger; extreme disorganization; noticeable changes in behavior; and homicidal/suicidal comments or threats (FBI, 2001). As in school settings, an atmosphere must be created where employees can feel free to come forward and report any disturbing behavior.

The risk of workplace violence and homicide increases during times of extreme job stress. Understaffed job sites, overworked employees, and times of downsizing or labor disputes will create a tense and potentially dangerous context for the development of violent behavior. Additionally, poor management, a high number of grievances, and the lack of employee access to counseling can contribute to violence and homicidal threat in the workplace (FBI, 2001). It is essential that workplace employers, particularly high-pressure workplaces or those undergoing turmoil, be mindful of the need for ongoing threat assessment and be proactive by providing support to employees.

Threat Level Assessment

Cornell (2007) points out that according to the U.S. Secret Service "anyone can make a threat but few individuals actually pose a threat" (p. 12). When a client has overtly indicated intent to harm others or has indirectly exhibited predictors or behaviors of violence and harm to others, the counselor must assess the level of threat. Threat level assessment is critically important to ensure the safety of others and to appropriately guide treatment decisions. While most people who make threats are unlikely to carry out a violent action, all threats must be taken seriously and evaluated (O'Toole, 2000). Threat assessment is the evaluation of the lethality of a threat through an examination of motive, risk factors, intent, and the means and ability to enact the threat. Cornell (2007, p. 13) presents a continuum of threats from highest to lowest :

- Warning of impending violence
- Attempts to intimidate
- Thrill of causing a disruption
- Attention-seeking, boasting
- Fleeting expressions of anger
- Jokes
- Figures of speech

Counselors must ascertain whether or not an individual is expressing frustration through a figure of speech or a joke, or is intent upon causing harm.

When evaluating lethal intent, the NCAVC provides specific guidance on areas for evaluation. O'Toole (2000) explains that threat assessment should involve exploration of the following questions: What are the details of the threat? Are the victims identified? Are the details logical, plausible, and spelled out in a specific manner (time of day, method)? Does the client have the means to carry out the threat? What is the emotional state of the client? While emotionality does not specifically indicate lethality, knowing the affective condition of the client provides important assessment and diagnostic information. Are there stressors or triggers that might predispose a client to violence? Is the level of threat low, medium, or high? NCAVC delineates threat levels as follows:

Low Level of Threat: A threat that poses a minimal risk to victim and public safety.

- The threat is vague and indirect.
- Information contained within the threat is inconsistent.
- The threat lacks realism.
- The content of the threat suggests the person is unlikely to carry it out.

Medium Level of Threat: A threat that could be carried out, although it may not appear to be entirely realistic.

- The threat is more direct and more concrete than a low-level threat.
- The wording in the threat suggests that the person issuing the threat has given some thought to how the act will be carried out.
- There may be a general indication of a possible place and time (though these signs still fall well short of a detailed plan).
- There is no strong indication that the person who issued the threat has taken preparatory steps, although there may be a veiled reference or ambiguous or inconclusive evidence pointing to that possibility—an allusion to a book or movie that shows planning of a violent act or a vague general statement seeking to convey that the threat is not empty: "I'm serious!" or "I really mean this!"

High Level of Threat: A threat that appears to pose an imminent and serious danger to the safety of others.

- The threat is direct, specific, and plausible.
- The threat suggests that concrete steps have been taken toward carrying it out—for example, statements indicating that the person who issued the threat has acquired or practiced with a weapon or has had the victim under surveillance. (O'Toole, 2000, pp. 8–9)

The process of threat assessment must be conducted in an environment that will calm the client, facilitate the de-escalation of intense emotions, and assist in the attainment of precise information regarding the level of threat intent. Tishler et al. (2000) note that the assessment of violence is similar to the assessment of other symptoms in that the client's history of violence, family and medical history, mental status, and drug use must be investigated. They also emphasize that a calm demeanor and basic rapport-building communication skills are necessary to create a constructive environment for assessment.

VOICES FROM THE FIELD 5.4
Leaving No Stone Unturned

Cheryl Lewellen

When assessing for homicidal ideation for potential clients to our nonprofit women's residential substance abuse treatment facility, we begin by using a state assessment issued by the Department of Mental Health. I'm sure most states have a similar standardized assessment. It takes more than an hour to perform and assesses for multiple factors, with both suicidal and homicidal ideation included.

Given the nature of clients struggling with addictions, it is important to continue to verbally assess for both suicide and homicide during individual sessions throughout the 90 days they are here. One of the main factors for this is that many of the women come into the program insufficiently detoxed and it takes

a while for them to gain a clear perspective on their lives. As they begin treatment and open up to aspects of their lives that caused them to use drugs and alcohol in the first place, the clients become aware of the multitude of emotions they had attempted to numb. Many of the clients have suffered abuse on multiple levels either before or during their drug use. Therefore, it is always important to monitor their potential ideation of both suicide and homicide.

As with assessment of suicidal ideation, assessment of the homicidal client involves asking questions to establish whether or not an individual has thoughts about harming or killing another person, if they have a plan, and to what extent the plan could be enacted.

Counselors should avoid quick movements and be mindful of personal space when assessing an agitated, potentially homicidal client. Once the client has calmed down, the counselor can delve into precise questions to obtain detailed information about the intent of the client to harm another, the extent and intrusiveness of the homicidal thoughts, and the ability of the client to acquire the means to implement homicide plans. When dealing with a client expressing homicidal intent, crisis counselors must always keep the ethical obligation of public safety and the duty to warn at the forefront of their minds, even with low-threat clients. Furthermore, while assessing homicidal ideation, the counselor should also assess for suicidal ideation as homicide and suicide may co-occur.

CASE STUDY 5.3

CLIENT: I hate my supervisor at work. My life would be better if that jerk was dead.

COUNSELOR: You're so angry at your supervisor that you wish he was dead. Have you had thoughts about harming him?

CLIENT: Sure, I think about killing him.

COUNSELOR: Have you come up with a plan to kill him?

CLIENT: A plan? I mean I've got a 45 at home but, no not a plan exactly.

COUNSELOR: Are there times when you feel you might act on these thoughts?

CLIENT: Ha, whenever I'm drunk.

Discussion Questions

1. What level of threat is indicated so far?
2. What other information does the counselor need to assess the threat level?
3. If the counselor determines the supervisor is in danger, what steps should the counselor take?

Referral

Because of the danger to others and the possible existence of mental disorders in homicidal clients, counselors usually refer clients to or work collaboratively with other mental health providers, particularly psychiatrists, when treating clients who pose a threat to others. Violent clients often need the help of specialists in forensic mental health, and it is a good idea for crisis counselors to be familiar with forensic specialists in their local area.

Clinical assessment of low-threat-level clients may reveal the need for psychiatric evaluation and treatment with psychotropic medication; however, it is imperative that clients with homicidal ideation who are assessed at the high and medium threat levels be referred for psychiatric evaluation and possible treatment with medications. Because of imminent danger to others, high-threat-level clients require immediate law enforcement involvement and probable voluntary or involuntary commitment (O'Toole, 2000). Medium-threat-level clients need to be monitored closely and may need to be hospitalized. In instances with out-of-control and impulsive clients, homicidal and suicidal ideation may coexist, and therefore, such a client poses a threat to both self and others. The procedures for voluntary and involuntary commitment discussed previously in this chapter in relation to suicide should be followed for homicide cases, with the inclusion of law enforcement in high-threat-level situations. Personal safety of the crisis counselor should always be a priority. A counselor should never attempt to physically stop a resistant client from leaving. If the client is intent on leaving, it is best to get as much information as possible about the client and request law enforcement to intervene.

What is the relationship between mental illness and homicide? Individuals with diagnosed mental disorders are at a higher risk than the general population for violent or homicidal behavior (Laajasalo & Hakkanen, 2004). It should be noted, however, that this risk is not present across the board and that an elevated threat to others is mainly associated with certain diagnoses (Eronen, Angermeyer, & Schulze, 1998). An increased risk of violent behavior has been found with diagnoses of schizophrenia and other psychotic disorders, but the highest risk of violent and homicidal behavior has been found in individuals with a dual diagnosis of antisocial personality disorder and substance use disorder. Substance abuse repeatedly emerges as a major risk factor for violent behavior and homicide; the comorbidity of substance abuse and any mental disorder will increase the likelihood of violence and should be taken into account when assessing and treating violent clients.

Treatment Options

The establishment of a strong therapeutic alliance through counseling microskills is essential in all counseling relationships and is discussed thoroughly in Chapter 4. A therapeutic alliance is particularly imperative with potential homicide offenders, since client investment in treatment compliance is necessary for public safety. Tishler et al.

(2000) note that mental health providers may struggle with achieving empathy and may experience fear when working with homicidal clients. While such reactions are understandable, it is important to remember that homicidal behaviors are symptoms of a client's illness and that open displays of fear and distaste will undermine rapport building and impair treatment outcomes.

Once the immediate homicidal crisis has been dealt with, the safety of others has been assured, and appropriate medical treatment has begun, long-term treatment planning can proceed. Ongoing assessment of the client is crucial to both treatment outcomes and public safety; therefore, assessment must remain foremost in the crisis counselor's mind. One concern in assessment is the tendency for violent offenders to be less than forthright about the facts surrounding violent acts (Carroll et al., 2004; Towl & Crighton, 1997). Crisis counselors should thoroughly examine client history and obtain external substantiation of client facts. Hillbrand (2001) cautions that suicidal ideation and homicidal ideation often co-occur and stresses the importance of assessing the risk of both suicide and homicide in clients who have thoughts of harm to self or others.

In addition to ongoing assessment, homicidal and violent client treatment plans typically include anger and stress management, medication, substance abuse treatment (when indicated), and limitation of access to weapons (Hillbrand, 2001). Treatment should also include the identification of factors that increase and decrease violent ideation. Brems (2000) discussed several aggression-motivating and -mitigating factors that should be assessed and addressed during treatment of violent clients:

- *Habit Strength:* Assessment of the degree to which past violence has worked for the client indicates whether this type of behavior has been reinforced. Clients who have gotten their way through aggression and violence in the past are more likely to use these behaviors in the future.
- *Inhibitions:* A client without inhibitions will be more likely to become aggressive; however, inhibitions may act to moderate aggressive acting out. Examples of inhibiting factors include personal morality and values, impulse control, fear of being caught, and fear of negative consequences. By exploring past times when the client did not resort to violence, a crisis counselor can identify inhibiting factors that can be integrated into treatment.
- *Situational Factors:* Exploration of context can yield important data for treatment. If a client is more likely to engage in violent action in certain circumstances, the treatment plan can include avoidance of triggering settings.

By understanding how aggression may have been reinforced in the client's past and by exploring any inhibiting factors and situational contexts, crisis counselors and clients can identify thoughts and behaviors that may lessen violent behavior in the future. The client can begin to learn other ways to cope with anger and aggression.

Klott and Jongsma (2004, p. 324) suggested the following long-term treatment goals for assaultive/homicidal males:

- Terminate the use of violence to meet social, psychological, and environmental needs.
- Enhance access to emotions and a capacity for empathy toward the needs, feelings, and desires of others.
- Develop adaptive coping strategies and problem-solving skills.

- Enhance personal resiliency, flexibility, and a capacity to manage crises and failures.
- Develop a supportive social network and the ability to engage in intimate relationships based on mutuality.
- Develop a sense of self-acceptance and the capacity for self-affirmation.

In addition to these goals, Klott and Jongsma suggest a goal of impulse resolution for males with both homicidal and suicidal ideation.

Compliance with treatment—in particular, compliance with medication—must be stressed with homicidal clients. Nordstrom, Dahlgren, and Kullgren (2006) studied convicted homicide offenders who had been diagnosed with schizophrenia. The majority of offenders were found to have been noncompliant with medication and treatment at the time of their crimes, resulting in active hallucinations and delusions during the homicidal crisis. Therefore, it is essential that crisis counselors conduct ongoing evaluations of medication compliance throughout treatment.

Family involvement in the treatment of homicidal clients is critical as a support for ongoing treatment compliance. Families can communicate to counselors if clients stop taking medication and can also report observed behaviors of concern that might indicate elevated risk (Carroll et al., 2004). Additionally, families provide a social network foundation that can facilitate client coping. In some instances, family members need to be given information to ensure their own safety. Family members and friends, rather than strangers, were the most frequent victims of homicide offenders with a diagnosis of schizophrenia (Laajasalo & Hakkanen, 2004). This fact highlights the need for families to be an active part of collaborative treatment and ongoing evaluation of homicidal clients.

Early environmental factors influence the development of mental disorders and violent behavior; thus, early intervention with children at risk and their families may deter the development of future antisocial behavior, including homicide (Laajasalo & Hakkanen, 2004). Schools provide the first opportunity for intervention with children who are exhibiting behavioral problems and struggling with academics, both of which are associated with violence. Farmer, Farmer, Estell, and Hutchins (2007) recommend a service delivery structure that supports intervention and prevention in order to promote academic achievement and social skills, intervention with at-risk youth, and developmental systemic prevention strategies. It should be noted that such a delivery structure can be achieved by the full implementation of *The ASCA National Model: A Framework for School Counseling Programs* (American School Counselor Association [ASCA], 2012).

CASE STUDY 5.4

Assessing for Level of Lethality

Judy is a 43-year-old single woman who has been placed on two weeks' administrative leave from her job as a research and development technician at a chemical company. Over the years, she has had many personality conflicts with other workers, but her expertise is valuable, and these conflicts have always been smoothed over and worked out. Recently, she "lost it" with her boss and flew into a rage when she was denied time off in compensation for working late the previous week; this incident was the basis for her administrative leave. Her family doctor has prescribed antidepressants for her and has referred her to you for counseling.

Judy expresses anger and a sense of hopelessness about her situation. She is distraught and has to drink wine every night just to go to sleep. Judy is convinced that she will be fired and that the boss is using these two weeks to build a case against her. She expresses to you how valuable she is to the company and how much knowledge she has, including her knowledge of tasteless but deadly poisons. She states, "Just one minute in the break room is all someone would need; just slip it in the coffee and they wouldn't know what hit them."

Discussion Questions

1. What level of threat is indicated in this case?
2. Are there factors that increase the homicide risk in this client?
3. What actions should you take?

Homicide Survivor Needs

In the aftermath of a homicide, the family, friends, and sometimes even the community of the victim experience impediments to healing as the mourning process is complicated by the brutality and abruptness of their loss. Hatton (2003) estimates that there are at least 50,000 bereaved homicide survivors every year in the United States. Unfortunately, homicide survivors may underutilize available services and may also have their grief and trauma compounded during subsequent crime investigations and legal proceedings (Horne, 2003). Homicide survivors often find themselves isolated as members of their social network withdraw due to distress and uneasiness over the terrible circumstances surrounding the loss (Currier et al., 2006) or due to stigmatizing circumstances surrounding the death (Hatton, 2003). This lack of community support can be thought of as a secondary victimization that further complicates the grief process. Collins and Collins (2005) point out that the common grief and loss reactions—such as anger, guilt, and self-blame—are amplified in homicide survivor cases.

Homicide is a violent loss, and survivor grief is complicated and multifaceted (Currier et al., 2006). In essence, violent death rocks the foundations of a survivor's worldview and impedes the ability to make sense of the death or to find meaning within the loss. The bereavement experienced after loss to homicide or suicide usually falls within the category of complicated grief—a grieving process that can occur when a death is sudden, developmentally unexpected, or violent. According to the Mayo Clinic (2008), several symptoms may accompany complicated grief:

- Extreme focus on the loss and reminders of the loved one
- Intense longing or pining for the deceased
- Problems accepting the death
- Preoccupation with your sorrow
- Bitterness about your loss
- Inability to enjoy life
- Depression or deep sadness
- Difficulty moving on with life
- Trouble carrying out a normal routine
- Withdrawing from social activities

- Feeling that life holds no meaning or purpose
- Irritability or agitation
- Lack of trust in others

Homicide survivors are almost certain to experience complicated grief. Asaro (2001) recommends the following treatment interventions for homicide survivors: (1) promote feelings of safety within the counseling relationship, (2) discuss the specifics of the murder and allow the client to review the murder as needed, (3) address any co-occurring conditions (e.g., substance abuse), (4) normalize and reframe the myriad feelings the client is experiencing, and (5) refer the client to support groups or other resources.

Armour (2005) promotes a constructivist, meaning-making approach to working with homicide survivors. To heal from violent loss, survivors need to feel able to openly express what has happened to them and to fight for change in a system where they have felt injustice. It is also important that survivors find meaning in the death of their loved one by working to benefit others experiencing similar circumstances; this gives meaning to the loss as well as purpose to the survivor.

The support experienced in group counseling is especially healing for homicide survivors and cannot be underestimated as a treatment modality (Piper, Ogrodniczuk, McCollum, & Rosie, 2002). Hatton (2003) found that homicide survivors found support group counseling to be one of the most helpful interventions in the bereavement process. Support groups give the participants an opportunity to express their feelings without the fear of alienation and stigmatization. Participants can openly talk about their experiences with others who have shared similar experiences and can offer informed support. The U.S. Department of Justice's Office for Victims of Crime (OVC, 2006) has links to support organizations and resources across the nation at www.ojp.usdoj.gov/ovc/help/hv.htm.

Crisis counselors responding to the crisis of homicide should be prepared for complex and varied reactions and symptoms from individual survivors. Individuals and entire communities can be altered by homicide. At college campuses where homicide has taken place, students no longer feel safe, and the stress and anxiety affect their academic achievement (Carr, 2005). Communities touched by homicide are altered by the brutal reality of murder within their midst; a coordinated community counseling response and activation of resources will serve to facilitate healing. Additionally, crisis counselors should be sensitive to cultural differences in grief expression. Clients from expressive cultures will show more outward signs of grieving. A lack of outward grief expression may be indicative of a more emotionally restrictive culture, and crisis counselors should not underestimate the inner grief state of less expressive clients (Cavaiola & Colford, 2006).

CASE STUDY 5.5

Treatment for Families of Homicide

Debbie, a 19-year-old college freshman, didn't show up for classes or for her job one day. When she didn't answer her cell phone or come home that night, her roommate was worried and contacted Debbie's family, who decided to report her as a missing person. After three weeks of searching and televised pleas for her return, Debbie's decomposing body was found in a wooded area 30 miles from her apartment. She had been sexually assaulted and strangled. DNA found on her body was a match with DNA from a man out on parole from a previous rape conviction. He was accused in Debbie's murder. The killer claimed that he had consensual sex with Debbie in his car and that she was fine when he dropped her off at campus. Debbie's parents were appalled when the killer's defense team attempted to portray Debbie as a wild, out-of-control college student who partied too much, had multiple sex partners, and put herself at risk. The trial ended with a hung jury, and there is uncertainty about when there will be a new trial. Debbie's parents have come to you for grief counseling.

Discussion Questions

1. What factors have contributed to the parents' complicated grief?
2. What emotions and reactions might you expect from the parents in this case?
3. What treatment goals and interventions are called for in this case?

VOICES FROM THE FIELD 5.5
Reacting in Crisis Situations

Gregory Pollock

The calm of the day was interrupted by the loudspeaker calling a code for violent behavior being exhibited by a client. I quickly dropped what I was doing and responded to the code. As I approached the area, the commotion of the situation became louder and louder, as my adrenaline levels increased quickly with each step closer to the area. I felt my breath become shallower, my stomach dropped, and my body became tense. I had to consciously step back and take a breath and attempt to relax prior to entering the room where the client in question was out of control and becoming violent. How many of us as counselors have been faced with these similar situations?

I have learned the hard way that approaching situations such as these while hyped up and excited only adds to the tension and worsens the situation. I think back to my early days in this field where I witnessed staff enter crisis situations in a frustrated state and saw how this exacerbated the situation in very negative ways, at times leading to the staff or client becoming injured.

It is imperative to remain calm when reacting in crisis situations so that we do not add to the situation at hand. I frequently hear from counselors in training that they do not feel that they could remain calm in a crisis situation and that when faced with a crisis they seem to "forget" all of their skills. On

the contrary, their skills are not forgotten, but often masked with anxiety, fear, adrenaline, and stress reactions. So how is it possible to remain calm and keep our wits about us when faced with a crisis? Our training programs do a great job of preparing us for a variety of situations through the use of counseling skills and techniques. Not all counselors have equal opportunities to practice in crisis situations, and those working in situations where crises are more common will have a greater comfort level in dealing with crisis incidents.

It is helpful to remain mindful of ourselves and recognize what is going on internally as we enter situations, whether entering a regular counseling session or a crisis situation. How aware are we of our feelings and thoughts when walking into crisis situations? It is important to control our emotions as we enter crisis situations with the best interest of the client at heart, much like a regular counseling session. There are great consequences to not remaining mindful lest we lose sight of what is needed to best remedy the situation we are faced with.

I refer to a yogic phrase, *Ahisma,* meaning to do no harm. This is a great term to keep in mind as we prepare for and enter into crisis situations. The best way to ensure that we do no harm to ourselves in yoga is by being aware of ourselves and staying in touch with our bodies to make sure that we do not strain ourselves. It may be difficult to understand the amount of influence that we have on situations, and controlling our emotions goes a long way in enabling us to enter stressful situations in a calm manner.

Maintaining awareness on a daily basis becomes very difficult, especially in light of our listening to and taking on the issues and circumstances of our clients, leaving us vulnerable to compassion fatigue, which in turn can lead to a loss of control in crisis situations. Self-care is vitally important to help us deal with underlying frustrations so that we can maintain our emotional stability.

The most important thing to focus on in crisis situations is maintaining safety of self, the client, and other staff. We also need to focus on what the client needs in crisis situations, and we need to be open to empathizing, understanding, and meeting the needs of the client in a respectful, nonharming manner, while approaching these situations with compassion and a calm even temperament.

Summary

Suicide and homicide are both crisis situations that counselors who are emergency first responders and who provide more long-term treatment are almost certain to be called on to address. These are critical incidents across the span of a professional career. Suicide rates are increasing among all segments of our population, and this trend is expected to continue despite the elaborate prevention efforts ongoing at school, local, state, and national levels.

In the treatment of suicide as a crisis, counselors and other response-oriented personnel may find that their own anxiety surrounding this topic affects their approach to helping clients resolve their own situations. Periodic self-examination is therefore necessary to maintain an adequate degree of separation from the client's crisis, to prevent transference of the crisis counselor's anxieties onto the client, and to avoid damaging the potential for a positive counselor-client relationship. No universally recognized standard of care is in place with regard to response to suicide and suicide attempts and to treatment of those with suicidal ideation, but professional concepts of foreseeability and assessment of risk have been established to guide and protect crisis counselors as they work with this population.

Three primary goals are presented for the crisis responder to set in dealing with crises of suicide or homicide: (1) to ensure client safety, (2) to assist the client in achieving immediate short-term mastery of self and situation, and (3) to connect the client with formal and informal supports. There are a variety of models presented to help the crisis responder achieve these goals. When the intervention spans more than one contact, as it often does for counselors, additional tools, such as Jobes's Collaborative Assessment and Management of Suicidality (CAMS) approach, are an effective way to achieve meaningful and maintainable client improvement and progress. A knowledge of suicide risk factors, warning signs, and protective factors is essential for the crisis counselor to make a justifiable assessment of suicide risk in clients who are struggling with this issue. Once the client is assessed, the counselor makes a decision regarding level of risk and actively monitors the client as he or she makes progress or subsequent events affect the client's disposition. Documentation of the entire process is an increasingly important part of the assessment and treatment cycle; it is emphasized that documentation is the single most important factor in justifying and defending a particular course of treatment action.

A variety of treatment options are in place to respond to those struggling with the issue of suicide, including inpatient hospitalization, partial hospitalization programs, and outpatient care. As managed care operations become the norm in American mental health treatment protocols, a comprehensive risk management plan becomes an essential part of cost-effective and medically justifiable care. The risk management plan typically consists of six components: (1) ensuring that all of the included professionals understand the statutes relevant to suicide treatment, confidentiality, and informed consent;

(2) having a detailed risk management policy; (3) ensuring clinical competency of staff members; (4) maintaining adequate documentation of treatment; (5) implementing a tracking system for follow-up actions; and (6) establishing and maintaining relevant resources.

Responding to incidents of homicide presents many of the same kinds of challenges as responding to a suicide incident does, although many crisis counselors underestimate the need for readiness to respond to homicide. In fact, since instances where homicide must be responded to in the counseling setting are becoming more frequent, crisis counselors must prepare themselves to engage with this crisis in a professional, defensible way. Crisis counselors may find themselves in a position of potential influence over those who might become capable of homicide, so the *Tarasoff v. Board of Regents of the University of California* case, which clarified the duty to warn individuals who may be in peril, applies to counselors; it is critical that crisis counselors be aware of their legal duties in these situations.

As with suicide risk assessment and management, counselors may be confronted with homicide risk factors, and violence capable of escalating to homicide must be examined in the educational arena and in the workplace. Crisis counselors must use a threat-level assessment to gauge the need for treatment and implement an appropriate treatment option that includes ongoing assessment of risk.

Homicide survivors usually experience complicated grief. They may feel stigmatized, isolated, and retraumatized by the legal system. Treatment of survivors should address their complicated grief issues and help them find resolution and meaning. Support groups for homicide survivors have been found to be a highly effective method of treatment.

6

Understanding and Treating Substance Use Disorders with Clients in Crisis

William R. Sterner

PREVIEW

This chapter provides an overview of substance use disorders and a crisis counselor's role in working with clients facing crisis situations. Etiological factors of substance use disorders and various models of addiction are reviewed. Those sections in the chapter dealing with treatment are arranged to help understand the sequential treatment process. Special issues such as relapse, support groups, co-occurring disorders, and cultural considerations are discussed. Case studies and activities are provided throughout the chapter to help the reader integrate and apply the material.

SUBSTANCE USE AND SOCIETY

Throughout history substances, many of which are now considered illegal in many countries, have been used as an integral component of social activities, religious ceremonies, spiritual rituals, and cultural practices. Along with intended sociocultural purpose, substances have also been sought out to alter mood and enhance sensory experience and pleasure. Individuals have continually experimented with mood altering substances, as well as heuristic routes of administration that both maximize the delivery to and enhance the effects on the brain. The list of mood altering substances is as varied as it is long and includes well known substances such as marijuana (the most commonly used illicit drug in the United States), cocaine, heroin, tobacco, and ethyl alcohol (one of the most widely used and easily accessible mood altering substances).

Data from the *2009 National Survey on Drug Use and Health* (Substance Abuse and Mental Health Services Administration [SAMHSA], 2010) revealed that nearly 52% of

Americans age 12 years and older (approximately 131 million) are current consumers of alcohol and nearly 70 million use tobacco products. Nearly 17 million reported using marijuana without a prescription, an increase of nearly 3 million from 2007. A growing problem is the nonmedical use of prescription-type drugs, especially pain medications. A majority (55.3%) of those reporting use of nonmedical prescription-type drugs indicated the source was family and friends. Of the 23.5 million who reported needing treatment for an illicit drug or alcohol problem, only 2.6 million (11%) received treatment (SAMHSA, 2010). In 2007, the economic cost of illicit drug use in the United States was over $190 billion (U.S. Department of Justice, 2011).

Based on this data the conclusion might be that substance use has evolved beyond sociocultural practices to more self-serving and unhealthy motives. However, what is not clear is the primary intent for use. Reasons for using substances can be quite varied and complex, as evidenced by the numerous theories developed to explain use and addiction. Prevailing attitudes, however, may not fully acknowledge factors beyond pleasure-seeking motives, factors such as stress, psychopathology, crisis response, and grief and loss responses to traumatic events such as natural and human-generated disasters, emergencies, and tragedies. Unfortunately aggregate data do not delineate the extent to which substance use may in fact be as much about pleasure-seeking as it is about compensating for psychosocial, psychopathological, and sociocultural problems.

Classification of Drugs and Terminology

The number of different drugs that exist worldwide is unknown. To gain some perspective, the 2011 *Physicians' Desk Reference* lists over 1,100 commonly prescribed FDA-approved medications. Anecdotal reports estimate the number of different drugs worldwide may be as high as 100,000. Rather than attempting to quantify drugs, a more effective methodology is to classify substances based on the specific physiological and psychological effects. Current drug classifications include cannabinoids (e.g., marijuana, hashish, dronabinol), depressants (e.g., alcohol, tranquilizers, barbiturates, sleeping pills, inhalants), stimulants (e.g., cocaine, amphetamines, methamphetamine, caffeine), hallucinogens (e.g., LSD, phencyclidine, ketamine, mescaline, psilocybin), opiates (e.g. heroin, morphine, OxyContin, codeine, methadone), nicotine, and psychotherapeutics (e.g., Prozac, Zoloft, Ativan, Xanax, BuSpar, Cymbalta, Abilify, lithium, Geodon, Zyprexa, Risperdal). Other drugs can have multiple effects and may fall under several classifications. For example, Ecstasy (3,4-methylenedioxymethamphetamine or MDMA), a designer drug popular in the club and bar scene during the mid-1990s, has both stimulant and hallucinogenic effects. Dextromethorphan (also known as DX or DXM), a drug found in many over-the-counter cough syrups, can have both depressant and mild hallucinogenic effects if taken in large doses.

The Comprehensive Drug Abuse Prevention and Control Act of 1970 classified drugs into five schedules based on a continuum for potential for abuse, accepted medical use, and potential for dependence. Drugs listed under Schedule I have the highest potential for abuse and dependence and have no current medical application in the United States (e.g., heroin, LSD, marijuana), whereas drugs listed under Schedule V have the lowest potential for abuse and dependence and have an established medical application (e.g., cough syrups with codeine).

Throughout this chapter, various terms will be used related to substance usage and crisis. *Substance use* is "the intake of a chemical substance into the body with the goal of somehow altering one's state of consciousness. Use may or may not cause problems" (Lawson, 1984, p. 37). *Substance abuse* is the "use of a substance in a manner, amounts, or situations such that the drug use causes problems or greatly increases the chances of problems occurring" (Hart & Ksir, 2011, p. 6). *Substance dependence* is defined as "a cellular change that occurs with the increased use of most depressant drugs. The primary clinical features are the development of tolerance and the development of withdrawal symptoms upon removal of the drug" (Lawson, 1984, p. 37).

Differentiating between substance use, abuse, and dependence is an important consideration as these terms are often used interchangeably, yet they have distinct differences. Many substance abuse counselors have found that delineating between these terms is best accomplished when viewed along a continuum with abstinence at one end and dependence (addiction) at the other. Understanding where a client is along this continuum provides counselors with a reference point with respect to the progression of the substance use pattern, as well as perspective as to how best to approach treatment and which interventions may be most applicable.

Current Research on Substance Use, Crisis, and Society

Several recent studies have documented the relationship between natural and human-generated disasters and patterns of substance use and abuse. A meta-analysis of over 30 studies investigating substance use following terrorist attacks in the United States found an increased use of substances in the two years following terrorist events and the rates of use were likely higher than estimated (DiMaggio, Galea, & Li, 2009). One month following the September 11 attacks on the World Trade Center, increased use of marijuana, alcohol, and cigarettes was reported in Manhattan (Vlahov et al., 2002) and just over 2% (130,000) of the more than 6 million adults living in New York City had more alcohol problems 6 months post-9/11 than prior (Vlahov et al., 2006). Women used more alcohol post-9/11 compared to those who were surveyed prior to this event (Richman, Wislar, Flaherty, Fendrich, & Rospenda, 2004).

Understanding how crisis situations affect those with preexisting conditions has important implications for substance abuse counselors. Examining the effects of substance use following the Oklahoma City bombing of April 19, 1995, a majority of survivors did not develop new substance abuse disorders; however, a majority of those survivors who did use substances excessively had a preexisting substance use disorder (North, 2010). Compared to a control community, alcohol consumption in the year following the Oklahoma City bombing was 2.5 times greater than for a control community (Smith, Christiansen, Vincent, & Hann, 1999). For evacuees of Hurricane Katrina in August 2005, treatment for preexisting psychiatric illnesses, not increased substance use issues, was the main concern (North, 2010). Those dealing with multiple assaults are at increased risk for both alcohol and drug use (Kilpatrick, Acierno, Resnick, Saunders, & Best, 1997). NDCHealth compiled data on the use of antianxiety medication following 9/11 in the New York City and Washington, DC, metropolitan areas. Data revealed in the two weeks post-9/11 prescriptions for Xanax, Ativan, and Valium increased in all three regions (Okie, 2001). Regarding adolescent patterns of substance use, changes in

ACTIVITY 6.1

Imagine a person with substance dependence. Describe some of the problems he or she may be facing. What images or biases come to mind when you think of one who is addicted to a substance?

usage status for adolescents exposed to Hurricane Katrina were noted with 15% shifting from cigarette nonuse pre-Katrina to use post-Katrina, 9% with marijuana, and 25% with alcohol (Rowe, La Greca, & Alexandersson, 2010). Adolescents not in close proximity to the events of 9/11 experienced increased marijuana use (Costello, Erkanli, Keeler, & Angold, 2004).

ETIOLOGY AND RISK FACTORS OF SUBSTANCE ABUSE AND DEPENDENCE

The most widely accepted belief is that addiction, alcohol specifically, is biologically based; however, alternative hypotheses continue to be developed and debated. One reason for the diversity of theoretical perspectives likely stems from the fact that while research continues to make inroads linking addiction to neurobiological mechanisms, no conclusive evidence of a specific biological relationship exists (Craig, 2004). Given the nature and complexity of addiction, other theories and models will likely evolve to help explain biological, psychological, and sociological factors. The National Institute on Drug Abuse (NIDA, 1980) published a compendium of over 40 models and theories of addiction to create a forum for discussion of diverse theoretical perspectives, as well as a tool to help practitioners compare and contrast the various theoretical approaches. Understanding etiology of substance abuse and addiction is especially critical for counselors working with clients dealing with crisis situations. Awareness of which theoretical model(s) are highly associated with client crisis and substance use may help minimize or ameliorate the physiological and psychological symptoms as well as provide counselors with a targeted treatment framework. Several of the more commonly accepted models are discussed in this section.

Disease (Medical) Model

In the mid-20th century, the disease concept of alcoholism became a viable alternative to the long-standing view that alcoholism was essentially a moral problem. An early pioneer in the disease model was Magnus Huss, a Swedish physician, who in 1849 coined the term *alcoholic* to describe behaviors and consequences associated with heavy alcohol use (Miller & Hester, 2003). E. M. Jellinek developed the disease concept of alcoholism from research conducted with males who identified as alcoholic. Jellinek (1960) considered alcoholism as much a disease as other maladies such as cancer or diabetes. Like other diseases, Jellinek believed individuals with alcoholism present a specific set of characteristics: (1) lack of control over drinking and primary symptoms are directly attributed to alcohol consumption, (2) symptoms are progressive, and (3) continued use would result in death. Jellinek (1946) viewed alcoholism as a chronic and irreversible condition where the individual progresses through four defined stages: (1) *prealcoholic* (alcohol is used to relieve tension), (2) *prodromal* (preoccupation with alcohol use, physical symptoms begin to appear), (3) *crucial* (loss of control over alcohol, evidence of withdrawal, interpersonal problems, drinking becomes primary focus), and (4) *chronic* (severe psychological, social, and biological problems). Because alcoholism is a chronic and progressive disease, the only treatment option is complete abstinence from alcohol use. Moderation is not considered an option given the progressive nature of the disease. Continued drinking will ultimately result in death. Jellinek's work influenced the American Medical Association (AMA) to classify alcoholism as a disease in 1956 (Doweiko, 2009). The AMA currently defines alcoholism as a "primary, chronic disease with genetic, psychosocial, and environmental factors influencing its development and manifestations. The disease is often progressive and fatal. It is characterized by impaired control over drinking, preoccupation with the drug alcohol, [and] use of alcohol despite adverse consequences" (Morse & Flavin, 1992, p. 1012).

Moral Model

The underlying premise of the moral model is the belief that individuals' personal choice related to substance abuse is morally wrong or deficient. Individuals make a personal choice to become addicted, which is viewed as the wrong choice, a sign of moral weakness, or a sin, rather than making an alternative choice to not use, which is the morally and spiritually correct decision. The moral model is rooted in the religious ideology of good versus evil and that addiction is caused by a spiritual deficit and thus is violating societal rules. Those who espouse the moral model discount the scientifically accepted position that addiction is biologically based (Capuzzi & Stauffer, 2012).

Genetic and Biological Models

GENETIC MODELS Genetic and biological models emphasize that addiction is caused by a genetic predisposition or physiological factors (Miller & Hester, 2003). These models assume that causality for addiction is rooted within a person's DNA or other inheritable biological condition that influence the metabolism of substances. Relationships between genetic predisposition and family patterns of alcoholism have been demonstrated (Craig, 2004). Arguments for the genetic model are evident throughout the literature. Sons of fathers who are alcoholic had a fourfold increase in developing alcoholism compared to sons of fathers who were not alcoholic (Goodwin, Schulsinger, Hermansen, Guze, & Winokur, 1973). First-degree relatives of parents who are alcoholic have a sevenfold risk for developing alcoholism compared to first-degree relatives whose parents did not report alcoholism (Merikangas, 1990). Koopmans and Boomsma (1996) found a similar pattern with genetic factors explaining 43% of the variance between parent and child alcoholism. Genetic and biologically based models view the course of addiction and treatment from a medical model perspective (Capuzzi & Stauffer, 2012) while deemphasizing the role of moral choice, sociocultural factors, or environmental influences.

NEUROBIOLOGICAL MODELS The basis of neurobiological models is that many psychoactive drugs have specific effects on neurotransmitter activity specifically on the limbic system, which influences emotions (Capuzzi & Stauffer, 2012) and the medial forebrain bundle where alcohol and drugs activate pleasure and reward centers (Hernandez et al., 2006). As substance use continues, the brain produces less of the targeted neurotransmitter (e.g., dopamine) within the pleasure center as the drug mimics the effects of the neurotransmitter. This homeostatic process results in addiction as the individual must now substitute substances for the depleted neurotransmitter thus leading to addiction. Proponents of this theory argue that addressing addiction involves using prescribed drugs to restore healthy neurotransmitter activity (Capuzzi & Stauffer, 2012). Despite the scientific advances in genetic and biological research on addiction, causality between addiction and the specific genetic and biological mechanisms has not been fully established (Craig, 2004).

Social Learning Model

The social learning model states that people learn from each other through observation, imitating, and/or modeling behaviors (Bandura, 1977)

GENERAL SYSTEMS MODEL In order to explain addiction from a general systems perspective, one must examine how an individual's behavior is influenced by and as part of a related system. The behaviors of an individual are best understood in relation to other members of the system. For example, when a family member is addicted to a substance, this model assumes that an individual's patterns of actions and behaviors are maintained and reinforced by other members within the established system (homeostasis). This model also assumes that individual problems are more systems-based rather than individual-based. Treatment involves working not only to change the problematic actions and behaviors of the individual but the dysfunction within the system (Miller & Hester, 2003).

COGNITIVE MODEL The cognitive model applies the basic tenets of cognitive learning. Simply stated, a person's beliefs about substance use influence expectations related to its use. If individuals believe that alcohol and other drug (AOD) use can result in positive outcomes, then this expectation will motivate them to increase the amount and frequency of the substance (Brown, 1993).

SOCIOCULTURAL MODEL A broader approach to AOD addiction is viewed from a cultural or societal perspective. The basic premise of this model is that the more acceptable and available the substance, the more members of the societal or cultural group will consume (Miller & Hester, 2003). This model addresses the role that culture, subculture, and society plays in how individuals perceive substance use and abuse. The sociocultural model views abuse and addiction based on cultural or societal expectations of acceptable patterns of use, ease of access, and relative availability of substances. Expectations related to substance use can be heightened or diminished based on cultural or subcultural attitudes toward a specific substance. For example, alcohol use continues to be a socially accepted and expected part of the college experience as many social activities revolve around alcohol and often view its use as a rite of passage.

Psychological Model

PSYCHODYNAMIC MODEL The psychodynamic model views substance abuse as originating with problems in childhood development. Issues such as attachment disorders, inadequate parenting, ego deficiencies, and development adjustment issues are at the source of eventual abuse and addiction problems. Those who view psychodynamic models as a possible cause for addiction believe that (1) basic psychopathology is likely the root cause of substance problems, (2) individuals who use substances may do so because of problems with affect regulation, and (3) problematic object relations may eventually influence the onset of substance problems (Dodgen & Shea, 2000).

CONDITIONING MODEL   Based on the concepts of classical and operant conditioning, this model views substance abuse problems as a learned habit, a response to a specific behavior(s). When an external stimulus produces a reward or positive experience, then the association is reinforced, increasing the likelihood that repeated actions or behaviors will result when the stimulus is presented again (Miller & Hester, 2003). When an individual drinks alcohol and experiences stress relief, feels more relaxed, or is less socially inhibited, a positive association is created between alcohol and symptom reduction that is expected when alcohol is consumed again. As the positive association is reinforced, repeated use of the substance continues. Treatment approaches using this model apply the same process to unlearning a behavior. Examples of treatment strategies include aversion therapies (e.g., disulfiram to treat alcohol addiction) or community reinforcement approach (e.g., increased exposure to recovery activities that are contingent on maintaining abstinence) (Miller & Hester, 2003).

Multicausal Model

Given that the cause of addiction is complex and often overlapping, single etiological models pose limitations since they neither account for the multiple factors that contribute to this phenomenon nor provide evidence explaining why some individuals become addicted when others do not. The multicausal model expands opportunities to better explain causal factors because it examines the unique individual experiences associated with addiction.

BIOPSYCHOSOCIAL MODEL   The biopsychosocial model views addiction from a biological, psychological, and sociological perspective. The biological component focuses on biological causes and requires specific medical or psychopharmacological interventions to address symptoms and behaviors. The psychological component focuses on maladaptive thoughts, emotional dysfunction, and habitual patterns that may factor into addiction. The sociological component examines the environmental aspects that contribute to addiction such as poverty, cultural beliefs and attitudes, social settings, and lack of social supports.

Factors That Increase Risk for Substance Abuse and Dependence

Numerous risk factors have been identified as contributing to initial substance use. Since initial use often occurs during adolescence, most of the commonly identified risk factors reflect events and issues relevant to that developmental stage. Some of the more

---

ACTIVITY 6.2

After reading through the various models of addiction, which model(s) do you think best explain the etiology   of substance use disorders and which one(s) do you not agree with?

common factors include poor academic performance, AOD availability, peer pressure, living in dysfunctional family environments, and undiagnosed pathology such as learning disabilities. Even though initial use is typically associated with adolescence, AOD use and abuse can occur at any age and can be triggered by various issues such as trauma, disasters, or other emergencies.

Differentiating between risk factors for initial use and substance abuse and dependence is an important consideration given that a majority of those who report experimenting or engaging in recreational use do not develop problematic usage behaviors. If that were the case, AOD data would yield a much bleaker picture. For individuals who develop substance abuse and dependence, counselors need to be aware of other potential risk factors such as self-esteem and self-worth issues, isolation, intimacy and fear of rejection issues, poor coping mechanisms, and impulsivity and compulsivity patterns.

Counselors must also be knowledgeable of co-occurring patterns between psychopathology and substance abuse/dependence. Several key psychiatric disorders that co-occur with substance use disorders (SUD) include major depressive disorders, post-traumatic stress disorder, schizophrenia, bipolar disorder, and certain personality disorders (e.g., borderline and antisocial personality disorders). Other risk factors that can lead to abuse and dependency problems include low socioeconomic status, cultural and subcultural factors/expectations, criminality, history of abuse, and a family history of substance abuse and psychopathology.

SCREENING, ASSESSMENT, AND DIAGNOSIS OF SUBSTANCE USE DISORDERS

A critical step in the treatment process is properly evaluating the degree to which substance use is problematic and the extent to which is has influenced the individual, especially for those clients who are dealing with crisis or trauma situations. Careful screening, assessment, and diagnosis not only provide an accurate clinical picture but also help the counselor conceptualize applicable theoretical models, formulate preliminary treatment goals, and implement techniques and approaches that will align with the client's presenting issue(s) and motivation for change.

Success at this stage of the treatment process is greatly influenced by the therapeutic relationship that has been established. A strong therapeutic working alliance between counselor and client can help create a trusting and safe environment enabling the client to feel more at ease when discussing substance history, especially sensitive, shameful, or embarrassing information. Creating a collaborative counselor-client relationship can reduce client resistance and ambivalence while increasing motivation to change. Counselors who instill a sense of optimism or hope and focus on the client's strengths and successes are more inclined to find clients open to exploring options. Seeing the client as more than his or her addiction can be critical to this process.

Screening

The first step in the evaluation process is to rule out AOD problems. Screening clarifies if there is sufficient evidence of problematic substance use and if this use warrants further investigation (assessment). Screening is brief in nature and often entails simple screening questions or brief measures related to substance usage. Questions are designed to determine patterns of use and often focus on frequency, quantity, and problem areas. Examples of frequency and quantity questions that might be asked during the screening process include "During the past 30 days, how many days per week did you drink alcohol or use drugs?" or "On a day when you did drink alcohol or use drugs, how many drinks did you have?"

Regarding the quantity question, the counselor must also determine the client's interpretation of a drink. The following example underscores the importance of clarification of the quantity question:

COUNSELOR (C):   Bob, during the past 30 days, how many days per week did you drink alcohol or use drugs?

BOB (B):   I've never used any drugs in my life but I do enjoy drinking alcohol. During the past 30 days, I would say I drank an average of two or three days each week and that was mainly on weekends.

C: On those days when you do drink, how many drinks do you consume?

B: I only have a couple beers.

C: By a couple do you mean two?

B: Actually, three or four.

Note that if the counselor completed the questioning at this point, the only information he or she would have is the number of drinks per episode and how many episodes occurred the past 30 days. The counselor may conclude there is no need for further evaluation. But what if the counselor probed further?

C: So on those days when you drink it is often three or four beers.

B: Yes.

C: Tell me about the number of ounces in a typical beer. (*The counselor notices a defensive shift in client's posture and his nonverbal facial expression is one of frustration. Client responds in an angry tone.*)

B: Why do you need to know this? I like a few beers, and that's no one's business! (*A period of silence follows.*) Okay, so I drink three or four '40s. It's not a big deal.

Making assumptions about the size of the drinks may lead to inaccurate information and miss a potential problem. In this example, the assumption may be the client consumes three or four 12-ounce beers per occurrence when in reality the client is consuming over three times that amount. Using the consumption question may be more telling than using more extensive questioning (Fleming, 2003). From a sample of men and women, Williams and Vinson (2001) found that asking the question "when was the last time you had more than four drinks (women) or five drinks (men)?" problem drinking or criteria for abuse or dependence was detected in nearly 9 out of 10 sampled. Self-administered screening instruments can also provide valuable information about substance patterns. Given the information presented in the example above, continued evaluation appears warranted.

Assessment

Assessment is defined as "the collection and use of information to obtain an understanding of an individual, usually for purposes of treatment planning, modification, and evaluation" (Maisto & Connors, 1990, p. 233). The purpose of assessment is to gather more detailed client information on different domains (e.g., medical, legal, education, employment history, family history, psychiatric history) to get an accurate clinical picture. Assessment provides context to the magnitude of the problem and the extent to which the problem is isolated to just the client. In addition to understanding the depth of the problem, assessment assists counselors in diagnoses, helps examine whether co-occurring disorders may exist, provides a mechanism for communication across treatment personnel, and aids in the development of treatment planning (Craig, 2004). When conducting a substance abuse assessment, counselors should also evaluate the client's current level of mental functioning, which is often done using the Mental Status Exam (MSE). The purpose of the MSE is to investigate signs and symptoms of impaired affect, behavior, cognition, and intellectual functioning related to one's mental state. The MSE can also be valuable in differentiating between substance and nonsubstance impaired mental symptoms and for ruling out co-occurring disorders (Buelow & Buelow, 1998).

One of most commonly used methods for conducting substance abuse assessment is the clinical interview, a document that contains extensive and detailed questions regarding various content domains. When counselors are conducting the clinical assessment, it is inevitable that clients indicate how they define their substance use. As mentioned earlier, some clients may be inclined to overestimate or underestimate use or information. Clients may indicate that they fit into certain categories (e.g., social drinkers or recreational users) despite information to the contrary. Therefore, counselors may need to ask additional questions or clarify client responses.

Scenario 1: Challenging a Client's Definition of Social Drinking

COUNSELOR (C): John, you mentioned earlier in our session that you drink daily and often drive when you know you shouldn't. Help me understand how you see your drinking.

JOHN (J): Well, I don't see it as a problem. I never had a DUI and had only minor issues with my wife when I've gotten home late or with my boss when I've missed time at work because I'm hung over. I guess I see myself as a social drinker because I only drink when I go out after work with my friends.

C: So you classify your drinking as social because it is the location and you have not had any significant consequences.

J: That's how I see it.

C: Tell me how you might view this definition if you got arrested for a DUI, the relationship with your wife got much worse, or you got fired from your job because of your drinking. (*This probe helps the client examine his usage knowing that any one of these scenarios is a real possibility even as a "social drinker."*)

Scenario 2: Differentiate Between Recreational Use and Substance Abuse

BILL (B):   I only smoke pot recreationally as a way to relax and have some fun.

COUNSELOR (C):   How would you classify your pot use?

B: I share a joint or two with some friends once a month. It's not a big deal.

C: You mentioned that you only use marijuana occasionally yet when you were discussing your medical and legal history you alluded to using it more regularly.

B: Just 'cause I have breathing problems and had a few run-ins with the law doesn't mean I have a problem!

C: I sense you're upset right now because we're talking about whether you're use is really recreational. My intent is not to judge or be critical of your choices around marijuana. Rather I'm concerned that your use may be causing problems in other areas of your life.

B: Sometimes I use it more as a way to have fun.

Diagnosis

A well-conducted, thorough assessment should yield sufficient data to make accurate diagnoses and establish the degree of impairment. The purpose of diagnosis is to identify the specific condition(s) or disorder(s) that are causing the impairment and provide a basis with which treatment interventions can be applied. According to Jacobson (1989), accurate diagnoses should lead to "a clearer understanding of the etiology, development, expression, and purpose of the alcoholism [and drug addiction]; the formulation of adequate and appropriate treatment plans and programs; some notion of prognosis; and full appraisal of the efficacy and outcome of the treatments" (p. 21). The main diagnostic tool used for substance use disorders is the fifth edition of the *Diagnostic and Statistical Manual of Mental Disorders* (DSM-5; American Psychiatric Association [APA], 2013). In the DSM-5 substance use and addictive disorders are organized into a number of categories. The two of primary interest here are alcohol use disorder and substance use disorder, the latter covering a variety of addictive substances, such as amphetamines, cocaine, and inhalants. For all substance-related disorders, it is imperative that counselors are competent in accurately assessing differences between abuse and dependence criteria and differentiating substance-induced disorders from other pathology.

The DSM-5 defines substance abuse "as a maladaptive pattern of substance use leading to clinically significant impairment or distress. . . occurring within a 12-month period" (APA, 2013). In order to be diagnosed with a substance use disorder, clients must demonstrate evidence that substance use is causing problems in at least two of the following areas: (1) significant problem exists at home, school, or work, (2) physical hazards occur due to repeated episodes of impaired driving or operating machinery while under the influence, (3) substance use results in recurring legal problems (e.g., public intoxication), (4) tolerance increases, (5) withdrawal occurs, (6) increasing amounts are taken over time, (7) failure to reduce usage levels, (8) spending a lot of time acquiring the substance, (9) reduced social or work activities due to recovery from effects of the substance, (10) continued use despite interpersonal and physical effects , and (11) craving, urges, or desire for the substance.

Commonly Used Screening and Assessment Instruments

Counselors using screening/assessment measures should carefully weigh the advantages and disadvantages to these assessment tools given the information gathered during the screening/assessment phase. If screening/assessment measures are deemed necessary to gain additional information into the client's substance use, the counselor must decide which measure is most efficient in maximizing clinical information while minimizing client time and frustration. Other considerations when using measures include having the client sign an informed consent (e.g., address purpose of measure, risks, benefits, how information will be used, client right to refuse, interpreting results), seeing the client as more than the results (it is only one of many pieces of the clinical picture), ensuring the measure is applicable and appropriate for the population it was designed to measure, training and competency in administering the instrument, and interpreting the results (Stauffer, Capuzzi, & Tanigoshi, 2008). Four commonly used screening/assessment instruments include the Alcohol Use Disorders Identification Test (AUDIT), Michigan Alcoholism Screening Test (MAST), Substance Abuse Subtle Screening Inventory-3 (SASSI-3), and the CAGE.

The AUDIT was developed as a collaborative project by the World Health Organization from a six-nation study to identify early detection of problematic drinking patterns and behaviors (Saunders, Aasland, Babor, de la Fuente, & Grant, 1993). The AUDIT is comprised of 10 items (drawn from a 150 items) and divided into three domains: alcohol consumption, alcohol dependence, and alcohol-related problems. Questions 1–3 address alcohol consumption patterns, questions 4–6 focus on dependency issues, and questions 7–10 address problems associated with alcohol use. The AUDIT questions use a 5 point Likert-type scale (0–4) and total scores can range from 0–40. A total score of > 8 points indicates a pattern of harmful or hazardous drinking. Of those diagnosed with harmful or hazardous drinking, 92% had scores > 8 points. Of those who were not diagnosed with problematic drinking, 94% had scores < 8 points. Based on total scores, counselors may incorporate certain interventions. The use of education and reduction approaches is suggested for those scoring 8–15. Individuals scoring 16–19 likely would benefit from brief interventions or counseling and follow-up. Individuals scoring over 20 are at high risk and should be assessed for alcohol dependence and more intensive treatment (Babor, Higgins-Biddle, Saunders, Monteiro, & World Health Organization, 2001).

The MAST is a 25-item measure that uses true-false responses (Selzer, 1971). Each question is scored using a weighted response of 0, 1, 2, or 5. The original scoring indicated clients who scored ≥ 5 points were alcohol dependent, those scoring 4 points were at risk of developing alcoholism, and individuals who scored < 3 points would not be considered alcoholic. Other scoring systems indicated individual scores of > 7 would be classified as alcohol dependent; 5–6 are borderline alcohol dependent, and < 4 points are not currently at risk for alcohol dependence (Hedlund & Vieweg, 1984). The MAST continues to be used extensively, and the scoring and interpretation are easy to understand. Variations of the MAST have been developed. These include the MAST-R, which modified the language, resulting in 22 items; the Short MAST (SMAST; Selzer, Vinokur, & Van Rooijen, 1975), which contains 13 items; and the MAST-G, a geriatric version (Blow et al., 1992).

The Substance Abuse Subtle Screening Inventory-3 (SASSI-3) was developed as an easy-to-use tool for clinical assessment and treatment to help identify those who have a high probability of developing substance use disorder (Miller, 1985). The inventory has 10 subscales. Eight subscales are comprised of 67 true-false questions on non-substance related issues. There are two subscales with 26 items addressing alcohol and other drugs using a self-report format. Scoring is done by using decision rules related to client recognition of abuse or dependence, defensiveness/denial, personality style similar to those with alcohol dependence, and characteristics associated with those misuse substances. The more decision rules that apply, the greater the probability of substance dependence (Miller, 1999). Psychometric data support the SASSI-3 as yielding reliable and valid scores for substance use disorder detection. Of the measures available, the SASSI-3 has also been an important and highly valued tool and has been used extensively by addictions counselors (Juhnke, Vacc, Curtis, Coll, & Paredes, 2003)

The CAGE (Ewing, 1984) is a simple four-question screening tool that can be incorporated into a clinical interview. It is used only with adult and adolescent clients, and it is intended to identify behaviors related to alcohol use only. Each letter in the acronym CAGE represents one of the four questions: Have you ever felt the need to **C**ut down on your drinking? Have people **A**nnoyed you by criticizing your drinking? Have you ever felt bad or **G**uilty about your drinking? Have you ever had a drink first thing in the morning to steady your nerves or to get rid of a hangover (**E**ye opener)? Each *yes* response to these questions receives a score of 1 point. Scores 0–1 do not reflect any apparent problems, and scores ≥2 are a possible indication of alcohol dependence. One concern with the CAGE is the wide variability in accurately diagnosing alcohol use disorders.

Assessing a Client's Readiness to Change

Assessing a client's readiness to change is an essential function during the assessment phase. Evaluating resistance to change allows the counselor to match treatment techniques and motivational approaches to the level of client ambivalence. Several change models have appeared within the field of psychotherapy since the 1970s (Connors, Donovan, & DiClemente, 2001) but Prochaska and DiClemente's (1992) five-stage change model focused mainly on change patterns associated with substance abuse and reflects identifiable stages individuals go through as they are attempting to change substance use behaviors.

Prochaska and DiClemente identified these five changes: (1) *precontemplation*: characterized by resistance to change or denying that a problem exists; (2) *contemplation*: evidence of ambivalence exists and the client is contemplating the effects of substance abuse as well as weighing the advantages and disadvantages of continued use; (3) *preparation*: resistance has waned and the client has made a decision to change but is uncertain how to go about this process; (4) *action*: the client is committed to making a change and has demonstrated specific goals and behaviors toward this end; and (5) *maintenance*: the client has maintained a period of abstinence and is working on maintaining recovery and addressing relapse issues and triggers.

Transitioning across stages is rarely a smooth, straightforward process. Clients may move from one stage to the next or make movement across several stages only to experience a setback. Moving back to an earlier stage is not unexpected given that change is difficult and clients will likely experience much frustration and discouragement during the process. Motivational support becomes an integral component to assist in the change process. Understanding the importance of instilling motivation as an antidote for ambivalence and resistance, Miller and Rollnick (2002) integrated their motivational interviewing (MI) approach into the stage of change model based on the belief that motivation is not intrinsically driven as part of one personality or personal trait but is rather developed through interpersonal interactions. They identified motivational interviewing as a client-centered, directive, transtheoretical approach emphasizing empathic communication to bring about client's intrinsic motivation to change that aligns with his or her values and beliefs. MI was developed as an alternative to the directive

---

VOICES FROM THE FIELD 6.1
Working with Substance Abuse

Rachel M. Hoffman

"Addiction is an issue with which I never want to work! I don't want to work with clients who don't want to change!" That quote, or something very close to it, was uttered by me at some point (or maybe more) during my graduate counselor training experience. Before being exposed to the field of addiction counseling, I mistakenly believed that addiction was a disorder from which people really had to "hit rock bottom" before they could recover. Now, many years and a lot of education later, I have a completely different view of addictions, and I honestly couldn't imagine working with any other population.

Addiction is a complex phenomenon. Many researchers now believe that addiction is a brain disease that results in neurological adaptations with prolonged substance use. After spending the past several years working in an agency that specialized in addiction, I've learned that it is important to use interventions appropriate for the clients' stage of change. Assessing clients' stage of change (i.e., precontemplation, contemplation, preparation, action, and maintenance) allows the counselor to develop interventions based on the clients' readiness to change a particular behavior or situation.

In my work with clients, I've appreciated the ability to use motivational interviewing techniques to help the client move through the stages of change. I respect my clients' abilities to make changes that align with their stated goals and desired outcomes. Adopting this strength-based approach to working with clients has helped me avoid frustration, burnout, and anger in my work with this difficult population. Although I did not initially intend to work with this population, I find my daily work with addictions immensely satisfying and rewarding and I'm thankful that my career path has led me in this direction.

and confrontational approaches that were widely used and accepted in treating addiction for decades. Four guiding principles facilitate the change process: (1) expressing empathy, (2) working with client resistance, (3) developing discrepancies (i.e., addressing cognitive dissonance), and (4) supporting client self-efficacy.

Treatment Admission and Placement

Information gathered during the assessment phase assists the crisis counselor in determining not only treatment planning but also the appropriate level of care. Clients who present with significant substance dependence issues will likely require an intensive treatment protocol compared to clients who are abusing a substance. The American Society of Addiction Medicine (ASAM; 1996) developed a comprehensive guideline for placement, continued stay, and discharge. The ASAM guidelines divide placement into increasing levels of care starting with Level V (early intervention), Level I (outpatient), Level II (intensive outpatient/partial hospitalization), Level III (residential/inpatient treatment), and Level IV (medically managed intensive inpatient treatment). Each level also has a detoxification designation that aligns with client tolerance and withdrawal potential.

Within each level are six dimensions that are used to provide rationale/justification for that level of care: (1) acute intoxication and/or withdrawal potential; (2) biomedical conditions and complications; (3) emotional, behavioral, and emotional conditions and complications; (4) readiness to change; (5) relapse, continued use, or continued problem potential; and (6) recovery/living environment. Case Study 6.1 highlights the ASAM placement process.

CASE STUDY 6.1

Using the Six ASAM Assessments

Rick is a 42-year-old, White male brought to the city hospital following a DUI accident that resulted in him breaking his nose and arm. Rick's blood alcohol level (BAL) was .36 at the time of his arrest, and this was his second DUI in the past 12 months. Rick's BAL for his first DUI was .12, and he was approved for Accelerated Rehabilitative Disposition (ARD), a pretrial intervention program for nonviolent offenders with no prior record. During the trial for the second DUI, the judge requested a substance abuse evaluation and is considering remanding Rick to treatment in lieu of incarceration. The counselor completed the evaluation using the six ASAM assessment dimensions and made the following recommendation:

Dimension 1: Intoxication/Withdrawal Rick demonstrated increased tolerance. Based on reported usage, he is at elevated risk for physiological withdrawal. Concerns exist given his pattern of continued use, his high BAL, and his inability to stop drinking on his own. Meets criteria for Level III-D (residential/inpatient detoxification).

Dimension 2: Biomedical Conditions/Complications With the exception of his current medical complications, Rick did not present any specific health problems or complications due to alcohol. He is not on any medications. Meets criteria for Level I (outpatient treatment).

Dimension 3: Emotional/Behavioral/Cognitive Rick has problems managing anger and often fighting with spouse and coworkers, especially when he is drinking. He lacks coping skills and can be quite reactive when confronted about his alcohol use. Interpersonal skills, especially communication skills are poor. He does not take responsibility for his actions and tends to blame others for his problems. He lacks self-efficacy, motivation, and cognitive awareness to make the necessary changes at this point. Meets criteria for Level III.3 (clinically managed, medium intensity residential treatment/ adult level only).

Dimension 4: Readiness to Change Rick is at the precontemplative stage of change. He does not see his use as a problem and believes he can control his drinking without any assistance. He feels others are not understanding him and is in denial about his usage and amount. He is defensive when discussing his alcohol use. Meets criteria for Level III.3.

Dimension 5: Relapse/Continued Use/Continued Problem Potential Rick's potential for relapse is very high without intensive treatment. He lacks skills and resources to maintain sobriety. He denies having any friends who do not drink or who provide positive support systems. Without intensive treatment and an established supportive network, his prognosis for maintaining sobriety is very poor. Meets criteria for Level III.3.

Dimension 6: Recovery Environment Rick has alienated his wife and family. He does not have a good relationship with his wife and does not care what she thinks about his drinking. He has refused to attend 12-step meetings and thinks they are a waste of time. His current support system cannot assist in helping him maintain recovery. His social activities revolve around drinking. Meets criteria for Level III.3.

Recommendation to the Judge Rick meets criteria for Level III for five of the six dimensions. Treatment recommendations are as follows: complete inpatient/residential treatment detoxification protocol followed by Level III.3 residential treatment (adult level only). Length of stay will depend on progress on all six dimensions and should be reevaluated after 4 weeks. Step down to Level II intensive outpatient treatment following successful discharge from Level III care.

SUBSTANCE-ABUSE TREATMENT AND CRISIS

Treating substance use disorders becomes more complex when the client is also experiencing crisis. Clients can be in crisis at any point along the substance use continuum and may require different interventions depending on their level of motivation, stage of change, the significance of the crisis event, intensity of the crisis response, coping capacity, resiliency, and existence of co-occurring disorders.

ACTIVITY 6.4

What counselor characteristics and counseling skills/ techniques do you believe are important when dealing with clients who use substances as a means to manage a crisis response?

VOICES FROM THE FIELD 6.2
Engaging the Client Who Uses Substances

Steve Zappalla

One of the most common traits of substance abuse clients is their denial system and strong habit to protect their substance of choice, often at any cost. For the counselor, it is important to relate to and understand their desire to use a substance. Using language, descriptions, and techniques they understand is helpful to gain their trust, respect, and confidence quickly. Meeting clients where they are is extremely important.

Listen carefully to the client's resistance, and use calm, reflective statements. Determine the main theme that is bothering the client and avoid attacking the drinking or using problem. It helps to hear what they're saying. Try to see things from the client's point of view, no matter how unreasonable or how irrational he or she seems. Your goal is to create a space

and help clients see that what they are doing is not working and try to get them to want to do something about it, not to win a confrontation. It could prove more beneficial to acknowledge different viewpoints.

Try to be encouraging and understanding. Clients often become hostile when they feel frustrated or confused. Clients with substance abuse tend not to have a very mature emotional coping system and will react quickly with what they know best. The most important thing to keep in mind is that there is a good chance the client does not know any other way. While small steps may seem a success early on, it is critically important to help clients feel and see the long-term benefit of this new behavior. It is most important to help clients see that what they are doing is not working and begin to help them take steps to do something about it.

Over the years, numerous treatment modalities have been implemented to address substance use disorders. Sorting out which treatments are effective has been no simple task. Decisions for treatment approaches have often been based on personal interest or counselor familiarity rather than on empirically supported evidence. Efforts to understand which treatments are effective have increased significantly over the past several decades. Traditional approaches such as confrontational approaches, aversion therapies, insight-based psychotherapy, and educational approaches have generally been ineffective (Miller, Wilbourne, & Hettema, 2003). A comprehensive review of various treatment modalities revealed that approaches such as brief interventions, motivational enhancement, GABA agonists and opiate antagonists, various behavioral treatments, community reinforcement, and social skills training were ranked the highest in terms of treatment efficacy (Miller et al., 2003).

Given that brief interventions and motivational enhancement approaches were two of the highest ranked effective approaches to address substance use disorders, integrating a crisis model that aligns with these approaches allows the counselor to effectively address both the crisis response and substance use disorder. Gilliland first developed the six-step model of crisis intervention in 1982. This intervention model includes three listening steps—(1) defining the problem, (2) ensuring client safety, and (3) providing support— and three action steps— (4) examining alternatives, (5) making plans, and (6) obtaining commitment (James, 2008). The listening steps involve building rapport through the use of empathy, genuineness, observing, attending, and active listening, and creating a nonjudgmental atmosphere. The action steps involve working collaboratively with the client in a nondirective manner to assess client needs and environmental supports.

Step 1, defining the problem, involves the counselor establishing rapport by engaging the client thorough attending behaviors and active listening skills (e.g., active listening, reflection of feeling, paraphrasing, probes, summarizing), creating warmth, expressing empathy and genuineness, and creating an atmosphere of acceptance. Establishing a trusting and safe therapeutic environment helps the client feel more at ease and comfortable with the counselor. Step 2, ensuring client safety, is of primary importance throughout the process. Establishing rapport and creating a safe environment provides the foundation from which the counselor can assess the crisis situation. James (2008) defined client safety as "minimizing the physical and psychological danger to self and others" (p. 21). The counselor may need to take a directive role when the crisis situation creates situations where the client presents a danger to self or others or when the client is so consumed by the events that he or she is unable to effectively engage in self-care behaviors. Step 3, providing support, must be directly conveyed to the client both in word and action. The counselor should not assume the client understands the attempts to establish rapport and trust. At this step the counselor reinforces the connections made during the first stage. The counselor makes it clear the intention to support is not conditional and is committed to helping the client through the crisis situation.

Step 4, examining alternatives, shifts the focus to initiating and discussing plans to help the client transition back to life precrisis. The counselor and client examine options that align with the unique factors associated with the client's presenting situation. A key counselor function is to assess client's coping mechanisms, identify specific support systems that can assist during the crisis transition, and evaluate congruence between cognitions and their appropriateness to realistic situations. James (2008) believed creating too many options serves no value; rather clients benefit most when well-conceived and appropriate choices match the reality of their situation. During step 5, making plans, counselor and client review alternatives developed in stage 4 and works collaboratively to develop a plan that involves specific external supports that can assist during the transitional process and well-defined coping strategies that the client understands and can implement. During step 6, obtaining commitments, the client takes responsibility and commits to implementing the collaborative plan that incrementally restores precrisis equilibrium.

CASE STUDY 6.2

Lenora: A Single Crisis Session

Lenora is a 23-year-old woman who was transported to the hospital during the early morning hours by her sister, Mary. Lenora presented as visibly upset, very angry, shaking, disheveled, and crying uncontrollably. Mary told the attending nurse that Lenora had been out drinking earlier that night and met a man. Mary explained that he was buying Lenora drinks and at one point must have slipped her a "roofie." Lenora did not recall what took place but when the drug wore off she found herself alone in a hotel room several blocks from the bar and unclothed. Lenora reported that she was sexually assaulted and raped several times. Mary also shared that Lenora "has been drinking a lot for the past six months" following the termination of a long-term relationship. You are a substance abuse counselor working for a local mental health agency that contracts with the hospital for evening and weekend crisis response calls. Explore how a counselor could integrate the six-step model of crisis intervention.

CASE STUDY 6.3

Crisis Intervention with a Substance Abuse Client

Francis is a 39-year-old married man who recently learned that his wife of 10 years is filing for divorce because of his marijuana and cocaine addiction. He also learned of an ongoing affair she is having with his best friend. Francis has been distraught for several days upon hearing this news and is contemplating suicide. At his mother's insistence, Francis begrudgingly decides to attend the initial appointment she made for him with a counselor who specializes in substance abuse and crisis issues at the local mental health agency. Francis has been aware that his drug use was causing some problems at home and has tried several times to stop but has been unable to maintain abstinence for more than a day. He reported that he was in counseling two years ago when his wife threatened to leave him but was not motivated to change and dropped out after a couple of sessions. He also did not feel the counselor was listening to him and was instead telling him what to do. He acknowledges his use has caused some problems and is really upset over his wife's affair with his best friend. He is coming to the realization that it is too late to save his marriage. He states to the counselor that he has no reason to live. Let's examine how the counselor may structure the first six sessions.

Session 1:

The counselor must undertake several tasks simultaneously. Understanding what was helpful and not helpful from the client's previous counseling experience can provide valuable information as to how the client views counseling, approaches that should be avoided or enhanced, a sense of motivation, and ways to conceptualize how best to establish a working alliance. Establishing a working relationship is essential given the client's fragile emotional state. While the counselor is working to establish rapport and create an environment where the client can feel supported, effort must be directed toward the client's message of desperation and suicide ideation. The counselor must assess the severity of the client's statement around self-harm. During this process, the counselor must assess the level of intent and determine both the subjective (client statements) and objective (specific concrete behaviors) messages (Rudd, 2006). Using direct language (direct questions versus reflective responses) is necessary to evaluate intent, means to carry out the intent, and a clearly developed plan. Conveying this information in an empathic manner creates a sense of care and concern that increases the likelihood the client will come back next session (Rudd, 2006). Let's look at the counselor-client dialogue related to examining intent.

COUNSELOR (C):	Francis, I appreciate your willingness to seek help and for being open with me. I want to ask you a few questions to help me better understand your emotional state.
FRANCIS (F):	Okay.
C:	Tell me about what you mean by not wanting to live anymore.
F:	My world has fallen apart. My wife has been upset about my drug use for some time, and I think it drove her to having an

affair. I'm really torn up by this and don't see any reason for living. I really screwed up.

C: You mentioned or alluded to a couple times today that you don't want to live. Before we talk about what is going on right now for you, let's discuss any previous suicidal thoughts or attempts. Have you made any suicide attempts previously?

F: No, never, but I've thought about it from time to time, especially after my wife and I got into fights about my drug use.

C: At that time did you have a plan to hurt yourself and, if you did, did you have the means to carry it out? (*Give examples of methods.*)

F: No, I didn't have a plan. It was just thoughts running around my head that I couldn't let go of. I got really scared of my thoughts because I didn't feel I had any reason to live. I felt that I'm no good to her or anyone. I felt overwhelmed and the pain was unbearable.

C: You felt so distraught and worthless because nothing seemed to matter anymore. The only solution in your mind was to commit suicide. Describe your intention to hurt yourself at that point.

F: I thought a lot in those moments about killing myself, but I didn't because I would have hurt more knowing my children and my mom would have to live with this.

C: Francis, you were aware of the painful outcomes killing yourself would have on loved ones. Help me understand more about your state of mind during that time. Did you think of or have a plan in place and if so did you have a means to carry out that plan?

F: No plan. I just wanted the pain to go away. I started to use more drugs to numb out.

C: Did you plan to use more drugs with the hope of killing yourself? (*Exploring drug use as a possible means to carry out suicide is important to assess as it can be easily overlooked with the focus on more acute means of lethality.*)

F: No. I never planned or intended to overdose or use drugs to kill myself. Only to take away the pain.

C: So you had no specific plan or means?

F: That's right. I guess I chickened out.

C: Choosing to live when you were facing incredible pain takes a lot of courage and strength. (*The counselor continues to use empathy to build support, rapport, and trust.*)

F: I guess, but I'm not feeling a lot of courage right now.

C: Describe your current thoughts about wanting to kill yourself. (*The counselor may use a 1–10 scale to help assess, with 1 being no intent, plan, or means to kill myself and 10 being a definite plan and means to kill myself.*)

F: Kind of like what we talked about before. Feeling really overwhelmed. Maybe a 3 or 4.

C: So a 3 or 4 would indicate feeling overwhelmed like what you felt before or is it more than before?

F: Pretty much the same.

C: Thank you for helping me understand. Francis, given these recent painful experiences, do you have a plan or means to kill yourself right now?

F: No. I just feel really awful. I just wish the pain would go away.

C: The pain feels really unbearable so much so that you think that the only way to reconcile it is by not existing anymore. (*If the client mentioned a plan and intent, the counselor would explore in detail the plan and means. The counselor would ask about specific sources to carry out suicide and continue to examine multiple methods until the client states that no other methods have been considered* (Rudd, 2006)].

F: Yes. (*Francis cries for several minutes.*) And I don't know what to do next cause nothing has worked out and my wife is leaving and screwing around with my best friend because of my drug use.

C: It sounds like you don't want to die, you just want your life to make sense. Right now you're uncertain what direction to go to alleviate the pain. You know that drugs have not helped the situation, but they have been the only thing that has helped to numb the pain.

F: Exactly! I know this is no way to live my life. I'm tired of feeling this way, but it's the only thing I know that works and I'm not sure I want to let go of using drugs at this point. (*The client's affect brightens a little and seems a little hopeful that he is being listened to. Something he complained his wife never did.*)

C: It sounds like the relationship with drugs is causing a lot of pain and problems but you're not ready to let it go. Maybe we can work together to examine this relationship and the costs/benefits of using versus not using.

F: It's something I've been thinking about. I've been trying to figure out why I keep doing this when it causes so many other problems, but I need it and I'm not sure I can give it up right now 'cause it hurts too much when I don't use drugs.

C: Let's not focus on all or nothing options related to use. Would you instead be open to examining your use and understanding what purpose it's serving for you?

F: I'd be open to talking about this.

C: To help initiate that conversation, I have some materials that others have found helpful as they attempted to understand similar issues you've been facing. Would you be interested in looking these over between now and our next session?

(F):   Yes, I'd be interested.

The counselor established that there was no chronic suicidality or previous attempts. Client responses indicate mild risk and the counselor should evaluate and monitor risk on an ongoing basis (Rudd, 2006). The client has difficulty when facing challenging situations, feels overwhelmed, often uses substances impulsively to manage emotional instability, and has a history of fleeting thoughts of suicide but no established intent, plan, or means. During the remainder of the session, the counselor will assess the client's drug use and motivation to change. The counselor is still concerned about the client's strained emotional state and will work to establish a plan in the event that the client's condition worsens before the next session. The counselor may consider using the Commitment to Treatment Statement (CTS), an agreement to commit to the treatment process and to living and a Crisis Response Plan that outlines specific behaviors the client will engage in if the crisis escalates (Rudd, 2006).

The counselor and client also work together to examine a realistic plan for substance use. It is evident the client is in the contemplative stage and the counselor wants to continue to enhance client understanding and awareness. The counselor also commits time in session to discussing the marital issues and explores the dynamics that have triggered this recent crisis situation. The client is feeling better at the end of the session and they agree to meet again in 4 days. At the end of this session the counselor must thoroughly document the session and provide specific content related to the suicidal ideation, established patterns, and current condition. The use of direct client quotes strengthens the record.

Session 2:

The counselor continues to build rapport and establish the therapeutic working alliance using basic reflective skills and advanced skills such as clarification and immediacy as needed while helping the client color in the details related to the presenting problem, including the implications of the affair. In this session the counselor assesses the client's emotional state and explores behaviors and activity during the past several days and evaluates whether different interventions are necessary. Using motivational enhancement approaches continue to serve as a building block for exploration of client's substance use and assist in shifting client's ambivalence toward change. Exploration and implementation of treatment options will align with the client's stage of change. Assessing cultural factors and their role in understanding a client's motivation level will be an important consideration during the second session. Also, the counselor discusses the bibliotherapy assignment and specific reactions, thoughts, insights, and how the client has integrated this information and any newly acquired knowledge into his situation. The counselor and client discuss additional options, including continued bibliotherapy options, and the possibility of listing advantages and disadvantages of current substance use for the next session. Concluding the session, the counselor and client both summarize salient issues and the counselor reminds the client of the behavioral plan in the event the crisis reemerges.

Sessions 3–6:

Evidence of a stronger therapeutic alliance is emerging with ease of rapport and signs that the client is trusting the counselor. The exploration of presenting problems continues. The counselor notices that the client has chosen options to help explore ambivalence, including a handwritten list of the advantages and disadvantages of drug use. The client reported he knew his substance use was a problem but did not understand the magnitude until he made this list. He reported that he wants to make changes and wants to end this relationship with drugs. He also realized how much he alienated his wife and, while still very hurt and upset over her affair, he understands how his drug use contributed to this process. He reported he wants to change but does not know where to begin. He also reported he has not used drugs for the past 12 hours and has been feeling a little rough, but he indicated he would like to be drug-free in the next month.

   The client's attitude has shifted from the first session and his behaviors indicate he is preparing to move toward making a change. The counselor recognizes this shift and works with the client to develop a plan to change and specific treatment options that align with the preparation. During this stage, the client's motivation aligns with specific behavioral approaches and the opportunity for the counselor to use other advanced skills such as challenging, advanced empathy, and immediacy. During these sessions, working with the client to establish a support system will be critical.

   At this point, the counselor would have a discussion about various types of supports and assess the client's willingness to explore each. It is important that the counselor be knowledgeable of different support options and help the client navigate this process. For example, integrating 12-step support groups is quite common, yet many counselors may not take the time to process the client's apprehensions or fears. Explaining what 12-step groups are about, types of meetings available, expectations, and what a typical meeting entails can do much to allay client fears. The counselor may suggest to Francis that to help ease into this process, it may be beneficial to see if a friend would be willing to accompany him the first time. Support is an essential step in enhancing motivation and creating an alternative to relying on drugs as a means of coping.

Relapse and Crisis

One of the more critical aspects of substance abuse treatment is addressing relapse. Relapse is often inevitable, especially for clients who have a chronic, long-term history of substance dependence. Despite efforts to address relapse as part of the treatment goals, relapse continues to be problematic for many clients. Estimates on rates of relapse for alcohol dependence range from 50% to 90% within 3 months post-discharge from treatment (Polivy & Herman, 2002). Numerous factors may contribute to this wide variance in relapse rates, such as treatment not addressing relapse issues, clients not following through with treatment goals, and clients dropping out of treatment. Those with substance use disorders may be at higher risk of relapsing when facing crisis situations. During treatment, counselors need to prepare for relapse by helping clients explore triggers and learn new cognitive and behavioral strategies. Techniques and approaches such as examining high risk behaviors, self-monitoring activities, developing coping skills, and different applications with progressive relaxation can be helpful in addressing relapse concerns (Lewis, Dana, & Blevins, 2002).

Counselors need to help clients differentiate when use is viewed as a "lapse" or a "relapse." A lapse is viewed as a single episode of using a substance following a period of abstinence. The individual often takes responsibility for this lapse and examines the specific experience or trigger(s) that resulted to build on recovery. A relapse is a return to sustained use of the same substance or another mood altering substance following a defined period of abstinence (Marlatt & George, 1984). Counselors need to be extra vigilant to potential warning signs, including client rationalization or denial (or using other defense mechanisms), clients not showing up for treatment, clients not attending meetings or working with their sponsor, clients demonstrating changes in attitudes, behaviors, or thoughts around substance use, and clients reconnecting with unhealthy people or environments. An established support system is an essential piece in addressing relapse during periods of crisis. Clients should be encouraged to seek support from 12-step groups, be aware of the need to commit more time to meetings, and work closely with sponsors.

Harm Reduction

For those with substance use disorders, the main goal of treatment is to establish and maintain abstinence while incorporating strategies for harm reduction. Getting to a place of abstinence is often a complex and difficult process. Counselors using various approaches may also find using harm reduction approaches is a valuable tool within the treatment protocol. Harm reduction is often misunderstood, and some believe it may encourage continued use. In reality, the ultimate goal of harm reduction is to achieve abstinence. Harm reduction is a component of treatment that is often used during the early stages of change when clients are expressing resistance. Harm reduction approaches are simply tools to help the client reduce the negative consequences associated with use, regardless of one's usage pattern. Clients in early stages of change are not going to be open to hearing about severing their relationship with their drug. Harm reduction can be helpful to find a common ground and meet clients where they are.

Marlatt (1998) identified five underlying principles of harm reduction: (1) strive for abstinence while considering alternative options to help minimize harm; (2) view prevention as a way to reduce the negative consequences or harmful outcomes associated with use but not focusing specifically on usage; (3) focus approaches on where the client is at that point in their use or addiction and develop approaches accordingly, (4) view harm

---

ACTIVITY 6.5

What are your thoughts, attitudes, and beliefs about relapse? What approach would you take if a client reported a lapse? What approach would you take if a client reported a relapse?

reduction as a community-oriented process where action is taken at the grass-roots level to advocate for change specific to the needs within that community; and (5) focus on minimizing harmful consequences and not about judging or criticizing client behavior. Using harm reduction approaches helps establish rapport because the counselor is working with client resistance and not targeting complete abstinence, but rather focusing on ways to reduce the harm associated with use. Clients are also more likely to buy into alternatives to reducing harm that can lead to lowered resistance. Harm reduction approaches may lead to an increased motivation for change while examining usage patterns. The dialogue that follows illustrates how the counselor can use harm reduction with a resistant client.

COUNSELOR (C):   Rick, you mentioned that you like to drink and you have no intention of stopping. Spending time out with your friends at the bar is an important part of your social life.

RICK(R):   Yes, so it's not really a good use of your time or mine if these sessions are going to be about you preaching to me about the ills of drinking. I don't have a problem and see nothing wrong with how I spend my time.

C: I appreciate your honesty. My intention is not to preach to you about your alcohol use. Rather, I was wondering if we might examine transportation options so that when you are out drinking you can avoid getting another DUI.

R: Well, now that I got my license back, I really don't want to risk losing it again. I need my license so I can get to work. I'm willing to discuss this, but I don't have an alcohol problem.

C: Fair enough. Let's brainstorm some possible transportation options together for the next time you go out with your friends. (*The counselor is not focusing on alcohol reduction at this point. The emphasis is on reducing the negative consequences associated with drinking and driving. By working together, the counselor not only is establishing the therapeutic alliance and working to reduce harm but also is helping the client feel comfortable and laying a foundation for later trust and change.*)

Support Groups

Support groups serve a valuable function within the treatment process. Clients with substance use disorders often find that as the condition progresses they become alienated and isolated from family, friends, and coworkers as they spend more time in relationships with their substances and those who enable the behavior. When clients enter treatment, some are often faced with the hard and painful reality that life is empty and too much damage has been done to repair some relationships. Another obvious issue is that clients often have poor social and coping skills, so engaging in social contact can be difficult. A common treatment goal is to learn to establish social and coping skills, which are critical components in developing and maintaining abstinence. Support groups play an instrumental role in facilitating and practicing these skills. The most common and best known support groups are Alcoholics Anonymous (AA) and

ACTIVITY 6.6

Clients unfamiliar with 12-step meetings are often reluctant or resistant to attend because they have misconceptions and fears about what to expect. Addictions counselors can help allay client concerns by educating them about these meetings. For this ac- tivity, attend an open meeting of the 12-step group of your choice. Note the sequence of events, format, and structure of the meeting, and other pertinent in- formation. How would you explain these meetings to a client?

Narcotics Anonymous (NA), which are both based on a philosophy that addiction is a disease and individuals are powerless over its effects. In order to recover they come to understand that they are powerless over the effects of the substance and cannot recover under their own volition and must turn their will and power over to a higher power.

The underlying mechanism of AA and NA are the 12-steps, a series of sequen- tial action steps that help individuals acknowledge their powerlessness over alcohol or other drugs and move toward accepting responsibility for their recovery. Several common misconceptions exist with respect to 12-step meetings, including the belief that AA and NA are religious-based and that these meetings serve as treatment for a person's addiction. Counselors encouraging clients to attend 12-step meetings should educate clients on the purpose and mission of 12-step meetings, as well as the variety of group options, meeting formats, and meeting structure. Encouraging support group attendance should align with the client's stage of change. Clients may also report feel- ing discouraged or frustrated after attending a meeting and should be encouraged to try out different meetings to find out which ones best match client needs. Clients may find other groups like SMART (a four-point program that emphasizes self-reliance and empowerment), Double Trouble (for those dealing with mental health and substance use disorders), Al-ANON (for families of those with substance addiction), Overeaters Anonymous, Sex and Love Addicts Anonymous, and Gamblers Anonymous as options.

Co-occurring Disorders and Crisis

Substance abuse is the most common co-occurring disorder with severe mental illness. The Center for Substance Abuse Treatment (2005) defined a co-occurring disorder as "one or more disorders relating to the use of alcohol and/or other drugs of abuse as well as one or more mental disorders. A diagnosis of co-occurring disorders occurs when at least one disorder of each type can be established independent of the other" (p. xvii).

Co-occurring disorders were first identified in the early 1980s, and treatment out- comes often had poor results as traditional approaches for treating substance abuse were integrated into existing mental health services (Drake, Mueser, Brunette, & McHugo, 2004). Clients who are diagnosed with a co-occurring disorder may find cri- sis situations will not only present challenges to maintain abstinence from substances but also may trigger symptoms associated with a mental health diagnosis. Counselors working with clients with co-occurring disorders have to be competent in understand- ing each disorder as well as how to integrate treatment so as to ensure that both are addressed simultaneously. Unfortunately, integrated treatment options within many communities may not be widely available (National Alliance of Mental Illness, n.d.).

ACTIVITY 6.7

What type of clients, characteristics of clients, or specific cultural differences would you feel most uncomfortable or fearful working with? Discuss the reason(s) for your concern.

MULTICULTURAL PERSPECTIVES, SUBSTANCE ABUSE, AND CRISIS

One of the many issues counselors must consider when working with clients is the significance of culture in shaping their identity. Pedersen (1991) emphasized the importance of cultural diversity within the counseling relationship and the recognition that all counseling is multicultural counseling. Counselors working with clients with substance use disorders who are in crisis need to understand how the culture of substance use influences each client's worldview. Historically treatment has focused on reduction or abstinence goals often with little consideration for understanding the role that culture plays in etiology or maintenance of use. Relapse considerations often emphasize exploring both intrapersonal and interpersonal factors yet may not fully explore the implications of culture on substance use behavior.

Counselors must be knowledgeable about multicultural counseling competencies. Sue, Arredondo, and McDavis (1992) outlined three characteristics—counselor awareness of own cultural values and biases, awareness of client's worldview, culturally appropriate intervention strategies—that each include three dimensions—attitudes and beliefs, knowledge, and skills. Regarding counselor awareness of values and biases, substance abuse counselors want to examine what cultural values and biases may interfere with their work with clients along with understanding any attitudes, values, or biases associated with specific substances and substance usage patterns or behaviors. For example, if a counselor has specific values or beliefs regarding clients exchanging sex for drugs, which may be a common practice within some drug-using subcultures, judgment and biases may spill over into therapy. The counselor also wants to be aware of the client's cultural worldview and the role substances play as part of that identity. For example, the counselor working with adolescent males should understand if certain substance use coincides with cultural expectations or rites of passage. Integrating cultural awareness into substance abuse treatment accounts for unique cultural perspectives that better align treatment approaches with cultural considerations.

Counselors must also consider the significance of the client's worldview and cultural influence during the assessment phase when evaluating motivation and ambivalence. Motivation for continued substance use is comprised of a complex and varied set of factors and circumstances often manifesting as client ambivalence and resistance. In some instances, ambivalence may be less about mood altering and getting high and more about maintaining a client's beliefs, customs, or rituals associated with substance use as it relates to cultural identity or tradition. Assessing cultural meaning as it relates to substance use provides a broader understanding of the cultural dynamics that may help explain ambivalence. Counselors should maintain a cultural focus when working with clients through the five stages of change. Triggers for relapse behavior should be examined from a cultural perspective.

CASE STUDY 6.4

Multicultural Consideration with Substance Abuse Clients

Van is a 26-year-old multiheritage male. Over the past 6 months, Van's use of alcohol and marijuana has increased significantly. His usage has coincided with his disclosure to his parents that he is gay, which conflicts with their beliefs and values. He feels he has let his parents down and feels depressed and isolated. Van has been attending counseling for the past month. In this session the discussion focused on understanding substance use and cultural expectations.

Counselor (C):	Van, we've been talking the last several sessions about your coming out process and how this has devastated your parents. You knew telling your parents that you're gay was going to be hard, but you didn't think it was going to be this painful. They are very angry and disappointed.
Van (V):	I didn't want to disappoint them, but I couldn't keep living this lie. They were pressuring me to settle down, get married, and have a family. They believe I'm making a choice to be gay as an act of defying them. The weight of their anger and disappointment sits heavy in my heart.
C:	I'm sensing your pain as we talk and the heavy toll it's taking on you. Tell me more about your parents' cultural beliefs about being gay.
V:	In my culture being gay has always been viewed as some sort of defect and has been looked down on. My parents don't support this lifestyle and believe it's sinful. They made it clear that they would never accept this lifestyle in any of their children. I was always fearful because I knew I was gay for a long time.
C:	You knew deep down that identifying as gay meant you'd never be accepted by your parents so you turned to alcohol and drugs as a way to numb the pain.
V:	Well, it's a lot easier to drink and get high to take away the pain than to feel it. Yet I still feel it and sometimes it only magnifies the feelings. Maybe I should just give them what they want because I see how much it is hurting them and me. It's so confusing and I don't know what to do.
C:	You're questioning yourself and thinking giving them what they want will make everything better. (*Van looks dejected, like he is feeling lost and confused. It is clear he is struggling with his truth versus family and cultural expectations.*)
V:	Yeah.

C: (*Using an advanced empathic statement to make the implicit message explicit.*) Van, as we've been talking today and over the last several sessions, might it be that you can't accept yourself as a gay man unless your parents can also accept you in that way as well, that you have struggled for a long time with the realization that being true to who you are means alienating your family? Knowing that you're disappointing them has led to alcohol and drugs as a way to numb the pain. Yet the pain never goes away.

V: (*Van sits for several minutes in silence reflecting on the counselor's response.*) I just wanted the pain to stop, but how can it as long as I keep denying who I am. I can't control how they see me, but I can control how I see myself and how I want to live my life. I'm really tired of feeling like I have to be something I'm not. I need to find other ways of dealing with this problem, and I realize using alcohol and drugs is not solving this problem.

C: You want to be true to yourself and find healthier ways of dealing with the pain. We can use our time together to explore what cultural expectations and messages you want to embrace while finding healthier ways to deal with painful emotions.

A multiculturally competent counselor examines any value conflicts and biases that arise as the client is telling his story and addresses them. The counselor also attempts to see the presenting problem from the client's worldview. Strategies for change will likely require exploration and resolution of conflicting cultural messages and healthier ways of coping as the client moves toward embracing his identity.

VOICES FROM THE FIELD 6.3
Substance Abuse and Crisis Issues

Meghan Brown
Recently, while sitting at my desk, one of the therapists on my team came to my office and noted that an 15-year-old female in her group was "acting out" and refusing to leave the women's restroom. I could hear the young girl yelling at her therapist and to all in the group to "leave me alone . . . my life is shit." The therapist returned to her group while I stood outside the restroom, nonchalantly pouring myself a cup of coffee. After a few moments the young woman came out of the restroom, joined me at the kitchenette and clearly stated, "No one can understand me . . . no one is me. I'd like to be a butterfly because butterflies are free." I immediately recognized that she was under the influence.

I asked the girl to enter into an open group room with me. I told her that she did not have to talk to me, but she was more than welcome to talk about anything as I was interested in what had her so upset. During the time she spoke, I was able to conduct an informal mental status exam, explore her judgment, assess her potential for suicide, and observe her behaviors to further assess what substance she had taken. The conversation was very interesting, but frightening due to hearing the girl repeatedly note that she has no reason to live, she wants to die, she will overdose to die, she has a history of psychiatric hospitalizations, she does not like her parents, and she enjoys her relationships with drugs. She remained disorganized in her thoughts, glared at me, was agitated, and demonstrated trouble regulating her breathing. Every few moments, it appeared as though she was gasping for air. I observed that her trouble breathing was not related to her crying, but potentially more a result of her using a system depressant. I quickly asked her therapist to give the rest of the group a break and to come and sit with her in the open group room while I contacted her parents.

The girl's parents arrived at the facility within minutes of our phone call. They were concerned and immediately defensive about their child's condition. The mother repeatedly noted that she does not think her daughter uses alcohol or other drugs, despite her being involved in chemical dependency treatment and testing positive in her most recent drug screen. I informed the parents that an ambulance had been called for their daughter due to her difficulty breathing and her high risk for suicide. The primary therapist and I worked with the client and the parents to try to keep everyone calm and provide the EMT's and police officer with the appropriate information.

The young woman repeatedly refused to cooperate with the EMT workers and the police officer. As a result of her refusal, the police officer stated to the young woman's parents that he could not take her to the hospital. Her parents, though initially resistant to the idea that their child was under the influence, noted that they were afraid to take their daughter home. They informed me that the police officer refused to "pink slip" their daughter and was going to send her home with them. It was at that point that I reminded the police officer what I had already told the EMT, that this young woman was clearly under the influence, stated she had no reason to live, and had the means to overdose if she wanted to die. It was only then that the officer agreed to mandate the girl be taken to the hospital for a 72-hour hold.

The entire length of this event was a total of 45 minutes, but looking back on it all, it seemed more like three hours. The situation required legal knowledge, sound ethics, and clinical judgment. I needed to be able to recognize the symptoms of a client under the influence of alcohol and/or other drugs, the risk factors and signs of suicide, and how to keep a client calm in a crisis situation to obtain the information needed to obtain appropriate care for the client. Had I not spent some time with the client to hear the words, "I want to die" and understand the means she had to kill herself, I would not have been able to gain the support of law enforcement to have the young woman mandated to receive care in an emergency room.

Summary

Substance use has been an integral part of the human experience and cultural identity throughout time. The reasons that people use drugs varies; however, specific biological, psychological, and sociological circumstances are key factors. Numerous models have been developed in an attempt to explain this complex phenomenon; yet there is still no consensus on the causality of addiction. Counselors having knowledge of different models and theories are better equipped to address the array of etiological considerations. In order to understand and treat clients with substance use disorders, especially those who are dealing with crisis, counselors must be competent in all aspects of assessment and diagnosis. Proper assessment and diagnosis are instrumental in establishing an effective treatment protocol. Treatment must consider both the level of motivation and the nature and severity of the crisis situation.

Understanding the stages of change within the crisis context can assist in developing both effective crisis response and quality therapeutic alliance. Implementation of crisis models allows for the client to return to a precrisis level of functioning and is the first step in treatment process, especially when crisis response involves increased use of substances or relapse. Counselors must understand that the risk of relapse is high when dealing with substance use disorders and can be magnified when clients are in crisis. Helping clients identify and address triggers is key part of treatment. Other issues that must be considered include co-occurring disorders and the involvement of support systems such as 12-step groups. Throughout the treatment process, the counselor must continually evaluate and challenge cultural values and biases that may interfere with the client's worldview.

7

Intimate Partner Violence

Amy L. McLeod, John Muldoon, and Danica G. Hays

PREVIEW

Intimate partner violence (IPV) is a major public health concern, and it is imperative that crisis counselors be able to recognize and respond to IPV survivors competently. This chapter provides an overview of the facts and figures associated with IPV, discusses the cycle of violence commonly experienced in abusive relationships, and explores various perspectives on survivors who stay in relationships with abusive partners. Common crisis issues experienced by IPV survivors, including dealing with physical injury, establishing immediate safety, and reporting IPV to the police, are also highlighted. In addition, this chapter explores special considerations regarding IPV in lesbian, gay, bisexual, and transgender (LGBT) relationships; relationships characterized by female-to-male violence; abusive relationships in racial and ethnic minority and elderly populations; and abusive dating relationships among adolescents and young adults. Guidelines for crisis counselors on conducting IPV assessment, responding to IPV disclosure, planning for safety, and addressing the emotional impact of IPV are provided. Finally, the goals, theories, and challenges associated with batterer intervention programs are discussed.

OVERVIEW OF INTIMATE PARTNER VIOLENCE

Intimate partner violence is the infliction of physical, sexual, and/or emotional harm to a person by a current or former partner or spouse with the intention of establishing power and control over the abused partner (Centers for Disease Control and Prevention, 2005a). IPV is an inclusive term that can be used to describe violence among heterosexual couples as well as LGBT couples. The term *intimate* does not imply that the couple is necessarily sexually intimate. IPV can occur in platonic dating as well as marital relationships.

CASE STUDY 7.1

Physical and emotional abuse

For days, Casey had taken extra precautions to make sure that nothing upset Jamie. Casey kept the house extra clean, had Jamie's favorite meals prepared for dinner every night, and tried to seem cheerful and upbeat. Still Casey couldn't get rid of the uneasy feeling that trouble was brewing with Jamie. It was eight o'clock, and Jamie still wasn't home from work. Casey was concerned. When Jamie walked in the door, Casey smelled whiskey.

"Where have you been? I was so worried!" Casey exclaimed.

Jamie's eyes narrowed. In a low, angry voice, Jamie growled "I'll go where I damn well please" and knocked Casey into the wall. Casey immediately apologized to Jamie, but it was too late.

"You constantly nag me," Jamie yelled and hit Casey hard across the face. Casey fell to the ground and sobbed.

Jamie walked into the kitchen and said, "I'm hungry."

Not wanting to make matters worse, Casey got up, walked into the kitchen, and started to warm up dinner. Casey's mind was racing, "I can't believe this is happening again. Jamie promised never again after the last time. Jamie promised!"

Discussion Questions

Take out a piece of paper and answer the following questions as quickly as possible:

1. Is Casey a female or male?
2. Is Jamie a female or male?
3. What do Casey and Jamie look like?
4. What is Casey's racial/ethnic background?
5. What is Jamie's racial/ethnic background?
6. Are Casey and Jamie heterosexual, homosexual, or bisexual?
7. Are they married?
8. Does either Casey or Jamie have a disability?
9. Are Casey and Jamie religious?
10. What does Jamie do for a living?
11. What does Casey do for a living?
12. Are Casey and Jamie upper, middle, or lower socioeconomic status (SES)?
13. Whom do you blame for the violence in this relationship?
14. How do your answers to these questions reflect your biases about IPV?
15. How may this influence your work with clients?

Statistics regarding IPV vary due to the range of IPV definitions and methods of data collection used by researchers. It is also important to note that most instances of

IPV are never reported, so the available facts and figures are likely an underestimation of the extent of the IPV crisis. Regardless of which statistical estimates are consulted, it is clear that IPV is a major public health concern and a common cause of injury that disproportionately affects women. The Centers for Disease Control and Prevention (2011) reported that approximately 25% of women and 14% of men experienced severe physical violence by an intimate partner. IPV affects women and men in all racial, ethnic, socioeconomic, and religious groups; and some studies suggest that individuals who are members of multiple oppressed groups (e.g., lower-SES women of color) are at increased risk of harm due to IPV because of their multiple oppressed social positions (Sokoloff & Dupont, 2005).

The tremendous emotional, social, and physical consequences of IPV for survivors are well documented. For example, IPV results in more injuries to women than do automobile accidents, muggings, and rapes combined (Keller, 1996), totaling nearly 2 million injuries and 1,300 deaths in the United States each year (Centers for Disease Control and Prevention, 2003). Annual health care and lost productivity costs of IPV against women exceed $8.3 billion. In addition, 11% of homicide victims from 1976 to 2002 were murdered by a current or former partner or spouse (Fox & Zawitz, 2004). The magnitude of the consequences of IPV calls for a greater understanding of the dynamics of IPV and the experiences of survivors of abuse. Increased understanding can assist crisis counselors in using more effective and appropriate interventions when working with IPV survivors (Hays, Green, Orr, & Flowers, 2007).

CYCLE OF VIOLENCE THEORY

The cycle of violence theory was developed by Walker (1979), a psychologist who based her theory on interviews with hundreds of women who experienced IPV. Walker noted that the violence described by women in her research typically followed a three-phase pattern: (1) the tension-building phase, (2) the explosion or acute battering incident, and (3) the honeymoon phase of kindness and contrite, loving behavior (Figure 7.1) Each phase varied in time and intensity during each cycle of violence for the same couple and between different couples.

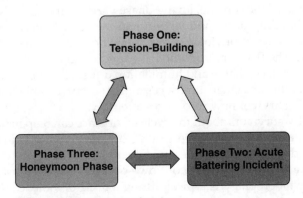

FIGURE 7.1 The Cycle of Violence

Phase 1: The Tension-Building Phase

Phase 1, the tension-building phase of the cycle of violence, is characterized by mounting pressure and strain in the relationship. The abused partner "walks on eggshells" around the abusive partner, becoming compliant, nurturing, or whatever it takes to keep the abusive partner's anger from escalating. This phase also involves minor battering incidents (Walker, 1979)—from insults and threats to actions such as throwing a dinner on to the floor and blaming the abused partner for overcooking the food. During the tension-building phase, the abused partner may cope with the minor battering incidents by denying anger about the incident, rationalizing the abuse to himself or herself (e.g., thinking that he or she did something to deserve this), or making excuses for the abuser. Following each minor battering incident, the tension and stress in the relationship build.

Phase 2: The Acute Battering Incident

Phase 2 of the cycle of violence occurs when tensions build to the point of explosion in an acute battering incident that is characterized by unpredictability, uncontrollable rage, brutality, and seriously damaging consequences (Walker, 1979). The acute battering incident is typically triggered by an external event (e.g., stress at work) or the abusive partner's internal state and can last for a number of hours to a number of days. During an acute battering incident, survivors have reported dissociative experiences, such as feeling as though they are outside their own bodies and watching themselves being thrown into a wall, choked, or raped. Following an acute battering incident, many survivors enter a state of shock and disbelief. Both partners may make attempts to rationalize the violence.

Phase 3: The Honeymoon Phase

Phase 3 in the cycle of violence is characterized by loving and repentant behavior from the abusive partner. The abuser may shower the IPV survivor with gifts, beg for forgiveness, and promise never to be violent again. During the honeymoon phase, the abusive partner may also attempt to persuade the survivor with guilt the survivor into staying in the relationship with statements such as "I would be lost without you" and "Don't make our kids grow up without me in their lives." The honeymoon phase results in the IPV survivor feeling needed and loved, leading to a renewed commitment to the relationship. The length of the contrite, loving phase varies, although it is typically shorter than the tension-building phase and longer than the acute battering incident (Walker, 1979). After repeated cycles of violence, the honeymoon phase may shorten or eventually be eliminated. The IPV survivor who has experienced numerous cycles of violence may experience increased shame and humiliation during the honeymoon phase due to the realization that the abuse will almost certainly reoccur, despite the batterer's promises, which the IPV survivor now recognizes as empty.

Educating IPV survivors about the cycle of violence can help in naming experiences as abusive. For example, some clients may not define their relationships as abusive because violence doesn't occur frequently. Other clients may see the batterer's apologies and gifts as a unique indication of how special their relationship is until learning that the honeymoon phase is typical during a cycle of violence (McLeod, Hays, & Chang, 2010).

THE DULUTH MODEL

The Duluth model was developed in 1984 by a group of intimate partner violence activists and is based on the actual experiences of female IPV survivors. The central component of the Duluth model is the Power and Control Wheel, a visual representation of the most commonly experienced abusive tactics, including economic abuse; using male privilege; using children; minimizing, denying and blaming; isolation; emotional abuse; intimidation; coercion and threats; and physical and sexual violence (Domestic Abuse Project, 2013). The Power and Control Wheel can be used to help female IPV survivors normalize and understand their experiences. It can also assist abusive partners in identifying violent behaviors as part of a batterer intervention program. Another component of the Duluth model is the Equality Wheel, which is a visual representation of the changes needed to move from an abusive relationship to a nonviolent relationship.

LEARNED HELPLESSNESS THEORY

The concept of learned helplessness originates from the research of Seligman (1975), in which dogs were locked in a cage and administered random electric shocks. The dogs quickly learned that none of their responses and attempts to escape were successful in eliminating the unwanted stimulus and therefore submitted passively to the shocks. Later the cages were opened, providing the dogs with an opportunity to escape, yet the dogs did not attempt to do so. In other words, the dogs learned to believe they were not in control of their situation, so even when they actually had the opportunity to control the outcome (i.e., avoid shocks by leaving the cage), the dogs responded with learned helplessness.

Learned helplessness theory has been used to explain why IPV survivors remain in abusive relationships. During the tension-building phase of the cycle of violence, the abused partner behaves in an accommodating manner in an attempt to avoid escalating the abusive partner's anger. Eventually, the tension builds to an explosive battering incident, and the survivor learns that his or her attempts to control the situation were unsuccessful. An IPV survivor may reach out for help from family, friends, or the police, yet the battering still continues. Again, the survivor receives the message that efforts to control the situation are ineffective. Repeated incidents of uncontrollable violence diminish the survivor's motivation to respond, leading to passivity and learned helplessness (Walker, 1979).

Alternatives To Learned Helplessness Theory

Opponents of the application of learned helplessness theory to IPV survivors argue that the theory pathologizes the survivor, places the responsibility for ending abuse on the survivor while ignoring the larger sociocultural context, and implies that leaving the relationship ensures the survivor's safety (Humphreys & Thiara, 2003; Peled, Eisikovits, Enosh, & Winstok, 2000; Werner-Wilson, Zimmerman, & Whalen, 2000). Ecological theory offers an alternative explanation for why the IPV survivor stays in a relationship with an abusive partner and states that the sociocultural system (the ideological and institutional patterns of a culture), the institutional-organizational system (the agencies, policies, programs, and professional groups), the interpersonal system (the survivor's

---

ACTIVITY 7.1

IPV in the Movies

Watch and critique a movie that depicts IPV. You may choose a movie from the following list or select a movie of your choice as long as IPV is a central issue in the film. Movies depicting IPV include *A Streetcar Named Desire* (1951), *Petulia* (1968), *The Burning Bed* (1984), *Crimes of the Heart* (1986), *Sleeping with the Enemy* (1991), *What's Love Got to Do with It* (1993), and *Enough* (2002). How does the movie you chose portray the abusive partner and the IPV survivor? Is the cycle of violence evident in the film? What stereotypes or myths are perpetuated by the film? What messages does the film send about staying in an abusive relationship? What positive or awareness-raising messages about IPV, if any, are present in the film? What was your reaction to watching the movie from a personal perspective? What was your reaction to watching the movie from a counseling perspective?

---

direct interactions with the abusive partner, children, family, and friends), and the individual system (the survivor's perceptions, meanings, and actions) all play roles in the survivor's decision (Peled et al., 2000).

The contextual model of family stress proposed by Boss (2003) in Rolling and Brosi (2010) also provides a more comprehensive view of intimate partner violence than learned helplessness theory. This model considers the interaction of the stressor event, available resources, an individual's perception of IPV, the external family context (culture, history, economy, development, and heredity), and the internal family context (family boundaries and rules, understanding of a stressor event, and family values, beliefs, and assumptions). This model allows for in-depth understanding of the survivor's experiences as well as for intervention in multiple domains.

Constructivist theorists argue that the decision to stay with an abusive partner could result from a rational decision-making process based on weighing the costs and benefits of ending the relationship. The survivor who decides to stay in the relationship, instead of being viewed as powerless and helpless, is viewed as choosing to confront violence from within the relationship. In addition, researchers have rejected the notion that the survivor who stays in the relationship is helpless and have focused on the inner resources (e.g., resilience, sense of humor, hope, spirituality) and survival strategies of the IPV survivor who chooses to stay with an abusive partner (Davis, 2002; Watlington & Murphy, 2006; Werner-Wilson et al., 2000). Crisis counselors are advised to consider how their interventions with survivors and perpetrators of IPV may be influenced by their beliefs about IPV and why victims stay in abusive relationships.

COMMON CRISIS ISSUES

The intense emotional and physical stress caused by IPV can often exceed the perceived coping resources of the abused partner. As a crisis counselor responding to an IPV crisis, the goal is to empower survivors to solve problems effectively. Crisis counselors should conduct a triage assessment in order to determine which aspects of the situation require immediate intervention. In addition, crisis counselors should work with IPV survivors in crisis to increase perceived options, mobilize resources, and identify sources of continued support after the crisis is stabilized (Greenstone & Leviton, 2002). Common crisis issues that emerge when working with IPV survivors include attending to physical injury, establishing immediate safety, and deciding whether or not to report IPV to the police.

Attending to Physical Injury

Many IPV survivors receive treatment in emergency rooms and doctors' offices for injuries inflicted by an intimate partner; yet health care providers often fail to assess the cause of the injuries they are treating (L. E. Tower, 2006; M. Tower, 2007). Just as it is imperative for health care providers to screen for IPV, it is also essential that crisis counselors ask about physical injuries and facilitate medical care when necessary. Physical injury resulting from IPV can range from scrapes and bruises to permanent disfigurement, disability, and death (Kramer, Lorenzon, & Mueller, 2004). Emergency medical treatment may be required before any further counseling intervention can occur; therefore, crisis counselors should be prepared to refer and arrange transportation to appropriate medical facilities. They should also be aware of free and low-cost medical resources, since survivors may not have health insurance. In addition, since IPV can take the form of sexual assault and rape, crisis counselors should be aware of medical facilities that specialize in rape. Advising the survivor of what to expect during use of a rape kit can help reduce anxiety and allow the survivor to make an informed decision about consenting to the procedure (Walker, 1994). Also, when a referral to a medical facility is necessary, crisis counselors should ensure continuity of care by communicating that they are not abandoning the survivor, checking to make sure that the survivor arrives at the medical facility safely, and advising the survivor that counseling is available for continued support once medical needs are addressed.

Establishing Immediate Safety

During an IPV crisis, establishing physical safety and preventing further harm to the survivor are paramount. Time is of the essence, and crisis counselors must gain thorough and accurate information quickly by conducting a detailed assessment of the situation, including violence severity, available resources, and barriers to accessing resources (McCloskey & Grigsby, 2005; Walker, 1994). The crisis counselor must also directly assess the survivor for suicide and homicide risk and be prepared to take protective measures if needed (e.g., to act on the duty to warn, to arrange for involuntary psychiatric hospitalization of the survivor or perpetrator in severe cases). In some situations, the survivor may not be able to return home safely, so the crisis counselor must arrange for emergency shelter. Provisions for children and pets at risk of harm may also be necessary (Walker, 1994). A detailed description of how to construct a safety plan is provided later in the chapter.

Reporting IPV to the Police

The decision about whether or not to report an IPV incident to the police is complex. It is clear that the majority of IPV incidents are not reported to the police (France, 2002; Fugate, Landis, Riordan, Naureckas, & Engel, 2005; Walker, 1979). A survivor may choose not to contact the police due to the belief that the abuse was not serious enough to require police intervention, that the police will not be helpful, and that if the police are called, the relationship with the abusive partner will need to end (Fugate et al., 2005). In addition, survivors may fear the consequences of contacting the police, such as the loss of housing or the involvement of child protective services (Fugate et al., 2005; Liang, Goodman, Tummala-Narra, & Weintraub, 2005). Children who are exposed to intimate partner violence experience a wide range of negative outcomes, including post-traumatic stress disorder, decreased self-esteem, academic difficulties, and higher rates of aggressive behavior (Goddard & Bedi, 2008). In fact, exposure to IPV is a reportable form of child abuse. Mandated reporting of child abuse can result in the IPV survivor feeling victimized by the counseling agency. In order to minimize the survivor's loss of power, counselors should pay special attention to the informed consent process regarding limits of confidentiality and encourage the IPV survivor to report child abuse herself (Lewis, 2003).

For members of minority groups (e.g., gay, lesbian, and bisexual individuals; racial and ethnic minorities; immigrants), the decision to call the police may be further complicated by other factors discussed in greater detail later in this chapter. Survivors may also fear that calling the police will increase the risk of further harm from their abusers (Humphreys & Thiara, 2003; Lindhorst, Nurius, & Macy, 2005; Walker, 1979). Unless suicidality, homicidality, or child abuse is disclosed, crisis counselors are not required to report IPV incidents and should support the choice the survivor makes regarding police notification (Chang et al., 2005; France, 2002). The crisis counselor should discuss the pros and cons of police intervention with the survivor and then respect the survivor's autonomy as much as possible. Understanding the laws regarding domestic violence is also helpful for counselors so they can assist their clients in what is realistic based on the laws that govern law enforcement officers' actions. State laws differ which may impact arrest policies and charges. Police officers do not make laws; they enforce the laws that are made through legislation.

ACTIVITY 7.2
Self-Awareness Assessment: What Are Your Values and Beliefs About IPV?

Read the following statements and honestly evaluate whether you agree or disagree with each one:

1. IPV is a personal matter. People outside the relationship should not interfere.
2. Women who stay in abusive relationships are partially at fault for the treatment they receive because someone can only treat you as bad as you let them.
3. You cannot be raped by your spouse or partner.
4. It is okay to get a divorce if you have been emotionally, physically, or sexually abused by your partner.
5. It is justifiable to resort to physical violence if you find out your significant other has been unfaithful to you.
6. It is okay to be physically violent in self-defense.
7. It is never okay to hit a woman.

What has shaped your responses to these questions (e.g., messages from your family of origin, religious/spiritual teachings, the media)? In addition to the statements listed above, what other messages have you received about IPV? How may your beliefs and values affect your work with clients?

IPV IN SPECIAL POPULATIONS

Culture is important to consider in understanding and treating IPV. Culture guides how clients define, view, experience, and respond to IPV. Crisis counselors responding to IPV should attend to cultural dimensions such as gender, race, ethnicity, socioeconomic status, level of acculturation, language, religiosity, sexual orientation, ability status, and age. With the increased acknowledgment that IPV is a global problem, the social and cultural contexts of IPV are gaining much needed attention. Unfortunately, the impact of culture on the IPV experience, including the reporting of IPV and help-seeking behaviors, has been largely ignored in the counseling literature. The sections that follow highlight some of the social and cultural considerations relevant to the conceptualization, prevalence, and presentation of IPV, including (1) racial and ethnic minority concerns and the intersection of gender, social class, immigration status, and religiosity; (2) female-to-male violence; (3) LGBT concerns; (4) disability status; (5) elder abuse; and (6) dating violence among adolescent and young adult populations.

Race and Ethnicity

Race and ethnicity are important considerations in understanding and intervening in IPV. Table 7.1 presents lifetime victimization rates for men and women by race and ethnicity in terms of the prevalence of rape, physical assault, or stalking. While the survey data described in this table provide important information, they do not distinguish rates for IPV specifically or highlight complexities in within-group variation of violence victimization.

ACTIVITY 7.3

Identifying Abusive Acts Against Women

Review this list of intentional acts. Circle the acts you would consider abusive toward females, adding more acts to the list as appropriate.

Scratching	Pulling hair	Disrupting sleep
Using physical restraint	Biting	Slapping
Throwing objects	Burning with cigarette	Humiliating in front of others
Pushing	Grabbing	Forcing sex
Calling names	Withholding sex	Committing adultery
Threatening to leave	Threatening to kill self	Threatening to kill others
Poisoning	Kicking	Choking
Destroying property	Using jealousy	Isolating from others
Killing partner	Controlling a schedule	Punishing for no sex
Deciding how a partner dresses	Disrupting meals	Wounding with a knife

Review the list. Would your choices be different if you were considering IPV among racial and ethnic minorities? Toward a male? Toward someone from a more religious background? Toward someone with a disability? Toward someone identifying as LGBT?

Discuss how the behaviors you consider abusive may depend on the cultural makeup of the client.

TABLE 7.1 Lifetime IPV Victimization Rates by Race/Ethnicity

		Hispanic	Non-Hispanic				
			Black	White	Asian/ Pacific Islander	Native American/ Alaska Native	Multiracial
Physical violence	% (F/M)	35.2/26.5	40.9/36.8	31.7/28.1	*/8.4	45.9/45.3	50.4/38.8
	N (F/M)	5.32m/4.28m	5.96m/4.60m	25.75m/21.52m	*/428,000	399,000/ 365,000	683,000/ 513,000
Rape	% (F/M)	14.6/ *	22.0/*	18.8/1.7	*/*	26.9/ *	33.5/ *
	N (F/M)	2.2 m/*	3.19 m/*	15.23 m/ 1.29 m	*/*	234,000/ *	452,000/*
Other sexual violence	% (F/M)	36.1/26.2	41.0/22.6	47.6/21.5	29.5/15.7	49.0/20.1	58.0/31.6
	N (F/M)	5.44 m/4.26 m	5.97 m/ 2.82 m	38.6 m/ 16.51 m	1.67 m/ 802,000	424,000/ 162,000	786,000/ 413,000
Stalking	% (F/M)	15.2/ 5.1	19.6/ 6.0	16.0/ 5.1	*/*	22.7/*	30.6/*
	N (F/M)	2.30 m/ 829,000	2.85 m/ 750,000	12.99m/ 3.92m	*/*	197,000/*	414,000/*

Note: N = estimated number of IPV victims in millions (rounded to the nearest ten thousand, unless otherwise indicated);

* = not reported; F/M = female/male statistics; race and ethnicity were self-identified in the survey.

Source: Centers for Disease Control and Prevention (2011); *National Intimate Partner and Sexual Violence Survey.* Retrieved from http://www.cdc.gov/ ViolencePrevention/pdf/NISVS_Report2010-a.pdf

Other studies provide somewhat mixed findings regarding IPV prevalence by racial/ethnic group. In one study, African American women reported IPV at a rate 35% higher than that of White women and about 2.5 times that of women of other races (Rennison, 2002). Other findings show that White and African American women report more IPV than do Hispanic women (McFarlane, Groff, O'Brien, & Watson, 2005). However, the prevalence rates of IPV victimization among African Americans and Hispanics were similar in one study (14% and 10%, respectively), while African Americans were approximately twice as likely to report IPV perpetration (Lipsky, Caetano, Field, & Bazargan, 2005). Finally, Asian and Pacific Islander women have reported lower rates of physical assault and rape (12.8% and 3.8%, respectively), although other studies show lifetime rates for physical and/or sexual abuse as high as 41–60%, depending on the amount of time subgroups have resided in the United States (Asian and Pacific Islander Institute on Domestic Violence, 2008). The prevalence of IPV, as indicated by these data, can differ depending on the study; hence, reported data may not accurately indicate actual prevalence. This may occur for several reasons. First, some of these rates may be underreported due to cultural values or social factors, as will be discussed shortly. Second, there are flaws in reporting as individuals get "lumped" into larger racial and ethnic groups, ignoring great variation within each racial or ethnic group. Third, information is self-report data obtained from samples of convenience, samples that vary significantly depending on the setting in which they are obtained. Fourth, many studies gather IPV data from health departments and clinics that serve lower socioeconomic victims of IPV; whereas higher socioeconomic groups may be financially able obtain counseling services through private practices and who may be underreported in many studies.

IPV reporting trends may be associated with community services sought by different racial/ethnic minority groups. For example, non-Hispanic Whites and African Americans are more likely than other racial groups to use housing assistance and emergency department services. African Americans were more likely to use police assistance compared with Hispanic women in some studies (Kaukinen, 2004; Lipsky, Caetano, Field, & Larkin, 2006). However, African American and Hispanic women were more likely to use police than White women in another study (Pearlman, Zierler, Gjelsvik, & Verhoek-Oftedahl, 2003). Further, there seems to be an underuse of IPV mental health services by African Americans but a comparable use of shelters and medical personnel (Coley & Beckett, 1988). With the exception of seeking police assistance, the underuse of community resources may be highest by Hispanics (McFarlane et al., 1997; West, Kanter, & Jasinski, 1998).

Several factors should be considered as we examine cultural variations in IPV. Differences in reporting trends and help-seeking behaviors among racial/ethnic groups may occur for several reasons. First, IPV may be defined differently across groups and thus be tolerated differentially. For many cultures, the concept of IPV is unknown, partly due to a lack of terminology. For example, there is no term for *domestic violence* in many Asian languages (Lemberg, 2002); further, *domestic violence* was known in Japan as children's violence toward their parents (Kozu, 1999). Another example is that there are no terms synonymous with *batterer* or *rape* in Russian (Horne, 1999). In Chile, IPV is called *private violence* (McWhirter, 1999). Even with increased attention to IPV, having to consider IPV a crime makes it difficult for many racial/ethnic minority women to report the abuse, often leading them to report only severe cases of abuse.

Second, cultural issues may influence the timing, presentation, and sequencing of reporting. These might include cultural solidarity, family structure, gender role socialization, socioeconomic status, and religiosity, to name a few. Cultural factors such as social isolation, language barriers, economic barriers, dedication to family, shame, and a cultural stigma of divorce also influence IPV reporting. Some immigrants and refugees may also experience fear of deportation or may be familiar only with their home country's cultural mores surrounding IPV (see Table 7.2 for examples). In addition, they may be afraid of police or other legal authorities given their previous experiences with police, military, and government.

Finally, IPV-related resources may be unavailable in certain lower SES communities of color, affecting reporting and help-seeking trends (Lee, Thompson, & Mechanic, 2002). Various forms of oppression such as racism, heterosexism, classism, and ableism may intersect to further prohibit a sense of safety to report. Alternatively, the degree of cultural solidarity may perpetuate IPV. Strong cultural ties, particularly in smaller communities, may isolate women from outside resources, promote greater acceptance of gender inequities, and result in a stronger tradition of family secrecy. For example, cultural norms, particularly those in non-Western cultures, may restrict survivors from seeking legal or medical attention for IPV.

Regardless of the differences in IPV prevalence rates by race and ethnicity, there seem to be similar reasons for remaining in violent relationships. However, there are cultural subtleties in how IPV is recognized and addressed that affect reporting trends across racial and ethnic groups. The interrelated factors include patriarchal family structure, socioeconomic status, immigrant status, and religiosity.

TABLE 7.2 Examples of IPV from Around the World

Jordan: In a review of 89 criminal records for homicides in 1995, 38 were homicides involving women, with 23 reported as "honor crimes" (i.e., violence against a female by a male relative for alleged sexual misconduct that "violated the honor of the family"). This may be supported by Article 340 of the Jordanian Penal Code, which states:

1. He who catches his wife, or one of his (female) unlawfuls, committing adultery with another, and he kills, wounds, or injures them, is exempt from penalty.
2. He who catches his wife, or one of his (female) ascendants or descendants or sisters, with another in an unlawful bed, and he kills, wounds, or injures one or both of them, benefits from a reduction of penalty.

Russia: Some common Russian proverbs that seem to support IPV include these: "If he beats you, it means he loves you" and "Beat the wife for better cabbage soup." In addition, a common joke stated by males is "If I could think of a reason, I would kill you" (Horne, 1999).

Japan: It is commonly understood that internal family life is free from legal intervention in Japan. Further, one Japanese proverb roughly translates to illustrate the tradition of family secrecy and honor that perpetuates IPV: "A nail that sticks out will get struck down" (Kozu, 1999).

Chile: Until 1989, the Civil Code of Chile called for wives to obey their husbands and for a husband to have authority over a wife's possessions and person. Unfortunately, much resistance to the dissolution of the Civil Code still remains today. Also, Chile is the only country in the Western world in which divorce is illegal (McWhirter, 1999).

PATRIARCHAL FAMILY STRUCTURE Patriarchy denotes clear gender role assignments based on patrilineal descent. Feminists view patriarchy as the most important cause of IPV because there is a power imbalance between males and females, and abuse is used as a source of control. In patrilineal societies, where male honor is measured by female chastity and fidelity, IPV could be higher, since any male member of the patriline may be violent toward any female member of the patriline. Patriarchal societies oftentimes create violent environments for women and increased tolerance of IPV.

Traditional gender roles are characteristic of patriarchal family structure, creating cultural pressure to remain in violent relationships. For example, *marianismo* in Latin cultures is the value of having females be economically dependent on males, maintain the family unit above their own personal needs, and respect males as decision makers (Villalba, 2014). Furthermore, African American women are often socialized to be strong and may avoid the impression of "victim" (Sleutel, 1998). Japanese women may view sexual acts with shame and embarrassment and thus tend to underreport sexual abuse (Inman & Alvarez, 2013).

A final example illustrates practices in Arab cultures. The concepts of family honor (*sharaf*) and shame (*ird, ayb*) promote "manliness" of males, sexual purity of females, and fidelity of a wife or mother. This in turn creates norms and practices that shape social and sexual behavior among males and females and in some instances promotes IPV without criminal prosecution (Kulwicki, 2002). In Arab cultures, violence from husbands is often legitimized and accepted by women as occupational or domestic stress, with women tolerating some forms of IPV. For example, between 14% and 69% of Palestinian women support wife beating on "certain occasions" (e.g., when the wife refuses to have sex, disobeys the husband, or challenges the husband's manhood) (Haj-Yahia, 1998); 86% of Egyptian women, who are currently or have ever been married, agreed that wife beating is appropriate under certain circumstances (e.g., when the wife burns food, neglects the children, disobeys the husband, wastes money, refuses to have sex, or talks to other men) (El-Zanaty, Hussein, Shawky, Way, & Kishor, 1996); and some Jordanian women justified wife beating in cases where the wife commits sexual infidelity, challenges the husband's manhood, or insults the husband in front of others (Haj-Yahia, 2002).

SOCIOECONOMIC STATUS The role of lower socioeconomic status has been examined in relation to IPV. While accurate data may be difficult to obtain, poor women are more likely to be victims of IPV. Poverty is inextricably linked to limited resources, substance abuse, social isolation, pregnancy, and unemployment. These variables collectively create unhealthy environments that both initiate and perpetuate IPV. Some argue that it may be income or social inequality rather than poverty that is associated with IPV. That is, the wider the gap between the "haves" and "have nots," the greater the violence victimization of those with lower SES. For example, violence has increased with the widening SES gap among women, racial/ethnic minorities, and minority and majority communities in general (Hines & Malley-Morrison, 2005).

IMMIGRANT STATUS IPV is common among immigrants and refugees, as migration from one country to another often creates isolation that facilitates IPV. On a global level, 17–38% of the world's women have been physically assaulted by a partner, with as many as 60% of women in developing countries experiencing IPV (United Nations,

1995). For women not highly acculturated to the U.S. culture, there is an overall decrease in the use of social and health care services (Lipsky et al., 2006). Language barriers often prevent women in abusive relationships from seeking assistance. In addition, dissonance with gender roles may perpetuate IPV, as women often become the primary breadwinner in the family due to more restricted employment opportunities for male immigrants (Mattson & Ruiz, 2005). With many immigrant and refugee women entering the United States each year, it is imperative that crisis counselors acknowledge the prevalence and consequences of IPV in this population. It is suspected that undocumented illegal immigrant victims of IPV may be more hesitant to report IPV due to concerns with deportation.

RELIGIOSITY   Individuals may use religion to perpetuate or excuse IPV, although the prevalence of violence across religious groups is not known. Some examples of how more conservative religious beliefs and practices may perpetuate IPV include the following: male domination, superior male morality, the value of suffering, references in biblical text to "submission" to husbands, and the importance of marital reconciliation in Christianity (Foss & Warnke, 2003); references to husbands as *shujin* (meaning "master") and to the need to put aside work to care for a husband's elderly parents in Confucianism (Kozu, 1999); and Koran passages that highlight obedience and respect for the husband as a wife's duty (Haj-Yahia, 2002). Thus, religious texts have been used (and misused) to promote violence in intimate partnerships.

Religion may also serve as a protective factor against IPV and as a coping mechanism in recovering from its consequences. For example, increased religiosity may be associated with decreased IPV (Elliott, 1994) or decreased severity of violence (Bowker, 1988). In the African American community, prayer is used significantly for coping with IPV consequences (El-Khoury et al., 2004).

Female-to-Male Violence

All reviews of IPV statistics reveal that women are significantly more likely to report IPV than are men, no matter the type of abuse (e.g., rape, physical assault, stalking, verbal assault). In addition, there is no doubt that in comparing the groups, women report experiencing more severe forms of abuse than do men. Therefore, female-to-male violence, sometimes referred to as husband abuse, has received minimal attention in the counseling literature and is probably underreported. Some common methods of female-to-male violence involve burning, inflicting gunshot wounds, hitting with objects, poisoning, and threatening to withhold sex. Estimates indicate that 50–90% of males experience emotional abuse (Hines & Malley-Morrison, 2005).

Why might female-to-male violence be underreported? Gender norms may prevent males who suffer emotional, physical, or sexual abuse from reporting, as disclosure might "emasculate" them. For example, males may be less likely to report sexual abuse (typically occurring through female persuasion rather than force or threat) because of societal fears of homosexuality and rigid definitions of gender roles. There are gender differences in defining aggression and thus in reporting IPV. While women tend to report both intentional and unintentional violent acts, men are more likely to report only intentional acts of aggression or violence (Walker, 1999). For example, while females may report jealousy, pushing, or grabbing as aggressive, males may be more inclined to report only more severe forms of violence, such as throwing objects or attempting to poison, as abusive. Obviously, there are fewer resources for male victims of IPV. Most shelters are designated for women and serve only women and children. Funding and grants are often awarded to clinics and centers that assist women who are victims of IPV. Prevailing myths, discriminative training and education, and biased clinical practices based only on the feminist theory or accepted myths that men cannot be the victims of IPV may prevent many in the helping field from intervening or even asking males at intake about being victims of IPV.

LGBT Violence

The prevalence of IPV for LGBT individuals is similar to or greater than that in heterosexual couples (Messinger, 2011; National Coalition of Anti-Violence Programs, 2007; Peterman & Dixon, 2003; Potoczniak, Mourot, Crosbie-Burnett, & Potoczniak, 2003). Approximately one in three gay and lesbian individuals experience LGBT violence in intimate partnerships, although this figure may be an underestimation, since most research involves White, higher-SES samples (Griffin, 2008). Considering data on lifetime victimization of IPV, 50–90% of lesbians experience physical and/or emotional abuse, 12–30% of lesbians experience sexual abuse, and 12–33% of gay men experience sexual abuse (Hines & Malley-Morrison, 2005). Further, there may be increased violence for females in both lesbian and bisexual relationships compared with females in only lesbian relationships. Comparing rates among lesbians, gay men, and bisexual men and women, lesbians experience more physical abuse than do gay men, and bisexual women experience more abuse than do lesbians or gay men. Prevalence in the transgender community is harder to estimate, yet the problem seems to be more pervasive. While accounting for only 4% of LGBT cases, approximately 50% rape and physical assault victimization rates involve transgender individuals (National Coalition of Anti-Violence Programs, 2007). These figures should be reviewed with caution, as national figures on LGBT violence are difficult to obtain due to the disproportionate clustering of LGBT individuals in select U.S. regions.

Estimating the prevalence of LGBT violence presents difficulties similar to those encountered in estimating violence among racial/ethnic minorities and against males. Among the systems affecting LGBT disclosure of IPV are family and friends, mutual friends of the abused and abuser in the LGBT community, LGBT-affirmative shelters and crisis counselors, the legal system (i.e., attorneys, jurors, judges, laws), public policy, and societal myths based in gender norms, homophobia, and heterosexism (Potoczniak et al., 2003).

Is IPV a gendered problem, as many feminists assert? Can men be victims and women be batterers? Feminists' notion that IPV is caused by traditional gender role socialization in a patriarchal family structure often does not fit LGBT relationships. If IPV is explained as a result of patriarchy, gay and bisexual men cannot be abused, and lesbian and bisexual women cannot be abusive. Thus, feminist theory may leave those working with LGBT couples with little information about the causes of IPV. In addition, there is not a uniform definition of same-sex violence (Potoczniak et al., 2003).

Homophobia, the prejudice and discrimination toward LGBT individuals and their culture, may be another reason IPV is minimized in the LGBT community, which precludes many from seeking help from traditional IPV resources (e.g., shelters, community agencies, the legal system). These attitudes and behaviors are often based in heterosexism, the idea that heterosexuality is normative and thus superior to homosexuality. LGBT couples may internalize heterosexist ideas and thus feel responsible for protecting one another due to societal oppression and the resulting social isolation. When one partner is being abused, it is difficult to report for several reasons: (1) the abuser may threaten to "out" the abused if he or she discloses the IPV to anyone; (2) the abused may be fearful of disclosing sexual orientation in the process of disclosing the abuse; (3) the abusive partner may be the only source of support; (4) the abusive partner may share the same friends as the abused partner, and embarrassing the abuser may result in potentially losing the community in which the abused partner feels accepted for his or her sexual orientation; (5) the process of disclosure may reinforce or strengthen internalized homophobia in the abused partner; and (6) the desire to maintain the LGBT community's reputation for offering safety and advocating for equal rights (e.g., marriage, adoption) may outweigh the desire to assert there is "something wrong" in the community, such as IPV (Peterman & Dixon, 2003).

Taken together, these factors have contributed to a lack of resources for LGBT individuals. Lesbians seek help from friends, crisis counselors, relatives, police, religious advisors, and hotline/shelters in that order; heterosexual women rate shelters as the primary resource (Renzetti, 1992). Gay and bisexual men may have fewer resources than do lesbian and bisexual women. Few shelters accept gay and bisexual men due to the propensity toward aggression and homophobia of other male batterers who may be living in the shelter. Further, IPV survivors seeking services may be revictimized if their relationship is viewed as not being "real" or if they are subjected to other forms of homophobia and heterosexism. Those providing community resources are often placed in a difficult position: Since LGBT violence goes against the typical view of the causes and course of IPV, they are left to decide "who to believe" and thus who should receive assistance and who should be reprimanded. This creates many situations where victims are ignored, abusers are unintentionally allowed into similar shelters as those they abuse, and abusers are not prosecuted.

Furthermore, the lack of a uniform definition of LGBT violence leads to the lack of legal protection. For example, Vermont is the only state with an IPV statute to protect same-sex couples. Approximately 12 states preclude gays and lesbians from legal protection, with two directly stating so. Sodomy laws in approximately 12 states prevent disclosure for many gay men because raising IPV essentially forces them to admit to a criminality (Peterman & Dixon, 2003). In addition, abused lesbian women may feel it is difficult to hold violent women accountable and thus opt to keep the IPV secret (Griffin, 2008).

Disability Status

Other special populations that have received some attention are individuals with physical, cognitive, or emotional disabilities. Controlling for race, ethnicity, age, and SES, women with disabilities are physically or sexually assaulted at a rate double that of those without disability (Fiduccia & Wolfe, 1999). A disability in either the victim or the perpetrator can be a risk factor for IPV, or the disability may be a result of IPV toward the individual.

Vulnerability and powerlessness are prevalent for those in this population, as they often depend on their intimate partners to assist them with activities of daily living, such as providing medication, bathing, dressing, and running errands. Thus, partners could be considered abusive if they remove a battery from a wheelchair, withhold medication, demand a kiss or verbal expression of appreciation before a task, or engage in an unwanted sexual touch during bathing or dressing (Hassouneh-Phillips & Curry, 2002). Able-bodied women might not readily consider many of these acts abusive, as they do not experience them. Thus, women with disabilities are concerned not just with typical forms of abuse but also with those specific to disability accommodations.

Unfortunately, women with disabilities experience a higher risk of victimization than do able-bodied women. The risk of victimization increases if individuals experience multiple oppressions from racism and classism. When women with disabilities seek support, they often find there are inaccessible or insufficient shelters or other community services. Crisis counselors are strongly encouraged to ensure that agencies in which they work are prepared adequately for women with disabilities; this may include having physical items such as wheelchairs readily available and making referrals for physical health needs.

Elder Abuse

With the U.S. population living longer, IPV will increasingly affect those within the geriatric population. Elder abuse may occur within domestic partnerships as well as extended families. Available data suggest that approximately two million Americans age 65 years or older experience abuse from someone they are dependent on for care and protection (National Center on Elder Abuse, 2005). Other estimates indicate that 2–10% of the elderly experience abuse (Lachs & Pillemer, 2004). In addition to physical, sexual, and emotional abuse, types of elder abuse include neglect (e.g., malnutrition, poor personal hygiene, unsafe or unclean living conditions), abandonment (e.g., desertion of an elder at a facility or public location), financial or material exploitation (e.g., sudden changes in bank account practices, unpaid bills despite availability of resources, forgery), and self-neglect. Vulnerability and powerlessness can be common risk factors for elder abuse, similar to that experienced by individuals with disabilities.

Dating Violence Among Adolescents and Young Adults

IPV begins early for many—sometimes with their first dating experiences. During the transition from adolescence to young adulthood, approximately 30% of adolescents experience some form of victimization (Fincham, Cui, Braithwaite & Pasley, 2008; Halpern, Oslak, Young, Martin, & Kupper, 2001). Adolescents often witness and/or experience some form of domestic violence at home. They learn from these experiences that violence is a normal and "appropriate" outlet for conflict within intimate relationships, since the abuser seldom gets punished. By the time adolescents enter their first romantic relationship, ideas related to interpersonal skills, expectations, partner selection, pace of intimacy, and sexual behavior are well established. Thus, adolescents and young adults may be simultaneously witnessing IPV within the home and being abused in dating relationships, creating minimal outlets for support and making them less likely to report the victimization to others.

According to the national Youth Risk Behavior Survey, physical violence is similar across genders. Approximately 9.0% of male students and 9.3% of female students report experiencing dating violence in the form of being slapped, hit, or physically hurt by a partner (Centers for Disease Control and Prevention, 2005b). In a study of

ACTIVITY 7.4
Raising Awareness About Adolescent Dating Violence

Unfortunately, dating violence is a problem that affects many individuals at an early age. When adolescents are first beginning to explore dating relationships, many of them are unaware of what a healthy or unhealthy dating relationship looks like. Work individually or in groups to develop an awareness-raising brochure or poster that is developmentally appropriate for adolescents. Include information such as facts and figures on dating violence, how to recognize warning signs that a dating relationship may be unhealthy, and how to ask for help if experiencing dating violence. Consider how you may use the brochure or poster you developed in your future counseling practice.

2,320 high school students, a similar proportion of males and females reported having been subjected to physical aggression by their dating partners (Cascardi, Avery-Leaf, O'Leary, & Slep, 1999). By early adulthood, many similarities between the genders disappear, with males becoming more physically aggressive than females. Approximately 33% of females in grades 10–12 and 20–30% of female college students report at least one incident of physical or sexual abuse (Berry, 2000).

The consequences of dating violence are great and include higher rates of eating disorders, substance abuse, depression, anxiety, somatization, and suicidal thoughts and attempts (Ackard & Neumark-Sztainer, 2002; Amar & Gennaro, 2005; Holt & Espelage, 2005; Murray, Wester & Paladino, 2008) as well as poor academic performance (Hanson, 2002). In addition, adolescent and young adult females who experience dating violence are more likely to be revictimized and experience marital violence. Both male and female dating violence survivors are more likely to engage in delinquent or risky behaviors (Howard, Wang, & Yan, 2007).

THE CRISIS COUNSELOR'S RESPONSE TO IPV

Screening for IPV

Due to the prevalence of IPV, it is generally agreed that IPV screening should be universal. Just as crisis counselors assess for suicidal and homicidal ideation with every client, they should ask all clients directly about IPV. Most research on IPV screening focuses on assessment in doctors' offices and emergency rooms, since many IPV survivors require medical treatment for physical injury inflicted by an intimate partner but may not necessarily seek counseling to address the effects of IPV. Nevertheless, these studies provide important information for crisis counselors.

While acknowledging the need for intervention with IPV survivors, most health care providers fail to routinely screen for IPV (L. E. Tower, 2006; M. Tower, 2007). A primary barrier to universal IPV screening is the lack of knowledge of and training on how to ask about IPV, how to recognize symptoms that may indicate an individual is experiencing abuse, and how to respond if IPV is disclosed (Gerbert et al., 2000; L. E. Tower, 2006; M. Tower, 2007). Personal variables may also prevent health care professionals and crisis counselors from asking about IPV. For example, clinicians may have negative attitudes toward IPV survivors stemming from personal experiences with IPV or have prejudicial attitudes including racism, classism, ageism, and homophobia (L. E.

Tower, 2006; M. Tower, 2007). Health care workers may also avoid screening for IPV due to fear for their own safety, fear of offending their patients, or perhaps because they do not view intervention in domestic affairs to be part of their health care responsibilities (Gerbert et al., 2000; M. Tower, 2007). Institutional and professional barriers to IPV screening, such as the perception of powerlessness to help IPV survivors due to insufficient community resources and the fear of marginalization by colleagues, are also important variables to consider (L. E. Tower, 2006). However, the multitude of reasons for not asking about IPV does not outweigh the argument for IPV screening. Screening can help prevent injury and literally help save the lives of individuals who suffer from partner abuse.

The first step in screening for IPV is to create a safe environment that is conducive to disclosure. Disclosing IPV can be a very difficult and painful process for survivors due to shame, embarrassment, and fear of being judged. Survivors may also fear losing their children or being further abused by their partner as a result of IPV disclosure (Kramer et al., 2004; Lutenbacher, Cohen, & Mitzel, 2003). Crisis counselors can indicate that it is safe to talk about IPV by placing posters and other IPV awareness materials in their office (Chang et al., 2005). The crisis counselor's interpersonal style can also help to create a safe atmosphere. For example, IPV survivors report that crisis counselors who smile, demonstrate care through empowering statements, reduce the power differential by using personal self-disclosure, don't appear to be rushed, are easily accessible, and are easier to trust and to talk about IPV (Battaglia, Finley, & Liebschutz, 2003; Chang et al., 2005; Kramer et al., 2004; Lindhorst, Nurius, & Macy, 2005). The single most important thing to remember about IPV screening is that crisis counselors should never ask about abuse in the presence of the client's partner; doing so may greatly increase the risk of harm to the client (Chang et al., 2005; Keller, 1996; Kramer et al., 2004; McCloskey & Grigsby, 2005).

Once you establish a safe atmosphere and develop rapport with your client, you should ask directly about IPV, gathering as many concrete and specific details as possible. During initial screening, you can ask the potential survivor if anyone is hurting them, who is hurting them, how arguments usually begin, details of the most recent incident of violence, how long the most recent incident lasted, and what happened when the incident was over (Keller, 1996; McCloskey & Grigsby, 2005). The client's IPV history is important as well, including the first and worst incidents of violence, past attempts at intervention by others (e.g., family, friends, neighbors, police, the legal system), and the role of mental health and substance abuse issues in the IPV (McCloskey & Grigsby, 2005). Crisis counselors are also advised to complete a lethality assessment whenever IPV is disclosed in order to determine the degree of urgency necessary in responding to the crisis, which may range from developing a safety plan with the survivor to seeking immediate police intervention and hospitalization. A lethality assessment includes questions about the severity of violence, other criminal behaviors of the abuser (e.g., assaults or harassment of others, previous criminal charges), failed past interventions (e.g., multiple calls made to 911; abuser ignores court orders; family, friends, and neighbors have tried to intervene, yet violence continues), obsessive or stalking behaviors, psychological risk factors (e.g., previous homicidal or suicidal threats or attempts, substance abuse issues, external life stressors, severe depression), perceived threats to the relationship (e.g., survivor planning to leave, separation or divorce, infidelity), access to weapons, and behaviors that prevent the survivor from accessing emergency resources.

Throughout the process of IPV assessment, be mindful of the phrasing of IPV screening questions, and take care to ensure that you are not inadvertently conveying judgment or blame. Also, remember that survivors may initially deny that they are experiencing abuse. If this occurs, make sure to revisit questions about IPV in later sessions.

The following intake provides an example of how to conduct an initial IPV screening.

COUNSELOR (C): Akia, we have talked a lot about your relationship with your boyfriend. I know the two of you have been through a lot and your relationship is really strained right now. I need to ask you if he has ever hurt you in any way.

AKIA (A): (*30 seconds of silence while looking down.*) Not really.

(C): I know it can be really hard to talk about. Take your time and know that I'm not judging you in any way.

(A): Are you going to call the cops if I talk about this?

(C): As we've discussed before, there are a few situations that would require me to break confidentiality in order to protect you or someone else. I would need to take action if you disclosed suicidal ideation, homicidal ideation, or child abuse. Otherwise, what we talk about is between us. It would be your decision to report to the police.

(A): (*30 seconds of silence, crying.*) I feel so embarrassed to say it out loud. (*Crying for 30 seconds.*) Last weekend, we both had too much to drink. We started arguing about the same things we always fight about—the bills, his ex-girlfriend, chores around the house. He threw a beer bottle at me and it hit me in the head. I fell over and started crying. He started yelling, "Get up bitch!" He came over and kicked me in the stomach a few times and spat on me. Then he stormed out. He didn't come back home for two nights. When he came back, he had flowers and he cried and he told me he would never hurt me again. I still cannot believe it happened. I never thought he would hurt me.

(C): Akia, it took a lot of courage to share that experience with me. I can see how painful it is for you to talk about that night. I need to ask you a few more questions, but let's take it at a pace you feel comfortable with. How are you feeling now?

(A): I actually feel a little better just sharing it with someone else.

(C): I can see that you're relaxing a little. Akia, no one deserves to be hurt. You didn't do anything to bring this violence on yourself.

(A): I don't know what to do. I love him. I know he really does love me too. I just never imagined this could happen to me.

(C):	Let's talk about that. How comfortable do you feel going home today?
(A):	I'm not sure.
(C):	You know sometimes when someone experiences something as shocking and devastating as what you've gone through, they have thoughts about hurting themselves or hurting the person who hurt them. Have you had those thoughts?
(A):	No. I would not ever hurt myself. . . .or him. I love him. I would never want to make him feel this awful. The not wanting to go home is more about worrying it could happen again. And just feeling so embarrassed.
(C):	Okay, we can talk about lots of different options. You're in control of how to handle this situation. I also want to give you some crisis resources in case he does get violent again. First, take me back to that night. Walk me through everything that happened. I know it will be really hard, but really dissecting the details of that night can help us come up with an effective safety plan for you.

Response to IPV Disclosure

Since nearly all counselors will work with an IPV survivor at some point, they must be prepared to respond when a client reports being abused by a partner. Immediately following an IPV disclosure, it is critical for the crisis counselor to validate the survivor's experience and communicate that the survivor is not to blame for the abuse (Dienemann, Glass, & Hyman, 2005). Documentation that the client is experiencing IPV is also important. IPV survivors indicate that it is helpful for crisis counselors or health care workers to make notes about the disclosure of IPV and to take pictures of physical injuries, which could later be used in court if the survivor chooses to take legal action. Using a diagram of a person to indicate where you visually see physical injuries and where the victim reports injuries can also be part of your notes.

Providing the survivor with resources and protection is another essential component of responding to an IPV crisis. Crisis counselors should have an extensive list of IPV resources available, including options for emergency shelter, transportation, food, child care, medical needs, mental health care, and legal aid. One such resource is the National Domestic Violence Hotline, which can be accessed 24 hours a day, 365 days per year at 1-800-799-SAFE or at www.thehotline.org. Crisis counselors may also consider providing a list of IPV resources to clients whether or not IPV is disclosed. Some agencies place small cards printed with IPV crisis resources in the restroom so that survivors may anonymously take the information and hide it if necessary (Chang et al., 2005).

While crisis intervention is typically more directive than traditional counseling, crisis counselors should strive to empower IPV survivors by giving them as much control over their situations as possible (Dienemann et al., 2005). Finally, survivors indicate that it is helpful to be informed that even if they initially choose not to access IPV resources, they can return to the agency and receive assistance if they ever decide to do so.

Safety and Harm Reduction Planning

Safety planning involves working with an IPV survivor to create a strategy for establishing physical and emotional safety that incorporates available resources and existing barriers. The safety plan is tailored to the unique situation of each IPV survivor; therefore, gaining concrete and specific information about the survivor's experiences is essential. It is also important to emphasize that a safety plan in no way guarantees the safety of the IPV survivor (McCloskey & Grigsby, 2005).

Safety plans can be developed for clients who do not intend to leave the abusive partner as well as for clients who are seeking to leave the relationship. Crisis counselors should be careful not to recommend ending the relationship as the only way to establish safety. In fact, the risk of harm to an IPV survivor may increase following separation from an abusive partner. Postseparation violence involves the

---

VOICES FROM THE FIELD 7.1

Safety Planning and IPV

Victoria E. Kress

"My boyfriend hits me....I've lost part of my hearing.... I have 2 missing teeth, and I've had two concussions.... I know I need to leave him, but I'm not sure I am ready.... He says he'll take the baby from me if I leave.... He's threatened to kill me if I leave." When I was in graduate school, I never learned what to say or do when counseling a person making these remarks. The first time I worked with a woman in a violent relationship my first reaction was to tell her to leave, to run to the nearest shelter and to get safe. My client's safety was a priority, of course, but I felt a personal need to protect her as well. As counselors we do have an obligation to encourage client safety, but we also have to balance this with clients' rights to autonomy; their right to make their own decisions on their own terms and schedule. So how do we respect a client's autonomy, while also facilitating their welfare?

While it may be difficult, I suggest that counselors working with clients in violent relationships should not suggest that clients leave the relationship but should instead encourage their clients to be as safe as possible. People in abusive relationships have typically been told by multiple others to leave, and they themselves have often thought about leaving. Counselors suggesting that clients leave a relationship may indicate an inability to understand the complexity of each client's situation. Maybe more importantly, suggesting that someone leave a relationship indicates that the counselor doesn't believe that the client can make autonomous choices.

Finally, at the time a woman leaves a violent relationship, her risk of being murdered escalates dramatically. So telling a woman to leave a relationship before she is prepared to do so can be dangerous.

Instead of focusing on the client leaving the relationship, I suggest counselors develop a thorough safety plan as a first step. When I develop safety plans, I encourage my clients to do specific things:

- Keep a purse and extra set of car keys in a place that is easy to access for quick escape.
- Identify at least two places where you can go the next time you need to leave the house or go somewhere safe.
- Tell friends or neighbors about the violence and request that they call the police if they get suspicious.
- Identify the safest rooms in your house where you can go if there is fear that an argument will occur.
- Develop and store somewhere safe and accessible an escape kit that includes a copy of a protection order, extra keys, money, checks, important phone numbers, medications, social security card, bank documents, birth certificates, change of clothes, bank and house information, etc.
- Process the safety plan with children when appropriate.
- Practice escape routes and identify rooms that are safe and not close to weapons.

batterer's attempts to regain control over the abused partner and may include physical assault, rape, stalking, harassment, and even homicide (Humphreys & Thiara, 2003). Research on nonlethal postseparation violence among heterosexual married couples indicates that the prevalence of IPV is nine times greater among women who are separated from their abusive husbands than among women who are still living with their husbands; IPV is four times more prevalent among divorced women than among women who are still married (Brownridge et al., 2008). Other research indicates that an estimated 76% of women experience some form of postseparation violence (Humphreys & Thiara, 2003) and that women are at the greatest risk of being killed by an abusive partner at the point of separation or after leaving the abusive partner (Wilson & Daly, 1992).

Intimate Partner Violence Shelters: Opportunities and Challenges

IPV shelters provide a safe haven for many abused women and their children. Not only do such shelters protect survivors from additional physical harm, but also they may be a place where emotional healing can begin. Shelter residents are often able to deeply connect with one another around their shared experiences. Shelter staff may provide much needed support and encouragement to survivors. Many IPV shelters also offer counseling services and provide survivors with comprehensive resources, including legal aid and assistance finding long-term housing and employment.

While IPV shelters are invaluable resources for many survivors, life in a shelter is certainly not stress-free, and it requires adherence to programmatic rules and regulations that may infringe on a survivor's sense of autonomy. In addition, survivors may not feel ready to address the emotional impact of their abuse, yet may be required to do so as part of the shelter program (Madsen, Blitz, McCorkle, & Panzer, 2003). Adjusting to a shared living environment may also present difficulties, particularly for survivors from cultural minority groups (Few, 2005). Finally, as a result of their traumatic experiences, some IPV survivors struggle with self-regulation and engage in behaviors such as verbal or physical altercations with shelter staff and residents or with substance abuse (Madsen et al., 2003).

Working as a crisis counselor in an IPV shelter can also be stressful. For example, crisis counselors may experience secondary traumatization from exposure to survivors' experiences. Crisis counselors must be sure to practice self-care in order to avoid burning out or taking a blaming attitude toward survivors. Crisis counselors may also experience the stress of dual roles (Madsen et al., 2003). For example, a counselor may deeply empathize with a survivor during an individual or group session and then later be required to enforce shelter rules (e.g., imposing a penalty for not completing a required chore, dismissing the survivor from the shelter for substance abuse).

In order for the survivor to leave the abusive partner as safely as possible, the crisis counselor and the survivor should work together to ensure that adequate personal and community resources are in place to provide protection and safety for the survivor. For clients who are not ready or who do not plan to leave the abusive partner, the goal of safety planning is harm reduction. For example, the IPV survivor may strategize to avoid rooms with no outside doors that contain weapons (e.g., bathrooms, kitchens) when they anticipate violence (McCloskey & Grigsby, 2005). Other ideas for safety

ACTIVITY 7.5
Create an IPV Resource Manual

Work individually or in groups to compile a list of IPV resources that are available in your community. Consider the multitude of needs of someone who is leaving an abusive partner (e.g., shelter, food, transportation, clothing, child care, employment assistance, legal aid, medical care) as well as the barriers to accessing resources that a survivor may encounter (e.g., having no Internet access, having to sneak out of the house to go to counseling, having limited financial resources). Gather specific information about how to access these community resources (e.g., hours of operation, cost of services, criteria for assistance). If possible, obtain written materials or brochures from community organizations that could be provided to IPV survivors. What was your experience like when trying to gather information? Were resources hard to identify? Were the agencies that you contacted helpful? How might your experiences identifying resources be similar to or different from those of an IPV survivor in crisis?

planning include developing a code word or signal to let friends and neighbors know when they need help, creating a signal for children when they need to stay in their bedrooms or flee to a neighbor's house for safety, and hiding a bag filled with essential items (e.g., clothes, cash, documents, extra sets of keys) in case the survivor needs to leave the house hurriedly.

Safety plans may also include self-care techniques that can help relieve some of the emotional pain caused by the abuse. For example, survivors report taking a quiet walk, listening to music, and reading self-care books helped in coping with IPV (McLeod et al., 2010). The key to safety planning is creativity in mobilizing community and personal resources.

Addressing the Emotional Impact of IPV

The emotional consequences of IPV are equally as devastating as the physical consequences. High rates of depression and low self-esteem are common among IPV survivors (Mechanic, Weaver, & Resick, 2008), and IPV is a major predictor of female drug and alcohol abuse (Clark & Foy, 2000). Many IPV survivors experience symptoms of post-traumatic stress disorder (PTSD), including a reexperiencing of the trauma (e.g., intrusive recollections, nightmares, flashbacks), avoidance/numbing (e.g., restricted range of affect, anhedonia, social withdrawal, inability to recall aspects of the trauma), and increased arousal (e.g., hypervigilance, exaggerated startle response, difficult falling or staying asleep) (Riger, Raja, & Camacho, 2002; Walker, 2006). In addition to the symptoms traditionally associated with PTSD, Walker (2006) argues that IPV survivors often experience a cluster of symptoms referred to as battered woman syndrome, which includes disrupted interpersonal relationships, difficulties with body image/somatic concerns, and sexual or intimacy problems.

When working with IPV survivors, it is essential to consider their trauma history in constructing a treatment plan or making a diagnosis. Unfortunately, many survivors are misdiagnosed and prescribed inappropriate medications by mental health care providers who fail to account for the effects of IPV. Survivors may be empowered by learning that the symptoms they are experiencing are a normal response to a traumatic event (McLeod et al., 2010).

CASE STUDY 7.2

Counseling an IPV Survivor: Melinda's Journey

Melinda, a 25-year-old, middle-class, African American female, first came to counseling for depression. During the initial intake interview, Melinda reported experiencing difficulty sleeping, frequent crying spells, low self-esteem, and feelings of hopelessness. Melinda's counselor, Candace, screened for suicidal ideation, homicidal ideation, and IPV as a routine part of the initial interview. Melinda denied suicidal and homicidal ideation and said that she had never been abused by her current boyfriend. At the end of the initial session, Candace provided Melinda with a packet of materials that she distributes to all new clients, which included a pamphlet on IPV.

Over the next two sessions, Melinda and Candace developed a strong rapport. During her third session, Melinda tearfully disclosed that her live-in boyfriend sometimes pushes or hits her when he has been drinking. Candace listened empathically to Melinda and let her know that the abuse was not her fault and that she believed her. After Melinda's disclosure, Candace asked for more information about the abuse, including how arguments usually begin, details of the most recent incident of violence, and Melinda's history of experience with IPV. Melinda reported that the last time her boyfriend hit her was a week ago, when he came home drunk from a party. Melinda sustained a split lip but did not require stitches.

Candace also completed a lethality assessment and determined that Melinda's boyfriend had never threatened to kill her, did not have a criminal record, and did not have a gun in the house. Melinda stated that she had never feared for her life when her boyfriend became abusive. She indicated that she did not want to break up with her boyfriend and that she did not think the abuse was serious enough to report to the police. Candace respected Melinda's autonomy and provided her with additional educational materials about IPV and information on 24-hour IPV crisis resources that Melinda could use in case of an emergency. Since Melinda reported that her boyfriend typically drank every weekend, Candace scheduled another appointment with Melinda before the upcoming weekend in order to develop a safety plan. Melinda and Candace collaboratively developed the following safety plan in order to minimize the risk and impact of IPV:

1. Plan to be away from the house when boyfriend comes home drunk.
2. If boyfriend comes home drunk unexpectedly, stay away from the bathroom and kitchen.
3. Pack and hide an emergency bag with clothes, cash, and an extra set of keys in case of the need to flee the house quickly.
4. Program IPV crisis hotline number into cell phone.

Melinda and Candace also discussed ideas for building coping resources, including engaging in self-care activities like reading empowerment books and joining a women's support group at church.

Over the next several months, Candace and Melinda met once a week for counseling. They continued to discuss and evaluate Melinda's safety. Despite her efforts to avoid physical violence from her boyfriend, the incidents of abuse became more frequent over time. Melinda had now sustained several injuries, including a broken arm and a broken rib. A turning point occurred when Melinda learned that she was eight weeks pregnant with her first child. Melinda decided that she did not want to raise a child in an abusive home. She was ready to leave. Candace and Melinda discussed the risks associated with leaving an abusive partner and tips for ensuring a safe escape. Together, they decided that an IPV shelter was the best option, since Melinda had no trusted family or friends in the area. Candace arranged for transportation to the shelter straight from her office and waited with Melinda until help arrived.

Discussion Questions

1. Are there other considerations that will need to be implemented into the treatment of Melinda?
2. What are some short-term and long-term therapeutic considerations?
3. What are some case management issues that must be addressed?
4. What referrals need to be made for Melinda?

BATTERER INTERVENTION

IPV response has two aspects, survivor advocacy and batterer intervention; both are valid attempts to end partner abuse. One model of attending to the needs of both IPV survivors and batterers is a coordinated community response, which involves the collaboration of local organizations in developing a method of addressing IPV incidents. Response teams are formed from representatives of local businesses, churches, law enforcement agencies, and mental health care professionals. These teams meet periodically to refine and process responses to IPV crises, sponsor training sessions, and develop protocols for IPV intervention. These response teams strive to create an infrastructure that will facilitate systems-level and ultimately societal-level change (Salazar, Emshoff, Baker, & Crowley, 2007). In addition to the efforts of community organizations, many states have developed standards to ensure that batterer intervention programs (BIPs) hire qualified staff, follow a structured curriculum, and have policies and procedures for referral, admission, and dismissal of program participants.

Batterer intervention programs (BIPs) have three primary goals: (1) ensuring the safety of IPV survivors, (2) stopping future acts of partner violence, and (3) increasing offenders' accountability for their behavior. In addition, batterer intervention programs strive to help offenders increase healthy expression of emotions, improve communication and anger management skills, decrease control in relationships, recognize the dynamics of abuse and the effects of violence on children, and understand social factors that condone power and control.

ACTIVITY 7.6
Crisis Counselor Self-Care

Working with survivors of IPV can vicariously traumatize crisis counselors; therefore, self-care is essential. Start practicing self-care now. Make a list of self-care activities that you find personally renewing. Plan to incorporate at least one self-care activity into each day of the upcoming week. Keep a brief journal about your self-care experiences.

Safety

The primary goal of batterer intervention programs is to ensure the safety of the abused partner and any children who may be involved. Steps to ensuring safety include assessment of the resources that are available to IPV survivors, assessment of the severity and repetition of violent incidents, and assessment of the effects on children who were exposed to IPV. Depending on the aforementioned factors, offenders may need to reside separately from the survivors. If law enforcement has been notified and an arrest has been made, incarceration of the offender may provide temporary safety.

Cessation of Violence

The second goal of batterer intervention programs is stopping all forms of violence, including verbal, emotional, physical, and sexual abuses. One of the first steps toward this goal is acknowledgment of one's violent behavior. Such an acknowledgment means discarding denial (e.g., "I didn't do it"), minimizing (e.g., "I only hit her"), and blaming (e.g., "She should have been home on time"). It also means accepting that threats, coercion, and emotional abuses—the types of violence where there is no physical contact—qualify as IPV.

Researchers have investigated which aspects of batterer intervention programs are most helpful in stopping violence. In one study, participants reported that developing supportive relationships with other program participants and the facilitators of the batterer intervention group enabled them to successfully address their violence. In addition, participants reported that learning specific strategies for violence cessation (e.g., taking a time-out, sharing feelings rather than holding feelings inside) was helpful (Rosenberg, 2003). Research also indicates that participation in a pro-feminist, cognitive-behavioral batterer intervention group may lead to a positive change in attitudes toward women and abusive behavior (Schmidt et al., 2007). For example, batterers who participated in this program were less likely to endorse statements in support of IPV (e.g., "Smashing things is not abusive, it's just venting") and more likely to endorse statements in support of nonviolent relationships (e.g., "I cannot be provoked into being violent").

Accountability

The third goal of batterer intervention is increasing individual accountability for IPV in the form of accepting responsibility for one's behavior. Simply saying "I'm sorry," especially if that's been said on multiple occasions, is not enough. Developing alternatives to battering is an essential component of increasing accountability. One alternative strategy involves understanding and subsequently changing negative self-talk to positive self-talk. Negative self-talk involves destructive comments made when challenged with an uncomfortable or threatening situation. For example, a batterer might say, "I'm so mad that my partner doesn't have dinner ready." The idea is to change this statement to something more constructive, such as "Since dinner isn't ready yet maybe I can help." A second task in becoming accountable is to learn to recognize triggers or cues leading to violent behavior. Triggers can be words, phrases, or statements that either the individual or partner uses (e.g., profanity, degrading comments); situations that typically create arguments (e.g., payday, drinking/drug use); and physiological changes (e.g., muscle tension, headaches, increased blood pressure/pulse). The identification of triggers enables IPV offenders to be responsible for initiating behaviors that will decrease their level of anxiety, frustration, and anger and thereby prevent any further acts of IPV.

THEORIES/APPROACHES TO BATTERER TREATMENT

Counselors who work with IPV perpetrators may use a wide variety of counseling theories and approaches. Some of the theories most commonly applied to batterer intervention include power and control theory (Domestic Abuse Project, 1993), moral development theory (Kohlberg, 1984), attachment theory (Bowlby, 1980), and feminist-informed cognitive-behavioral theories.

Power and Control Theory

The predominant model that influences both survivor and offender services is the power and control theory (Domestic Abuse Project, 1993). Essentially, this theory states that IPV occurs when individuals in intimate relationships influence their partner's behavior by controlling them with violence or the use of power. Violence may include verbal taunts or threats, psychologically demeaning statements or actions, physical assaults, and sexual violence.

VIOLENCE IS A LEARNED BEHAVIOR   According to the first principle of power and control theory, violence is a learned behavior. There is no genetic predisposition for violence or existence of a violence gene; instead, people learn violence from many sources, including the media and community dysfunction but primarily from parents or guardians.

VIOLENCE IS A CHOICE   The second principle of power and control theory is that people choose to be violent. Violence occurs because people are aware of a situation, understand potential rewards and consequences, and then choose to be violent. Sometimes people choose violent behavior because they are not aware of other behavioral options. Similarly, people might be unconsciously aware of behavioral alternatives but are not able to access these behaviors in a crisis situation. To that end, one can choose to "unlearn" violence through training in recognizing pending violence and in replacing violent behaviors with positive coping strategies.

ENDING VIOLENCE IS A PROCESS   The third principle of power and control theory asserts that violence can be stopped when the generational cycle of violence is understood and paired with nonviolent alternative behaviors. People who are seeking to end their violent behavior eventually begin to comprehend that learning to be nonviolent is a process. An individual does not awake one morning and vow to be nonviolent. There are occasional setbacks that require additional learning.

One assumption is that all participants in a batterer intervention program (BIP) understand that their violence was related to power and control, especially after education about this dynamic. Counselors leading BIP groups need to be flexible in ensuring that adhering to one theory may distance some participants. If they empower all participants about the use of positive power and control, they may facilitate the identification and naming of abusive behavior and assist batterers to grasp what they have done to harm the physical and emotional well-being of their partner(s) and children. Counselors might ask BIP participants "What personal power or personal control do you possess that you can use to change your role in partner violence?" With new self-awareness, batterers can gradually change their thoughts, attitudes, and behaviors and begin to stop blaming counselors, their partner(s), or criminal justice personnel for their current circumstance and consequences (Muldoon & Gary, 2011).

Moral Development Theory

Some batterer intervention programs apply Kohlberg's (1976) theory of moral reasoning to individuals that batter. According to Kohlberg, moral development occurs over time and in stages, moving from simple to higher-order moral reasoning. Kohlberg's (1984) moral development model is organized into three levels: preconventional, conventional, and postconventional.

PRECONVENTIONAL LEVEL   The majority of children under nine years of age, some adolescents, and most juvenile and adult criminal offenders operate at the preconventional level, which is characterized by moral decision making based on being afraid of authority, avoiding punishment, and satisfying personal needs. An IPV offender at the preconventional level of development may attend IPV treatment to avoid going to jail.

CONVENTIONAL LEVEL   The majority of adolescents and adults function at the conventional level of moral development, a level at which they behave in order to win approval and meet the expectations of their immediate group or to uphold laws for their own sake. Right behavior is equated with doing one's duty and abiding by the social order (Rich & DeVitis, 1985). A batterer at the conventional level of moral development may make statements such as these: "I don't argue with my wife because she'll get upset" (abiding by the conduct of the social order) or "I admit I hit her because she was cheating; I have to accept the penalties just like anyone else" (taking responsibility for a wrong act).

POSTCONVENTIONAL LEVEL   A minority of adults reach the postconventional level of development, which is characterized by a belief in equality and mutual obligation within the democratic order and by comprehension of the relativism of personal values. In group settings, procedural rules are followed in reaching consensus. Individual principles of conscience are comprehensive and universal, and rightness is determined by conscience in accord with ethical principles (Rich & DeVitis, 1985). A statement such as "I'm speaking to groups of adolescents about how to treat a partner with respect; I encourage other men to seek help when they're mistreating their partners" would be characteristic of an IPV offender who has reached the postconventional level of moral reasoning.

Empirical evidence suggests that moral development is universal among people of diverse cultural backgrounds (Kohlberg, 1984), and moral education programs are effective in raising levels of moral reasoning (Buttell, 2001), which may result in reduced criminal activity. Batterer intervention programs using a moral education approach do not focus solely on Kohlberg's theory but may educate participants about the levels of moral development, present them with moral dilemmas, and structure discussions that allow them to challenge one another. In a batterer's group, the discussion should be organized around preconventional reasoning (e.g., "I'm here because my probation officer told me I had to come here" or "I don't want to go to jail") and as ideas and concepts from this level of moral reasoning are deliberated and discarded as ineffective, the discussion should proceed to include conventional-level ideas and concepts (e.g., "What are some ways that you can create a healthier relationship with your partner?" or "How will you ensure your children will not witness more violence, so they don't have to see you get arrested again?"). One benefit of incorporating a moral development component into BIP treatment is the empirical evidence suggesting that both African American and White batterers would benefit from moral education. Another benefit is that the moral dilemma scenarios used could be organized around culturally sensitive topics, such as racism and discrimination (Buttell, 2003).

Attachment Theory

According to attachment theory, excessive interpersonal dependency among abusive men is a consequence of insecure attachment in childhood (Dutton, 1995; Holtzworth-Monroe, Bates, Smultzer, & Sandin, 1997). In brief, attachment theory proposes that the overall quality of the infant-caretaker relationship during infancy and early childhood is both the primary determinant of dependent traits in adulthood (Ainsworth, 1969) and a model for later interpersonal relationships (Bowlby, 1980). The paradox, according to Holtzworth-Monroe et al. (1997), is that happily married men as well as violent men are dependent on their wives, but dependency is a problem only for the violent men. Relative to the development of excessive interpersonal dependency among batterers, Dutton (1995) argued that battered mothers cannot adequately attend to the demands of the attachment process while simultaneously attempting to negotiate a hostile and dangerous home environment. Consequently, children in this situation become insecurely attached and in adulthood exhibit excessive dependency on their partners (Dutton 1995; Holtzworth-Monroe et al., 1997; Murphy, Meyer, & O'Leary, 1994). In addition, people with battering issues have difficulty initiating and maintaining an emotionally supportive relationship. As a result, they simultaneously desire closeness with their partners but, given their inability to achieve emotional closeness, engage in violent and controlling behaviors to ensure physical closeness instead (Murphy et al., 1994).

Similar to incorporating moral development into batterer intervention programs, a batterer program using attachment theory does not focus entirely on attachment issues. A typical BIP session on attachment initially might include a discussion of healthy and unhealthy relationships, particularly referencing the parental relationships that members observed in their childhood. A description of the types of attachment might follow as members are asked to identify the types of attachment they observed as children. The session then might focus on members' current relationships, which may be the relationships within which they had their IPV incident, and they might be again asked to identify the type of attachment. Members might then be asked to discuss the connection between the type of attachment they observed as children and the type they experienced in the relationship within which the IPV event took place. A discussion of the unhealthy and illegal consequences of unhealthy attachment types might follow. The session may then conclude by asking members to identify what they will contract to do to begin progressing toward secure attachments with their partners.

Feminist-Informed Cognitive-Behavioral Theory

Most treatment programs for batterers employ a feminist-informed cognitive-behavioral treatment approach (Bennett & Williams, 2001). Feminist theory asserts that IPV involves a wide range of behaviors aimed at maintaining an imbalance of power in a relationship, IPV is a violation of human rights, and IPV is supported and maintained by sexism and homophobia (Schmidt et al., 2007). Many types of cognitive and behavioral therapies—for example, Ellis's (1962) rational emotive behavior therapy and Glasser's (1965) reality therapy—operate under the tenets of feminist theory used in batterer intervention.

In BIP groups, participants would receive education about healthy communication, anger/stress management, positive and negative self-talk, cues to violence, and others topics. Each of these topics would typically include worksheets where participants would reflect on the incident that led to their referral and write positive alternatives to their problematic thoughts and behaviors. In addition, most BIPs would also include sessions specifically focusing on domestic violence, such as costs and payoffs of IPV, effects of IPV on children, understanding violence and relationships and the cycle of violence (Domestic Abuse Project, 1993).

CHALLENGES IN BATTERER INTERVENTION

Counselors who work with IPV perpetrators encounter numerous challenges, including the underreporting of IPV incidents, the need to distinguish batterer intervention programs from anger management programs, limited financial resources, and completion rates. Working with the victim of IPV is only part of stopping incidents and the repeated acts of IPV. The field needs counselors who are also willing to work on ending the perpetration of IPV which may assist in ending generations of abuse.

Underreporting of IPV Incidents

One of the biggest challenges regarding batterer intervention is that most program participants are court mandated. In order for a judge or probation officer to refer an IPV

VOICES FROM THE FIELD 7.2
Working in Batterer Intervention

John Muldoon

I was the director of a batterer intervention program for almost seven years. While my body sometimes cringed at statements men would make, I also saw the trauma that some male offenders experienced as a result of growing up with inappropriate or absent male role models and the interconnection of substance use and IPV. My experiences raised my awareness about the lack of equality inherent in batterer intervention. Many of the batterers that chose to attend our program in order to avoid incarceration were either unemployed or working in blue-collar jobs. IPV offenders with higher income

levels were often able to hire an attorney to dispute the criminal charges at the time of the incident. I also saw the lack of consistency from one jurisdiction to another and even from one judge or probation officer to another in terms of willingness to understand the general mission of batterer programs and to collaborate with our program. To this end, I know there are pockets of places that are committed to seeing that something is being done to end IPV. Overall, there is much work that still needs to be done regarding educating people about IPV, which is a social crisis that is greatly unknown and misunderstood, except to those who experience it.

offender to treatment, someone must first report an IPV incident. Survivors may choose not to report IPV or not to seek community-based assistance for many reasons, including feelings of shame and embarrassment, a desire to protect the abusive partner and preserve the relationship (Dutton, Goodman, & Bennett, 1999), the belief that assistance is not needed or is not useful (Fugate, Landis, Riordan, Naureckas, & Engel, 2005; Gondolf, 2002), a lack of resources such as money, transportation, child care, and insurance (Fugate et al., 2005; Gondolf, 2002), and fear of retaliation from the abusive partner (Fugate et al., 2005). Although many of these reasons are valid, if an IPV incident is not reported, batterer intervention is nearly impossible.

IPV and Anger Management

The misconception that anger management problems and IPV are synonymous terms is another challenge to batterer intervention. Persons with an anger management problem are unable to control their temper regardless of why or at whom they become angry or even when they become angry. Persons with a battering problem are able to control their anger when it is advantageous to do so, and then they impose that anger on an intimate partner. For example, consider the person who becomes angry at his supervisor at work for not receiving a deserved promotion. If he has an anger problem, he will probably express his anger inappropriately to his supervisor at that time. If he has a battering problem, he will withhold his anger in the moment and later direct that anger at his intimate partner.

The distinction between anger management programs and batterer programs is important when marketing a batterer program. Generally, it would be better to market batterer programs to look more like anger management programs because anger management programs are more socially acceptable. Many participants are reticent to enroll in a batterer program, believing it implies that they are chronic offenders who leave bruises on their partners or beat their partners to the point of requiring medical attention. Similarly, donors might not want to give money to a batterer program, believing it could reflect negatively on the organization or business. The distinction between anger management programs and batterer intervention programs is also important because some states and jurisdictions refer offenders specifically to batterer intervention programs and others do not. If there is not a specific referral, individuals are highly likely to enroll in anger management programs that they believe can be completed in less time, cost less money, and may be covered by insurance. However, it is doubtful that traditional anger management programs cover the IPV issues that need to be addressed to prevent the reoccurrence of partner abuse.

Financial Resources

The financial aspect of batterer intervention is also a challenge. A significant number of batterer programs charge fees for services in order to sustain the program's existence. Most federal and state monies for IPV go to battered women's programs—and rightly so. However, if we do not intervene with batterers and reeducate them, IPV will likely never end. Therefore, it is left to the batterer program staff to solicit referrals from judges and probation officers. Unfortunately, potential referral sources often refuse to make appropriate referrals to batterer intervention programs due to their cost. Some judges and probation officers do not want to require someone to attend a program for a minimum of 26 weeks (or sometimes less in some states) and pay money (generally $20 to $30 per session) because of one reported incident of IPV. Ironically, many IPV offenders are bailed out of jail for about as much money as it would cost to attend a batterer intervention program.

Completion Rates

Treatment refusal, overt or passive resistance, and premature termination (i.e., dropout), are common therapeutic issues confronted by counselors in the typical batterer intervention program (Kistenmacher & Weiss, 2008). Numerous authors have reported treatment noncompliance and client attrition rates ranging between 40% and 70% (Buttell & Pike, 2003; Chang & Saunders, 2002; Eckhardt, Holtzworth-Munroe, Norlander, Sibley, & Cahill, 2008). These statistics and accompanying therapeutic challenges suggest negative therapeutic outcomes for many batterers. Complicating matters further, outcome research on treatment compliance may be defined differently by clients, counselors, and researchers (Arias, Dankwort, Douglas, Dutton, & Stein, 2002). For instance, does "compliance" mean completing a prescribed treatment program in earnest or completing it with minimal psychic energy and investment? Does it mean completing a prescribed treatment program *and* experiencing behavioral change, as in the decrease or cessation of battering?

If BIP counselors are successful in penetrating the batterer's barrier of resistance to treatment, the prognosis for treatment compliance and behavior change improves. Researchers (Rosenberg, 2003; Snyder & Anderson, 2009) reported that positive treatment outcomes and reduced incidents of violence are related to the frequency and regularity of session attendance. Moreover, Levesque, Gelles, and Velicer (2000) and Kistenmacher and Weiss (2008) concluded that those batterers who overcome their resistance and complete treatment programs in earnest report the reduction or cessation of violence and the reduction of victim-blaming, when compared to resistant batterers or those just beginning treatment. Finally, Shepard, Falk, and Elliott (2002) reported that female partners of batterers described reductions in physical abuse by men who had completed the prescribed intervention. The women also reported reductions in physical and emotional abuse when the offender had been mandated to treatment by criminal justice personnel.

Coulter and VandeWeerd (2009) concluded that recidivism rates for batterers were substantially lower for those who completed intervention programs when compared to those who stopped attendance prematurely. These authors also reported that re-arrest rates were substantially lower for batterers who completed treatment than are generally found in the literature on batterer recidivism. These findings offer optimism for counselors willing to address the batterer's resistance as a major component of treatment planning.

CASE STUDY 7.3

An Ethical Dilemma

You are a counselor who is leading groups in a batterer intervention program for men. One afternoon a woman whose partner is enrolled in the program calls to ask what the program is teaching about violence. During the course of your conversation, the woman discloses that her partner, the program's client, threatened her the night before. Consult the *ACA Code of Ethics* (American Counseling Association, 2005) to inform your discussion of the dilemma.

Discussion Questions

1. What additional questions do you ask?
2. What referrals do you offer?
3. What, if anything, do you do with this information, knowing that confronting your client might cause additional violence to the partner?

CASE STUDY 7.4

Responses to Domestic Violence Crisis Calls

It's about 2:45 on a weekday afternoon. You receive a phone call from a woman who explains that her husband is abusive to her. She also notes that he is not at home, which is why she is making the call now. She further states that she is not sure what he would do if he knew she was talking to someone about the violence. After about 10 minutes on the phone, she becomes erratic and excited, stating that her husband has come home and she cannot talk any longer. She hangs up the phone.

Discussion Questions

1. What do you do?
2. What can you do?

CASE STUDY 7.5

Intervening with an IPV Solution

It's between 5:45 and 6:00 p.m. on a Tuesday afternoon. You are the counselor for this evening's BIP group, which starts at 6:00 p.m. Participants have begun checking in and paying their fees. One of the participants has already taken a seat in the group. You are aware that he received a phone call and left the building. A few moments later you hear yelling outside and go out to see what is happening. Upon walking outside, you notice the BIP member standing in the doorway very calmly. A woman, whom the participant states is his estranged partner, is yelling and screaming and pointing an accusatory finger at him.

Discussion Questions

1. What do you do with/for the BIP participant?
2. What do you do with/for the woman?
3. What conclusions can you hypothesize from what you observed?
4. What questions will you/must you ask the BIP participant?
5. What questions will you/must you ask the woman?

Summary

IPV is a crisis all too commonly experienced. As a result, crisis counselors must be prepared to respond to the needs of IPV survivors. Understanding the cycle of violence is a critical first step for crisis counselors. The cycle of violence consists of the tension-building phase, the acute battering incident, and the honeymoon phase, which is characterized by contrite, loving behavior. It is also important for crisis counselors to examine their beliefs about why IPV survivors stay in relationships with abusive partners. In this chapter, two explanations for staying with an abusive partner were offered: learned helplessness theory and the ecological theory of IPV.

Common crisis issues for IPV survivors were highlighted, including attending to physical injury, establishing immediate safety, and deciding whether or not to report the IPV to the police. When addressing IPV crises, crisis counselors should strive to empower survivors to problem solve effectively and respect survivors' autonomy as much as possible. When addressing IPV in racial and ethnic minority and LGBT communities, crisis counselors must be aware of the compounded effects of IPV on these populations due to oppression stemming from racism, classism, and homophobia. In addition, issues specific to female-to-male violence, dating violence, and violence against a disabled partner must also be considered.

This chapter discussed barriers to IPV screening and argued that due to the prevalence of IPV, universal screening is necessary.

IPV screening includes gathering concrete and specific details about the client's IPV history and conducting a lethality assessment in order to determine the degree of urgency that is required in responding to the IPV crisis. When IPV is disclosed, the crisis counselor should validate the survivor's experience, document that IPV is occurring, and provide resources and continued support to the survivor. A specific component of IPV response is safety planning, which involves constructing a detailed strategy for reducing harm caused by the abusive partner based on the resources available to the survivor and the barriers to accessing these resources. Finally, when responding to IPV, the crisis counselor should consider the emotional consequences of abuse and be careful not to pathologize a normal response to the trauma of IPV.

The chapter concludes with a discussion of the various aspects of batterer intervention. The goals of batterer intervention programs include ensuring the safety of IPV survivors, stopping future violence, and increasing the batterers' accountability for their behavior. Batterer intervention programs are based on power and control theory, moral development theory, attachment theory, and feminist-informed cognitive-behavioral theories. Common challenges encountered in batterer intervention include the underreporting of IPV, the confusion surrounding the differences in anger management problems and battering behavior, and limited financial resources.

8

Sexual Assault

Robin Lee and Jennifer Jordan

PREVIEW

Sexual assault is an underreported crime, with survivors facing a number of potential physical, psychological, cognitive, behavioral, and emotional consequences. Crisis counselors who work with survivors of sexual assault need to be aware of the multitude of challenges these individuals face, best practices for treatment, and support services available in the local community. In this chapter, sexual assault will be defined, signs and symptoms described, treatment interventions discussed, and guidelines for working with law enforcement provided. In addition, the final section of this chapter addresses sexual offenders, their patterns of behavior, and common treatment options.

SEXUAL ASSAULT

According to the Rape, Abuse and Incest National Network (RAINN, 2012a), a sexual assault occurs every 2 minutes in the United States. Within 1 year, slightly more than 213,000 people are victims of rape, attempted rape, or sexual assault. According to the Federal Bureau of Investigation (FBI), in 2009 approximately 81, 280 forcible rapes were reported (U.S. Department of Justice, 2012b), which constitutes 6% of all violent crimes reported (i.e., murder and nonnegligent manslaughter, forcible rape, robbery, and aggravated assault). Although instances of rape and sexual assault have declined by more than 60% since 1993, rape and sexual assault are still the most underreported crimes, with more than half of all instances not reported.

The women's movement was responsible for first drawing attention to sexual assault in the late 1960s and early 1970s (Largen, 1985). Women began to gather in

ACTIVITY 8.1

Internet Activity

Visit the Rape, Abuse and Incest National Network (RAINN) website at www.rainn.org. Explore the web- site to learn more about how the organization benefits victims of sexual assault.

communities to discuss problems they were facing, including experiences of sexual assault. Because these women had remained mostly silent until this point, it became evident that this was a problem that needed attention. In the 1970s, the National Organization for Women (NOW) drew attention to the issue of sexual assault by developing rape task forces, which were designed to investigate and document the problems rape victims experienced in their communities. Based on this documentation, these task forces began advocating for change in public policies and for change in social institutions, including court systems, public education, and law enforcement agencies.

In the 1970s, the National Organization for Victim Assistance (NOVA) was also formed, which led to the development of the National Coalition Against Sexual Assault (NCASA). In 1975, Brownmiller published *Against Our Will*, which also brought attention to the issue of rape and sexual assault. Later, in the 1980s, attention was given to acquaintance rape after an article on campus sexual assault was published in *Ms.* magazine (Warshaw, 1988). This article, based on research conducted by Koss (1993), challenged the myth that stranger rape was the most common form of sexual assault. In fact, RAINN (2012a) currently reports that two-thirds of perpetrators are known to the victim. In 1994, the Violence Against Women Act (VAWA) was passed, the first federal legislation that focused specifically on violent crimes (including sexual assault) specifically committed against women and children (Roe, 2004). VAWA was reauthorized in 1999 and more recently in 2005.

PREVALENCE OF SEXUAL ASSAULT

In the United States, 1 in 6 women and 1 in 33 men are victims of sexual assault (Tjaden & Thoennes, 2000). According to RAINN (2012a), over 17 million women have been victims of rape or sexual assault. It is estimated that between 14% and 20% of women are at risk of being a victim of a sexual assault in a lifetime (Kilpatrick & Resnick, 1993; Koss, 1993; Tjaden & Thoennes, 2000). According to the 2009 National Crime Victimization Survey (U.S. Department of Justice, 2012a), 90% of rape survivors were female. In addition, women with a history of rape before the age of 18 years were two times as likely to be raped when they were adults.

Statistics reveal little difference between Whites and persons of color in prevalence of rape or sexual assault (Tjaden & Thoennes, 2000). However, when the statistics of the sexual assaults of people of color are examined more closely, they reveal that American Indian and Alaska Native women were more likely to report having experienced rape, sexual assault, or stalking than were Caucasian, African American, Hispanic American, Asian American, or Pacific Islander women.

DEFINITIONS AND TERMS RELATED TO SEXUAL ASSAULT

According to the Bureau of Justice Statistics in the U.S. Department of Justice (2008), sexual assault is defined as an attack or attempted attack involving unwanted sexual contact, either forcibly or nonforcibly. An attack does not have to be completed in order to be considered a sexual assault. Also, a sexual assault consists of both forcible attacks and attacks where consent is not or cannot be given (e.g., due to intoxication, being below the age of legal consent, being mentally incapacitated). A forcible sexual assault may be violent. Forcible sexual assaults are frequently reported in the media and are easily identified and agreed on. However, nonforcible sexual assault is less understood and less identifiable, and it occurs when the person who is attacked lacks the capacity to give consent. Individuals who may lack the capacity to give consent include minors, people with mental disabilities, and people who may be incapacitated due to intoxication. In such cases, the diminished capacity of the individual makes consent impossible. A final factor in defining sexual assault is the types of contact that can occur, which can include grabbing, fondling, exhibitionism, verbal threats, and penetration.

The DSM-5 (American Psychiatric Association, 2013) includes four criminal paraphilias that fit the definition of sexual assault: (1) frotteurism, the act of touching, fondling, or rubbing someone without their consent; (2) pedophilia, the attraction to and sexual activity with a minor under the age of 16 years by an adult at least five years older than the victim; (3) sexual sadism, sexual excitement gained at the expense of another's mental or physical torment; and (4) voyeurism, the attainment of sexual satisfaction from observing others in the nude or in the act of intercourse.

There is much contention surrounding the inclusion of paraphilia in the DSM, including the validity of such diagnoses based on relevant empirical studies and differences in clinical opinion between degrees of mental illness and criminal intent in these diagnoses. The fear is that the DSM confuses the diagnosis of a paraphilia or mental disorder with criminal action. Previous editions of the DSM required that the diagnosis be given only if the client experienced distress or dysfunction of some kind. The DSM-5 takes those criteria away, creating a blur between pathology and criminal intent. Moser and Kleinplatz (2005) support the removal of most paraphilias from the DSM in order to focus on criminal intent preventing perpetrators from becoming accountable and answerable for their crimes. First and Halon (2008) stress the fact that only a small number of perpetrators who commit sexual offenses also have a diagnosible paraphilia responsible for the sexual offense, and an even smaller number of those with a paraphilia are unable to control their harmful desires.

It is significant to mention that "rape" was removed as a diagnostic criterion in the DSM-3 in order to diminish any confusion between mental illness and criminal conduct. The concept of adding "Paraphilic Coercive Disorder" to the DSM-5 has recently been debated and since rejected for inclusion (Frances, 2011). Rape is often considered a specific category of sexual assault, defined as forcible sexual intercourse, perpetrated by either psychological coercion or physical force (U.S. Department of Justice, 2012a). In many states, penetration is an act that distinguishes rape from other types of sexual assault. Penetration can occur vaginally, anally, or orally, with either a person's body part or an object. While these definitions are typically standard, terms may vary from state to state. New legislation has modified how the FBI defines rape for statistical purposes. The previous statistics included only "carnal knowledge of a female forcibly and against her will," whereas the new definition includes male victims, all cases in which children are victims unable to consent, and cases that include threats of violence (Rape, Abuse and Incest National Network, 2012b).

Definitions and Types of Rape

Different types of rape are discussed in the sections that follow. First, definitions of the different types of rape are presented, followed by a discussion of three types of rape motivators defined by Groth (2001).

ACQUAINTANCE RAPE   One of the most prevalent acts within the area of sexual assault and rape is acquaintance rape. This term has evolved over the past several decades from what was once described as date rape. This semantic change helps distinguish sexual assault and/or rape that occurs between people who are in an intimate or dating relationship from sexual assault and/or rape that occurs between people who are not (see Chapter 7, Intimate Partner Violence). The term *acquaintance* indicates that while the victim may know the assailant, the victim is not necessarily in an intimate relationship with the perpetrator. Although acquaintance rape occurs within the general population, it is most prevalent on college campuses. According to RAINN (2012a), females in early adulthood are four times more likely to be sexually assaulted than females in other age groups. Shockingly, few of these rapes are reported. According to *The Sexual Victimization of College Women*, a report published by the National Institute of Justice, fewer than 5% of rapes, either completed or attempted, that occurred among college-aged females were reported to law enforcement (Fisher, Cullen, & Turner, 2000). This report found that more than half of college-aged females surveyed indicated they share these experiences with friends, often not reporting the experiences to family member, campus officials, or law enforcement. Fisher et al. also found that 9 in 10 women knew their attackers, who included boyfriends, ex-boyfriends, classmates, friends, coworkers, and other acquaintances. Four main factors emerged that increased the risk of college-aged women being a victim of a sexual assault and/or rape: (1) frequent intoxication to the point of incapacitation, (2) single status, (3) previous sexual victimizations, and (4) residing on campus.

When addressing acquaintance rape on college campuses, education is a primary focus. According to Franiuk (2007), college students had difficulty identifying situations as sexual assaults, even when these assaults met legal definitions. In this study, students were more likely to label the incident as a sexual assault when physical force was present or the victim was drugged. When consent was at issue, including incidents involving self-intoxication, however, students had more difficulty identifying incidents of sexual assault. In order to address college students' inability to correctly identify ambiguous situations as sexual assault, many college campuses conduct awareness weeks aimed at providing education on the subject. For detailed guidelines on conducting a campus-wide prevention campaign, see Lee, Caruso, Goins, and Southerland (2003).

VOICES FROM THE FIELD 8.1
Advocacy and Working Toward Prevention on College Campuses

Michele E. Caruso

The more things change, the more they stay the same. Or so the saying goes. For all of the awareness and prevention efforts, research on effective treatment methodologies, and laws that were enacted, retracted, and enacted again, in many ways substantial challenges remain in working with sexual violence. This is true when working with the victim/survivor directly and with those indirectly affected by it, as well as the countless individuals hiding behind the "it only happens to *those* people" blindfolds or lost in the "ignorance is bliss" places.

I have been involved with this kind of work in some capacity with college students for over 20 years. The fears, anxieties, somatic headaches, depression, and pain are the same. The faces are different. I wouldn't expect, though, the clinical experiences or victim responses to change. We are all human beings, after all, who were not born to be violated in such a manner. What I would have expected to see shift by now is the cultural setup for sexual violence, the cultural response to sexual violence, and the cultural treatment of the victims of sexual violence.

We all know sexual violence does not happen in a vacuum. Nobody wakes up one day and thinks, "Hmmm. I'm bored. I think I'll rape someone today." We allow, condone, and even celebrate behaviors, attitudes, activities, and certainly entertainment that perpetuate sexist, racist, and heterosexist roles that devalue, objectify, silence, and oppress. I would even posit that there has been an escalation in this in the last 20 years. College students are bombarded and saturated with it. We could say there aren't enough conversations to the contrary, but there are. They just aren't getting through the noise. Is it any wonder?

For every college student who "gets it" and is willing to use his or her voice, there are 100 who haven't heard of it, another 100 who don't want to hear of it, and another 100 who have heard of it but are too afraid, confused, or "fill in the blank" to use their voice. These are individuals with great potential to facilitate the needed cultural shift and bring the generations behind them along for the ride. For all of the advocacy, services, and research that take place on college campuses, college students are still vulnerable to the cultural perpetuation of sexual violence. Not only are traditional age college students still the most at risk for being victims of sexual violence, but they are also very vulnerable to the cultural perpetuation of all the factors that contribute to sexual violence.

So, working with college students through prevention efforts or victims services has changed in some ways but has remained the same in many other ways. We might have more dedicated staff on campus to address violence, but the effort is still significantly underfunded. We might have more sexual assault awareness events, but we still have entertainment on the TV in the student unions that contributes to victims/survivors being doubted. We might use social networking to spread the word more efficiently than ever about how to assist friends who are victimized, but social networking is also used to spread hateful, disparaging, and damaging sentiments about victims, potential victims, and student advocates just as efficiently. We might have more students looking for a place to find and use their voice to address sexual violence, but we still have boxes we keep people in where voices are not allowed.

I do absolutely remain hopeful and certainly inspired by those on the front lines and behind the scenes in all of the fields that address sexual violence, from counselors and advocates to lawmakers and law enforcement, and everyone in between. However, the challenges in breaking through the cultural noise to access and help victims/survivors and to shift the paradigm of the upcoming generations in a way that would actually reduce sexual violence remain.

CASE STUDY 8.1

Sexual Assault

You have been working as a counselor at a university counseling center. Cindy—an 18-year-old college student who recently began seeing you for problems she is having in her classes—has come to see you and reports that she is failing most of her classes. She recently took her midterm exams and did not pass any of them. In addition, she did not even take two of the exams. She graduated at the top of her high school class, even receiving an academic scholarship covering the majority of her tuition. She reports that she is in jeopardy of losing her scholarship. She is also concerned because her grades will be sent home to her parents in the next few weeks. They have always expected her to excel in school, and she feels they will be very disappointed with her, possibly even insisting she return home to her small rural town, which she was trying to escape.

At your first meeting with Cindy, she also reports that she is having trouble going to her classes because she is sleeping through most of them. She reports wanting to sleep all the time, having a depressed mood, and avoiding her friends, who have ultimately convinced her to attend counseling. Cindy's appearance is disheveled, and she is wearing what seem to be dirty clothes.

During the first two sessions, Cindy cries frequently and rarely shares information. Finally, she reveals to you that one month ago she attended a party at an off-campus apartment. The apartment belonged to the man who is dating Cindy's best friend. Although Cindy reports that she is not a big drinker, while at the party she had a few drinks with Dennis, a guy from her sociology class, whom she has been interested in dating since the beginning of the semester. They were having a great time, talking and laughing, until she felt dizzy. She reported that the next thing she remembered was waking up in Dennis's bed with no clothes on, feeling sore in her "private area," and bleeding slightly. She quickly put her clothes on while Dennis was in the bathroom and ran out of the apartment. She told no one what happened. She has not been back to the sociology class that she has with him.

Discussion Questions

1. Does this case meet the legal definition of sexual assault?
2. In this situation, how would you proceed with your work with Cindy?
3. What are the legal and ethical guidelines that will drive your work with Cindy?

DRUG-FACILITATED SEXUAL ASSAULT   As mentioned earlier, intoxication may increase the risk for sexual assault occurrences. With this knowledge, perpetrators have been known to use drugs, often referred to as "date rape drugs," to prepare for the sexual assault. Most often given to victims without their knowledge these drugs impair their ability to guard themselves from being assaulted. The three most common drugs used to facilitate sexual assault are Rohypnol, GHB, and Ketamine (Womenshealth.gov, 2012).

Rohypnol, also known as roofies, can cause a myriad of effects, including dizziness, loss of muscle control, confusion, lack of consciousness, and, in severe cases, death. Rohypnol's effects can last for more than a few hours (Womenshealth.gov, 2012). Gamma-Hydroxybutyric acid (GHB) is a powerful drug used to treat narcolepsy, yet it is often made on the streets. GHB can cause blackouts, dreamlike feelings, seizures, coma, and possibly death. Ketamine is a legal anesthetic mostly used on animals. Like most anesthetics it can cause symptoms such as numbness, loss of coordination, memory problems, and depression, to name a few.

SPOUSAL RAPE   Spousal rape—defined as sexually assaulting one's partner with force—is rarely reported and most often classified as domestic violence. However, when it is reported, police officials enforce these cases the same way they would any other reported rape.

STATUTORY RAPE   A person who has been charged with statutory rape has no defense that can overturn the verdict. Statutory rape differs with each state due to differing laws that may allow minors to marry, allow minors within a certain age range to have consensual sex, and exclude emancipated minors from statutory offenses. For this reason, it is important to have an understanding on the laws in your state regarding statutory rape and age of consent (also known as Romeo and Juliet laws) to become familiar with statutory rape guidelines.

TYPES OF RAPE   Groth (2001, p. 2) defines rape as a "pseudosexual act, complex and multidetermined, but addressing issues of hostility (anger) and control (power) more than passion (sexuality)." Sex occurs during rape but it is also the method by which aggression is expressed. Groth discovered three basic motivators of rape: (1) power, (2) anger, and (3) sadism. Power accounts for the majority of rapes committed (55%), while anger accounts for 40%, and sadism accounts for 5%. Understanding the types of rape is important for understanding treatment for victims and perpetrators.

POWER   The power-motivated rape, the most common, is one in which "sexuality becomes an expression of conquest" (Groth, 2001, p. 13). Power is the ultimate form of gratification for the rapist. Victims are viewed as possessions that are obtained through sex. Having sexual intercourse with the victim is the goal rather than only achieving power and control. Unlike anger or sadistic rapists, the power rapist may use only the amount of force necessary to subdue his victim. Methods used to subdue the victim may include verbal threats (telling the victim that she will be hurt if she does not cooperate), intimidation using a weapon, and physical violence when the victim does not cooperate. Victims may often be kidnapped, held captive, and subjected to repeated assaults.

ANGER   In the anger-motivated rape; the sexual encounter is considered a hostile act, often leading to physical brutality (Groth, 2001). The force used in the rape may exceed what is necessary to subdue the victim and achieve the goal of sexual penetration. The perpetrator attacks the victim, often exhibiting strong forms of violence (e.g., grabbing, hitting, beating, tearing clothes). This type of attack may take two forms: (1) a surprise attack, catching the victim off guard, or (2) a manipulated approach during which the perpetrator demonstrates a charisma and confidence to make the victim feel secure, only to change, suddenly becoming angry and aggressive. Anger-motivated rapes are typically brief, with the primary objectives of hurting, humiliating, and demeaning the victim.

SADISM   The sadistic rapist, the most brutal but least common of the types identified by Groth, commits an act in which anger and power are eroticized. This type of rape integrates sexuality and aggression to form a "single psychological experience known as sadism" (Groth, 2001, p. 44). The main goal of the sadistic rapist is to achieve sexual gratification through inflicting pain. The assault may be a bizarre encounter, often including bondage or types of ritualistic incidents such as body washing of the victim, dressing a certain way, burning, or biting. Parts of the victim's body, other than the sex organs, may become the focus of injury by the rapist, and foreign objects may be used to penetrate the victim. Homicide may be the end result of the encounter, even leading to necrophilia (i.e., sex with dead bodies). Victims' bodies may be mutilated either during the rape or after they are killed. Sadistically motivated rapes are typically premeditated, with the rapist often preying on victims regarded as promiscuous. Based on the current diagnostic criteria in the DSM-5 (American Psychiatric Association, 2013), a rapist, regardless of motivational type, may be misdiagnosed as a sexual sadist. However, there is no support in the literature that suggests a sexual sadist is more likely to be a rapist.

CASE STUDY 8.2

What Is Sexual Assault?

You are a counselor in a mental health center. You have a new client named Sherry, who is a 25-year-old female who made an appointment for depression and anxiety she has been experiencing. During the initial session, Sherry reports that she received an associate's degree at a local technical college in nursing assistance 6 years ago. Since receiving her degree, she has worked primarily as a nursing aide in several rehabilitation centers. She recently quit her job abruptly due to an incident at the rehabilitation center where she was employed for 2 years. Sherry reports experiencing sleeplessness and weight loss. She has difficulty getting out of bed every morning and has not looked for a new job since she left.

Sherry recently ended a 5-year relationship with her boyfriend, although the couple was scheduled to be married in 6 months. She describes several episodes where she has been forced to leave public places after being unable to catch her breath and feeling as if she is being judged by others. After several sessions, she reveals that while at the rehab center, she was sexual assaulted at the center by a 32-year-old male patient named James, who became a paraplegic after a car accident that left him paralyzed below the waist. Sherry began to spend extra time with James after learning that he had very little to no family support and typically had no visitors. On several occasions, James began to ask questions about Sherry's dating life, and he eventually asked her to date him. James then began asking Sherry to help him deal with his frustrating involuntary erections and ejaculations. When she laughed-off this suggestion, James began to become more suggestive and aggressive with Sherry. He would talk about his previous sexual activities prior to being injured. Eventually, James's behavior turned to sexual advances, such as groping Sherry and suggesting that they should have sex. After enduring his advances for several weeks, Sherry finally complained to her supervisor and asked to be moved to another wing. Her request was denied due to a shortage of staff. She was encouraged to remain professional and told that James was harmless. One day while Sherry was helping James bathe, James overpowered her and sexually assaulted her with a shampoo bottle. Due to her shock, Sherry left the rehab center that day and never returned. She did not report it to her supervisor or the police.

Discussion Questions

1. Does Sherry's experience meet the definition of sexual assault? Why?
2. What are some of the additional problems Sherry might develop resulting from her sexual assault?
3. Keeping these circumstances in mind, how would you proceed to work with Sherry?
4. What are the legal and ethical guidelines that will drive your work with Sherry?

ACTIVITY 8.2

Interviewing Activity

Determine if your community has an agency that specifically deals with victims of sexual assault. Request an interview with an agency official to obtain answers to these questions: What services are provided to victims in the community? Who provides these services? How can victims access these services?

Rape Myths

One reason sexual assault is one of the most underreported crimes may be the social stigma of being a sexual assault victim. For many years, myths about sexual assault were commonly accepted, but with continued research and awareness-raising, many of these myths have been dispelled. Some of the more common myths about rape and sexual assault include the following:

- *Myth 1: Rape is about sex.* Rape is typically about the perpetrator's need to exert power and control over another individual, with sex as the weapon of choice.
- *Myth 2: Victims of rape deserve to be raped due to their appearance or their neglect of safety issues.* Although sexual assault and rape awareness have improved over the years, many individuals still believe that victims are to blame for their assault. Some may believe that victims incite a rapist because of provocative dress, appearance, or behavior. Others may blame the victim if they perceive that the victim did not take appropriate safety precautions to guard against an attack. As discussed later in this chapter, sexual predators will often rape someone with little or no cause to do so—regardless of how a person dresses or behaves.
- *Myth 3: Victims of sexual assault often make false reports based on revenge.* According to statistics from the Uniform Crime Reporting Program of the FBI (2005), just under 5,000 of the 90,518 forcible rapes reported in the United States in 2006 were determined to be unfounded—either false or baseless complaints. This constitutes 5.4% of forcible rapes reported in 2006.
- *Myth 4: Only strangers lurking in dark alleys commit sexual assaults.* According to the U.S. Department of Justice (2008), approximately 65% of all sexual assaults and/or rapes were committed by nonstrangers; 35% were committed by strangers. Sexual perpetrators are no longer thought of as mentally ill sociopaths who victimize strangers. Those who sexually assault others come from diverse socio-economic, racial, geographic, and educational backgrounds.

EFFECTS OF SEXUAL ASSAULT

Burgess and Holmstrom (1974) first coined the term *rape trauma syndrome* to describe the cluster of symptoms reported by women who were raped, shown in Table 8.1 (Burgess, 1985). Burgess, a psychiatric nurse, and Holmstrom, a sociologist, conducted research with women who presented in the emergency room after having experienced a rape. Burgess and Holmstrom described two distinct phases of women's response to sexual assault: (1) the acute phase and (2) the reorganization phase. During the acute phase, the survivor experienced a heightened stress level, lasting from several days to multiple weeks.

TABLE 8.1 Symptoms of Rape Trauma Syndrome

- Continuing anxiety
- Severe mood swings
- Sense of helplessness
- Persistent fear or phobia
- Depression
- Rage
- Difficulty sleeping (nightmares, insomnia, etc.)
- Eating difficulties (nausea, vomiting, compulsive eating, etc.)
- Denial
- Withdrawal from friends, family, activities
- Hypervigilance
- Reluctance to leave the house and/or go places that remind the individual of the sexual assault or perpetrator
- Sexual problems
- Difficulty concentrating
- Flashbacks

Source: From *National Sexual Assault Hotline* (Rape, Abuse & Incest National Network, 2008a). Retrieved from www.rainn.org/get-help/national-sexual-assault-hotline.

The reorganization phase was a longer-term process of integration, during which the victim regained a sense of control over life. In conceptualizing rape trauma syndrome, Burgess and Holmstrom found commonalities consistent with post-traumatic stress disorder (PTSD), including a significant stressor, intrusive thoughts about the sexual assault, and decreased involvement in their environment (e.g., feeling emotionally numb), as well as various other symptoms such as sleep disturbances, hypervigilance, guilt, impaired memory, and fears about reoccurrence of the sexual assault.

Physical Effects of Sexual Assault

Physical reactions to sexual assault can manifest in varying somatic complaints, including sleep disturbances, hyperalertness, and impaired memory. Sleep disturbances may range from sleeplessness or frequent waking to excessive amounts of sleeping. Victims may deal with other physical issues as a result of the sexual assault, including headaches, pregnancy, sexually transmitted infections (STIs) contracted during the assault, or permanent physical injuries sustained during the attack.

Emotional/Psychological Effects of Sexual Assault

Emotional and psychological reactions to a sexual assault may be either expressed or controlled. Victims who demonstrate more expressed reactions openly show emotions by crying, screaming, yelling, or even laughing. Those who demonstrate more controlled reactions may show little outward emotion or remain completely silent. Victims may experience a wide range of emotions: (1) guilt about surviving the attack, (2) self-blame about not being able to stop the attack, (3) shame if they chose not to report the assault, (4) humiliation with family and friends, (5) anxiety about another attack, and (6) depression that manifests as an inability to return to normal functioning in daily life. Victims may report feeling emotionally numb and being unable to reconnect with the world around them.

Cognitive/Behavioral Effects of Sexual Assault

Victims of sexual assault may experience cognitive or behavioral problems and may have impaired memory and/or concentration, including memory loss or the inability to recall certain details in their lives. They may have a marked inability to concentrate on work tasks and other activities of daily living. Victims of sexual assaults may change addresses or telephone numbers to try to ensure safety. They may find themselves in a state of hyperalertness, which can manifest as paranoia (e.g., feeling as if they are being followed), compulsive behaviors (e.g., constantly checking the house for intruders), or displaying an imaginary audience (e.g., thinking that others can tell they were sexually assaulted by looking at them).

INTERVENTIONS WITH SURVIVORS OF SEXUAL ASSAULT

Early evaluation and intervention are vital for victims of sexual assault. There are typically two facilities that provide intervention and evaluation services for victims. The first is the emergency room, where many victims of sexual assault first present themselves after having been physically injured during an attack. Once victims enter the health care system, they are treated for a variety of possible health concerns (e.g., pregnancy, STIs, HIV/AIDS, hepatitis B). The second treatment facility for victims of sexual assault is the crisis center, which is typically in a different location from the emergency medical facility and can be a self-contained unit, providing all services on-site. The majority of these crisis centers have 24-hour crisis telephone services through which victims can make initial contact. Often, if victims of sexual assault present to a law enforcement facility, they will be taken to either an emergency room or a crisis center, depending on which facility typically handles these types of cases in the local community. Services that are provided at emergency rooms or crisis centers may include (1) evidence collection, (2) medical interventions to treat possible health concerns, and (3) examinations by sexual assault nurse examiners (SANE nurses), who are specially trained to work with victims of sexual assault. The crisis center may use trained, on-call volunteers to assist victims of sexual assault when victims present at the crisis center, police department, or emergency room. Crisis counselors may participate in this volunteer program, often by providing the services during regular hours and by preparing, supporting, and supervising volunteer workers. The most important function of these volunteers is to support victims during the process of reporting and help prepare them for future steps. Crisis counselors and volunteers help victims understand the medical examination and evidence collection process, anticipate legal requirements, and develop safety plans. The crisis center may also offer additional services, including short-term or long-term counseling, education, and legal assistance. Although these may be the two most prevalent places rape victims take themselves or are taken, it is important for all counselors to have an understanding of the process and what may occur during medical examinations.

Medical examinations are a crucial crisis intervention strategy when dealing with sexual assault. The medical exam, however, can be both uncomfortable and overwhelming to a victim. Victims have experienced a violation that is both physically and psychologically intrusive, and many may fear that the medical exam required to collect evidence may lead to reliving the trauma they experienced.

It is important for crisis counselors to become familiar with the medical exam process to help victims understand and prepare for the exam. By offering information about what to expect during the process, the counselor can allow the victim to gain some control. The Office on Violence Against Women (OVW) in the U.S. Department of Justice (2004) developed a national protocol for sexual assault forensic exams (SAFEs) to recognize the sensitive needs of sexual assault victims and preserve evidence vital to the successful prosecution of offenders. Once a victim presents to an emergency room or crisis center, a SAFE is conducted by a trained medical professional such as a SANE nurse. The SAFE typically takes about four hours to complete and involves collecting biological samples, including blood, urine, hair, and saliva and obtaining oral, vaginal, and anal swabs and smears that may be used for DNA analysis and comparison. Urine samples help to determine if victims were drugged during the sexual assault. Clothing and any foreign materials on the body are collected, and many crisis centers provide donated clothing to victims once their clothing has been collected for evidence. For evidence preservation purposes, it is important for victims not to bathe, wash their hands, or brush their teeth; crisis counselors should be knowledgeable about the need for collecting urine samples in case victims are unable to wait until the forensic examiner arrives. A final aspect of the medical exam involves treating any potential medical conditions that occur due to the sexual assault (e.g., pregnancy, STIs, HIV/AIDS, hepatitis B). These conditions are treated with oral medications during the exam. The Centers for Disease Control (CDC) recommends follow-up testing for STIs 1 to 2 weeks after the assault and for syphilis and HIV 6, 12, and 24 weeks after the assault (U.S. Department of Justice, Office on Violence Against Women, 2004).

Because law enforcement may be an entry point for some victims of sexual assault, many police departments have begun offering specific training and specialized units for working with survivors of sexual assaults. The first step for many departments is to train personnel to understand the dynamics of rape and sexual assault. This training may range from basic one-day training to a more extensive course to help officers develop a deeper understanding of how to handle sexual assaults. Training should include understanding the victims they will encounter, common reactions and responses victims may have, types of violence that may occur during assaults, and patterns of perpetrators. Officers need to be aware of services available to victims and how to help victims who have been sexually assaulted access those services.

Once the first responders have connected sexual assault victims to the health care system, the next step for law enforcement officials is the investigation, which may be handled by specialized units that are trained in investigating sexual assaults, including procedures for interviewing survivors and collecting evidence. After the conclusion of the investigation, the case may be turned over to the local prosecutor's office, which may then develop a case to present to a judge and/or jury. Victims may be referred to a victims' assistance program to help deal with the personal impact of the trial.

These programs can help victims understand their rights regarding the court case. In 2004, President George W. Bush signed the Justice for All Act, which allows victims to write, submit, and/or present impact statements (U.S. Department of Justice, Office for Victims of Crime, 2006). Impact statements may be one of the first steps toward empowerment for victims of sexual assault or abuse. According to the National Center for Victims of Crimes (2009), a victim impact statement allows the victim of a crime to share the effect(s) of the crime. Statements typically focus on the harm that the offense caused, including physical, emotional, and financial harm as well as harm to family and other significant relationships. Statements are most often given in either written or oral forms and used at sentencing.

TREATMENT OF SURVIVORS OF SEXUAL ASSAULT

As discussed earlier, rape trauma syndrome is an adaptation of PTSD used to understand symptoms experienced by survivors of sexual assault. Because there are significant similarities between rape trauma syndrome and PTSD, crisis counselors should familiarize themselves with both. PTSD, acute stress disorder, and other related diagnoses were discussed in more depth in Chapter 1.

Short-term/Immediate Interventions

Decker and Naugle (2009) stress the importance of victims determining their own needs and voicing them before any intervention begins. They found little empirical evidence for immediate intervention after sexual assault. After a thorough investigation of the literature, they found that Psychological First Aid (PFA)—a systematic set of skills known for working with victims of recent traumatic events—is the most favorable approach for immediate intervention with sexual assault victims. It is a practical set of actions that are meant to be used immediately, within 24 hours, following a trauma. According to Ruzek and colleagues (2007) PFA consists of eight essential measures referred to as "core actions": (1) contact and engagement, (2) safety and comfort, (3) stabilization, (4) information gathering, (5) practical assistance, (6) connection with social supports, (7) information on coping support, and (8) linkage with collaborative services. The benefits of PFA are that it can be used by anyone trained in the application of the core actions.

CONDUCTING THE FIRST SESSION OR MEETING USING THE PFA APPROACH   Approach the victim gently and introduce yourself. Allow the victim to determine what role you can play for him or her and respect her wishes. You can begin by explaining some of the things you could offer—for example, comfort items such as a blanket—or your willingness to just sit quietly with the client. It is essential to be aware of the factors that can impede the medical exam process, such as not allowing the victim to brush his or her teeth, eat, drink, shower, or change clothes before the exam. While supporting the client continually, assess his or her wish for your level of involvement. It is crucial to allow the victim to feel in control of this process. Offer to accompany the victim to the medical exam, if appropriate in your position. In some agencies and in most school and private practice settings, it may be more appropriate for support systems to be contacted to assist in this role. Ask the victim if she or he would like you to explain the exam process step by step. Let the client lead the conversation; do not push or direct the dialogue, especially toward the incident. If the victim does wish to speak about the assault, it is crucial to be supportive; do not doubt or blame the victim. Support through active listening and empathic statements have the most impact at this stage. After the exam and any necessary protocol, such as speaking with law enforcement, assess the client's need for safety. Determine the best place for the victim to go and determine what types of support are necessary and begin putting these supports in place.

Long-term Interventions

After victims have survived the immediate aftereffects of the attack (e.g., medical interventions), long-term counseling services should be considered. Crisis counselors should perform a thorough evaluation to determine the most appropriate treatment plan (Foa & Rothbaum, 1998). Several assessments exist that may be helpful when collecting information related to the assault, including the Assault Information and History Interview (AIHI; Foa & Rothbaum, 1998), the Clinician-Administered PTSD Scale (Blake et al., 1995), and the PTSD Symptom Scale (Foa, Riggs, Dancu, & Rothbaum, 1993). Self-report measures include the Impact of Event Scale (Horowitz, Wilner, & Alvarez, 1979) and the Rape Aftermath Symptom Test (Kilpatrick, 1988). As with any crisis situation, a risk assessment should be completed.

A second consideration is the length of the treatment program. Although survivors have already experienced short-term interventions (e.g., medical examinations, involvement with law enforcement), longer-term counseling may help them to deal with the effects that occur long after the sexual assault. Foa and Rothbaum (1998) offer these suggestions to crisis counselors when working with survivors: (1) provide support to the survivor for other issues being dealt with (e.g., involvement in the legal system, family considerations, job stress), (2) take and maintain a nonjudgmental attitude; (3) show a level of comfort with the traumatic events described; (4) demonstrate competence with rape trauma syndrome; (5) feel confident about the treatments chosen; (6) focus on personal resources; and (7) normalize the response to the assault.

A meta-analysis conducted by Russell and Davis (2007) examined 41 studies over a 25-year period to determine the strength and quality of each intervention used in the treatment of sexual assault. They found the most efficacious treatment protocols used either cognitive-behavioral therapy (CBT), exposure therapy, or a combination of the two. The other therapies studied included assertion training, cognitive experiential reprocessing, cognitive processing therapy, cognitive restructuring, eye movement desensitization, eye movement desensitization and reprocessing (EMDR), educational video (shown at medical exam), imaginal exposure, imagery rehearsal, minimal attention, prolonged exposure, supportive counseling, systematic desensitization, stress inoculation, stress inoculation training, and visual-kinesthetic dissociation. Overall, they found that all of the treatments researched had at least minimal positive effects.

Cognitive-Behavioral Approaches

Cognitive-behavioral approaches are well researched and have been shown to have positive results for survivors of sexual assault (e.g., Bryant, Harvey, Dang, Sackville, & Basten, 1998; Foa, Hearst-Ikeda, & Perry, 1995; Foa & Rothbaum, 1998; Foa, Rothbaum, Riggs, & Murdock, 1991; Jaycox, Zoellner, & Foa, 2002; Kubany, 1998; Muran & DiGiuseppe, 1994; Resick & Schnicke, 1992). Foa et al. (1995) conducted a study to examine the use of brief prevention programs designed to treat PTSD symptoms with sexual assault survivors. This program, like many abuse-focused cognitive-behavioral therapies , included techniques such as exposure, relaxation training, and cognitive restructuring. Treatments for sexual assault survivors, including exposure therapy, anxiety management programs, and psychoeducation, are discussed in the sections that follow. Some of these techniques or approaches may require additional training and education. Counselors should never practice outside their scope or position.

TRAUMA-FOCUSED COGNITIVE-BEHAVIORAL THERAPY   Created by Cohen, Mannarino, and Deblinger (2006), trauma-focused cognitive behavioral therapy (TF-CBT) is specifically geared toward working with children, adolescents, and their families. It consists of eight components characterized by the acronym PRACTICE: (1) **P**sychoeducation; (2) **R**elaxation and stress management skills; (3) **A**ffective expression and modulation; (4) **C**ognitive coping and processing; (5) **T**rauma narration; (6) **I**n vivo mastery of trauma; (7) **C**onjoint child-parent sessions; and (8) **E**nhancing future safety and development. TF-CBT has been shown to decrease the symptoms of PTSD as well as other symptoms caused by assault. The treatment also provides relief for caregivers of the victim providing secondary gain for all those involved. Additional information can be found in the *How to Implement TF-CBT Manual* at http://www.nctsnet.org/nctsn_assets/pdfs/TF-CBT_Implementation_Manual.pdf (National Child Traumatic Stress Network, 2012).

EXPOSURE THERAPY   According to Foa and Rothbaum (1998), exposure therapy is considered the most appropriate treatment for PTSD symptoms related to sexual assault. It is a form of systematic desensitization that calls for repeated exposure to a traumatic event in order to reduce the fear, anxiety, and pathology associated with the event. During exposure therapy, clients, with eyes closed, are encouraged to recall the traumatic event in the safety of a counselor's office. These sessions are often audiotaped to allow the client to review them at home in order to continue the repeated exposure to the memories, with the intent of continuing to lessen the fear and anxiety associated with the event. Although this treatment may be stressful, it is considered the most effective intervention for treating sexual assault survivors. Another form of exposure therapy, *in vivo* therapy, involves repeated exposure to real-life situations and/or places that remind the survivor of the event in order to restore feelings of safety. It is important to note that exposure therapy has been criticized in the literature for being ineffective, dangerous, and increasing dropout rates (Pitman et al., 1991). However there are no research findings that support such claims (Foa, Zoellner, Feeny, Hembree, & Alvarez-Conrad, 2002).

EYE MOVEMENT DESENSITIZATION AND REPROCESSING   Eye movement desensitization and reprocessing (EMDR) attempts to help clients process memories of their abuse that cause psychological and psychosomatic symptoms that interfere with their daily living. EMDR processes parts of the abuse and uses bilateral stimulation such as eye movement, tapping, or sounds to change the way the brain is processing a memory. EMDR uses eight phases of treatment to identify and deal with the trauma that creates a person's current distress.

ANXIETY MANAGEMENT TRAINING PROGRAMS   There are several anxiety management training (AMT) programs that are effective for treating PTSD symptoms following a sexual assault. AMT programs are designed to help equip clients with tools to better handle anxiety (Foa & Rothbaum, 1998). AMT treatments that have been found to be most successful working with sexual assault survivors include stress inoculation training and relaxation training.

STRESS INOCULATION TRAINING   Stress inoculation training (SIT) was developed by Meichenbaum (1996) as a treatment to help clients deal with a stressful event and to prevent or "inoculate" them against future stressors. According to Meichenbaum, SIT has three phases: (1) conceptualization, (2) skills acquisition and rehearsal, and (3) application and follow-through. In the conceptualization phase, the counseling relationship is developed, stressors are evaluated to determine severity, problem-solving methods are employed to determine stressors that can be changed, and goals are set. In the acquisition and rehearsal phase, coping skills are taught and rehearsed in the clinical setting so they can be applied in stressful situations. These coping skills include emotional regulation, self-soothing, relaxation training, problem-solving skills, communication tools, and social support networks. In the application and follow-through phase, the client applies the coping skills developed through modeling and role playing. In this final phase, ways to prevent relapse are discussed.

RELAXATION TRAINING   Relaxation techniques can be incorporated in any treatment plan when working with survivors of sexual assault. Victims can learn to know how and when to use relaxation techniques and apply this technique to times when they are triggered by the traumatic event causing dysfunction. These techniques include deep breathing, deep muscle relaxation, and cue-controlled relaxation which involve teaching the client to recognize body tension, using it as a cue for employing relaxation techniques (Foa & Rothbaum, 1998).

PSYCHOEDUCATION AND OTHER TREATMENTS   During the process of recovery, survivors must learn many things related to sexual assault. They may need help understanding the myths that surround sexual assault, and they may need to be educated about negative thoughts they may experience and any triggers associated with the assault. They need to understand several common reactions to sexual assault: (1) fear and anxiety, (2) re-experiencing the trauma through nightmares or flashbacks, (3) increased arousal such as impatience or irritability, (4) avoidance of situations that remind the client of the assault, (5) numbness, (6) anger, (7) guilt and shame, (8) depression, (9) negative self-image, and (10) problems with intimate relationships, including issues with sexual pleasure.

GROUP THERAPY   Group therapy is a common treatment modality for survivors of sexual assault. Most rape crisis center and abuse shelters offer some form of group therapy. The most common and most beneficial types of group for survivors of sexual assault are support and therapy groups. The group format allows survivors to share their stories with others in a supportive environment and gain an understanding of their symptoms and concerns. Group therapy encourages the feeling of belonging and facilitates the growth process. Jacobs, Masson, Harvill, and Schimmel (2012) recommend screening clients prior to entering a support or therapy group for sexual assault. They stress the importance of the client having had individual therapy and being at a point in their process where the clients are dedicated to moving forward in the treatment process.

VOICES FROM THE FIELD 8.2
Working with Victims of Sexual Assault in Mental Health Settings

Alissa Sawyer

After working in a variety of clinical settings, I have had my share of clients who are sexual assault victims. I can recall that only a few weeks into my first "real job" in counseling at a community mental health center, I was both shocked and heartbroken at the overwhelming number of clients who reported being sexually assaulted. I have found since then that this is a global issue with far too little awareness. I have gone through various training programs in order to better treat these clients.

Common themes exist among many sexual assault victims. One such commonality is knowing who their abuser is prior to the sexual assault(s). I find this frequently among children, adolescents, and adults alike. There have been fewer than a handful of clients over the years who I have encountered who did not know their abuser prior to the sexual assault(s). A second commonality is repeated sexual assault by different people. This is a phenomenon I am still attempting to understand. The best way I can frame this in my own mind is that sexual assault victims lose a sense of self, self-respect, and self-esteem, and thus are more vulnerable to those who prey on others sexually than those who exude more confidence and self-respect.

A final common theme I have found among sexual assault victims is a willingness to "own" the responsibility for the assault(s). Attackers are very adept at making a victim feel responsible for the assault. They will fuse logic with lies to confuse the victim into believing that he or she is fully responsible for the attack. This is a pivotal issue to address in counseling, even if a client initially denies ownership of the attack.

One of the most important aspects of counseling sexual assault victims is helping them realize and accept that the assault was not their fault and that it was only the fault of their attacker. An equally important aspect of counseling with sexual assault victims is talking about the assault(s). Many victims are tired of discussing it and believe that if they could just "leave it behind" they would be able to "move on." However, this is far from reality. The more that victims of sexual assault attempt to repress memories and feelings about their assaults, the more their minds and bodies will remind them, and the more fearful they are likely to be. The best way I can describe this to my sexual assault victim clients is to compare their situation to a broken bone. If a child breaks his leg and allows it to heal on its own, it will heal improperly and will give the child incredible pain and lack of mobility. If the child then goes to the doctor, the doctor will have to first break the bone again in order to set it to heal properly. This is very similar to working with sexual assault victims. They must go back to the point of pain, look at it in truth and hurt again, now in a safe place, in order to best heal and move forward with their lives.

One of the approaches that I often use with sexual assault victims is eye movement desensitization and reprocessing (EMDR), an effective way for clients to reprocess past trauma so it is no longer in the forefront of their minds. Another approach I frequently use with sexual assault victims is trauma-focused cognitive-behavioral therapy (TF-CBT). I have found both EMDR and TF-CBT to be very effective tools for those who have suffered sexual assault, especially as it comes to owning too much responsibility for the assault(s).

Jacobs et al. draw attention to the fact that many survivors early in the recovery process are still trying to make sense out of the assault and have not yet dealt with the guilt and shame that accompanies such abuse, and they are therefore not ready to enter into the group therapy process.

ETHICAL AND LEGAL ISSUES REGARDING SEXUAL ASSAULT

Ethical and legal issues regarding sexual assault include confidentiality, release of information, counselor competence, and personal values. When working with victims of sexual assault, a crisis counselor may experience ethical dilemmas related to confidentiality, which may conflict with personal values. It may be quite obvious to the crisis counselor that reporting the assault may be in the best interest of the client. However, the crisis counselor is both ethically and legally obligated to maintain confidentiality even if it is counterintuitive to the client's needs. In addition, the crisis counselor is ethically obligated to avoid imposing personal values on the client (American Counseling Association, 2005). The crisis counselor must not persuade clients to report sexual assaults or endure forensic examinations against their will. Particularly after something as intrusive as a sexual assault, empowering clients to make decisions about what happens to their bodies is important.

According the *ACA Code of Ethics* (American Counseling Association, 2005, p. 9), crisis counselors "practice only within the boundaries of their competence, based on their education, training, supervised experience, state and national professional credentials, and appropriate professional experience." Although working with survivors of sexual assault is not considered a specialty area, crisis counselors must develop knowledge and skills specific to dealing with sexual assault survivors to help these clients improve through counseling. Counselors should gain competence in treatment modalities applicable to sexual assault issues (e.g., cognitive-behavioral approaches, exposure therapy, anxiety management programs) and develop skills related to rape trauma syndrome and PTSD prior to working with this population. Competence can be gained by attending workshops, seminars, or training sessions focused on how to work with sexual assault survivors. Crisis counselors can choose to read literature about sexual assault or conduct conjoint counseling with another counselor who is experienced in working with sexual assault survivors.

Because many sexual assault survivors are involved in the legal system, it is important to recognize that they may be particularly sensitive to having their information disclosed. Voluntary release of information forms should be in place to allow crisis counselors to share information with attorneys, medical personnel, and law enforcement. If a survivor chooses not to sign these documents, information cannot be revealed unless the crisis counselor is legally required to do so (i.e., by subpoena and court order). It is important to recognize that just because a counselor receives a subpoena does not mean that information is automatically shared. Many subpoenas are not considered official subpoenas. Crisis counselors are encouraged to seek legal counsel in any situation in which the legal system is involved. Legal representatives can help crisis counselors prepare for possible court testimony and become familiar with state laws pertaining to crisis counseling.

Spirituality and Religious Issues Related to Sexual Assault

Integration of spirituality and religious beliefs in counseling has gained significant focus in recent years. Spirituality as a means to improved mental health has long been an accepted practice in dealing with substance abuse issues (as demonstrated by Alcoholics Anonymous). According to Cashwell and Young (2011), the spiritual and/or religious life of clients can be crucial to their development, particularly when dealing with their personal problems. Clients often create a spiritual existence that provides meaning, peace, and tranquility to their lives, which needs to be acknowledged and accepted by the counselor. Although research has been conducted to determine if a person's spirituality and religious beliefs can be a way of coping with stressful events, particularly when dealing with trauma, the findings of these studies are inconsistent. More specifically, people may engage in either and/or both positive or negative religious coping behaviors. Examples of positive coping behaviors include (1) using religion to find meaning, comfort, and support, (2) engaging in good deeds and helping others, and (3) involvement in church activities and/or attending religious services. Examples of negative coping behaviors include (1) using religion to avoid dealing with problems, (2) making bargains with God to make things better, and (3) feeling dissatisfied with religion after the assault (Ahrens, Abeling, Ahmand, & Hinman, 2010). Fallot and Heckman (2005) conducted research to examine the spirituality and religious coping behaviors used by women who had experienced personal traumas. According to their findings, participants in the study relied more on positive religious coping behaviors than the general population. However, one important finding in the study was that the more severe the trauma, the more participants engaged in negative religious coping behaviors. In a study conducted by Kennedy, Davis, and Taylor (1998), 70 inner city, predominately minority women who had been sexually assaulted in the past 9 to 24 months were surveyed to understand the role that spirituality and religious beliefs played in dealing with the sexual assault. According to the results, 60% of the participants reported an increased reliance on their spiritual beliefs to deal with their sexual assault. Ahrens et al. (2010) conducted a study of approximately 100 sexual assault survivors who reported a belief in God. According to their findings, sexual assault survivors who used positive religious coping behaviors experienced improved well-being and less depression than those who used negative religious coping behaviors. It is important to note that ethnicity played a significant part in the focus on religious coping behaviors. African American survivors tended to rely more heavily on their religious beliefs than White survivors (Ahrens et al., 2010; Kennedy, Davis & Taylor, 1998).

In working with survivors of sexual assault who may have strong religious and/ or spiritual beliefs, it is important to recognize that clients should be able to initiate a discussion of religion when they choose and that counselors should avoid imposing personal religious beliefs on the client. According to the *ACA Code of Ethics* (American Counseling Association, 2005, pp. 4–5), "Counselors are aware of their own values, attitudes, beliefs, and behaviors and avoid imposing values that are inconsistent with counseling goals. Counselors respect the diversity of clients, trainees, and research participants."

When working with survivors of sexual assault who view their religious beliefs as a significant part of their lives, counselors should consider the following guidelines:

1. Do not ignore the strong spiritual/religious beliefs of clients. These beliefs are just as important as any other beliefs that clients may have. However, counselors should refrain from imposing their own religious beliefs onto clients.
2. Help clients see the benefits of their religious/spiritual beliefs to their wellness and recovery process.
3. If clients are experiencing negative religious coping skills (e.g., using religion to avoid dealing with problems, bargaining with God, feeling dissatisfied with religion), help them develop more positive religious coping skills (e.g., find meaning through their religious beliefs, helping others, becoming involved in religious activities).

The Association for Spiritual, Ethical, and Religious Values in Counseling (ASERVIC), a division of the ACA, developed *Competencies for Addressing Spiritual and*

Religious Issues in Counseling to help counselors understand the skills and knowledge necessary to develop spiritual and religious sensitivity when working with clients (Cashwell & Watts, 2010). A discussion of all the competencies can be found at the ASERVIC website at http://www.aservic.org/resources/spiritual-competencies/.

Multicultural Issues and Victims with Special Needs

According to the ACA *Code of Ethics* (American Counseling Association, 2005, p. 10), counselors should be cognizant of the influence of individual differences based on "age, culture, disability, ethnicity, race, religion/spirituality, gender, gender identity, sexual orientation, marital status/partnership, language preference, socioeconomic status, or any basis proscribed by law." In addition, counselors are encouraged to use appropriate language clearly understandable by clients. When difficulty with a client's ability to understand occurs, counselors should "provide the necessary services (e.g., arranging for a qualified interpreter or translator)" to help clients comprehend information (American Counseling Association, 2005, p. 4). Addressing individual needs and services for victims of sexual assault who present with special needs is a crucial part of a crisis counselor's work.

According to the President's DNA Initiative Sexual Assault Medical Forensic Examinations (2008), crisis counselors who are working with victims of sexual assault should educate themselves about various populations in their communities in order to increase the quality of services provided to victims with special needs. Examples of special services may include (1) interpreters for hearing-impaired victims; (2) special equipment and supplies to perform the sexual assault forensic exam for victims with physical disabilities (e.g., a hydraulic lift exam table); and (3) interpreters for non-English-speaking victims.

Other special services may include an understanding of the influence of cultural values on the response of victims to a sexual assault. Examples include (1) cultural values that discourage a woman from disrobing in the presence of the opposite sex, particularly during any medical examinations; (2) the belief that the loss of virginity prior to marriage is disgraceful to the entire family and causes the victim to be undeserving of an honorable marriage; and (3) an awareness that certain cultures (e.g., Indian tribes) may have their own laws and regulations addressing sexual assault. In addition to understanding cultural beliefs, crisis counselors need to be aware of victims' personal needs and beliefs that may be different from their overall cultural beliefs. For example, some victims may choose to have friends and/or family present during any services provided, but victims with disabilities may be reluctant to report a sexual assault due to their ability to remain independent being challenged by family members. Special populations such as male, LGBT, disabled persons, and vulnerable adult victims may present with unique reactions after a sexual assault. It is important for crisis counselors to treat clients as individuals and try to understand their unique needs. Confidentiality may need to be specifically emphasized with male victims who are fearful of the effect any public disclosures may have due to social stigmas associated with male sexual assault. Crisis counselors should work to develop comprehensive services to meet the needs of male victims, including becoming visible in the male community. Crisis counselors should honor a male victim's wishes to have a particular gender provide services. Male victims are often very reluctant to seek support from friends and families and should be encouraged to seek professional help when needed.

PERPETRATORS OF SEXUAL ASSAULT

When discussing sexual assault, it is important to consider not only the survivors but also the perpetrators. In the sections that follow, the prevalence, characteristics, and treatment options regarding perpetrators of sexual assault are described.

Prevalence and Characteristics of Sexual Assault Perpetrators

It is common knowledge that the majority of sexual assault perpetrators are male. According to the Bureau of Justice Statistics (U.S. Department of Justice, 2008), almost 98% of offenders are male, with only 2% being female. More than 40% of male offenders are over the age of 30 years. The vast majority (85%) of these perpetrators used no weapons during the assaults. In the assaults that used weapons, firearms were typically used. According to the Bureau of Justice Statistics, an examination of four datasets (i.e., arrests in the FBI's Uniform Crime Reports, state felony court convictions, prison admissions, and the National Crime Victimization Survey) reveals that sex offenders are older (early 30s) and more likely to be White than other violent offenders.

According to Groth (2001), several myths exist regarding rapists: (1) rapists are sexually compulsive males who see women as provocative and malicious; (2) rapists are sexually frustrated males reacting to repressed stress; and (3) rapists are "demented sex-fiends" who harbor perverted desires. These myths assume that the perpetrator's primary motivation is based on sexual needs and desires and that rape is the method for gratifying these desires. In reality, the rape of an adult is based on the nonsexual needs of the perpetrator, which include power and control rather than sexual needs. The basic characteristics of perpetrators who commit power, anger, and sadistically motivated rapes are detailed below.

PERPETRATORS OF POWER-MOTIVATED RAPE A power-motivated rapist may be attempting to validate strength and control in compensation for feelings of inadequacy. Like the perpetrator of the anger rape, a power rapist finds little sexual gratification with the act; unlike the anger rape perpetrator, however, the power rapist may have fantasized about or planned the event. The fantasy may include a desire that the victim will not protest and will find the sexual prowess difficult to resist. When the victim does resist, the act is disappointing to the perpetrator because the fantasy does not come to fruition. At this point, the aggressor may feel the need to experience another rape in order to continue to pursue the fantasy. The power rape diverges from the anger rape in that the power rape may be premeditated, with the perpetrator often searching for victims or acting on opportunities. Victims of the power rape may be the same age or younger than the perpetrator and are based on availability, accessibility, and vulnerability. The power rapist may deny that the encounter was forced, often believing that the victim actually enjoyed the encounter. The rapist may attempt to show a kind gesture following the encounter as a way to discredit the victim.

PERPETRATORS OF ANGER-MOTIVATED RAPE As described earlier in the chapter, the purpose of an anger-motivated rape is to hurt, humiliate, or demean the victim. Methods employed by an anger rapist include both physical violence and verbal aggression. This rapist, however, finds that physical and verbal aggressions alone do not meet the desired needs for power and control, and sex becomes a weapon by which to release anger. Anger rape may also include other acts thought of by the rapist to be particularly objectionable, such as sodomy or fellatio, or humiliating, such as urinating or ejaculating onto the victim. This rapist may have difficulties with an erection and may find little sexual gratification with the act. Anger-motivated rapes are typically brief, often unplanned by the rapists, and not a focus of the rapist's fantasies prior to the act.

PERPETRATORS OF SADISTICALLY MOTIVATED RAPE   The sadistically motivated rapist finds pleasure with the torment, anguish, suffering, and pain of the victim. The main goal of the sadistic rapist is to achieve sexual gratification through inflicting pain, even finding pleasure in the victim's futile resistance. The sadistic motivated rape is often premeditated, and the perpetrator goes to great lengths to avoid detection, often wearing gloves, wearing disguises, or blindfolding victims. A sadistic motivated rapist is frequently considered a psychopath, although the perpetrator is often married and employed and can appear personable and friendly.

Treatment of Sex Offenders

Because there is no evidence-based guidance about the most effective approaches to working with female sexual offenders (Center for Sex Offender Management, 2007), the primary focus of this treatment section will be on male offenders, with "sex offender" referring to males unless specifically stated otherwise. When considering treatment for sex offenders, crisis counselors should consider three aspects: (1) client dynamics, (2) treatment setting, and (3) treatment modality (Groth, 2001). First, client dynamics must be assessed through a comprehensive psychological evaluation that includes demographics, family background, medical history, education level, military history, interpersonal development (e.g., social, sexual, and marital information), occupational history, and criminal history. In addition, assessments should include behavioral observations, field investigations, medical examination, and psychometric examinations. The clinical assessment must obtain information about the perpetrator's sexual behavior, including premeditation, victim selection, style of attack, accompanying fantasies, role of aggression, sexual behavior (contact, duration, dysfunction), mood state, contributing factors (stressors), acceptance of responsibility, and recidivism and deterrence.

Second, appropriate treatment settings should be considered (Groth, 2001). Most offenders enter the mental health system through either the criminal justice or the health care system. The perpetrator may have been hospitalized for a mental illness or referred by the courts for treatment. Treatment facilities may typically specialize in the treatment of sex offenders and offer either inpatient or outpatient treatment. Group counseling may be the primary method of delivery of services in order to provide confrontation to a client population that may be prone to denial.

Lastly, there are specific treatment modalities that may be effective when treating sex offenders. However, it is important to recognize that no single treatment modality has been found to be the most effective treatment for sex offenders (Groth, 2001). Crisis counselors should consider court requirements and the specific needs of each client to determine a course of treatment and possibly combine treatments in order to find a successful plan of action. Available treatment modalities include chemotherapy, psychotherapy, psychoeducation, behavior modification and cognitive-behavioral approaches, incapacitation, and family systems counseling.

CHEMOTHERAPY   The use of chemotherapy in the treatment of sexual offenders includes administering an antiandrogen hormone to reduce interest in sexual activity. The most commonly used forms of chemotherapy include medroxyprogesterone acetate (MPA), available in the United States, and cyproterone acetate (CPA), available in Canada and Europe. This medical intervention is based on the use of synthetic progesterones designed to decrease testosterone levels, which has been shown to lessen deviant sexual fantasies and behaviors as well as reducing libido, erections, and ejaculations (Grossman, Martis, & Fichtner, 1999).

PSYCHOTHERAPY   Various methods of counseling are used to treat sex offenders. Individual counseling, group counseling, and family and marital counseling are all used to help clients develop insight into their inappropriate behavior and choices, which are typically thought to be based on internal and emotional conflicts (Groth, 2001). Although counseling may be the most common treatment for sex offenders, it has several limitations. First, there is no clear evidence that this type of treatment works, particularly in isolation. Second, clients' intellectual functioning can affect their ability to develop insights related to their behavior; in addition, their ability to think abstractly, as well as their level of self-awareness, is crucial to the success of counseling. Third, the ability to develop a counseling relationship with clients is important. It is highly possible that this population is distrustful of any professional perceived as punitive. If clients have been required to attend counseling by a third party (e.g., by a judge), the challenge of developing a relationship increases.

PSYCHOEDUCATION   Life-skills training involves focusing on several areas where deficiencies may exist, such as sex education, social skills, empathy skills, and emotional regulation (Groth, 2001). Sex education can help the sex offender understand normal sexual functioning, as most experience sexuality in a dysfunctional way. Social skills training allows sex offenders to understand healthy relationships and develop improved interpersonal skills. Empathy-building skills help the sex offender develop sensitivity to people and recognize the needs of others. Emotional regulation is important for helping sex offenders cope with anger and aggression, which they typically release via a sexual assault. Relaxation techniques may also be used to address their feelings of frustration.

BEHAVIOR MODIFICATION AND COGNITIVE-BEHAVIORAL APPROACHES   Behavior modification for sex offenders primarily involves aversive conditioning in which a sexual response (such as an erection) is repeatedly paired with a noxious event, such as an electric shock or unpleasant smell (Groth, 2001). One example of behavior modification is to have an offender masturbate to ejaculation while fantasizing about an appropriate, nondeviant sexual encounter and partner; then, postorgasm, to have the offender continue to masturbate for an additional hour to a fantasy involving his preferred (and deviant) partner or sexual encounter, thus pairing the pleasurable experience with a socially appropriate partner and the uncomfortable experience with the behavior to be extinguished (Miller-Perrin & Perrin, 2007). Another behavior modification technique for treating sex offenders is covert sensitization in which guided imagery is used to help the client imagine his offense and then imagine a frightening or disgusting event. In both of the treatment modalities, repeating the techniques until the behavior is extinguished is the key to success. Although this is a commonly used approach, there is debate over whether aversion therapy produces permanent results (Laws & Marshall, 2003).

Cognitive-behavioral therapy (CBT) has also been used to treat offender populations, targeting cognitive distortions, deviant sexual practices and preferences, concurrent nonsexual behavioral and social challenges, and relapse prevention (Miller-Perrin & Perrin, 2007). The Sex Offender Treatment and Evaluation Project (SOTEP) is a cognitive-behavioral treatment program for sex offenders in California (see Marques, 1999; Marques, Wiederanders, Day, Nelson, & van Ommeren, 2005) that has tracked participants longitudinally for 8 years. Results are mixed, with no statistical difference in rates of recidivism between participants and nonparticipants; however, the treatment has been associated with a significant reduction of reoffending in individuals who complete program goals, suggesting that there is potential for cognitive-behavioral approaches to reduce reoffending with at least some segment of sex offenders (Marques et al., 2005).

INCAPACITATION Incapacitation for the sex offender can take several forms, including neurosurgery, surgical castration, and imprisonment/institutionalization. Neurosurgery involves removing parts of the hypothalamus, which decreases male hormone production and diminishes sexual arousal and impulsive behaviors. Surgical castration involves a sex offender losing the functions of his testes. Sex offenders may voluntarily undergo this procedure to help lessen sexual drives. Involuntary castration is extremely controversial, based on legal, moral, and ethical ambiguity. Imprisonment is the most common type of incapacitation (Groth, 2001), in which the confinement of the sex offender prevents commission of future acts.

CASE STUDY 8.3

How Do You Work with a Perpetrator?

Refer back to Case Study 8.2, and now consider that James presents at the mental health center as your next appointment. Although he has not been charged with a sexual assault, he is disturbed by what he did to Sherry. After the incident, he was afraid Sherry would report him to the staff and that he would be asked to leave the rehab center. He knew he did not have any other place to go and would probably end up homeless if forced to leave. He asked the rehab center staff to make an appointment for him at the local mental health center. He reported the incident to you in detail. Although he can discuss the details of what he calls "the incident," he reports feeling as if he was outside of his body looking down at what was going on. He says he doesn't know why he did that to Sherry, who is someone he really cared about. He had tried to call Sherry but she will not answer the phone. He would like to apologize to her but he is concerned she will never talk to him again. He is asking you to help him figure out what to do.

Discussion Questions

1. What additional information would you like to know about James through your initial interview? What information would be helpful in understanding how you will work with James?
2. In this case, how would you proceed to work with James?
3. Discuss any ethical issues you need to consider when working with James.

TREATMENT FOR FEMALE OFFENDERS   Although there is little evidence-based guidance regarding treatment of female sex offenders, female perpetrators have higher rates and more severe experiences of sexual victimization than do male perpetrators (Center for Sex Offender Management, 2007). Treatment, therefore, may need to address the trauma that these female perpetrators (and male perpetrators who may have sustained similar sexual abuse) have encountered. Thus, while addressing victimization issues, it is important for clinicians to be empathetic regarding the abuse that perpetrators have sustained without minimizing or excusing the sexual offenses that they have committed. In treating any perpetrator of rape, the priority of treatment must be focused on the perpetrated act in the attempt to decrease the rate of recidivism.

Summary

Survivors of sexual violence are a significant proportion of society, with some reports estimating that at least 20% of women and up to 10% of men are sexually victimized in their lifetime. Although the definitions of sexual assault and statutory rape may differ by state, it is important for crisis counselors to be aware of legislation, resources, and best practices for working with survivors of sexual violence. Primarily, the need for empathetic understanding, for the use of abuse-specific cognitive-behavioral strategies, and for the connection of survivors to resources in the community that best fit their needs is vital. It is also important to understand that not all victims of sexual violence will react the same way. While some may show immediate physical, cognitive-behavioral, or psychological signs, others may appear without symptoms. It is a crisis counselor's responsibility to provide support to clients in keeping with ethical and legal guidelines, respecting a client's right to decide whether or not a sexual assault is reported

In addition, sexual offenders who perpetrate sexual assault are often perceived as a highly difficult population to treat. Through education about the motivations of these individuals, crisis counselors may be able to better implement treatment strategies or programs to rehabilitate sexual offenders.

9

Child Sexual Abuse

Carrie Wachter Morris and Elizabeth Graves

PREVIEW

Child sexual abuse is one of the most underreported crimes, with survivors facing a number of potential physical, psychological, cognitive, behavioral, and emotional consequences. Crisis counselors who work with survivors of child sexual abuse need to be aware of the multitude of challenges these individuals face, best practices for treatment, and support services available in the local community. In this chapter, child sexual abuse will be defined, signs and symptoms described, treatment interventions discussed, and guidelines for working with law enforcement and child protective services personnel provided. In addition, the final section of this chapter addresses sexual offenders, their patterns of behavior, and common treatment options.

CHILD SEXUAL ABUSE

Child sexual abuse (CSA) affects children, families, and communities worldwide (Krug, Dahlberg, Mercy, Zwi, & Lozano, 2002). Despite national efforts in the United States through the National Child Abuse and Neglect Data System (NCANDS) and the National Incidence System (NIS), exact statistics regarding the number of children and families affected by CSA are difficult to derive (Berliner & Elliott, 2002; Johnson, 2008). Estimates of annual CSA cases range from 83,810 (U.S. Department of Health & Human Services, 2007) to 180,500 (Sedlak et al., 2010), and even these reports are thought to be underestimates. NCANDS data include only the reports of state Child Protective Services (CPS) workers, while the NIS contains data from CPS agencies and community professionals from nationally representative, randomly sampled counties. The NIS–4, which is thought to be the most comprehensive collection of child abuse and neglect data, does not include incidences of sexual abuse by perpetrators who are not in parental or caregiving roles. Although most of the sexual abuse cases that come to the attention of CPS involve intrafamilial relationships, it should be noted that on average only about one third of CSA cases involve family members, with the remainder involving nonfamily (extrafamilial) individuals known to the child or strangers (U.S. Department of Health & Human Services, 2007). Of the extrafamilial CSA incidences, only 5–15% are perpetrated by strangers (Berliner & Elliott, 2002), meaning that the vast majority of extrafamilial CSA occurs at the hands of individual(s) whom the child or adolescent knows. Thus, many CSA cases would not fall into the definitions used for data collection of these national samples, leading to an underestimate of CSA incidents.

In addition to those victims who do not meet an agency definition, children who fail to come to the attention of these agencies and individuals are not included in estimates. Children and adolescents who have been sexually abused but have not disclosed the abuse, those who have disclosed the abuse but have not had that disclosure come to the attention of CPS, and those who have disclosed the abuse but have not had it substantiated are not included in the official count.

Studies have found that typically only about 33% of females (Ullman, 2003) and 0–15% of males (Collings, 1995) who reported being sexually abused as children disclosed that abuse. Thus, the incidence rates of CSA reported by government agencies are likely to be significantly lower than the true incidence rate. Also, it should be noted that although the average percentage of substantiated child maltreatment cases that involved CSA was only 9.3%, state reports of substantiated cases of CSA ranged from 2.7% to 62.5% of all substantiated child maltreatment cases (U.S. Department of Health and Human Services, 2005). This suggests a wide variability of substantiation among states and perhaps points to an underlying variability in the veracity with which these charges are pursued.

Prevention of Child Sexual Abuse

It is widely recognized by child advocates that the best way to keep these staggering numbers low is for those agencies, institutions, and individuals who serve children and families to focus their efforts and resources on preventing CSA. Schools and some community organizations across the United States have responded to this charge by offering annual group instruction to students in recognizing potentially dangerous adult behaviors, enforcing personal physical and psychological boundaries, getting away from those who violate those boundaries, and reporting odd adult behavior and boundary violations to caring and trusted adults. Although programs such as "Stranger Danger" and "Funny Tummy Feelings" have increased the number of after-the-fact disclosures of sexual abuse, it is unclear as to whether such programs are effective in preventing abuse. Researchers have shown, however, that when children themselves are involved in role playing or participant modeling exercises, behavior changes in children are more likely to occur (Allen, Barrett, Doherty, & Hunt, 1990). Therefore,

VOICES FROM THE FIELD 9.1
Typical Sexual Abuse?

Barbara
One thing I try to remember is that there is no "typical" kid who suffers sexual abuse. Black or white, male or female, skinny or heavy, outgoing or shy, academically gifted or slower learner, younger or older—sexual predators simply seek out children. It is our own biases or misunderstandings that guide us to be sensitive to sexual abuse in one group over another. But it is happening in all of them.

those seeking to prevent sexual abuse in children should use prevention programs that involve children acting out for themselves and demonstrating for other children how to enforce personal boundaries with, get away from, and report such persons.

Prevalence of CSA by Gender, Age, Race, and Ability

Females appear to be the victims of CSA more frequently than males (Putnam, 2003). To date, this trend has been consistent over time, with multiple iterations of the NIS reporting rates and retrospective studies underscoring this gender differential. It should be noted, however, that over 30 years ago researchers predicted that rates of CSA in males would one day match those in females (Finkelhor, 1979), a conjecture that has come closer to realization with each passing decade. In fact, a recent study found that about 40% of college undergraduate females and 31% of males reported a history of CSA (Young, Harford, Kinder, & Savell, 2007). Presently in the United States approximately 1 in 3 females and 1 in 6 males have experienced sexual abuse as children (Hopper, 2010; Loeb et al., 2002). When considering gender of victims, however, it is also important to keep in mind that males are significantly less likely to disclose CSA than are females (Sorsoli, Kia-Keating, & Grossman, 2008), and therefore, the statistics may not yet represent the true differential in rates of victimization.

Reports of average ages of victimization vary, with sources reporting the mean age of onset between 7 and 12 years of age (Berliner & Elliott, 2002; Trickett, 2006), but national statistics indicate higher rates of substantiated abuse at higher ages—e.g., 12–15 years of age (U.S. Department of Health & Human Services, 2005a). Therefore, it appears that individuals may be at risk for CSA across their childhood and adolescent years.

Unlike gender and (potentially) age, race does not appear to be a differentiating characteristic in occurrence of CSA, with consistent rates of CSA victimization in children of all races (U.S. Department of Health and Human Services, 2009). White children, however, had a slightly higher proportion of sexual abuse at the hands of biological parents than did children of other racial backgrounds. This could be due to higher incidence rates, but it could also be linked to factors such as a greater distrust of the systems involved in child protection or a reliance on less formalized support systems to address issues of CSA. Reporting by this group may also be higher.

Finally, children with certain disabilities appear more likely to be sexually victimized than other children. Specifically, children who are at increased risk are those with blindness, deafness, mental retardation, and other disabilities that serve to increase their susceptibility to abuse while decreasing their perceived credibility in the eyes of adults to whom they might disclose (Putnam, 2003; Westcott & Jones, 1999). This appears to be especially true in boys (Sobsey, Randall, & Parrila, 1997).

VOICES FROM THE FIELD 9.2
Advice from the Doctor

I don't think that most people who work with kids really have the awareness that 18% of the boys and 33% of the girls they teach or coach or counsel have been sexually abused. America has been in denial about this for so long. If we aren't aware, then we can't talk with kids about these dangers or help them know what to do if trouble arises. We owe them our raised awareness.

DEFINITION OF CSA AND RELATED TERMS

In addition to the difficulty in tracking children and adolescents who have been sexually abused, there is no agreed-on definition of CSA (Haugaard, 2000). Further complicating the process of defining CSA is how to distinguish it from statutory rape. In the section that follows, CSA and statutory rape are defined, with an explanation of the distinction between statutory rape and CSA and how statutory rape may be handled differently.

Definitions of Child Sexual Abuse

There is no universally accepted definition of child sexual abuse, with definitions varying from state to state and from one research project to the next. Some broader definitions include "any sexual activity or contact with a child where consent is not or cannot [for reasons of age or power differential] be given" (Berliner & Elliott, 2002, p. 55). More narrow definitions used by some states or research groups may include only specific sexual behaviors (e.g., penetration), specific perpetrator groups (e.g., intrafamilial), or specific ages or age differences (e.g., an age difference of four years) and refer to other sexual acts (e.g., showing pornography to a child, exposing one's genitalia to a child) or perpetrator groups (e.g., neighbors, acquaintances, strangers) in categories such as child exploitation, child molestation, or statutory rape. In the Child Abuse Prevention and Treatment Act (CAPTA; Public Law No. 93-247), child abuse and neglect are limited to "a parent or caretaker," and CSA is defined as

> the employment, use, persuasion, inducement, enticement, or coercion of any child to engage in, or assist any other person to engage in, any sexually explicit conduct or simulation of such conduct for the purpose of producing a visual depiction of such conduct; or...the rape, and in cases of caretaker or inter-familial relationships, statutory rape, molestation, prostitution, or other form of sexual exploitation of children, or incest with children. (p. 44)

CAPTA specifies that "child" is specific to all individuals under the age of 18 years for sexual abuse.

Although CAPTA does give a definition of CSA, age of consent differs from state to state, and even within the same state, ages of consent may differ for heterosexual and homosexual relationships and for males and females. It is important for clinicians working with children and adolescents to be aware of the most recent legislation for the state(s) within which they practice regarding CSA, age of consent, mandatory reporting laws regarding sexual behaviors, and relationships involving individuals under the age of consent. For the purposes of this chapter, child sexual abuse is defined as any sexual

---

ACTIVITY 9.1

Internet Activity

Find the legislation for three different states, including the one in which you hope to practice, regarding CSA, statutory rape, and the age of consent for opposite and same-sex relationships for males and for females. Note not just definitional aspects of the law but also who the laws identify as prosecutable perpetrators of CSA, rape, and sexual victimization. Pay particular attention to issues of gender, age discrepancies, and legal guardianship/designated caretakers.

contact, behavior, or exposure for the purposes of sexual gratification of another individual that involves a child who is unable or unwilling to give consent.

Statutory Rape

Complicating the definition of CSA further is the delineation between CSA and statutory rape. Legally, CSA usually includes only those individuals who are in parental or caretaking roles (e.g., babysitter, teacher, coach) with the child or adolescent. Statutory rape, however, refers primarily to a relationship "between a juvenile and an adult that is illegal under the age of consent statutes, but that does not involve the degree of coercion or manipulation sufficient to qualify under criminal statutes as a forcible sex crime" (Hines & Finkelhor, 2007, p. 302). Just as age of consent statutes may vary from state to state, legal definitions and terminology for statutory rape also vary between states (Mitchell & Rogers, 2003).

CYCLE OF CHILD SEXUAL ABUSE

CSA typically develops through a cycle of behavior (Lanning, 2001; Terry & Tallon, 2004). This process begins when a perpetrator identifies a child who may be an easy target, due to some sort of neediness, passivity, or suggestibility. Once a child has been identified, the perpetrator will begin "grooming" the child for sexual abuse by starting with nonsexual contact and behavior and progressing slowly to more sexual activity and behavior, which the perpetrator normalizes. Through a system of reinforcement (e.g., toys, candy, ice cream, attention) and punishment (e.g., anger, threats against the child or the child's loved ones), the child is coerced into entering into and remaining in a sexually exploitive relationship with the perpetrator and keeping the relationship hidden from others.

Another way in which cycles tend to manifest in CSA pertains to intergenerational abuse. Although it may seem that adult men and women who were sexually abused as children should have a lower rate of CSA incidence in their own children due to increased vigilance and heightened awareness of the danger of victimization, the converse appears to be true. As compared with the children of parents who were not subject to CSA in childhood, sexual abuse is sometimes more common in children whose parents have a history of CSA. The reason for these higher rates is not necessarily that they, in turn, abuse their own children. In fact, only one fourth of male victims of CSA and one tenth of female victims experience sexual interest in children as adults; even fewer become CSA perpetrating adults (Romano & DeLuca, 1997). There are several reasons for this heightened risk. First, since interfamilial CSA perpetrators tend to abuse children across several generations of family members, children in such families are often at greater risk (Duncan, 2004). Another reason may be that, having had their own physical and psychological boundaries violated as children, these parents may be less apt to know and teach appropriate boundaries to their own children, or to detect when their children are already caught in the grooming process. Furthermore, because CSA can affect victims' ability to establish and maintain intimate bonds well into adulthood, those who experienced CSA as children sometimes may be less able to develop the parent-child bond than other parents (Main, 1996) and, therefore, may be less able to detect that something is amiss.

SIGNS AND SYMPTOMS OF CHILD SEXUAL ABUSE

Children and adolescents who have experienced CSA may respond and react in a variety of ways, ranging from nonresponse to more severe reactions, including PTSD symptomology (e.g., Miller-Perrin & Perrin, 2007). Given this range of reaction, it is important to view children or adolescents in the context of developmentally appropriate behavior patterns, giving special attention to significant deviations from those norms and from typical developmental behaviors and milestones.

For example, a kindergarten-aged boy who touches his penis in class or a 4-year-old girl who lifts up her dress in a grocery store may be exhibiting developmentally normal behavior. If that kindergarten boy, however, accompanies the touching of his penis with moaning or thrusting behaviors or if the 4-year-old girl lifts up her dress and rubs up against another individual in a seductive manner, those behaviors are not developmentally appropriate and may signify that those children have witnessed sexual behaviors or been the victims of CSA.

Furthermore, researchers have suggested that an effective method of evaluating children's sexual behaviors as normal or concerning is to evaluate the motivation behind the behavior (Chaffin et al., 2008). If the motivation appears to be curiosity and the behavior falls within a developmentally appropriate range, there may be little to fear. However, if the motivation appears to be coercion or compulsion, or if it is accompanied by physical or psychological distress, there may be good cause for alarm (Kellogg, 2010). Table 9.1 provides summaries of cues that may indicate child sexual abuse.

Although most research has indicated that CSA outcomes and symptoms in boys and girls tend to be remarkably similar (e.g., Dube et al., 2005), there is also a fair amount of evidence that suggests otherwise. When gender differences present, it tends not to be in terms of severity or magnitude but rather in the manner in which they manifest. Specifically, boys tend to act out or *externalize* their symptoms, while girls tend to *internalize* their symptoms. This means that boys may be more likely to engage in aggressive, violent, or risky behaviors, while girls may be more likely to present with depression, anxiety, or self-harming behaviors.

Finally, it is important to note that researchers have reported children who were victims of CSA but who were without symptoms at the time of their evaluations (Putnam, 2003). Reasons for these asymptomatic presentations may include narrowness of symptomology being studied, symptoms that have not yet manifested, or children's perceptions that the CSA was not intolerable, was not threatening, or did not exceed their normal functioning. Nevertheless, what researchers in this field call *sleeper effects*—the tendency of symptoms to present over time and across many phases of lifespan development—tend to be the norm for children who are either symptomatic or asymptomatic for CSA. As a result, it is the standard of practice that, regardless of symptom presentation, sexually victimized children receive psychoeducational treatment that helps them to express their feelings, understand their feelings as normal, create a plan to prevent revictimization, and educate their caregivers (Putnam, 2003).

INTERVENTION STRATEGIES FOR VICTIMS OF CSA

When working with victims of CSA, it is important that clinicians know and understand the dynamics of not only their own personal work with the client but also how the counseling process might affect the legal and social services processes and professionals that

TABLE 9.1 Cues That May Indicate Child Sexual Abuse

Symptom Domain	Potential Signs of CSA	
Behavioral cues	Difficulty in walking or sitting	Talk about being damaged
	Frequent vomiting	Attempting to run away
	Sexually explicit drawings/writing	Cruelty to animals (especially those that would normally be pets)
	Sexual interaction with others	
	In-depth sexual play with peers	Fire-setting
	Sexual interactions with animals/toys	Eating disordered behavior
		Self-injurious behavior
	Exceptionally secretive behavior	Use of sexual language inappropriate to developmental level
	Extreme compliance or withdrawal	
	Overt aggression	
	Extremely seductive behavior	Sexual victimization of others
	Sudden nonparticipation in school activities	Masturbation (if masturbation behaviors include masturbating to point of injury; masturbating repetitively or obsessively; being unable to stop masturbating; making groaning or moaning noises while masturbating; thrusting motions while masturbating)
	Crying without provocation	
	Regressive behaviors (e.g., thumb sucking, clinging, separation anxiety)	
	Sudden onset of wetting or soiling	
	Sudden phobic behavior	
	Suicide attempt	
Cognitive cues	Drop in school performance	
	Suicidal ideation	
	More sexual knowledge than is appropriate	
	Fear of males or fear of females	
Physical cues	Complaints of genital or anal itching, pain, or bleeding	
	Blood or discharge on undergarments	
	Frequent psychosomatic illnesses	
	Pregnancy at young age	
	Sexually transmitted infections at young age	
	Older, more sexualized appearance than peers	
	Sleep disturbances, nightmares, night terrors	
Psychological cues	Feelings of low self-worth	
	Depression	
	Anxiety	
	Guilt	
	Shame	
	Hostility	
	Flashbacks	
	Nightmares	

might also be working with the child and family. Crisis counselors must understand how the therapeutic relationship will act in concert with other support services for the child from the initial interview through the reporting and counseling process. Without a thorough understanding, crisis counselors may impede the progress of legal proceedings. In the sections that follow, intervention strategies are discussed, but it is strongly recommended that crisis counselors become familiar with the local legal and social services entities and professionals with whom they will be interacting so as to understand local procedures and laws regarding CSA.

Initial Disclosure and Interviewing for CSA

When working with a child or adolescent who has recently disclosed CSA, it is critical to both the success of treatment and potential prosecution of the perpetrator that counselors respond to the disclosure with informed intention—the intent to do no further psychological harm to the victim with statements that may be perceived as blaming. This includes the verbal and nonverbal responses made directly to survivors as well as the steps taken in the aftermath of the disclosure to respond appropriately. According to Whiffen and MacIntosh (2005), the worst long-term outcomes for clients with histories of CSA are consistently found in those children who met with unsupportive verbal or nonverbal responses following their disclosure of sexual abuse. All too often, common responses to such disclosures tend to be disbelief (e.g., "It is hard to believe that Coach would do such a thing—everyone knows he's so good with kids"), blame ("If it was so awful for you, then why did you go back to that house the next day?" or "Perhaps if you weren't so flirtatious with her, this wouldn't have happened"), shame ("That is disgusting—I can't believe you were involved in all that"), or catastrophizing ("You're damaged goods now —you'll never be the same again"). The result of such responses tends to be that the feelings of guilt, self-blame, and low self-worth initiated during the grooming process and reinforced in the abuse process are further deepened and internalized in the victim. Both short-term and long-term outcomes for those receiving responses like these are poor.

The same is true for nonverbal responses to disclosure. Looks of skepticism, rolling of eyes, or a disapproving shaking of the head communicate disbelief, blame, and disgust. Affirmative responses to a child's disclosure of CSA includes attentive body posture, empathic facial expression, nodding head with belief, and refraining from expressions of alarm or shock. When children receive affirmative responses such as these, they sense that they have done the right thing in reporting the abuse, feel trust that the adult they told will respond appropriately, and have hope that the abuse will cease.

VOICES FROM THE FIELD 9.3
What Not to Ask

I have learned the hard way not to ask a lot of questions when kids disclose to me about their abuse. First of all, it scares kids and doesn't communicate empathy. But secondly, it also can lose the case for the prosecution when the defense team asserts that you are the one who put all this in the children's heads. Now I ask the bare minimum questions and then call the mandated agencies if what I'm hearing is suspect. I let the experts handle all that. My concern is the child's wholeness and wellness, not investigating the validity or details of the story.

Similarly, it is important that the clinicians receiving the disclosure follow appropriate procedural guidelines. Clinicians should not ask leading questions regarding the veracity or nature of the abuse. There are specific protocols that Child Protective Services (CPS) workers and law enforcement officers use when working with children and adolescents who have reported abuse, and members of those agencies should be responsible for the investigation of the alleged abuse. Many communities have child advocacy centers in which trained forensic interviewers work in concert with CPS, law enforcement, medical officials, and counselors to interview the child only once and document the interview.

Therefore, while it may be appropriate to ask some general probing questions, crisis counselors should not suggest or make inferences that CSA has occurred. A question such as "It sounds like this was a difficult weekend for you, and you seem really upset. Is there some way I can help you?" is an appropriate prompt. Conversely, "Did someone sexually abuse you this weekend?" or "Sometimes daddies touch little girls and make them feel uncomfortable. Did that happen to you?" are inappropriate prompts.

As crisis counselors, it is important to be sensitive to the fear, emotional fragility, or flat affect of children and adolescents who are making a disclosure of CSA. Often they may be afraid of making the disclosure because of the potential ramifications of the disclosure. These fears may be the result of a promise of retaliation by the perpetrator for the disclosure (e.g., a threat to harm the child or a family member), a belief that the perpetrator may go to jail, a fear that the victim will be blamed for the perpetrator's removal from the home, and feelings of loyalty, attachment, or love for the perpetrator. In addition, the child may appear to have an inappropriately flat affect or a matter-of-fact attitude. Reasons for such presentations may include their belief that the abuse is normal (e.g., a form of sex education, a ritual to initiate one into manhood/womanhood) or their preferred manner of coping with the abuse (dissociative responses).

It is important when working with a child or adolescent who is disclosing abuse to help the child maintain a sense of control of the information that he or she gives and understand the steps involved in the reporting process. This could include involving the child or adolescent, as appropriate, in making the report to CPS or describing the steps in the process as clearly as possible. It is very important not to make promises that cannot be guaranteed or kept, and crisis counselors may find it helpful to involve appropriate individuals (e.g., CPS social worker, law enforcement officer) in helping lay out when the child can expect to be interviewed, what the potential consequences may be for the perpetrator of the abuse, and what sort of process will be involved if the child is, in fact, removed from the home. Equally important is reiterating, even multiple

VOICES FROM THE FIELD 9.4
The Denial of Boys

In all my years in law enforcement, the number of times boys have disclosed that they are being sexually abused I could count on one hand. Usually they deny it long after we have already found evidence like photos and videotape of the abuse. When told that the evidence is already in hand, they get angry, saying that they aren't gay. I have never understood that. Sexual abuse isn't sex—its abuse. Sexual orientation has nothing to do with it. Still, I think that's why they don't tell—the fear of being called gay.

times, that the child is not at fault, not in trouble, and not to blame in any way. This can help the child maintain some sense of control and stability, even in an unfamiliar circumstance. Case Study 9.1 provides insight into what this process might look like.

CASE STUDY 9.1

Crisis Intake with a Child Sexual Abuse Client: Eliminating Blame

Eight-year-old Marcus has been seeing Justin, his clinical mental health counselor, for the past 3 months. Marcus was referred to Justin by the boy's mother, who expressed concern that her son began wetting his bed about 10 months ago, responding to the slightest criticism with emotions incongruent with the situation at hand, and refusing to play with other children at home or school. While routinely discussing his week at the start of the session, Marcus discloses to Justin that his stepfather "hurt my penis again." Although Justin is stunned, he remains outwardly calm and focuses on simply reflecting Marcus's words as a prompt for the child to continue.

MARCUS:	Yeah. All that happened last week. And then…my stepdad hurt my penis again.
JUSTIN:	Your stepfather sometimes hurts your penis . . .
MARCUS:	Yeah . . . (*Long silence ensues.*)
JUSTIN:	(*Says nothing, but inclines his head downward as if to scoop up Marcus's eyes, which are fixed on the floor.*)
MARCUS:	It really hurts when he does it. But I'm not allowed to talk about it or else he'll hurt me worse. And he said he'd tell mama what I've done to him if I tell anyone.
JUSTIN:	He has told you that, if you tell, bad things will happen to you— that your mama will blame you for it all.
MARCUS:	(*Suddenly raising fear-filled eyes to meet Justin's; he is nodding emphatically.*) She will too. I get blamed for everything bad that happens even when it's not my fault.
JUSTIN:	You're afraid that your mama won't understand—that she'll get mad at you. (*Pause.*) Here's the thing, Marcus. You and I know that it's not your fault. It's your stepdad's fault because he is the adult who is supposed to take good care of you—not hurt you. It's never okay for people to do what he's been doing to you.
MARCUS:	Yeah, but he makes me do stuff. Stuff that makes me feel sick. It's really bad what he makes me do—and I have to do it. I have to do whatever he says. (*He drops his eyes to the floor.*)
JUSTIN:	You're really scared of your stepdad. You do whatever he tells you so he won't hurt you worse. That tells me that you

sure mustered up a lot of courage when you decided to tell me this today—and that was the right thing to do. (*Short silence.*) Although I'm really sad that your stepdad has been hurting you, I also feel really glad that you told me because that tells me that you trust me to do the right things to keep you safe.

MARCUS: (*Nodding, but with some uncertainty in his eyes.*) Does that mean you're going to tell mama? (*His expression conveys a look of both anxiety and hopefulness.*)

JUSTIN: (*Nodding.*) Your mama needs to know this has been happening to you because it is her job to keep you safe. There are also some other people who need to know too—people whose job it is to protect kids when adults do things like hurt little boys' penises and do stuff that's wrong. Sometimes it takes a few important people knowing this stuff for it to stop and stay stopped.

MARCUS: (*Lets out a soft but high-pitched whine and starts to shake and cry.*)

JUSTIN: (*Leaning forward.*) I know it seems pretty scary right now to think about your mom finding out that this has been going on. I also know that, together, we can figure out the best way for her to learn this news today. I'll be right here with you, Marcus.

MARCUS: (*Continues to cry quietly as Justin waits; after a minute or so, he nods and lifts his head.*)

JUSTIN: I wonder if it would help to stand up and take a deep breath so we can think clearly about how best to do this…

Justin and Marcus stand up and do some breathing exercises that Justin often does with his minor clients to help them calm and center themselves. Justin explains that kids have told him things like this in the past and asks Marcus if he'd like to know what typically happens after they do. Marcus indicates he would like to know. Justin explains that he has a friend named Joan in the CPS (and/or law enforcement office) that he tells these things to, that she takes kids' stories like this very seriously, and that she sometimes helps moms understand that it's never the kid's fault.

Justin explains that both Marcus's mom and Justin's friend Joan need to hear his story and asks how he would like for them to find out (who should tell the story, who should find out first). Marcus decides that he wants Justin to tell his mom for him, but that he wants to be in the room while he does. He says he doesn't care who talks to Joan or when she is told. Because Justin is not sure about how Marcus's mother will react, Justin decides to tell Marcus that he thinks it is a good idea to tell Joan first because she might be able to come over either now or sometime soon and help. Justin calls the designated law enforcement officer with whom he has a relationship of trust while Marcus is in the room, telling her that there is a little boy with him right now who has told him something that worries him and that she needs to hear. The officer is available and agrees to come to Justin's office.

Justin explains that he needs to speak to Marcus's mother now. The counselor reinforces that the child has done the right thing by telling Justin and that his job as Marcus's counselor is to make sure that Marcus's mother understands it is not her son's fault. Justin goes to the lobby to meet the mother. Together, Justin and Marcus tell the mother that Marcus's stepdad has been "hurting his penis." When her look of shock turns to anger and she demands to know details, Justin intervenes to help the mother understand that Marcus is very afraid that she will be mad at him and that part of why he hasn't told this in the past is that he is afraid of being blamed for this—that the step-dad has told Marcus that all this is the boy's fault. Justin tells the mother that, in accordance with a state mandate, he has called the local law enforcement authorities and that they will be on their way soon to come to the office to help Marcus and his mother get through the next few days.

It should be noted that Justin took pains to do several things correctly. First, when the boy was disclosing the abuse to him, he merely reflected the boy's own words, careful not to sabotage a potential prosecution by requiring the boy to tell his story in detail. In this case, the counselor gathered only enough information as was absolutely necessary to substantiate his own reasonable suspicions that the boy might have been sexually abused and then made the mandated report to the proper agency. He did not ask questions or pump the child for details about when, where, how often, etc., the abuse had occurred. Rather, he focused on the feelings the boy was having, validated those feelings, reinforced the boy's decision to disclose the abuse, supported him by letting him know that it was not his fault, and reassured him that he would help him through the process of telling and reporting.

Second, Justin did not use the word *abuse*. Knowing that this is a term that boys can sometimes find emasculating and disempowering, Justin chose only to use the boys own words in very concrete (rather than euphemistic) terms such as "he hurt your penis."

Third, Justin remained calm and matter of fact, while communicating empathy with his tone and body language. The message this manner conveyed to the child was that adults can handle these things calmly without the response of blame or anger, which can be scary for children; that they care; and that they should be told in order to keep children safe.

Finally, Justin gave Marcus as many choices as he could. Some of those choices were who to tell first, who should do the telling, and where the telling should happen. This facilitated the child's sense of empowerment, restored to the child confidence in his choices and, by proxy, reinforced his sense of self-worth.

In the weeks immediately following, Justin maintained consistent contact with Marcus's mom, the assigned CPS caseworker, law enforcement, and local children's advocacy center. Although agreed to see Marcus twice a week, the boy was very reluctant to talk about his abuse. Justin therefore decided that play therapy might be the best course of treatment. They undertook about 20 sessions of child-centered play therapy before Marcus's original presenting symptoms, and his later anxiety, depression, and anger dissipated.

It should be noted that each case of child abuse differs and while some counselors may not want to scare a child by introducing what could be perceived as scary questions, others may be able to gather crucial information that is often requested by CPS when filing a report. Depending on the unique situation and disposition of the child and the experience of the counselor, more information could be obtained (perpetrator name, place where alleged incident occurred, when the abuse took place, type of alleged abuse, knowledge of other children in the house) to provide CPS reviewers more information that may be needed for their processing and decision making on the case. Similarly, it is important for crisis counselors to weigh the safety of the child in determining if family members should be contacted about the abuse.

Discussion Questions

1. What questions do you need to collect for CPS?
2. How can you determine the safety of other family members?

Reporting CSA

In the United States, every state has mandated reporting of CSA. Mandated reporters may differ by state and typically include mental health professionals, educational personnel, law enforcement officers, and medical personnel (U.S. Department of Health & Human Services, 2009). Despite the legal responsibility to report child abuse and neglect, there are times when professionals choose not to report such information. This, however, can put the professional in conflict with legal and ethical guidelines such as CAPTA (American Counseling Association, 2005) that require disclosure of suspicion of CSA. It is important for individuals serving children and adolescents to be knowledgeable of a counselor's legal and ethical responsibilities regarding CSA. This includes knowing not only the laws governing the reporting of CSA and the statutes of limitations for their particular state(s) but also the policies of the agency, organization, or school in which they practice (Table 9.2).

TABLE 9.2 Policies to Know Regarding Child Sexual Abuse

- Whom do you notify?
- What specific information do you need to know in order to report?
- What other agency/school personnel should be involved?
- Who makes the report to CPS? How?
- Is there a time frame for making a verbal report followed by a written report?
- Who is responsible for monitoring or receiving feedback from CPS once the report is filed?
- What information should be included in the report? (This is dictated by state law and CPS policy.)
- What does the protocol indicate regarding confidentiality?
- Is the written report kept in a separate location from the client's normal file or cumulative folder?
- What follow-up is expected on reported cases?
- What role will you play in possible community or child protection teams?

ACTIVITY 9.2
Interviewing Activity

Contact a member of Child Protective Services or a member of local law enforcement with experience in working with children and adolescents who have been sexually abused. Interview that individual about the process of making reports, including agency procedures when CSA has been reported, the process involved in interviewing and investigating CSA, and the timeline during which major events occur (e.g., initial interview of child, interview of family and/or alleged perpetrator, filing of legal charges, removal from home).

The mandate for reporting suspicion of CSA can make it difficult to determine when steps should be taken, especially in cases where a child has not disclosed abuse but rather has exhibited some behaviors that seem to demonstrate a potential history of sexual abuse. For clinicians working with children and adolescents, one way to help provide some clarification is to develop professional relationships with contacts within the local CPS agency and local law enforcement, preferably prior to having a client who may be a victim of CSA. This can help the clinician understand the process of local agencies as well as provide an individual or individuals with whom that clinician can discuss hypothetical cases and appropriate action(s) or reporting procedures. This can be especially helpful in cases where the line between CSA (and thus mandated reporting) and statutory rape (for which reporting is not typically mandated) is blurred.

CPS traditionally works with CSA cases involving parents or caregivers, especially those in the home. While CPS may be involved in other CSA cases, CPS's primary focus will typically be on parent/caregiver cases. Law enforcement agencies will typically handle extrafamilial cases or those that involve individuals who are not in a caretaking role. Important information to include in a CSA report is presented in Table 9.3. When making an initial CSA report to CPS, it is important for the mental health professional to

---

TABLE 9.3 Information to Include in an Initial Report of Child Sexual Abuse

- Child's name
- Age
- Sex
- Address
- Parent's name and address
- Nature and extent of the condition observed
- Actions taken by the reporter (e.g., talking with the child)
- Where the act occurred
- Issues of potential risk for the child (e.g., Is the perpetrator in the home? Is there a threat of physical abuse for the child disclosing information? Might the child be kicked out of the home for reporting?)
- Are there other children who might be at risk from the alleged perpetrator?
- Reporter's name, location, and contact information

VOICES FROM THE FIELD 9.5
The Resilience of Youth

Rather than catastrophizing about a child's abuse after it is discovered, I think we need instead to be intentional about approaching the child in therapy from the assumption that kids are capable of remarkable resilience. Because it is our responsibility and privilege to help them get there, we have no business doubting that they can get there. They need our hope, our expectations of healing.

document that the report was made, including to whom the report was made (both the agency and the name of the individual taking the report).

CPS reports may be filed anonymously. Even if an anonymous report is made, however, counselors are mandated reporters and should document their reports. The documentation should include the report made, the date and time the report was made, and the name of the individual to whom the report was made. It should be cautioned that by reporting anonymously, the only record of obligated reporting is from your notes, not from CPS since they will not have your identity.

Reporting Past Incidents of CSA

When working with adults who disclose past child sexual abuse, there are multiple factors that need to be taken into consideration. Crisis counselors need to consider adult clients in their own context, regarding desired treatment outcomes (e.g., is the client presenting with sexual dysfunction, relationship issues, difficulty in regulating mood, PTSD), client abuse history (e.g., Who was the perpetrator? When did the abuse take place? What was the duration of the abuse?), as well as factors that might necessitate involving law enforcement or CPS (e.g., Is the abuser still alive? If so, does the abuser have access to children or adolescents who might also be victimized?). Another factor to consider in treatment planning is whether or not clients have previously disclosed their abuse, and, if so, what the outcomes were of the disclosures. Is there documentation to substantiate a report being made? Crisis counselors should empower and respect the autonomy of the adult CSA survivor while also taking necessary steps to protect any children or adolescents who might be at risk as outlined by the laws of their practicing state. Because reporting past child sexual abuse differs according to the laws in each state, counselors and adult survivors should consult their state laws regarding reporting past abuse.

Treatment of Survivors of CSA

There are a number of difficulties in identifying evidence-based practices for effectively treating survivors of CSA, based in part on the range of symptomology presented; the challenges that children have verbalizing their current mental, emotional, and physical states; and the reliance on parent and teacher reports, which may differ substantially both from each other and from the experience of the child (Saywitz, Mannarino, Berliner, & Cohen, 2000). Although children and adolescents who have survived sexual abuse are usually served through a combination of individual and group counseling (Swenson & Chaffin, 2006), the type of counseling offered can vary widely.

At the present time, the standard of practice in serving this population leans heavily in the direction of cognitive-behavioral therapy (CBT). Because CBT approaches are the primary evidence-based practice for treating children and adolescents with posttraumatic symptomology (Chaffin & Friedrich, 2004), such therapies may be most beneficial to children and adolescents who are struggling with posttraumatic stress or depression after being sexually abused. The most popular of these, trauma-focused CBT (Cohen, Mannarino, & Deblinger, 2006) employs strategies that combine psychoeducation, anxiety management, prolonged exposure, cognitive restructuring techniques, and family-based interventions. In fact, many mental health agencies across the United States which serve children now have clinicians who have a significant amount of training in trauma-focused CBT.

One potential caveat for mental health personnel employing abuse-specific CBT or any type of treatment using exposure therapy is that the process of exposure and systematic desensitization or cognitive restructuring around sexual abuse needs to be done carefully in order to reduce any potential distortion in the child's story that could affect court testimony or a CPS investigation (Saywitz et al., 2000). Crisis counselors should consult with CPS workers and law enforcement officers and avail themselves of training opportunities and continuing education for working with CSA survivors.

Another potential caveat for the use of CBT in counseling is that several researchers conducting meta-analyses found CBT to be no more effective than any other treatment modality (e.g., Nurcombe, Wooding, Marrington, Bickman, & Roberts, 2000). In response to this, one group of researchers has suggested that the type of therapy employed should depend upon the developmental level and the presenting complaints displayed by the child (Hetzel-Riggin, Brausch, & Montgomery, 2007). For example, since CBT appears to be most successful with children who present with behavior problems, group counseling with those children with low self-concept or depression, and play therapies with those children with deficits in social functioning, the therapy modality should be tailored to the specific needs and characteristic of the child.

Another popular and effective approach in treating children with histories of CSA is play therapy (e.g., Aarons, 2004; Green, 2008; Johnston, 1997). Although it may lack the plethora of efficacy studies that trauma-focused CBT enjoys at the present time, many counselors who have extensive experience in working with children prefer play therapy (including the authors of this chapter). Particularly with young children who may not yet have the necessary cognitive and verbal skills to get the most benefit from trauma-focused CBT, play therapies and expressive arts therapies may be particularly indicated. In choosing a particular approach to play therapy (e.g., Jungian, Child-Centered, Adlerian, Theraplay), both the needs of the child and family context should be carefully considered.

CASE STUDY 9.2

Denial in Child Sexual Abuse Victims

Erica is a shy, bright four-year-old who has been referred for counseling by the local children's advocacy center following the investigation and prosecution of her former preschool teacher for sexual abuse. Several of Erica's classmates disclosed their abuse, but despite the presence of several typical behavioral and physical indicators, Erica has denied any abuse. The nurse practitioner trained in forensic investigation who examined Erica confirmed that she had been sexually abused. Although her parents made the decision not to participate in the prosecution proceedings brought by her classmates' parents, the teacher eventually was found guilty and sent to prison.

Tamika is the counselor to whom Erica has been referred. Her parents' primary concern is that the little girl has been having night terrors that are alleviated only by sleeping with them in their fully lighted bedroom. No one is getting any sleep. Tamika is trained in both trauma-focused CBT and Jungian play therapy. Although she has used both approaches with young, sexually abused children, she decides that play therapy may be the more efficacious approach in working with Erica given her commitment to denial (and/or her possible dissociation) of the abuse event.

At their first session, Erica takes her time touring the play room and choosing a book to read with Tamika. As soon as the story is over, Erica walks to the art supplies station and settles down to draw, gathering her crayons and paper from the bins. She proceeds to color for the next 35 minutes on one drawing without any verbal interaction with Tamika. Tamika sits at the table with Erica observing the child's intensity and absorption in her task, but refrains from interrupting Erica's process with observations or interjections of her own. At the end of the session, Erica takes her drawing to Tamika and pronounces that Tamika should keep it for her, but that it is Erica's and should not be looked at until she finishes drawing it. Over the course of several months, Erica continues to draw during her sessions with notable focus for a child her age. Tamika is eventually given permission to look at Erica's *spontaneous drawings,* and eventually they settle into a routine where they talk about the drawings before Erica leaves the session.

Over time, Tamika notices that certain features exist in every drawing as do certain colors. As a Jungian play therapist, she is sensitive to compensatory and excitatory symbols that often present in the art of abused children. She understands that these symbols often hold the metaphorical key to the child's healing process by pointing to the area of the unconscious mind that is most avoided as well as to that region that holds the key to activating their self-healing process. Using a phenomenological approach, Tamika explores the child's inner meaning-making and language around the symbols by asking Erica to externalize the explanatory inner dialogue she has created around them or attributed to them.

One *compensatory symbol* which appears to be consistent in Erica's art is the bright yellow sun that fills any outdoor sky or indoor windows that she has drawn with radiant light. When asked about the yellow, Erica tells Tamika that the sun is always warm and makes you feel safe and happy—that bad things don't happen when the sun is looking.

Also notable in each drawing is a consistent *excitatory symbol*. Without fail, a small, very dark area about the size of a dime is located in the lower central region of the page she is drawing. Sometimes it is full of black color and sometimes it appears that some object has been drawn inside the dark spot. Usually, however, Erica tries to color over the black spot with a white crayon, a process that leaves gray smudges around the dark spot. These smudges seem to cause the child more distress at some times than others. When asked about the black spot, she sometimes wordlessly shrugs, emits a guttural sort of giggle that lacks humor or joy, or ignores Tamika's question altogether.

During one session, however, Erica begins to cover the paper with yellow from top to bottom. When reaching the lower central portion, however, she stops. Putting her yellow crayon down, she searches the crayon bin carefully for a particular crayon. Evidently not finding what she is looking for, she rests her elbows on the table and puts her face in her hands. "It feels yucky. Don't like it there. But…Maybe Teacher gets out, goes out of here, don't goes here again, and she can't stay so sun stays warm. It hurts her when I not come, but I not come. Sun is nice. Can I tell mommy sun is nice? I not come to Teacher anymore?" Inviting Erica's mother into the room, Tamika explains that Erica has a message for her. The child climbs onto her mother's lap and explains to her rapt mother the same thing she has told Tamika. Although the language the child uses is difficult to understand, her meaning is not. Her eyes are wide with emphasis and her tone sounds hopeful and bright.

At their next session, Erica's mother informs Tamika that the child is sleeping through the night again. She has stopped climbing in bed with her parents in the middle of the night. The nightmares that once left her terrorized have all but vanished. Tamika continues to see Erica for another two sessions before suggesting to the parents that termination seems indicated. The parents, however, emphatically express their unease about termination because of how much more at peace their daughter appears when seeing Tamika. In response, Tamika decides that the best course of action may be to teach Erica's parents filial play therapy so that they can continue to stay engaged with their daughter in therapeutic ways, seeing gains in Erica's recovery across time and within the context of their strong family bonds. Upon completion of this goal, Tamika terminates counseling with Erica and her family.

In addition to these strategies, the inclusion of the nonoffending parents in the treatment of children who have experienced sexual abuse has been related to a reduction in children's acting out or other problematic behaviors (Deblinger, Lippman, & Steer, 1996) and an increase in parent support (Berliner & Elliott, 2002). Abuse-specific CBT strategies tailored to parent needs are particularly effective in reducing problem behaviors (Cohen & Mannarino, 1997) and internalizing symptoms (Cohen & Mannarino, 1998). At this point, there is little experimental research on other therapeutic approaches besides CBT for the inclusion of nonoffending parents (Berliner & Elliott, 2002). It is important, therefore, that crisis counselors continue to follow the professional literature on counseling strategies for CSA survivors and their families. The benefit of including nonoffending fathers is at this time inconclusive, due in part to a lack of research on this population (Swenson & Chaffin, 2006).

Coping Strategy Considerations and Their Impact Upon Treatment Planning

One particularly critical issue in the treatment and recovery of children with CSA is the method of coping that the child assumes in the wake of their abuse. It has long been the case that the worst outcomes are seen in those children and adolescents who choose avoidant, as opposed to approach, coping strategies (Fortier et al., 2009). *Avoidant coping* can be characterized by verbal or psychic denial of the abuse, withdrawal from one's social network, dissociation, or dissociative forgetting of the abuse. Conversely, *approach* coping can be characterized by reaching out to others for support, disclosing the abuse, or discussing the abuse with friends, family, and/or counselors.

Although this is likely to make intuitive sense to helping professionals such as crisis counselors, researchers have consistently found that that this is not always the case (Chaffin, Wherry, & Dykman, 1997; Oaksford & Frude, 2003). In fact, the use of avoidant coping in the immediate wake of traumatic CSA, followed thereafter by the use of approach coping strategies, appears to produce the best outcomes for those traumatized by their abuse. Bessel van der Kolk, a scholar in the field of traumatic dissociation, hypothesized that the psychic stress resulting from various traumas may exceed a child's ability to cope. This causes the child's psyche to dissociate the abuse in order to survive intact (van der Kolk, 1994; van der Kolk & van der Hart, 1989). Therefore, if children have been traumatized by their abuse, clinicians should allow for a period of stabilization of the child's life, safety, and routines before attempting to facilitate treatment that directly addresses the abuse. Many scientist-practitioners who specialize in trauma treatment have addressed this dynamic by allowing for a period of safety-building and life-stabilization in treatment plans for traumatized clients (e.g., Rothschild, 2000, 2010).

CASE STUDY 9.3

The Role of a School Counselor in the Disclosure of Sexual Abuse

Eleven-year-old Alicia arrives in her school counselor's office one day in tears. She is accompanied by a friend who holds her hand and speaks for her. The friend explains to Cherise, the school counselor, that something really bad is happening to Alicia and that it's got to stop because Alicia can't take it anymore. Because Cherise knows Alicia well from years of working with all her students in classroom guidance and small groups, she asks Alicia if she feels okay to talk about it with her alone. After the friend leaves, Alicia discloses that her grandfather has been sexually abusing her for at least the past year.

After making the proper reports to the authorities and helping Alicia tell her parents about the abuse, Cherise makes a referral for community mental health services. Several months go by with Cherise checking on Alicia and checking in with Alicia's teachers and family. All seems to be going well. One day, however, Alicia's mother, Georgia, calls Cherise in tears, begging her to see Alicia for counseling at school. Alicia's mother informs the school counselor of the long list of mental health counselors that she and her husband have taken their daughter to see (indeed, every counselor on the list that Cherise provided the family) and explains that Alicia has flatly refused to speak about her abuse to anyone she doesn't know. She has told her mother that Cherise is the only counselor she trusts.

Cherise agrees to invite Alicia to see her for six half-hour sessions over the next several weeks until Georgia can find a suitable counselor with whom Alicia will work. Although Cherise prepares to talk with Alicia about peripheral issues secondary to the abuse that directly pertain to her school life, Alicia arrives after lunch one day for her session, plops down on Cherise's office easy chair, and declares that she wants to write her story so she can finally get it out of her head and stop thinking about it and feeling sick to her stomach all the time. Cherise affirms Alicia's determination and courage to work on this goal, but she also expresses her concern that discussing these sensitive events at school might bring into the school some bad feelings that might get in the way of Alicia's ability to focus on her schoolwork and be her usual self around her friends. Alicia dismisses this and reaches for a stack of copy paper, folds it in half, creases the paper, punches two staples into the crease and starts decorating the front cover of her book.

Over the course of the next 6 weeks, Alicia and Cherise work together to get Alicia's story down on paper. In keeping with tenets of some narrative therapies, Cherise suggests that they write the ending to the story first. Following some discussion, Alicia decides that she wants her story to end when she is 25 years old and has a family of her own, that her story has a happy ending, and that her dad (whose own father would eventually serve a modest jail sentence for taking indecent liberties with a minor) would one day love and accept her again and be able to look her in the eye with pride. At the end of their sessions together, Cherise agrees to invite Alicia's parents to school so that their daughter can read her story to them. The family enjoys listening to Alicia's story, crying healing tears, and affirming their love for and pride in their daughter. Alicia's parents then get permission for their daughter to leave school to have a celebratory lunch together. Alicia did eventually see a counselor the following year after moving on to middle school, but her school performance never suffered the drop that her parents expected and doctors predicted. Throughout her secondary school years her academics continued to be a place where Alicia felt strong, supported, known, and accepted.

PERPETRATORS OF SEXUAL ASSAULT AND CHILD SEXUAL ABUSE

When discussing sexual assault and child sexual abuse, it is important to consider not only the survivors but also the perpetrators. In the sections that follow, the prevalence, characteristics, and treatment options regarding perpetrators of sexual assault and child sexual abuse are described.

The Prevalence and Characteristics of Child Sexual Abuse Perpetrators

Perpetrators of CSA are both male and female, and they commit sex crimes against children for a variety of reasons. Some of these may be parallel to the reasons of sexual assault perpetrators, but some are distinctly different. In the following section, male and female perpetrators of CSA are described, with a focus on the motivation that may drive behavior that is sexually abusive toward children or adolescents.

MALE PERPETRATORS OF CHILD SEXUAL ABUSE   Like sexual assault perpetrators, individuals who sexually abuse children are predominantly male. Indeed, males are the perpetrators in 75–96% of reported child victimization cases (McCloskey & Raphael, 2005; U. S. Department of Health & Human Services, 2005a). Unlike sexual assault perpetrators, individuals who sexually abuse children fall along a continuum of motivation for committing the sexual abuse, ranging from situational to preferential (Lanning, 2001). Situational perpetrators commit sexual abuse because they are driven by basic sexual *and* nonsexual (e.g., power, anger) needs. In the case of situational offenders, the preferred sexual partner is not typically a child; rather, the child is available when the individual perceives that he has a sexual or power-related need that must be met. Thus, the child serves as a sexual substitute and may be part of a larger pattern of abusive behavior. In contrast, preferential perpetrators are compulsive and driven by fantasies about their victims; they may participate in behaviors that groom their potential targets. Preferential perpetrators are more likely than situational perpetrators to sexually abuse children or adolescents. In his behavioral analysis of child molesters, Lanning (2001) describes this continuum as well as subcategories of situational and preferential perpetrators. These motivations and subtypes are meant not to provide clinical treatment or diagnosis but rather to help law enforcement officials recognize, identify, and gather relevant evidence about individuals who sexually abuse children.

Lanning (2001) identified three patterns of situational perpetrators of sexual abuse: (1) regressed, (2) morally indiscriminate, and (3) inadequate. A situational offender who follows a regressed pattern is driven by a precipitating stressor and may find a readily available child to serve as a sexual substitute for a preferred adult partner. A situational offender who fits a morally indiscriminate pattern abuses all or many types of individuals, so the sexual abuse of a child is less a specific preference for children than the result of a sociopathic level of indiscriminate abuse of people regardless of their age or background. Finally, the inadequate pattern of situational perpetrators is typically followed by an individual perceived as nonmainstream, perhaps with preexisting mental or emotional problems, who may sexually abuse a child out of insecurity or curiosity about sexual behavior.

Those individuals who fall toward the preferential side of the motivation continuum tend to sexually abuse children or adolescents either because children and/or adolescents are their preferred sexual partners or because children and/or adolescents are less threatening individuals with whom they can participate in sexual behaviors that are more bizarre or more shameful to the perpetrator (Lanning, 2001). Not all preferential perpetrators, therefore, are pedophiles; many, however, have a paraphilia, which is defined in the DSM-5 as a strong sexual preference for nonhuman objects, nonconsenting individuals, or the suffering and/or humiliation of themselves or their partners (American Psychiatric Association, 2013). Not all individuals who have a paraphilia (including pedophilia) commit child sexual abuse; therefore, it is important that clinicians not assume that all, most, or even many individuals who have a paraphilia will sexually abuse children.

In addition to identifying three patterns of situational perpetrators, Lanning (2001) identified four patterns of preferential perpetrators: (1) seduction, (2) introverted, (3) diverse, and (4) sadistic. Sexual abuse perpetrators who fit the seduction pattern of preferential motivation form the largest group of acquaintance child molesters and are characterized by an ability to identify with children and groom potential victims. When grooming children, the perpetrator will adorn them with gifts and positive attention, making them feel loved and understood to the point where they may willingly participate in sexual acts. Unlike individuals who fit the seduction pattern, perpetrators who fit the introverted pattern lack the verbal and social skills to seduce children and may resort to the traditionally stereotypical behaviors of lurking around playgrounds or abducting children with whom there is no prior relationship. This pattern parallels the inadequate pattern of situational offenders, but with a specific preference for children. Individuals who fit the diverse pattern of preferential motivation are interested in sexual experimentation, and they choose a child target because of the novelty or taboo, or because the child is a more vulnerable partner with whom sexual experimentation can take place. Finally, individuals who fit the sadistic pattern of preferential motivation are a small percentage of perpetrators, but they are the most likely to abduct or kill their victims. The sadistic perpetrator is aroused by the infliction of pain, humiliation, and suffering in his victims.

FEMALE PERPETRATORS OF CHILD SEXUAL ABUSE   Female perpetrators of sexual abuse appear to be fewer in number than their male counterparts, but there are several factors that must be considered when working with female perpetrators of CSA. First, females are still socially accepted as the primary caregivers in society; therefore, they can bathe and touch children without arousing the same type of suspicion as a male who performs comparable activities (Miller-Perrin & Perrin, 2007). Second, there is more of a social media acceptance of older females seducing younger males (e.g., the *American Pie* series of movies, the songs "Stacy's Mom" and "That Summer") than there is of similar relationships between older males and adolescent females (e.g., *Lolita*). Law enforcement officers, criminal justice personnel, and mental health providers must be aware of their own biases and stereotypes about the demographic characteristics of sex offenders so as to understand the severity of abuse for the victim and to properly treat the female perpetrator.

Due to the relatively smaller numbers of female perpetrators, the literature on female perpetrators is still sparse compared to that on their male counterparts. In groundbreaking research, Mathews, Matthews, and Speltz (1989) clustered female offenders into three subtypes: (1) male-coerced, (2) predisposed, and (3) teacher/lover. Male-coerced females tend to abuse children in concert with a dominant male partner, and they may grant access to children out of a fear of abandonment by a dominant male partner. Predisposed female abusers typically act alone in victimizing their own children or other easily accessible young children. They are typically survivors of incestuous relationships with continued psychological problems and deviant or paraphilic sexual fantasies. Teacher/lover female perpetrators have a more regressed pattern of behavior, have strained peer relationships, and perceive themselves as being in romantic relationships or as sexually mentoring their victims, therefore resisting the idea that their actions might be criminal in nature.

Since then, Vandiver and Kercher (2004) and Sandover and Freeman (2007) analyzed larger samples of female sex offenders in Texas and New York, respectively. Both studies reported finding six clusters of female offenders, differing on characteristics that included offender age, victim age, victim gender, total number of arrests, any drug arrest, any incarceration term, and whether the offender was rearrested after the arrest for a sexual offense. Although the two studies had some differences in identified clusters, in both, the average female sex offender was a Caucasian in her early 30s, and the average victim age was just under 12 years old (Sandover & Freeman, 2007). In the Sandover and Freeman study, all six clusters targeted victims under 18 years old. It is important to note, however, that these clusters are inclusive only of women who had been arrested for sex offences and labeled as sex offenders, and thus may not be inclusive of female perpetrators of child sexual abuse who have not been arrested or identified. The six categories identified by Sandover and Freeman (2007) are criminally limited hebephiles, criminally prone hebephiles, young adult child molesters, high-risk chronic offenders, older nonhabitual offenders, and homosexual child molesters.

Treatment of Sex Offenders

Because there is no evidence-based guidance about the most effective approaches to working with female sexual offenders (Center for Sex Offender Management, 2007), the primary focus of this treatment section will be on male offenders, with "sex offender" referring to males unless specifically stated otherwise. When considering treatment for sex offenders, crisis counselors should consider three aspects: (1) client dynamics, (2) treatment setting, and (3) treatment modality (Groth, 2001).

First, client dynamics must be assessed through a comprehensive psychological evaluation that includes demographics, family background, medical history, education level, military history, interpersonal development (e.g., social, sexual, and marital information), occupational history, and criminal history. In addition, assessments should include behavioral observations, field investigations, medical examination, and psychometric examinations. The clinical assessment must include information about the perpetrator's sexual behavior. This information should include premeditation, victim selection, style of attack, accompanying fantasies, role of aggression, sexual behavior (contact, duration, dysfunction), mood state, contributing factors (stressors), acceptance of responsibility, and recidivism and deterrence.

Second, appropriate treatment settings should be considered (Groth, 2001). Most offenders enter the mental health system through either the criminal justice or the health care system. The perpetrator may have been hospitalized for a mental illness or referred by the courts for treatment. Treatment facilities may typically specialize in the treatment of sex offenders and offer either inpatient or outpatient treatment. Group counseling may be the primary method of delivery of services in order to provide confrontation to a client population that may be prone to denial.

Third, there are specific treatment modalities that may be effective when treating sex offenders. However, it is important to recognize that no single treatment modality has been found to be the most effective treatment for sex offenders (Groth, 2001). Crisis counselors should consider court requirements and the specific needs of each client to determine a course of treatment, and they may choose to combine treatments in order to find a successful plan of action. The available treatment modalities include chemotherapy, psychotherapy, psychoeducation, behavior modification, and incapacitation, which were discussed in Chapter 8, as well as family systems counseling, which is described in the section that follows.

FAMILY SYSTEMS COUNSELING   In the case of incestuous CSA, a family systems approach to treatment may be taken (e.g., the Child Sexual Abuse Treatment Program; see Hewitt, 1998). This systems-oriented counseling may involve individual counseling for the child, the nonoffending parent(s), and the perpetrator; marital therapy; counseling with the nonoffending parent(s) and child; counseling with the offender and the child; group counseling; and family therapy with the purpose of retaining or reunifying the family (Miller-Perrin & Perrin, 2007). It should be noted that family counseling with the offender and the child would need to be undertaken with great care and is not common practice.

FEMALE OFFENDERS   Virtually no current evidence-based guidance regarding treatment of female sex offenders of CSA exists in the literature. Most modes of treatment for male offenders have been applied to female offenders, taking into account the unique

VOICES FROM THE FIELD 9.6
The Troubled Family

Sherdene Simpson

As I entered the lobby of my office building, I heard the sounds of the phone ringing and noticed an array of people sitting around talking. Even though the environment appeared normal, I noticed that there was a man and woman sitting stoically in the corner of the waiting room. I noticed that the woman had two little girls sitting next to her. Two boys stood near the man; both stood motionless. As I walked by, I offered an enthusiastic, "Good morning." The parents looked up with tears in their eyes and said "hello." The children in an almost rehearsed manner waved and looked away. I entered my office and stood still for a moment. Something about my interaction with them had felt uncomfortable. The phone rang; it was a call from the office manager calling to say that there was a family in the lobby who needed to be seen immediately. She shared that the man expressed that they were not leaving until they met with me. I told her that I would see them, and instructed her to give them the intake paperwork. At first, I did not find the situation to be that unusual. I work on a church staff, so it is not uncommon for parishioners to stop into our Counseling Center and request to see me without a scheduled appointment.

After they completed the paperwork, I invited the family into my office. The parents stood up to come with me, and all four children remained positioned on the sofa like minifigurines. I looked back several times as the parents and I left the waiting area, but the children remained motionless. I was taken aback because even the youngest child, who appeared to be about 3 years old, sat perfectly still.

I intended to facilitate my usual routine of conducting a thorough clinical assessment, but the father dominated the next few minutes by explaining that he wanted help for his family but was afraid to share with me. The mother said that she did not want anyone "to go to jail." The father interrupted his wife, saying that he was angry and did not know what to do. I immediately felt that they had experienced a tragedy. My thoughts starting running as I considered the word "jail" and all that word could imply.

I quickly stopped them both from sharing and reviewed in great detail my informed consent procedures and the limits to confidentiality. When I stopped talking, I felt that they stopped breathing. The room felt thick with silence and I could hear every movement in the hallway. It felt like we sat in silence for days. In a harsh voice, the man uttered, "I thought we were safe coming to our church." As I began to talk, a scream came from the chair across from me that changed the entire climate of the room. The woman, gripping her chair, yelled, "I'm not leaving here. We're getting help or else." The husband sat back with streams of tears falling from his eyes. He began to share their story.

He explained that his 10-year-old daughter was being sexually abused by her brother, aged 12. As he spoke, his voice faded in and out. He shared his confusion, frustration, and feelings of failure. He continued to report the anger and disdain that he felt toward his son. The wife chimed in and expressed her feelings of grief and numbness. Sadly, in graduate school, no one had taught me what to do when emotionally charged crisis situations like this emerge. As a grief recovery specialist, I knew that this family needed a heart with ears. So, I listened, and I listened, and I listened.

I invited the 10-year-girl into my office and heard the stories of sexual abuse that she had endured over the past 2 years. She was very candid in her emotions and shared the anger and disappointment she felt for her brother. She also said that she forgave him for his "sinful" behavior and was hopeful that God would heal her heart. The resilience that this child possessed left me in awe. After she left the room, I continued to hear her small voice saying, "I know that God will heal my heart."

Afterward, I invited the 12-year-old brother into my office; he appeared overwhelmed with fear and nervousness. I told him quickly that I was a counselor, not a police officer. He settled in and shared with me stories of his journey through pornography and masturbation and ultimately described the sexual urges that led him to abuse his sister. He appeared remorseful and said that he never meant to hurt his sister and that he is hopeful that she will forgive his behavior. He said in an almost adult manner, "I need to be healed from my sexual desires."

Nothing could have prepared me for the stories that I was exposed to by this family. The graphic depiction of the sexual abuse and the emotional devastation of this family will ring in my memories for years to come. What do you do when the victim and the perpetrator are siblings? How do you manage having such a close connection to all of the players involved in a situation such as this?

The emotionally drained father looked at me and asked, "Will my family ever be healed?" This was the first time in years of practicing as a counselor that I was utterly speechless. Because we were in a church setting and their resource as a family was their religion and faith, I pulled on this source of strength and reinforced their belief that their faith, combined with counseling, would glue their family back together.

The layered complexity of the situation and its immediacy was affecting me on multiple levels.

In the midst of all these emotions, as a counselor, I knew that legally and ethically I had to report this case. Emotionally, I empathized with their pain. Professionally, I needed to explore support services for this family. Cognitively, I was perplexed. There were layers of presenting concerns that emerged in the stories of sexual abuse.

This situation, while overwhelming, taught me the importance of being calm in crisis situations. It also taught me that clients find a sense of stability in counselors' comportment and composure in crisis situations. Finally, it taught me the importance of building upon clients' strengths and resources in times of crisis.

VOICES FROM THE FIELD 9.7
Protecting Shelby

Maegan Vick

Seven-year-old Shelby sat down with me as usual and traced the blisters she got on her palms from the monkey bars. By now, I was accustomed to Shelby asking to see me. We would talk about anything—from what she did at recess that day to how she was not getting along with her sister. However, I always felt she left something unsaid, something much bigger. During this session, she was really trying to convey to me she did not want to go to her father's house for her usual weekend visit. She took a deep breath and finally said that her father had touched her bottom and that he got naked in front of her. She said she closed her eyes

because she did not want to see. He made her get in the shower with him as well. I praised Shelby for being brave enough to share that information with me and promised I would get her some help, so her father would never do that again. She was apprehensive and worried her father would be in trouble. I eased her fear by saying that the people I would call would help him, because what he was doing was not OK. Our bodies belong to us and no one should ever touch us where our swimsuits cover our private areas. I contacted child protective services and then referred Shelby to Owens's House, a nonprofit organization that helps children who are sexually abused and exploited.

issues leading a female to offend in CSA situations. If the female was also a victim of CSA, a portion of the treatment may need to address the trauma that these female perpetrators encountered. While addressing victimization issues, it is important for clinicians to be empathetic regarding the abuse that perpetrators have sustained without minimizing or excusing the sexual offenses that they have committed. In treating any perpetrator of CSA, the priority of treatment must be focused on the perpetrated act in the attempt to decrease the rate of recidivism over the perpetrator as victim.

Summary

Survivors of sexual violence are a significant minority of society, with some reports estimating that at least 20% of women and up to 10% of men are sexually victimized in their lifetime. Although the definitions of sexual assault, child sexual abuse, and statutory rape may differ by state, it is important for crisis counselors to be aware of legislation, resources, and best practices for working with survivors of sexual violence. Primarily, the need for empathetic understanding, for the use of intervention strategies tailored to the developmental needs of the child, and for the connection of survivors to resources in the community that best fit their needs is vital. It is also important to understand that not all victims of sexual violence will react the same way. While some may show immediate physical, cognitive-behavioral, or psychological signs, others may appear without symptoms. It is a crisis counselor's responsibility to provide support to clients in keeping with ethical and legal guidelines, respecting adult clients' right to decide whether or not a sexual assault is reported, and making proper reports to Child Protective Services regarding the sexual abuse of children.

In addition, sexual offenders who perpetrate sexual violence against youth or adults are often perceived as a highly difficult population to treat. When crisis counselors educate themselves about the motivations causing sexual abuse, they may be able to better implement treatment strategies or programs to rehabilitate sexual offenders.

10

Emergency Preparedness and Response in the Community and Workplace

Jason McGlothlin

PREVIEW

Emergency preparedness and effective responses by crisis counselors are reviewed in this chapter. Given the emphasis that the Council for Accreditation of Counseling and Related Educational Programs (CACREP) has put on training counselors to work with crises, disasters, and emergencies, this chapter will focus on crisis intervention models and clinical implications of disasters and hostage situations, and the role of the crisis counselor. However, the content of this chapter infuses information found in previous chapters to allow readers to synthesize what they have previously read.

STANDARDS FOR CRISIS COUNSELING PREPARATION

Given recent terrorist attacks, national disasters, and crisis situations, the notion of crisis intervention and emergency response has been heavily ingrained in counselor training standards. The most recent curriculum standards of CACREP (Council for Accreditation of Counseling and Related Educational Programs, 2009) place a heavy emphasis on the training of counselors in crisis intervention and emergency response. For example, all master's level training programs must have curriculum pertaining to the following:

> Counselors' roles and responsibilities as members of an interdisciplinary emergency management response team during a local, regional, or national crisis, disaster or other trauma-causing event (Standard II.G.1.c)...effects of crises, disasters, and other trauma-causing events on persons of all ages (Standard II.G.3.c)...[and]...crisis intervention and suicide prevention models, including the use of psychological first aid strategies. (Standard II.G.5.g)

In addition, CACREP includes the following curricular standards for different types of counselors:

Addiction Counseling

- Understands the impact of crises, disasters, and other trauma-causing events on persons with addictions (Standard A.9).
- Understands the operation of an emergency management system within addiction agencies and in the community (A.10).
- Understands the principles of intervention for persons with addictions during times of crises, disasters, and other trauma-causing events (Standard C.8).

Career Counseling

- Understands the impact of crises, emergencies, and disasters on a person's career planning and development (Standard C.3).

Clinical Mental Health Counseling

- Understands the impact of crises, disasters, and other trauma-causing events on people (Standard A.9).
- Understands the operation of an emergency management system within clinical mental health agencies and in the community (Standard A.10).
- Understands the principles of crisis intervention for people during crises, disasters, and other trauma-causing events (Standard C.6).
- Understands appropriate use of diagnosis during a crisis, disaster, or other trauma-causing event (Standard K.5).
- Differentiates between diagnosis and developmentally appropriate reactions during crises, disasters, and other trauma-causing events (Standard L.2).

Marriage, Couple, and Family Counseling

- Understands the impact of crises, disasters, and other trauma-causing events on marriages, couples, families, and households (Standard A.7).

School Counseling

- Understands the operation of the school emergency management plan and the roles and responsibilities of the school counselor during crises, disasters, and other trauma-causing events (Standard A.7).
- Understands the potential impact of crises, emergencies, and disasters on students, educators, and schools, and knows the skills needed for crisis intervention (Standard C.6).
- Knows school and community collaboration models for crisis/disaster preparedness and response (Standard M.7).

Student Affairs and College Counseling

- Understands the impact of crises, disasters, and other trauma-causing events on people in the postsecondary education community (Standard A.11).
- Understands the operation of the institution's emergency management plan and the roles of student affairs professionals and counselors in postsecondary education during crises, disasters, and other trauma-causing events (Standard A.12).

- Demonstrates an understanding of the psychological impact of crises, disasters, and other trauma-causing events on students, faculty, and institutions (Standard B.7).
- Understands the principles of intervention for people in the learning community during times of crises and disasters in postsecondary education (Standard C.4).
- Demonstrates skills in helping postsecondary students cope with personal and interpersonal problems, as well as skills in crisis intervention in response to personal, educational, and community crises (Standard D.3).

Counselor Education and Supervision (Doctoral Standards)

- Theories pertaining to the principles and practice of counseling, career development, group work, systems, consultation, and crises, disasters, and other trauma causing events (Standard II.C.1).
- Understands the effectiveness of models and treatment strategies of crises, disasters, and other trauma-causing events (Standard IV.G.4).
- Understands models, leadership roles, and strategies for responding to community, national, and international crises and disasters (Standard IV.I.4).

LEADERSHIP ROLES IN A MULTIDISCIPLINARY CRISIS RESPONSE TEAM

Multidisciplinary crisis response teams (MCRTs) have various names—first responder teams, primary and emergency health care teams, school response teams, community emergency response teams (CERTs), etc. The hallmark of MCRTs is that they are comprised of multiple individuals from different professions, each serving a specific function, who work together to provide different perspectives on the crisis or disaster. A similar concept that counselors are familiar with is a multidisciplinary treatment team, in which counselors, social workers, vocational workers, psychiatrists, and nurses, work to treat a client. In the case of MCRTs, the client is in crisis. Members of a MCRT work with individuals, families, and groups in a variety of different roles not only to help individuals but also to help reduce the impact of the crisis or disaster on the community.

Depending on the type of crisis or disaster, and the type and organization of the MCRT, there are various leadership roles that must be present. Police, firefighters, and SWAT members provide leadership in instilling safety and rescue. Medical personnel (e.g., physicians, nurses, EMTs) lead the effort to treat physical trauma. Mental health clinicians (e.g., counselors, social workers, psychiatrists, psychologists) provide crisis intervention and emotional support. Counselors on a MCRT may also be designated to fulfill any of the following leadership roles:

- *Media liaison:* a team member who effectively communicates with the media and other inquiring bodies (e.g., the government, FEMA, families, loved ones).
- *Mortality liaison:* in some crises or disasters, the loss of life is so great or impactful that a member of the MCRT must be designated to accurately convey loss of life to families.
- *The MCRT leader:* in every MCRT, a leader is designated to oversee how the team responds to the crisis or disaster, delegate who is responsible for what, and evaluate the effectiveness of the response.

VOICES FROM THE FIELD 10.1

Crises in the Workplace

Scott Baker

During my time as a crisis counselor on a mobile crisis response team, it was not unusual to encounter workplace emergencies. In a large city in the Southwest, the mobile crisis counseling teams had been specially trained by the local fire department to assist with disaster situations. One afternoon, we were called upon by the fire department to assist with such a scenario.

Upon arrival, we were informed that a young man had jumped from a high-rise building. Despite the fire department's best efforts, there was no way to hide the gruesome scene. Our first intervention was for ourselves, taking deep breaths and focusing on the job at hand, reminding ourselves of our training and creating a mental checklist of the steps that we would follow. The first step was to coordinate with other responding teams to identify clients and responsibilities.

The person in charge of the crisis response informed us that our job was to assist the employees who had been working in the high rise. Those employees had evacuated the building when the young man accessed the roof, setting off the fire alarms throughout the building. Thinking the alarm was a test or the result of some minor incident, the employees were certainly not prepared for what they witnessed as they evacuated the building. The young man was falling and screaming, "Get out of the way!" He hit the ground, surrounded by those who had been working inside.

As is common in workplace crises, the situation was more complicated than it seemed. In this case, the employees working inside the building were managers of the large company that owned the building. There had been a labor dispute, and the regular workers were striking. In response, the company had sent managers to staff the building. This added to the horror of the employees, as a rumor quickly spread that the suicidal man was a displaced worker, causing many to feel extreme guilt. It became very important to stop the spread of this rumor, and, once the information became available, to inform the employees that the suicide was unrelated to the labor dispute.

Each crisis team was assigned to conduct a group intervention with 8–10 employees. While one team member encouraged the employees to discuss what they had experienced, the other monitored for individual needs. My role was the latter, and I quickly identified my client, a large, middle-aged man who looked very pale, but otherwise unaffected. I spoke with him individually. He proceeded to explain that he was one of the first people outside, and he described, in horrific detail and with very little emotion, what he had seen. After purging his traumatic memory, he looked directly at me and matter-of-factly said, "Well, I guess I'd better get back to work." He started to stand up, but he seemed unsteady on his feet and about to fall over.

I directed him to sit down, explained that he would not be returning to work, and attended to his basic needs. I alerted an EMT, who monitored my client's shock response. We made a list of the things he had to do for the rest of the day, including taking his medication, eating dinner, and avoiding use of alcohol. We made a second list of what symptoms he might expect, how he might cope with each, and what he should do if coping was not working. We identified who would take him home, who would help him through the evening, and where he would go for continued assistance.

When the response was over and all immediate needs met, we returned to the office. Though our shift was over, we stayed and engaged in critical incident stress debriefing (CISD). Even with careful attention to this postcrisis intervention, it was several weeks before I stopped driving past that high rise on my way home from work.

CHARACTERISTICS OF AND RESPONSES TO DISASTERS, TERRORISM, AND HOSTAGE SITUATIONS

An elevated level of stress is a natural response to a crisis, whether it is a natural disaster, an act of terrorism, or mass destruction. Reactions to a natural disaster, terrorism, and, to some degree, hostage situations create two distinct forms of trauma. Individual trauma affects a person's mental and emotional states and requires the person to react to the event in some compensatory manner. On the other hand, collective trauma occurs on a communitywide level whereby communities either join together and prevail or fragment and possibly create isolation and further conflict. Whether the trauma results from a disaster or act of terrorism, James (2008) provided a timeline of reactions and interventions needed to handle the traumatic event, as illustrated in Table 10.1. For the purposes of this section, the term disaster will stand for a natural disaster or an act of terrorism.

TABLE 10.1 Timeline for Intervening in a Disaster

Time	Possible Response	Intervention Needed
Initial disaster strikes	• Shock • Fear/panic • Self-preservation • Family preservation • Helplessness/hopelessness • Denial/disbelief • Confusion/disorientation	• Evidence of resources available • Evidence of chaos reduction
Hours after disaster	• Same as above • Anger • Grief • Energy/emotion • Action without efficiency • Rumination of disaster	• Evidence of resources available • Evidence of chaos reduction • Organization/control • Ventilation • Problem solving • Connection with loved ones
Days after disaster	• Fear • Denial/disbelief • Anger • Emotion • Rumination of disaster • Cohesion of community • Optimism • Thoughts of predisaster life • That which does not kill me makes me stronger!	• Gathering information about loved ones, neighborhoods, etc. • Crisis intervention therapies • Financial/government support
First month after disaster	• Stop talking about disaster • Rumination of disaster • Resiliency • Setbacks can occur	• Prevention of acute stress disorder and possibly posttraumatic stress disorder • Promotion of wellness model • Life is different but can go on
Months after disaster	• Disappointment • Physical and emotional fatigue • Possible onset of panic disorder, anxiety disorder, suicide, depression, etc. • Moving on!	• Psychotherapy • Resources • Continual support from loved ones

(Continued)

TABLE 10.1 Timeline for Intervening in a Disaster

Time	Possible Response	Intervention Needed
One year after disaster	• Significance of anniversary • Family disputes if family members are not on the same level of recovery from disaster • Move on!	• "Life will go on" focus of counseling • Family therapy
Reflection of disaster	• Move on! • Literally move and rebuild? • Grow and build life	• Support • Validation of safety

Source: Compiled from *Crisis Intervention Strategies,* 6th ed., by R. K. James, 2008, Belmont, CA: Brooks/Cole.

Initially, when a disaster strikes, people experience feelings of shock, fear, panic, confusion, and, possibly, disorientation. Statements such as "I can't believe this is happening" and "This can't be happening" are typical. Almost immediately after the disaster occurs, people transition into preservation mode. Thoughts quickly enter the mind regarding the safety of self and family. During this initial time of the disaster, people need to know or be assured that basic survival resources (e.g., safety, food, water) are available. People also need to know that the chaos created by the disaster (e.g., physical or material destruction, communitywide or groupwide panic) will subside. At this point in the disaster, first responders must be visible to increase a sense of hope and reduce feelings of helplessness.

Hours after a disaster strikes, the same emotions and reactions that occurred at the onset of the disaster may continue, although these reactions would likely be decreased, even if the decrease is minimal. Feelings of anger and grief may continue, and people may experience an inability to stop thinking about the disaster. Powerful emotions typically prevent victims from organizing an effective response. Likewise, if the crisis turns to chaos, people may not be able to either provide or receive help.

Hours after the disaster first responders should help people regain a sense of safety in their lives. First responders can be of substantial help by providing basic problem-solving strategies. Individuals may not be able to solve large or complex problems until personal safety needs have been met. Providing resources is crucial, such as connecting people with family members and providing them with resources to meet basic needs such as shelter and safety.

After a few days, people may still experience thoughts of fear, denial, disbelief, anger, heightened emotions, and continual rumination over the disaster. However, some people may begin to see optimism in getting past the disaster and moving on with life. Communitywide efforts may start to emerge to address disaster-related issues. Community efforts instill hope in moving past the disaster and even getting back to a predisaster life (e.g., going back to work, buying groceries). First responders should continue to help people gather information about loved ones, neighbors, pets, and others that victims are concerned about. At this point, first responders can use specific crisis intervention counseling strategies with a focus on rebuilding life to a predisaster state. Also, financial and government support is needed by victims within days after the disaster.

Months after the disaster, people may stop talking about the disaster as life begins to mirror how life was before the disaster occurred. Resiliency is a positive sign of healthy adjustment. However, some people continue to ruminate over the disaster. Rumination can be a precursor to post-traumatic stress disorder (PTSD) or acute stress disorder. Setbacks to resiliency can occur because some factors are still out of the control of many people (e.g., government assistance does not occur in a timely fashion).

Helping people a month after a disaster requires transition from the role of a first responder to that of a crisis counselor or other mental health clinician. Clinicians at this point should assess for and intervene to address acute stress disorder and prevent PTSD. Clinicians should promote a wellness philosophy that helps people reestablish physical, emotional, and spiritual health and reinforces the perspective that life can continue, although somewhat differently since the disaster.

The months that follow a disaster represent a time when people can either thrive or become stagnant. People who thrive are those who learned from the events surrounding the disaster and feel as if they are stronger because they survived. These individuals do not perceive the disaster as uncontrollable, often possess effective coping skills, and/or have a good support system. People who become stagnant at this point can experience physical, emotional, and spiritual exhaustion. If this exhaustion persists, it can lead to thoughts of suicide or to symptoms of depression or intense anxiety, especially if life has not returned to a predisaster state.

Whether people are thriving or stagnating several months after the disaster, it is critical that family and other loved ones show continual support for those who experienced the disaster and that resources are available to help them move on with their lives. Also at this point, people may need to begin formal individual or group psychotherapy in order to prevent or manage symptoms of PTSD, suicide, depression, panic disorder, anxiety disorder, or other feelings that may impair their functioning.

At the one-year anniversary of the disaster, some victims may have moved on with their lives. However, family disputes may occur when a family member continues to focus on the disaster and continually talks about the events surrounding it, while other family members have moved on with their lives. Because such conflicts can create distance between some family members, family counseling may be warranted, or individual counseling that focuses on wellness, symptom reduction, and the finding of meaning in life.

One year after the disaster, most individuals will have moved on with life. However, those who were significantly devastated by the disaster may need to relocate their residence in order to either distance themselves from the daily reminder of the disaster or rebuild their lives. With these individuals, crisis counselors need to focus on support, validation of safety issues, and possibly continued care connections to counselors in the area where the victims may relocate.

Overall, the results of a disaster can have short- and long-term consequences for people that may be perfectly normal. Everly and Mitchell (1999), along with Alexander (2005), summarized the typical responses to disaster:

- *Cognitive reactions:* blaming, uncertainty, poor troubleshooting abilities, poor concentration, disorientation, lessened self-esteem, intrusive thoughts or rumination of the disaster, hypersensitivity, confusion, nightmares, blaming others, and difficulty with memory.

- *Physical reactions:* increased heart rate, tremors, dizziness, weakness, chills, fainting, reduced libido, headaches, vomiting, shock, fatigue, sweating, and rapid breathing.
- *Emotional reactions:* apathy, feelings of being overwhelmed, depression, irritability, anxiety, agitation, panic, helplessness, hopelessness, anger, grief, fear, guilt, loss of emotional control, and denial.
- *Behavioral reactions:* difficulty eating and/or sleeping, restlessness, conflicts with others, withdrawal from others, lack of interest in social activities, and increased drug/alcohol use.

Those who work over a period of time with people who have experienced a disaster need to be able to recognize when "normal reactions" to disaster become substantially debilitating. In order to prevent those normal reactions from becoming debilitating, an immediate response to those exposed to a disaster is critical. The goal of such a response is also to reduce panic and chaos.

Everly and Mitchell (1999) proposed that three essential elements need to take place in order to prevent panic and chaos immediately following a disaster. First, a command post needs to be established in order to help people locate and recognize one centralized location of leadership and organization in a time of chaos and disarray. Second, connections need to be made between those exposed to the disaster and needed resources. Third, it is essential to communicate with those in need and create an atmosphere in which feelings of helplessness are extinguished.

INTERVENTIONS AFTER A DISASTER OR ACT OF TERRORISM

Little literature exists on the types of therapeutic strategies that are most effective when working with victims of a disaster. Regardless of the modality of intervention, the essential crisis intervention microskills (presented in Chapter 4) are critical to building a therapeutic foundation with clients in crisis. Some argue that cognitive-behavioral therapy (CBT) or eye movement desensitization and reprocessing (EMDR) can be highly effective due to the positive outcomes for adult clients with PTSD (Bradley, Greene, Russ, Dutra, & Westen, 2005; Hamblen, Gibson, Mueser, & Norris, 2006). Hebert and Ballard (2007) state that play therapy is the most beneficial approach with children because it allows children to express the trauma. In contrast, Harper, Harper, and Stills (2003) contend that meeting a child's basic human needs should be the main concern. Perhaps the most appropriate intervention could be developmental, such as responding initially with a Rogerian approach to allow the client to feel accepted and heard, followed by an existential approach to help the client establish or redefine meaning in his or her life. No matter what type of intervention is implemented, most agree that early interventions increase personal recovery from a disaster (Bonanno, Galea, Bucciarelli, & Vlahov, 2007; Shalev, 2004).

Fortunately, the literature does provide insight into some models for intervening in times of disaster. Psychological First Aid (PFA), Critical Incident Stress Management (CISM), and the Crisis Counseling Program (CCP) have appeared in the literature as models that have been successfully implemented in recent disasters such as the terrorist attacks on September 11, 2001, and Hurricane Katrina. A discussion of these models follows.

Psychological First Aid

Psychological First Aid (PFA) is grounded in evidenced-based research and provides mental health clinicians with tools to help reduce the beginning stress and trauma caused by a crisis or disaster. The underpinnings of PFA are rooted in the notion that individuals are resilient to some degree and that severe trauma does not necessarily develop into long-term mental health problems. PFA is a practical approach that emphasizes the treatment of individuals' experiencing a variety of emotional, psychological, behavioral, spiritual, and physical reactions to a crisis or disaster. PFA has been shown to work with individuals of all ages as well as in group settings.

According to the National Child Traumatic Stress Network (2010), the basics of PFA include the following guidelines:

- Be compassionate and provide emotional comfort.
- Connect with individuals in a nonintrusive and non-threatening manner.
- Recognize that the relationship between the individual and the clinician is important.
- Empower individuals to believe in the notion that they are safe and that they will continue to be safe.
- Encourage individuals to be concrete in their immediate needs.
- Focus on heightened emotional states with individuals and attempt to reduce feelings of being overwhelmed and hopeless.
- Help individuals reduce feelings of isolation by connecting them to their family and friends as soon as possible.
- Be aware of cultural and spiritual differences as they may play a large role in reaction to and coping with trauma.
- Provide individuals with realistic resources and the practicalities of such resources (i.e., when and where they are available).

When delivering PFA, begin by observing the situation; do not approach individuals until you observe how they are behaving in the moment. Once that is accomplished and you believe that your presence would not be too intrusive, ask the person in crisis how you could be helpful and about their immediate needs (e.g., something to eat, medical attention). Typically at this point, individuals will either act shy and avoid you or bombard you with information. Remain calm with the client and speak slowly. Be empathetic and take your time. If individuals want to talk, then simply listen and try and pick up on the subtle resources they might need.

At this early point in the conversation, you want to focus on the positive accomplishments that have kept them alive, safe, etc. Because PFA focuses on immediacy, try to keep the conversation on what the individual wants to accomplish in the moment and in the immediate future (i.e., the next hour or day). Although it may be easy to get the individual to recount the events of the trauma and it is okay for some of this dialogue to occur, PFA would stress that you focus less on the traumatic event and more on the recovery from the event. The goal of this interaction is to reduce stress, provide resources, empower with hope, and promote positive functioning.

In an attempt to provide an overview of PFA, Everly and Flynn (2005) reported that PFA begins with helping those in need to meet their basic physical needs (e.g., safety, food, water, shelter). After those physical needs are met, or are about to be met, a crisis counselor practicing PFA attempts to help meet the client's psychological needs (e.g., emotional and behavioral support, empathy, consolation). Next, connecting the client with friends, family, and other loved ones must take place. In addition, measures to decrease a victim's isolation must occur. Lastly, clinicians practicing PFA should provide avenues for follow-up care. The above steps were successfully used by direct responders after the September 11, 2001, terrorist attack in New York City.

PFA has developed into the hallmark of crisis response. Compared with other types of crisis response, PFA is a gentler approach that allows for open communication, immediate support, focus on the positive, and empowerment. While some other approaches of debriefing are seen as intrusive or dictating that individuals need help, PFA is offered to people inquiring how help can be provided.

Everly, Phillips, Kane, and Feldman (2006) stated that PFA "is emerging as the crisis intervention of choice in the wake of critical incidents such as trauma and mass disaster" (p. 130). According to Ruzek et al. (2007, p. 17), PFA is

> a systematic set of helping actions aimed at reducing initial post-trauma distress and supporting short- and long-term adaptive functioning. Designed as an initial component of a comprehensive disaster/trauma response, PFA is constructed around eight core actions: contact and engagement, safety and comfort, stabilization, information gathering, practical assistance, connection with social supports, information on coping support, and linkage with collaborative services.

PFA is typically an individual approach to treatment; however, Everly et al. (2006) have suggested that group approaches can also be beneficial to those experiencing crisis. Overall, the goals of PFA are to provide resources, education, and information to those in need; promote help-seeking behaviors (especially mental health services); provide empathy and support during the crisis; and aid in moving those in immediate crisis to a precrisis state of adjustment (Everly & Flynn, 2005).

Critical Incident Stress Management

The fundamental components of Critical Incident Stress Management (CISM) are set out in the work of Everly and Mitchell (1999). This model begins with choosing potentiating pairings—specific crisis interventions (e.g., venting, debriefing) to best meet the needs of each client. Once such interventions are identified, the crisis counselor specifically chooses catalytic sequences—the order to use the potentiating pairings. Lastly, the polythetic nature of the situation emerges—how one implements the potentiating pairings and the catalytic sequences based on the individual needs of each situation or disaster. Essentially, CISM is an eclectic approach to crisis intervention that takes into consideration the client's individual needs, the interventions available, and the nature of the situation.

According to Castellano and Plionis (2006), CISM was successfully implemented to augment established individual counseling through the following six components:

- *Component 1—Acute Crisis Counseling Provided by Peer Counselors:* Crisis counselors and law enforcement officers with crisis intervention skills provided crisis intervention to law enforcement officers who initially responded to the 9/11 terrorist attack in New York. Component 1 lasted 3 months after the attack and consisted of traditional crisis intervention techniques.

- *Component 2—Executive Leadership Program:* Because so many senior/superior police officers saw their lower-ranked colleagues die or become devastated by the 9/11 terrorist attack, specific crisis intervention services and educational seminars were developed and delivered to this population.
- *Component 3—The Multidisciplinary Team:* A multidisciplinary team delivered trainings around the clock for everyone working at the site of the 9/11 attack. Crisis intervention seminars and counseling sessions were called "trainings" at the time because they would be better received and attended by those who may have stereotypes about mental health services.
- *Component 4—Acute Traumatic Stress Group Training Sessions:* For the large number of those in need of crisis intervention, two-day psychoeducational group sessions helped to decrease isolation, normalize emotions and reactions to the attack, decrease guilt, and increase coping mechanisms.
- *Component 5—Hotline:* Telephone crisis hotlines were highly emphasized and used to help those who responded to the 9/11 attack. Hotlines are seen as a 24/7 resource that can provide support and information in times when others may not be available. In fact, hotlines are considered to be a necessity in many crisis intervention plans (Wunsch-Hitzig, Plapinger, Draper, & del Campo, 2002).
- *Component 6—Reentry Program:* 9/11 responders who directly witnessed death, carnage, and destruction were deemed to be at high risk and identified as individuals who would have difficulty going back to their jobs and families. The reentry program focused on such high-risk responders to help them get back to their "normal" life.

Crisis Counseling Program

According to Castellano and Plionis (2006), the Crisis Counseling Program (CCP) is frequently used for responses to natural disasters. The CCP model consists of the following components:

- *Assess Strengths:* The crisis counselor must identify not only what the problems are (e.g., stranded people, postdisaster crime) but also what human and material resources are available.
- *Restore Predisaster Functioning:* The key to restoring life to what it was before the disaster (especially emotional status) is to attempt to reduce the chaos of the disaster.
- *Accept the Face Value:* Crisis counselors must help clients to reorganize life to accommodate for the impact of the disaster (e.g., "Your home was completely destroyed by the hurricane; now how can you move on?").
- *Provide Validation:* The provision of unconditional positive regard, acceptance, and validation is critical to the growth of disaster victims.
- *Provide a Psychoeducational Focus:* The provision of psychoeducation (on both a group and an individual level) regarding the normal (and abnormal) reactions to disaster can play a central role in helping disaster victims monitor their own recovery.

NATURAL DISASTERS

The consequences of natural disasters come in many forms, ranging from power outages resulting from high winds to mass casualties and staggering death tolls resulting from a tsunami. Many crisis intervention strategies such as PFA, CISM, and CCP can be used. However, when responding to a natural disaster, crisis counselors must be aware of the dynamics of the specific disaster to be better prepared for what to expect from their clients and the environment in the aftermath of the disaster.

In Chapter 2, emphasis was placed on the safety concerns and precautions of crisis counselors and their reactions to crises. This is especially critical when responding to a natural disaster. In a natural disaster, crisis counselors who are at the disaster site may see death and dismemberment, experience remarkable emotional reactions to the crisis, and be exposed to harmful situations. Chapter 2 discussed proactive approaches that a crisis counselor could take when working with clients in crisis. When reading the remainder of this section, reflect back on Chapter 2 and relate what you learned to natural disasters.

In the sections that follow, a brief overview of specific natural disasters is presented, covering issues that crisis counselors must keep in mind. This information is especially important because many crisis counselors may not have experienced many natural disasters.

Winter Storms

There are many components to a winter storm, and its definition varies in different parts of the United States and the world. However, the consistent elements of a winter storm include heavy snow in a short period of time, high winds, ice (i.e., sleet, freezing rain, accumulated ice), winter flooding due to large amounts of snow melting, and extreme cold temperatures. Winter storms can be localized to a few towns or affect several states (Community Emergency Response Team, 2003).

The consequences of a winter storm include heart attacks and exhaustion (mostly due to overexertion from shoveling snow), frostbite, hypothermia (mostly in elderly individuals), asphyxiation (due to improper use of heating fuels), and house fires (due to improper use of heating devices). Automobile accidents are also a significant result of winter storms and can be considered the leading cause of death resulting from a winter storm. Winter storms can also close transportation routes (e.g., roads and airports), prolong response time by emergency personnel, create damage to residential and commercial structures, and have a significant economic impact on communities (Community Emergency Response Team, 2003).

When crisis counselors work in such conditions, they should be mindful of taking care of their own needs to stay warm and hydrated. They should not stay outdoors for long periods of time; when outdoors, they should make sure all body parts are covered, especially the neck and wrist areas; and they should eat and drink on a regular basis to conserve energy and warmth. Lastly, crisis counselors should be aware of the local resources to counter the effects of a winter storm.

Earthquakes

Earthquakes are caused by movement in the earth's crust. The damage that results from such disasters can range from mild tremors that have little effect to strong shocks that destroy buildings. Depending on its intensity and location, an earthquake can cause power outages, damage to roads and bridges, fires and explosions, structural instability or destruction to buildings, landslides, avalanches, and even tsunamis (Community Emergency Response Team, 2003). The vast physical effects of earthquakes include adult respiratory distress syndrome, asphyxiation, burns, death, drowning, extremity injuries, myocardial infarctions, skin injuries, and head trauma (Jones, 2006).

After the initial earthquake, aftershocks often occur. In addition, one or more earth tremors will occur initially after the earthquake and up to several weeks after (Community Emergency Response Team, 2003). If you experience an earthquake or aftershock , drop to the floor and cover your head. Also, be aware of the unstable environment. Depending on the location, you should act accordingly:

- If indoors, stay inside; don't run outdoors.
- If outdoors, go to an area away from buildings, bridges, power lines, trees, and the like.
- If in a car, stay in the car, but pull over to the side of the road.
- If in a multistory building, don't use the elevators to leave. Also, keep in mind that alarms or sprinklers may be activated. (Community Emergency Response Team, 2003)

Regardless of their location, crisis counselors need to be mindful not only of the environment during an earthquake situation but also of their clients and themselves. They need to make sure that steps are taken to protect themselves and their clients from future aftershocks, check for injuries, and inquire with clients about the location of family members who may be trapped or removed due to the earthquake.

Floods

Floods are caused by heavy rains (either long periods of rain or a very intense rain), poor soil absorption of rain, snowmelt, and failures in dams or levees (Community Emergency Response Team, 2003). Floods have been known to cause a variety of physical problems among flood victims, including asphyxiation (by some means other than drowning), drowning, hepatitis A, physical trauma, respiratory infections, suicides, and tetanus (Jones, 2006).

When responding to victims of flooding, crisis counselors need to be prepared for additional flash floods. The best response to a flood is to get to higher ground. It is also important not to walk or drive through any floodwaters (even if the water does not look deep), and to avoid potentially flood-prone areas (e.g., low-lying areas, ditches, storm drains) (Community Emergency Response Team, 2003).

The most distinguishing aspect of floods is the psychological effect it has on victims. In the wake of fires, earthquakes, tornados, and other disasters, many of the victim's belongings are completely destroyed and disintegrated—gone—and any remains are not intact. Victims of these natural disasters may have a sense of finality or closure with the notion that "my things are gone and I need to get new things." However, the psychological toll is different for flood victims in that they can see their belongings and how they have been damaged by the flood. Their belongings are not disintegrated and gone, though they are destroyed. Crisis counselors need to pay close attention to how flood victims respond emotionally to revisiting their homes and rebuilding their lives.

Heat Waves

A heat wave is an extensive period of time with excessively high temperatures and high humidity. The consequences of a heat wave can include muscular pains and spasms, heat cramps, heat exhaustion, dehydration, and, ultimately, heatstroke or sunstroke, which is a life-threatening condition in which the body cannot regulate its proper temperature. Such heat waves are especially devastating to the very young and the elderly because their bodies are not physically equipped to work harder to regulate body temperature.

When crisis counselors are working in such conditions, they should attempt to work in air-conditioned facilities, wear lightweight and light-colored clothing, not overexert by doing physical activities, and frequently drink fluids. Also, they should inquire about the client's family members and friends (especially those who are very young or elderly) to ensure their safety.

Hurricanes

Hurricanes consist of high winds, intense rain, and storm surges. They can destroy buildings, damage communities' utility systems, erode the ground, cause tornados and/ or floods, displace communities, and devastate the economy (Community Emergency Response Team, 2003). Hurricanes have been known to cause a variety of physical problems among their victims, including carbon monoxide poisoning, congestive heart failure, diarrheal disease, drowning, pulmonary conditions, extreme heat exposure, myocardial infarction, injuries to skin and soft tissue, suicide, and trauma (Jones, 2006).

One of the most destructive hurricanes in recent times was Hurricane Katrina, which in August 2006 devastated the economy, infrastructure, communities and neighborhoods, and way of life for residents of New Orleans and along the Gulf Coast. The devastation of this hurricane created posttraumatic mental health issues that will need to be addressed for years to come (Madrid & Grant, 2008). Therefore, for crisis counselors who respond to large-scale hurricane sites such as Katrina, it is important for them to be able to follow up with their clients and connect them with long-standing mental health treatment.

Crisis counselors need to know that, because of the intense damage that hurricanes create, dangerous situations can persist after the initial impact of the hurricane. Therefore, in order to stay safe, they should work only in areas that officials have declared as being safe, not approach or be around downed power lines, and not get separated from others (Community Emergency Response Team, 2003).

Tornados

Tornados are powerful funnels of intense circular wind that can be accompanied by severe weather, hailstorms, and gusting winds. Depending on the intensity of the tornado, it can destroy buildings and structures, move cars, destroy utilities, break glass, move concrete blocks, uproot trees and shrubs, and destroy communities (Community Emergency Response Team, 2003).

Crisis counselors must be cautious of working near a site at which a tornado touched down because it can be a dangerous environment. Broken glass, rubble, sharp objects, jagged metal, and unstable structures could be present. When working with a client who has suffered loss due to a tornado, uncertainty about the future and physical heath are the issues of most concern. However, those living in tornado-prone areas (typically known as "tornado alleys") could have existential concerns about when a tornado is going to happen again and why this destruction is happening to them.

Wildfires

There are essentially three types of wildfires: (1) surface fires, which are slow moving and burn the forest floor and trees; (2) ground fires, which are typically started by lightning and burn below the forest's floor, and (3) crown fires, which are quickly spreading fires that start unnoticed and burn trees, homes, and brush. Depending on the type and intensity of the fire, it can cause asphyxiation, heat exhaustion, smoke damage, burns, and damage to communities and homes (Community Emergency Response Team, 2003).

Crisis counselors need to keep safe by staying abreast of how the fire is progressing. Some fires move very quickly, and crisis counselors need to make sure they are staying away from the fire's path. Crisis counselors need to be aware of a client's perception of actual and perceived loss. In other words, some clients might know that their home or community was destroyed by the fire (actual loss). Other clients may have been evacuated before the fire came to their community, so they may not know if their home is gone but they anticipate its loss (perceived loss). This actual or perceived loss includes not only material possessions but also loved ones, pets, and the like. For more information on loss, refer to Chapter 12.

With any natural disaster, there are transitions, displacement, relocation, and rebuilding that must occur. The psychological toll that such situations take on victims is monumental, and crisis counselors need to be aware of all the consequences of natural disasters (Schuh & Laanan, 2006). For example, in the aftermath of Hurricane Katrina, job sites were gone, colleges and schools were gone, grocery stores were gone, and homes were gone, and victims had to face many questions: Where will I live? Where will I go to school? How will I finish my college degree? Where will I work? How will I get food? A critical task for crisis counselors is to get clients to become aware of and use resources and follow-up services. In addition, helping clients to triage the priorities in their lives is a key element in the direct aftermath of a natural disaster (Dugan, 2007).

Besides natural disasters, crisis counselors may be called on to respond to disastrous events that are the result of human factors: for example, house fires or structural fires, chemical spills, nuclear disasters or nuclear meltdowns, contagion, and natural gas explosions. As with natural disasters, crisis counselors need to ensure their own safety as well as attending to the needs of their clients who have experienced these human-caused disasters.

CASE STUDY 10.1

Dealing with a Flood

Anton, a 50-year-old Brazilian man, lives in rural Missouri. He has lived alone there for the past 30 years, working in his home as a typesetter. Anton does not have any family left and rarely talks to anyone except his clients. Two years ago his hearing began to diminish, and now he has no hearing in his left ear and only 15% of his hearing in his right ear.

For the past 6 days, torrential rains have plagued his town. The local news and emergency broadcast system warned of flooding and urged residents to evacuate. Rather than evacuating, Anton began to place sandbags around his home to keep the water out. Unfortunately, the water rose too quickly and spilled over the sandbags. Now Anton's home and business are 7 feet under water. He was rescued by the local fire and rescue unit yesterday evening.

As a crisis counselor, you are meeting Anton for the first time just 22 hours after he was rescued. You are meeting him in a school gymnasium that has been converted into a shelter for flood victims.

Discussion Questions

1. As a crisis counselor, what would be your priority with Anton?
2. What might be Anton's thoughts, feelings, and behaviors?
3. What resources do you think Anton needs to be connected with?
4. What might be some multicultural considerations for Anton, located in rural Missouri?
5. What might be some long-term effects of this flood on Anton's professional and personal life?
6. What might be some barriers to his recovery?
7. What would be some key counseling skills to use with this client? See Chapter 4 for information on such skills.
8. Referring back to Chapter 5, contemplate this client's suicidality. Could Anton be suicidal? If so, at what level of lethality do you think he might present with? Discuss various ways to assess Anton for suicide, and think of follow-up strategies to keep Anton safe.

CASE STUDY 10.2

Dealing with a Residential Fire

The Zhang family—Kane, the 32-year-old father; Miya, the 28-year-old mother; Asa, the 7-year-old daughter; and Kenji, the 3-month-old son—lives on the sixth floor of a 9-story apartment building in a major metropolitan area. Last week there was an electrical fire in their neighbor's apartment. As a result, their entire floor caught fire, as did parts of the floors above and below them. The majority of the building experienced significant smoke damage. The Zhang family was awakened at 2:30 a.m. by fire alarms and the smell of smoke. They barely escaped the fire; Kane and Asa both got second-degree burns and Miya got third-degree burns on 10% of her body. All four family members also experienced significant smoke inhalation.

After the fire was extinguished, the tenants were taken to the hospital and treated. The building was declared to be unsafe, and the Zhang family and the rest of the tenants were told that they could not move back into the building.

As a crisis counselor, you are meeting with the entire Zhang family for the first time three weeks after the fire. They are living with family nearly 40 miles away from their previous home and did not recover any of their belongings from the fire.

Shortly after the fire, Kane started to drink heavily (a minimum of 8 beers a day and a maximum of a fifth of bourbon a day). You are meeting them in a group room in a local mental health clinic.

Discussion Questions

1. As a crisis counselor, what would be your priority with the Zhang family?
2. What might be some of their thoughts, feelings, and behaviors?
3. Consider the appropriateness of individual, group, or family counseling for this family. How might each be conducted if found to be appropriate?
4. How might you facilitate growth in this family?
5. What might be some developmental concerns for each of the family members?
6. What might be some multicultural considerations for the family?
7. What physical concerns might you have for each of the family members?
8. Consider the reaction and consequence of Kane's recent drinking.

In Case Studies 10.1 and 10.2, no one died, but there was a tremendous amount of loss. What might be some emotions related to loss and grief in each of the case studies? Even though there was no loss of life, could the individuals in the case studies progress through different stages of grief and loss? If so, discuss your responses.

HOSTAGE SITUATIONS

Hostage situations are rare in the United States; however, there are specific ramifications of such situations that mental health practitioners need to consider, given that over 50% of hostage takers have a mental or emotional disorder. Literature on hostage negotiation is vast, and a thorough discussion of specific negotiation strategies is beyond the scope of this chapter. However, a brief discussion of hostage situations may allow mental health practitioners to gain some insight into the experiences of hostages and hostage takers.

There are essentially four stages of a hostage situation (Strentz, 1995): (1) alarm, (2) crisis, (3) accommodation, and (4) resolution, as shown in Table 10.2. The alarm stage occurs at the initial onset of the hostage situation and is typically the most volatile and dangerous period of time. Hostage takers believe that terror must be instilled in the hostages in order to keep them under control, and any hint of panic by hostages creates extreme overreactions by hostage takers. During this stage, hostage takers are highly emotional, aggressive, irrational, and abusive.

During the alarm stage, hostages are confused by the sudden turn of events and feel victimized. They suddenly feel like there is no escape from the situation and become paralyzed not only due to threats of physical harm but also due to the severe shock resulting from aggressive actions by the hostage takers. Similar to the experiences of disaster victims, hostages during this stage express denials such as "I can't believe this is happening." As a result of the events that take place during the alarm stage, survivors of hostage situations share similar characteristics with abused children, abused women, and concentration camp survivors (Herman, 1995).

As the alarm stage ends, the crisis stage begins. During this time, hostage takers begin to realize the magnitude of the situation and continue to be highly dangerous and volatile but realize that they must secure their surroundings from authorities and

TABLE 10.2 Stages of Typical Hostage Situations

Stage	Characteristics of Hostage Takers	Characteristics of Hostages
Alarm	• Volatile • Dangerous • Highly emotional • Highly aggressive • Highly irrational • Abusive to others • Signs of panic create overreactions	• Most traumatized • Confused • Victimized • Shock • Helpless/defenseless • Denial • Paralyzed
Crisis	• Initial reason • Volatility • Danger • Grandiose/ridiculous demands • Rants • Securing the area and hostages • Fear of authorities/paranoia • Need for attention • Verbal abuse followed by violence	• Relationship with hostage taker is central to outcome • Denial • Increased fear if hostage taker is unpredictable • Fugue episodes • Claustrophobia • Reliance on hostage takers • Hopelessness
Accommodation	• Long-lasting time period • Fatigue • Increased control of hostages	• Time stands still • Boredom • Brief feelings of terror • Fatigue • Passivity • Possible Stockholm syndrome
Resolution	• Fatigue • Realization of lost expectations • Contemplation of outcome • Suicide becomes possible outcome	• Fatigue • Seeing closure

attempts by hostages to escape. The crisis stage also begins the hostage takers' interactions with the authorities, with the hostage takers frequently making grandiose or ridiculous demands with the expectation that the authorities will meet such demands. Hostage takers during this stage need attention, which they use as a means to show that they are in power. Typically, this showing of power begins with yelling or verbal abuse of the hostages but can quickly escalate to violence.

During the crisis stage, hostages begin to develop a relationship with the hostage takers. They rely on them for everything—from food and water to permission to use the restroom. Hostages soon learn that the more cooperative they are, the less violent the hostage takers will be toward them. If a hostage shows panic or contradicts a hostage taker, then violence may occur. Hostages still experience hopelessness, denial, and fear, though fear drastically increases if hostage takers are unpredictable or appear disorganized. Occasionally, hostages will experience a significant loss of time or go into a fugue state as a defense mechanism to cope with the trauma. They may also experience a sense of claustrophobia and may feel the need to get out of their situation even though they know there could be dangerous consequences if they do take such action.

The third stage of a hostage situation is the accommodation stage, which is marked by time standing still and fatigue for both the hostages and the hostage takers. Overall, this stage is somewhat peaceful because dominance over the hostages is established and acts of violence may not be deemed necessary by the hostage takers. Hostages become passive and bored. They may even experience Stockholm syndrome, a situation in which hostages develop positive feelings for the hostage takers and negative feelings for the authorities, while hostage takers gain concern and positive feelings for the hostages. Everyone is emotionally and physically exhausted. Typically, this is the longest of the four stages of a hostage situation.

The resolution stage is the last stage in a hostage situation. Hostage takers and hostages alike are weary and see that a resolution (whether good or bad) is nearing. Both realize that this situation will not last forever. Hostage takers begin to realize that their demands, or their initial expectations, are not going to be met. The hostage takers contemplate suicide, killing the hostages and themselves, or ending the situation peacefully. No matter what the outcome is, the hostage takers and the hostages typically know that the situation is ending.

Once the hostage situation is over, significant deescalation, ventilation, and self-preservation issues need to be addressed through crisis intervention strategies provided to the hostages and possibly to the hostage takers. Long-term individual and group therapy may need to be implemented to provide preventative measures for PTSD to the hostages.

CASE STUDY 10.3

A Commercial Hostage Situation

In a small convenience store located in an Appalachian town, two men, wearing masks, attempt to rob the store. Both men have guns. Besides the two gunmen, the people in the store are the owner, who is behind the checkout counter, and six customers, located in different aisles in the store. The gunmen ask for money from the cash register, but the owner denies their request. While the gunmen and the owner are arguing, one of the customers calls the police from his cell phone, and within 4 minutes, a police car pulls up in front of the store. One of the gunmen locks the store's front door, and the robbery has quickly turned into a hostage situation. The hostage situation lasts for 7 hours. Given the information presented earlier, imagine what goes on during those 7 hours.

Discussion Questions

1. Discuss how the hostage takers and the hostages think, feel, and act during the different stages of the situation.
2. What would be some follow-up resources for the hostages?

3. What might be some multicultural considerations for the hostages?

4. What would be some key counseling skills to use with the hostages? See Chapter 4 for information on such skills.

CASE STUDY 10.4

A Family Hostage Situation

Martin is a 38-year-old construction worker who has been married four times and has four children. He has one child (Pat, aged 20 years) with his first wife, and three boys (Ben, aged 10 years; Todd, aged 6 years; and Sig, aged 4 years) from his current wife, Michelle. Within the past 3 weeks, Martin broke his wrist while working, he lost his job because of his anger outbursts and his pushing one of his coworkers after an argument, and he was notified that he needs to pay $22,000 in back taxes to the Internal Revenue Service. Earlier today, Michelle told him that she was leaving him and she was taking the children with her. During this conversation, the police were called because neighbors were concerned about the yelling they heard. When the police arrived, Martin did not answer the door and told the police that he had a gun and "no one is coming out unless they are in a body bag."

Martin kept Michelle and her three children at gunpoint for 3½ hours. During this time, he yelled, talked as if he was in a rant, cried uncontrollably, put his gun to Michelle's head and threatened to pull the trigger, and slapped Michelle and Ben in the face. After talking to a police negotiator on and off for over 2 hours, Martin shot himself in the head in front of Michelle and his children.

When the police and the hostage negotiator entered the house, they found Michelle holding her husband's hand, while he lay dead on the floor. Two of her children were sitting on the couch, still afraid to move, while Ben ran out the door into the hands of the police. Michelle and her children spent the next 4 hours debriefing with the hostage negotiator and other support staff. Later Michelle saw a counselor twice a week for 8 months, then once a week for 4 months, and then once a month thereafter.

Discussion Questions

1. Overall, what do you think Michelle experienced during this situation? What about her children?

2. How do you think Michelle and the children experienced each stage of the hostage situation as described above?

3. What would be some of the emotions, behaviors, and thoughts felt by this family immediately after the hostage situation ended?

4. How should Martin's son Pat (from his first marriage) be informed of this situation? What should be said?

5. What would be the crisis counselor's initial treatment goals with Michelle and her children?

6. How might treatment differ for Michelle, Ben, and the other two children taken hostage?

7. What do you think was the reason Michelle was able to decrease treatment over time?

Summary

This chapter began by describing typical responses to disaster and how people's reactions to disaster evolve over time. It could be said that exposure to disaster or trauma plays an important role in a person's mental, emotional, cognitive, behavioral, social, and physical functioning. The difficult part of treating individuals is identifying when "normal" responses become significantly detrimental to their functioning.

Various models of crisis intervention have been discussed in this book, and they all have merit. However, the common thread among these models is that the key to treatment of those who experienced disaster (in all forms) is early intervention. The sooner crisis counselors respond, reduce panic or chaos, create a sense of hope and support, and establish connections between those in need and appropriate resources, the better.

As with disasters, there are many systematic factors and evolutionary components of a hostage situation. Though hostage situations are relatively rare, those providing mental health services should be aware of the unique characteristics of those who have experienced a hostage situation because it could influence the approach to treatment.

All crises evolve through different stages—and then end. Those who experience crisis, disaster, or trauma also evolve in that they, hopefully, resolve or at least experience a lessened impact of the situation. Crises affect lives in systemic ways; every aspect of a person's life can be affected by a crisis.

Emergency Preparedness and Response in Schools and Universities

Michele Garofalo and Bradley T. Erford

PREVIEW

Emergency preparedness and effective responses by crisis counselors in schools and universities are reviewed in this chapter. Mitigation and prevention strategies are emphasized as critical elements in the school environment. Crisis preparedness, response, recovery, and debriefing procedures are applied to school and university settings. Special emphasis is given to strategies for how to help students and parents during and after a crisis event. Finally, numerous case studies are provided to help prepare counselors-in-training for potential crisis situations encountered in academic environments. Like Chapter 10, the content of this chapter infuses information found in previous chapters to allow readers to synthesize what they have previously read.

CHARACTERISTICS OF AND RESPONSES TO SCHOOL CRISES

Schools are called upon to respond to a variety of crises both on a local and national level. As these crises occur, it becomes the responsibility of the school community to respond in a timely manner so that accurate information is provided, while helping students, teachers, administrators, parents, and communities cope with the crisis. Kerr (2009, p. 9) defines a school crisis as a "temporary event or condition that affects a school, causing individuals to experience fear, helplessness, shock, and/or horror [and] requires extraordinary actions to restore a sense of psychological and physical security." Crises do not need to occur on school property to have a devastating effect on the school community.

Johnson (2000, p. 3) contends that a school crisis brings chaos that affects perceptions of safety and stability for an entire school community. It exposes students and staff to "threat, loss, and traumatic stimulus" and undermines their "security and sense of power." School is a place where students, families, and school staff expect stability and safety. When a crisis occurs, it is understood that school personnel will react in a professional manner to make certain that information, support, and counseling services are provided. Everyone in the school community needs to feel informed, supported, and safe. School personnel play a vital role in managing crises and providing coping strategies to restore the school to a stable and safe environment. The approach must be organized and sensitive to the needs of diverse students, teachers, parents, administrators, and other community members.

Crises affecting schools can happen on a continuum with a wide range—from the individual level to national and international levels. On the individual level, for example, 1 in 7 youths in the United States seriously consider suicide each year. Of all deaths occurring in 2009 in the 15–24 year old age bracket, 14.4% were suicides (http://www.cdc.gov/nchs/data_access/vitalstatsonline.htm). Furthermore, one youth dies of suicide every 2 hours, and six youths survive a suicide attempt every 2 hours. Whether a crisis occurs at the national level (e.g., September 11, 2001, or Hurricane Katrina) or the local level (e.g., the death of a student/teacher as a result of an automobile accident, illness, or suicide), it will certainly have an impact on the school community. The school's response must be planned, organized, and coordinated effectively in order to provide the necessary support and services. A secondary goal is to prevent additional crises stemming from the initial crisis. For example, if there has been a suicide, school officials need to address the immediate impact of the suicide, but they must also attempt to reduce the possibility of any related suicide attempts.

The Office of Safe and Drug-Free Schools in the U.S. Department of Education (2003) identified four phases of a comprehensive school crisis plan: (1) mitigation and prevention, which addresses what schools can do to reduce or eliminate risk to life and property; (2) preparedness, which refers to the process of planning for a crisis; (3) response, which refers to the actions taken during the crisis; and (4) recovery, which refers to restoring the school environment after a crisis. Each of these phases will be addressed in turn.

Mitigation and Prevention

Mitigation is any sustained action taken to reduce or eliminate long-term risk to life and property from a hazard event. Mitigation encourages long-term reduction of hazard vulnerability (Federal Emergency Management Agency, 2012). Mitigation and prevention involve assessing the dangers in a school and community and identifying strategies to prevent and reduce injury and property damage. Both the school and community must work together in preventing crises. The Federal Emergency Management Agency (FEMA) has done extensive work to help communities with their mitigation planning. Mitigation procedures strive to decrease the need for subsequent responses rather than simply increasing response capability. FEMA has outlined five action steps for mitigation and prevention in schools:

1. *Know the school building.* Regular safety audits of the physical plant must be carried out along with an assessment of any potential hazards on campus. Parking lots, playgrounds, driveways, outside structures, and fencing should be examined. The information collected is then used for mitigation and prevention planning.

2. *Know the community.*   It is necessary to work with local emergency management officials to assess hazards in the community. The probability of natural disasters (e.g. hurricanes, tornadoes, earthquakes, floods) and industrial and chemical accidents (e.g., fuel spill, water contamination) must be considered. Potential hazards related to terrorism should also be carefully assessed (e.g., geographic location, government buildings).

3. *Bring together regional, local, and school leaders.*   Schools must work collaboratively with state and local governments to ensure support of their mitigation efforts.

4. *Make regular school safety and security efforts part of the mitigation/prevention practices.*   Schools must conduct needs assessments regularly to identify the types of incidents that are common in the school and continually refine the school safety plan.

5. *Establish clear lines of communication.*   Communication among stakeholders is critical as agencies and schools work together. It is necessary for families and the community to understand that schools and local governments are working together to ensure the safety of the school community and the larger community. Schools must keep families informed about the safety measures being developed.

Preventive efforts begin with an awareness of all activities occurring in the school environment, as well as the emotional climate of the school. School personnel must be aware of what is occurring in the hallways, restrooms, cafeteria, etc., in order to assess any risk that may be present (e.g., bullying, gang activity, talk of intended violence or harm). Steps should be taken to secure the building from outside intruders—for example, by employing a school resource officer, implementing a sign-in procedure for visitors, supervision in all parts of the building (including the playground and playing fields), surveillance cameras, keeping entrances to the building locked, and in some instances metal detectors. It would be wise for schools to work in conjunction with local law enforcement agencies to consult on additional ways to maintain safety and security.

All prevention efforts must also include education for everyone in the school community. Training of faculty and staff to develop knowledge, attitudes, and skills is an effective component of any crisis intervention program. Prevention programs on the topics of bullying, substance use/abuse, suicide, drinking and driving, depression, intimate partner violence, stress management, and conflict resolution should be carried out for students at a developmentally appropriate level. School counselors are instrumental in delivering classroom guidance presentations and small group counseling sessions on these topics. Character education programs also are in place in most schools and help to foster a positive school climate.

Attention to building a positive school climate is critical in prevention efforts. The University of South Florida (2012) proposed that school climate refers to the physical, aesthetic, and psychological qualities within a school. School personnel can help foster school climate by facilitating connectedness, participation, academic success, and safety as well as through training, policies, and positive concern for all participants in the educational process. Schools should provide extracurricular activities (e.g., clubs, activities, organizations), involve students in school decisions, promote safety and cleanliness of the facilities, promote high academic standards, reduce bullying, and equivalently enforce disciplinary standards. In other words, a positive school climate aimed at preventing school crises is respectful, caring, and supportive of all stakeholders in the school community.

VOICES FROM THE FIELD 11.1
On Call

Tricia Uppercue

It is Sunday evening, and I'm relaxing before the start of a new week when the phone rings. It is the supervisor of school counseling, who informs me that a high school student in the county died over the weekend. He drowned in a local swimming area, surrounded by friends who tried to save him. She asks me to report on Monday morning to the high school that the student attended to provide counseling to the students, staff, and faculty as part of the county crisis team.

On Monday morning, I arrive at the school. The mood is somber and I see many students crying in the hallways. All of the appropriate personnel are assembled in the library, the designated area for students and staff to report if they are upset and need support. Chairs are arranged in groups in the main library and in a small room next to the library to accommodate students who need one-on-one counseling as well as those who may want to be in a group setting with others.

Many students make their way to the library. Most are friends of the victim, some were at the scene where he died; others students knew of the victim, and some may not have known the victim but the tragedy of his death reminds them of a personal trauma they have experienced. They are shaken and saddened by the loss of their classmate. I become part of a group of students who are concerned about their friends who were at the scene of the drowning. Feelings of anger, sorrow, and guilt are evident as they discuss the details of the drowning, death of loved ones, and memories of their deceased friend.

Everyone grieves differently, and members of the crisis team are prepared to deal with individual needs. Some students stay home to be with family members, and others come to school to be surrounded by friends. Being with loved ones is a necessary part of the grieving process. Others may want to be involved in an activity, such as making cards for the victim's loved ones. Most, I found, may need time with a counselor, either individually or in a group, to process their thoughts and feelings.

As a counselor, being a part of the crisis team is an important role. I am able to provide support, and allow students to work through the grieving process and express their thoughts and feelings. I have learned that whether I am involved in a crisis within the school in which I work or if I am called to another school where the students may not know me, many students just need someone to listen and support them, and they are grateful to have that opportunity within the school setting.

Training programs for teachers and staff (including coaches, bus drivers, cafeteria workers and janitors) must be implemented to make all employees aware of warning signs/symptoms (risk factors) and appropriate methods for intervention. Prevention-based curricula generally promote awareness, but should also train gatekeepers (all faculty and staff) as to the signs of suicide or threat, as well as screening for those students who present as high risk. While much has been written about risk factors contributing to suicide and other threats, from a strengths-based perspective it is important to consider and promote protective factors, including family cohesion, support from adults, connectedness to the school, stable living environment, responsibilities for others (e.g., siblings, pets), participation in sports and other extracurricular activities, and positive peer and adult relationships (University of South Florida, 2012).

Preparedness and Advanced Planning

Preparedness and advanced planning has a positive impact on crisis response. When planning for a crisis policies and procedures must always be considered. Kerr (2009, p. 17) defined a policy as a "brief written expression of guiding ideas, derived from regulations, mandates, or an organization's philosophy." A crisis policy provides guidance to those responding to the crisis and authorizes a course of action. In contrast, procedures provide detailed implementation protocols or step-by-step crisis plans.

PLANNING FOR A CRISIS   Every school must have a crisis plan in place that is shared with all teachers and staff prior to any crisis event, implemented quickly in a crisis, reviewed annually and after a crisis event, and updated as needed. National data from the *School Survey on Crime and Safety* (U.S. Department of Education, National Center for Education Statistics, 2004) indicated that the majority of schools has written crisis plans. Many times schools are faced with responding to crises as they are unfolding (e.g., intruder in the school building, terrorist attack, natural disaster). During the planning phase, it is important to predict and describe the types of crises the plan will address in the school based on needs and vulnerabilities.

CRISIS TEAM   The first step in crisis planning is to establish a crisis team. This team should include a team leader (usually the principal), professional school counselors, teachers, school social worker, school psychologist, school security officer, school nurse, custodian or building manager, staff members, and communications coordinator. The team should also include individuals who have specialized training in crisis intervention and grief/loss counseling as well as professional counselors, social workers, psychologists, and psychiatrists from the community.

Kerr (2009, pp. 36–37) suggested that responsibilities be shared among the following team members:

1. *Crisis team leader:*   usually the principal or another administrator.
2. *Crisis team leader designee:*   a person who takes over if the team leader is absent.
3. *Offsite manager:*   a senior staff member without direct student responsibilities who can prepare in-shelter facilities in an evacuation.
4. *Security coordinator:*   a school resource officer, security guard, or other staff member who can work with others to secure the school until law enforcement arrives.
5. *Medical responder:*   usually the school nurse or a staff member with medical training.
6. *Communications coordinator:*   someone who manages the communications until the designated spokesperson takes over. This person may need to work with additional individuals who can translate information to be relayed in all languages represented in the school community.
7. *Mental health specialist:*   a school counselor, psychologist, or social worker who is responsible for providing counseling support and services.
8. *Facilities manager:*   a custodian or building manager who can address utility needs, direct traffic, and provide floor plans to public safety responders.
9. Other staff members, including teachers.

Riley and McDaniel (2000) asserted that during times of crisis, the role of the school counselor is critical. School counselors are expected to provide counseling for students, coordinate all counseling activities, communicate with teachers and parents, seek support from the crisis team and contact neighboring schools. The position statement on immediate response prepared by the American School Counselor Association (2000) stated that school counselors provide direct counseling services during intervention and postvention phases of the crisis. They are also expected to serve students and school personnel during times of crisis by providing individual and group counseling; to consult with administrators, teachers, parents, and professionals; and to coordinate services with the school and the community (American School Counselor Association, 2012).

The crisis team should be provided with extensive training that occurs on an ongoing basis. Crisis teams should meet at the beginning of each school year to review procedures and receive training. In addition, the crisis team should meet several times during the school year to receive additional training and discuss case scenarios and appropriate responses. Contact information should be updated at these training sessions so that team members can be reached quickly and easily in the event of a crisis. These training sessions provide an opportunity for team members to become acquainted and share strategies to be implemented if a crisis occurs. These sessions are also a time to assign specific responsibilities to each team member and to reassign responsibilities if necessary. For success, it is critical that the crisis team have the full support of the school administration.

CRISIS PREPARATION The Center for Mental Health in Schools at UCLA (2008) recommends steps that could be taken in preparation for a crisis:

- Post on the wall of each classroom an outline of emergency procedures and crisis team information.
- At the beginning of each school year, distribute updated information to all school personnel explaining the crisis plan and responsibilities of the crisis team.
- Provide in-service training for all school staff at the beginning and midpoint of the school year.
- Perform disaster/crisis drills (e.g., lockdown, shelter-in-place, evacuation, hurricane, tornado, intruder in the building).

While full-scale disaster drills may be difficult to carry out, a practical method and alternative to a full-scale drill is the tabletop exercise, which is designed so that district and school crisis teams, first responders, and other community partners come to the table to evaluate whether written plans would work in an actual emergency. In this exercise, a hypothetical scenario is discussed to assess how school and community partners would respond to the situation. Based upon the results of the tabletop exercise, revisions to the crisis plan may be made (Trump, 2009).

When preparing for drills, it is important to contact representatives from local schools, law enforcement, and emergency response agencies. Inquire about kinds of crisis situations that have happened or are likely to happen in your area so that you may consider them as you are developing your drill. It would be extremely important for the crisis team to present an in-service training to all school personnel, including bus drivers, administrative assistants, custodians, food services staff, and anyone employed by the school. Professionals from the local community who have expertise in crisis counseling should also be invited to participate in the training.

IMPLEMENTING THE WRITTEN CRISIS PLAN The crisis team is responsible for implementing a written crisis plan that outlines the school's response to crises. This plan should detail exact steps to be taken in the event of a crisis situation. Although most school districts will have a general plan, each school would need to adapt the plan to its needs. Often, schools are called upon to respond to crises as they are unfolding (e.g., intruder in the building, violent event in the building, natural disaster, terrorist attack). Each school should have a plan for responding to such situations, and each classroom teacher should know how to implement the plan. This plan should be shared with everyone in the school community so that they are aware of response procedures. This information must be translated in all languages represented in the school community. Parents/guardians must be informed of the plan prior to any crisis. A letter or brochure (written in all languages spoken by families) should be developed and sent to parents/guardians explaining this plan so everyone will understand what will occur during a crisis situation (e.g., lockdown, shelter in place, evacuation). While the letter or brochure should not describe specific actions or locations in detail in case a parent/guardian might be the intruder, it should provide a general overview so that parents/guardians are secure in the knowledge that their children are safe at school. Parents/guardians must be informed so that they understand that the school has planned for crises and to reassure them that the school has a plan to keep all students safe.

FEMA (2012) recommends the following action steps in developing the crisis plan: (1) identify and involve stakeholders; (2) consider existing efforts; (3) determine what the crisis plan will address; (4) define roles and responsibilities; and (5) develop methods for communicating with the staff, students, families, and the media. Decisions need to be made regarding how the school will communicate with individuals who are directly or indirectly involved in the crisis. Because crisis team members and staff will need to have several means of communication (e.g., walkie-talkie, cell phones, intercom), it is important to obtain necessary equipment and supplies ahead of time. Staff must also be given the necessary equipment to respond in a crisis, such as emergency response guide, phones, radios, contact information for families, student rosters, first aid supplies, food, and water.

When a crisis occurs, it is imperative to determine as quickly as possible whether students and staff need to be evacuated from the building, returned to the building, or locked down in the building. Evacuation requires all students and staff to leave the building. The evacuation plan should include backup buildings to serve as emergency shelters (e.g., religious institutions, community centers, businesses, or other schools). Agreements for using these spaces should be confirmed prior to the beginning of each school year. Evacuation plans should also include contingencies for weather conditions as well as transportation methods for students.

Sometimes an incident may occur while students are outside, and they will need to return to the building. Once inside the building, the situation may call for a lockdown. Lockdowns are appropriate when a crisis occurs outside of the school and an evacuation would be dangerous. A lockdown may also be necessary when there is a crisis within the school, such as an intruder or shooter. In a lockdown, all exterior doors are locked and students and staff stay in their classrooms. Windows may need to be covered and classroom doors locked to prevent an intruder from gaining access to potential victims. Alternatively, "shelter-in-place" may need to be used when there is not time to evacuate or when it may be harmful to leave the building (because of hazardous material spills, hurricane, flooding, etc.).

In the event of a crisis, emergency responders need to know exact locations of everything in a school. Site maps should include information about classrooms, hallways, and stairwells, location of utility shut-offs, and potential staging sites. Emergency responders should have copies of this information in advance. In addition to maps, it is essential to designate locations for emergency responders to organize, for medical personnel to treat the injured, for the public information officer to brief the media, and for families to be reunited with their children.

During a crisis, it is imperative to account for all students, staff, and visitors. Before a crisis occurs, families should be informed of release procedures. Finally, drills and crisis exercises for staff, students, and emergency responders must be carried out frequently whether in large scale or using tabletop exercises.

A key consideration in any crisis intervention plan is the method for communicating with students, staff, families, and the media. FEMA (2012) recommends that one of the first steps in planning for communication is to develop a mechanism to notify students and staff that an incident is occurring and to instruct them on what to do. This communication should cover the methods available to reunite students with their families as quickly as possible and to provide factual information for the school community. The crisis plan should indicate what information will be shared and who is responsible for conveying the information (U.S. Department of Education, 2003).

When sharing information, it is necessary to consider and provide for language and cultural differences. Information should be shared in all languages represented at the school. In addition, there should be individuals available who speak these languages to respond to parents' questions. Information may be shared by activating emergency response messages to phones via text, voice message, e-mail, website, telephone tree, or letter. In addition, a crisis plan should address how to implement these services:

- Return the school to its normal routines.
- Provide physical and emotional support to all those affected by the crisis.
- Identify and refer those at risk for unhealthy behaviors and reactions.
- Provide care for the crisis team. One strategy to help prevent burnout would be to assign crisis team members on a rotating basis. (Knox & Roberts, 2005)
- Evaluate responses to refine and improve future responses.

Specific crisis plans should be developed for a variety of crisis situations, as each crisis may require different responses. Plans should be developed for the following, at a minimum:

- Natural disasters (weather)
- Intruder in the building
- Emergency in neighborhood
- Facilities issues (electrical outage, heating, plumbing)
- Individual accidents and illnesses
- Hostage situations
- Death of student, teacher, or other school personnel
- Terrorist attack
- Suicide
- Bomb threat
- Events outside school that affect the school community (students/staff witnessing an accident, crime, etc.)

I. ASSESSMENT
___A. Identify problem and determine degree of impact on school.
___B. Take steps to secure the safety and security of the site as needed.
___C. Make incident report to district administrator.
___D. Determine if additional support is needed.
    ___1. Call school police and/or city police.
    ___2. Call Cluster Crisis Team.
    ___3. Call other district crisis personnel.
___E. Alter daily/weekly schedule as needed.

II. INTERVENTION: COMMUNICATION
___A. Set up a Command Center.
___B. Establish Sign-In Procedures at ALL campus entry sites.*
___C. Administrator/designee/crisis manager should:
    ___1. Review facts/determine what information should be shared.
    ___2. Consider police investigation parameters.
    ___3. Notify family with sensitivity and dispatch. (Consider a personal family contact.)
___D. Develop and disseminate a bilingual fact sheet (written bulletin).
    ___1. Faculty
    ___2. Students
    ___3. Parents/community
___E. Begin media interactions.
    ___1. Identify a media spokesperson. (Office of Communications may be utilized.)
    ___2. Designate a location for media representatives.*
___F. Contact neighboring schools.
___G. Contact schools of affected students siblings.
___H. Organize other communication activities.
    ___1. Classroom presentations/discussions
    ___2. Parent/community meetings
    ___3. School staff meeting
___I. Provide for rumor control.
    ___1. Keep a TV set or radio tuned to a news station.
    ___2. Verify ALL facts heard.
    ___3. Update fact sheet as needed.
    ___4. Utilize student leaders
        (a) as sources knowledgeable of rumors among students.
        (b) as peer leaders to convey factual information.
        (c) as runners (written bulletins should be sealed when necessary).

III. INTERVENTION: FIRST AID AND EMERGENCY RELEASE PLAN
___A. Initiate First Aid Team procedures.
___B. Designate Emergency Health Office location.*
___C. Initiate Emergency Release Plan procedures.
___D. Designate student check-out location.*

IV. INTERVENTION: PSYCHOLOGICAL FIRST AID/COUNSELING
___A. Logistics: Designate rooms/locations/areas.**
    ___1. Individual counseling—location:_____**
    ___2. Group counseling—location: _____**

FIGURE 11.1 A Sample Crisis Plan Developed by the Los Angeles Unified School District.

___3. Parents—Location: _____ **

___4. Staff (certificated and classified)—location:_____ **

___5. Sign-in for support services—location: _____

___B. Initiate the referral process, including procedures for self-referral.

    ___1. Identify a crisis team member to staff all locations.**

    ___2. Provide bilingual services as needed.

    ___3. Distribute appropriate forms for student counseling referrals to staff.

    ___4. Disseminate student referral information to teachers and other staff.

___C. Identify and contact high-risk students.

___D. Identify and contact other affected students, staff, and personnel.

___E. Initiate appropriate interventions:

    1. Individual counseling

    2. Group counseling

    3. Parent/community meetings

    4. Staff meetings (ALL staff)

    5. Classroom activities, presentations

    6. Referrals to community agencies

IV. INTERVENTION: DISSEMINATE APPROPRIATE HANDOUTS TO STAFF/PARENTS

V. INTERVENTION: DEBRIEFING

___A. Offer daily and mandatory debriefing.

___B. Organize crisis intervention activities.

    ___1. Review the actions of the day.

    ___2. Identify weaknesses and strengths of crisis interventions.

    ___3. Review status of referred students.

    ___4. Prioritize needs/personnel needed the next day.

    ___5. Plan follow-up actions.

___C. Allow time for emotional debriefing.

*Logistics/room designations/space allocations.

**Support personnel needed for these locations

Source: Center for Mental Health in Schools at UCLA,. (2008). *Responding to a Crisis at a School.*
Los Angeles, CA: Author. Retrieved from http://smhp.psych.ucla.edu/pdfdocs/crisis/crisis.pdf

FIGURE 11.1 (*continued*)

Response

According to Trump (2009), the terms *emergency* and *crisis* are often used inter-changeably in schools. However, the two terms have different meanings. An emergency refers to actions taken immediately to manage an event that may threaten the safety of all parties with the goal of stopping or minimizing the event. Emergency guidelines would be implemented when there is an event that threatens the safety of the school community (e.g., intruder in the building, shooting in the building, natural disaster, fire, bomb). A crisis involves actions taken after an emergency situation is under control to deal with the emotional needs of all parties affected by the event. By separating these concepts, schools are able to create concise and clear guidelines to use as references.

According to FEMA (2012), in the event of an emergency school personnel should take the following steps:

- Assess the situation and choose the appropriate response.
- Notify the appropriate emergency responders and then the school crisis team and school board administration.
- Decide whether to evacuate or lock down the school.
- Provide emergency first aid to those in need.
- Keep supplies nearby and organized at all times.
- Trust leadership of the crisis team and emergency responders. This trust will help to minimize the chaos that occurs during a crisis.
- Communicate accurate and appropriate information to stakeholders and the media.
- Activate the student release system.
- Allow for flexibility in implementing the crisis plan.
- Document steps taken. Write down every action taken during the response to provide a record of appropriate implementation of the crisis plan.

At times, a crisis affects a large number of students, and a systematic response from the school is required (American School Counselor Association, 2000; Trusty & Brown, 2005). Examples of crises that may dictate a systemic response include student homicide or suicide, unexpected death, and natural disasters. Although crises are, unfortunately, an uncontrollable aspect of school life, the manner in which school professionals respond to crisis can be controlled. Professional school counselors often play leadership roles in helping schools develop and implement a systemic crisis plan, which is comprehensive and well planned, mobilizes resources, and operates quickly (Steigerwald, 2010b).

Crisis response plans should exist both on a district level and on an individual-school level. Professional school counselors may be members of the district and school critical response teams or solely members of the school-level response team. In either case, the professional school counselor takes a leadership role in the prevention, intervention, and postincident support of school critical responses (American School Counselor Association, 2000). In this role, professional school counselors provide individual and group counseling; consult with administrators, teachers, parents, and professionals; and coordinate services within the school and the community (Allen et al., 2002; American School Counselor Association, 2000).

Crisis plans need to be put in place before a crisis occurs. Crisis response planning committees and crisis response teams (CRTs) are instrumental in planning for, coordinating, and implementing a systemic crisis response. James (2008) recommended the following minimum requirements for a school crisis plan:

- *Physical requirements:* Identify locations for temporary counseling offices. An operations/communications center should be identified where crisis intervention procedures are monitored, needs are assessed, and information for the media is disseminated. Other suggestions include a break room, a first-aid room, and an information center designed to handle media personnel and to facilitate parent communication.

- *Logistics:* Address specific areas that need consideration as an intervention plan is implemented. For example, attention needs to be given to the manner in which on-site and off-site communication will take place. Other logistics that need attention include providing (1) procedural checklists to ensure that the intervention plan is being followed, (2) building plans for emergency personnel, and (3) food and drink for crisis personnel.
- *Crisis response:* Prepare a sequential plan for crisis response that includes gathering and verifying the facts, assessing the impact of the crisis to determine what assistance is needed, providing triage assessment to determine who is most in need of immediate attention, providing psychological first aid as a first-order response, having a model in place, providing crisis intervention, and following through by briefing, debriefing, and demobilizing.

In response to a crisis, team members should first strive to ensure student safety and simultaneously send for help from support personnel (inside or outside of the school as appropriate). Crisis counselors should listen actively, be direct and honest, know their limits, help keep the students informed at each intervention step, and inform parents as soon as possible. They also should not panic, rush, or lose patience with students, act shocked, judge, underreact, or preach (University of South Florida, 2012). In the midst of a school crisis that the University of South Florida faced (in this instance, a death on campus), the following steps, which can be modified for other types of crises, were suggested:

1. The school principal should contact the police or medical examiner in order to verify the death and get facts surrounding the death.
2. Inform the superintendent of the school district of the death.
3. Prepare and activate procedures for responding to the media.
4. Notify and activate the school's crisis response team.
5. Contact the family of the deceased.
6. Schedule a time and place to notify faculty members and all other school staff.
7. Contact community support services.
8. Arrange a meeting for parents/caregivers.
9. Meet with all students in small groups.
10. Provide additional survivor support services, such as suicide bereavement support groups.
11. Members of the school's crisis team should have knowledge of the victim's classes to gauge which students may need intervention.
12. Establish support stations or counseling rooms.
13. Debrief staff.
14. Reschedule any immediate stressful academic exercises.
15. In the case of a suicide, avoid flying the school flag at half-mast in order to avoid glamorizing the death.
16. During any memorialization, focus on prevention, education, and living.
17. Collaborate with students to utilize social media effectively to disseminate information and promote suicide prevention efforts.
18. Inform local crisis telephone lines and local mental health agencies about the death.

19. Provide information about visiting hours and funeral arrangements to staff, students, parents, and community members.
20. Encourage the family of the deceased to schedule the funeral after school hours.
21. Arrange for students, faculty, and staff to be excused from school to attend the funeral.
22. Follow up with students who are identified as at-risk.

It is essential for professional school counselors to be familiar with their district and school crisis response plans. If no such plan is in place, professional school counselors will want to work with administrators and other school personnel to create and implement a plan to respond to crises. Moreover, professional school counselors can be instrumental in leading workshops in the school and community to communicate the plan to others. A helpful resource that provides information and guidance for crisis planning is *Crisis Communications Guide and Toolkit* (www.nea.org/crisis), produced by the National Education Association (2002). The University of South Florida (2012) also provides sound suggestions for how to respond to and work with the media during crises.

Recovery

The goal of recovery is to return the school to a stable, precrisis environment and return students to learning as quickly as possible. However, FEMA (2012) cautions that healing and recovery may take months or even years depending on the traumatic event. School personnel need to understand that healing is a process that will take time. It is necessary to plan for recovery during the preparedness phase so that roles and responsibilities of everyone who will participate in the recovery process are defined. There are different models for implementing services and support during the recovery process. Many school systems will have a system-wide crisis intervention team that will go to the school where the crisis has occurred and provide counseling and support for days/weeks following the crisis. Other schools may have the in-school crisis team provide counseling and services for the school community.

During the recovery phase, school personnel need to keep students, families, and the media informed. It is imperative to clearly state what steps have been implemented to provide for student safety. In addition, families and community members need to be informed about services being provided for students and families at school and in the community. Cultural differences should be considered when composing letters or announcements to parents. It may be necessary to translate letters and other forms of communication into the languages represented at the school.

While in the recovery phase, remember to focus on the building as well as the people. There may be damage to the building that needs to be repaired. FEMA (2012) recommends conducting safety audits to assess the building and develop plans for repairs. In addition to assessing the damage to the building, it is critical to continue to assess the emotional needs of all students and staff to determine who will need the services of the school counselor, social worker, school psychologist, or other mental health professionals. Specific suggestions for interventions with students, school staff, and families will be discussed later in this chapter.

Debriefing

Debriefing is a time for the crisis team members to gather and share their unique experiences of the crisis in a private and safe environment. It is extremely important to allow some time for the crisis team members to share their thoughts and feelings. Team members may have been the teachers, counselors, and mentors of the victims. Or the event may have triggered some other unresolved crisis in their lives. Hence, support for the crisis team is critical. It is important for the team leader to invite team members to share what happened, what the experience was like, what memory stands out in their mind that is hard to erase, and what each can do to take care of themselves during and after the crisis. Fitzgerald (1998) offered the following suggestions for self-care after a crisis:

- Debrief with partner, team members, or supervisor.
- Attend regular support meetings.
- Find ways to relax such as music, exercise, meditation, hobbies, reading, or sports.
- Maintain a healthy balance in life and separate work from leisure time.
- Acknowledge personal feelings.
- Spend quality time with family and friends who are not connected with your crisis work.
- Visit a place that is peaceful such as a church, synagogue, park, or art gallery.
- Write in a journal.

Evaluation of the crisis response and recovery efforts is a necessary part of the crisis plan. FEMA (2012, pp. 5–6) suggests conducting interviews with the crisis team, emergency responders, families, teachers, students, and staff in order to determine what efforts were successful along with changes that are necessary. The following are examples of questions to ask:

- Which classroom-based interventions proved most successful and why?
- Which assessment and referral strategies were the most successful and why?
- What were the most positive aspects of staff debriefings and why?
- Which recovery strategies would you change and why?
- Do other professionals need to be tapped to help with future crises?
- What additional training is necessary to enable the school and the community at large to prepare for future crises?
- What additional equipment is needed to support recovery efforts?
- What other planning actions will facilitate future recovery efforts?

Helping Students During and After School Crises

Students will need to talk about what they have experienced during the crisis and it is important to offer a variety of counseling services for students so that they feel supported and receive needed help. Individual counseling and small-group counseling give students an opportunity to express their feelings and receive support. Classroom guidance lessons and class meetings may also be extremely helpful and can provide a forum for students to express emotions, obtain accurate information, and ask questions. Brock (1998) developed an intervention program for use in classrooms following a school crisis. The program focuses on providing facts and dispelling rumors, sharing

VOICES FROM THE FIELD 11.2
Dealing with a School Suicide

Nicole Adamson

As part of a class assignment during my first semester as a school counseling master's student, I enthusiastically decided to shadow the high school counselor in my hometown. My connections with the members of my rural community run deep and many of the students at the school were younger siblings of my high school friends. Many Friday nights were spent caring for these students when their parents went out to celebrate their anniversaries or birthdays. Needless to say, I was truly excited to return to the high school and experience the culture from a different vantage point.

As I walked into the building, I immediately sensed something was wrong; the tension was palpable. I approached the school counselor's office only to find several sobbing students. When the school counselor saw that I had come to shadow her, she met with me privately and informed me that she was dealing with a crisis situation. A male student had passed away the previous evening as a result of suicide.

To further complicate the situation, I knew the student personally, as his family lived next door to one of my closest friends. This news greatly affected me and I was torn between a desire to mourn and a desire to help the young students who knew and loved this student. The minimal training I'd had at that point had not prepared me to handle a situation such as this. I did not know how to integrate my personal reactions with my emerging professional role.

The school counselor handled the situation with confidence. First, she called a local agency to assist in meeting with students who needed individual assistance. She then continued to meet with students until the external agency's counselors arrived. When these counselors came and met individually with students, I had an opportunity to learn from these observations.

Later that day, as I processed these events, I gained an awareness of the complexities of a school counselor's job. I had previously understood the classroom guidance, student planning, and system support aspects of the school counselor's responsibilities, but on that day I gained an understanding of school counselors' important role in managing responsive services. I learned that my own emotions were natural and could help me empathize with the thoughts and feelings of students in a crisis. I also learned that counselors must sometimes set aside their own needs in order to best help others.

Although that day was filled with pain and struggle, it informed and colored my experience as an emerging counselor. I gained an acute understanding of the complexities of the school counseling profession, and I learned the value of crisis response preparedness. I also learned from an excellent school counselor how to identify and use resources in order to respond appropriately and effectively to a crisis.

stories, sharing reactions, empowering students, and providing closure. Younger children may not be able to articulate their feelings but will benefit from opportunities to draw, paint, or participate in other creative activities. Adolescents should be encouraged to talk about their feelings in small group discussions or through writing about their experiences.

Helping Parents/Guardians During and After a School Crisis

When there is a crisis at school, parents/guardians must receive accurate information along with appropriate suggestions for assisting their children. It is very helpful to send a letter to parents/guardians that includes accurate information, symptoms, common and uncommon reactions they might observe in their children, and suggestions to help children who are experiencing distress as a result of the crisis. Figure 11.2 presents a sample letter to parents/guardians related to the death of a student. These letters

Dear Parents/Guardians:

I regret to inform you of the death of one of our students. Laurie Jones, a fifth grader, died on January 15 of leukemia. I know that you join me in my concern and sympathy for the family.

The students were told of Laurie's death today by their classroom teachers. Crisis counselors visited each class and provided an opportunity for students to talk, ask questions, and share their feelings. Those children who were most upset met privately with counselors for additional counseling and support. Counseling services will continue to be made available to students this week and in the future as needed.

Notes and cards may be sent to the family at the following address: Mr. and Mrs. Jackson Jones XXX Elm Street, Arlington, VA 222XX. A memorial service will be held at St. John's Church on Monday, January 19 at 9:00 a.m. The church is located at 1500 Main Street, Arlington, VA 22207. In lieu of flowers, the family requests that donations be made to the Leukemia and Lymphoma Society.

Your children may experience a wide range of emotions as a result of Laurie's death. The following suggestions may be useful as you help your children cope with their grief:

- Encourage your children to talk about their feelings or to draw pictures to express their emotions.
- Offer support and let your children know that you are available to talk with them and answer questions.
- Allow your children to be sad and to cry.
- Reassure your children that they are healthy, and discuss fears they may have about their own death or the death of a family member.
- Explain the ritual of funerals and memorial services. If children express a desire to attend the memorial service, it is recommended that you accompany them.
- Monitor your child's emotional state and behavior. If you notice prolonged sadness, withdrawal from social contact, changes in eating or sleeping habits, or other behavior unusual for your child, please contact Ms. Smith, our professional school counselor, who will be available to offer support and resources to you and your child. She can be reached at XXX-555-3607 or Jaclyn.Smith@xxx.k-12

If you have questions or concerns, please don't hesitate to contact me.
Sincerely,
Mrs. Helen Smith, Principal
XXX-555-2438, Helen.Smith@xxx.k-12

FIGURE 11.2   Sample Letter to Parents/Guardians.

should be developed before a crisis so that, when a crisis occurs, they can be quickly adapted to the uniqueness of the existing crisis and then copied and distributed. These letters can be sent home and put on the school's website; however, the website should never be the only means of communication, since there are many families without this technological resource. The letters should be written in all languages that are represented in the school community.

Depending on the nature of the crisis, it may be necessary to invite parents/guardians to a group meeting at school so that they can receive accurate information, share feelings and questions, and learn ways to support their children during and following the crisis. The goals of the family/community meeting are to impart information and to assist the family and community members in processing their reactions to the crisis (Poland & McCormick, 1999). At this meeting, the crisis team can offer support and suggestions, while also passing along information about services that are available in the community (American School Counselor Association, 2003).

The National Association of School Psychologists (NASP) offers the following guidelines to help teachers, parents, and other caregivers support children who have experienced loss:

- Give children the opportunity to tell their story and be a good listener.
- Recognize that all children are different and their views of the world are unique and shaped by different experiences.
- Understand that "grieving is a process, not an event." Parents and schools need to allow adequate time for each child to grieve in whatever way they choose. Also, remember that encouraging children to resume "normal" activities without the opportunity to deal with their emotional pain may cause negative reactions.
- Provide honest information about the tragic event in developmentally appropriate ways.
- Encourage children to ask questions about loss and death.

Notifying Students of a Death, Accident, or Event

In addition to guidelines in the crisis plan, the following steps should be followed for situations where students are being notified of a death, accident, or event.

- Gather the crisis team members for a planning meeting. The team members should obtain and verify the facts of the incident and designate the person who will continue to gather factual information. At this time, the team should decide on the format for conveying the information to teachers, students, school staff, parents (e.g., large-group meetings, classroom meetings, emergency alert/texts/e-mails/letters to parents).
- Conduct a meeting for teachers and school staff before school begins to inform them of the situation and to give them information about how the crisis plan will be implemented.
- Form teams that can announce the crisis event via individual classroom sessions, meetings of smaller groups of students, general assemblies, or announcements to larger groups. Keep in mind that meeting with smaller groups and holding general assemblies are the preferred methods for passing along the information. The public address system should be used only if absolutely necessary.
- The leader of the crisis team should determine the assignments for crisis team members, taking into account team member strengths and comfort levels. Possible roles for team members include direct contact with groups of students, individual counseling sessions, and administrative tasks. Crisis intervention should never be done alone. Team members should always work in pairs. Two crisis team members should observe the class and look for high-risk students. Having two team members working together allows one team member to escort a distressed child out of the room for private counseling, while the other team member continues working with the group. Team members who are experiencing the same intervention are able to debrief each other and can monitor each other's stress levels and react accordingly.

- Introduce crisis team members to the students. Even if students know the staff, teachers, school counselors, and administrators from other interactions, students must be made aware that these people are also crisis team members and be apprised of the team members' roles during the crisis event.
- Ask students if any of them have heard about the event. Allow students to tell what they know or have heard about the event. This will not only allow the sharing of information but will also allow any rumors to be discussed in the group so the team can verify or deny them publicly.
- Deliver the facts of the event in developmentally appropriate terms, and clarify any rumors or incorrect information. Allow enough time for students to ask questions.
- When appropriate, allow children to tell their stories about this experience or similar ones. List all the feelings voiced on the blackboard and spend some time talking about the normalcy of these feelings.
- In crises that may involve another student, allow students to talk about memories each has of the absent student.
- If the event involves a student who may be able to return to school, it is important to discuss what they may encounter when the student returns and how they can help the student.
- If the event involves the death of a student, keep in mind the additional issues to address—for example, what to do with the empty desk. Often, the desk will be left vacant for a period of time; however, a time limit should be established and shared with the other students so they understand that the desk eventually will be removed. It is crucial to involve the students in this process.
- If developmentally appropriate, share information regarding the funeral, including the type of funeral and cultural rituals.
- Provide information regarding the resources that are available at school and in the community and provide additional handout materials that can be helpful to the students in working through the crisis.

SCHOOL RESPONSES TO NATIONAL CRISES

Many crises occur miles away from our schools or even in other states or countries (e.g. hurricanes, earthquakes, terrorist attacks, school shootings, war). However, such crises may have a tremendous impact on our students in schools throughout the nation. School personnel must always respond in a way that reassures students, teachers, staff, and parents/guardians. It is important that they follow these guidelines:

- Present accurate information in developmentally appropriate ways.
- Give students opportunities to express feelings and ask questions.
- Provide information for teachers and parents/guardians so that they can help students.
- Organize service activities so that students and all members of the school community can provide assistance to victims (e.g., collect money/clothing for victims, organize fund raisers, correspond with children who were affected).

TABLE 11.1 Resources and Websites

- Responding to Crisis at a School: UCLA Resource Aid Packet http://smhp.psych.ucla.edu/pdf-docs/crisis/crisis.pdf
- FEMA for Kids: FEMA website for children to help them understand and prepare for disaster www.fema.gov/kids/
- Center for Mental Health Services: Tips for talking about disaster www.mentalhealth.org/cmhs/emergency services/after.aps
- National Association of School Psychologists: Provides information on helping children, youth, parents, teachers, and schools cope with crisis www.nasponline.org
- U.S. Department of Education: Tips for helping students recover from traumatic events www.ed.gov/parent/academic/help/recovering
- U.S. Department of Education, Office of Safe and Drug-Free Schools: Provides crisis planning to create drug-free schools www.ed.gov/admins/lead/safety/crisisplanning.html
- U.S. Department of Education, Office of Safe and Drug-Free Schools: Practical Information on Crisis Planning: A Guide for Schools and Communities. To order copies e-mail request to ed-pubs@inet.ed.gov or call 1-877-433-7827
- Emergency Response and Crisis Management (ERCM) Technical Assistance Center www.ercm.org
- UCLA Center for Mental Health in Schools: Basic information on responding to crisis in schools http://smhp.psych.ucla.edu
- American Red Cross www.redcross.org
- American Hospice Foundation: Information and activities for children and adolescents coping with loss/disaster/crisis www.americanhospice.org
- National Education Association—NEA Health Information Network www.nea.org/crisis/bihome.html#response
- American School Counselor Association : Resource section offers articles/activities that can be used to assist schools in responding to crisis and the needs of the school community www.schoolcounselor.org

Table 11.1 provides a listing of resources and websites with additional helpful information about dealing with crises on school and university campuses. Case Studies 11.1 through 11.6 apply the skills learned thus far in the chapter.

CASE STUDY 11.1

A Student with a Terminal Illness

Laurie was a fifth grader diagnosed with leukemia within the past year. During this time, she was absent from school while receiving chemotherapy treatment for her cancer and had lost her hair. The students were aware of her condition. Her parents just called the school and reported that Laurie died. The principal asks you to call a meeting of the crisis team, teachers, and appropriate staff to discuss how to best approach the other students about Laurie's death. As the leader of this team, consider these questions.

Discussion Questions

1. Who needs to be contacted before offering any news? What do you need to know?
2. How do you decide what groups are the priority to received intervention?
3. Who are some typical groups?
4. What questions would you expect to have from students?

CASE STUDY 11.2

Natural Disaster

A tornado hit and destroyed the school building and many homes in a small Midwest town. There were only a few students and teachers in the school at the time the tornado hit. They took cover and were not injured. The school was destroyed and must be entirely rebuilt. Homes and businesses in the town were destroyed and 25 deaths occurred.

Discussion Questions

1. Discuss how the crisis team would be used and how the crisis plan would be implemented.
2. How should the school intervene with the students, teachers, staff, parents/guardians, and community?

CASE STUDY 11.3

School Shooting

A 17-year-old male enters the cafeteria, takes out a gun and begins shooting at students seated at tables. Eight students are hit before the gunman runs out of the building. You are the school counselor and come into the cafeteria just after the shooting has occurred.

Discussion Questions

1. What immediate steps should be taken to insure the safety of everyone in the school?
2. Discuss how the crisis team would be involved and how the crisis plan would be implemented.
3. How should the school intervene with students, teachers, staff, parents, and community?

CASE STUDY 11.4

Stabbing as a Student Exits the Bus

A 10th-grade student is the first one to exit the school bus. Just after he steps onto the sidewalk, another student walks up to him, starts screaming, and stabs him. The student falls to the ground and later dies. All of the students on the bus and in front of the school, along with the bus driver, witness the event.

Discussion Questions

1. What immediate steps should be taken to ensure the safety of everyone in the area?
2. Discuss how the crisis team would be involved and how the crisis plan would be implemented.
3. How should the school intervene with students, teachers, staff, parents, and community?

CASE STUDY 11.5

Death of a Teacher

It is 8:00 a.m. and the principal calls you, the elementary school counselor, to his office to say that a teacher died suddenly last evening.

Discussion Questions

1. Discuss how you might react to this situation.
2. What steps should be taken to inform the teachers, staff, students, and parents?
3. Discuss how the crisis team would be involved and how the crisis plan would be implemented.
4. How should the school intervene with students, teachers, staff, and parents?

CASE STUDY 11.6

Student Threatening Violence

The high school counselor has been alerted that there are two students in the school parking lot with rifles and a box of explosives. The students were overheard saying: "We're going to get everyone who has been bullying us for years. We're going to shoot up the school and make everyone pay."

Discussion Questions

1. If you were the counselor, discuss how you would feel/react?
2. What steps should be taken to ensure the safety of the school community?
3. Discuss how the crisis team would be involved and how the crisis plan would be implemented.
4. How should the school intervene and support students, teachers, staff, and parents?

VOICES FROM THE FIELD 11.3
My Last Day

Tori Stone

It was the last day of school. I was wrapped up in last-day-of-school thoughts: saying goodbye to my eighth-grade students; the adaptation of *A Midsummer Night's Dream* the eighth grade students were presenting; the faculty luncheon that afternoon. I remember sending the girls who would take the class passes to the main office for an errand, but they returned because they wanted me to give them stickers. That stands out in my mind: the innocence of the girls returning for the stickers. I was handing them the stickers when the principal came running through, yelling "Lock it down, lock it down, lock it down!" I can still remember the sound of his voice. It was clear that something was very wrong.

I pushed the girls into my office, closed the door and turned off the lights. I had the girls crawl under my desk and hide themselves in the corner furthest from the door. I pulled the phone onto the floor and called my guidance director to find out what was going on. She told me there was a student with several rifles and ammunition in the office. I remember thinking to myself, "I can't call these parents and tell them that their children are dead. If someone has to die, it will have to be me." This sounds heroic, but it wasn't. I was more scared than I had ever been in my life. It occurred to me that I didn't want to die; that I might want to have children; that wooden doors are not bullet proof. When one of the girls started to panic, I talked to her calmly about other things. I gave her tissues and patted her back. I told the girls I would protect them. This statement still has the weight of a lie in my head. I knew there was little I could do to protect them.

Time passed, but I'm still not sure how long exactly. Finally, someone pounded on the door and yelled, "SWAT police, come out with your hands up!" The girls cried; I was scared as well. When we opened the door there were SWAT team members in riot gear surrounding my office. They pointed guns at our heads and yelled at us to run. I was afraid, the girls were crying, and I felt angry. I yelled at the SWAT team to stop yelling at the children. They did not stop yelling. They told us to "Shut up and run!" We ran. There were kids in costumes because of the play. I remember seeing little girls dressed like fairies with bare feet. The juxtaposition of SWAT members pointing guns at children in tutus will stay with me forever.

Things I learned: stay calm; follow procedure; act like you are okay in front of the children, even if you are not. Schools should conduct lockdown drills more than once per school year. It should be second nature to staff members to secure their classrooms. Once a building is evacuated for a gunman incident, the building is a crime scene. You cannot reenter. We had 1,100 children outside for more than four hours on a 95 degree day; we had no water and very little shelter from the sun. Some children were overcome by fear, others by the heat. If you work in a small district, ask questions about where students will be moved to in the event of an emergency. Getting to another large venue where kids can have access to water and restrooms, and where parents can pick them up, is essential.

The next day we returned to school and everything was eerily just as we left it. The stickers were still on my desk, balls stood in place on the gymnasium floor, there were shoes in the hallways because kids literally ran out of their shoes. Initially, parents were kind and supportive, but eventually, in search of a reason that could resurrect their sense of security, they wanted to place blame. As a staff we faced many questions—from "Why are there no metal detectors?" to "Why wasn't there water and sunscreen buried someplace on the campus in case of this kind of event?" Parents were scared, and their fear turned quickly to anger; anger that an incident such as this could happen and because we could not promise that it would not happen again. I think back to myself as young and naïve, and never expected the anger and the blame, so I wasn't prepared for it. The truth is, a barricaded hostage event, or worse, a school shooting, could happen at any time, at any school in the country. As school counselors, we are trained to handle critical incidents, and that training is invaluable, but it does not make us impenetrable to random acts of violence. That may very well be the most valuable lesson I learned from this event.

RESPONDING TO CRISES IN HIGHER EDUCATION SETTINGS

Colleges and universities strive to keep campuses safe so that students may grow intellectually and personally. However, this is a constant challenge. All higher education settings must prepare for crises and have plans in place to ensure the safety and well-being of all students, faculty, and staff. The four phases identified by the U.S. Department of Education's Office of Safe and Drug-Free Schools (2003) serve as a model for crisis planning at the college/university level. Discussed earlier in this chapter, they include: mitigation/prevention; preparedness, response, and recovery. Indeed, most of the information presented in this chapter and throughout this book can be applied to university campuses with appropriate modifications.

Colleges and universities must be prepared to respond to the death of any member of the community (student or faculty); natural disasters; terrorist attacks; bomb threats; fire, and other acts of violence. A response for each of these events should be developed and a crisis plan should be prepared and practiced. Everyone who is a member of the campus community (including parents) should be aware of emergency procedures and crisis plan. These procedures and plans should be described on the website and should be discussed with students, faculty, and staff. All campuses should have an alert system (e.g., text, e-mail, website, phone message notification) in place whereby the students, faculty, and staff can be alerted to potential emergencies on campus.

In an effort to prevent acts of violence, many institutions of higher education have created threat assessment teams. These teams are usually composed of representatives from various departments including academic affairs, student affairs, legal counsel, mental health services, and public safety. The threat assessment teams evaluate persons of concern who may pose a potential risk of violence. Drysdale, Modzeleski, and Simons (2010, p. 27) defined a three-step process in threat assessment:

- Identify individuals whose behavior causes concern or disruption on or off campus affecting students, faculty, or staff.
- Assess whether the identified individual possesses the intent and ability to carry out an attack against the community, and if the individual has taken steps to prepare for the attack.
- Manage the threat posed by the individual, to include disrupting potential plans of attack, mitigating the risk, and implementing strategies to facilitate long-term resolution.

Now apply the skills and knowledge learned in this chapter to Case Studies 11.7and 11.8.

CASE STUDY 11.7

Shooting of Students in a Dormitory

The Dean of Students at a large university has just been informed that two student have been shot in a dormitory and have been taken to the hospital. The gunman has not been identified or captured.

Discussion Questions

1. If you were the Dean of Students how would you feel/react?
2. What steps should be taken to ensure the safety of everyone on campus?
3. What steps should the university take to inform and protect students, faculty, staff, and campus employees?
4. How should parents be informed?
5. What should occur in the hours/weeks after the event has occurred?

CASE STUDY 11.8

A Flood on Campus

Recent storms have caused local rivers to overflow and the entire town (including the college campus) is experiencing extreme flooding. Students are unable to leave their dormitories, libraries, or classrooms.

Discussion Questions

1. What steps should be taken to ensure the safety of everyone on campus?
2. What steps should the university take to inform and protect students, faculty, staff, and campus employees?
3. How should parents be informed?
4. What should occur in the hours/weeks after the event has occurred?

VOICES FROM THE FIELD 11.4
Collaboration in the Midst of a Campus Crisis

Kyoung Mi Choi

Because most of the students had returned home for Thanksgiving break, the campus seemed very quiet. Just as I finished my Thanksgiving dinner with friends and was ready to relax, I received a phone call from my supervisor at the Center for International Student Services. With some trepidation, I answered the phone: "Hi, there's been a really bad car accident, and four international students were involved. I'm not sure of the exact situation yet, but would you be able to accompany the DPS [Department of Public Safety] officers to the hospital? They need someone who can speak Korean and communicate with the survivors and their families in Korea. I'll update you with more detailed information later." My heart stopped; I knew something was seriously wrong.

Instead of DPS officers, the Vice President of Student Affairs came to my apartment gate. I briefly greeted him and followed him to the car. As we arrived at the hospital, we were directed to the emergency area. There were two students lying on the beds in two small separate rooms. I was wondering about what happened to the other two students.

Shortly after, I found out that the driver and one of the passengers were the only survivors and the other students were killed in the car accident. The one survivor could not even say a word; tears were rolling down her cheeks. These two students were there—by themselves—wondering about their friends' safety.

Because of the traumatic incident, the students had difficulty communicating in English, a nonnative language for them. I tried to comfort them in Korean while simultaneously translating between the students and the DPS officers, the Victim Protective Services, and the hospital staff. What was even more difficult was that I also had to call the students' parents in Korea; delivering this information to parents who were half-way around the world from their children was difficult.

As a counselor on a college campus, I have worked with international students as a peer mentor, consultant, and educator for international students. Working with international students requires much collaboration and relationship building within all of the functional areas in Student Affairs. Especially, when a crisis happens, the first person contacted is often not the student's parents, but college staff, oftentimes counselors.

At last, the four students' parents were contacted, flights were arranged, and the families arrived on campus. The community, especially ethnic churches and organizations, were actively involved in the funeral preparations and services. The Korean Student Association also set up meetings to support the survivors and the deceased students' families. The campus counseling services provided the survivors and other students who were affected by this incident with individual and group counseling sessions. The Residence Life staff also assisted the deceased students' parents in collecting their children's belongings. The whole campus worked together to support the survivors, mourn the losses, and educate students about safety.

Summary

This chapter provided a detailed overview of crises in schools and how to respond to such crises. An emphasis was placed on how to create a network of support because school systems have so many stakeholders to address (e.g., students, parents, school staff, principals). The components of a comprehensive school crisis plan include determining the composition of the crisis team, gathering the crisis team members for a planning meeting, deciding how to announce the event and discuss or review classroom activities, and holding a team debrief-

ing. This is accomplished through developing effective mitigation and prevention, preparedness, response, recovery, and debriefing strategies. Numerous case studies are provided to allow counselors to apply knowledge and skills gained. All crises evolve through different stages— and then end. Those who experience crisis, disaster, or trauma also evolve in that they, hopefully, resolve or at least experience a lessened impact of the situation. Crises affect lives in systemic ways; every aspect of one's life can be affected by a crisis.

Grief and Loss

Lourie W. Reichenberg

PREVIEW

This chapter covers approaches to crisis counseling with mourners, theories of grieving, and the variables that affect how a bereaved person mourns. It also addresses how timing, the cause of death, and the role the relationship played in a person's life all mediate the mourning process, followed by a discussion that distinguishes between "normal grief" and complicated mourning. Finally, the chapter details how the mourner's belief system (faith, spirituality, and religion) are integral to coping, preventing dysfunction, and finding meaning in life after a loss.

HISTORICAL PERSPECTIVES AND MODELS OF GRIEF WORK

Nearly two and a half million Americans die each year (Kung, Hoyert, Xu, & Murphy, 2008), leaving behind millions of husbands, wives, mothers, fathers, sisters, brothers, children, friends, coworkers, uncles, and aunts to mourn their losses. How the person died, whether it was sudden and unexpected or the result of a prolonged or chronic illness, affects the way the grieving process will unfold. So, too, do the cultural and spiritual backgrounds of the bereaved; their temperaments, life circumstances, and previous experiences with death and loss; and the order of death (e.g., whether it is a grandparent at the end of a long life or a young person just starting out in life).

Of course, grief and loss reactions are not solely related to issues of death and dying. Feelings of loss may occur after many developmentally or situation-related changes. This chapter focuses on many of the different types of losses people encounter but does not address every type of loss specifically. Although there has been an increased deployment of crisis counselors to respond to natural disasters, acts of terrorism (New York, Pennsylvania, and the Pentagon on September 11, 2001), hostage situations, and school shootings, it more likely that a crisis counselor will intervene with a client or family experiencing a recent death or a situational or developmental loss that affects the individual or family.

Working with grieving clients is an important part of both crisis counseling and traditional counseling. Many people seek counseling specifically to help them cope with a recent loss. But far more frequently the client has been in counseling for a while for issues unrelated to death and then experiences the death of a family member or has memories of a previous death triggered by the counseling. At such points, what was previously career counseling or couples counseling may become crisis intervention as the crisis counselor helps the client through the initial impact of the death. For some clients, that will be all that is needed, and they will return to their previous treatment plan. However, for other clients, more extensive counseling may be necessary to help them make sense of the loss and find meaning in life once again.

VOICES FROM THE FIELD 12.1
Mourning the Loss of a Sister

At the age of 53, my older sister, Susie, underwent surgery to remove a benign cyst on her liver. During the surgery, her daughter and I passed the time happily looking through her recent wedding photos. Hours later a nurse led us into a small private room. The doctor, still in his scrubs, his shoes and pant legs covered with blood spatters, came in to inform us that my sister was much sicker than he had realized. When he attempted to remove the tumor, he said, she had "bled out," and despite his best efforts, there was nothing he could do to control the bleeding. My sister had died in the operating room.

The news was unfathomable. One minute we were happily passing the time, and the next moment my 30-year-old niece was wailing, keening back and forth in a state of disbelief. As I put my arms around her to comfort her, it felt surreal, as if I were watching the events unfold from a distance. It seemed as though someone had hit the slow motion button on my internal DVR and everything was proceeding in front of me like a movie, albeit at a slower, choppier pace. This feeling of numbness and unreality stayed with me for days as I went through the rituals of mourning—informing family members about Susie's death, helping to make funeral arrangements, comforting my elderly father, and delivering my sister's eulogy.

When people talked to me, it seemed like I would catch conversations halfway through, as if my head had been underwater and I'd just come up for air. Weeks after the funeral I sat at a football game and felt completely dissociated from the game, as if I weren't really there. For weeks, I would wake up each morning, and within seconds, as the reality of what had happened came back to me, I would stifle a visceral urge to scream. Eventually, as the shock and numbness wore off, I was able to talk about my sister's untimely death with friends and family. By working through the pain I was able to grieve and eventually accept the reality of what had happened.

More than 10 years have passed, my sister's children now have families of their own, and we talk about her frequently. Looking back, I see that the numbness and dissociation that I initially experienced were my body's way of shielding me from feeling the full force of the shock of my sister's death. It was only when the numbness wore off and I was able to feel the pain outright, that the healing process could begin. I will always feel sad at not being able to make new memories with her or simply to have an everyday conversation with my only sister. I have, however, integrated her death into my life, and I often imagine what she would say to me in any given situation. I am thankful for having had her in my life and for the continuing effect that she has on me. I often think of a quote attributed to Rose Kennedy: "Birds sing after a storm; why shouldn't people feel as free to delight in whatever sunlight remains to them?"

In his work *Mourning and Melancholia* (1917), Freud proposed what was probably the first psychoanalytic theory of grieving. Mourning occurs when the libido psyche stubbornly hangs on to a lost object, refusing to give it up. Grieving ends, according to Freud, when the client lets go of attachment to the lost object and becomes free to devote his or her libido to another love object. Although drive theory is not as accepted today as it once was, Freud's writings on mourning provided the basis from which grief work later evolved.

Lindemann's Approach

In what is perhaps the first research conducted on sudden death, Lindemann (1944) studied the 1942 Cocoanut Grove nightclub fire in Boston. Lindemann identified three tasks of mourners: (1) emancipation from the bond to the deceased, (2) readjustment to a life in which the deceased is missing, and (3) formation of new relationships (Berzoff & Silverman, 2004). Like Viktor Frankl's (1959) later work with concentration camp survivors, Lindemann observed feelings of intense guilt in many people who survived the fire.

Adjustment required letting go of the deceased. Lindemann believed that grief was resolved when the mourner severed the relationship with the deceased and moved on to form new attachments. For many years, Lindemann's work remained the main resource on bereavement.

The Death Awareness Movement: Kübler-Ross

Beginning in the 1960s, Elizabeth Kübler-Ross was credited with creating the death awareness movement. Her works, including *On Death and Dying* (1969) and *Death: The Final Stage of Growth* (1975), affected a core change in attitudes toward and education about the dying process and helped to reduce the taboo surrounding the discussion of death in the United States. Kübler-Ross was famous for her work with terminally ill patients, which led to her development of the five stages of dying: (1) denial, (2) rage and anger, (3) bargaining, (4) depression, and (5) acceptance. Kübler-Ross later applied the stages of dying to grief.

Rather than proceeding through the stages as one would proceed from hole to hole on a golf course, people experience the stages of death and dying as more of a spiral, moving forward and then circling back over time. Kübler-Ross (1969, p. 216) also warned that what people experience is far more than mere stages. It is not enough to identify the stages, she wrote. "It is not just about the life lost but also the life lived."

The five stages of death and dying developed by Kübler-Ross have given countless caregivers a framework to understand dying patients. Many crisis counselors base grief counseling on these early works on death and dying. They are presented here with the following caveats. Kübler-Ross's work does not apply to catastrophic or sudden death because there is no time to say good-bye and the dying person is not able to go through the stages of grieving. Nor did Kübler-Ross consider the stages to be concrete or contiguous; rather, her writings were based on observations of common emotions experienced by people in the midst of the dying process (1969, 1972, 1975).

- *Stage I: Denial.* "Not me." "I am not dying." "A miracle will happen." Such comments are typical reactions to being told of a terminal illness. According to Kübler-Ross, denial serves a protective function in the initial stages by cushioning the blow that death is inevitable.

- *Stage II: Rage and anger.* "Why me?" The seemingly arbitrary nature of the news of one's impending death almost always causes one to erupt into anger and rage. Such anger is often targeted at those who are living and will survive as well as at God for handing down the death sentence. Kübler-Ross believed such feelings were not only acceptable but also inevitable.
- *Stage III: Bargaining.* "Yes me, but. ..." In the bargaining stage, one begins to accept the inevitability of death. But one bargains for more time by offering to do good deeds or change in a specific way.
- *Stage IV: Depression.* "Yes, me." The depression stage is the beginning of acceptance. Initially, the person mourns previous regrets and losses, but this turns into an acceptance of the impending death and what is referred to as "preparatory grief" (Kübler-Ross, 1975). During this time, the dying person begins to face any unfinished business and prepares to "let go" peacefully.
- *Stage V: Acceptance.* "Death is very close now, and it's all right." Some people are able to cope with the news of a terminal illness and work through the anger and sadness to reach an emotional equilibrium that allows them to live out their final weeks and months with inner peace.

Research shows that a person's ability to cope with major life stressors in the past is predictive of the manner in which the person is likely to cope with chronic illness and face death. Other factors that facilitate the process of death acceptance include having lived a full life, harboring few regrets about the way in which one lived, being able to talk frankly about the terminal illness with family and medical personnel, holding hope for a life after death, having a close relationship with a significant other, and being concerned for one's children and close friends (Carey, 1975). Fear at the end of life seems to be mostly related to how people view the actual process of their dying: anxiety surrounding their pain and being able to cope with it, their desire not to become a burden to one's family, and their uncertainty about how loved ones will survive after they are gone.

Kübler-Ross did not believe that everyone reached the stage of acceptance of his or her own death, but she firmly believed in open communication, with supportive physicians and family members telling the person about the impending death and facilitating the process of emotional adjustment as much as possible. With terminally ill patients, adequate pain management can be the most frequent predictor of emotional adjustment at the end of life.

Multiple parallels exist between the stages of death and dying and the ways in which people adapt to other losses in life (e.g., ending a relationship, leaving a job, experiencing any other sudden crisis). In *On Grief and Grieving* (Kübler-Ross & Kessler, 2005), published after Kübler-Ross's death, the authors wrote specifically about the internal and external world of grief.

Kübler-Ross wrote that the stages of dying "apply equally to any significant change (e.g., retirement, moving to a new city, changing jobs, divorce) in a person's life" (1975, p. 145); these are commonly called developmental or situational changes. Further, Kübler-Ross believed that if people could accept the ultimate knowledge of their own death and integrate this knowledge into their lives, they could learn to face productively the challenges and losses that come their way and face death with peace and joy as the final stage of growth.

ACTIVITY 12.1

Your Feelings and the Grieving Process

Draw a circle and divide it into slices like a pie, based on your feelings about death (e.g., grief, regret, hope, sadness). The size of each slice should accurately depict the amount of that emotion you are feeling.

Over the years, a broader approach to death education has focused on the unique needs and perspectives of the individual. Workshops, support groups, and end-of-life planning, all serve to educate the individual about transitions at the end of life. Berzoff and Silverman (2004) categorized death education as prevention (i.e., preparing for the inevitable), intervention (i.e., dealing with the immediate), and postvention (i.e., understanding the crisis or experience). A good example of effective death education was an event sponsored by a local church that offered a 5-week workshop that examined the music of Brahms's *Requiem* along with Kübler-Ross's five stages of death and dying. Such workshops often help reduce death anxiety. Now assess your reaction to Kübler-Ross's perspectives on grief and loss by completing Activity 12.1.

VOICES FROM THE FIELD 12.2

Grief and Loss

Kami Wagner

When entering a helping field, one of the challenging emotional responses that is hard to be prepared for is loss of clients or students. As professionals, our first responsibility is to appropriately help those we serve. In cases when the loss of someone with whom we are working occurs, it is helpful to have thought about our own feelings on grief and loss. It is something that you likely haven't experienced in this context previously, but separating your own emotions and the ability to help others work through their grief is important. It is also critical to recognize when your own feelings of loss are too overwhelming for you to be a support for others. There are certainly times when your personal connection to someone requires you to step aside and let others care for those around you, and you must focus on helping yourself process and grieve.

Unfortunately, in my 6 years as a high school counselor, there were multiple crises I had to handle—from the death of a student to the death of a coworker's daughter. Managing my own emotions—not pushing them aside but finding an appropriate way to deal with them—while helping others work through their pain is a challenge. In addition to death, there are other losses in our field that we must process. For example, the incarceration of a student or firing of a teacher for inappropriate actions may also be considered losses that we must process as professionals and as humans. Helping others work through their grief is often a way to better understand yourself and process your own feelings, but you must do your best to maintain appropriate boundaries and not use someone else's counseling session as a time for you to process your own issues. Making sure you have resources in place to help yourself grieve is critical to helping yourself and those whom you are serving.

The profession we have chosen poses an interesting challenge of showing empathy for and helping those struggling to deal with loss while putting aside one's own need to process emotions until a more appropriate time. We are often asked to teach others about the process of grief, which can be a great reminder to ourselves as we walk through the pain ourselves. It is critical to remember that if you are not in a healthy place, you are not in a position to help others get to a healthy place. Accepting our own weaknesses and vulnerability to crises must be a part of our continual self-evaluation in order to best serve our students and clients.

Worden's Task Model of Grieving

According to Lewis (1961, p. 38), grieving "is not a state, but a process." In a significant move away from stage theories, Worden (2009) proposed a task model of grieving that empowers the bereaved to accomplish the following four tasks:

- *Accept the loss:* After a period of disbelief, the person must begin to accept that the death is real. A pervasive sense of shock, numbness, or unreality may be felt for a long time. A sudden death, or a death far away, makes it particularly difficult to grasp that death has occurred. As people begin to work through this task, they start to accept the reality of the facts surrounding the death of their loved one and the meaning behind the loss and to accept that the person is not coming back. People who remove pictures or otherwise avoid any reminders of their loss are hindering themselves from the task of accepting the loss.

- *Experience the pain:* Working through the pain of grief is the second task Worden believes people must undergo. Some people may dissociate from the pain, immersing themselves in work, cleaning, and any other methods of keeping busy. Still others may feel overwhelmed by their sorrow. Recognizing and labeling the pain rather than avoiding it, helps them to grieve and to move forward through the pain and grieve successfully.

- *Adjust to an environment without the person:* To accomplish this task, people must learn to continue on despite the loss of a love object in their world. While it is impossible to clearly delineate precisely what has been lost, the void of grief is often deep. Coming home to an empty house, missing the communication and companionship of a loved one, and celebrating special holidays, birthdays, and milestones in other people's lives can all serve to increase the pain associated with loss. To successfully work through this task, mourners must learn to cope and adjust to the many different voids left after the loss of a loved one.

- *Reinvest emotional energy in other relationships:* Grieving persons are called on to emotionally relocate the lost person and to move on with life, while still honoring their loved one (Toray, 2004). Worden (2009, p. 46) considers it a "benchmark of a completed grief reaction" when the person is "able to think of the deceased without pain."

Like a physical illness or wound, grief takes time to heal. Therefore, Worden does not assign time periods to grief. Parkes and Prigerson (2009) indicate that widows may take three or four years to move through the grief process and achieve stability in their lives. During that time, they are working to return to a level of equilibrium. Grieving requires effort, and those who do not take the time to work through the tasks of mourning will delay the grief process (Worden, 2009). Case Study 12.1 provides an example of a delayed grief process.

CASE STUDY 12.1

An Example of Delayed Grieving

I once had an aunt whom I loved and treasured no less than my biological mother until she was taken away from me by the devastating, disturbing disease of breast cancer. I spent most of my childhood at her house. She was the one who taught me how to walk, ride a bicycle, cook, and differentiate right from wrong. The day I lost her I was in denial and refused to accept the fact that she was gone and that I would never see her again. I was not able to go to her funeral because she lived in Ethiopia when she passed away.

Ever since her death, I had panic attacks whenever I passed by a cemetery, and it became my biggest fear. Two years after her death my best friend's mother passed away, and I was not able to attend her funeral. I was hurt and frustrated by the fact that I couldn't face my fears. I spent the entire day crying and started thinking how I would feel if my best friend did the same thing to me.

Seven years after my aunt's death I had an opportunity to go to Ethiopia, but I refused to go because I knew I would have to face her grave once I got there. It was not something that I was ready to do. I spoke with my friends about the struggle I was facing, and each of them tried to help me. They told me that death was a part of life and that I just had to accept it and move on. The feedback they gave me made me realize that I still had not accepted my aunt's death and that it was playing a huge part in my fear.

Earlier this year I had another opportunity to go back to Ethiopia. At this point, it had been almost 10 years since my aunt passed away and more than 12 years since I had been in Ethiopia. I told myself I would just have to find someone to help me. I decided to talk with a counselor. He told me that facing my aunt's grave would give me closure to her death. He also talked to me about where my aunt could be now and helped me to slowly try to process it. I started looking at old pictures and even videos. I realized that she was in a more peaceful place since she struggled for so long with the sufferings connected with her cancer. It was killing her while she was still alive.

I boarded the airplane to Ethiopia. During my 18-hour flight, I remember processing what I had learned about my aunt's death. My counselor told me to go visit her grave first so that I could enjoy the rest of my visit home. When I got there, I was ready to face the reality. I rested for two days and then went to visit her grave on the third day. The closer I got, the more nervous I became. My body was shaking, and I actually had such a hard time walking that my cousin had to help me. But once I got to my aunt's grave, I let all of my emotions out, asking her why she had to go. I realized she was in a better place. I remembered what my teacher had told me. His words gave me strength and helped me to overcome my fear. I prayed and told my aunt how much I had missed her and asked her to keep looking over me. My experience was overwhelming to my cousins because they could not believe that I was still in denial over my aunt's death. For them, it was something that happened a long time ago. It had become a part of their lives, and they had moved on. I now feel okay, and happy with the fact that I have faced her grave.

Attachment and Loss

Past history and current research indicate that most mourners do not believe that the relationship ends with the death of their loved one. This is contrary to the medical view of grief, in which mourning is a phase from which people should recover. The distinction between normal grief and clinical depression is important and will be discussed in depth later in this chapter. For most people, grief is an accepted and normal part of the life cycle, from which they eventually return to their previous level of equilibrium.

> Intimate attachments to other human beings are the hub around which a person's life revolves, not only when he is an infant or toddler or a schoolchild but throughout his adolescence and his years of maturity as well, and on into old age. From these intimate attachments a person draws his strength and enjoyment of life and, through what he contributes, he gives strength and enjoyment to others. (Bowlby, 1980, p. 442)

Drawing on the works of Ainsworth, Parkes, Winicott, Seligman, and others, Bowlby produced a three-volume series that became the seminal work on attachment and loss (1960, 1973, 1980). Bowlby (1980) noted four phases of the mourning process: (1) numbing, which lasts from a few hours to a week; (2) yearning or searching for the lost figure, lasting for months or even years; (3) disorganization or despair; and (4) some degree of reorganization.

The numbing phase is often expressed as being stunned or shocked at the news of a death. The yearning phase is seen by Bowlby as normal and may result in efforts by the bereaved to locate the lost person. Such searching may include motor restlessness—the inability to slow down or to control continuous movement—or scanning the environment. The bereaved may develop a sense that the person is present with them or may construe sights or sounds to be an indication that their loved one is near. In a study of widows, Parkes (1975) found that half of the widows felt drawn toward objects they had associated with their husbands, and many located a person in a specific portion of the environment (e.g., the chair he used to sit in). Many continued to talk to their spouses one, two, and even three years after they had died. Cultural background affects the expression of grief. For example, a 50-year old Iranian woman who lived with her adult son and his family sought treatment 10 years after the death of her husband. She continued to be sad and expressed the desire to return to his grave "and dig him up" with her hands. Her son and his wife only wanted her to be happy, and live out her years with them and her grandchildren. Culturally sensitive counselors must be aware of any cultural traditions or family expectations that affect the grieving process.

Disorganization or despair often takes the form of irritability or bitterness. In most cases in which there is a target of the anger, it may be clergy, doctors, or surviving family members. Self-reproach is also common and can be intense and unrelenting. Anger associated with grief must be discussed. Anger falls along a continuum from anger to rage to violence. Anger that is externalized, spoken, and processed is less likely to manifest itself in negative behaviors, which can mask the underlying feelings of grief and loss.

Bowlby noted that in most instances of disordered mourning, the loss was almost always of an immediate family member—most notably, a parent, child, or spouse. In other words, the strength of the attachment bond and the closeness of the relationship are important variables that profoundly affect the grieving process. In earlier research Lindemann (1944) noted that severe reactions seemed to occur in mothers who had lost young children.

Bowlby saw mourning as a time of transition during which mourners adapt to the loss, reorganize their lives, and find new roles for themselves. During this period, it is necessary for the bereaved to experience sadness and despair. C. S. Lewis (1961, p. 59) wrote extensively about the loss of connection following the death of his wife—"So many roads once; now so many cul-de-sacs"—expressing not only his deep feelings but also the loss of cognitions and actions that were formerly shared and now must be reworked. During the period of reorganization, so much work must be done by the bereaved. Where one previously defined oneself as part of a couple, he or she is now single. Those once connected to a mother as a child now see themselves as orphans. Bowlby notes that this redefinition of self is a painful but necessary process. The bereaved can reestablish themselves and develop plans for the future only when they have recognized that their loved one will not return.

Pathology tends to result when people do not take the time to grieve or do not grieve properly, resulting in devolution of the natural process of mourning into clinical depression. Loss can be a provoking agent that increases the risk of an emotional disorder developing, or the person may have a preexisting vulnerability that increases his or her sensitivity to loss. Either can result in a pattern of disorganized mourning.

Bowlby noted that depression-prone individuals deal with death differently than do those who do not become depressed. Numbness, for example, is common to all mourners. After an initial few days or a week of numbness, however, the healthy mourner may begin to talk about the pain and suffering of the deceased and express frustration at not having been able to do more to help. In contrast, depression-prone mourners may experience numbness that lasts indefinitely and may dissociate themselves from feelings of grief. When thoughts of the deceased do arise, they may focus on self-centered ruminations about their own loss, rather than expressing sadness at the loss of their loved one. Bowlby (1980, p. 249) noted that "depression-prone individuals possess cognitive schemas having certain unusual but characteristic features which result in their construing events in their lives" in idiosyncratic ways. Seligman (1973) wrote that such people have often failed to solve problems in their lives and, when confronted with loss, revive the cycle of "learned helplessness."

UNDERSTANDING GRIEF

In the DSM–5 (American Psychiatric Association, 2013), bereavement has been narrowly defined as the loss of a loved one. More expansive (and historically accurate) definitions are likely to embrace the concept that *any* negative life event serious enough to affect a person's thoughts, emotions, or important areas of life can be considered a loss. Even changes in role or position, such as the birth of a baby, relocation, or retirement, can trigger feelings of loss or grief. Life is filled with "little deaths" of what we give up and what we learn (Kübler-Ross, 1969). Grief is a natural and universal reaction to those developmental or situational losses.

Even though there are many similarities, every grief experience is different. In Western culture, grief is an intensely personal experience that affects not only the individual but also the entire family system and in some situations (e.g., September 11, natural disasters, school shootings) the entire community. Grief reactions vary by culture, individual, and relationship to the deceased. All of these factors should be considered as mediators of the mourning process and will be discussed in greater detail.

Cultural Similarities in Grieving

Cross-cultural research has found similarities in intrapersonal experiences of grief. In a study of 78 different cultures, Rosenblatt, Walsh, and Jackson (1976) found that people in all cultures express grief through tears, depressed affect, anger, disorganization, and difficulty performing normal activities. Every culture has "rules" for acceptable grieving that prescribe the behavior that is expected and allowed but does not address the internal emotions that are felt. For instance, widowed women in some Middle Eastern cultures are expected to become incapacitated by their demonstrations of grief whereas widows in Bali are strongly discouraged from crying. In many Hispanic cultures, it is believed that the deceased wants something from the living.

An awareness of cultural variations in mourning should lead a culturally competent crisis counselor to inquire about the cultural traditions, rituals related to death, what behaviors would be culturally proscribed or prohibited, the client's beliefs about where the person is now, and what they expect their continued relationship with the deceased to be like.

Helping people to find meaning in the lives of their loved ones, individually and in what they meant for society, can be an important part of coming to terms with the loss. In collectivist societies, death affects the entire village or community. For example, bereavement, known as "sorry business," is a very important part of Aboriginal culture. Funerals can involve entire communities, and the expression of grief can include self-injury. The grieving relatives may live in a specially designated area, the sorry camp, for a period of time. The relatives may also cut off their hair or wear white pigment on their faces (Australian Academy of Medicine, 2012).

Guilt is not always a part of loss but is more common in suicide, sudden death, or other situations in which people have not been able to say good-bye, have left something unsaid, or feel that they somehow could have done something to change the outcome (Hooyman & Kramer, 2008). Recent and ongoing research distinguishes between normal (or uncomplicated) grief and complicated mourning, which may require additional grief work or additional steps before the grief work can begin.

Delayed or masked grief reactions can complicate the mourning process. According to Worden (2009), grief that is repressed or denied can result in aberrant behavior or can cause physical symptoms. He notes that pain can be a symptom of repressed grief and that many people who are treated for somatoform disorders are really experiencing the pain of loss. This is particularly noticeable if the physical symptoms are similar to those experienced by the deceased. Similarly, unexplained depression, acting-out behavior on the part of adolescents, and overly intense grief reactions that occur after seemingly minor losses can all be indications of repressed grief. Thorough assessment and clinical skills are required to identify the problem. Complicated grief will be discussed later in this chapter.

ACTIVITY 12.2

Think about your own religious, cultural, and ethnic background in relation to death and dying. Is there one tradition, ritual, or attitude that is different from others who do not share your background? What seems unusual about it? What do you say to explain the tradition or ritual to others who are unfamiliar with your custom?

Ambiguous Loss and Disenfranchised Grief

Doka (2002) and Boss (2006) expanded the concept of grief to include loss that is ambiguous or disenfranchised. Included in this definition are relationships that are not recognized (e.g., gay and lesbian relationships, lovers, friends, coworkers), loss that is not recognized (e.g., perinatal loss, abortion, pet loss), grievers who are not recognized (e.g., the very old, the very young, persons with developmental disabilities), and disenfranchised death (e.g., murder, suicide, AIDS). Coping with a loss that is an experience rather than the actual death of a person (e.g., children who are kidnapped, family members who disappear, or soldiers who are missing in action) can also be considered an ambiguous loss. As Boss noted, one of the primary tasks of a family is to come together to grieve the loss of a family member. Not knowing whether the person is dead or alive prevents any type of grieving from beginning. The person is physically gone from their lives, but little support is available, and in many instances, friends and family do not understand the depth of the loss or know what to say.

In such situations the primary mission of the crisis counselor is to understand the stress of the situation, the ambiguity surrounding decision-making processes, and the manner in which this stress and ambiguity affect the family relationships, and then to help the family develop resilience (Boss, 2006). Long-term effects of living with ambiguous loss can include depression, anxiety, guilt, ambivalence, and interpersonal conflicts. Each client heals at his or her own pace. After an ambiguous loss, the client may take years, even decades, to develop the perspective necessary to become centered again and to create a healthy and fulfilling life. During that time within a couple's relationship, the partnership is at risk. It is not uncommon for couples to initially reach out to each other in their pain, but since each person is apt to grieve differently and at a different pace, the couple may begin to find fault and blame each other. During infertility treatments, after a miscarriage, or after the loss of child, couples should seek couples counseling. An example of an ambiguous loss through miscarriage and infertility is provided in Case Study 12.2, which poignantly reflects the experience of a young woman who desperately wanted to have a baby and was told she never would.

CASE STUDY 12.2

Miscarriage and Infertility: Ambiguous Losses

What followed for Aisha was a self-described "week of hell"—the emergency room trip, a stomach pump, the nurse who rebuked her, saying, "You tried to kill yourself. You don't deserve sympathy." This humiliation preceded commitment in a private mental hospital, a court hearing to determine her sanity, and the requirement that, before leaving the hospital, Aisha schedule an appointment with a counselor. That's how she found me.

Aisha and her husband of three years were facing not only the reality of never giving birth to their own children but also the possibility of a diagnosis of cancer. It was too much to bear, and after a day spent drinking with her husband and friends to calm down, Aisha went home and "tore the kitchen apart," broke her arm against the wall, swallowed a bottle of antianxiety medication the doctor had given her, and then called her mother. She sat down to wait for the emotional help she so desperately needed. No one was listening to Aisha. No one had grasped the totality of her pain. "I just want someone who can understand what I am going through," she cried. From the moment she learned she could never bear a child, Aisha was grieving the loss of future plans that would never be realized. She would never be a mother, never hold her infant, and never have a family. All of those holidays, birthdays, years stretching out ahead of her, alone and barren.

She feared that her husband would leave her for someone younger, who could give him children, and that she could never look at children again without being reminded of her loss. All she had ever wanted was to be married and raise a family. Now that dream was shattered.

How to go on? Why go on? The existential questions stretched like open fields for miles in front of her—questions that were not easily answered by the meaningless mantra of well-meaning friends and relatives: "You can adopt," or "Relax, you'll get pregnant."

More than losing her footing, Aisha had her future plans yanked right out from under her in one horrible afternoon. She needed time just to accept the reality of her loss before she could even start to think about the future. It was months before she was able to accept the diagnosis. It was even longer before Aisha could start to dream again about the color, the texture, and the design she would weave into the rug of her new life.

When working with women who have recently miscarried or are coping, like Aisha, with infertility, hollow reassurances and suggestions about the future are ineffective, I find that only empathy, being with the person as they experience the pain, and being a witness to their grief will help them cope with the loss will be capable of moving the grieving process forward.

The loss of the ability to have children is similar to the loss of your future. In Aisha's case, the professionals failed her. A nurse shamed her suicide attempt. A psychiatrist and a counselor gave her platitudes instead of helping her to come to the terms with and process her loss. Even the physician who gave Aisha the bad news failed to ensure she received adequate counseling. He focused on saving her body but ignored how she felt about the prospect of living life without children. Once Aisha was able to define the loss she was feeling—the need to nurture a baby—she was able to find an appropriate outlet by volunteering to rock babies in the hospital nursery. Years later she was able to see that there were actually benefits of not having children of her own. She and her husband were able to take trips their friends could only dream of. Her husband was able to fill his parenting need by coaching a boy's basketball team. The couple ruled out adoption but was able to build a fulfilling life that included friends and nurturing others' children.

Discussion Questions

1. What are some losses experienced by the couple and by them as individuals?
2. What are some things to consider in looking at possible crises in the future?

When helping clients adjust to an ambiguous loss, the first step is to acknowledge the depth of the loss, not to minimize the pain. Find out exactly what having a baby meant to each partner. In the case study, Aisha felt isolated because none of her friends knew what to say. There are no greeting cards expressing sorrow for infertility. None

ACTIVITY 12.3
Looking for Death

In American culture, death is frequently hidden. Look for personal and cultural images of death in the media and your immediate environment. Discuss your findings with the class or a peer.

of the men in her life was comfortable talking about reproduction. In addition to her grief over the loss of the future she had envisioned and over her inability to provide a child for her husband, Aisha felt depressed and hopeless about her future. When hope is gone, the risk of suicide increases.

Whether childless by choice or happenstance, at midlife, women who chose a lifestyle of childlessness may feel a resurgence of ambivalence surrounding not having had children. While friends are discussing the "empty nest," those without children have difficulty relating. As one woman said, "How can you discuss the empty nest when your nest was never feathered?" As others take pleasure at the birth of grandchildren, those without children may feel further isolated and begin to doubt their place in life. "It didn't occur to me," one woman told me, "that they live on through their children and their children's children, for generations. But my life stops with me."

Coping with this type of loss involves helping people to clarify the missing role and then to find other outlets and activities that provide a meaningful substitute. Those who feel isolated could be referred to Resolve, the national infertility association (www. resolve.org), to find information, research, and support groups for people working through infertility. Online support is also available for women who experience loss through a miscarriage. BellaOnline (bellaonline.com) provides a clearinghouse of information and online blogs.

Someone who feels isolated and alone, for example, may benefit from adopting or rescuing a dog. Those who feel they have much to give to children may find meaning by volunteering at an elementary school, becoming a foster grandparent, or tutoring children after school. Younger men or women who are missing children in their lives can be encouraged to become a special aunt or uncle to a niece or nephew, become a Big Brother or Big Sister, become foster parents, or house an exchange student from another country. Activity 12.3 will help you become more sensitized to the way grief and coping with grief are hidden in American culture.

MEDIATORS OF THE MOURNING PROCESS

Bowlby (1980) notes five conditions that affect the course of grieving that may be used in the crisis intervention assessment: (1) the role of the person who died, (2) the age and gender of the bereaved person, (3) the cause and circumstances surrounding the death, (4) the social and psychological circumstances affecting the bereaved at that time of loss, and (5) the personality of the bereaved, especially as it relates to one's capacity for making attachments and for coping with stressful situations. The role of the person who died and the circumstances surrounding the death are examined in the sections that follow. Readers are encouraged also to take into consideration other conditions listed here that may affect the bereaved.

Relationship: The Role of the Person Who Died

Just as every relationship in a person's life is unique, so, too, is every death. The closeness of the relationship, whether the person who died was a spouse of 30 years or a distant uncle, is a key ingredient in how the death is perceived and mourned and what the length of the grieving process will be. It is important to define the unique attachment or loss associated with the death so that if a referral is needed, this information can be transferred as well.

Some of the most difficult deaths to accept are those of people we are the closest to: our children, our parents (especially if the death is experienced by a child), and our spouses or life partners. The death of a sibling, too, can have a tremendous effect on a family. Each of these relationships is discussed in more detail below. Crisis counselors are encouraged to consider other deaths that may be particularly difficult to accept.

DEATH OF A CHILD The death of a child reverses the natural generational order of death and can have a devastating influence on the entire family. Children play multiple roles in their parents' lives—socially, psychologically, and genetically. So the death of a child disrupts the parents' attachment not only to the child in the moment but also to their dreams and expectations for the future, as well as to the child's place in the generational structure of the family.

"The death of an only child, only son or daughter, or the last of a generation leaves a particular void" (Walsh & McGoldrick, 2004, p. 20). Epidemiological studies have found that the death of a child leaves parents more susceptible to depression, illness, and premature death due to changes in the immune system.

Many authors write of the differences in grief responses between men and women, with a focus on the impact of grief on a woman's continuing relationship with her surviving children (Walsh & McGoldrick, 2004; Wang, 2007). Unfortunately, little research is available that is specific to fathers. In general, men are less likely to express their grief by verbalizing or expressing their emotions; rather, they tend to stay busy and become task oriented (Wang, 2007).

When there is a death in the family, parents are not the only grievers. Siblings, too, may be distraught by the loss and experience survivor guilt. Often, a parent's coping response may be functional for him or her but may have a negative influence on his or her partner or surviving children. Sometimes a parent's behavior toward surviving children may change. The research indicates that the grieving process is determined to a large extent by the quality of the parents' relationship. Maternal depression, marital discord, and separation are likely to result in additional psychological fallout for the remaining children. Previously well-adjusted siblings commonly develop symptoms of anxiety, school refusal, depression, and severe separation anxiety (Bowlby, 1980). Some parents may withdraw from their surviving children, while others may turn to another child as a stand-in for the deceased. Both coping styles are fraught with problems. A stable, secure environment in which both parents nurture each other as they go from one stage of mourning to the next, while also helping their surviving children to express and cope with their own feelings, seems likely to foster the best outcome.

Losing an adult child is rare. Only 10% of adults over 60 years of age experience the death of an adult child. Parents who lose a child in their later years are at a significant disadvantage; since it is rare, very few other people can empathize with their loss.

In addition, these parents experience a sense of failure; it does not seem natural to them to bury their own children (Bryant, 2003).

DEATH OF A PARENT   Children mourn differently than adults. The way in which children mourn depends on their age, level of cognition, emotional development, relationship to the deceased, and the quality of the support network available to them. Clinicians working with children need to take these factors into account when developing individualized treatment programs for bereaved children or adolescents. Five- to seven-year-olds are especially vulnerable due to their lack of cognitive ability to understand fully the concept and permanence of death. Complications may result, and these children may develop a fear of losing the other parent. Preadolescents and adolescents are strongly influenced by their peers and the need to belong. They may feel isolated and different from their friends who have not experienced the death of a parent. Particularly vulnerable are teenage daughters who lose their mothers.

SIBLING LOSS   Losing a sibling at any age or stage of life is difficult. But often the loss of a brother or sister is a silent loss. When a sibling dies, parents or children are often viewed as the primary mourners, and sibling grief is often forgotten. In fact, when a sibling dies, one loses more than the relationship; one loses a part of oneself. A 60-year-old client whose brother had recently died said, "It was like losing my hard drive," because no one else shared her childhood memories and experiences, nor was there anyone she could talk to about her parents, family history, and other childhood recollections.

The effect of sibling loss is complicated by factors such as the age of the child, the inability to accept death, and the inability to discuss emotions. Eighty-three percent of children who die leave behind at least one sibling (Doka, 2002). The death of a child can disrupt the entire family system. Ultimately, it is the manner in which the parents cope with the death that is the most relevant to the surviving children's ability to cope. Whenever there is a question of whether a child should be referred for counseling or not, err on the side of caution and seek professional help with someone experienced in child psychology and grief.

Charles and Charles (2006) note the importance of working with families who have lost a child to help them develop coping skills that allow them to facilitate the grieving process in their other children. Even young adolescents and teens who appear on the surface to be coping well may really be presenting a facade. This failure to grieve can have a deleterious effect on normal childhood and adolescent development and may even affect future generations. "Without intervention, unresolved trauma tends to be passed along from generation to generation" (Charles & Charles, 2006, p. 86). Somatic symptoms are particularly common in children experiencing grief and loss. Stomachaches, headaches, and loss of appetite are common. It is also common for young children to regress to an earlier form of behavior during this time. Sleep disturbances, nightmares, and enuresis may occur, as might a drop in school performance, lack of concentration, and school refusal. Adolescents may begin using alcohol or drugs as a way of self-medicating their feelings. Professional help should be sought for substance abuse problems as well as for any grief that turns into severe depression or is accompanied by hopelessness or suicidal ideation. In addition, Fox (1988) identifies the following four indications for referral of a child for grief counseling: (1) children who have a life-threatening or serious illness themselves, (2) children who have previously been identified as emotionally disturbed, (3) children who have a developmental disability and may not understand the concept of death, and (4) children who remain "stuck" in grief or shock after others have moved on.

LOSS OF A SPOUSE The loss of a spouse can be devastating. The effect is compounded when the person is elderly. More than 75 percent of deaths occur in the over-65-years age bracket. The death of a spouse therefore frequently occurs at a time when losses associated with health, retirement, and decreased independence and mobility have a cumulative effect. When a spouse dies, the surviving spouse is at increased risk for heart attack or stroke.

Guilt over "what could have been" in the relationship, as well as guilt about surviving when one's loved one died, is a normal part of the grieving process. When we consider that four out of every five survivors are women and that the average age of women who lose their husbands is 53 years of age, we can see that many women are living alone long after the death of their spouses (Rock & Rock, 2004). For most of these women, making meaning of the rest of their lives becomes a primary focus.

As we have discussed, the need to make sense of the death of a loved one has been considered one of the necessary conditions for adjustment or recovery (Neimeyer, 2001). However, recent studies have shown that a widow who lost a spouse and had not found meaning in the death by 5 months was not likely to have found meaning at 18 months (Carnelley, Wortman, Bolger, & Burke, 2006). Especially at the end of life when losses are frequent, a bereaved person may not have enough time to work through the death of a loved one before another loss occurs. Such back-to-back losses are called *grief overload*.

THE LOSS OF ANIMAL COMPANIONS Pets can play important roles in people's lives by reducing loneliness and isolation for the elderly, providing a purpose in life, and even replacing the loss of a human social contact. For some people, losing a pet can be as difficult as losing a family member. For these reasons, pet loss is included in this discussion of grief and loss.

More than 62% of American households and 70% of families with children live with pets. Pets have become so common in the United States that more people now live with a pet than live with children (American Pet Products Association, 2008). Toray (2004) notes that some people—particularly those who live by themselves, have no children in the household, and are socially isolated—may be at higher risk for prolonged or intense grief. Grief over the loss of a pet can be magnified due to lack of support by society for the loss of a pet.

For children, however, the loss of a pet is frequently their first experience with death. If handled sensitively, the loss of a pet can provide a valuable opportunity to learn about death and to be involved in the grieving process. Children may express anger at their parents or the veterinarian for not being able to save their pet. They may also express fear and concern that others may be taken from them as well. Burial or other rituals are particularly important for children and help them feel involved in the grieving process.

Elderly people who live alone may become especially distraught after the death of a pet. Companion animals provide unconditional love and help owners maintain a daily schedule. It is critical to take such losses seriously and to help seniors cope with their loss and begin to find a new sense of purpose.

According to Toray (2004), the optimal pet loss counselor is one who recognizes the human-animal attachment and is skilled in bereavement and grief counseling. As with other types of loss, the primary goal of counseling is to validate the person's loss; reduce the pain, regret, guilt, and sadness that follow the death of a pet; and help the person resume a healthy level of functioning. Some people may decide to get another pet, while others may take the time to reassess the commitment necessary to raise another pet.

Cause of Death

It seems to be human nature to scan the obituaries looking for causes of death. An immediate flurry of questions results when someone dies. How did he die? When? How long did he know? What did he do to prevent it? What happened? By gathering the details associated with the cause of death, questioners are distancing themselves from death and assessing the potential likelihood of the same type of death happening to them. Such distancing does nothing to help the bereaved and often leaves them feeling alienated and alone. By blaming the victim for his or her own demise (e.g., "He smoked cigarettes," "She didn't wear a seat belt," "He had a family history of heart disease") or projecting blame onto others, people are actually reassuring themselves: "This will never happen to me." The effect of this reaction is to leave the bereaved feeling alone in their grief. To be supportive, crisis counselors should acknowledge that the death could have happened to any one of us.

TERMINAL ILLNESS   When the dying process has been prolonged by treatment for a chronic, long-term illness, families may have to grapple with difficult financial, legal, religious, and ethical decisions about treatment. Questions about who makes the final decision, what the patient would want, how long to continue life support, and other ethical issues may arise. An extended illness can deplete a family's financial and emotional resources.

Helping families to shift from the fighting spirit so necessary to battle an illness and adopt an attitude of acceptance or "letting go" can provide a valuable opportunity to create the sacred space in which the dying person can approach life's end on his or her own terms. When the focus shifts from curative efforts to end-of-life care, dying persons should have the following four needs met: (1) freedom from pain: physically, the focus should be on comfort care and reducing fear; (2) legal and ethical issues: they should have the opportunity to put affairs in order, to allow a natural death, and to experience a more humane transition; (3) emotional support: they deserve to have a sacred space in which acceptance of the coming separation from their loved ones is acknowledged, they are given the opportunity to grieve, to make amends, and to say goodbye to loved ones; and (4) social support: they deserve to have people around them, to have family support for themselves and for the other members of their family (Corr, Nabe, & Corr, 2012).

In their work with dying people and their families, crisis counselors can be instrumental in creating the space necessary to allow families to experience appropriate end-of-life care. Over the past few decades, the hospice movement has provided many new resources and opportunities to facilitate end-of-life decisions, provide quality care, and help people experience a good death. In his book *Dying Well*, Ira Byock (1997), a physician and former president of the American Academy of Hospice and Palliative Medicine tells the story of his own father's death from pancreatic cancer. The family gathered at his father's bedside, providing comfort care and medication for pain, sometimes laughing and sometimes crying as they recounted stories from their childhood. As his father drew his last breath, the family held his hands, complete in the knowledge that these were precious moments and that they were honored to be sharing this final experience with their beloved father. They remained in his room for an hour, crying and holding each other, before calling the mortuary. As Byock reported, "It was real, and yet so unreal. Dad was dead. The world had forever changed, yet it still turned; the sun still came up. The next day Mom and I boarded a plane and took Sy home" (p. 24).

As more and more people forgo heroic efforts at life's end and elect instead to allow a natural death, social workers and crisis counselors will be called upon to help families through the transition from medical interventions to palliative care and, eventually, death. Crisis counselors can help families share their feelings about the complicated situation, consider different options, and accept the ambivalence that can result from the conflicting emotions, involving relief that the person is no longer suffering. Crisis counselors may be instrumental in helping family members deal with any guilt or regrets over their actions and eventually come to peace with the loss.

SUDDEN DEATH   Sudden death creates special problems for survivors. Unlike a death following a prolonged illness, sudden death denies family members the opportunity to come to terms with unfinished business, to prepare for the loss, and to say good-bye. According to Doka (1996), sudden loss often leads to intensified grief. The world as the survivor knew it has been shattered. Concurrent crises and secondary losses such as lost income, a lost home, or even the loss of spiritual beliefs may also occur. Doka listed several factors that should be taken into consideration when working with survivors of sudden loss: (1) natural versus human-made losses (e.g., heart attacks and tsunamis are examples of natural causes; hostile actions and bombings are human made), (2) the degree of intentionality (e.g., accident versus drunk driving), and (3) how preventable the death was.

SUICIDE, HOMOCIDE, AND COMMUNITY LOSSES: SCHOOL SHOOTINGS, TERRORIST ATTACKS, AND NATURAL DISASTERS   Losses connected with suicide, homicide, and various types of disasters pose unique grief issues. These issues are discussed in more detail in other chapters of this text.

Normal Versus Complicated Bereavement

Bereavement, which most people experience several times over the course of a lifetime, is considered a normal response to the death of a loved one. Prolonged or complicated bereavement occurs when symptoms are of unusual duration or severity and interfere with life activities. Both of these conditions are defined and addressed below.

NORMAL BEREAVEMENT   According to the DSM–5, bereavement is the normal reaction to the death of a loved one, lasts no longer than 2 months, and includes some symptoms of a major depressive episode such as sadness or somatic symptoms; the symptoms and duration can be expected to vary across cultures. In general, bereaved individuals experience the depressed mood as "normal." Classic somatic symptoms that a mourner may experience include interrupted sleep, lack of energy, and appetite disturbances.

These symptoms are also found in depression, and yet clinical depression differs from the sadness of grief in several important ways. Any guilt associated with grief tends to be very specific to the loss and does not permeate all areas of life, as depression does. Neither does grieving generally lower the self-esteem of the bereaved.

Depression may co-occur with bereavement, particularly if the person has a previous history of clinical depression. Worden (2009) notes that in such cases the person should be referred for medication management, along with continuation of grief counseling. Antidepressants will decrease the emotions experienced in grief by numbing the pain but will not help the person come to terms with the attachment loss (Seligman & Reichenberg, 2011); therefore, referral for medical treatment should be done only when the loss affects the normal functioning of the individual and the loss is perceived as exceeding the current coping skills or resources. Crisis counselors are crucial when assessing and referring individuals in their immediate grief. The grief process is a normal process, and often individuals do not want to feel the normal reaction to their loss. However, in order to move forward in the healing process, it is important to experience the feelings associated with the loss and not to deaden the feelings through medication. This will only prolong or delay the grief process.

COMPLICATED BEREAVEMENT Although most bereavement reactions fall into the "normal" category, will quickly resolve, and will soon return the bereaved to previous levels of functioning, 10 to 15% of people will go on to experience more enduring grief reactions (Bonanno et al., 2007). Grief that is comorbid with depression, anxiety, or other, more severe symptoms is diagnosed as a more serious disorder (e.g., mood disorder, anxiety disorder, adjustment disorder, PTSD).

Individuals displaying symptoms of normal bereavement may subsequently be diagnosed as having a major depressive disorder if the symptoms are long-standing (i.e., last more than 2 months), cause severe impairment, and include such signs of a major depression as strong feelings of guilt and worthlessness, suicidal ideation and preoccupation with death, psychomotor retardation, and loss of contact with reality (other than seeing or hearing the deceased). PTSD may be diagnosed following a violent death by homicide or suicide if the survivor was present at the death or following a natural disaster or terrorist attack (Bonanno et al., 2007). People with few support systems and those with coexisting medical or psychological problems are at particularly high risk for severe reactions to a death (Seligman & Reichenberg, 2011).

Currently, diagnosing complicated grief is done in one of two ways: Either the client comes into therapy with problems related to the process of grieving a death or the client is completely unaware that what he or she is struggling with is the result of a loss. Worden (2009) suggests "clues" that may indicate unresolved grief: (1) the person cannot speak of the deceased without becoming distressed, (2) a relatively minor event may trigger an exaggerated grief reaction, (3) themes of loss may repeatedly come up in therapy, (4) the person may be unable to let go of any of the possessions of the deceased, or (5) the person may develop physical symptoms similar to those experienced by the deceased before he or she died. Imitation of the dead person may also indicate an inability to grieve. A good example here would be a 36-year-old single woman who, after her mother's death, took to wearing her mother's outdated shoes and clothes. She also joined her mother's garden club, and for months, her only form of social activity was entertaining her elderly neighbors. Clearly, she was not grieving well. Other symptoms—such as isolating oneself from friends and family members, becoming phobic about illnesses (especially the illness that killed the deceased), engaging in self-harming behaviors and suicidal ideation, and developing subclinical depression or intense guilt—indicate that the person should be referred for treatment (Worden, 2009).

In the near future it may be possible to identify people at risk of developing complicated grief. By administering the Beck Depression Inventory (Beck, Steer, & Brown, 1996) along with an additional question ("Even while my relative was dying, I felt a sense of purpose in my life") asked at 8 weeks after the loss of a loved one, Guldin, O'Connor, Sokolowski, Jensen, and Vedsted (2011) were able to predict those who were at risk for developing complicated grief.

According to the literature, clients with symptoms of complicated grief may benefit from earlier intervention, as these symptoms portend a less favorable outcome and may result in increased medication, job-related problems, the development of psychopathology, and even death (Guldin et al., 2011). The DSM-5 (American Psychiatric Association, 2013) includes criteria for distinguishing between, normal bereavement and complicated grief. Complicated grief is a separate category with specific symptoms and diagnostic criteria. As we have already discussed, different relationships, different causes of death, and other mediators can increase the length of time for and complicate the bereavement process. For example, a married woman who loses her spouse of 50 years can be expected to experience bereavement for years. Or a father who lost his only son in a tragic school shooting may not recover his equilibrium in the 2 months considered "normal" by current DSM standards.

Other losses in life can result in symptoms similar to both "normal" bereavement and complicated grief. A survey of survivors of Hurricane Katrina found that 58% had severe hurricane-related loss, and only 3.7% had lost a loved one. The bulk of the loss was related to tangible losses that resulted from the hurricane, such as jobs, homes, and support networks. Researchers found that predictors of later development of complicated grief included prehurricane variables such as lack of social support, ethnic-minority status, and preexisting psychopathology (Shear et al., 2011).

Other losses such as separation or divorce, being fired from a job after 20 years, or even retirement can lead to loss of meaning in life. Horwitz and Wakefield (2007) suggested that as many as 25% of people who are diagnosed as having a major depressive disorder could actually be experiencing "normal" sadness reactions as the result of a major loss.

Until additional research is conducted and better definitions of bereavement and complicated bereavement are established, clinicians must carefully assess the symptoms of their bereaved patients to distinguish between the normal sadness reactions to death and other losses and the more prolonged symptoms of complicated grief, adjustment disorder, major depressive disorder, or PTSD.

INTERVENTIONS FOR GRIEF AND LOSS

In the past decade, growing controversy over the effectiveness of grief work has necessitated taking a closer look at the empirical evidence related to such work. Several articles published in notable journals have suggested that grief work, especially with normal bereavement, could actually do more harm than good. Larson and Hoyt (2007) investigated such claims and found no evidence to support a harmful effect of bereavement counseling. Rather, they noted that previous claims of harm were actually based on misrepresentations of several meta-analyses and subsequent republication of erroneous results.

Despite limited research on effective interventions for the grieving process, it has become fairly common practice to help clients "work through" their grief. This is not to suggest that there is a linear, preferred method or manner in which to do this; rather, as memories and thoughts come up, the bereaved client addresses the feelings, accepts them, and moves on.

Worden (2009) notes that one of the most important benefits of grief counseling is educating the client about the dynamics of the grieving process. Crisis counselors should help clients understand that there is no set period of time for the mourning process, that sadness and grief are normal, and that the process is not linear but rather comes and goes like waves. Specifically, holidays, birthdays, and the first-year anniversary may be particularly difficult. Some people may also experience increased sadness during the change of the seasons and may not feel appreciably better until an entire year has gone by and anniversary dates begin to include new memories of life after the loss of their loved one. An effective intervention is to help the person realize that such times may be difficult and to plan ahead for additional support during holidays, birthdays, and anniversaries of the death.

When working with bereaved clients, Wang (2007) underscored the need for the crisis counselor to join with the client empathically and "from the utmost genuine spot" (p. 77). To quote Carl Rogers (1980): "I find that when I am closest to my inner, intuitive self, when I am somehow in touch with the unknown in me, when perhaps I am in a slightly altered state of consciousness, then whatever I do seems to be full of healing. Then, simply my presence is releasing and helpful to the other" (p. 129). By practicing the necessary conditions of unconditional positive regard, genuineness, and empathy first set forth by Rogers, the client feels heard and no longer alone, and the crisis counselor, who cannot do anything to solve the client's grief or bring the loved one back, *can* do the one thing available—be there in an empathic, genuine, respectful, and honest way.

Restoring Life's Meaning

Helping people focus on re-creating a meaningful existence is the most important function of the grieving process. Vaclav Havel, former president of the Czech Republic, wrote about hope as a dimension of the human spirit that comes from "elsewhere" and gives us the courage to live even in conditions of despair. Hope is an orientation of the spirit. "It is not the conviction that something will turn out well, but the certainty that something makes sense, regardless of how it turns out" (Havel, 2004, p. 24). The biggest job of the crisis counselor when working with bereaved clients is to help them make sense of the loss, accept the changes that they did not wish for or create, and restore meaning to their lives. Working on meaning and purpose often becomes the goal of long-term counseling after the crisis is stabilized

Spirituality, religion, or faith-based practices are also an important part of a person's coping strategies and help to give life meaning. Having a spiritual bent can often help people to transcend suffering and adapt to life's difficulties when they occur. Crisis counselors, who may or may not be grounded in a religious tradition of their own, must approach clients with respect and dignity, without proselytizing about their own faith, and with recognition of the boundary between crisis counseling and spiritual counseling.

By following a theoretical model that addresses issues of spirituality and religion, crisis counselors can improve client rapport and more accurately assess and work with people in all stages of development and with diverse types of crises. Acknowledging a person's belief system can also provide a source of strength and support and shed light on areas in which matters of faith may be contributing to suffering. Some examples in which adherence to religious doctrines may actually add to the pain mourners experience might occur surrounding issues of suicide, gay or lesbian relationships, and married interracial couples.

Everyone has a faith story that illustrates (or narrates) their spiritual beliefs, and these stories are often brought up in the counseling session. A question frequently asked by clients is some version of "What religion are you?"—which can be a great starting point for a much broader discussion of the role that faith, religion, or spirituality has in a client's life. I recognize that behind the question is curiosity, respect and tolerance for alternative beliefs, a desire not to offend, and also an attempt to find common ground for discussion. It is also, at its core, an invitation by clients to be understood on a deeper and more meaningful level, to be known for the beliefs and values that underscore their decision-making, and to create an atmosphere in which they are comfortable discussing all aspects of their lives. This is especially true in the area of crisis counseling in which people are struggling to find meaning after a personal loss or tragedy. People need to know that it is okay to address their spiritual, philosophical, and moral dilemmas in the counselor's office.

Spiritually competent crisis counselors who have effectively incorporated spirituality into their counseling practices can appreciate a richer assessment of the entire person (mind, body, and spirit), a deeper rapport, and a fuller understanding of the person's beliefs, goals, and life's purpose (Borneman, Ferrell, & Pulchaski, 2010). People who identify with a particular religious belief system and those who may be skeptical about counseling in the first place, are frequently reassured and more comfortable with the process if the clinician incorporates spirituality and meaning-making into the assessment process.

Much has been written about the importance of incorporating spirituality into the counseling process (Cashwell & Young, 2011; Pargament, 2007; Parker, 2011; Sperry & Shafranske, 2005), but less has been written about how to do it. In general, crisis counselors should be familiar with the stages of faith development as well as cognizant of ethical boundaries related to discussing spiritual issues with clients. Being aware of one's own spiritual attitude, and keeping that attitude out of the counseling process, also helps. People want and need to be able to discuss aspects of their faith with clinicians. In recognition of that need, Christine Pulchaski, a physician, developed the FICA assessment, a four-step process that clinicians can use to quickly assess a patient's spiritual attitude using the following four question sets:

1. *Faith, Belief, Meaning:*   Do you consider yourself a spiritual or religious person? Where do you find meaning in life?
2. *Importance and Influence:*   How important is your faith to your life? How do your beliefs help you to cope in times of stress?
3. *Church and Community:*   Are you a part of a faith-based or religious community? If so, what type of support does this community provide?
4. *Apply and Address:*   How would you like me to address or apply this information in our work together? (Borneman et al. 2010)

Using the FICA assessment tool is just one way in which the importance of spirituality can be assessed and seamlessly incorporated into the therapeutic process to provide a richer, more integrated, and more positive experience for the client. Crisis counselors should also have an understanding of the developmental stages of faith.

Faith development theory (FDT) is a cognitive-structural model of spiritual and religious development that counselors can use to assess the client's stage of spiritual growth and development and to identify any developmental crisis that may be occurring. FDT is nonsectarian and allows clinicians to "work with the client's faith structures without having to endorse or challenge specific religious beliefs" (Parker, 2011, p. 112). Like Kohlberg's (1976) stages of moral development, Fowler's (1981) model of faith development views faith as a universal human activity that manifests differently over the course of a lifetime. The stages range from childhood to later life with most people growing through the stages developmentally, although not all will achieve the final stage in which faith is universalized. FDT incorporates the following six stages:

- *Stage 1— Intuitive-Projective Stage:* An egocentric stage that is most often seen in childhood (ages 3 to 7 years), where fantasy and reality are intertwined. The imagination is powerful and images can be either positive and enforcing of values or destructive and terrorize the child (e.g., monsters in the closet at night). The emergence of concrete operational thinking and the child's desire to know how things work and to distinguish between what is real and what is imagined often marks the transition to Stage 2.
- *Stage 2—Mythic-Literal Stage:* A narrative is used to give meaning to life at this stage, where logic, cause and effect relationships, and a sense of justice begin to emerge as well as the seeds of taking another's perspective. The child begins to take on the beliefs, stories, and symbols of his or her community or family. Story-making becomes a way of making sense of the world. In this stage, a person may become too literal and goodness and evil may be seen as a black and white duality.
- *Stage 3—Synthetic-Conventional Stage:* Personal identity is formed at this stage, and worth tends to be determined by the approval of others. Generally, this occurs in adolescence, but for many it may provide the faith balance they hold for the rest of their lives. Fowler (1981) refers to this as a conformist stage in which faith and values mesh nicely with the expectations and judgments of others. When the emergence of autonomy gives rise to critical reflection on how one's beliefs and values were formed, or how one loses faith in leaders or the establishment, the transition to Stage 4 may begin. Leaving home, establishing one's own identity, and other experiences that result in self-examination of values are also likely precursors to transitioning to Stage 4.
- *Stage 4—Individuative-Reflective Stage:* The recognition at this stage of the worldviews and experiences of others leads to critical reflection of one's own beliefs and outlook. For some, this occurs in young adulthood, with the rise of responsibility for personal beliefs, attitudes, commitments, and lifestyle. For others, this occurs later in life (late 30s to 40s) if at all. Highlights of Stage 4 include tension between individuality and group membership; a recognition of injustice

(sexism, racism, nationalism); demythologization of symbols; and a broadening of worldview.

- **Stage 5—Conjunctive Stage:** This stage moves beyond the logic of prior stages and begins to view truth as multidimensional and relative. These exceptions lead one to search for deeper spiritual meanings and a justice worldview that extends beyond family, state, or religious denomination. There is a danger that people in this stage may become cynical or passive, firmly planted in the physical world and unable to transcend or to act upon their newfound beliefs. Those who are able to act are likely to put their efforts toward creating a better world.

- **Stage 6—Universalizing Faith Stage:** Although Fowler (1981) believed this stage is rarely achieved, those who do reach this level of faith development believe in the inclusiveness of all beings. They may rise above religious boundaries and social or political structures, and they may become radicalized in their attempts to help humanity. People in this stage recognize the impermanence of everything, are free of ideological bonds and are sometimes honored and revered for their beliefs.

By incorporating the stages of faith development, the crisis counselor is better able to understand the effects of the crisis on the client and to help the client identify and work through any faith stage transition that coincides with the ongoing crisis. Identifying the client's stage of faith development can lead to an identification of transitions between stages in contrast to stable periods, and it can help to determine how current life crises may be intersecting with faith stages in a beneficial or disharmonious way.

Crises, both physical and metaphysical, can happen in life at any time. Helping clients to recognize and distinguish a faith stage transition from a life crisis can help to normalize the experience, provide a manner of looking at the two crises separately, and help the client understand the effect one has on the other. For example, a client who is proceeding with a divorce and then finds he is being excommunicated from the religious institution he has belonged to for 20 years must come to terms with the loss of not only his marriage but also his supportive faith-based community. Helping him to separate the two types of grief, and acknowledge and work through the loss of each, can help this client to move forward and perhaps find others who are struggling with similar issues. Walsh (2012) believes counselors have an ethical obligation to rise above their own sectarian religious or spiritual beliefs to provide safe places in which clients can explore their opinions, feelings, and beliefs. Having a faith development perspective can increase counselor competency in working with spiritual and religious issues and can help to assess the role of spirituality or religion in a client's life, regardless of religion or denomination (Parker, 2011). Activities 12.4 and 12.5 provide further insight into how you can integrate spirituality into grief work with clients.

ACTIVITY 12.4

Consider Fowler's stages of faith development. What stage best fits your spiritual development? Are you currently in a stable period or in a period of transition? How has your faith affected other areas of your life (work, relationships, decision-making)? How might your stage of religious or spiritual development positively affect your role as a crisis counselor? What might be some limitations?

ACTIVITY 12.5

This chapter has discussed how to use the FICA assessment tool to gently inquire about a client's spirituality and Fowler's faith development theory to assess the stages of faith development. Would you be comfortable incorporating these tools into your clinical work? Do you consider meeting the client's spiritual needs as part of your responsibility as a clinician? Are you prepared to listen for clues to spiritual suffering and to approach clients about spiritual issues? How do your own religious and spiritual issues affect your work with patients in the area of death and dying?

VOICES FROM THE FIELD 12.3
Working with Clients Experiencing Loss and Grief

Randall M. Moate

One of the primary tenets of Buddhist philosophy is the idea that suffering is a part of the human condition. While at first glance this idea may sound bleak, it is not intended in that way. Simply put, this idea refers to the notion that whatever brings us pleasure or happiness also has the capacity to bring us pain. Another way to understand this idea is to consider the things that fill up our lives with meaning or happiness, such as careers, personal interests, family, children, friendships, romantic relationships, possessions, good health, goals, and personal values. While the presence of these things gives our lives meaning, purpose, and pleasure, loss of any of them can create a void that causes fear, confusion, and sadness. How we experience loss and grief is personal to each of us, yet experiencing loss and grief is something that is common to all humans. This is something that binds us together as part of the human experience.

As a counselor, something that I have had to overcome is a natural reaction to want to dive in and pull my clients out of their grief. When someone has experienced a loss and is submerged in grief, my initial reaction is, "How can I help my client feel better as soon as possible?" In other words, I want to help my client move out of the sad or painful place, and bring my client toward a happier place in the present. What I have come to learn is that this is precisely the wrong thing to do. Clients experiencing acute grief, or a vacuum of meaning after a major loss, need space and time to grieve and to settle into this painful space. I have found that clients will move forward from their grief and loss on their own time, when they are ready to do so. Attempting to move clients from this place before they are ready is almost guaranteed to turn out badly. It has been my experience that clients resent, or take poorly to, feeling ushered out of their state of grief by their counselors.

When working with clients who have experienced loss and grief, I have found that these individuals want several things. They want me to deeply listen to their story, experience a compassionate and human connection with me, and sense that I have understanding and empathy for their experience. But how does one achieve these things? To counter my knee-jerk reaction to want to dive in and save my clients, I have developed a personal maxim I use in counseling that I call "*less is more*" —which refers to *less* questioning, *less* intervention, *less* technique, and *less* direction on my behalf. This results in my coming across to my client as being *more* helpful, *more* compassionate, and *more* understanding. Clients in deep grief are not looking for a magic solution from me. In truth, even if they were, I posses no magic solutions or answers that could fill the void from their loss. What I can do, however, is carefully listen to my clients, help them sit with their grief, and through my body language and presence communicate a sense of compassion and respect.

Perhaps the most valuable thing I do when working with a client who is experiencing grief, or coping with loss, is sharing hope. Sometimes after major losses and when grief is at its apex, a client may experience a loss of hope. From the perspective of the place that they are in, it seems as if things will never get better. I have witnessed some of my clients make profound changes in their lives and overcome huge obstacles. I hold onto these memories in a special place within me, as they remind me that people are resilient and have the capacity to change. Amidst the despair, confusion, and sadness my client may present during session, these memories act as a lighthouse for me and orient me toward a sense of hope and optimism. I then in turn, try to act as a lighthouse for my clients and help orient them toward the hope and optimism I feel for their situation. While I rarely find it appropriate to verbalize this during a session, I believe that my clients can sense it nonetheless.

Interventions

Grief is an individual, subjective experience with many different facets. There is no single model of grief counseling because grief work must consider the importance of culture, background, religious and spiritual issues, and family history as well as the individual qualities, circumstances, and personalities of the mourner. Helping people focus on re-creating a meaningful existence becomes the most important function of the grieving process.

By taking into account individual grieving styles, crisis counselors can tailor appropriate interventions. Doka (2005) identified a continuum of grieving styles ranging from intuitive to instrumental. People who are intuitive respond to grief affectively, while instrumental grievers are more likely to react cognitively or behaviorally.

Doka (2005) suggested that recovery from a loss may not be possible or desirable and instead described amelioration of grief, a return to similar (or better) levels of functioning with diminished pain. The bereaved maintain connections to the deceased through memory, biography, legacy, and spirituality. Crisis counselors face the challenge of helping the bereaved to celebrate connections, while avoiding potential problems, such as an inability to grow or move forward.

The emotional impact of the loss of a family member, especially the death of a spouse, can linger for years, even decades, depending on circumstances, age and cause of death, social support, and other mediators. Because loss of a family member can have detrimental effects on the health and mental health of survivors, a thorough assessment that includes the physical, psychological, cognitive, and spiritual effects of the loss should be conducted with these clients.

Crisis counselors should routinely ask how their clients found out about the death. Especially in sudden loss, including suicide, the survivors should be encouraged to talk about what happened as often as possible, to have their reactions validated and believed, and to be with others who have been through similar experiences. What is not helpful is to be told that they need medication or that they should not think about it or to be referred to support groups prematurely (Lord, 1997). Grassroots organizations such as Compassionate Friends, Parents of Murdered Children, and Mothers Against Drunk Driving can offer support and information for survivors.

For the treatment of complicated grief, cognitive behavior therapy has been found to be more effective than other types of therapy. Mindfulness-based cognitive therapy has also shown promise in helping people to accept what has happened to them, and stay focused in the moment without dwelling on the past or worrying about the future. Mindfulness-based practices such as meditation, focused breathing, and body scans can also help people in crisis to reduce their distress and can promote long-term well-being (Humphrey, 2009).

Boelen, de Keijser, van den Hout, and van den Bout (2007) found that cognitive distortions and maladaptive behaviors not only are common in complicated grieving but also actually contribute to its creation. In one study, they compared cognitive behavior therapy with supportive counseling. The results indicate that six sessions of pure cognitive restructuring combined with six sessions of exposure therapy were more effective than supportive counseling. Since avoidance and negative thinking are central to the creation of complicated grief, Boelen et al. (2007, p.283) concluded that "encouraging patients to confront and work through the loss is important to treating complicated grief and more helpful than targeting thinking patterns."

Writing a life history or creating a personal narrative as one approaches the final stage of life can help to give life meaning and can provide a valuable integration of the totality of one's life. Butler (1963) was the first to describe the universal occurrence of life review in older people. Butler noted that the "looking-back process" was set in motion by the nearness of death, coupled with the additional time available for self-reflection that is a by-product of retirement. Dreams and thoughts of death and of the past are reported to increase in the seventh and eighth decades of life.

Congruent with Erikson's (1980, 1997) psychosocial crisis of stage 8 (i.e., integrity versus despair), Butler (1963) found that, depending on the environment and the individual's character, life review can increase reminiscences and mild nostalgia, which can result in adaptive and positive integration of one's life, or it can result in increased anxiety, depression, and despair. Those who cannot integrate, comprehend, and realistically accept their lives as adequate run the risk of inner turmoil, increased rumination, depression, and possibly suicide. The research suggested that it is not the process of life review but the achievement of integrity that promotes successful aging (Butler, 1963).

Other interventions such as logotherapy (Frankl, 1959), narrative therapy (Neimeyer, 2001), expressive therapy through art, music or journaling; mindfulness meditation (Davidson et al., 2003), and other types of counseling that address spiritual needs, can all contribute to meaning-making and can be effective tools for working with people in crisis. As in all therapy, the role of the crisis counselor is to provide empathy, to detect suffering and address it, and to provide psychoeducation about what lies ahead in the next stage of development. Counselors who are able to do this in a culturally and spiritually competent manner can help to relieve distress and improve a person's quality of life, no matter what the crisis or which stage of faith development the person is experiencing. In general, the mourning process concludes when the person feels more hopeful, experiences a renewed interest in life, is able to discuss the loss without extreme emotion, and responds to condolences with gratitude rather than avoidance.

Group Support

Short-term bereavement support groups can sometimes provide a positive adjunct to individual grief work, especially when the type of loss results in feelings of isolation (e.g., suicide, homicide, HIV, miscarriage, infertility). As with all therapeutic groups, clients should be screened prior to participation to ensure that they are appropriate for the group. Parents who have lost a child should not be put in groups with those who have miscarried. People who have lost a grandparent should not be grouped with people who have lost a spouse or a child. As much as possible, the makeup of support groups should be homogeneous. Looking ahead to Case Study 12.3, which follows later in the chapter, Shayna felt comfortable in a support group for young adults (aged 23–29 years) who had lost a spouse, fiancé, sibling, or parent. During each week of the 6-week group, they were asked to process a different aspect of their loss. In week 1, clients were asked to talk about the person they lost. In week 2, attendees were asked what surprised them most about the grieving process. In week 3, they had a type of "show and tell," with each person bringing in an object and explaining its relationship to the person. Week 4 was devoted to rituals, and each person in turn lit a candle as he or she spoke of rituals that had proved helpful. During the final two sessions, the group members processed their feelings toward one another and the connection they had made, vowing to continue meeting outside of the hospice environment. As with all other groups, it is important to screen clients beforehand for readiness for the group experience. In general, most people will not be ready to join a support group in the first month after a loss.

Support groups for survivors of suicide should help members focus on the unique elements of their loss. Many survivors are eager to know why their loved one ended his or her life, so reconstructing the final days, looking for clues, and talking about their last telephone call may be integral to the grieving process. Absolving guilt is another important aspect. Processing these feelings together as a group helps normalize the feelings so that the guilt frequently begins to dissipate. Another distinctive goal of survivor support groups is to prevent future suicides. The research shows that family members and friends of a person who has completed a suicide are more likely to attempt suicide themselves. The reason is unclear, but it may be that once the taboo of suicide has been breached, it becomes an acceptable alternative to life. Another possibility is that the survivor empathizes with the other's despair. Whatever the reason, interventions with survivors of suicide have been shown to prevent future suicides.

Working with Children

According to Worden (2009, p. 235), "the same tasks of grieving that apply to the adult obviously apply to the child." But such tasks have to be modified to meet the social, cognitive, emotional, and developmental stages of the child. Preparing children, first-time funeralgoers, or people from cultures not familiar with the concept of viewings and funerals in traditional American society for what to expect can help decrease additional crisis or anxiety. A child attending a funeral for the first time may have extreme reactions to specific funeral customs (e.g., open caskets, touching the dead body, graveside burial), but if explained appropriately, these customs can help the healing process.

Following the death of a parent, children need support, continuity, and nurturance. In a two-year study of 125 schoolchildren who experienced the loss of a parent, Worden (2001) found that 80% were coping well by the first or second anniversary of their parent's death. The stability of the remaining parent was the greatest predictor of the level of a child's adjustment to a parent's death. Based on the study, the following needs of bereaved children were identified:

1. Bereaved children need to have their questions answered in an age-appropriate way. They need to know that they were not responsible in any way for their parent's death. Frequently asked questions on children's minds include the circumstances surrounding the death: "How did my mother [or father] die?" "Where is my dad [or mom] now?" If the parent died from disease or cancer, the concept of contagion may need to be explained to children who think they might contract their parent's illness: "Will it happen to me?"

2. Children need to feel involved. Developing a ritual, allowing children to be involved in the funeral, and including them in decision making are important. For example, having a child place a memento in the casket, light a candle, or decide which dress mommy will wear allows a child of any age to be included in the rituals of mourning.

3. Children's routines should be kept as consistent as possible. This can be difficult for the grieving parent, but research has shown that children do better when they know what to expect, can rely on the remaining parent for support and nurturance, and have families that exhibit an active rather than a passive coping style. Families

in which the surviving parent is not coping well, is young, is the father, becomes depressed, or begins dating within one year of the spouse's death are likely to have children who have more anxiety, lower self-esteem, and less self-efficacy and who exhibit more acting-out behavior.

4. Children need a way to remember the deceased. Photographs, scrapbooks, and memory books filled with stories or pictures of the deceased can all help children remember. Such books may be referred to again and again as they grow older.

Due to their limited life experiences and coping skills, children may have more difficulty mourning than adults do. Children's reality is often formed through fantasy and play. They are likely to fill in the blanks with assumptions or partial truths suited to their developmental age. They have a limited understanding of the world around them; therefore, they need playtime to act out their feelings of anger, anxiety, or fear. If a child regresses or participates in acting-out behavior, a thorough assessment may be in order. A screening instrument for identifying bereaved children who are at increased risk can be found in Worden's book *Children and Grief: When a Parent Dies* (2001). Interventions that have been found to be especially useful in helping children of all ages come to terms with their grief include play therapy, expressive art therapies, peer support groups, camps, and bibliotherapy with books such as *Tear Soup* or *Waterbugs and Dragonflies* (Corr & Balk, 2011; Stickney & Nordstrom, 2010).

Mourning may be a lifelong process for children who lose a parent. Feelings may be reactivated during adulthood when life events (e.g., weddings, other deaths or losses, reaching the same age as the parent who died) trigger the memory of loss. Recognition of these potentially vulnerable times allows people to actively plan their grief work.

Family Interventions

Walsh (2012) recommends that a systems approach be taken with the loss of any family member. This approach views the interactions among relationships, family processes, and the extended family as key to understanding how the death has affected the entire family system. Connectedness, communication, and mutual support and respect among members of the family seem the most likely to engender a balanced response to the loss. Two extremes run the risk of developing dysfunctional patterns: (1) families in which grief is avoided and pain is hidden and (2) families that cannot eventually work together to pick up the pieces and begin to form new attachments. Such patterns can affect the family for generations to come.

Finding meaning in the loss can help family members begin to heal. For example, those who have lost a loved one to suicide might invite crisis counselors or crisis line workers to attend the funeral, pass out literature delineating the warning signs of suicide, and offer grief counseling for those who need it. In this way, families can find a purpose and begin to create something good out of a traumatic experience.

DIFFICULTIES IN GRIEF COUNSELING

Withdrawal

When the survivor feels that no one understands or when the circumstances of the death or loss are so rare that no one in the survivor's social network has experienced such a loss before, the result can be withdrawal and isolation. This loss of empathy and connection causes the person to withdraw to make sense of the tragedy. The person may be overwhelmed with feelings of loss, guilt, anger, shame, or vulnerability. And yet no one in the person's support network can share in his or her specific form of loss. The person feels alone and, in this aloneness, may lose faith in all he or she believed to be true. An example of withdrawal is provided in Case Study 12.3. Then complete Activities 12.6 and 12.7.

CASE STUDY 12.3

Shayna

Shayna, a woman in her mid-20s, presented for counseling several months after the death of her fiancé, Jerod, from a rare viral infection. While hospitalized for the virus, Jerod had a heart attack, lapsed into a coma, and died several days later. He was 25 years old. Shayna was distraught, as was Jerod's family. The death was completely unexpected— and making sense of it was deferred for months as they awaited autopsy results. It was only after the autopsy that they discovered that a rare and fatal virus had crystallized in Jerod's organs, and one by one his organs failed. Even then, the cause of death was not fully comprehensible. It did not make sense. His mother and father were in their 40s; his younger brothers and sisters still lived at home. His death was out of chronological order. Shayna was sad and could not stop searching for answers. She sought out her minister and a psychic, and she even attended new age healing sessions in her efforts to make sense of the tragedy. She had a large support network of college friends and co-workers of her own age. While initially supportive of her grief, many of her friends had never experienced the death of a loved one, and one by one, they stopped asking about her loss and began to focus instead on their latest career moves, graduate school plans, and other day-to-day activities. Shayna stopped returning their calls. She began to isolate herself from friends and family and, other than going to work, did not leave her house. She reported, "No one can understand what I am going through." She could no longer relate to the trivial matters that made up the drama of her young friends' lives. "Only someone who has experienced death can appreciate the fragility of life," Shayna said.

We worked to help Shayna build a bridge back to her life. At first, her days were filled with yearning to have her boyfriend back, while at night she dreamed about him but could not communicate with him. Each morning she awoke sad and frustrated. Those first sessions early in therapy were very painful as Shayna recounted the story of her fiancé's death. I could do nothing to help except be present, empathic, and bear witness to her pain. This gave her comfort in the knowledge that someone else was accompanying her on this painful journey. She was not alone.

We began to discuss the unconscious needs reflected in her dreams and the importance of establishing rituals to honor her fiancé. Each night she would light a candle and talk to his picture. This gave her comfort and a newfound way to communicate with him. We also talked about the goals she and her fiancé had for the future. She decided to continue on the same path for awhile and to move ahead with one of their goals—to get a dog. The puppy proved to be source of solace and support over the days and months.

Shayna continued to go to work as an accountant, although she had many physical symptoms including anxiety, waking up in the middle of night, loss of interest in food and daily routines, and poor concentration. We began doing cognitive behavioral therapy to help her identify and rate her anxiety. I taught her how to do breathing exercises to regulate her breath and ward off panic attacks, and how to conduct a simple body scan meditation at night to help her relax and get back to sleep.

Gradually, Shayna began to confide in two coworkers who checked in with her regularly. The trust and support she found in these two women helped her begin to integrate the trauma into her life and start to reconnect with the community. When she was ready, she participated in a support group, run by a local hospice specifically for young people who were widowed or had lost siblings or significant others. Finally, she found a group of people of her own age who could relate to her, and she began to tell her story in an empathic, supportive environment. "I no longer feel like I'm a freak," she said. "I looked at the men and women in that room and realized that every person has baggage. Everyone has some trauma or some deep dark secret that they're living with. I'm not alone." Within a year, Shayna was ready to continue on the path she had set for herself prior to the death. She applied to graduate schools, was accepted, and the following year moved to New York.

Discussion Questions

1. What symptoms of grief did Shayna exhibit?
2. What facts surrounding the death of her fiancé made recovery more difficult?
3. What other questions would you ask about Shayna's life to help in your clinical decision making?
4. What type of treatment would you recommend?

Counseling the Crisis Counselor

Working with grieving clients can raise some of our own issues surrounding grief, loss, and mortality. Walsh (1998, p. 206) wrote: "There is no safe boundary between clients and therapists; we all must experience and come to terms with our own losses and mortality. Forming caring and therapeutic bonds in the face of loss deepens our humanity and offers a model to clients of living and loving beyond loss." However, to avoid secondary traumatization or compassion fatigue, counselors learn to establish healthy boundaries, seek supervision, and recognize transference (Renzenbrink, 2011). Appropriate self-care is particularly important for crisis counselors, as we have seen in Chapter 2.

ACTIVITY 12.6
Your Attitudes About End of Life Issues

It's been said that we all come into the world in the same way, but the way in which we die is different for everyone. Think about all that you have read in this chapter related to death and dying. What experiences have you had with families that are grieving or people who are facing their own deaths? Which of the experiences that you have read about here would be the most difficult for you? Which would be easier? How could you best educate yourself in preparation for addressing future clients' needs surrounding issues of death and dying that might arise in the course of your professional work?

ACTIVITY 12.7
A Counselor Death Awareness Exercise

Worden (2009) recommends that all counselors, prior to working with grieving clients, take an honest look at their own histories of loss. Grief counseling is not the place for counselors to work out their own unresolved issues, and those who find themselves in acute grief should first seek their own counseling before trying to help others. However, people who have worked through their own grief successfully can be instrumental in helping others work through their grief. Think back on your earliest experience with death. How old were you? How did you feel? What helped you to cope with the loss? Now think of a more recent loss you experienced. Again, what coping skills did you develop? Look into your future. What do you expect will be the most difficult death for you to accept? How will you cope? What thoughts arise when you think about your own death?

When working with grieving clients, Worden (2009) warns against cutting counseling short because of the counselor's own frustration or anger. He offers that nothing is more frustrating for a crisis counselor than not being able to help a client, and yet, in the case of the death of a loved one, there is nothing a counselor can do. Participating in a client's grieving process has a profound effect on crisis counselors, who must make sure that their own issues do not get in the way. Worden is particularly concerned about three areas that might affect a crisis counselor's ability to be helpful: (1) counselors who have had a similar loss that they have not worked through, (2) counselors working with a client's loss when they fear a similar loss of their own (such as the death of a parent or child), and (3) existential fears resulting from the counselor's failure to come to terms with his or her own mortality. The last issue can be addressed if counselors are willing to explore their own history of loss and fine-tune their death awareness.

VOICES FROM THE FIELD 12.4
Grief and Loss Case Study: Hanna

Nadine Hartig

I was providing individual counseling for Hanna at a college counseling center. Hanna was an 18-year-old female college freshman who attended Columbine High School and was present during the shooting on April 20, 1999. She was close to one of the teachers who was killed on that day and was friends with some of the students who were injured or murdered. Hanna began college in fall 1999, and she described coming to college as a surreal and sad time.

Hanna was experiencing daily panic attacks, insomnia, gut-wrenching sadness, nightmares, and debilitating grief. She cried our entire first session and felt devastated, lost, and, confused. She also experienced survivor's guilt and often asked, "Why did I live when these other people did not?" This was supposed to be an exciting time in her and her classmates' lives, but instead she felt "dead inside."

Our first step was to process her intense emotions. I am person-centered by nature and used this approach to develop rapport and process the depth of Hanna's emotions. Accurate empathic understanding and immediacy allowed me to help Hanna feel understood and deepen her awareness of the impact of the trauma. For example, Hanna often wanted to focus on the sadness and loss of the experience, yet I could sense an underlying anger in her. I was able to non-judgmentally reflect her anger, because she felt robbed of her worldview that the world is a safe place. As a result, Hanna was able to explore this part of her grief and loss, and she was able to acknowledge her intense anger and resentment toward the shooters in the incident. Her enhanced insight helped her understand her reactions to the crisis.

In addition to processing emotions, I also used cognitive behavioral techniques to help contain the flooding of emotion that was interfering with her daily functioning. Part of Hanna's panic was related to her fear that something like this would happen again. Essentially, she did not feel safe anymore. We worked on decatastrophizing the likelihood of this tragedy reoccurring, but we also worked on creating a safety plan since the unbelievable had indeed happened to her.

Hanna found grounding techniques, such as focusing on her breath and progressive relaxation, to be very helpful to her when she became overwhelmed and paralyzed with panic. We practiced these techniques in session and she would also practice them on her own. We also identified the most common triggers for her panic, which included doors slamming in her residence hall (the sound reminded her of gun shots), people making jokes about the Columbine tragedy, and the sight of blood. We developed a plan to deal with these triggers, which included moving to a calmer residence hall and leaving campus on rambunctious weekends.

Eventually, Hanna began to heal after this tragedy and to make sense of her life. She started to feel less "dead inside" and found joy in some parts of college life. However, with each new milestone came sadness as she thought of those who would not experience these milestones. She still felt intense anger toward the shooters, but was able to view them as unstable and hurting people. Hanna continued to view the shooting as a senseless tragedy, but she was able to let go of some of her survivor's guilt. She found support from friends and family and found a vocational purpose that made her feel like she could make a difference in others' lives. At termination, Hanna stated, "I am a changed person forever, and I wish this had never happened. All I can do now is to be the best person I can be." Hanna sought counseling for one academic year with me. She re-entered counseling the following year during the weeks before and after the anniversary of the Columbine shooting.

During my time working with Hanna, I sought regular supervision about this case. Her grief felt palpable to me, and she encountered many setbacks during our counseling relationship. I found it necessary to process my own feelings about Hanna's grief and the Columbine tragedy to prevent projecting my emotions onto Hanna.

Clinicians working with dying patients frequently have difficulty with one or more types of death. Perhaps one of the most important traits for crisis counselors to possess is knowledge of their own limitations and recognition of their own unresolved issues. By recognizing that not every counselor can work with every issue, they are better prepared to help those they can help and provide appropriate referrals for those they can't. Counselors who do grief work or who work with dying clients should (1) recognize their own limitations and accept these limitations with compassion and without judgment, (2) work to prevent burnout by practicing mindfulness meditation and active grieving, and (3) know how to ask for help, seeking supervision when necessary (Halifax, 2011; Renzenbrink, 2011; Worden, 2009). Working in pairs, when possible, can help relieve some of the stress.

VOICES FROM THE FIELD 12.5
My Client, My Teacher: "Let go, Let Love"

Jessica Headley

My client, Ms. B., disclosed that all formative figures in her life had passed. She had come to me for counseling, not only to deal with these unresolved losses, but also to deal with the loss of a former, healthy self. She was struggling in a fight with cancer—a lengthy battle in which she had experienced more lows than highs. She felt alone. When asked what she hoped to gain from therapy, Ms. B. disclosed that she wanted to "let go, let love." This mantra served as a guidepost of healing for Ms. B. in therapy, and one that I, too, took to heart as we worked together.

Letting go for Ms. B. meant allowing herself to share her painful thoughts and emotions surrounding the death of her loved ones. It also meant reframing the notion that asking for help was a sign of weakness; instead it was a sign of strength. As she began to do this, Ms. B. began to let love: she focused on strengthening her relationship with God, building connections with members of her church, showing kindness and affection to anyone she interacted with, accepting herself, and embracing her strengths.

Simultaneously, I myself was growing. Letting go for me meant allowing myself to also depart from rigid guidelines and plans so that I could be present in the moment with Ms. B. Once I was able to demonstrate this mindfulness, together we worked on forgiving the past, and trusting the future. Letting love, for me, involved the use of prayer, therapeutic touch, crying with my client, and allowing her to be the guide.

Through the course of therapy, Ms. B. and I experienced the powerful interaction of faith, hope, and love. These, I believe, are the key ingredients to grief therapy. On the last day of our sessions, I will never forget when Ms. B. referred to me as her sister, "You have taught me, and I have taught you." She will forever be an inspiration to me.

Summary

This chapter on grief and loss reviewed several different psychological theories of grief, including Freud's original drive theory, Kübler-Ross's groundbreaking work on death and dying, and the task model put forth by Worden. The importance of attachment across the lifespan was discussed in relation to the work of Bowlby and to Ainsworth on the role of attachment and loss. More recently, Walsh and McGoldrick have added a family systems perspective, illuminating the intergenerational layers involved in the grieving process. Coping skills and the role of religion and spirituality were examined with Fowler's faith development theory, and the acronym FICA was discussed as a useful tool for exploring the role of spirituality in the client's life.

We are all born the same way, but each of us dies differently. Death can come peacefully at the end of a life well lived, or it can be untimely, traumatic, or life-changing for the bereaved. As in the case of infertility, Alzheimer's, or missing persons, loss can also be ambiguous. It is not possible in this space to create specific interventions for every possible grief experience; an extensive list of references is included for readers to conduct additional research. Rather, the goal is to help professionals learn about grief, be able to identify the nuances between normal and complicated grief, and understand and address any continuing issues of their own concerning death and dying.

Type of relationship, attachment, cause of death, and timing are unique to each situation and require individually tailored responses. Professionals who work with crisis intervention, and particularly death and dying, would do well to follow the basics set forth by Rogers: to be fully present and responsive to the needs of the bereaved, to be open to familial and cultural adaptations to loss, to encourage and foster strength and resilience, and to take into account any spiritual or religious values that the client values. The ultimate goal should be to provide appropriate and timely interventions during times of crisis so that people can experience and process their grief in a healthy manner and not become stuck in patterns that lead to depression, complicated bereavement, or result in more serious pathology. If successful, we will have helped our clients forge a path through their grief and once again find meaning in their lives.

Military Deployment and Reintegration Issues

Seth C. W. Hayden

PREVIEW

Serving the needs of military personnel and families presents unique challenges for counselors working in a variety of settings. Whether providing services in a community agency, a K–12 or post-secondary school setting, or in a rehabilitation context, there is a high likelihood of encountering military personnel and/or families in need of assistance. Military families are a significant part of our communities, with more than two thirds residing in the larger civilian community and the remainder on military bases (Hoshmand & Hoshmand, 2007). The anticipated mental health needs and increases in access of counselors to military and family members requires an understanding of military culture in addition to effective methods to support this population. This chapter provides an in-depth discussion of the military experience and offers various approaches to assist military service members and their families.

RELEVANCE OF MILITARY PERSONNEL AND FAMILIES TO COUNSELORS

Military personnel and families comprise a significant segment of the U.S. population. As of 2012, more than 1.4 million people were on active duty in the military (U. S. Department of Defense, 2012). An additional 1,267,309 service members comprise the National Guard and Reserve components (Military Leadership Diversity Commission, 2010). The impact of serving in combat and effects of deployment on our military and family members have been the focus of the media and research since the Authorization for Use of Military Force Against Iraq Resolution was passed in 2002 and Operation Iraqi Freedom began in March

20, 2003. Statistics on fatalities and physical injuries are staggering and continue to rise even with decisions made for troop withdrawal. As of May 29, 2012, according to the U.S. Department of Defense (http://www.defense.gov/releases/default.aspx) there were 4,409 total fatalities (including killed in action and nonhostile action) and 31,928 wounded in action (WIA). Of the total reports of fatalities, 98% were male; 91% noncommissioned officers; 82% active duty; 11% National Guard; 74% Caucasian; 9% African American; 11% Latino; 54% under the age of 25 years; and 72% from the U.S. Army. Of the total number of wounded troops reported, 20% include serious brain or spinal injuries. This total of wounded troops excludes psychological injuries.

When considering that 55% of those deployed to Operation Enduring Freedom (OEF) and Operation Iraq Freedom (OIF) are married, millions of spouses and children within military families comprise an additional segment significantly affected by the military experience. Within military service, deployment affects a large portion of service members and their families. Roughly 1 million service members have children, with 48% having children 5 years old or younger (Office of the Deputy Under Secretary of Defense, 2005). Since 2001, over 1.9 million people have been deployed in conjunction with Operation Iraqi Freedom and Operation Enduring Freedom (Institute of Medicine, 2010). This ever-expanding community of those associated with the military experience demonstrates the need for counselors to understand the unique needs of this population as it relates to wellness and healthy functioning.

RELEVANCE OF MILITARY POPULATION TO COUNSELORS

While counselors have a long history of working with military men and women and their families in various capacities, the current and anticipated need has necessitated military systems such as the Veteran's Administration to formally incorporate licensed mental health counselors into the treatment mechanism of the organization. The Veterans Benefits, Healthcare, and Information Technology Act of 2006 established explicit recognition of both mental health counselors and marriage and family therapists within the Veteran's Administration (Public Law 109-461). While this development provided the needed emphasis for counselors to operate with the military mental health apparatus, an occupational code to allow the Veteran's Administration to hire counselors was not created until late in 2008. This has since been addressed, which means that positions for licensed mental health counselors are now posted within the federal government for the purposes of providing direct counseling services to military personnel and families.

In addition to access, counseling is also a frequently used resource by military families experiencing deployment. A survey by the National Military Family Association (2006) reported that half of the military dependents surveyed about deployment-related needs have used, or would use, counseling services. Access and utilization of services necessitates counselors having an understanding of various aspects of the military experience to provide competent assistance to service members and their families.

Military Culture

There exists within the military a culture consisting of shared values that significantly affect both service members and their families. Military culture exists by virtue of the use of specific language, symbols, and hierarchy present in formations of armed forces, which are critical to military effectiveness (Ulmer, Collins, & Jacobs, 2000). Central themes within military culture are loyalty, teamwork, leadership, obedience, and hierarchy (Green, Buckman, Dandeker, & Greenberg, 2010). Though these values can all be found, to some extent, within nonmilitary cultures, military culture is distinct in that it demands subordination of the self to the group, which requires military individuals to make sacrifices for others, including, in the extreme, giving of one's life (Dandeker, 2000). This is a unique context in which military service members and families function, and it can significantly affect the work of counselors.

CULTURAL DIFFERENCES IN THE MILITARY   When discussing military culture, it is important to consider the within-group differences as opposed to viewing the military as a monolithic entity. There are cultural differences among branches (i.e., Army, Navy, Air Force, Marines, and Coast Guard), and each has its own operational structure and procedures, which can present issues during joint operational missions (Green et al., 2010). Counselors encountering a service member or family would benefit from learning the specific organization, common language, hierarchy, and unique characteristics of their affiliated branch of the military.

RESERVISTS AND NATIONAL GUARD VERSUS CAREER ACTIVE DUTY MILITARY   There are also cultural differences between regular service members and National Guard/reservists. The recent conflicts in Iraq and Afghanistan have utilized the reservists in unprecedented numbers, requiring ongoing contact between reservists and their families with the regular military culture. Oftentimes, reservists maintain ideas of fairness and equality learned in civilian culture as compared to regular military service members who tend to focus on military concepts that can affect how each group perceives particular events (Greene et al., 2010; Howard, 2006). Reservists often experience sudden changes in cultural context, which can be difficult for them and their families. The military culture tends to favor total immersion, creating the potential for reservists to feel more isolated from active military despite serving in a similar manner (Greene et al., 2010). Counselors encountering reservists would benefit from assessing the degree to which their issues may be related to this cultural dynamic but also how they differ.

Apart from the cultural dynamic, reservists had higher rates of mental health and behavioral problems than their regular military personnel peers (Hoge et al., 2004; Hotopf et al., 2006; Milliken, Auchterlonie, & Hoge, 2007). Counselors working with reservists and their families should be aware of the unique aspects of this population's experience within the military to properly address their needs. Reservists may receive less support and possibly decreased benefits after the deployment ends.

Mental Health and Military Stigmatization

An additional aspect related to military culture that may affect supporting military service members and families is a perceived stigma within the military related to receiving mental health services. In a study by Hoge et al. (2004) regarding barriers to help-seeking within the military population, findings indicated that out of those who were screened to have major depression, generalized anxiety, and PTSD, only 38% to 45% had interest in receiving help and only 23% to 40% of that group actually sought medical health care. Some reasons for not seeking assistance were fears of being stigmatized by others along with military-specific reasons for not seeking services, such as not wanting to be treated differently by unit leadership and desiring to maintain the confidence of fellow unit members. Being passed over for possible promotions may also be a reason to not seek mental health services. There still remains a stigma of weakness among many in the military.

Not only is the service member influenced by this stigma, but accessing services within the military family can also be hindered by the stigma associated with seeking mental health assistance. Military families cope with various stressors in a structured environment that pressures families to behave a certain way (Drummet, Colman, & Cable, 2003). Military spouses and children are viewed as informally carrying the rank of their spouse or parent, which includes guidelines for behavior and pressure to conform. It is often believed that service members' career advancement can be detrimentally affected by the behavior of their family members (Albano, 2002). The stigma attached to receiving services can be a challenge for counselors working with service members and families.

The Cycle of Deployment

Deployment is an experience not shared by other segments of our population. The deployment cycles in the conflicts in Iraq and Afghanistan are unique in the acceleration of typical deployment rotations (Lincoln, Swift, & Shorteno-Fraser, 2008). The length of deployment, which was once fairly predictable, has been uncertain in the face of frequent deployment extensions and multiple deployments in a short period of time to Afghanistan and Iraq. The deployment cycle is not solely the service members' time in theater, since military are also involved in predeployment and postdeployment processing requirements (Erbes, Polusny, MacDermid, & Compton, 2008). Logan first conceptualized deployment as a cycle as opposed to a singular event (Lincoln et al., 2008), involving five distinct phases: (1) predeployment (from notification to departure), (2) deployment (from departure to return), (3) sustainment, (4) redeployment, and (5) postdeployment (Pincus, House, Christensen, & Adler, 2005). Each phase can affect both service members and their families.

During predeployment, partners prepare to rely on alternative sources of social support (Erbes et al., 2008) and form new roles and norms for the household. Children within the family require significant logistical arrangements as the nondeployed wwb: care-giver likely will function as a single parent for an extended period of time. There also exists the potential that the serving member may not return on time, requiring additional preparation and coping by the family.

During deployment, it is typical for both partners to worry about the safety and well-being of family members in addition to concern for maintaining the relational bond (Erbes et al., 2008). Current technology allows for unprecedented communication between service members and family members, but these interactions do not always prevent stress. Issues experienced by both the deployed service member and the nondeployed partner still occur apart from each other without full engagement in problem solving due to distance. Children in the family may also struggle with the absence of a caregiver. Celebrations and milestones are often missed by the deployed member, which may cause a sense of isolation and disconnect within the family.

Postdeployment (or reintegration) presents the potential for a wide range of concerns regarding the adjustment of having the service member return to the family (Erbes

ACTIVITY 13.1

Imagine you are working with a family who is seeking counseling prior to the deployment of a family member. You may have only one session to work with the family. What would you discuss to prepare the family for the separation? What questions would be important to ask?

et al., 2008), adapting to new roles and rules in the family, reinforcing one's authority in the house, and sensing internal or external blame or guilt for the absence. The reintegration period requires that the service member and partner reconstruct their relationship and roles at home as both have inevitably changed as a result of the deployment. The family must also adjust to the resumption of roles as partner and parent (Lincoln et al., 2008) as changes in caretaking roles, discipline, and other familial functions often are changed as well.

This cycle of deployment presents significant elements to consider when assisting military personnel and families. The majority of families possess the skills to successfully cope with deployment, but some do struggle with the stress and experience negative consequences (Chandra et al., 2010b; McNulty, 2003). The deployment, when conceptualized as a cycle, provides a more accurate framework within which to consider the challenges of service members and their families as related to their time in the military.

ISSUES FOR MILITARY PERSONNEL AS IT RELATES TO DEPLOYMENT

For the first time in history, the number of psychological casualties related to combat far outstrips the number of physical injuries or deaths (Sammons & Batten, 2008). Some projections of the current rate of psychological issues resulting from active service estimate that over 30% of combatants will develop symptoms consistent with a mental health diagnosis. Currently, 40% of Operation Enduring Freedom (OEF) in Afghanistan and Operation Iraqi Freedom (OIF) in Iraq veterans have or are currently accessing services at the Department of Veterans Affairs Medical Center for mental health concerns, including post-traumatic stress disorder, anxiety, and depression. As was common with veterans from the Vietnam War, PTSD increases significantly over time (Batten & Pollack, 2008). These numbers illustrate the high volume of negative mental outcomes related to active duty military in Iraq and Afghanistan.

Apart from the high prevalence of mental health issues, traumatic brain injury (TBI) is especially significant in recent military conflicts. This type of injury has become known as a "signature wound" of Operation Enduring Freedom and Operation Iraqi Freedom with the incidence of TBI being higher in these conflicts than in previous conflicts (Bagalman, 2011). In the fiscal year of 2010, 45,606 service members were diagnosed with TBI–related conditions at VA medical facilities. Within Department of Defense health care systems, 30,703 service members sustained TBI and an estimated 20% of OEF and OIF have suffered some form of a TBI (Tanielian & Jaycox, 2008). The prevalence of TBI within our military population increases the likelihood a counselor will encounter this issue when working with service members. Appropriate referrals should be made to medical professionals to ensure the treatment of the whole person. While injuries and issues may increase over time, there is also an indication that symptoms of combat-related mild traumatic brain injury or PTSD may disappear or be significantly reduced after returning from combat. A study by Milliken, Aucheterlonie, and Hoge (2007) found that as many as half of service members experiencing PTSD after deployment do not exhibit any symptoms after 3 months at home. Hoge et al. (2004) reported several service members who have mild traumatic brain injury (MTBI), sometimes referred to as a concussion, seemed to not experience symptoms within 4 to 12 weeks postdeployment. A counselor encountering these issues would benefit from determining both the symptomatology related to PTSD and MTBI, the time frame associated with the injury, and the past and current treatment implemented to address these issues.

Other physical injuries may also be present at the same time as mental health and other medical issues. Many service members may return with polytraumatic injuries, including traumatic brain injury, injuries to several body systems (e.g., skin/soft tissue, eye injuries), complex pain syndromes, and PTSD (Collins, & Kennedy, 2008). This reality presents a special clinical situation in which counselors may need to work closely with other providers who are serving military members and their families to address complex issues of mental and physical injuries related to their experiences during deployment.

In addition, there has been a fair amount of media attention given to the growing rate of suicide among service members (Roan, 2012). Additional analysis has determined a significantly higher rate of suicide between veterans and the nonveteran population (Kaplan, McFarland, Huguet, & Newsom, 2012). Service members are also at risk for substance use problems (Jacobson et al., 2008) and short-term readjustment reactions manifesting as difficulty sleeping, irritability, and difficulty concentrating (Shea, Vujanovic, Masfield, Sevin, & Liu, 2010).

Women service members face additional stressors. A study of women veterans in the military who have sought services for PTSD found that 23% reported military sexual trauma (Skinner et al., 2000). The high rate of military sexual trauma presents a unique challenge for women who serve in the military. Thus, counselors must have an understanding of the potential risks with which service members may present for counseling. In addition to service members, family members also encounter issues associated with the military life.

ISSUES FOR MILITARY FAMILIES RELATED TO DEPLOYMENT

It is important to recognize that many military families display a high level of resilience regarding the stress of deployment (Jensen, Xenakis, Wolf, & Bain, 1991). Though many successfully manage the situation, military families experience problems meeting the challenges. The following section discusses the ways military families may struggle with the deployment experience.

Familial Stress Associated with Deployment

Given the high rate of veterans who are married and have children, it is important to consider the influences deployments have on family members. Previous studies indicated deployment was associated with increased stress among nondeployed parents (Gibbs, Martin, Kupper, & Johnson, 2007; Haas, Pazdernik, & Olsen, 2005; McNulty,

2003). Nondeployed parents who are left with the responsibilities of maintaining the household and raising children are also concerned with the well-being of their spouse at war. There is evidence of higher rates of separation and divorce as well as incidents of domestic violence with OEF/OIF combat veterans (Sayers, Farrow, Ross, & Oslin, 2009).

Extensions in deployment and multiple deployments because of extended conflicts in Iraq and Afghanistan have affected nondeployed spouses and deployed spouses and partners. SteelFisher, Zaslavsky, and Blendon (2008) found that spouses who experienced deployment extensions reported higher rates of mental health issues and evaluated the Army more negatively than previous spouses who did not experience extensions. A counselor who assists families experiencing multiple deployments may encounter high levels of stress and frustration within the family and expressions of frustration with the military structure related to the prolonged deployments.

In families with children, research indicates that child maltreatment and neglect occur in higher rates during deployment (Gibbs et al., 2007). Deployment exacerbates a parent's struggle to fulfill children's needs. While the caregivers' interactions with their children may be affected by deployment, the mental health of the children is also a concern. Barker and Berry (2009) found that children unable to cope with a deployed parent often demonstrated increased behavior problems at deployment and attachment problems at reunion compared with children whose parents had not recently deployed. Research indicates that the mental health of children and adolescents is influenced by the stress of a parent's deployment (Lincoln et al., 2008). Dealing with the unavailability of a parent for an extended period of time, along with the heightened stress within the family, can contribute to emotional issues that manifest in children of deployed service members. Family members may also worry about the physical and mental well-being of the returning service member and a potential subsequent deployment (Chandra et al., 2010a, 2010b, 2011; Pincus et al., 2005).

Reunification

In addition to the time apart, challenges exist during the reunification of the service member with the nondeployed spouse and family. Previous research regarding reunification has indicated potential struggles within the family (Chandra et al, 2010a. 2010b, 2011; Pincus, House, Christensen, & Adler, 2005). There may be conflict associated with familial roles and boundaries, which requires renegotiation. There may be conflict over ways the house was managed and the loss of the spouses' newfound independence. Military family members may also struggle with adjusting to new relationships that have been developed during deployment. Feelings of abandonment during the prolonged separation may also exist. Unresolved issues may also reemerge and occur

ACTIVITY 13.2

You are working with a couple who is seeking counseling for marital difficulties. They report that the husband has just come home from his second deployment in Afghanistan, with each having lasted 13 months. The presenting issue is centered around the husband not feeling involved in the family and the kids not listening to his authority. During the session, he states that he feels restless and has difficulty sleeping, an inability to concentrate, headaches, and dizziness. What are your primary and secondary priorities?

simultaneously with new issues related to readjustment to the new familial dynamic. Family members may also struggle with negotiating a balance between the support networks formed during deployment and independence. Children within the family may reject, be apathetic, or have anxiety around the newly returning family member. Children may also display loyalty toward the nondeployed parent while also being resistant to the disciplining of the returning parent (Chandra et al., 2010a, 2010b, 2011; Pincus et al., 2005).

Finally, it is important to consider the relational quality of the military couple. Divorce rates of service members have been on a continual rise since 2001. The annual divorce rate in 2001 was 2.65% and rose to 3.7% in 2011 (Bushatz, 2011), reflecting a steady and consistent increase in marital issues. A counselor working with a military family should evaluate the relational satisfaction within the marriage or determine ways to enhance relational bonds prior to prolonged periods of separation.

Military Families and Traumatic-Brain Injury

Though we have already addressed the impact that a traumatic brain injury may have on service members, families of the injured service member are also affected by this new reality. There are special considerations for families confronting a traumatic brain injury (Landau & Hissett, 2008). A significant reorganization within the family is needed to adjust to the new reality of a loved one who is not the same as before deployment. A counselor encountering a service member with a TBI should include the family as part of the recovery process to assess the well-being of the service member and family members.

COUNSELOR INTERVENTION WITH MILITARY SERVICE MEMBERS

The U.S. Department of Defense and the Veteran's Health Administration provide myriad services designed to support military personnel and families. While these organizations strive to support service members and their families, there is recognition of the need for quality interventions from community-based organizations and personnel to address the ongoing needs of this population (Burnam, Meredith, Tanielian, & Jaycox, 2009). Despite the counselor's setting or primary focus, there is a strong possibility of encountering service members and veterans in one's counseling practice.

The discussion of interventions that follows will largely focus on systemic interventions as opposed to viewing an issue in isolation. In addition, this section will provide specific strategies to address common issues among military personnel, such as PTSD, TBI, suicide, and family issues. Collaboration between civilian and military counselors is the wave of the future (Hoshmand & Hoshmand, 2007), and this is especially true for crisis counselors. Though there are evident barriers to this approach, integration of support services by military family service providers is useful when assisting families (Hayden, 2011).

The approaches reviewed below are by no means an exhaustive list of ways to support military personnel and families. This discussion is intended to provide tangible means to intervene in crisis situations. Collaboration and service integration are key, but clinical expertise and experience will be a preeminent resource for assisting this population as you consider the unique needs of this population.

Interventions for Post-Traumatic Stress Disorder

When addressing post-traumatic stress disorder (PTSD), collaborating with other service providers is a critical component of effective intervention. A counselor addressing various issues associated with PTSD would benefit from considering the previously mentioned aspects of the military context in which military members and their families operate. This involves acquiring general knowledge of the cultural realities of this population via education, training, and supervision. Lack of awareness of the culture of the military can be a therapeutic barrier within counseling. Counselors willing to learn about the context within which military personnel and families function will enhance the counselors' ability to join with service members in counseling. The interventions that follow were chosen because of empirical evidence to support their use. The goal is to provide the reader with some tangible interventions to address common issues within this population.

RESILIENCE RELATED TO PTSD   There has been a focus within military mental health on building preventive resilience to PTSD prior to exposure to traumatic events. Evidence for this approach is ample when focusing on psychoeducational discussions of resilience, enhancing awareness of emotional and physical experiences, and attention to positive emotional experiences and social bonds (Kent, Davis, Stark, & Stewart, 2011). Working with service members to develop resilience when it is apparent they are likely to be exposed to traumatic events provides a preventive approach as opposed to addressing PTSD. Prevention is an important aspect in crisis intervention. Education and counseling prior to a deployment can assist in decreasing crises, in this case PTSD.

TRAUMA-FOCUSED COGNITIVE-BEHAVIORAL THERAPY   One intervention often used to address PTSD is trauma-focused cognitive-behavioral therapy (TF-CBT), an approach endorsed in clinical practice guidelines by the Veterans Administration (VA) and Department of Defense (DoD) Clinical Practice Guideline Working Group (2010). These guidelines provide evidence-based practices related to commonly encountered mental health issues within the military population. Trauma-focused CBT involves confronting the memories of the traumatic events and the feared and avoided external situations that remind clients of the events (Creamer, Wade, Fletcher, & Forbes, 2011). These maladaptive interpretations and beliefs associated with the events interfere with adaptation and recovery (Forbes et al., 2007). This cognitive behavioral approach offers a framework within which to address PTSD.

Some trauma-focused CBT approaches have evidence of effectiveness. Prolonged exposure techniques such as those used by Foa, Rothbaum, Riggs, and Murdock (1991), where the service member is subjected to the avoided or feared event *in vivo*, have demonstrated effectiveness in the treatment of PTSD (Powers, Halpern, Ferenschak, Gillihan, & Foa, 2010). Crisis counselors implementing this intervention must be cautioned to ensure that they are competently trained in this technique due to the intensity and affective elements associated with exposure to traumatic stimulus.

COGNITIVE-PROCESSING THERAPY   Cognitive processing therapy (CPT) has shown positive effects for addressing PTSD. CPT focuses on the range of emotions, in addition to anxiety, that may result from traumatization (e.g., shame, sadness, anger). A benefit of this approach to PTSD is that CPT can be generalized to comorbid mental health conditions and day-to-day problems, and it is in a manualized format allowing for widespread dissemination (Monson et al., 2006). CPT can be implemented using a 12-session, manualized approach (Resick, 2001) focused primarily on cognitive interventions. The following brief overview of this approach will assist with providing an understanding of how to implement this intervention. Crisis counselors should know who is able to provide these services (i.e., make a referral) if the services cannot be provided during a limited exposure to the military client.

A counselor begins CPT by offering psychoeducational information related to the symptoms of PTSD, keeping in mind the cognitive and information processing aspects of the condition (Monson et al., 2006). After the initial session, clients are asked to write an "impact statement" in which they detail the meaning of the traumatic event, including beliefs about why the event happened. This statement is then discussed in subsequent sessions with the counselor evaluating various problematic beliefs and cognitions. The service member is then taught to identify the connection between events, thoughts, and feelings with homework assignments related to understanding the relationship among these elements. The counselor then follows up with the client on the homework. Various activities, such as having the service member consider current stressful events and gradually processing these events, are aspects through which the counselor guides the service member through a reprocessing of various experiences. The counselor challenges problematic beliefs and cognitions when clinically appropriate. Typical homework assignments involve worksheets in which the service members process their day-to-day lives to enable analysis and modification of various maladaptive beliefs and cognitions. Therapy concludes with the consolidation of treatment gains.

Family Involvement in the Treatment of PTSD

Family involvement in treatment with service members is a vital component of addressing various issues. As previously discussed, families are significantly affected by deployment and military life (Gibbs et al., 2007; SteelFisher et al., 2008). In addition to being affected by this experience, families engaged in mental health treatment have been associated with improved treatment outcomes when addressing a variety of psychological disorders (Falloon, Roncone, Held, Coverdale, & Laidlaw, 2002). Veterans themselves have also expressed a desire to have family members involved in their treatment for PTSD (Batten et al., 2009). This indicates a need on the part of a counselor to include family members when assisting a service member recovering from PTSD.

COGNITIVE–BEHAVIORAL CONJOINT THERAPY.   Monson, Guthrie, and Stevens (2003) reported evidence supporting the use of cognitive-behavioral conjoint therapy (CBCT) when addressing PTSD within military families. This systems approach recognizes that a couple's behaviors and belief systems interact and PTSD has an impact on all family members (Monson, Guthrie, & Stevens, 2003). CBCT for PTSD involves 15 sessions comprising three phases of treatment. The first phase provides treatment orientation and psych education about PTSD relating it to intimate relational problems. The second phase provides behavioral communication skills training. The third and final phase focuses on cognitive interventions for the couple to address PTSD. After the initial phase, the conjoint behavioral interventions are aimed at overcoming experiential avoidance and improving communication skills. The implemented cognitive interventions are used to modify core interacting schemas associated with the development and/or maintenance of PTSD and relational discord. Further discussion of this approach can be found in Monson, Guthrie, and Stevens (2003). This approach focuses on PTSD in the context of the intimate relationship and involves the partner in the therapeutic process. Viewing PTSD in the context of the relationship can be a more effective manner of addressing this issue.

Traumatic Brain Injury

Due in large part to improvised explosive devices (IEDs), traumatic brain injury has become the signature injury of the current military conflict in Iraq (Eden, Stevens, & Institute of Medicine, 2006). In addition, people with mild TBI are more likely to use counseling and/or rehabilitation services as compared with medical services, even for acute care (Kraus et al., 2005). The severity of TBI injuries range from mild—involving a brief change in mental status and consciousness—to severe—involving an extended period of unconsciousness or amnesia after the injury (Centers for Disease Control and Prevention, 2006). Due to the potential for being undiagnosed or misdiagnosed, a clinician should inquire about any sort of head trauma when working with service members who may come to counseling for other issues, such as PTSD or anxiety or depression (Landau & Hissett, 2008). The most frequent unmet needs of this population are improving memory and problem-solving, managing stress and emotional upsets, controlling anger, and improving job skills . Several of these issues fall within the realm of counseling, heightening the likelihood of counselor involvement in treatment. Asking about direct or indirect exposure to IED's is crucial to treat the whole person and make appropriate referrals to medical professionals.

COGNITIVE-BEHAVIORAL THERAPY   Certain interventions are effective when assisting a service member with TBI. Cognitive-behavioral therapy approaches to TBI are concrete and direct (Mateer, Sira, & O'Connell, 2005). An additional significant benefit of this approach with military personnel is the apparent reduction in post-traumatic stress reactions with clients who have experienced a mild TBI (Bryant, Moulds, Guthrie, & Nixon, 2003), which often occurs simultaneously. Various deficits may lead to negative self-statements, which the counselor can challenge with statements of positive self-efficacy (Patterson & Staton, 2009). A key component of the CBT approach when addressing TBI is to inform the client that negative self-statements can potentially erode one's sense of control and dictate behavior (Mateer, Sira, & O'Connell, 2005).

BRIEF THERAPY   Brief therapy may be implemented to address issues with TBI and focuses on listening to, understanding, and validating the client's story (Patterson & Staton, 2009). In the process of setting goals, the counselor listens to the service member's story and reflects meaning, placing the problem in the past tense while also communicating the language of a healthy and positive future (Presbury, Echterling, & McKee, 2002). The clinician engages in what is called relabeling regarding the language that the service member uses related to his or her injury and identity. As opposed to allowing the client to use negative self-identifiers such as being a "bum," the clinician would relabel this term as "not feeling productive" (Patterson & Staton, 2009). The relabeling is continually reinforced throughout therapy. This assigns meaning to the negative statements and then allows a behavioral plan to be integrated into the short-term counseling.

Another aspect of the brief therapy approach that seems useful when working with service members with TBI is to enhance their sense of agency (Patterson, & Staton, 2009). Using techniques such as externalizing the problem to avoid negative internalization of limited functionality related to the injury is a tangible method of enhancing a sense of agency within the service member. This limits the identification related to the injury and helps service members understand that the TBI does not control them. Brief therapy presents a useful and effective approach to working with service members who have suffered a TBI. Often, it is this brief therapy that may be implemented in crisis intervention. Small accomplishments at this level may open the military member for longer-term counseling.

Risk Assessment

Given the higher rates of suicide in the military population (Kaplan, McFarland, Huguet, & Newsom, 2012), it is important to keep this potential issue in mind when working with service members. Equally important in this assessment, although less evident, is the risk of harm to others. Assessing for the potential to harm oneself and assessing for indications of isolation are critical to ensure the safety of the client. Once a service member has been identified with a potential of harm to self or others, a counselor should decide on the best plan of intervention based on the level of lethality (Martin, Ghahramanlou-Holloway, Lou, & Tucciarone, 2009).

Joiner's interpersonal-psychological theory of suicide has relevance (Brenner et al., 2008) to this population. Joiner's theory holds that people who die by suicide may perceive themselves as a burden to others, have a thwarted sense of belonging, and have the capability to engage in a lethal act as a result of experiences that caused pain and fear (Joiner, 2005). There is evidence that these three elements collectively differentiate between living and suicide samples of Air Force personnel (Nademin et al., 2008). It is critically important to remove or restrict access to lethal means (Martin et al., 2009), such as weapons, because a decrease in suicide risk occurs when this safety measure was enacted. A counselor can also address the misperception of being a burden to others and a thwarted sense of belonging when assisting service members at risk for suicide. Exploring or helping to develop a new sense of meaning after a deployment may also be an essential aspect to decrease lethality.

Supporting Military Families

As previously stated, military families may be affected by deployment and by the potential physical and mental health issues service members develop related to their combat experiences. This highlights the need to continually consider the family when working with service members. It is essential for civilian and military providers to collaborate with each other to ensure that the family's needs are being effectively addressed (Hoshmand & Hoshmand, 2007).

Hayden (2011) surveyed service providers in U.S. Army Family Centers and found frequent collaboration between military and civilian providers. Military family support professionals indicated collaboration enhanced their awareness of services, increased access to services for family members, and enhanced continuity of care. Continuity of care is critical given the frequent mobility of this population. Service providers also indicated collaboration could be expanded through outreach between civilian and military providers in addition to reorganizing support services to lower barriers among branches of the military. Since the family system within the military is continually experiencing change, professional intervention should be systems-oriented and multilayered (Huebner, Mancini, Wilcox, Grass, & Grass, 2007).

A leadership summit of military professionals was held to focus on military families and offered several recommendations related to supporting military families of deployments (Booth, Segal, & Place, 2009). The participants at this summit decided to begin evaluating support programs to learn which models are effective and build on those that are successful. Communicating critical information and establishing collaborative partnerships was a key recommendation in serving military families. The summit identified a need to address psychological health needs of military family members and to develop and implement programs that support military children and youth.

Adaptation Within Military Families

Counselors can promote adaptation within military families by linking them to resources within the community. There is evidence that a familial adaptation program within the Air Force focused on community-based prevention efforts instills a sense of community (Bowen, Mancini, Martin, Ware, & Nelson, 2003). In this approach, interventions expand beyond the clinical services and educational seminars to include advocacy and social change, citizen participation, community development, resource mobilization, and collective action (Rothman, 1999). Counselors working with military families can work within the communities to enhance communal connection and action.

Bowen et al. (2003) also found it useful to work with unit leaders around unit-based and unit-supported initiatives to sustain the social fabric of military units. This may need to be facilitated by the counselor who has access to unit leadership. Again, it is important to consider the formal and informal supports for service members and their families when considering preventative and/or remediation interventions.

Lincoln, Swift, and Shorteno-Fraser (2008) offer empirically validated interventions for supporting children and families. First, they suggest providing enhanced support services for military families during periods of increased stress. A counselor can assess whether various programs and procedures are in place that work toward improving communication, mitigating stress, and resolving crises during key time frames—for example, following redeployment and reintegration. Another recommendation is to identify children and families including, reservists' families, who are at an increased risk during predeployment and intensify education and services as part of deployment preparation. A counselor should also identify those deployed parent-soldiers who appear at an increased risk for postdeployment integration issues because of physical injuries, psychological trauma, and substance abuse. A counselor can develop and sustain resources for the children and families of at-risk soldier parents prior to postdeployment and develop a treatment plan for addressing concerns.

ACTIVITY 13.3

Over the next week, investigate the clinical mental health, rehabilitative, religious/spiritual, and medical resources that are available for military members and family members in your community to develop your understanding of community resources for potential referrals.

An additional intervention is to develop programs that integrate education and training for families of injured service members who are being followed throughout the military medical services or VA hospitals. Acting in collaboration with military medical services and VA hospitals, specific community mental health specialists with specific training and expertise in treating children and families of military personnel is important. Lincoln et al. (2008) have also suggested building interdisciplinary trainings for community-based mental health professionals with the goal of normalizing expectations regarding psychological reactions to deployments, clinical problems associated with all phases of deployment, interventions, and resources available to children and families of service members. A counselor is uniquely positioned to be a critical asset to military service members and families by addressing healthy adaptation, resilience, and additional issues when they arise.

SPIRITUALITY AND RELIGIOUS NEEDS OF DEPLOYED MILITARY SERVICE MEMBERS

An area receiving even less attention in the literature has been how the lack of, or inclusion of, spiritual and religious practices may affect mental health during predeployment, deployment, and reintegration. However, one comprehensive study found that spiritual and religious practices among Americans is strong; 96% of people living in the United States believe in a higher being, 90% report to praying, 69% state they are members of a religious organization, and 43% state they have attended their religious institution in the past 7 days (Princeton Religious Research Center, 2000). In a study conducted with approximately 200 deployed military in Iraq, Jackson-Cherry and Sterner (2012) found religious and spiritual practices to be reflective of the general population and a reported area of strength for many deployed military who indicated a positive view of a faith tradition or spirituality. In fact, many of those who were surveyed stressed the importance of their practices to work through many of the existential and relationship struggles they encountered while deployed. In taking a preventative approach, it would seem essential to evaluate effective and positive coping mechanisms that have been helpful in noncombat situations and make available those strategies while in combat.

The wellness approach proposes that a "well" person is one who has balanced six essential dimensions: (1) intellectual, (2) emotional, (3) physical, (4) social, (5) occupational, and (6) spiritual. Indeed, spiritual and religious beliefs and practices have been viewed as influencing worldviews and behaviors, and they are relied upon by many as a coping mechanism through religious ceremonies and services (Biema, 2001). Spiritual practices, having a strong support system, assigning meaning to traumatic events, and overall positive thinking may be linked to decreasing post-traumatic stress (Meisenhelder, 2002). Prayer, meaning, and positive faith have been linked to reduced symptoms of posttraumatic stress in those service members directly and indirectly exposed to the trauma. Gerber, Boals, and Schuettler (2011) found positive religious coping practices were directly related to posttraumatic growth and inversely related to posttraumatic stress. In a study of deployed military personnel, Harris et al. (2011) found individuals who perceived their spirituality as a source of validation and acceptance were more likely to find healthy meaning in their deployment and recover from trauma. Jackson-Cherry and Sterner (2012) found that having a sense of purpose and meaning in the deployment, maintaining healthy relationships during deployment, and integrating religious and/or spiritual practices can be essential to decreasing symptoms of anxiety and depression while deployed.

VOICES FROM THE FIELD 13.1

Anonymous Responses from Deployed Military in Combat

• **What makes you feel at peace?**

"After praying and talking to my younger children and seeing them happy and innocent brings peace."

"Knowing that in my mind God or a higher power is there with me and he will only give me what I can handle."

• **What events tested your faith/spirituality?**

"When I knew soldiers who were killed in combat, and some of them were Christians and others were not.

It's just conflicting for me personally when thinking about someone I know (who was a good person and a good soldier) and wondering whether or not he's in Heaven."

"Death of soldiers, close call with husband, marriage issues all had me questioning 'why' but it wasn't for long that I got my answer from His word (the Bible)."

"When the bridge was blown up, it made me thank God as soon as we got a second to stop and think."

VOICES FROM THE FIELD 13.2

A Warrior's Story

Tracy Roberts

Working as a rehabilitation counselor with a U.S. Marine Corps veteran of Iraq recently provided me with the opportunity to hear about his combat experience and blast injuries and learn about what it is like for him to live with mild traumatic brain injury (MTBI), post-traumatic stress disorder (PTSD), chronic pain, and vision impairment. Our work together came to focus on identifying his goals for his post injury civilian life and creating strategies together, ultimately implementing them while integrating recommendations from our entire team of treating medical professionals and discipline specific specialists, such as occupational, physical, and speech therapists. Re-entering civilian life as a food ministry volunteer worker was one of

his goals. To accomplish it, we implemented systematic desensitization as one treatment to treat his PTSD, first driving by the facility, next visiting it while it was empty, then again for a short period of time when operational, and ultimately returning weekly to volunteer on a regular basis. We identified and used cognitive interventions for MTBI like written instructions, pain management tools such as a special portable stool, and visual aids such as specially filtered sunglasses for photosensitivity. All the while, my client and I processed his grief over significant loss and his awareness of the challenges and rewards specific to finding the strength, courage, and spirit to continue to engage life as fully as possible.

Summary

Serving the needs of military personnel and families presents unique challenges for counselors working in a variety of settings. The chance of counseling a military member who has been deployed or working with family members during deployment continues to rise. Many military members will take advantage of services provided in their military communities. More are seeking counseling with civilian counselors because over two thirds of service members live in civilian neighborhoods. This is also true for reservists who make up a large segment of individuals deployed. Understanding military cultural norms and expectations is essential in treating the whole person. Deployments offer a unique experience not known to civilians never deployed or exposed to deployments. Many deployed military service members may encounter physical or mental health issues requiring collaboration and services from counselors. Families left behind during deployment also may experience mental health concerns requiring professional counseling services. Predeployment, deployment, and postdeployment each bring about changes and require adjustments. Most service members and their families make adjustments and do not encounter individual or family crises. Others may require some additional assistance to deal with the deployment or reintegration back into the family and culture. In taking a preventative approach, counselors who are working with military prior to deployment may find it helpful to the service member to treat the whole person and explore all the aspects on the wellness wheel, including spirituality and religious practices. This chapter offered an overview of the common problems encountered by military and families and strategies to assist with mental health issues.

14

Death Notifications

Lisa R. Jackson-Cherry

PREVIEW

Death notifications are viewed as the least favored responsibility for any professional. Notifying someone of a loved one's death can be difficult, not only for the one receiving the news but also for the one providing the death notification. Receiving a poorly executed death notification can increase confusion and anger, and it can negatively impact the grief process. At the same time, a death notification given with empathy, calmness, and accuracy of information can assist the grieving person with a sense of control—not over the death but over the process of finding reliable information to start effectively implementing plans and moving forward in the healing process. The information in this chapter will assist crisis counselors to be prepared and equipped when called upon to either give or assist with a death notification. Stewart, Lord, and Mercer (2000) found that 40% of the 70% of professionals who had given at least one death notification had no formal training in providing such a notification. In crisis intervention, it is better to be prepared ahead of time than to learn "on the job" for the first time and risk negatively affecting a person who is already in crisis. Effective death notifications will decrease the need for intense debriefings, complicated grief process, and burnout. Although agencies and schools may have a protocol for issuing a death notification, which should be followed, the steps outlined in this chapter can be infused into any environment, professional or personal, as a "best practice" in giving a notification of death.

VOICES FROM THE FIELD 14.1

A Death Notification in Elementary School

Maegan Vick

It was after school during a faculty meeting when the police showed up. Most of the staff was already in the meeting. I just happened to be in my office, about to head that way, when I got called to the front office. When I walked in, I noticed Eric, one of our first grade students, who had suffered a traumatic brain injury when he was a toddler. Eric was still waiting with his teacher for his father to pick him up in the front office. I said hello to Eric and then noticed a police officer in the corner speaking with the secretary. The policeman introduced himself and walked with me to my office without saying a word. I knew something was terribly amiss. The police officer sat down with me and said Eric's father had been killed in a car accident on the way to pick him up from school that day. This was especially tragic because Eric's mother had been killed in a car accident when Eric was a toddler. Eric was in the car with his mother during that fatal car accident and that was how Eric got traumatic brain injury. Now, with both parents deceased, Eric was all alone.

Eric's teacher, Ms. Smith, waited anxiously in the front office after she saw the police officer walk with me to my office. As we returned, I watched her glistening eyes search my face for any indication of what was happening. When my eyes met hers, it was as if she already knew her fear had come true. While Eric waited in the office with the secretary, I pulled his teacher to the hallway where we could be alone. "I'm sorry to have to tell you this," I said to her, "but Eric's father's was killed in a car accident on the way to pick him up today." Ms. Smith sank to the floor with a muffled scream, "No, no, no! It's just not fair...his mother was killed this way...I just..." There were not any words that could comfort her at this moment. All

I could do was hold her and tell her we would take care of Eric. He would be okay. During the next couple of hours, we tried to contact Eric's closest relative, his uncle Matt.

The following day Eric's uncle, Matt, came to meet with me. He wasn't sure how to tell Eric about his father. It's hard enough for any first grader to understand that his mother and father are both dead, much less a child with traumatic brain injury. I encouraged Eric's uncle to be as honest and as concrete as possible. He asked me if we could tell Eric together. We did.

"Daddy will not be coming home. He died. His heart stopped beating. His eyes will not open. Daddy loved you, but he will not be back."

"Eric bad?" Eric asked.

"Daddy mad?"

"No, you were not bad," I said, "You are a good boy. Daddy died. He cannot come back. He loved you very much. You'll go home with Uncle Matt, Jayne, and Ally."

Only the slightest sign of revelation appeared on Eric's face. "I go home with Jayne and Ally?"

We then read a short children's story about "Elmo remembering his daddy." I gave this book to Eric's uncle so that Eric could read it at their house. Eric's uncle called a few days later asking if Eric should attend the funeral. I encouraged him to make a decision with which he felt comfortable. Some believe that allowing a young child to attend a funeral can help provide closure. Uncle Matt took Eric to the funeral.

In the end, Eric adjusted well to his new home and new school. His uncle grew more confident with his ability to help Eric grieve and understand. Our school learned to cope with a tragedy. I will always remember Eric.

EFFECTIVE DEATH NOTIFICATIONS

Historically, crisis counselors seldom acted as first responders in the death notification process, although in their personal lives, death notifications were inevitable. Often when the notification is someone close, all the counseling skills one has learned and practiced may not be as effective as one would expect. In a professional role, counselors traditionally have become involved with clients after a death notification to assist individuals in dealing with the grieving and healing process. In crisis intervention, it is likely a crisis counselor will intervene when the death of a loved one causes so much stress to the surviving significant other that it affects their normal daily functioning and in some cases may increase suicide lethality. It is likely in every situation outlined in this text that a counselor may be called to give a death notification or provide support for someone who is the primary death notifier. As roles and job opportunities become more diverse in the communities for crisis counselors (e.g., police departments, fire departments, military settings, religious settings, chaplaincies, crisis centers, hospitals, and other agencies such as Red Cross, Green Cross, and Hospice), the likelihood of participating in a death notification increases. With the increase of counselors as first responders during recent national crises (e.g., Hurricane Katrina, Hurricane Isabel, terrorist attacks on September 11, 2001), counselors have been placed in the role of giving or being part of giving death notifications more frequently.

Even if a counselor intends to work in a private practice, it is not unforeseen to be asked to assist with a death notification or to be consulted about how to tell another family member about a death. No two death notifications are ever the same due to the actual event, unique relationships, ecological determinants, and perception of the death by the survivor. However, the level of preparedness of the crisis counselor in the notification process may affect the initial situation of the notification, how a survivor responds during the crisis state, and whether a person seeks professional counseling in the future. That said, crisis counselors rarely notify anyone of a death unless they are given permission to do so. Such permission is to be given by someone who is either their supervisor or team leader.

Although no crisis counselor who provides a death notification can ever be fully prepared for the response of the person receiving the notification, there are several components that should be included in order to provide a foundation for an effective death notification. As outlined in the training protocol for the Maryland State Police (2001), but adapted for the training of crisis counselors for this section, death notifications should be provided in person and in pairs, in an appropriate time frame, in plain language, and with compassion.

ACTIVITY 14.1

Reflect on your own personal losses and where you are in the grief process. If you were called to provide a death notification or act as a support counselor in this process, could you be present with the bereaved to support them in their loss?

ACTIVITY 14.2

Take a few minutes and reflect upon a time when you were notified of a death. Who was the person who died? Who provided the death notification? What were the circumstances? How was the death relayed to you? What were some of your initial feelings or thoughts? What kind of influence did the actual process of the death notification have on you? What made the notification process helpful? What could have made the death notification process better?

In Person and in Pairs

Whenever possible, death notifications should be made in person, not by telephone. The human presence during the notification of the death of a loved one is essential. The presence of a crisis counselor can be crucial if the survivor has a reaction that requires assessment of self-risk or the need for immediate medical attention. Crisis counselors can assist clients during the initial shock, which may be devastating and demobilizing and may interrupt intact normal thought processes. Counselors can also help the survivor formulate a plan for informing others close to the deceased. It is helpful to work in pairs in case questions need to be answered, multiple survivors are present with various needs (age and developmental appropriateness), and for safety precautions of the notifying team members. If possible, when there are children in the same room, take the specified adults into a private area to notify them of the death. It would be helpful for the crisis worker to have information on hand to share with those receiving the notification on the grieving process and developmental grieving of children.

Team members may be a combination of law enforcement officers, professional counselors, pastoral counselors, medical staff, clergy, school counselors, case managers, other family members, or friends of the victim . For example, in homicide/suicide cases the team ordinarily would consist of law enforcement and possibly a clergy member, and/or a professional counselor. More and more police departments are working together with crisis agencies that use professional counselors for these situations. In a hospital setting, the team may consist of a medical doctor, nurse, chaplain, professional counselor, or social worker. In a school setting, the team may consist of the school counselor, administrator, and teachers. In the military, depending on the branch of service, the team would consist of a Casualty Assistance Officer (CAO) and possibly a chaplain. Depending on the setting and circumstances of the death in each example, outside professional counselors may be included to assist with any crisis situations or death notifications.

In our society, family members do not always live in the same community or even in the same state as one another, which makes the process of the death notification being done "in person" often impossible. Depending on the setting, crisis counselors may not be able to offer an "in person" notification. In these circumstances, contact can be made with a medical examiner, law enforcement department, religious clergy, or other friend or family member in the survivor's home area to deliver the notification in person to the next of kin. This first notification of a death announcement would preferably be given to someone who has contact but is not as emotionally involved as the person for whom the death notification is intended. In other cases these persons may be called to act as a physical support while the notification is done by phone.

In Time and with Accurate Information

Timeliness of a death notification is essential so that a person is informed in person by the appropriate individual rather than by hearing it from outside persons. At the same time it is imperative to first verify the accuracy of the information to be sure that the correct information regarding the correct person is being given to a survivor. This must be done in a short amount of time given the nature of the event. For example, in law enforcement cases it is important that relatives (next of kin) be notified in a timely manner and with accurate information so that relatives do not see or hear the news of the death on the television or radio. When there is a death on campus or in a school, it is also important for those closest to the deceased to be notified initially. In these instances, it would be preferable for administrators, crisis counselors, and faculty to receive the information first so as to prioritize who should be notified (e.g., team members, classmates, close friends) and in what manner (e.g., small groups, team players, homerooms, LISTSERVs). This also allows for those giving the notifications to be able to assess if more intervention is needed for some individuals. Prior to any event, agencies and school settings should designate a contact person or alternate person who will be responsible for collecting and dispensing information. Even if a team is formed to gather information, only one person should be designated as the communicator so differing accounts or information are not relayed. Inaccurate or differing information from several sources could cause confusion, chaos, or panic.

Accuracy of the information does not necessarily mean a crisis counselor has to have the full details, as this depends on the situation. For example, the sudden and tragic death of one of our graduate students was reported by a student to faculty the morning following the incident. Although essential to provide information in a timely manner, it would have been premature to inform other students without receiving confirmation of the student's death from the family member or another firsthand source. At the same time, it was not as crucial to have the details of the circumstances (e.g., drunk driving case) as it was to confirm and provide accurate information as to the identity of the student so we could formulate a response to the students. For other situations, more detailed information may be needed at the time of the death notification.

It is essential to make an accurate notification. Mistaken death notifications may cause undo trauma and in some cases has caused medical complications for the person being informed. Before the notification, move quickly to gather information by contacting family members for confirmation and to issue condolences. Be sure that the victim's identity has been confirmed. If administrators need to report the death via electronic communications, be sure the entire name of the deceased has been verified (first names alone are not sufficient) so as not to cause any further chaos or generate rumors. For example, in the above situation, all the students could not be contacted individually although faculty advised students in their classes. The student LISTSERV needed to be utilized. When using a LISTSERV and providing follow-ups on the events (e.g., services, memorial services) through this format, the one person appointed to communicate information should provide frequent updates and give first and last names in all correspondences. It should not be assumed just because previous e-mails were sent out that all previous messages have been read by the receivers. Messages may seem redundant but accuracy should be consistent. Correspondences with university administration (Vice President for Academic Affairs, President, Dean, Student Services) should be made to ensure university policies are followed. Contact with the Campus Ministry and Counseling Center should be made, and these services should be relayed and made available to students, faculty, and staff in an appropriate time frame. Evaluating the uniqueness of the situation is imperative in order to provide any other interventions. In the university student case, the student was enrolled in a practicum placement. Contact with the on-site supervisor was necessary not only for notification but to ensure a plan for the deceased student's clients. Furthermore, the religious beliefs of the family needed to be explored and conveyed to the students

VOICES FROM THE FIELD 14.2
Learning from Mistakes

Lisa R. Jackson-Cherry

In working with a police department counseling center during an internship experience, I was asked to ride along on my first death notification for added support. A briefing was conducted with the team as we traveled to a small rural town. When we reached our destination, the team leader knocked on the front door, which was opened by an elderly woman. After the leader introduced us, he asked the woman if she was Mrs. Smith. "Yes" she replied. The leader continued, "I'm sorry to be the one to inform you that there was a car accident and your husband, Bill, was killed. He did not survive his injuries." She appeared visibly shocked and started to sob uncontrollably. As we sat down to continue to talk, another woman came running from the adjacent yard. The leader turned to the woman and said, "Would you be willing to stay with Mrs. Smith until we can contact her family? Her husband, Bill, was in a car accident and he died." This woman also began shaking and sobbing and said, "This is my mother-in-law. I'm also Mrs. Smith and Bill

is my husband. My husband, Bill, is her son." At this time, we knew we had the correct family but the next of kin we were informing was not the correct person.

In all of our preparation, we did not go over the unique issues that we may encounter in a small rural town. In this case, most of the family members lived on the same street and many shared the same names. In not asking for the complete name of the woman we were notifying and asking the relation of Bill to her, we not only gave devastating news of her son's death (not her husband's death) but then gave a less than full and compassionate notification to the actual wife of the deceased. Needless to say, we did follow through with debriefing and put into practice necessary procedures to insure a mistake like this never happened again. This is one reason why I believe counselors should be prepared to assist with death notifications and why it is imperative to include this information in the text. I think of this family often and wonder the impact of this notification on them as it still weighs heavy on my mind over 20 years later.

before attending the funeral service. In this example, flowers were prohibited, and there were specific expectations due to religious beliefs during the service, including prohibiting any outward expressions of emotions that were believed to prevent the passing of the deceased from this world to the next. In the end, students needed an extra debriefing with faculty after the service to work through their unexpressed grief.

In Plain Language

It is important that the death notification be given to the survivor in a calm, direct, and simple manner by the crisis counselor. Too much information or vague information can cause survivors to panic before getting the information. A crisis counselor can demonstrate care by stating the notification in clear and concise language. For example, "I have some very bad news to tell you," or a similar statement allows a brief but crucial moment for the survivor to prepare for the shock. The follow-up statement should also be provided in plain language, such as "Your daughter, Jill, was in a car crash and she was killed." It is important to avoid vague statements such as, Jill was "lost," "hurt," or "passed away." It is important to include a definitive conclusion of what occurred such as " . . . and she was killed" or " . . . there were no survivors." This prevents conveying a message of false hope of survival. It is important to refer to the victim by name to provide another level of verification and also to personalize the deceased.

One of the most important gifts a crisis counselor can offer to a survivor is the gift of the crisis counselor's control and calmness during the death notification. Overemotional crisis counselors can increase the potential for panic or chaos. Survivors often have many questions and some questions may be asked multiple times. Like a child's experience with a death notification, survivors will often ask the same question for verification of facts. It is crucial to patiently answer questions about the circumstances regarding the death that a crisis counselor may be privy to, such as the location of the deceased's body, how the deceased's body will be released and transported to a funeral home, and whether an autopsy will be performed. However, the sharing of this information should always take into consideration the developmental stage and clinical assessment of how much can be handled by the survivor at the time of the notification. Oftentimes, crisis counselors may not know the answer, and it is better for them to acknowledge this to survivors rather than give false information. It is important for crisis counselors to state that they will attempt to find the answers to the questions they cannot answer. If there are questions they have offered to explore, it is imperative that they follow-up directly with the survivor even if another agency or office will be contacting them to provide the information.

With Compassion

Presence and compassion may be the only resources crisis counselors can provide during the initial death notification process. It is important for them to accept the survivor's reactions and emotions to the death notification and also important to recognize their own emotions associated with the notification. Although overemotional crisis counselors can increase confusion and possible panic with survivors, it is better for a crisis counselor to express appropriate emotion than to appear cold and unfeeling. It is important to relay to survivors that death is a personal event and that due to the unique situation they may feel various emotions, including sadness, anger, frustration, relief, and guilt, to name a few. Normalizing the vast array of emotions survivors may experience during the grief process is an important resource. Print resources that reveal the grieving process, reactions to grief, explaining death to a child (if appropriate), and referrals for mental health counseling or a funeral home may be helpful and can be left with the victim. Imposing personal religious beliefs is also not helpful and could be harmful. Statements such as, "This was God's will," "She led a full life," and "I understand what you are going through" do not demonstrate compassion or regard for the person's unique grief experiences associated with loss.

If the crisis counselor is part of a team, it is essential to take time to provide information, support, and direction to the survivor. Never simply provide a death notification and leave. Information about funeral planning, normal grief process, and referrals for counseling is important to offer. The bereaved may not be ready for counseling at that moment but may be in need of counseling in the near future. Also, it is not recommended that the crisis team take a victim's personal belongings during the death notification. Survivors often need time before accepting the victim's belongings, but eventually survivors will want to take possession of the items. Likewise, crisis counselors should never transport survivors (to the hospital or home or to other agencies) unless law enforcement is a part of the notification team. No one can ever truly predict the emotional reaction to the death of a loved one, and the safety of the crisis counselor is always a priority.

Follow-up

Crisis counselors should always leave their names and phone numbers with survivors, and a follow-up contact with the survivor should be scheduled for the following day, since most funeral arrangements must be made soon after the death. Some individuals, depending on their social support system, may request assistance from team members for funeral arrangements. If a crisis counselor is asked by the survivor to help with these plans, it is imperative to assist the survivor based on the customs, traditions, religious beliefs, and personal preferences of the family. Most survivors are confused at the initial notification, and others may feel abandoned after the notification. Many survivors will want clarifications or may need more direction on necessary arrangements.

Following up is an important last step in completing the death notification process and may be a crucial factor enabling a survivor to reach out for continued mental health services. Often, counseling services are necessary for clients to work through the extended or complicated grieving process. A death notification event may be the first exposure a survivor has to a mental health professional, so the interaction could encourage or discourage further connections with crisis counselors. The members of the notification team should be clear with one another on any follow-up assignments.

Debriefing with Team Members

Debriefing with team members should occur immediately after the death notification. This debriefing time should be used to plan for any follow-up with the survivors and to review how the death notification process was implemented and received. Processing what went well and what could be improved upon will be helpful for future death notifications. In addition, death notifications can be stressful and emotionally draining to the individuals involved in the notification process. Team members should share concerns with one another. It is important to discuss feelings or thoughts associated with the death notifications that may have triggered personal unresolved grief issues. Taking care of oneself is essential when taking care of another person's initial grief. The stages of grief and loss can certainly take place among crisis counselors. When debriefing, it is important to take into consideration that crisis counselors experience grief and should be encouraged to process that grief. As a final activity, choose either Case A or Case B in Activity 14.3 and prepare a death notification strategy as an individual, in small groups, or as a total class activity.

ACTIVITY 14.3
Practice Cases for Death Notifications

Case A: Community Setting

You are part of a crisis team that has been called to give a death notification to the next of kin for a person who was killed during a random shooting. You are not sure how the person was involved or became a victim of the shooting. Work with your team to plan what needs to be addressed and then role-play a death notification to the family.

Case B: School Setting

The principal of your high school contacts you in the morning and states that there was a phone message left the night before that a ninth grade student (John) was killed in an automobile accident. As a school counselor and a member of the crisis response team for the school, work with your team and decide what needs to be addressed in this process and to whom notifications will be made.

Summary

Death notifications are often viewed as the least favored duty for any professionals. Notifying someone of a loved one's death can be difficult, not only for the one receiving the news, but also for the one providing the death notification. It is always important to make sure the person providing the notification is one who is not experiencing personal unresolved grief issues and who can provide a sense of calmness and compassion in the notification. Death notifications can be unpredictable since no one ever knows how another person may react in receiving such news. As outlined in the chapter on grief and loss, individuals may respond with a continuum of responses—from numbness, excessive sadness, and melancholy to anger in some cases. Unknown circumstances may lead a person to project their feelings to the person providing the notification. It is always important to understand that reactions will differ and to keep your personal safety in mind when providing a death notification.

Although the likelihood of a counselor being involved in providing a death notification has increased over the years due to expanded job responsibilities and employment settings, research suggests there is little preparedness in this area. Indeed counselors have more often been involved in this process in their personal lives, but this does not mean the process was effective. Counseling programs offer little to no formal training in this area. Although we can never train counselors how to respond to every crisis situation, and knowing that death is a natural part of the life process, it is an appropriate part of clinical training to include information on providing a death notification. The level of preparedness of the professional counselor in the notification process may affect the reaction and the traumatic impact of the delivery on the survivor, reduce professional burnout, affect the bereavement process, and influence whether a person seeks professional counseling in the future.

REFERENCES

Aarons, J. D. (2004). The use of play therapy with child victims of sexual abuse. *Journal of Student Social Work, 12,* 227–234.

Ackard, D. M., & Neumark-Sztainer, D. (2002). Date violence and date rape among adolescents: Associations with disordered eating behaviors and psychological health. *Child Abuse and Neglect, 26,* 455–473.

Ahrens, C. E., Abeling, S., Ahmad, S., & Hinman. J. (2010). Spirituality and well-being: The relationship between religious coping and recovery from sexual assault. *Journal of Interpersonal Violence, 25,* 1242–1263.

Ainsworth, M. (1969). Object relations, dependency and attachment: A theoretical review of the infant-mother relationship. *Child Development, 40,* 969–1025.

Albano, S. (2002). What society can learn from the U.S. military's system of family support. *National Council on Family Relations Report, 47*(1), F6–F8.

Alexander, D. A. (2005). Early mental health intervention after disasters. *Advances in Psychiatric Treatment, 11,* 12–18.

Allen, A., Barrett, W., Doherty, N., & Hunt, S. (1990). The prevention of child sexual abuse. *Nursing Standard (Royal College of Nursing Great Britain), 4*(27), 28–30.

Allen, M., Burt, K., Bryan, E., Carter, D., Orsi, R., & Durkan, L. (2002). School counselors' preparation for and participation in crisis intervention. *Professional School Counseling, 6,* 96–101.

Amar, A. F., & Gennaro, S. (2005). Dating violence in college women: Associated physical injury, healthcare usage, and mental health symptoms. *Nursing Research, 54,* 235–242.

American Association of Suicidology. (2005). *Assessing and managing suicide risk: Core competencies for mental health professionals.* Washington, DC: Author.

American Association of Suicidology. (2006a). *Assessing and managing suicide risk.* Washington, DC: Author.

American Association of Suicidology. (2006b). *Suicide in the United States.* Retrieved from www.suicidology.org

American Counseling Association. (2005). *ACA code of ethics.* Alexandra,VA: Author.

American Counseling Association. (2011). *Task force on counselor wellness and impairment.* Retrieved from http://www.counseling.org/wellness_taskforce/index.htm

American Foundation for Suicide Prevention. (2012). Latest suicide data: An analysis. Retrieved from http://www.afsp.org/index.cfm?fuseaction=home.viewPage&page_ID=04EA1254-BD31-1FA3-C549D77E6CA6AA37

American Pet Products Association. (2008). *2007–2008 APPA national pet owners survey.* Retrieved from www.americanpetproducts.org/press_industrytrends.asp

American Psychiatric Association. (2003). *Practice guidelines for the assessment and treatment of patients with suicidal behaviors.* Retrieved from www.psych.org/psych_pract/treatg/pg/pg_suicidalbehaviors.pdf

American Psychiatric Association. (2004). *Committee on Psychiatric Dimensions of Disaster: Disaster psychiatry handbook.* Retrieved from www.psych.org/Resources/DisasterPsychiatry/APADisasterPsychiatryResources/DisasterPsychiatryHandbook.aspx

American Psychiatric Association. (2008). *Psychiatric practice.* Retrieved from www.psych.org/MainMenu/PsychiatricPractice.aspx

American Psychiatric Association. (2013). *Diagnostic and statistical manual of mental disorders* (5th ed.). Washington, DC: Author.

American Red Cross. (2005). *Foundations of disaster mental health participants workbook.* Washington, DC: Author.

American School Counselor Association. (2000). *Position statement: Critical incident response.* Alexandria, VA: Author.

American School Counselor Association. (2003). *Counselor immediate response guide.* Retrieved from www.cc.ain.com/asca.crisis.htm

American School Counselor Association. (2008). *The role of the professional school counselor.* Retrieved from www.school-counselor.org/content.asp?pl=325&sl=133&contentid=240

American School Counselor Association. (2012). *The ASCA National Model: A framework for school counseling programs* (3rd ed.). Alexandria, VA: Author.

American Society of Addiction Medicine. (1996). *Patient placement criteria for the treatment of substance-related disorders* (2nd ed.). Washington, DC: Author.

Anderson, R. (1974). Notes of a survivor. In S. B. Troop, & W. A. Green (Eds.), *The patient, death, and the family* (pp. 73–82). New York, NY: Scribner.

Andriessen, K. (2009). Can postvention be prevention? *Crisis, 30*(1), 43–47.

Arias, I., Dankwort, J., Douglas, U., Dutton, M. A., & Stein, K. (2002). Violence against women: The state of batterer prevention programs. *The Journal of Law, Medicine, and Ethics, 30,* 157–169.

Armour, M. (2005). Meaning making in the aftermath of homicide. *Death Studies, 27,* 519–540.

Arthur, G. L., Brende, J. O., & Quiroz, S. E. (2003). Violence: Incidents and frequency of physical and psychological assaults affecting mental health providers in Georgia. *Journal of General Psychology, 130*, 22–45.

Asaro, M. R. (2001). Working with adult homicide survivors: Part II: Helping family members cope with murder. *Psychiatric Care, 37*(4), 115–126.

Australian Academy of Medicine. (2012). *Bereavement, known as sorry business, is a very important part of Aboriginal culture.* Retrieved from http://www.aams.org.au/mark_sheldon/ch7/ch7_sensitive_areas.htm

Babor, T. F., Higgins-Biddle, J. C., Saunders, J. B., Monteiro, M. G., & World Health Organization (2001). *AUDIT The Alcohol Use Disorders Identification Test: Guidelines for use in primary care* (2nd ed.). Geneva, Switzerland: World Health Organization. Document # WHO/MSD/MSB/01.6a.

Bagalman, E. (2011). *Traumatic brain injuries among veterans* (Report No. R40941). Retrieved from http://www.nashia.org/pdf/tbi_among_veterans_may_2011.pdf

Bandura, A. (1977). *Social Learning Theory.* New York: General Learning Press.

Barbee, P. W., Ekleberry, F., & Villalobos, S. (2007). Duty to warn and protect: Not in Texas. *Journal of Professional Counseling: Practice, Theory, and Research, 35*(1), 18–25.

Barboza, S., Epps, S., Bylington, R., & Keene, S. (2010). HIPAA goes to school: Clarifying privacy laws in the education environment. *Internet Journal of Law, Healthcare and Ethics, 6*(2). Retrieved from http://www.ispub.com/journal/the-internet-journal-of-law-healthcare-and-ethics/volume-6-number-2/hipaa-goes-to-school-clarifying-privacy-laws-in-the-education-environment.html.

Barker, L. H., & Berry, K. D. (2009). Developmental issues impacting military families with young children during single and multiple deployments. *Military Medicine, 174*, 1033–1040.

Battaglia, T. A., Finley, E., & Liebschutz, J. M. (2003). Survivors of intimate partner violence speak out: Trust in the patient-provider relationship. *Journal of General Internal Medicine, 18*, 617–623.

Batten, S. V., Drapalski, A. L., Decker, M. L., DeViva, J. C., Morris, L. J., Mann, M. A., & Dixon, L. B. (2009). Veteran interest in family involvement in PTSD treatment. *Psychological Services, 6*, 184–189.

Batten, S. V., & Pollack, S. J. (2008). Integrative outpatient treatment for returning service members. *Journal of Clinical Psychology: In Session, 64*, 928–939.

Beck, A. T., Steer, R. A., & Brown, G. K. (1996). *Manual for the Beck Depression Inventory–II.* San Antonio, TX: Psychological Corporation.

Bedi, R. P. (2006). Concept mapping the client's perspective on counseling alliance formation. *Journal of Counseling Psychology, 53*, 26–35.

Bennett, L., & Williams, O. (2001). Intervention program for men who batter. In C. Renzetti & J. Edleson (Eds.), *Sourcebook on violence against women* (pp. 261–277). Thousand Oaks, CA: Sage.

Berliner, L., & Elliott, D. M. (2002). Sexual abuse of children. In J. E. B. Myers, L. Berliner, J. Briere, C. T. Hendrix, C. Jenny, & T. A. Reid (Eds.), *The APSAC handbook on child maltreatment* (2nd ed., pp. 55–78). Thousand Oaks, CA: Sage.

Berman, A. L. (2006). Risk management with suicidal patients. *Journal of Clinical Psychology, 62*, 171–184.

Berry, D. B. (2000). *The domestic violence sourcebook* (3rd ed.). Los Angeles, CA: Lowell House.

Berzoff, J. N., & Silverman, P. R. (Eds.). (2004). *Living with dying: A handbook for end-of-life healthcare practitioners.* Irving, NY: Columbia University Press.

Biema, D. V. (2001, October 8). Faith after the fall. *Time, 158*, 76.

Blake, D. D., Weathers, F. W., Nagy, L. M., Kaloupek, D. G., Gusman, F. D., Charney, D. S., & Keane, T. M. (1995). The development of a clinician administered PTSD scale. *Journal of Traumatic Stress, 8*(1), 75–90.

Bland, D. (1994). *The experiences of suicide survivors 1989–June 1994.* Baton Rouge, LA: Baton Rouge Crisis Intervention Center.

Blauner, S. R. (2002). *How I stayed alive when my brain was trying to kill me—One person's guide to suicide prevention.* New York, NY: HarperCollins.

Blow, F. C., Brower, K. J., Schulenberg, J. E., Demo-Dananberg, L. M., Young, J. P., & Beresford, T. P. (1992). The Michigan Alcoholism Screening Test-Geriatric Version (MAST-G): A new elderly-specific screening instrument. *Alcoholism: Clinical and Experimental Research, 16*, 372.

Boelen, P. A., de Keijser, J., van den Hout, M. A., & van den Bout, J. (2007). Treatment of complicated grief: A comparison between cognitive-behavioral therapy and supportive counseling. *Journal of Consulting and Clinical Psychology, 75*, 277–284.

Boelen, P. A., van den Bout, J., & de Keijser, J. (2003). Traumatic grief as a disorder distinct from bereavement-related depression and anxiety: A replication study with bereaved mental health care patients. *American Journal of Psychiatry, 160*, 1339–1341.

Bonanno, G. A., Galea, S., Bucciarelli, A., & Vlahov, D. (2007). What predicts psychological resilience after disaster? The role of demographics, resources, and life stress. *Journal of Counseling and Clinical Psychology, 75*, 671–682.

Bonanno, G. A., & Mancini, A. D. (2008). The human capacity to thrive in the face of extreme adversity. *Pediatrics, 121*, 369–375.

Bonanno, G. A., Neria, Y., Mancini, A., Coifman, K. G., Litz, B., & Insel, B. (2007). Is there more to complicated grief than depression and post-traumatic stress disorder? A test of incremental validity. *Journal of Abnormal Psychology, 116,* 342–351.

Booth, B., Segal, M. W., & Place, N. (2009). *Final report on National Leadership Summit on Military Families.* College Park, MD: University of Maryland.

Borneman, T., Ferrell, B., & Pulchaski, C. M. (2010). Evaluation of the FICA tool for spiritual assessment. *Journal of Pain and Symptom Management, 40,* 163–173.

Boss, P. G. (1988). *Family stress management.* Newbury Park, CA: Sage.

Boss, P. G. (2002). *Family stress management: A contextual approach* (2nd ed.). Thousand Oaks, CA: Sage.

Boss, P. G. (2006). *Loss, trauma, and resilience: Therapeutic work with ambiguous loss.* New York, NY: Norton.

Bowen, G. L. Mancini, J. A., Martin, J. A., Ware, W. B., & Nelson (2003). Promoting the adaptation of military families: An empirical test of a community practice model. *Family Relations, 52*(1), 33–44.

Bowker, L. H. (1988). Religious victims and their religious leaders: Services delivered to one thousand battered women by the clergy. In A. L. Horton, & J. A. Williamson (Eds.), *Abuse and religion: When praying isn't enough* (pp. 229–234). Lexington, MA: Lexington Books.

Bowlby, J. (1960). *Attachment and loss: Attachment* (Vol. I). New York, NY: Basic Books.

Bowlby, J. (1973). *Attachment and loss: Separation, anxiety, and anger* (Vol. II). New York, NY: Basic Books.

Bowlby, J. (1980). *Attachment and loss: Loss, sadness and depression* (Vol. III). New York, NY: Basic Books.

Bradley, R., Greene, J., Russ, E., Dutra, L., & Westen, D. (2005). A multi-dimensional meta-analysis of psychotherapy for PTSD. *American Journal of Psychiatry, 162,* 214–227.

Brems, C. (2000). *Dealing with challenges in psychotherapy and counseling.* Belmont, CA: Wadsworth/Thompson Learning.

Brenner, L. A., Gutierrez, P. M., Cornette, M. M., Betthauser, L. M., Bahraini, N., & Staves, P. J. (2008). A qualitative study of potential suicide risk factors in returning combat veterans. *Journal of Mental Health Counseling, 30,* 211–225.

Brock, S. E. (1998). Helping classrooms cope with traumatic events. *Professional School Counseling, 2,* 110–116.

Brock, S., Sandoval, J., & Lewis, S. (2001). *Preparing for crises in the schools: A manual for building school crisis response teams* (2nd ed.). New York, NY: Wiley.

Brown, S. A. (1993). Drug effect expectancies and addictive behavior change. *Experimental and Clinical Psychopharmacology, 1,* 55–67.

Brownmiller, S. (1975). *Against our will.* New York, NY: Ballantine Books.

Brownridge, D. A., Chan, K. L., Hiebert-Murphy, D., Ristock, J., Tiwan, A., Leung, W., & Santos, S. C. (2008). The elevated risk for non-lethal post-separation violence in Canada: A comparison of separated, divorced, and married women. *Journal of Interpersonal Violence, 23,* 117–135.

Bryant, C. D. (Ed.). (2003). *Handbook of death and dying* (Vol. 1). Thousand Oaks, CA: Sage.

Bryant, R. A., Harvey, A. G., Dang, S. T., Sackville, T., & Basten, C. (1998). Treatment of Acute Stress Disorder: A comparison of cognitive-behavioral therapy and supportive counseling. *Journal of Consulting and Clinical Psychology, 66,* 862–866.

Bryant, R. A., Moulds, M., Guthrie, R., & Nixon, R. D. V. (2003). Treating acute stress disorder following mild traumatic brain injury. *American Journal of Psychiatry, 160,* 585–587.

Buelow, G. D., & Buelow, S. A. (1998). *Psychotherapy in chemical dependence treatment: A practical and integrative approach.* Pacific Grove, CA: Brooks/Cole.

Bureau of Justice Statistics (2012). BLS: News Release (September 20, 2012). *National Census of Fatal Occupational Injuries in 2011* (Preliminary Results) www.bls.gov/news. release/pdf/cfoi.pdf

Burgess, A. W. (Ed.). (1985). *Rape and sexual assault: A research handbook.* New York, NY: Garland.

Burgess, A. W., Hartman, C. R., McCausland, M. P., & Powers, P. (1984). Response patterns in children and adolescents exploited through sex rings and pornography. *American Journal of Psychiatry, 141,* 656–662.

Burgess, A. W., & Holmstrom, L. L. (1974). Rape trauma syndrome. *American Journal of Psychiatry, 131,* 981–986.

Burnam, M., Meredith, L., Tanielian, T., & Jaycox, L. (2009). Mental health care for Iraq and Afghanistan war veterans. *Health Affairs, 28,* 771–782.

Bushatz, A. (2011, December 11). *Military divorce rates continue steady climb.* Retrieved from http://www.military.com/news/article/military-divorce-rates-continue-steady-climb.html

Butler, R. N. (1963). The life review: An interpretation of reminiscence in the aged. *Psychiatry, 26,* 65–76.

Buttell, F. P. (2001). Moral development among court-ordered batterers: Evaluating the impact of treatment. *Research on Social Work Practice, 11*(1), 93–107.

Buttell, F. P. (2003). Exploring the relevance of moral development as a treatment issue in batterer intervention. *Social Work Research, 27,* 232–241.

Buttell, F. P., & Pike, C. K. (2003). Investigating the differential effectiveness of a batterer treatment program on outcomes for African American and Caucasian batterers. *Research on Social Work Practice, 3,* 675–692.

Byock, I. (1997). *Dying well: Peace and possibilities at the end of life.* New York, NY: Berkley Publishing Group.

Carnelley, K. B., Wortman, C. B., Bolger, N., & Burke, C. T. (2006). The time course of grief reactions to spousal loss: Evidence from a national probability sample. *Journal of Personality and Social Psychology, 91*, 476–492.

Campbell, F. (2005). *Intention style and survival outcome.* Baton Rouge, LA: ASIST Trainers.

Campos-Outcalt, D. (2004). How does HIPAA affect public health reporting? *Journal of Family Practice, 53*, 701–704.

Caplan, G. (1961). *An approach to community mental health.* New York, NY: Grune and Stratton.

Caplan, G. (1964). *Principles of preventive psychiatry.* New York, NY: Basic Books.

Capuzzi, D., & Stauffer, M. D. (2012). History and etiological models of addiction. In D. Capuzzi, & M. D. Stauffer (Eds.), *Foundations of addiction counseling* (2nd ed.; pp. 1–15). Upper Saddle River, NJ: Pearson.

Carey, R. G. (1975). Living until death: A program of service and research for the terminally ill. In E. Kubler-Ross (Ed.), *Death: The final stage of growth* (pp. 73–86). New York, NY: Simon and Schuster.

Carr, J. L. (2005). *American College Health Association campus violence white paper.* Baltimore, MD: American College Health Association.

Carroll, A., Lyall, M., & Forrester, A. (2004). Clinical hopes and public fears in forensic mental health. *Journal of Forensic Psychiatry and Psychology, 15*, 407–425.

Cascardi, M., Avery-Leaf, S., O'Leary, K. D., & Slep, A. M. S. (1999). Factor structure and convergent validity of the Conflict Tactics Scale in high school students. *Psychological Assessment, 11*, 546–555.

Cashwell, C. S., & Watts, R. E. (2010). The new ASERVIC competencies for addressing spiritual and religious issues in counseling. *Counseling and Values, 55*, 2–5.

Cashwell, C., & Young, J. (Eds.). (2011). *Integrating spirituality and religion into counseling* (2nd ed.). Alexandria, VA: American Counseling Association.

Castellano, C., & Plionis, E. (2006). Comparative analysis of three crisis intervention models applied to law enforcement first responders during 9/11 and Hurricane Katrina. *Brief Treatment and Crisis Intervention, 6*, 326–336.

Cavaiola, A. A., & Colford, J. E. (2006). *A practical guide to crisis intervention.* Boston, MA: Lahaska.

Center for Mental Health in Schools at UCLA. (2008). *Responding to a crisis at a school.* Los Angeles, CA: Author.

Center for Sex Offender Management. (2007). *Female sex offenders.* Retrieved from www.csom.org/pubs/female_sex_offenders_brief.pdf

Center for Substance Abuse Treatment. (2005). *Substance abuse treatment for persons with co-occurring disorders.* Treatment Improvement Protocol (TIP) Series 42 (DHHS Publication No. [SMA] 05-3922). Rockville, MD: Substance Abuse and Mental Health Services Administration.

Center for Substance Abuse Treatment. (2009). *Addressing suicidal thoughts and behaviors in substance abuse treatment.* Treatment Improvement Protocol (TIP) Series 50. HHS Publication No. (SMA) 09-4381. Rockville, MD: Substance Abuse and Mental Health Services Administration.

Centers for Disease Control and Prevention. (2003). *Costs of intimate partner violence against women in the United States.* Retrieved from www.cdc.gov/ncipc/pub-res/ipv_cost/ipv.htm

Centers for Disease Control and Prevention. (2005a). Intimate partner violence injuries: Oklahoma, 2002. *Morbidity and Mortality Weekly Report, 54*(41), 1041–1045.

Centers for Disease Control and Prevention. (2005b). *Youth risk behavior surveillance—United States, 2005.* Retrieved from www.cdc.gov/mmwr/PDF/SS/SS5505.pdf

Centers for Disease Control and Prevention. (2006). *Fact sheet on traumatic brain injury.* Retrieved from http://www.cdc.gov/ncipc/tbi/factsheets/facts_about_tbi.pdf

Centers for Disease Control and Prevention. (2007). *Suicide facts at a glance.* Retrieved from www.cdc.gov/ncipc/dvp/Suicide/SuicideDataSheet.pdf

Centers for Disease Control and Prevention. (2011). *National Intimate Partner and Sexual Violence Survey.* Retrieved from http://www.cdc.gov/ViolencePrevention/pdf/NISVS_Report2010-a.pdf

Centers for Disease Control and Prevention. (2012). *Ten leading causes of death and injury.* Retrieved from http://www.cdc.gov/injury/wisqars/LeadingCauses.html.

Cerel, J., & Campbell, F. (2008). Suicide survivors seeking mental health services: A preliminary examination of the role of an active postvention model. *Suicide and Life Threatening Behavior, 38* (1), 30–34.

Chaffin, M., Berliner, L., Block, R., Johnson, T. C., Friedrich, W., Louis, D…Silovsky, J. (2008). Report of the ATSA Task Force on Children with Sexual Behavior Problems. *Child Maltreatment, 18*, 199–218.

Chaffin, M., & Friedrich, B. (2004). Evidence-based treatments in child abuse and neglect. *Children and Youth Services Review, 26*, 1097–1113.

Chaffin, M., Wherry, J. N., & Dykman, R. (1997). School age children's coping with sexual abuse: Abuse stresses and symptoms associated with four coping strategies. *Child Abuse & Neglect, 21*, 227–240.

Chandra, A., Lara-Cinisomo, S., Jaycox, L. H., Tanielian, T., Burns, R. M., Ruder, T., & Han, B. (2010a). Children on the homefront: The experience of children from military families. *Pediatrics, 125*, 16–25.

Chandra, A., Martin, L., Hawkins, S., & Richardson, A. (2010b). The impact of parental deployment on child social and emotional functioning: Perspectives of school staff. *Journal of Adolescent Health, 46,* 218–226.

Chandra, A., Lara-Cinisomo, S., Jaycox, L. H., Tanielian, T., Han, B., Burns, R. M., & Ruder, T. (2011). *Views from the homefront: The experiences of youth and spouses from military families.* Santa Monica, CA: RAND Corporation.

Chang, H., & Saunders, D. G. (2002). Predictors of attrition in two types of group programs for men who batter. *Journal of Family Violence, 17,* 273–292.

Chang, J. C., Decker, M. R., Moracco, K. E., Martin, S. L., Petersen, R., & Frasier, P. Y. (2005). Asking about intimate partner violence: Advice from female survivors to healthcare providers. *Patient Education and Counseling, 59,* 141–147.

Charles, D. R., & Charles, M. (2006). Sibling loss and attachment style. *Psychoanalytic Psychology, 23,* 72–90. *Child Abuse Prevention and Treatment Act* (CAPTA), Pub. L. No. 93-247. Retrieved from www.acf.hhs.gov/programs/cb/laws_policies/cblaws/capta03/capta_manual.pdf

Chiles, J. A., & Strosahl, K. D. (1995). *The suicidal patient: Principles of assessment, treatment, and case management.* Washington, DC: American Psychiatric Press.

Chung, K., Chung, D., & Joo, Y. (2006). Overview of administrative simplification provisions of HIPAA. *Journal of Medical Systems, 30*(1), 51–55.

Clark, A. H., & Foy, D. W. (2000). Trauma exposure and alcohol use in battered women. *Violence Against Women, 6,* 37–48.

Cohen, E. D., & Cohen, G. S. (1999). *The virtuous therapist: Ethical practices of counseling and psychotherapy.* Belmont, CA: Wadsworth.

Cohen, J. A., & Mannarino, A. P. (1997). A treatment study for sexually abused preschool children: Outcome during a one-year follow-up. *Journal of the American Academy of Child and Adolescent Psychiatry, 36,* 1228–1235.

Cohen, J. A., & Mannarino, A. P. (1998). Factors that mediate treatment outcome of sexually abused preschool children: Six- and 12-month follow-up. *Journal of the American Academy of Child and Adolescent Psychiatry, 37,* 44–51.

Cohen, J. A., Mannarino, A. P., & Deblinger, E. (2006). *Treating trauma and traumatic grief in children and adolescents.* New York, NY: Guilford Press.

Coley, S. M., & Beckett, J. O. (1988). Black battered women: A review of empirical literature. *Journal of Counseling and Development, 66,* 266–270.

Collings, S. J. (1995). The long-term effect of contact and non-contact forms of child sexual abuse in a sample of university men. *Child Abuse and Neglect, 19,* 1–6.

Collins, B. G., & Collins, T. M. (2005). *Crisis and trauma developmental-ecological intervention.* Boston, MA: Houghton Mifflin/Lahaska Press.

Collins, R. C., & Kennedy, M. C. (2008). Serving families who have served: Providing family therapy and support in interdisciplinary polytrauma rehabilitation. *Journal of Clinical Psychology: In Session, 64,* 993–1003.

Community Emergency Response Team. (2003). *Instructor guide for the Federal Emergency Management Agency (FEMA) Emergency Management Institute, United States Fire Administration.* McLean, VA: Author.

Connors, G. J., Donovan, D. M., & DiClemente, C. C. (2001). *Substance abuse treatment and the stages of change.* New York, NY: Guilford Press.

Conte, J. R., & Schuerman, J. R. (1987). Effects of sexual abuse on children: A multidimensional view. *Journal of Interpersonal Violence, 2,* 380–390. doi: 10.1177/088626058700200404

Coombs, D., Harrington, J. A., & Talbott, L. L. (2010). Youth suicides in Alabama: A focus on gun safety. *Alabama State Association for Health, Physical Education, Recreation, and Dance Journal, 31*(1), 31–35.

Corey, G., Corey, M., & Callahan, P. (2007). *Issues and ethics in the helping professions.* (7th ed.). Belmont, CA: Thomson.

Cornell, D. G. (2007). *Best practices for making college campuses safe* (statement before the U.S. House Committee on Education and Labor, May 15, 2007). Retrieved from www.youthviolence.edschool.virginia.edu/prevention/congress/testimony%202007.htm

Corr, C. A., & Balk, D. E. (2011). *Children's encounters with death, bereavement, and coping.* New York, NY: Springer.

Corr, C. A., Nabe, C. M., & Corr, D. M. (2012). *Death and dying: Life and living* (7th ed.). Belmont, CA: Wadsworth/Thomson Learning.

Costello, E. J., Erkanli, A., Keeler, G., & Angold, A. (2004). Distant trauma: A prospective study of the effects of September 11th on young adults in North Carolina. *Applied Developmental Science, 8,* 211–220.

Coulter, M., & VandeWeerd, C. (2009). Reducing domestic violence and other criminal recidivism: Effectiveness of a multilevel batterer's intervention program. *Violence and Victims, 24,* 139–152.

Craig, R. J. (2004). *Counseling the alcohol and drug dependent client: A practical approach.* Boston, MA: Pearson.

Creamer, M., Wade, D., Fletcher, S., & Forbes, D. (2011). PTSD among military personnel. *International Review of Psychiatry, 23,* 160–165.

Currier, J. M., Holland, J. M., & Neimeyer, R. A. (2006). Sensemaking, grief and the experience of violent loss: Toward a meditational model. *Death Studies, 30,* 403–428.

Dandeker, C. (2000). On the need to be different: Recent developments in military culture. In H. Strachan (Ed.), *The British Army manpower and society in the twenty-first century* (pp. 173–190). Portland, OR: Frank Case London.

Dansby-Giles, G., Giles, F. L., Frazier, W., Crockett, W. L., & Clark, J. (2006). Counselor ethics circles and sources of ethics information. In G. R. Waltz & R. K. Yep (Eds.), *VISTAS: Compelling perspectives on counseling 2006* (pp. 195–197). Alexandria, VA: American Counseling Association.

Darby, P. J., Allan, W. D., Kashani, J. H., Hartke, K. L., & Reid, J. C. (1998). Analysis of 112 juveniles who committed homicide: Characteristics and a closer look at family abuse. *Journal of Family Violence, 13*, 365–375.

Daughhetee, C., Puleo, S., & Thrower, E. (2010). Scaffolding of continuing competency as an essential element of professionalism. *Alabama Counseling Association Journal, 36*(1), 15–22.

Davidson, R. J., Kabat-Zinn, J., Schumacher, J., Rosenkranz, M., Muller, D., Santorelli, S. F., …Sheridan, J. F. (2003). Alterations in brain and immune function produced by mindfulness meditation. *Psychosomatic Medicine, 65*, 564–570.

Davis, R. E. (2002). "The strongest women:" Exploration of the inner resources of abused women. *Qualitative Health Research, 12*, 1248–1263.

Deblinger, E., Lippman, J. T., & Steer, R. (1996). Sexually abused children suffering post-traumatic stress symptoms: Initial treatment outcome findings. *Child Maltreatment, 1*, 310–321.

Decker, S., & Naugle, A. (2009). Immediate intervention for sexual assault: A review with recommendations and implications for practitioners. *Journal of Aggression, Maltreatment, and Trauma, 18*, 419–441.

Despenser, S. (2005). The personal safety of the therapist. *Psychodynamic Process, 11*, 429–446.

Despenser, S. (2007). Risk assessment: The personal safety of the counselor. *Therapy Today, 18*(2), 12–17.

Diem, C., & Pizarro, J. M. (2010). Social structure and family homicides. *Journal of Family Violence, 25*, 521–532.

Dienemann, J., Glass, N., & Hyman, R. (2005). Survivor preferences for response to IPV disclosure. *Clinical Nursing Research, 14*, 215–233.

DiMaggio, C., Galea, S., & Li, G. (2009). Substance use and misuse in the aftermath of terrorism. A Bayesian meta-analysis. *Addiction, 104*, 894–904. doi: 10.1111/j.1360-0443.2009.02526.x

Dodgen, C. E., & Shea, W. M. (2000). *Substance use disorders: Assessment and treatment.* San Diego, CA: Academic Press.

Doka, K. J. (1996). *Living with grief after sudden loss: Suicide, homicide, accident, heart attack, stroke.* New York, NY: Taylor and Francis.

Doka, K. J. (Ed.). (2002). *Disenfranchised grief: New directions, challenges, and strategies for practice.* San Francisco, CA: Jossey-Bass.

Doka, K. J. (2005, May). New perspectives on grief. *Counseling Today*, 56–57.

Domestic Abuse Project. (1993). *Men's group therapy manual.* Minneapolis, MN: Author.

Doweiko, H. E. (2009). *Concepts of chemical dependency* (7th ed.). Belmont, CA: Brooks/Cole.

Drake, R. E., Mueser, K. T., Brunette, M. F., & McHugo, G. J. (2004). A review of treatments for people with severe mental illnesses and co-occurring substance use disorders. *Psychiatric Rehabilitation Journal, 27*, 360–374.

Drummet, A. R., Colman, M., & Cable, S. (2003). Military families under stress: Implications for family life education. *Family Relations, 52*, 279–287.

Drysdale, D., Modzeleski, W., & Simons, A. (2010). *Campus attacks: Targeted violence affecting institutions of higher education.* Washington, DC: U.S. Secret Service, U.S. Department of Homeland Security, Office of Safe and Drug-Free Schools, U.S. Department of Education, and Federal Bureau of Investigation, and U.S. Department of Justice.

Dube, S. R., Anda, R. F., Whitfield, C. L., Brown, D. W., Felitti, V. J., Dong, M., & Giles, W. H. (2005). Long-term consequences of childhood sexual abuse by gender of victim. *American Journal of Preventive Medicine, 28*, 430–438. doi: 10.1016/j.amepre.2005.01.015

Dugan, B. (2007). Loss of identity in disaster: How do you say goodbye to home? *Perspectives of Psychiatric Care, 43*(1), 41–46.

Duncan, K. (2004). *Healing from the trauma of childhood sexual abuse: The journey of women.* Westport, CT: Praeger.

Dunkley, J., & Whelan, T. A. (2006). Vicarious traumatisation: Current status and future directions. *British Journal of Guidance and Counseling, 34*(1), 107–116.

Dutton, D. (1995). *The batterer: A psychological profile.* New York, NY: Basic Books.

Dutton, M., Goodman, L., & Bennett, L. (1999). Court-involved battered women's response to violence: The role of psychological, physical, and sexual abuse. *Violence and Victims, 14*, 89–104.

Earley, P. (2006). *Crazy a father's search through America's mental health madness.* New York, NY: Penguin Group.

Eckhardt, C., Holtzworth-Munroe, A., Norlander, B., Sibley, A., & Cahill, M. (2008). Readiness to change, partner violence subtypes, and treatment outcomes among men in treatment for partner assault. *Violence and Victims, 23*, 446–476.

Eden, J., Stevens, R., & Institute of Medicine. (2006). *Evaluating the HRSA Traumatic Brain Injury Program.* Washington, DC: National Academies Press.

Egan, G. (2002). *The skilled helper: A problem-management and opportunity-development approach to helping* (7th ed.). Pacific Grove, CA: Brooks/Cole.

El-Khoury, M. Y., Dutton, M. A., Goodman, L. A., Engel, L., Belamaric, R. J., & Murphy, M. (2004). Ethnic difference in battered women's formal help-seeking strategies: A focus on health, mental health, and spirituality. *Cultural Diversity & Ethnic Minority Psychology, 10*, 383–393.

Elliott, D. M. (1994). Impaired object relations in professional women molested as children. *Psychotherapy, 21*, 79–86.

Ellis, A. (1962). *Reason and emotion in psychotherapy*. New York, NY: Lyle Stuart.

El-Zanaty, F., Hussein, E. M., Shawky, G. A., Way, *A. A.*, & Kishor, S. (1996). *Egypt demographic and health survey—1995*. Cairo, Egypt: National Population Council.

Enarson, E., Fothergill, A., & Peek, L. (2006). Gender and disaster: Foundations and possibilities. In H. Rodriguez, E. Quarantelli & R. Dynes (Eds), *Handbook of disaster research* (pp. 130–146). New York, NY: Springer.

Erbes, C. R., Polusny, M. A., MacDermid, S., & Compton, J. A. (2008). Couple therapy with combat veterans and their partners. *Journal of Clinical Psychology: In Session, 64*, 972–983.

Erford, B. T., Lee, V. V., Newsome, D. W., & Rock, E. (2011). Systematic approaches to counseling students experiencing complex and specialized problems. In B. T. Erford (Ed), *Transforming the school counseling profession* (pp. 288–313). Columbus, OH: Pearson Merrill.

Erikson, E. H. (1980). *Identity and the life cycle*. New York: Norton.

Erikson, E. H. (1997). *The life cycle completed*. New York: Norton.

Eronen, M., Angermeyer, M. C., & Schulze, B. (1998). The psychiatric epidemiology of violent behavior. *Social Psychiatry and Psychiatric Epidemiology, 33*(Suppl.), 13–23.

Essex, N. L. (2004). Confidentiality and student records. *Clearing House, 77*, 111–113.

Evans, D. R., Hearn, M. T., Uhlemann, M. R., & Ivey, A. E. (2008). *Essential interviewing: A programmed approach to effective communication*. Belmont, CA: Brooks/Cole.

Everly, G. S., & Flynn, B. W. (2005). Principles and practices of acute psychological first aid after disasters. In G. S. Everly, & C. L. Parker (Eds.), *Mental health aspects of disasters: Public health preparedness and response* (rev. ed., pp. 79–89). Baltimore, MD: Johns Hopkins Center for Public Health Preparedness.

Everly, G. S., & Mitchell, J. (1999). *Critical incident stress management* (2nd ed.). Ellicott City, MD: Chevron.

Everly, G. S., Phillips, S. B., Kane, D., & Feldman, D. (2006). Introduction to and overview of group psychological first aid. *Brief Treatment & Crisis Intervention, 6*, 130–136.

Ewing v. Goldstein, 120 Cal. App. 4th 807 (2004).

Ewing, J. A. (1984). Detecting alcoholism: The CAGE questionnaire. *Journal of the American Medical Association, 252*, 1905–1907.

Falloon, I. R. H., Roncone, R., Held, T., Coverdale, J. H., & Laidlaw, T. M. (2002). An international overview of family interventions: Developing effective treatment strategies and measuring their benefits for patients, careers, and communities. In H. P. Lefley & D. L. Johnson (Eds.), *Family interventions in mental illness: International perspectives* (pp. 3–23). Westport, CT: Praeger/Greenwood.

Fallot, R. D., & Heckman, J. P. (2005). Religious/spiritual coping among women trauma survivors with mental health and substance use disorders. *Journal of Behavioral Health Services and Research, 32*, 215–226.

Farmer, T. W., Farmer, E. M. Z., Estell, D. B., & Hutchins, B. C. (2007). The developmental dynamics of aggression and the prevention of school violence. *Journal of Emotional & Behavioral Disorders, 15*, 197–208.

Farrow, T. L. (2002). Owning their expertise: Why nurses use no suicide contracts rather than their own assessments. *International Journal of Mental Health Nursing, 11*, 214–219.

Federal Bureau of Investigation, National Center for the Analysis of Violent Crime. (2001). *Workplace violence: Issues in response*. Retrieved from www.fbi.gov/publications/violence.pdf

Federal Bureau of Investigation. (2010). *Crime in the United States*. Retrieved from http://www.fbi.gov/about-us/cjis/ucr/crime-in-the-u.s/2010/crime-in-the-u.s.-2010/tables/10shrtbl02.xls

Federal Emergency Management Agency (FEMA). (2006). *FEMA national US&R response system structural collapse technician*. Retrieved from www.fema.gov/pdf/emergency/usr/module1b.pdf

Federal Emergency Management Agency. (FEMA). (2012). *National preparedness guidelines*. Retrieved from www.fema.gov/pdf/government/npg.pdf

Few, A. L. (2005). The voices of Black and White rural battered women in domestic violence shelters. *Family Relations, 54*, 488–500.

Fiduccia, B. W., & Wolfe, L. R. (1999). *Violence against disabled women*. Retrieved from www.centerwomenpolicy.org

Figley, C. R. (2002). Compassion fatigue: Psychotherapists' chronic lack of self care. *Journal of Clinical Psychology, 58*, 1433–1441.

Fincham, F. D., Cui, M., Braithwaite, S., & Pasley, K. (2008). Attitudes toward intimate partner violence in dating relationships. *Psychological Assessment, 20* (3), 260–269. doi: 10.1037/1040-3590.20.3.260

Finkelhor, D. (1979). *Sexually victimized children*. New York, NY: Free Press.

Finkelhor, D., & Berliner, L. (1995). Research on the treatment of sexually abused children: A review and recommendations. *Journal of the American Academy of Child and Adolescent Psychiatry, 34*(11), 1408.

First, M., & Halon, R. (2008). Use of DSM paraphilia diagnosis in sexually violent predator commitment cases. *Journal of the American Academy of Psychiatry and the Law Online, 36*, 443–454.

Fisher, B. S., Cullen, F. T., & Turner, M. G. (2000). *The sexual victimization of college women: Research report*. Washington, DC: U.S. Department of Justice.

Fitzgerald, H. (1998). *Grief at school*. Washington, DC: American Hospice Foundation.

Flannery, R. B., & Stone, P. S. (2001). Characteristics of staff victims of patient assault: Ten-year analysis of the assaulted staff action program. *Psychiatric Quarterly, 72*, 237–248.

Fleming, M. F. (2003). Screening for at-risk, problem, and dependent alcohol use. In R. K. Hester & W. R. Miller (Eds.), *Handbook of alcoholism treatment approaches: Effective alternatives* (3rd ed.) (pp. 64–77). Boston, MA: Allyn and Bacon.

Foa, E. B., Hearst-Ikeda, D., & Perry, K. J. (1995). Evaluation of a brief cognitive-behavioral program for the prevention of chronic PTSD in recent assault victims. *Journal of Consulting and Clinical Psychology, 63*, 948–955.

Foa, E. B., Riggs, D. S., Dancu, C. V., & Rothbaum, B. O. (1993). Reliability and validity of a brief instrument for assessing Post-traumatic Stress Disorder. *Journal of Traumatic Stress, 6*, 459–473.

Foa, E. B., & Rothbaum, B. O. (1998). *Treating the trauma of rape: Cognitive behavioral therapy for PTSD*. New York, NY: Guilford Press.

Foa, E. B., Rothbaum, B. O., Riggs, D. S., & Murdock, T. (1991). Treatment of Posttraumatic Stress Disorder in rape victims: A comparison between cognitive behavioral procedures and counseling. *Journal of Consulting & Clinical Psychology, 59*, 715–723.

Foa, E. B., Zoellner, L., Feeny, N., Hembree, E., & Alvarez-Conrad, J. (2002). Does imaginal exposure exacerbate PTSD symptoms? *Journal of Counseling and Clinical Psychology, 70*, 1022–1028.

Forbes, D., Creamer, M., Phelps, A., Bryant, R., McFarlane, A., Devilly, G….Newton, S. (2007). Australian guidelines for the treatment of adults with acute stress disorder and post-traumatic stress disorder. *Australian and New Zealand Journal of Psychiatry, 43*, 637–648.

Fortier, M. A., DiLillo, D., Messman-Moore, T. L., Peugh, J., DeNardi, K. A., & Gaffey, K. J. (2009). Severity of child sexual abuse and revictimization: The mediating role of coping and trauma symptoms. *Psychology of Women Quarterly, 33*, 308–320. doi: 10.1111/j.1471-6402.2009.01503.x

Foss, L. L., & Warnke, M. A. (2003). Fundamentalist Protestant Christian women: Recognizing cultural and gender influences on domestic violence. *Counseling and Values, 48*, 14–23.

Fowler, J. W. (1981). *Stages of faith*. New York, NY: Harper Collins.

Fox, J. A., & Zawitz, M. W. (2004). *Homicide trends in the United States*. Washington, DC: U.S. Department of Justice.

Fox, S. (1988). *Good grief: Helping groups of children deal with loss when a friend dies*. Boston, MA: New England Association for the Education of Young Children.

France, K. (2002). *Crisis intervention* (4th ed.). Springfield, IL: Charles C. Thomas.

Frances, A. (2011, May 26). *DSM 5 rejects coercive paraphilia*. Retrieved from http://www.psychologytoday.com/blog/dsm5-in-distress/201105/dsm-5-rejects-coercive-paraphilia

Franiuk, R. (2007). Discussing and defining sexual assault: A classroom activity. *College Teaching, 55*(3), 104.

Frankl, V. (1959). *Man's search for meaning*. Boston, MA: Beacon Press.

Friedrich, W. N., Urquiza, A. J., & Beilke, R. (1986). Behavior problems in sexually abused young children. *Journal of Pediatric Psychology, 11*, 47–57.

Freud, S. (1917). *Mourning and melancholia*. London, UK: Hogarth Press.

Fugate, M., Landis, L., Riordan, K., Naureckas, S., & Engel, B. (2005). Barriers to domestic violence help seeking: Implications for intervention. *Violence Against Women, 11*, 290–310.

Gamino, L. A., & Ritter, R. H. (2009). *Ethical practice in grief counseling*. New York, NY: Springer.

Gerber, M. M., Boals, A., & Schuettler, D. (2011). The unique contributions of positive and negative religious coping to post traumatic growth and posttraumatic stress disorder. *Psychology of Religion and Spirituality, 3*, 298–307.

Gerbert, B., Capsers, N., Milliken, N., Berlin, M., Bronstone, A., & Moe, J. (2000). Interventions that help victims of domestic violence. *Journal of Family Practice, 49*, 889–895.

Gibbs, D. A., Martin, S. L., Kupper, L. L., & Johnson, R. E. (2007). Child maltreatment in enlisted soldiers' families during combat-related deployments. *Journal of the American Medical Association, 298*, 528–535.

Gladding, S. T. (2010). *The counseling dictionary: Concise definitions of frequently used terms* (5th ed.). Upper Saddle River, NJ: Pearson.

Gladding, S. T., & Newsome, D. W. (2010). *Clinical mental health counseling*. Columbus, OH: Pearson Merrill.

Glasser, W. (1965). *Reality therapy: A new approach to psychiatry*. New York, NY: Harper and Row.

Goddard, C., & Bedi, G. (2010). Intimate partner violence and child abuse: A child-centered perspective. *Child Abuse Review, 19*, 5-20. doi: 10.1002/car.1084

Gondolf, E. (2002). Service barriers for battered women with male partners in batterer programs. *Journal of Interpersonal Violence, 17*, 217–227.

Goodwin, D. W., Schulsinger, F., Hermansen, L., Guze, S. B. & Winokur, G. (1973). Alcohol problems in adoptees raised apart from alcoholic biological parents. *Archives in General Psychiatry, 28,* 238–243.

Gould, M. S. (2010). Schools and suicide: Latest and best school-based strategies. Webinar hosted by WellAware and the Wyoming Department of Health.

Grafanki, S., Pearson, D., Cini, F., Goldula, D., Mckenzie, B., Nason, S., & Anderegg, M. (2005). Sources of renewal: A qualitative study on the experience and role of leisure in the life of counsellors and psychologists. *Counselling Psychology Quarterly, 18*(1), 31–40.

Granello, D. H., & Granello, P. F. (2007). *Suicide: An essential guide for helping professionals and educators.* Boston, MA: Pearson.

Green, E. J. (2008). Reenvisioning Jungian analytical play therapy with child sexual abuse survivors. *International Journal of Play Therapy, 17,* 102–121. doi: 10.1037/a0012770

Green, T., Buckman, J., Dandeker, C., & Greenberg, N. (2010). The impact of culture clash on deployed troops. *Military Medicine, 175,* 958–963.

Greenberg, L. S., & Pascual-Leone, A. (2006). Emotion in psychotherapy: A practice friendly review. *Journal of Clinical Psychology: In Session, 62,* 611–630.

Greenstone, J. L., & Leviton, S. C. (2002). *Elements of crisis intervention: Crises and how to respond to them* (2nd ed.). Pacific Grove, CA: Brooks/Cole.

Griffin, R. M. (2008). *Breaking the silence: Sociologist studies woman-to-woman sexual violence.* Retrieved from www.snbw.org/articles/womantowomansexualviolence.htm

Grossman, L. S., Martis, B., & Fichtner, C. G. (1999). *Are sex offenders treatable? A research overview.* Retrieved from www.psychservices.psychiatryonline.org/cgi/reprint/50/3/349.pdf

Groth, A. N. (2001). *Men and rape: The psychology of the offender.* New York, NY: Basic Books.

Guldin, M., O'Connor, M., Sokolowski, I., Jensen, A. B., & Vedsted, P. (2011). Identifying bereaved subjects at risk of complicated grief: Predictive value of questionnaire items in a cohort study. *BMC Palliative Care, 9,* 1–9.

Haas, D. M., Pazdernik, L. A., & Olsen, C. H. (2005). A cross-sectional survey of the relationship between partner deployment and stress in pregnancy during wartime. *Womens Health Issues, 15*(2), 48–54.

Haj-Yahia, M. M. (2002). Beliefs about wife-beating among Palestinian women: The influence of their patriarchal ideology. *Violence Against Women, 12,* 530–545.

Halifax, J. (2011). *Being with dying: Cultivating compassion and fearlessness in the presence of death.* Boston: MA: Shambhala.

Halpern, C. T., Oslak, S. G., Young, M. L., Martin, S. L., & Kupper, L. L. (2001). Partner violence among adolescents in opposite-sex romantic relationships: Findings from the national longitudinal study of adolescent health. *American Journal of Public Health, 91,* 1679–1685.

Hamblen, J. L., Gibson, L. E., Mueser, K. T., & Norris, F. H. (2006). Cognitive behavioral therapy for prolonged post-disaster distress. *Journal of Clinical Psychology: In Session, 62,* 1043–1052.

Hanson, R. F. (2002). Adolescent dating violence: Prevalence and psychological outcomes. *Child Abuse and Neglect, 26,* 447–451.

Harper, F. D., Harper, J. A., & Stills, A. B. (2003). Counseling children in crisis based on Maslow's hierarchy of basic needs. *International Journal for the Advancement of Counselling, 25*(1), 11–25.

Harrington, J. A. (2007, March). Obstacles in effective suicide intervention in suicide: Responding to the emergency. Training workshop for Chilton Shelby Mental Health Center, Birmingham, AL.

Harrington, J. A. (2011, September). Safety plan design with notes for mental health professionals. Suicide training session with Gateway Family Services, Birmingham, AL.

Harris. J. I., Erbes, C. R., Engdahl, B. E., Thuras, P., Murray-Swank, N., Grace, D... Le, T. V. (2011). The effectiveness of a trauma-focused spiritually integrated intervention for veterans exposed to trauma. *Journal of Clinical Psychology, 67,* 425–438.

Hart, C. L., & Ksir, C. (2011). *Drugs, society and human behavior* (14th ed.). New York, NY: McGraw-Hill.

Hassouneh-Phillips, D., & Curry, M. A. (2002). Abuse of women with disabilities: State of the science. *Rehabilitation Counseling Bulletin, 45,* 96–104.

Hatton, R. (2003). Homicide bereavement counseling: A survey of providers. *Death Studies, 27,* 427–448.

Haugaard, J. J. (2000). The challenge of defining sexual abuse. *American Psychologist, 55,* 1036–1039.

Havel, V. (2004). An orientation of the heart. In P. R. Loeb (Ed.), *The impossible will take a little while* (pp. 82–89). New York, NY: Basic Books.

Hayden, S. (2011). Addressing needs of military families during deployment: Military service providers' perceptions of integrating support services. University of Virginia. ProQuest Dissertation and Thesis Abstracts (UMI No. 3485316).

Hays, D. G., Green, E., Orr, J. J., & Flowers, L. (2007). Advocacy counseling for female survivors of partner abuse: Implications for counselor education. *Counselor Education and Supervision, 46,* 186–198.

Health Insurance Portability and Accountability Act of 1996 (HIPAA). (2011). 42 U.S.C. § 1320d-9 (2011).

Hebert, B. B., & Ballard, M. B. (2007). Children and trauma: A post-Katrina and Rita response. *Professional School Counseling, 11*(2), 140–144.

Hedlund, J., & Vieweg, B. (1984). The Michigan Alcoholism Screening Test (MAST): A comprehensive review. *Journal of Operational Psychiatry, 15,* 55–64.

Herbert, P. B., & Young, K. A. (2002). Tarasoff at twenty-five. *Journal of the American Academy of Psychiatry and the Law, 30,* 275–281.

Herman, J. L. (1995). Complex PTSD: A syndrome in survivors of prolonged and repeated trauma. In G. S. Everly & J. M. Lating (Eds.), *Psychotraumatology: Key papers and core concepts in posttraumatic stress* (pp. 87–100). New York, NY: Plenum.

Hernandez, P., Gansei, D., & Engstrom, D. (2007). Vicarious resilience: A new concept in work with those who survive trauma. *Family Process, 46,* 229–241.

Hernandez G., Hamdani S., Rajabi H., Conover K, Stewart J, Arvanitogiannis A, & Shizgal P. (2006). Prolonged rewarding stimulation of the rat medial forebrain bundle: Neurochemical and behavioral consequences. *Behavioral Neuroscience, 120,* 888–904. doi: 10.1037/0735-7044.120.4.888

Hetzel-Riggin, M. D., Brausch, A. M., & Montgomery, B. S. (2007). A meta-analytic investigation of therapy modality outcomes for sexually abused children and adolescents: An exploratory study. *Child Abuse and Neglect, 31,* 125–141. doi: 10.1016/j.chiabu.2006.10.007

Hewitt, S. K. (1998). *Small voices: Assessing allegations of sexual abuse in preschool children.* Thousand Oaks, CA: Sage.

Hill, R. (1949). *Families under stress.* Westport, CT: Greenwood Press.

Hill, R. (1958). Social stresses on the family: Generic features of families under stress. *Social Casework, 39,* 139–150.

Hillbrand, M. (2001). Homicide-suicide and other forms of co-occurring aggression against self and others. *Professional Psychology: Research and Practice, 32,* 626–635.

Hines, D. A., & Finkelhor, D. (2007). Statutory sex crime relationships between juveniles and adults: A review of social scientific research. *Aggression and Violent Behavior, 12,* 300–314.

Hines, D. A., & Malley-Morrison, K. (2005). *Family violence in the United States: Defining, understanding and combating abuse.* Thousand Oaks, CA: Sage.

Hoge, C. W., Castro, C. A., Messer, S. C., McGurk, D., Cotting, D. I., & Koffman, R. L. (2004). Combat duty in Iraq and Afghanistan, mental health problems, and barriers to care. *New England Journal of Medicine, 351,* 13–22.

Holt, M. K., & Espelage, D. L. (2005). Social support as a moderator between dating violence victimization and depression anxiety among African American and Caucasian adolescents. *School Psychology Review, 34,* 309–328.

Holtzworth-Munroe, A., Bates, L., Smultzer, N., & Sandin, E. (1997). A brief review of the research on husband violence. *Aggression and Violent Behavior, 2,* 65–99.

Horne, C. (2003). Families of homicide victims: Utilization patterns of extra- and intrafamilial homicide survivors. *Journal of Family Violence, 18*(2), 75–82.

Horne, S. (1999). Domestic violence in Russia. *American Psychologist, 54,* 55–61.

Horner, J., & Wheeler, M. (2005). HIPAA: Impact on clinical practices. *American Speech-Language-Hearing Association Leader, 10*(12), 10–23.

Hooyman, N. R., & Kramer, J. (2008). *Living through loss: Interventions across the lifespan.* New York, NY: Columbia University Press.

Hopper, J. (2010). *Sexual abuse of males: Prevalence, possible lasting effects, and resources.* Retrieved from http://www.jimhopper.com/male-ab/

Horowitz, M. J., Wilner, N. J., & Alvarez, W. (1979). Impact of Events Scale: A measure of subjective stress. *Psychosomatic Medicine, 41,* 209–218.

Horvath, A. O., & Bedi, R. P. (2002). The alliance. In J. C. Norcross (Ed.), *Psychotherapy relationships that work: Therapist contributions and responsiveness to patients* (pp. 37–69). New York, NY: Oxford University Press.

Horwitz, A. V., & Wakefield, J. C. (2007). *The loss of sadness: How psychiatry transformed normal sorrow into depressive disorder.* New York, NY: Oxford University Press.

Hoshmand, L. T., & Hoshmand, A. (2007). Support for military families and communities. *Journal of Community Psychology, 35,* 171–180.

Hotopf, M., Hull, L., Fear, N., Browne, T., Horn, O., Iversen, A… Bland, D. (2006). The health of UK military personnel who deployed to the 2003 Iraq war: A cohort study. *Lancet, 367,* 1731–1741.

Howard, D. E., Wang, M. Q., & Yan, F. (2007). Psychosocial factors associated with reports of physical dating violence among U.S. adolescent females. *Adolescence, 42,* 311–324.

Howard, J. L. (2006). The role of culture in shaping perceptions of discrimination among active duty and reserve forces in the U.S. military. *Employee Rights and Responsibilities, 18,* 171–187.

Huebner, A. J., Mancini, J. A., Wilcox, R. M., Grass, S. R., & Grass, G. A. (2007). Parental deployment and youth in military families: Exploring uncertainty and ambiguous loss. *Family Relations, 56,* 112–122.

Humphrey, K. M. (2009). *Counseling strategies for loss and grief.* Alexandria, VA: American Counseling Association.

Humphreys, C., & Thiara, R. K. (2003). Neither justice nor protection: Women's experiences of post-separation violence. *Journal of Social Welfare and Family Law, 25,* 195–214.

Huprich, S. K., Fuller, K. M., & Schneider, R. B. (2003). Divergent ethical perspectives on the duty-to-warn principle with HIV patients. *Ethics and Behavior, 13*, 263–278.

Inman, A., & Alvarez, A. (2014). Individuals and families of Asian descent. In D. G. Hays & B. T. Erford (Eds.), *Developing multicultural counseling competence: A systems approach* (2nd ed, pp. 246–276). Boston, MA: Pearson.

Institute of Medicine. (IOM). (2010). *Returning home from Iraq and Afghanistan: Preliminary assessment of readjustment needs of veterans, service members, and their families.* Washington, DC: National Academies Press. Retrieved from http://books.nap.edu/openbook.php?record_id=12812&page=R1

International Association for Suicide Prevention. (2000). *Guidelines for suicide prevention.* Retrieved from www.med.uio.no/iasp/english/guidelines.html

Ivey, A. E., & Ivey, M. B. (2007). *Intentional interviewing and counseling: Facilitating client development in a multicultural society* (6th ed.). Belmont, CA: Brooks/Cole.

Jackson-Cherry, L., & Sterner, W. (2012). Spiritual and religious needs of deployed military: Voices from the field. Unpublished manuscript.

Jacobs, D. G. (Ed.). (1999). *The Harvard Medical School guide to suicide assessment and intervention.* San Francisco, CA: Jossey-Bass.

Jacobs, E., Masson, R., Harvill, R., & Schimmel, C. (2009/2012). *Group counseling: Strategies and skills* (7th ed.). Belmont, CA: Brooks/Cole Cengage Learning.

Jacobsen, I. G., Ryan, M. A., Hooper, T. I., Smith, T. C., Amoroso, P. J., Boyko, E. J...Bell, N. S. (2008). Alcohol use and alcohol-related problems before and after military combat deployment. *Journal of the American Medical Association, 300*, 663–675.

Jacobson, G. R. (1989). A comprehensive approach to pre-treatment evaluation: I. Detection, assessment, and diagnosis of alcoholism. In R. K. Hester, & W. R. Miller (Eds.), *Handbook of alcoholism treatment approaches: Effective alternatives* (pp. 17–53). New York, NY: Pergamon.

James, R. K. (2008). *Crisis intervention strategies* (6th ed.). Belmont, CA: Brooks/Cole.

Jaycox, L., Zoellner, L., & Foa, E. (2002). Cognitive-behavior for PTSD in rape survivors. *Psychotherapy in Practice, 58*, 891–906.

Jellinek, E. M. (1946). Phases in the drinking history of alcoholics: Analysis of a survey conducted by the official organ of Alcoholics Anonymous. *Quarterly Journal of Studies on Alcohol, 7*, 1–88.

Jellinek, E. M. (1960). *The disease concept of alcoholism.* New Brunswick, NJ: Hillhouse Press.

Jensen, D. G. (2003). HIPAA overview. *Therapist, 15*(3), 26–27.

Jensen, P. S., Xenakis, S., Wolf, P., & Bain, M. W. (1991). The "military family" syndrome revisited. *Journal of Nervous Mental Disease, 179*, 102–107.

Jobes, D. A. (2006). *Managing suicidal risk: A collaborative approach.* New York, NY: Guilford Press.

Jobes, D. A. (2008). Collaborative assessment and management of suicidality. Training seminar hosted by Health Education, Birmingham, AL.

Johnson, K. (2000). *School crisis management: A hands-on guide to training crisis response teams* (2nd ed.). Alameda, CA: Hunter House.

Johnson, K. R. (2004). Black kinesics: Some nonverbal communication patterns in Black culture. In R. L. Jackson (Ed.), *African American communication and identities* (pp. 39–46).Thousand Oaks, CA: Sage.

Johnson, R. J. (2008). Advances in understanding and treating childhood sexual abuse: Implications for research and policy. *Family and Community Health, 31*(Suppl. 1), S24–S34.

Johnston, S. M. (1997). The use of art and play therapy with victims of sexual abuse: A review of the literature. *Family Therapy, 24*(2), 101–113.

Joiner, T. E. (2005). *Why people die by suicide.* Cambridge, MA: Harvard University Press.

Jones, J. (2006). Mother Nature's disasters and their health effects: A literature review. *Nursing Forum, 41*(2), 78–87.

Jordan, J. R. (2006). *Suicide survivors defining needs and interventions.* Retrieved from http://webdev.sprc.org/featured_resources/trainingandevents/conferences/no/presentation.

Juhnke, G. A., Vacc, N. A., Curtis, R. C., Coll, K. M., & Paredes, D. M. (2003). Assessment instruments used by addictions counselors. *Journal of Addictions and Offender Counseling, 23*, 66–72.

Kalafat, J., Gould, M. S., & Munfakh, J. L. H. (2005). Final progress report: Hotline Evaluation and Linkage Project Category II. Washington, DC: Substance Abuse and Mental Health Services Administration.

Kanan, L. M. (2010). When students make threats. *Tech Directions, 70* (5), 31–35.

Kaplan, M., McFarland, H., Huguet, N., & Newsom, J. (2012). Estimating the risk of suicide among U.S. veterans: How should we proceed from here? *American Journal of Public Health, 102*(S1), S21–23.

Kaukinen, C. (2004). The help-seeking strategies of female violent-crime victims, the direct and conditional effects of race and the victim-offender relationship. *Journal of Interpersonal Violence, 19*, 967–990.

Keller, E. L. (1996). Invisible victims: Battered women in psychiatric and medical emergency rooms. *Bulletin of the Menninger Clinic, 60*(1), 1–21.

Kellogg, N. D. (2010). Sexual behaviors in children: Evaluation and management. *American Family Physician, 82*, 1233–1238.

Kennedy, J., Davis, R., & Taylor, B. (1998). Changes in spirituality and well-being among victims of sexual assault. *Journal for the Scientific Study of Religion, 37*, 322–328.

Kent, M., Davis, M., Stark, S., & Stewart, L. (2011). A resilience-oriented treatment of posttraumatic stress disorder: Results of a preliminary randomized clinical trial. *Journal of Traumatic Stress, 34*, 591–595.

Kerr, M. M. (2009). *School crisis prevention and intervention*. Columbus, OH: Pearson Merrill Prentice Hall.

Kilpatrick, D. G. (1988). Rape aftermath symptom test. In M. Hersen & A. S. Bellack (Eds.), *Dictionary of behavioral assessment techniques* (pp. 366–367). New York, NY: Pergamon Press.

Kilpatrick, D. G., Acierno, R., Resnick, H. S., Saunders, B. E., & Best, C. L. (1997). A 2-year longitudinal analysis of the relationships between violent assault and substance use in women. *Journal of Consulting and Clinical Psychology, 65*, 834–847.

Kilpatrick, D. G., & Resnick, H. S. (1993). PTSD associated with exposure to criminal victimization in clinical and community populations. In J. R. T. Davidson & E. B. Foa (Eds.), *PTSD in review: Recent research and future directions* (pp. 113–143). Washington, DC: American Psychiatric Press.

Kistenmacher, B. R., & Weiss, R. L. (2008). Motivational interviewing as a mechanism for change in men who batter: A randomized control trial. *Violence and Victims, 23*, 558–570.

Kleespies, P. M. (1998). *Emergencies in mental health practice*. New York, NY: Guilford Press.

Klott, J., & Jongsma, A. E. (2004). *The suicide and homicide risk assessment and prevention treatment planner*. Hoboken, NJ: Wiley.

Knapp, S., & VandeCreek, L. (1982). *Tarasoff*: Five years later. *Professional Psychology, 13*, 511–516.

Knox, K. S., & Roberts, A. R. (2005). Crisis intervention and crisis team models in schools. *Children and Schools, 27*(2), 93–100.

Kohlberg, L. (1976). Moral stages and moralization: The cognitive-developmental approach. In T. Lickona (Ed.), *Moral development and behavior: Theory, research, and social issues* (pp. 41–59). New York, NY: Holt, Rinehart, and Winston.

Kohlberg, L. (1984). *The psychology of moral development* (Vol. 2). San Francisco, CA: Harper and Row.

Koopmans, J. R., & Boomsma, D. I. (1996). Familial resemblances in alcohol use: Genetic or cultural transmission? *Journal of Studies on Alcohol, 57*, 19–28.

Koss, M. P. (1993). Detecting the scope of rape: A review of prevalence research methods. *Journal of Interpersonal Violence, 8*, 198–222.

Kozu, J. (1999). Domestic violence in Japan. *American Psychologist, 54*, 50–54.

Kramer, A., Lorenzon, D., & Mueller, G. (2004). Prevalence of intimate partner violence and health implications for women using emergency departments and primary care clinics. *Women's Health Issues, 14*, 19–29.

Kraus, J., Schaffer, K., Ayers, K., Stenehjem, J., Shen, H., & Afifi, A. A. (2005). *Journal of Head Trauma Rehabilitation, 20*, 239–256.

Krug, E. G., Dahlberg, L. L., Mercy, J. A., Zwi, A. B., & Lozano, R. (Eds.). (2002). *World report on violence and health*. Geneva, Switzerland: World Health Organization.

Kubany, E. S. (1998). Cognitive therapy for trauma-related guilt. In V. M. Follette, J. I. Ruzek, & F. R. Abueg (Eds.), *Cognitive-behavioral therapies for trauma* (pp. 124–161). New York, NY: Guilford Press.

Kübler-Ross, E. (1969). *On death and dying*. New York, NY: Collier Books.

Kübler-Ross, E. (1972). *Questions and answers on death and dying*. New York, NY: Simon and Schuster/Touchstone.

Kubler-Ross, E. (1975). *Death: The final stage of growth*. Englewood Cliffs, NJ: Prentice-Hall.

Kubler-Ross, E. & Kessler, D. (2005). *On grief and grieving*. New York, NY: Scribner.

Kulwicki, A. (2002). The practice of honor crimes: A glimpse of domestic violence in the Arab world. *Issues in Mental Health Nursing, 23*, 77–87.

Kung, H., Hoyert, D., Xu, J., & Murphy, S. L. (2008). *Deaths: Final data for 2005. National Vital Statistics Reports* (Vol. 56, no. 10). Retrieved from www.cdc.gov/nchs/data/nvsr/nvsr56/nvsr56_10.pdf

Laajasalo, T., & Hakkanen, H. (2004). Background characteristics of mentally ill homicide offenders: A comparison of five diagnostic groups. *Journal of Forensic Psychiatry and Psychology, 15*, 451–474.

Lachs, M. S., & Pillemer, K. (2004). Elder abuse. *The Lancet, 364*, 1192–1263.

Lambie, G. W. (2006). Burnout prevention: A humanistic perspective and structured group supervision activity. *Journal of Humanistic Counseling, Education and Development. 45*(1), 32–44.

Landau, J., & Hissett, J. (2008). Mild traumatic brain injury: Impact on identity and ambiguous loss in the family. *Families, Systems, and Health 1*, 69–85.

Lanning, K. (2001). *Child molesters: A behavioral analysis* (4th ed.). Alexandria, VA: National Center for Missing and Exploited Children.

Largen, M. A. (1985). The anti-rape movement—Past and present. In A. W. Burgess (Ed.), *Rape and sexual assault: A research handbook* (pp. 1–13). New York, NY: Garland.

Larson, D. R., & Hoyt, W. T. (2007). What has become of grief counseling? An evaluation of the empirical foundations of the new pessimism. *Professional Psychology: Research and Practice, 38,* 347–355.

Laux, J. M. (2002). A primer on suicidology: Implications for counselors. *Journal of Counseling and Development, 80,* 380–384.

Laws, D. R., & Marshall, W. L. (2003). A brief history of behavioral and cognitive behavioral approaches to sexual offenders: Part 1. Early developments. *Sexual Abuse: A Journal of Research and Treatment, 15,* 75–92.

Lawson, G. W. (1984). Characterizing clients and assessing their needs. In G. W. Lawson, D. C. Ellis, & P. C. Rivers (Eds.) *Essentials of chemical dependency counseling* (pp. 31–69). Gaithersburg, MD: Aspen.

Lawson, G., & Myers, J. E. (2011). Wellness, professional quality of life, and career sustaining behaviors: What keeps us well? *Journal of Counseling and Development, 89,* 163–171.

Lawson, G., & Venart, B. (2005). Preventing counselor impairment: Vulnerability, wellness, and resilience. In G. R. Walz, & R. K. Yep (Eds.), *VISTAS: Compelling perspectives on counseling 2005* (pp. 243–246). Alexandria, VA: American Counseling Association.

Lazarus, R. S. (1976). *Patterns of adjustment* (3rd ed.). New York, NY: McGraw-Hill.

Lazarus, R. S. (1993). Coping theory and research: Past, present, and future. *Psychosomatic Medicine, 55,* 234–247.

Leary, M. R., Kowalski, R. M., Smith, L., & Phillips, S. (2003). Teasing, rejection and violence: Case studies of school shootings. *Aggressive Behavior, 29,* 202–214.

Lee, J. B., & Bartlett, M. L. (2005). Suicide prevention: Critical elements for managing suicidal clients and counselor liability without the use of a no-suicide contract. *Death Studies, 29,* 1–19.

Lee, R., Caruso, M., Goins, S., & Southerland, J. (2003). Addressing sexual assault on college campuses: Guidelines for a prevention/awareness week. *Journal of College Counseling, 6* (1),14.

Lee, R. K., Thompson, V. L. S., & Mechanic, M. B. (2002). Intimate partner violence and women of color: A call for innovations. *American Journal of Public Health, 92,* 530–534.

Lee, S. M., Cho, S. H., Kissinger, D., & Ogle, N. T. (2010). A typology of burnout in professional counselors. *Journal of Counseling and Development, 88,* 131–138.

Lemberg, J. (2002, July 21). *Spouse abuse in South Asian marriages may be high.* Women's News. Retrieved from www.womensenews.org/article.cfm/dyn/979/context/archive

Levesque, D. A., Gelles, R. J., & Velicer, W. F. (2000). Development and validation of a stages of change measure for men in batterer treatment. *Cognitive Therapy and Research, 24,* 175–199.

Lewis, C. S. (1961). *A grief observed.* London, England: Faber and Faber.

Lewis, J. A., Dana, R. Q., & Blevins, G. A. (2002). *Substance abuse counseling* (3rd ed.). Pacific Grove, CA: Brooks/Cole.

Lewis, N. K. (2003). Balancing the dictates of law and ethical practice: Empowerment of female survivors of domestic violence in the presence of overlapping child abuse. *Ethics and Behavior, 13,* 353–366.

Liang, B., Goodman, L., Tummala-Narra, P., & Weintraub, S. (2005). A theoretical framework for understanding help-seeking processes among survivors of intimate partner violence. *American Journal of Community Psychology, 36,* 71–84.

Lichtenstein, R., Schonfield, D. J., Kline, M., & Speese-Lineham, D. (1995). *How to prepare for and respond to a crisis.* Alexandria, VA: Association for Supervision and Curriculum Development.

Lincoln, A., Swift, E., & Shorteno-Fraser, M. (2008). Psychological adjustment and treatment of children and families with parents deployed in military combat. *Journal of Clinical Psychology: In Session, 64,* 984–992.

Lindemann, E. (1944). Symptomatology and management of acute grief, *American Journal of Psychiatry, 101,* 141–148.

Lindhorst, T., Nurius, P., & Macy, R.J. (2005). Contextualized assessment with battered women: Strategic safety planning to cope with multiple harms. *Journal of Social Work Education, 41,* 331–352.

Linley, P., & Joseph, S. (2004). Positive change following trauma and adversity: A review. *Journal of Traumatic Stress, 17,* 11–21.

Lipsky, S., Caetano, R., Field, C. A., & Bazargan, S. (2005). The role of alcohol use and depression in intimate partner violence among Black and Hispanic patients in an urban emergency department. *American Journal of Drug and Alcohol Abuse, 31,* 225–242.

Lipsky, S., Caetano, R., Field, C. A., & Larkin, G. L. (2006). The role of intimate partner violence, race, and ethnicity in help seeking behaviors. *Ethnicity and Health, 11,* 81–100.

Loeb, T., Williams, J., Carmona, J., Rivkin, I., Wyatt, G., Chin, D., & Asuan-O'Brien, A. (2002). Child sexual abuse: Associations with the sexual functioning of adolescents and adults. *Annual Review of Sex Research, 13,* 307–346.

Loeber, R., Pardini, D., Homish, D. L., Wei, E. H., Crawford, A. M., Farrington, D. P. . . . Rosenfeld, R. (2005). The prediction of violence and homicide in young men. *Journal of Consulting and Clinical Psychology, 73,* 1074–1088.

Lord, J. (1997). *Death notification: Breaking the bad news with concern for the professional and compassion for the survivor.* Washington, DC: U.S. Department of Justice, Office for Victims of Crime.

Lutenbacher, M., Cohen, A., & Mitzel, J. (2003). Do we really help? Perspectives of abused women. *Public Health Nursing, 20* (1), 56–64.

Luthar, S. S. (2006) Resilience in development: A synthesis of research across five decades. In D. Cicchetti, & D. J. Cohen (Eds.). *Developmental psychopathology. Volume 3. Risk, disorder, and adaptation* (2nd ed.) (pp. 739–795). New York, NY: Wiley.

Luthar, S. S., Cicchetti, D., & Becker, B. (2000). The construct of resilience: A critical evaluation and guidelines for future work. *Child Development, 71*, 543–562.

Madrid, P. A., & Grant, R. (2008). Meeting mental health needs following a natural disaster: Lessons from Hurricane Katrina. *Professional Psychology: Research and Practice, 39* (1), 86–92.

Madsen, L. H., Blitz, L. V., McCorkle, D., & Panzer, P. G. (2003). Sanctuary in a domestic violence shelter: A team approach to healing. *Psychiatric Quarterly, 74*(2), 155–171.

Main, M. (1996). Introduction to the special section on attachment and psychopathology: Part II. Overview of the field of attachment. *Journal of Consulting and Clinical Psychology, 64*(2), 5–7.

Maisto, S. A., & Connors, G. J. (1990). Clinical diagnostic techniques and assessment tools in alcohol research. *Alcohol Health and Research World, 14*, 232–238.

Mann, J. J., Apter, A., Bertolote, J., Beautrais, A., Currier, D., Haas, A., . . . Hendin, H. (2005). Suicide prevention strategies: A systematic review. *Journal of the American Medical Association, 294*, 2064–2074.

Maris, R. W. (1992). Overview of the study of suicide assessment and prediction. In R. W. Maris, A. L. Berman, J. T. Maltsberger, & R. I. Yufit (Eds.), *The assessment and prediction of suicide* (pp. 3–22). New York, NY: Guilford Press.

Maris, R. W., Berman, A. L., & Silverman, M. M. (2000). *Comprehensive textbook of suicidology.* New York, NY: Guilford Press.

Marlatt, G. (1996). Harm reduction: Come as you are. *Addictive Behaviors, 21*, 779–788.

Marlatt, G. A. (Ed.). (1998). *Harm reduction: Pragmatic strategies for managing high-risk behaviors.* New York, NY: Guilford Press.

Marlatt, G. A., & George, W. (1984). Relapse prevention: Introduction and overview of the model. *British Journal of Addictions, 79*, 261–275.

Marques, J. K. (1999). How to answer the question, "Does sexual offender treatment work?" *Journal of Interpersonal Violence, 14*, 437–451.

Marques, J. K., Wiederanders, M., Day, D. M., Nelson, C., & van Ommeren, A. (2005). Effects of a relapse prevention program on sexual recidivism: Final results from California's Sex Offender Treatment and Evaluation Project (SOTEP). *Sexual Abuse: A Journal of Research and Treatment, 17*, 79–107.

Martin, J., Ghahramanlou-Holloway, M., Lou, K. & Tucciarone, P. (2009). A comparative review of U.S. military and civilian suicide behavior: Implications for OEF/OIF suicide prevention efforts. *Journal of Mental Health Counseling, 31*, 101–118.

Maryland State Police. (2001). *Recommended procedures for death notifications: The principles of death notifications.* Annapolis, MD: Author.

Mascari, J. B., & Webber, J. M. (2006). Salting the slippery slope: What licensing violations tell us about preventing dangerous ethical situations. In G. R. Waltz & R. K. Yep (Eds.), *VISTAS: Compelling perspectives on counseling 2006* (pp. 165–168). Alexandria, VA: American Counseling Association.

Masten, A. S., & Obradovic, J. (2008). Disaster preparation and recovery: Lessons from research on resilience in human development. *Ecology and Society, 13*(1), 9.

Mateer, C. A., Sira, C. S., & O'Connell, M. E. (2005). Putting Humpty Dumpty together again: The importance of integrating cognitive and emotional interventions. *Journal of Head Trauma Rehabilitation, 20*, 62–75.

Mathews, R., Matthews, J. K., & Speltz, K. (1989). *Female sexual offenders: An exploratory study.* Orwell, VT: Safer Society Press.

Mattson, S., & Ruiz, E. (2005). Intimate partner violence in the Latino community and its effect on children. *Health Care for Women International, 26*, 523–529.

Mayo Clinic. (2008). *Complicated grief.* Retrieved from www.mayoclinic.com/health/complicated-grief/DS01023/DSECTION=2

McClarren, G. M. (1987). The psychiatric duty to warn: Walking a tightrope of uncertainty. *University of Cincinnati Law Review, 56*, 269–293.

McCloskey, K., & Grigsby, N. (2005). The ubiquitous clinical problem of adult intimate partner violence: The need for routine assessment. *Professional Psychology: Research and Practice, 36*, 264–275.

McCloskey, K. A., & Raphael, D. N. (2005). Adult perpetrator gender asymmetries in child sexual assault victim selection: Results from the 2000 National Incident-Based Reporting System. *Journal of Child Sexual Abuse, 14*, 1–24.

McConnell, A., & Drennan, L. (2006). Mission impossible? Planning and preparing for crisis. *Journal of Contingencies and Crisis Management, 14*(2), 59–70.

McCubbin, H. I., & Figley, C. R. (1983). *Stress and the family volume I: Coping with normative transitions.* New York, NY: Brunner Mazel.

McCubbin, H. I., & Patterson, J. M. (1982). Family adaptation to crisis. In H. I. McCubbin, A. E. Cauble, & J. M. Patterson (Eds.), *Family stress, coping, and social support* (pp. 26–47). Springfield, IL: Charles C. Thomas.

McFarlane, J. M., Groff, J. Y., O'Brien, J. A., & Watson, K. (2005). Prevalence of partner violence against 7,443 African American, White, and Hispanic women receiving care at urban public primary care clinics. *Public Health Nursing, 22*, 98–107.

McFarlane, J., Soeken, K., Reel, S., Parker, B., & Silva, C. (1997). Resource use of abused women following an intervention program: Associated severity of abuse and reports of abuse ending. *Public Health Nursing, 14,* 244–250.

McKenry, P. C., & Price, S. J. (2005). *Families and change: Coping with stressful events and transitions* (3rd ed.). Thousand Oaks, CA: Sage.

McLeod, A. L., Hays, D. G., & Chang, C. Y. (2010). Experiences of female intimate partner violence survivors: Accessing personal and community resources. *Journal of Counseling and Development, 88,* 303–310.

McNulty, P. A. (2003). Does deployment impact the health care use of military families stationed in Okinawa, Japan? *Military Medicine, 168,* 465–470.

McWhirter, P. T. (1999). La violencia privada: Domestic violence in Chile. *American Psychologist, 54,* 37–40.

Mechanic, M. B., Weaver, T. L., & Resick, P. A. (2008). Mental health consequences of intimate partner abuse: A multidimensional assessment of four different forms of abuse. *Violence Against Women, 14,* 634–654. doi: 10.1177/1077801208319283

Meichenbaum, D. H. (1996). Stress inoculation training for coping with stressors. *Clinical Psychologist, 49,* 4–7.

Meisenhelder, J. B. (2002). Terrorism, posttraumatic stress and religious coping. *Issues in Mental Health Nursing, 23,* 771–782.

Melby, T. (2004). Duty to warn: A question of loyalty varies by state. *Contemporary Sexuality, 38*(1), 3–6.

Merikangas, K. R. (1990). The genetic epidemiology of alcoholism. *Psychological Medicine, 20,* 11–22.

Messinger, A. M. (2011). Invisible victims: Same-sex IPV in the National Violence against Women Survey. *Journal of Interpersonal Violence, 26,* 2228–2243.

Meyer, D., & Ponton, R. (2006). The healthy tree: A metaphorical perspective of counselor well-being. *Journal of Mental Health Counseling, 28,* 189–201.

Military Leadership Diversity Commission. (2010). *National Guard and reserve man-power.* Retrieved from http://mldc.whs.mil/download/documents/Issue%20Papers/53_Manpower.pdf

Miller, G. A. (1985). *The Substance Abuse Subtle Screening Inventory (SASSI) manual.* Springfield, IL: SASSI Institute.

Miller, G. A. (1999). *The SASSI Manual Substance Abuse Measures* (2nd ed.). Springfield, IL: SASSI Institute.

Miller, T., Clayton, R., Miller, J. M., Bilyeu, J., Hunter, J., & Kraus, R. F. (2000). Violence in the schools: Clinical issues and case analysis for high-risk children. *Child Psychiatry and Human Development, 30,* 255–272.

Miller, W. R., & Hester, R. K. (2003). Treating alcohol problems: Toward an informed eclecticism. In R. K. Hester & W. R. Miller (Eds.), *Handbook of alcoholism treatment approaches: Effective alternatives* (3rd ed.) (pp. 1–12). Boston, MA: Allyn and Bacon.

Miller, W. R., & Rollnick, S. (2002). *Motivational interviewing: Preparing people for change* (2nd ed.). New York, NY: Guilford Press.

Miller, W. R., Wilbourne, P. L., & Hettema, J. E. (2003). What works? A summary of alcohol treatment outcome research. In R. K. Hester & W. R. Miller (Eds.), *Handbook of alcoholism treatment approaches: Effective alternatives* (3rd ed.; pp. 13–63). Boston, MA: Allyn and Bacon.

Miller-Perrin, C. L., & Perrin, R. D. (2007). *Child maltreatment: An introduction* (2nd ed.). Thousand Oaks, CA: Sage.

Milliken, C. S., Auchterlonie, J. L, & Hoge, C. W. (2007). Longitudinal assessment of mental health problems among active and reserve component soldiers returning from the Iraq War. *Journal of the American Medical Association, 298,* 2141–2148.

Mitchell, C. W., & Rogers, R. E. (2003). Rape, statutory rape, and child abuse: Legal distinctions and counselor duties. *Professional School Counseling, 6,* 332–338.

Mitchell, R. (2001). *Documentation in counseling records* (2nd ed.). Alexandria, VA: American Counseling Association.

Moline, M. E., Williams, G. T., & Austin, K. M. (1998). *Documenting psychology essentials for mental health practitioners.* Thousand Oaks, CA: Sage.

Monson. C. M., Guthrie. K. A., & Stevens, S. P. (2003). Cognitive-behavioral couple's treatment for posttraumatic stress disorder. *Behavior Therapist, 26,* 393–402.

Monson, C. M., Schnurr, P. P., Resick, P. A., Friedman, M. J., Young-Xu, Y., & Stevens, S. P. (2006). Cognitive processing therapy for veterans with military-related posttraumatic stress disorder. *Journal of Consulting and Clinical Psychology, 74,* 898–907.

Monson, C. M., Schnurr, P. P., Stevens, S. P., & Guthrie, K. A. (2004). Cognitive-behavioral couple's treatment for posttraumatic stress disorder: Initial Findings. *Journal of Traumatic Stress 17*(4), 341–344.

Montgomery County Emergency Service, Inc. (2006). After a suicide: A postvention primer for providers. *MCES Quest Comprehensive Behavioral Health Services, 5*(2), 1–11.

Morse, R. M., & Flavin, D. K. (1992). The definition of alcoholism. *Journal of the American Medical Association, 268,* 1012–1014.

Moser, C. & Kleinplatz, P. L. (2005). DSM-IV-TR and the paraphilia: An argument for removal. *Journal of Psychology and Human Sexuality, 17,* 91–109.

Muldoon, J. P., & Gary, J. (2011). Motivating factors to enhance treatment compliance for male batterers: Getting them "in the door" and staying "in the room." *Journal of Mental Health Counseling, 33,* 144–160.

Muran, J. C., & DiGiuseppe, R. A. (1994). Patient pretreatment interpersonal problems and therapeutic alliance in short-term cognitive therapy. *Journal of Consulting and Clinical Psychology, 62*(1), 185–190.

Murphy, C., Meyer, S., & O'Leary, D. (1994). Dependency characteristics of partner assaultive men. *Journal of Abnormal Psychology, 103,* 729–735.

Murphy, G. (2010). *Following up with individuals at high risk for suicide: Developing a model for crisis hotline and emergency department collaboration.* New York, NY: National Suicide Prevention Lifeline.

Murray, C. E., Wester, K. L., & Paladino, D. A. (2008). Dating violence and self-injury among undergraduate college students: Attitudes and experiences. *Journal of College Counseling, 11,* 42–57.

Nademin, E., Jobes, D. A., Pflanz, S. E., Jacoby, A. M., Ghahramanlou-Holloway, M., Campise, R…Johnson, L. (2008). An investigation of interpersonal-psychological variables in Air Force suicides: A controlled-comparison study. *Archives of Suicide Research, 12,* 309–326.

National Alliance of Mental Illness. (n.d.). *Dual diagnosis and integrated treatment of mental illness and substance abuse disorder.* Retrieved from http://www.nami.org/ Tem-plate. cfm?Section=By_Illness&template=/ContentManagement/ ContentDisplay.cfm&ContentID=10333

National Center for Victims of Crimes. (2009). *Victim impact statements.* Retrieved from www.ncvc.org/ncvc/main.aspx? dbName=DocumentViewer&DocumentID=32515

National Center on Elder Abuse. (2005). *Elder abuse and prevalence.* Retrieved from http://www.ncea.aoa.gov/nceroom/ Main_Site/pdf/Publication/final Statis-tics050331.pdf

National Child Traumatic Stress Network. (2012). *TF-CBT implementation manual.* Retrieved from http://www.nctsnet.org/ nctsn_assets/pdfs/TF-CBT_Implementation_Manual.pdf

National Coalition of Anti-Violence Programs. (2007). *Lesbian, gay, bisexual and transgender domestic violence in the United States in 2006.* Retrieved from http://www.ncavp.org/common/ document_files/Reports/2006NationalDVReport(Final).pdf

National Education Association. (2002). *Crisis communications guide and toolkit.* Washington, DC: Author.

National Institute on Drug Abuse. (1980). *Theories on drug abuse: Selected contemporary perspectives.* NIDA Research Monograph 30. Washington, DC: U.S. Department of Health and Human Services.

National Military Family Association. (2006). *Report on the cycles of deployment: An analysis of survey responses from April–September 2005.* Alexandria, VA: Author.

National Suicide Prevention Lifeline. (2006). *Lifeline suicide risk assessment policy: Lifeline suicide risk assessment standards.* Washington, DC: Author.

Neimeyer, R. A. (2001). *Meaning reconstruction and the experience of loss.* Washington, DC: American Psychological Association.

Newell, J. M., & MacNeil, G. A. (2010). Professional burnout, vicarious trauma secondary traumatic stress and compassion fatigue: A review of theoretical terms, risk factors and prevention methods for clinicians and researchers. *Best Practices in Mental Health, 6* (2), 57–68.

Newman, C. (2012). Back from the brink: Using CBT to help suicidal patient to choose to live. Seminar for Canterbury Methodist Church training. Birmingham, AL.

Nordstrom, A., Dahlgren, L., & Kullgren, G. (2006). Victims' relations and factors triggering homicides committed by offenders with Schizophrenia. *Journal of Forensic Psychiatry and Psychology, 12,* 192–203.

Norris, H., & Rosen, C. S. (2009). Innovations in disaster mental health services and evaluation: National, state, and local responses to Hurricane Katrina (Introduction to the special issue). *Administrative Policy Mental Health 36,* 159–164.

North, C. S. (2010). A tale of two studies of two disasters: Comparing psychosocial responses to disaster among Oklahoma City bombing survivors and Hurricane Katrina evacuees. *Rehabilitation Psychology, 55,* 241–246. doi: 10.1037/ a0020119

Nugent, F. A., & Jones, K. D. (2009). *Introduction to the counseling profession* (5th ed.). Upper Saddle River, NJ: Pearson.

Nurcombe, B., Wooding, S., Marrington, P., Bickman, L., & Roberts, G. (2000). Child sexual abuse II: Treatment. *Australian and New Zealand Journal of Psychiatry, 34,* 92–97.

Nuttall, J. (2002). Modes of therapeutic relationship in brief dynamic psychotherapy. *Journal of Psychodynamic Process, 89,* 505–523.

Oaksford, K., & Frude, N. (2003). The process of coping following child sexual abuse: A qualitative study. *Journal of Child Sexual Abuse, 12,* 41–72. doi: 10.1300/J070v12n02_03

Office of the Deputy Under Secretary of Defense. (2005). 2005 *demographics report.* Retrieved from URL>http:// www.militaryhomefront.dod.mil/12038/Project%20 Documents/Military HOME-FRONT/QOL%20Resources/ Reports/2005%20Demographics%20Report.pdf

Okie, S. (2001, October 14). Use of anti-anxiety drugs jumps in US: Number of new prescriptions increases sharply in Washington and New York. *Washington Post,* A8.

Oppel, R.A. (2011). *Steady decline in major crimes baffles experts.* Retrieved from http://www.nytimes.com/2011/05/24/ us/24crime.html

O'Toole, M. E. (2000). *The school shooter: A threat assessment perspective.* Retrieved from www.fbi.gov/publications/school/ school2

Pabian, Y. L., Wefel, E., & Beebe, R. S. (2009). Psychologists' knowledge of their states' laws pertaining to Tarasoff-type situations. *Professional Psychology: Research and Practice, 40*(1), 8–14.

Pargament, K. (2007). *Spiritually integrated psychotherapy: Understanding and addressing the sacred.* New York, NY: Guilford Press.

Park, C. L., Cohen, C. H., & Murch, R. L. (1996). Assessment and prediction of stress-related growth. *Journal of Personality, 64,* 71–105.

Parker, S. (2011). Spirituality in counseling: A faith development perspective. *Journal of Counseling and Development, 89,* 112–119.

Parkes, C. M. (1975). Determinants of outcome following bereavement. *Omega, 6,* 303–323.

Parkes, C. M., & Prigerson, H. G. (2009). *Bereavement: Studies of grief in adult life* (4th ed.). New York, NY: Routledge.

Patterson, F. A., & Staton, A. R. (2009). Adult-acquired traumatic brain injury: Existential implications and clinical considerations. *Journal of Mental Health Counseling, 31,* 149–163.

Payne, S., & Delbert, E. (2011). Safe2tell. *New Directions for Youth Development, 129,* 103–111.

Pearlin, L. I., & Schooler, C. (1978). The structure of coping. *Journal of Health and Social Behavior, 19,* 2–21.

Pearlman, D. N., Zierler, S., Gjelsvik, A., & Verhoek-Oftedahl, W. (2003). Neighborhood environment, racial position, and risk of police reported domestic violence: A contextual analysis. *Public Health Reports, 118,* 44–58.

Pearlman, L. A., & MacIan, P. S. (1995). Vicarious traumatization: An empirical study of the effects of trauma work on trauma therapists. *Professional Psychology: Research and Practice, 26,* 558–565.

Pedersen, P. B. (1991). Multiculturalism as a generic approach to counseling. *Journal of Counseling and Development, 70,* 6–12.

Peled, E., Eisikovits, Z., Enosh, G., & Winstok, Z. (2000). Choice and empowerment for battered women who stay: Toward a constructivist model. *Social Work, 45*(1), 9–25.

Peterman, L. M., & Dixon, C. G. (2003). Domestic violence between same-sex partners: Implications for counseling. *Journal of Counseling and Development, 81,* 40–47.

Pincus, S. H., House, R., Christensen, J., & Adler, L. E. (2005). *The emotional cycle of deployment: A military family perspective.* Retrieved from http://www.hooah4health.com/deployment/familymatters/emotionalcycle.htm

Piper, W. E., Ogrodniczuk, J. S., McCollum, M., & Rosie, J. S. (2002). Relationships among affect, work and outcome in group therapy for patients with complicated grief. *American Journal of Psychotherapy, 56,* 347–362.

Pitcher, G. D., & Poland, S. (1992). *Crisis intervention in the schools.* New York, NY: Guilford Press.

Pitman, R. K., Altman, B., Greemnwald, E., Longpre, R. E., Macklin, M. L., Poire, R. E., & Steketee, G. S. (1991). Psychiatric complication during flooding for posttraumatic stress disorder. *Journal of Clinical Psychiatry, 52,* 17–20.

Poland, S., & McCormick, J. S. (1999). *Coping with crisis: A resource guide for schools, parents, and communities.* Longmont, CO: Sopris West.

Polivy, J., & Herman, C. P. (2002). If at first you don't succeed. *American Psychologist, 57,* 677–689.

Potoczniak, M. J., Mourot, J. E., Crosbie-Burnett, M., & Potoczniak, D. J. (2003). Legal and psychological perspectives on same-sex domestic violence: A multisystemic approach. *Journal of Family Psychology, 17,* 252–259.

Powell, J. (2004). *The use of judgmental language that promotes the stigma associated with suicide in speeches and literature by the suicide prevention organizations.* Retrieved from http://www.suicideperspective.com/stigma/the-use-judgmental-language/

Powers, M., Halpern, J., Ferenschack, M., Gillihan, S., & Foa, E. (2010). A meta-analytic review of prolonged exposure for posttraumatic stress disorder. *Clinical Psychology Review, 30,* 635–641.

Presbury, J. H., Echterling, L. G., & McKee, J. E. (2002). *Ideas and tools for brief counseling.* Upper Saddle River, NJ: Merrill Prentice Hall.

President's DNA Initiative Sexual Assault Medical Forensic Examinations. (2008). *Be aware of issues commonly faced by patients from specific populations.* Retrieved from http://samfe.dna.gov/overarching_issues/victim_centered_care/issues

Princeton Religious Research Center. (2009). *Center for the Study of Religion: Princeton University.* Retrieved from http://www.princeton.edu/csr/

Prochaska, J. O., & DiClemente, C. C. (1992). Stages of change in the modification of problem behaviors. In M. Hersen, R. M. Eisler, & P. M. Miller (Eds.), *Progress in behavior modification* (Vol. 28, pp. 183–218). Sycamore, IL: Sycamore Publishing.

Purcell, R., Powell, M. B., & Mullen, P. C. (2005). Clients who stalk psychologists: Prevalence, methods, motives. *Professional Psychology: Research and Practice, 36,* 531–543.

Putnam, F. W. (2003). Ten-year research update review: Child sexual abuse. *Journal of the American Academy of Child and Adolescent Psychiatry, 42,* 269–278.

Quinnett, P. (2012). *What is QPR? QPR Institute.* Retrieved from http://www.qprinstitute.com/about.html.

Range, L. M., Campbell, C., Kovac, S. H., Marion-Jones, M., Aldridge, H., Kogas, S., & Crump, S. (2002). No suicide contracts: An overview and recommendations. *Death Studies, 26,* 51–74.

Rape, Abuse & Incest National Network. (2012a). *Statistics.* Retrieved from www.rainn.org/statistics

Rape, Abuse & Incest National Network. (2012b). *FBI changes its definition of rape.* Retrieved from www.rainn.org/news-room/fbi-changes-rape-definition

Raphael, B. (2000). *Promoting the mental health and wellbeing of children and young people.* Retrieved from http://www.health.gov.au/internet/main/publishing.nsf/content/48F5C63B02F2CE07CA2572450013F488/$File/promdisc.pdf

Remley, T. P., & Herlihy, B. (2010). *Ethical, legal, and professional issues in counseling* (3rd ed.). Upper Saddle River, NJ: Pearson.

Rennison, C. M. (2002). *Intimate partner violence, 1993–2001* (Pub. No. NCJ-178247). Washington, DC: U.S. Department of Justice, Bureau of Justice Statistics.

Renzenbrink, I. (2011). *Caregiver stress and staff support in illness, dying, and bereavement.* New York, NY: Oxford University Press.

Renzetti, C. M. (1992). *Violent betrayal: Partner abuse in lesbian relationships.* London, England: Sage.

Resick, P. A. (2001). *Cognitive processing therapy: Generic version.* St. Louis, MO: University of Missouri–St. Louis.

Resick, P. A., & Schnicke, M. K. (1992). Cognitive processing therapy for sexual assault victims. *Journal of Consulting and Clinical Psychology, 60,* 748–756.

Rich, J. M., & DeVitis, J. L. (1985). *Theories of moral development.* Springfield, IL: Charles C. Thomas.

Richman, J. A., Wislar, J. S., Flaherty, J. A., Fendrich, M., & Rospenda, K. M. (2004). Effects on alcohol use and anxiety of the September 11, 2001, attacks and chronic work stressors: A longitudinal cohort study. *American Journal of Public Health, 94,* 2010–2015.

Riger, S., Raja, S., & Camacho, J. (2002). The radiating impact of intimate partner violence. *Journal of Interpersonal Violence, 17,* 184–205.

Riley, P. L., & McDaniel, J. (2000). School violence prevention, intervention, and crisis response. *Professional School Counseling, 4,* 120–125.

Roan, S. (2012, March 8). Suicides among army personnel up 80% in 4 years. *Los Angeles Times.* Retrieved from http://www.latimes.com/health/boostershots/la-heb-army-suicide-20120308,0,7002109.story

Rock, M., & Rock, J. (2004). *Widowhood: The death of a spouse.* Victoria, BC: Trafford.

Roe, K. J. (2004). *The Violence Against Women Act and its impact on sexual violence public policy: Looking back and looking forward.* Retrieved from www.nrcdv.org/docs/Mailings/2004/NRCDVNovVAWA.pdf

Roe-Sepowitz, D. (2007). Adolescent female murderers: Characteristics and treatment implications. *American Journal of Orthopsychiatry, 77,* 489–496.

Rogers, C. R. (1951). *Client-centered therapy.* Boston, MA: Riverside Press.

Rogers, C. R. (1980). *A way of being.* New York, NY: Houghton Mifflin.

Rolling, E., & Brosi, M. (2010). A multi-leveled and integrated approach to assessment and intervention of intimate partner violence. *Journal of Family Violence, 25,* 229–236.

Romano, E., & De Luca, R. (1997). Exploring the relationship between childhood sexual abuse and adult sexual perpetration. *Journal of Family Violence, 12,* 85–98.

Rosenberg, M. S. (2003). Voices from the group: Domestic violence offenders' experience of intervention. *Journal of Aggression, Maltreatment, and Trauma, 7,* 305–317.

Rosenblatt, P. C., Walsh, R. P., & Jackson, D. A. (1976). *Grief and mourning in cross-cultural perspective.* New Haven, CT: Human Relations Area Files Press.

Rothman, J. (Ed.). (1999). *Reflections on community organization: Enduring themes and critical issues.* Itasca, IL: F. E. Peacock.

Rothschild, B. (2000). *The body remembers.* New York, NY: Norton.

Rothschild, B. (2010). *Eight keys to safe trauma recovery.* New York, NY: Norton.

Rowe, C. L., La Greca, A. M., & Alexandersson, A. (2010). Family and individual factors associated with substance involvement and PTS symptoms among adolescents in greater New Orleans after Hurricane Katrina. *Journal of Consulting and Clinical Psychology, 78,* 806–817. doi: 10.1037/a0020808.

Rowe, L. P. (2005). What judicial officers need to know about the HIPAA privacy rule. *NASPA Journal, 42,* 498–512.

Rudd, M. D. (2006). *The assessment and management of suicidality.* Sarasota, FL: Professional Resource Exchange.

Rudd, M. D., Joiner, T. E., & Rajab, M. H. (2004). *Treating suicidal behavior: An effective, time-limited approach.* New York, NY: Guilford Press.

Russell, P., & Davis, C. (2007). Twenty-five years of empirical research on treatment following sexual assault. *Best Practices in Mental Health, 3*(2), 21–37.

Russo, C. J., & Mawdsley, R. D. (2004). Student records. *Education and the Law, 14,* 181–187.

Ruzek, J. L., Brymer, M. J., Jacobs, A. K., Layne, C. M., Vernberg, E. M., & Watson, P. J. (2007). Psychological first aid. *Journal of Mental Health Counseling, 29*(1), 17–27.

Salazar, L. F., Emshoff, J. G., Baker, C. K., & Crowley, T. (2007). Examining the behavior of a system: An outcome evaluation of a community coordinated response to domestic violence. *Journal of Family Violence, 22,* 631–641.

Sammons, M. T., & Batten, S. V. (2008). Psychological service for returning veterans and their families: Evolving conceptualization of the sequelae of war-zone experiences. *Journal of Clinical Psychology: In Session, 64*, 921–927.

Sandover, J. C., & Freeman, N. J. (2007). Typology of female sex offenders: A test of Vandiver and Kercher. *Sexual Abuse: A Journal of Research and Treatment, 19*, 73–89.

Saunders, J. B., Aasland, O. G., Babor, T. F., de la Fuente, J. R., & Grant, M. (1993). Development of the Alcohol Use Disorders Identification Test (AUDIT): WHO collaborative project on early detection of persons with harmful alcohol consumption. *Addiction, 88*, 791–804.

Savic-Jabrow, P. C. (2010). Where do counsellors in private practice receive their support? A pilot study. *Counselling and Psychotherapy Research, 10*, 229–232.

Sayers, S. L., Farrow, V. A., Ross, J., & Oslin, D. W. (2009). Family problems among recently returned military veterans referred for a mental health evaluation. *Journal of Clinical Psychiatry, 70*, 163–170.

Saywitz, K. J., Mannarino, A. P., Berliner, L., & Cohen, J. A. (2000). Treatment for sexually abused children and adolescents. *American Psychologist, 55*, 1040–1049.

Schmidt, M. C., Kolodinsky, J. M., Carsten, G., Schmidt, F. E., Larson, M., & MacLachlan, C. (2007). Short term change in attitude and motivating factors to change abusive behavior of male batterers after participating in a group intervention program based on the pro-feminist and cognitive-behavioral approach. *Journal of Family Violence, 22*, 91–100.

Shuchman, M. (2007). Falling through the cracks—Virginia Tech and the restructuring of college mindfulness to counseling students through yoga, meditation, qigong. *Journal of Counseling and Development, 86*, 47–56.

Schuh, J. H., & Laanan, F. S. (2006). Forced transitions: The impact of natural disasters and other events on college students. *New Directions for Student Services, 114*, 93–102.

Sedlak, A. J., Mettenburg, J., Basena, M., Petta, I., McPherson, K., Greene, A., & Li, S. (2010). *Fourth National Incidence Study of Child Abuse and Neglect (NIS–4): Report to Congress*. Washington, DC: U.S. Department of Health and Human Services, Administration for Children and Families.

Seligman, L., & Reichenberg, L. (2011). *Selecting effective treatments: A comprehensive, systematic guide for treating mental disorders*. New York, NY: Wiley.

Seligman, M. E. (1973). Fall into helplessness. *Psychology Today, 7*, 43–48.

Seligman, M. E. (1975). *Helplessness: On depression, development and death*. San Francisco, CA: Freeman.

Selye, H. (1956). *The stress of life*. New York, NY: McGraw Hill.

Selzer, M. L. (1971). The Michigan Alcoholism Screening Test: The quest for a new diagnostic instrument. *American Journal of Psychiatry, 127*, 1653–1658.

Selzer, M. L., Vinokur, A., & Van Rooijen, L. J. (1975). A self-administered Short Michigan Alcohol Screening Test (SMAST). *Studies on Alcohol, 36*, 117–126.

Sethi, S., & Uppal, S. (2006). Attitudes of clinicians in emergency room towards suicide. *International Journal of Psychiatry in Clinical Practice, 10* (3), 182–185.

Shalev, A. Y. (2004). Further lessons from 9/11: Does stress equal trauma? *Psychiatry, 67*, 174.

Shea, M. T., Vujaniovic, A. A., Mansfield, A. K., Sevin, E., & Liu, F. (2010). Posttraumatic stress disorder symptoms and functional impairment among OEF and OIF National Guard and reserve veterans. *Journal of Traumatic Stress, 23*, 100–107.

Shea, S. C. (2002). *The practical art of suicide assessment: A guide for mental health professionals and substance abuse counselors*. Hoboken, NJ: Wiley.

Shear, M. K., McLaughlin, K. A., Ghesquiere, A., Gruber, M. J., Sampson, N. A., & Kessler, R. C. (2011). Complicated grief associated with Hurricane Katrina. *Depression and Anxiety, 28*, 648–657.

Shen, J., Samson, L. F., Washington, E. L., Johnson, P., Edwards, C., & Malone, A. (2006). Barriers of HIPAA regulation to implementation of health services research. *Journal of Medical Systems 30*(1), 65–69.

Shepard, M. F., Falk, D. R., & Elliott, B. A. (2002). Enhancing coordinated community responses to reduce recidivism in cases of domestic violence. *Journal of Interpersonal Violence, 17*, 551–569.

Shrier, D., & Johnson, R. L. (1988). Sexual victimization of boys: An ongoing study of an adolescent medicine clinic population. *Journal of the National Medical Association, 80*, 1189–1193.

Simon, R.I. (2004). *Suicide risk: Guidelines for clinically based risk management*. Washington, DC: American Psychiatric Publishing.

Skinner, K., Kressin, N., Frayne, S., Tripp, T., Hankin, C., Miller, D., & Sullivan, L. (2000). The prevalence of military sexual assault among female veterans' administration outpatients. *Journal of Interpersonal Violence, 15*, 291–310.

Skovholt, T. M. (2001). *The resilient practitioner: Burnout prevention and self-care strategies for counselors, therapists, teachers and health professionals*. Boston, MA: Allyn and Bacon.

Slaikeu, K. A. (1990). *Crisis intervention: A handbook for practice and research* (2nd ed.). Boston: Allyn and Bacon.

Sleutel, M. R. (1998). Women's experience of abuse: A review of qualitative research. *Issues in Mental Health Nursing, 19*, 525–539.

Smith, D. W., Christiansen, E. H., Vincent, R., & Hann, N. E. (1999). Population effects of the bombing of Oklahoma City. *Journal of the Oklahoma State Medical Association, 92*, 193–198.

Snyder, C. M. J., & Anderson, S. A. (2009). An examination of mandated versus voluntary referral as a determinant of clinical outcome. *Journal of Marital and Family Therapy, 35,* 278–292.

Sobsey, D., Randall, W., & Parrila, R. (1997). Gender differences in abused children with and without disabilities. *Child Abuse and Neglect, 21,* 707–720.

Sokoloff, N. J., & Dupont, I. (2005). Domestic violence at the intersections of race, class, and gender: Challenges and contributions to understanding violence against marginalized women in diverse communities. *Violence Against Women, 11*(1), 38–64.

Sorsoli, L., Kia-Keating, M., & Grossman, F. (2008). "I keep that hush-hush": Male survivors of sexual abuse and the challenges of disclosure. *Journal of Counseling Psychology, 55,* 333-345. doi: 10.1037/0022-0167.55.3.333

Spencer, P. C., & Munch, S. (2003). Client violence toward social workers: The role of management in community mental health. *Social Work, 48,* 532–544.

Sperry, L., & Shafranske, E. (Eds.) (2005). *Spiritually oriented psychotherapy.* Washington, DC: American Psychological Association.

Stanford, E. J., Goetz, R. R., & Bloom, J. D. (1994). The no harm contract in the emergency assessment of suicidal risk. *Journal of Clinical Psychiatry, 55,* 410–414.

Stanley, B., & Brown, G. (2008). *Sample safety plan.* Retrieved from http://www.sprc.org/sites/sprc.org/files/library/SafetyPlanTemplate.pdf

Stauffer, M. D., Capuzzi, D., & Tanigoshi, H. (2008). Assessment: An overview. In D. Capuzzi & M. D. Stauffer (Eds.), *Foundations of addictions counseling* (pp. 76–100). Boston, MA: Allyn and Bacon.

SteelFisher, G. K., Zaslavsky, A. M., & Blendon, R. J. (2008). Health-related impact of deployment extensions on spouses of active duty army personnel. *Military Medicine, 173,* 221–229.

Steigerwald, F. (2010a). Crisis intervention with individuals in the schools. In B. T. Erford (Ed.), *Professional school counseling: A handbook of theories, programs, and practices* (2nd ed., pp. 829–841). Austin, TX: PRO-ED.

Steigerwald, F. (2010b). Systemic crisis intervention in the schools. In B. T. Erford (Ed.), *Professional school counseling: A handbook of theories, programs, and practices* (2nd ed., pp. 843–849). Austin, TX: PRO-ED.

Stewart, A., Lord, H., & Mercer, D. (2000). A survey of professional training and experiences in delivering death notifications. *Death Studies, 24*(7), 611–632.

Stickney, D., & Nordstrom, R. H. (2010). *Water bugs and dragonflies: Explaining death to young children.* Cleveland, OH: Pilgrim Press.

Strentz, T. (1995). Strategies for victims of hostage situations. In A. R. Roberts (Ed.), *Crisis intervention and time limited cognitive treatment* (pp. 127–147). Newbury Park, CA: Sage.

Substance Abuse and Mental Health Services Administration. (2010). *Results from the 2009 National Survey on Drug Use and Health: Volume I. Summary of National Findings* (Office of Applied Studies, NSDUH Series H-38A, HHS Publication No. SMA 10-586Findings). Rockville, MD: Author.

Substance Abuse and Mental Health Services Administration. (2012). *National registry of evidence-based programs and practices.* Retrieved from www.nrepp.samhsa.gov

Sue, D. W., Arredondo, P., & McDavis, R. J. (1992). Multicultural counseling competencies and standards: A call to the profession. *Journal of Counseling and Development, 70,* 477–486.

Suicide Prevention Resource Center. (2006). *Assessing and managing suicide risk: Core competencies for mental health professionals.* Retrieved from http://www.sprc.org/traininginstitute/amsr/core.asp

Suicide Prevention Resource Center, (2012). *Best practices registry.* Retrieved from http://www.sprc.org/bpr

Sullivan, A. M., Bezmen, J., Barron, C. T., Rivera, J., Curley-Casey, L., & Marino, D. C. (2005). Reducing restraints: Alternatives to restraints on an inpatient psychiatric unit utilizing safe and effective methods to evaluate and treat the violent patient. *Psychiatric Quarterly, 76*(1), 51–65.

Survivors of Loved Ones' Suicides, Inc. (SOLOS). (2006). *The suicide paradigm.* Retrieved from paradigmhttp://www.adph.org/suicideprevention/assets/SuicideParadigm.pdf

Swenson, C. C., & Chaffin, M. (2006). Beyond psychotherapy: Treating abused children by changing their social ecology. *Aggression and Violent Behavior, 11,* 120–137.

Tanielian, T., & Jaycox, L. (Eds.). (2008). *Invisible wounds of war: Psychological and cognitive injuries, their consequences and services to assist recovery.* Santa Monica, CA: RAND Corporation.

Tarasoff v. Regents of the University of California, 529 P.2d. 553, 118 Cal. Rptr. 129 (1974), *vacated,* 17 Cal. 3d 425, 551 P.2d 334, 131 Cal. Rptr. 14 (1976).

Tedeschi, R. G., & Calhoun, L. G. (2004). A clinical approach to post-traumatic growth. In P. A. Linley & S. Joseph (Eds.), *Positive psychology in practice* (pp. 405–419). Hoboken, NJ: Wiley.

Terry, K. J., & Tallon, J. (2004). *Child sexual abuse: A review of the literature.* Retrieved from http://www.usccb.org/nrb/johnjaystudy/litreview.pdf

Texas Association of Hostage Negotiators. (2003). *Suicide lethality checklist.* Retrieved from www.tahn.org

Thienhaus, O. J., & Piasecki, M. (1998). Assessment of psychiatric patients' risk of violence toward others. *Psychiatric Services, 49,* 1129–1130.

Thomas Nelson Publishers (1987). *New American Bible.* Boston, MA: Benziger.

Tishler, C. L., Gordon, L. B., & Landry-Meyer, L. (2000). Managing the violent patient: A guide for psychologists and other mental health professionals. *Professional Psychology: Research and Practice, 31*(1), 34–41.

Tjaden, P., & Thoennes, N. (2000). *Full report of the prevalence, incidence and consequences of violence against women: Findings from the National Violence Against Women Survey.* Washington, DC: U.S. Department of Justice.

Toray, T. (2004). The human-animal bond and loss: Providing support for grieving clients. *Journal of Mental Health Counseling, 26,* 244–259.

Tower, L. E. (2006). Barriers in screening women for domestic violence: A survey of social workers, family practitioners, and obstetrician-gynecologists. *Journal of Family Violence, 21,* 245–257.

Tower, M. (2007). Intimate partner violence and the health care response: A postmodern critique. *Health Care for Women International, 28,* 438–452.

Towl, G. J., & Crighton, D. A. (1997). Risk assessment with offenders. *International Review of Psychiatry, 9,* 187–193.

Townsend, L. L. (2006). *Suicide pastoral responses.* Nashville, TN: Abingdon Press.

Tribbensee, N. E., & McDonald, S. J. (2007). *FERPA allows more than you may realize.* Retrieved from http://www.insidehighered.com/views/2007/08/07/ferpa

Trickett, P. K. (2006). Defining child sexual abuse. In M. M. Feerick, J. F. Knutson, P. K. Trickett, & S. M. Flanzer (Eds.), *Child abuse and neglect: Definitions, classifications, and a framework for research* (pp. 123–150). Baltimore, MD: Brookes.

Trippany, R. L., White Kress, V. E., & Wilcoxon, A. S. (2004). Preventing vicarious trauma: What counselors should know when working with trauma survivors. *Journal of Counseling and Development, 82* (1), 31–37.

Trump, K. S. (2009). School emergency planning: Back to basics. *Student Assistance Journal, 1,* 13–17.

Trusty, J., & Brown, D. (2005). Advocacy competencies for professional school counselors. *Professional School Counseling, 8,* 259–265.

Twemlow, S. W. (2001). Interviewing violent patients. *Bulletin of the Menninger Clinic, 65,* 503–521.

Ullman, S. (2003). Social reactions to child sexual abuse disclosures: A critical review. *Journal of Child Sexual Abuse, 12,* 89–121. doi: 101300/J070v1201_05

Ulmer, W. F., Collins, J., & Jacobs, T. O. (2000). *American military culture in the twenty-first century: A report of the CSIS international security program.* Washington, DC: CSIS Press.

United Nations. (1995). *Report on the world's women 1995: Trends and statistics.* New York, NY: Author.

U.S. Department of Education, National Center for Educational Statistics. (2004). Crime and safety in America's public schools: Selected findings from the *School survey on crime and safety* (NCES 2004-370). Retrieved from www.nces.ed.go/ppubs 004/2004370.pdf

U.S. Department of Education, Office of Safe and Drug-Free Schools. (2003). *Practical information on crisis planning: A guide for schools and communities.* Washington, DC: Author.

U.S. Department of Health and Human Services. (2002). Standards for privacy of individually identifiable health information; Final rule. Retrieved from http://www.hhs.gov/ocr/privacy/hipaa/news/2002/combinedregtext02.pdf

U.S. Department of Health and Human Services. (2005a). *Child maltreatment 2003.* Washington, DC: U.S. Government Printing Office.

U.S. Department of Health and Human Services. (2005b). *Health information privacy: When does the Privacy Rule allow covered entities to disclose protected health in-formation to law enforcement officials?* Retrieved from http://www.hhs.gov/ocr/privacy/hipaa/faq/ disclo-sures_for_law_enforcement_purposes/505.html

U.S. Department of Health and Human Services. (2006). *Health information privacy: Can health care information be shared in a severe disaster?* Retrieved from http://www.hhs.gov/ocr/privacy/hipaa/faq/disclosures_in_emergency_situations/960.html

U.S. Department of Health and Human Services. (2007). *Child maltreatment 2005.* Retrieved from www.acf.hhs.gov/programs/cb/pubs/cm05/table3_6.htm

U.S. Department of Health and Human Services. (2008). *Hurricane Katrina bulletin: HI-PAA privacy and disclosures in emergency situations.* Retrieved from www.hhs.gov/ocr/hipaa/KATRINAnHIPAA.pdf

U.S. Department of Health and Human Services. (2009). *Mandatory reporters of child abuse and neglect: State statutes series.* Retrieved from www.childwelfare.gov/systemwide/laws_policies/statutes/manda.cfm

U.S. Department of Health and Human Services. (n.d.). *Health information privacy: Is the HIPAA Privacy Rule suspended during a national or public emergency.* Retrieved from http://www.hhs.g ov/ocr/privacy/hipaa/faq/disclosures_in_emergency_situations/1068.html

U. S. Department of Health and Human Services, Administration on Children, Youth and Families (2009). *Child maltreatment 2007.* Retrieved from http://www.acf.hhs.gov/programs/cb/pubs/cm07/cm07.pdf

U.S. Department of Justice. (2011). *The economic impact of illicit drug use on American society.* U.S. Department of Justice, National Drug Intelligence Center. Product No. 2011-Q0317-002. Washington, DC: Author.

U. S. Department of Justice. (2012a). *Sexual assault.* Retrieved from http://www.ovw.usdoj.gov/sexassault.htm

U. S. Department of Justice. (2012b). *Crime in the United States.* Retrieved from http://www2.fbi.gov/ucr/cius2009/offenses/violent_crime/forcible_rape.html

U.S. Department of Justice, Bureau of Justice Statistics. (2008). *Definitions.* Retrieved from www.ojp.usdoj.gov/bjs/abstract/cvus/definitions.htm#rape_sexual_assault

U.S. Department of Justice, Office for Victims of Crimes. (2006). *OVC fact sheets: The Justice for All Act.* Retrieved from www.ojp.usdoj.gov/ovc/publications/factshts/justforall/welcome.html

U.S. Department of Justice, Office of Violence Against Women. (2004). *A national protocol for sexual assault medical forensic examinations.* Retrieved from www.ncjrs.gov/pdffiles1/ovw/206554.pdf

U.S. Secret Service. (2010). *National Threat Assessment Center: Secret Service school initiative.* Retrieved from http://www.secretservice.gov/NTAC_ssi.shtml

University of South Florida. (2012). *Youth suicide school-based prevention guide.* Retrieved from http://theguide.fmhi.usf.edu/

Urquiza, A. A., Capra, M. M., & Hunter, M. (1990). The impact of sexual abuse: Initial and long-term effects. *Sexually Abused Male: Prevalence, Impact, and Treatment, 1,* 105–135.

Uses and Disclosures of Protected Health Information: General Rules, 45 C.F.R. §164.502 (2002).

Vaillant, L. M. (1997). *Changing character: Short-term anxiety-regulating psychotherapy for restructuring defenses, affects, and attachment.* New York, NY: Basic Books.

van der Kolk, B. A. (1994). The body keeps the score: Memory and the evolving psychobiology of posttraumatic stress. *Harvard Review of Psychiatry, 1,* 253–265.

van der Kolk, B. A., & van der Hart, O. (1989). Pierre Janet and the breakdown of adaptation in psychological trauma. *American Journal of Psychiatry, 146,* 1530–1540.

VandeCreek, L., Knapp, S., & Herzog, C. (1987). Malpractice risks in the treatment of dangerous patients. *Psychotherapy: Theory, Research, & Practice, 24,* 145–153.

Vandiver, D., & Kercher, G. (2004). Offender and victim characteristics of registered female sexual offenders in Texas: A proposed typology of female sexual offenders. *Sexual Abuse: A Journal of Research and Treatment, 16,* 121–137.

Veterans Administration (VA) and Department of Defense (DoD) Clinical Practice Guideline Working Group. (2010). *Management of post-traumatic stress.* Washington, DC: VA Office of Quality and Performance.

Villalba, J. (2014). Individuals and families of Latin descent. In D. G. Hays & B. T. Erford (Eds.), *Developing multicultural counseling competence: A systems approach* (2nd ed., pp. 277–300). Boston, MA: Pearson.

Vlahov, D., Galea, S., Ahern, J., Rudenstine, S., Resnick, H., Kilpatrick, D. & Crum, R. M. (2006). Alcohol drinking problems among New York City residents after the September 11 terrorist attacks. *Substance Use and Misuse, 41,* 1295–1311. doi: 10.1080/10826080600754900

Vlahov, D., Galea, S., Resnick, H., Ahern, J., Boscarino, J. A., Bucuvalas, M., Gold, J., & Kilpatrick, D. (2002). Increased consumption of cigarettes, alcohol, and marijuana among Manhattan residents after the September 11 terrorist attacks. *American Journal of Epidemiology, 155,* 988–996.

Walfish, S., Barnett, J. E., Marlyere, K., & Zielke, R. (2010). "Doc, there's something I have to tell you": Patient disclosure to their psychotherapist of unprosecuted murder and other violence. *Ethics and Behavior, 20,* 311–323.

Walker, L. E. (1979). *The battered woman.* New York, NY: Harper and Row.

Walker, L. E. (1994). *Abused women and survivor therapy: A practical guide for the psychotherapist.* Washington, DC: American Psychological Association.

Walker, L. E. (1999). Psychology and domestic violence around the world. *American Psychologist, 54,* 21–29.

Walker, L. E. (2006). Battered woman syndrome: Empirical findings. *Annals of the New York Academy of Sciences, 1087,* 142–157.

Walsh, F. (1998). *Strengthening family resilience* (2nd ed.). New York, NY: Guilford Press.

Walsh, F. (2012). *Normal family processes: Growing diversity and complexity.* New York, NY: Guilford Press.

Walsh, F., & McGoldrick, M. (Eds.). (2004). *Living beyond loss: Death in the family* (2nd ed.) New York, NY: Norton.

Wang, C. C. (2007). Person-centered therapy with a bereaved father. *Person-Centered Journal, 14,* 73–97.

Warshaw, R. (1988). *I never called it rape: The Ms. report on recognizing, fighting and surviving date and acquaintance rape.* New York, NY: Harper and Row.

Watlington, C. G., & Murphy, C. M. (2006). The roles of religion and spirituality among African American survivors of domestic violence. *Journal of Clinical Psychology, 62,* 837–857.

Weeks, K. M. (2001). Family-friendly FERPA policies: Affirming parental partnerships. *New Directions for Student Services, 94,* 39–50.

Welfel, E. R. (2013). *Ethics in counseling & psychotherapy* (5th ed.). Belmont, CA: Brooks/Cole.

Werner-Wilson, R. J., Zimmerman, T. S., & Whalen, D. (2000). Resilient response to battering. *Contemporary Family Therapy, 22,* 161–188.

West, C. M., Kanter, G. K., & Jasinski, J. L. (1998). Sociodemographic predictors and cultural barriers to help-seeking behaviors by Latina and Anglo American battered women. *Violence and Victims, 13,* 361–375.

Westcott, H. L., & Jones, D. P. (1999). The abuse of disabled children. *Journal of Child Psychology and Psychiatry, and Allied Disciplines*, 40, 497–506.

West-Olatunji, C., & Goodman, R. D. (2011). Entering communities: Social justice oriented disaster response counseling. *Journal of Humanistic Counseling, 50*, 172–182.

Whiffen, V. E., & MacIntosh, H. B. (2005). Mediators of the link between childhood sexual abuse and emotional distress. *Journal of Trauma, Violence, & Abuse, 6*, 24–39. doi: 10.1177/1524838004272543

Williams, R., & Vinson, D. C. (2001). Validation of a single screening question for problem drinking. *Journal of Family Practice, 50*, 307–312.

Wilson, M., & Daly, M. (1992). *Homicide*. New York, NY: Aldine de Gruyter.

WomensHealth.gov. (2012). *Date rape drugs fact sheet*. Retrieved from http://www.womenshealth.gov/publications/our-publications/fact-sheet/date-rape-drugs.pdf

Worden, J. W. (2001). *Children and grief: When a parent dies*. New York, NY: Guilford Press.

Worden, J. W. (2009). *Grief counseling and grief therapy: A handbook for the mental health practitioner* (4th ed.). New York, NY: Springer.

Wozny, D. A. (2007). "Living the ACA Code of Ethics" project: Integrating ethics in counselors' personal lives. In G. R. Walz & R. K. Yep (Eds.), *VISTAS 2007*. Alexandria, VA: American Counseling Association.

Wunsch-Hitzig, R., Plapinger, J., Draper, J., & del Campo, E. (2002). Calls for help after September 11: A community mental health hotline. *Journal of Urban Health: Bulletin of the New York Academy of Medicine, 79*, 417–428.

Young, M. E. (2008). *Learning the art of helping: Building blocks and techniques* (4th ed.). Upper Saddle River: NJ: Pearson Education.

Young, M. S., Harford, K. L., Kinder, B., & Savell, J. K. (2007). The relationship between childhood sexual abuse and adult mental health among undergraduates: Victim gender doesn't matter. *Journal of Interpersonal Violence, 22*, 1315–1331. doi: 10.1177/0886260507304552

Zalaquett, C., Carrión, I., & Exum, H. (2009). Counseling survivors of national disasters: Issues and strategies for a diverse society. In J. Webber (Ed.), *Terrorism, trauma, and tragedies: A counselor's guide to preparing and responding*. Alexandria, VA: American Counseling Association.

INDEX

AA. *See* Alcoholics Anonymous (AA)
Aarons, J. D., 234
AAS. *See* American Association of Suicidology (AAS)
Aasland, O. G., 138
ABC-X model of crisis, 5–6, 10
Abeling, S., 211
Ability, and CSA, 221
Absenteeism, 39
Abuse. *See* Child sexual abuse (CSA); Substance abuse
ACA. *See* American Counseling Association (ACA)
ACA Code of Ethics, 210, 211, 212
Accountability, for IPV
    See also Health Insurance Portability and Accountability Act
    batterer intervention and, 183–184
Acierno, R., 129
Ackard, D. M., 174
Acquaintance rape, 196
ACSA. *See* American School Counselor Association (ACSA)
Acute battering incident
    of cycle of violence theory, 160
Acute grief, 4
Acute risks, for suicide, 93–96
Acute Stress Disorder (ASD), 4, 14
    diagnostic criteria for, 14
Acute stressors, 8–9
Adamson, Nicole, 281
Adaptation, 15–16
    concept of, 6
    defined, 15
    by families, 16
    within military families, 339–340
Adaptational theory, 5
Addiction, 131. *See also* Substance abuse; Substance dependence
    counseling, 246
Adjustment Disorder, 311, 312
Adler, L. E., 330, 333, 334
Adolescents
    and young adults, dating violence among, 173–174
Adults
    and adolescents, dating violence among, 173–174
Adversity, 16
Afifi, A. A., 337
African Americans
    eye contact in counseling, 68–69
    IPV prevalence, 167
AFSP. *See* American Foundation for Suicide Prevention (AFSP)

Against Our Will (Brownmiller), 194
Age, and CSA, 221
Ahmad, S., 211
Ahrens, C. E., 211
Ainsworth, M., 186, 300, 326
Al-ANON, 152
Albano, S., 330
Alcohol and other drug (AOD) addiction, 132
Alcoholics Anonymous (AA), 151–152
Alcoholism. *See also* Substance abuse; Substance dependence
    characteristics, 130
    concept of, 130
    defined, 131
    stages, 130–131
Alcohol Use Disorders Identification Test (AUDIT), 138–139
Aldridge, H., 87
Alexander, D. A., 251
Alexandersson, A., 130
Alfred P. Murrah Federal Building bombing in 1995 (Oklahoma City), 8, 13
Allan, W. D., 112
Allen, A., 220
Allen, M., 277
Altman, B., 207
Alvarez, A., 169
Alvarez, W., 206
Alvarez-Conrad, J., 207
AMA. *See* American Medical Association (AMA)
Amar, A. F., 174
American Association of Suicidology (AAS), 86, 90, 92
American Counseling Association (ACA), 18, 48, 56, 61, 66, 190, 210, 211, 212, 231
    Code of Ethics, 56, 58, 59, 61, 62, 63
American Foundation for Suicide Prevention (AFSP), 86
American Medical Association (AMA), 131
American Pet Products Association, 308
American Psychiatric Association (APA), 4, 13, 14, 20, 101, 137, 195, 200, 239, 301, 312
American Red Cross, 20, 47, 63, 65, 285
American School Counselor Association (ACSA), 20, 121, 271, 272, 277, 283, 285
American Society of Addiction Medicine (ASAM), 141–142
AMT. *See* Anxiety management training (AMT) programs

Anda, R. F., 224
Anderegg, M., 42
Anderson, S. A., 189
Andriessen, K., 89
Anger
    externalized, 300
    grief and, 300–301
    management, IPV and, 188
Angermeyer, M. C., 119
Anger-motivated rape, 199
    perpetrators of, 213–214
Angold, A., 130
Anxiety management training (AMT) programs, 207–208
APA. *See* American Psychiatric Association (APA)
Applied Suicide Intervention Skills Training (ASIST), 89
Approach coping, 236, 237
Apter, A., 89, 103
Arias, I., 189
Armour, M., 123
Arredondo, P., 153
Arthur, G. L., 34
Arvanitogiannis, A., 131
ASAM. *See* American Society of Addiction Medicine (ASAM)
Asaro, M. R., 123
ASD. *See* Acute Stress Disorder (ASD)
ASERVIC. *See* Association for Spiritual, Ethical, and Religious Values in Counseling (ASERVIC)
ASIST. *See* Applied Suicide Intervention Skills Training (ASIST)
Assessment. *See also* Self-assessment
    defined, 136
    substance use disorders, 136–137
    suicide intervention, 92–93
Association for Spiritual, Ethical, and Religious Values in Counseling (ASERVIC), 211–212
Asuan-O'Brien, A., 221
Attachment
    described, 16
    intimate, 300
    loss and, 299–301
Attachment theory
    for batterer, 186
Attending skills, 68–72
    body position, 70
    eye contact, 68–69
    silence, 71–82
    vocal tone, 70–71
Attitudes, suicide prevention and, 90–91
Auchterlonie, J. L., 329, 332

AUDIT. *See* Alcohol Use Disorders
  Identification Test (AUDIT)
Austin, K. M., 60, 62
Australian Academy of Medicine, 302
Avery-Leaf, S., 174
Avoidance-focused coping, 15
Avoidant coping, 236, 237
Awareness
  death, 295–297
Ayers, K., 337

Babor, T. F., 138, 139
Bagalman, E., 331
Bahraini, N., 338
Bain, M. W., 332
Baker, C. K., 182
Baker, Scott, 248
Balk, D. E., 321
Ballard, M. B., 252
Bandura, A., 132
Barbee, P. W., 59
Barboza, S., 53
Barker, L. H., 333
Barnett, J. E., 111
Barrett, W., 220
Barron, C. T., 35
Basena, M., 219
Basic listening sequence
  open and closed questions, 72–76
  reflecting skills, 76–83
Basten, C., 206
Bates, L., 186
Battaglia, T. A., 175
Batten, S. V., 331, 336
Batterer intervention, 182–184
  accountability, 183–184
  attachment theory, 186
  challenges in, 187–189
  completion rates, 189
  feminist-informed cognitive-behavioral
    theory, 187
  financial resources and, 188–189
  moral development theory, 185–186
  power and control theory, 184–185
  safety, 183
  underreporting of IPV incidents,
    187–188
  violence cessation, 183
  vs. anger management programs, 188
Batterer intervention programs (BIPs),
  182
Bazargan, S., 167
Beautrais, A., 89, 103
Beck, A. T., 312
Becker, B., 16
Beckett, J. O., 167
Beck Scale for Suicide Ideation, 100
Bedi, G., 164
Bedi, R. P., 68, 79

Beebe, R. S., 59
Behavior modification, for sex offenders,
  215
Behaviors
  coping, 10, 14–15
  violent, 34
Belamaric, R. J., 170
Belislem, Hayden, 44
Bennett, L., 187, 188
Bereavement, normal *vs.* complicated,
  310–312
Beresford, T. P., 139
Berlin, M., 174, 175
Berliner, L., 219, 220, 221, 224, 233, 234
Berman, A. L., 60, 91, 92
Berry, D. B., 174
Berry, K. D., 333
Bertolote, J., 89, 103
Berzoff, J. N., 295, 297
Best, C. L., 129
Betthauser, L. M., 338
Bezmen, J., 35
Bickman, L., 234
Biema, D. V., 340
Bilyeu, J., 114
Biopsychosocial model
  substance abuse, 133
BIPs. *See* Batterer intervention programs
  (BIPs)
Blake, D. D., 206
Bland, D., 87, 329
Blauner, S. R., 107
Blendon, R. J., 333, 336
Blevins, G. A., 150
Blitz, L. V., 179
Block, R., 224
Blow, F. C., 139
Boals, A., 17, 174, 175, 341
Body position of counselor, 70
Boelen, P. A., 318
Bolger, N., 308
Bonadaptation, 7
Bonanno, G. A., 252, 311
Boomsma, D. I., 131
Booth, B., 339
Borneman, T., 314
Boss, P. G., 2, 6, 7, 8, 9, 10–11, 12, 13, 162,
  303
Bowen, G. L., 339
Bowker, L. H., 170
Bowlby, J., 184, 186, 300–301, 305, 306, 326
Bradley, R., 252
Braithwaite, S., 173
Brausch, A. M., 234
Brems, C., 120
Brende, J. O., 34
Brenner, L. A., 338
Brief therapy
  for service member with TBI, 337–338

Brock, S. E., 280
Brock, S., 280
Bronstone, A., 174, 175
Brosi, M., 62
Brower, K. J., 139
Brown, D., 277
Brown, D. W., 224
Brown, G., 102, 103
Brown, G. K., 312
Brown, Meghan, 155–156
Brown, S. A., 132
Browne, T., 329
Brownmiller, S., 195
Brownridge, D. A., 179
Brunette, M. F., 152
Bryan, E., 277
Bryant, C. D., 307
Bryant, R., 335
Bryant, R. A., 206, 337
Brymer, M. J., 205, 254
Bucciarelli, A., 252
Buckley, James L., 53
Buckley Amendment,. *See* Family
  Educational Rights and Privacy Act
  (FERPA)
Buckman, J., 329
Buelow, G. D., 136
Buelow, S. A., 136
Buffers, concept of, 98
Bureau of Justice Statistics, 111, 115, 195,
  213
Burgess, A. W., 201, 202
Burke, C. T., 308
Burnam, M., 334
Burnout, 39–40
Burns, R. M., 333, 334
Burt, K., 277
Bushatz, A., 334
Butler, R. N., 319
Buttell, F. P., 185, 186, 189
Bylington, R., 53
Byock, I., 309, 310

Cable, S., 330
CACREP. *See* Council for Accreditation
  of Counseling and Related
  Educational Programs (CACREP)
Caetano, R., 167, 170
CAGE, 138, 139
Cahill, M., 189
Calhoun, L. G., 7, 15
Callahan, P., 49, 56, 57, 59
Camacho, J., 180
Campbell, C., 87
Campbell, F., 88, 90, 91
Campise, R., 338
Campos-Outcalt, D., 51
CAMS. *See* Collaborative Assessment for
  Managing Suicide (CAMS)

Cannabinoids, 128
Caplan, Gerald, 4, 5
Capsers, N., 174, 175
Capuzzi, D., 131, 132, 138
Cardiopulmonary resuscitation (CPR), 89
Career counseling, 246
Care management
  suicidal client, 102–104
Carey, R. G., 296
Carmona, J., 221
Carnelley, K. B., 308
Carr, J. L., 114, 123
Carrión, I., 65
Carroll, A., 110, 120, 121
Carsten, G., 183, 187
Carter, D., 277
Caruso, M., 196, 197
Cascardi, M., 174
Cashwell, C., 210, 314
Cashwell, C. S., 212
Castellano, C., 254, 255
Castro, C. A., 329, 332
Catastrophic stressors, 8
Cavaiola, A. A., 56, 123
CBCT. *See* Cognitive-behavioral conjoint therapy (CBCT)
CBI. *See* Counselor burnout inventory (CBI)
CCP. *See* Crisis Counseling Program (CCP)
Center for Mental Health in Schools at UCLA, 272, 276, 285
Center for Sex Offender Management, 214, 217, 241
Center for Substance Abuse Treatment, 92, 152
Centers for Disease Control and Prevention, 86, 115, 157, 159, 166, 173, 204, 337
Cerel, J., 88
Chaffin, M., 224, 233, 234, 236, 237
Chan, K. L., 179
Chandra, A., 331, 333, 334
Chang, C. Y., 160, 180
Chang, H., 189
Chang, J. C., 164, 175, 177
Charles, D. R., 307
Charles, M., 307
Charney, D. S., 206
Chemical dependency counselors, 20
Chemotherapy, for sex offenders, 215
Child abuse hotlines, 23
Child Abuse Prevention and Treatment Act (CAPTA), 222
Child Protective Services (CPS), 219, 220
Children and Grief: When a Parent Dies, 321
Child sexual abuse (CSA)
  coping strategy, 236–237
  cues indicating, 225

cycle of, 223
defining, 222–223
incidence rates, 220
initial disclosure for, 226–228
nonoffending parents in treatment of, 236
perpetrators of, 238–240
prevention of, 220–221
reporting, 231–233
signs and symptoms of, 224
survivors, treatment of, 233–234
victims, intervention strategies for, 224, 226
Chiles, J. A., 91, 102
Chin, D., 221
Cho, S. H., 39
Choi, Kyoung Mi, 290–291
Christensen, J., 330, 333, 334
Christiansen, E. H., 129
Chronic risks, for suicide, 93–96
Chronic stage of alcoholism, 131
Chung, D., 51
Chung, K., 51
Cicchetti, D., 16
Cini, F., 42
CISM. *See* Critical Incident Stress Management (CISM)
Clark, A. H., 180
Clark, J., 48
Clayton, R., 114
Clients
  in crisis, 10, 23–24, 33–34
  ecological factors and, 10–11
  self-referred, dangers of, 32, 34
  stalking counselors, 34
  suicidal, 46, 95
  transportation, 31, 35
  traumatic experiences of, managing reactions to, 29
  violent, 34, 35
Client safety, defined, 144
Clinical mental health counseling, 246
Closed questions, 74–75
  vs. open questions, 75–76
Cocaine, 127
Cocoanut Grove nightclub, fire in, 4, 14, 295
Cognitive-behavioral conjoint therapy (CBCT)
  for PTSD, 336–337
Cognitive-behavioral therapy (CBT), 216, 234
  for complicated grief, 318
  for service member with TBI, 337
Cognitive model
  substance abuse, 132
Cognitive processing therapy (CPT)
  for PTSD, 335–336
Cohen, A., 175

Cohen, C. H., 7, 15
Cohen, E. D., 60, 111
Cohen, G. S., 60, 111
Cohen, J. A., 207, 233, 234, 236
Coifman, K. G., 311
Coley, S. M., 167
Colford, J. E., 56, 123
Coll, K. M., 139
Collaborative Assessment for Managing Suicide (CAMS), 100
Colleges/universities
  emergency preparedness and response in, 289–291
Collings, S. J., 220
Collins, B. G., 10, 13, 55, 58, 111, 112, 122
Collins, J., 329
Collins, R. C., 332
Collins, T. M., 10, 13, 55, 58, 111, 112, 122
Colman, M., 330
Communication. *See also* Listening
  attending skills, 68–71
  body position, 70
  good, 68
  paraphrasing, 76
  vocal tone, 70
Community
  emergency preparedness and response in, 245–264
  loss, 310
  social support from, 12
Community crises, 4
Community Emergency Response Team, 256, 257, 258, 259
Compassion
  death notification with, 349
Compassion fatigue, 39–40
Competencies for Addressing Spiritual and Religious Issues in Counseling, 211–212
Competency(ies)
  suicide prevention and, 90–91
Comprehensive Drug Abuse Prevention and Control Act of 1970, 128
Comprehensive Textbook of Suicidology, 92
Compton, J. A., 330–331
Conditioning model
  substance abuse, 133
Confidentiality, 61–62
  defined, 61
Connors, G. J., 136, 139
Conover, K., 131
Continuing education
  ethical practices and, 48
Co-occurring disorders
  defined, 152
  substance use disorders and, 152–153
Coombs, D., 103

Coping
  ability for, 296
  with ambiguous loss, 303, 305
  avoidance-focused, 15
  behaviors, 10, 14–15
  defined, 14–15
  emotion-focused, 15
  outcomes, 15
  problem-focused, 15
  resources of fortified, 6–7
  strategies, 10
Coping strategy, for CSA, 236–237
Corey, G., 49, 56, 57, 59
Corey, M., 49, 56, 57, 59
Cornell, D. G., 113, 114, 115
Cornette, M. M., 338
Corr, C. A., 309, 321
Corr, D. M., 309
Costello, E. J., 130
Cotting, D. I., 329, 332
Coulter, M., 189
Council for Accreditation of Counseling
    and Related Educational Programs
    (CACREP), 245
  standards for counselors, 246–247
Counseling. *See also* Crisis intervention
  addiction, 246
  career, 246
  clinical mental health, 246
  closed questions, 74–75
  for crisis counselors, 323–326
  crisis intervention as a unique form of,
    18–19
  CSA survivors, 224, 226–228, 233–234
  defined, 18
  difficulties in grief, 322–323
  ethical and legal considerations, 47–66
  family systems, 241
  FERPA and, 54–56
  grief, 293–294, 312–313
  group, 20
  HIPAA and, 51–52
  individual, 20
  in-home, 35
  marriage, couple, and family, 246
  open questions, 72–74
  open *vs.* closed questions, 75–76
  physical safety and crisis, 31–37
  in rural community, 30
  school, 246
  spirituality in, 314
  standards for preparation of, 245–247
  student affairs and college, 246–247
  summaries, 82
  supervision in, 44–45
  Tarasoff v. Regents decision and, 58–59
  traditional, 18–19
Counselor burnout inventory (CBI), 39
Counselor(s)

attending skills, 68–72
body position, 70
boundaries as set by, 34–35
chemical dependency, 20
complications of, responding to crisis,
  25
counseling for crisis, 323–326
crisis, 11
CSA survivors and, 224, 226–228
as culturally sensitive, 29–30
education and supervision, 247
effective responses to emergency by,
  245–264
emergency preparedness by crisis,
  245–264
emotional challenges, 37
empathic, 39
eye contact, 68–69
intervention with military service
    members, 334–340
in IPV shelter, 179
marriage and family, 19
microskills, 67–68
pastoral, 20
pet loss, 309
private practitioners, risks for, 31–32
professional, 19–20
referral mechanisms, 32
reflecting skills, 76–83
relevance of military personnel and
    families to, 327–328
relevance of military population to,
    328–331
response to IPV, 174–182
safety of, 27–37
safety precautions for, 33
school, 20
self-assessment (*See* Professional self-
    assessment)
silence, 71–82
as stalked by clients, 34
vocal tone, 70–71
wellness strategies for, 48
Countertransference, 38–39
Coverdale, J. H., 336
Covered entities, 50
CPR. *See* Cardiopulmonary resuscitation
    (CPR)
CPS. *See* Child Protective Services (CPS)
CPT. *See* Cognitive processing therapy
    (CPT)
Craig, R. J., 130, 131, 132, 136
Crawford, A. M., 112
Creamer, M., 335
Crighton, D. A., 120
Crisis Counseling Program (CCP), 255
Crisis(es). *See also* Crisis intervention;
    Transcrisis
  ABC-X model of, 5–6, 10

clients in, 10, 23–24, 33–34
cognitive-behavioral perspective, 5
in colleges and universities, 289–291
common issues by IPV, 162–164 (*See
    also* Intimate partner violence
    (IPV))
community, 4
complications of counselors
    responding to, 25
contextual factors influencing, 10–11
defined, 1–2
disequilibrium and, 5
Double ABC-X model of, 5–7
ecological factors of client and, 10–11
external stressors causing, 8
fundamentals of working with clients
    in, 23–24
hotline workers and, 22–23
key concepts, 12–17
mitigation and prevention in schools,
    268–670
as occurring, 1
as outcome of precipitating event, 5
planning, 27–28, 271, 276–279
preparedness, 27–28, 272
protecting confidentiality during, 54
relapse and, SUD and, 149–150
research on, 129–130
resilience, 16–17
responses to, 1, 27
response strategies, 12
response team, 28
roles of/collaboration between helping
    professionals during, 19–23
safety and, 27–46
in schools, 267–284
self-assessment of counselor during,
    38
self-care in, 27–46
signs for concern of clients in, 33–34
socioeconomic status and survivors
    of, 30
stressors causing, 8
substance abuse, 142–153, 155–156
in SUD, 142–153
systemic and ecosystemic theories of, 5
team, 271–272
theory, 7–10
written crisis plan implementation in
    schools, 272–276
Crisis intervention. *See also* Psychological
    First Aid (PFA)
  active, 71
  attending skills, 68–72
  basic listening sequence, 72–83
  closed questions, 74–75
  death notifications (*See* Death
    notifications)
  essential skills, 67–83

ethical and legal considerations (*See* Ethical and legal considerations)
local authorities and, 28–30
with low cognitive functioning clients, 110
microskills, 67–68
open questions, 72–74
open *vs.* closed questions, 75–76
overview, 1–2
reflective skills, 71, 76–83
study of, 3
termination in, 63–65
theory, 3–5
as a unique form of counseling, 18–19
as unscheduled, 19
Critical Incident Stress Management (CISM), 254–255
Crockett, W. L., 48
Crosbie-Burnett, M., 171
Crowley, T., 182
Crucial stage of alcoholism, 131
Crump, S., 87
Cui, M., 173
Cullen, F. T., 196
Culture
counselors as sensitive to, 29–30
differences in military, 328–329
grief and, 302
IPV prevalence and, 167–168
Curley-Casey, L., 35
Currier, D., 89, 103
Currier, J. M., 111, 122
Curry, M. A., 173
Curtis, R. C., 139
Cycle of violence theory, 159–160
acute battering incident, 160
honeymoon phase, 160
tension-building phase, 160

Dahlberg, L. L., 219
Dahlgren, L., 121
Daly, M., 179
Dana, R. Q., 150
Dancu, C. V., 206
Dandeker, C., 329
Dang, S. T., 206
Dankwort, J., 189
Dansby-Giles, G., 48
Darby, P. J., 112
Dating violence
among adolescents and young adults, 173–174
Daughhetee, C., 43
Davidson, R. J., 319
Davis, C., 206
Davis, M., 335
Davis, R., 211
Davis, R. E., 162
Day, D. M., 216

Death. *See also* Grief; Mourners
acceptance of, 296–297
awareness movement, 295–297
causes of, 309–310
of child, 306–307
looking for, 305
as marked by different cultures, 302
from natural disasters, 310
notifying students of, 283–284
of parent, 307
process of dying and, 296
of sibling, 307–308
of spouse, 308
stages as experienced of, 295–297
sudden, 295, 310
talking about, 320
Death: The Final Stage of Growth (Kübler-Ross), 295
Death notifications, 343–350
with accurate information, 346–348
in clear and concise language, 348–349
with compassion, 349
debriefing with team members, 350
in elementary school, 344
follow-up, 350
overview, 343
in person and in pairs, 346
practice cases, 350
timeliness of, 346–348
Deblinger, E., 207, 234, 236
Debriefing
in schools after crisis, 280
with team members, after death notification, 350
Decker, M. L., 336
Decker, M. R., 164, 175, 177
Decker, S., 205
De Keijser, J., 318
De la Fuente, J. R., 138
Delbert, E., 114
Del Campo, E., 255
De Luca, R., 223
Demo-Dananberg, L. M., 139
DeNardi, K. A., 236
Department of Veterans Affairs Medical Center, 331
Depressants, 128
Depression
death dealt with by people with, 301
Desire, concept of, 97
Despair, 300
Despenser, S., 31–32, 34
Devilly, G., 335
DeVitis, J. L., 185
DeViva, J. C., 336
Dextromethorphan, 128
DHHS. *See* U.S. Department of Health and Human Services (DHHS)

Diagnostic and Statistical Manual of Mental Disorders (DSM-5), 4, 14, 137
DiClemente, C. C., 139, 140
Diem, C., 111
Dienemann, J., 177
DiGiuseppe, R. A., 206
DiLillo, D., 236
DiMaggio, C., 129
Disability
IPV prevalence and, 172–173
Disasters. *See also* Natural disasters
interventions after, 252–255
responses to, 248–252
timeline for intervening in, 249–250
Disclosure, of CSA, 226–228
Disease (medical) model
substance abuse, 130–131
Disequilibrium, 5
"Disillusionment," 5
Distress, 12
Dixon, C. G., 171, 172
Dixon, L. B., 336
Documentation, 60–61. *See also* Record keeping
Dodgen, C. E., 133
Doherty, N., 220
Doka, K. J., 303, 307, 310, 318
Domestic Abuse Project, 161, 184, 187
Domestic violence, 1, 167
Domestic violence hotlines, 23
Dong, M., 224
Donovan, D. M., 139
Double ABC-X model of crisis, 5–7
Double Trouble, 152
Douglas, U., 189
Doweiko, H. E., 131
Drake, R. E., 152
Drapalski, A. L., 336
Draper, J., 255
Drennan, L., 28
Drug-facilitated sexual assault, 198
Drugs, classification of, 128–129
Drummet, A. R., 330
Drysdale, D., 289
DSM-3, 195
DSM-5, 195
Dube, S. R., 224
Dugan, B., 259
Duluth model, of IPV, 161
Duncan, K., 223
Dunkley, J., 40
Dupont, I., 159
Durkan, L., 277
Dutra, L., 252
Dutton, D., 185, 186
Dutton, M., 188
Dutton, M. A., 170, 189
Duty to consult principle, 58
Duty to protect, 57

Duty to warn, 57, 58, 59
Dykman, R., 237

Earley, P., 104
Earthquakes, 13
  damage from, 256–257
Echterling, L. G., 337
Eckhardt, C., 189
Economic status, stressor events and, 11
Ecosystemic theories of crisis, 5
Ecstasy (3,4-methylenedioxymethamphet
      amine (MDMA)), 128
Eden, J., 337
Education
  suicide prevention and, 89–90
Edwards, C., 51
Egan, G., 68, 70
Eisikovits, Z., 161, 162
Ekleberry, F., 59
Elder abuse
  IPV and, 173
El-Khoury, M. Y., 170
Elliott, B. A., 189
Elliott, D. M., 170, 219, 220, 221
Ellis, A., 187
El-Zanaty, F., 169
EMDR. *See* Eye movement
      desensitization and reprocessing
      (EMDR)
Emergency
  defined, 276
Emotional reaction, to sexual assault,
      202–203
Emotion-focused coping, 15
Emotions. *See also* Feelings
  coping strategies focused on, 10
Empathy, 39
Emshoff, J. G., 182
Enarson, E., 66
Engdahl, B. E., 341
Engel, B., 163, 164, 188
Engel, L., 170
Engstrom, D., 41
Enosh, G., 161, 162
Epps, S., 53
Erbes, C. R., 330–331, 341
Erford, B. T., 113
Erikson, E. H., 319
Erkanli, A., 130
Eronen, M., 119
Escape routes, 34, 35
Espelage, D. L., 174
Essex, N. L., 53
Estell, D. B., 121
Ethical and legal considerations, 47–66
  confidentiality, 61–62
  documentation and record keeping,
      60–61
  FERPA, 52–56

HIPAA, 49–52
  informed consent, 62–63
  negligence and malpractice, 60
  overview, 47
  primary prevention
    continuing education, 48
    supervision and peer consultation,
      48–49
    wellness, 48
  spiritual and multicultural
      considerations, 65–66
  Tarasoff v. Regents decision, 56–59
  termination in crisis intervention, 63–65
Ethnicity
  IPV intervention and, 165–170
Ethyl alcohol, 127
Eustress, 12
Evans, Amanda, 110
Evans, D. R., 79, 81
Everly, G. S., 251, 252, 254
Ewing, J. A., 139
Ewing v. Goldstein, 57
Exposure therapy, 207, 234
Exum, H., 65
Eye contact, 68–69
Eye movement desensitization and
      reprocessing (EMDR), 207

Faith-based practices, 313
Faith development theory (FDT), 315
  stages, 315–316
Falk, D. R., 189
Falloon, I. R. H., 336
Fallot, R. D., 211
Family Educational Rights and Privacy
      Act (FERPA), 52–56
  crisis counseling and, 54–56
  described, 53
  HIPAA and, interaction between, 55
  impact of, 53–54
Family(ies)
  adaptation by, 16
  adaptation within military, 339–340
  hostage situations and, 264
  military, TBI and, 334
  stress associated with military
      deployment, 332–333
  supporting military, 338–339
  in treatment of PTSD, 336–337
Family systems counseling, 241
Farmer, E. M. Z., 121
Farmer, T. W., 121
Farrington, D. P., 112
Farrow, T. L., 87
Farrow, V. A., 333
Fatigue
  compassion, 39–40
FBI. *See* Federal Bureau of Investigation
      (FBI)

FDT. *See* Faith development theory (FDT)
Fear, N., 329
Federal Bureau of Investigation (FBI),
      111, 112, 193
Federal Emergency Management Agency
      (FEMA), 28, 31, 247, 268, 273, 274,
      277, 279, 280, 285
Feelings
  grieving process and, 297
  of loss, 293
  reflecting, in counseling, 78–81
Feeny, N., 207
Feldman, D., 254
Felitti, V. J., 224
FEMA. *See* Federal Emergency
      Management Agency (FEMA)
Female offenders, treatment of, 241, 243
Female perpetrators
  of child sexual abuse, 240
  literature on, 240
  male-coerced, 240
  predisposed, 240
  teacher/lover, 240
Female-to-male violence, 170–171
Feminist-informed cognitive-behavioral
      theory
  for batterer, 187
Fendrich, M., 129
Ferenschack, M., 335
FERPA. *See* Family Educational Rights
      and Privacy Act (FERPA)
Ferrell, B., 314
Few, A. L., 179
FICA assessment tool, 314, 315
Fichtner, C. G., 215
Fiduccia, B. W., 172
Field, C. A., 167, 170
Figley, C. R., 40, 107
Fincham, F. D., 173
Finkelhor, D., 221, 223
Finley, E., 175
Fire. *See also* Wildfires
  in Cocoanut Grove nightclub, 4, 14, 295
  residential, 260–261
First, M., 221
Fisher, B. S., 196
Fitzgerald, H., 280
Flaherty, J. A., 129
Flannery, R. B., 35
Flavin, D. K., 131
Fleming, M. F., 135
Fletcher, S., 335
Floods, 13, 257
  dealing with, 259–260
Flowers, L., 159
Flynn, B. W., 254
Foa, E., 206, 335
Foa, E. B., 206, 207, 208, 335
Focusing summaries, 82

Follow-up
  death notification, 350
Forbes, D., 335
Forensic inpatient units
  risks for worker in, 35
Forrester, A., 110, 120, 121
Fortier, M. A., 236
Foss, L. L., 170
Fothergill, A., 66
Fowler, J. W., 315, 316
Fox, J. A., 159
Fox, S., 307
Foy, D. W., 180
France, K., 163, 164
Frances, A., 195
Franiuk, R., 196
Frankl, V., 319
Frasier, P. Y., 164, 175, 177
Frayne, S., 332
Frazier, W., 48
Freeman, N. J., 240
Freud, S., 5, 295, 326
Friedman, M. J., 336
Friedrich, B., 234
Friedrich, W., 224
Frotteurism, 195. *See also* Sexual assault
Frude, N., 237
F-5 tornado, 13
Fugate, M., 163, 164, 188
Fuller, K. M., 59

Gaffey, K. J., 236
Galea, S., 129, 252
Gamino, L. A., 63
Gansei, D., 41
Gary, J., 185
Gatekeeper strategy
  of suicide prevention, 89–90
Gelles, R. J., 189
Gender, and CSA, 221
General adaptation syndrome, 12
General crisis intervention hotlines for
      youth, 23
General systems model
  substance abuse, 132
Genetic models
  substance abuse, 131
Gennaro, S., 174
George, W., 150
Gerber, M. M., 17, 174, 175, 341
Gerbert, B., 174, 175
Ghahramanlou-Holloway, M., 338
Ghesquiere, A., 312
Gibbs, D. A., 332, 333, 336
Gibson, L. E., 252
Giles, F. L., 48
Giles, W. H., 224
Gillihan, S., 335
Gjelsvik, A., 167

Gladding, S. T., 19, 61
Glass, N., 177
Glasser, W., 187
Goddard, C., 164
Goins, S., 196
Goldula, D., 42
Gondolf, E., 188
Goodman, L., 164, 188
Goodman, L. A., 170
Goodman, R. D., 30
Goodwin, D. W., 131
Gordon, L. B., 34, 110, 117, 119
Gould, M. S., 89, 97, 103
Grace, D., 341
Grafanki, S., 42
Granello, D. H., 66, 87, 90, 92, 99, 104
Granello, P. F., 66, 87, 90, 92, 99, 104
Graney, Beth, 3, 17–18
Grant, M., 138
Grant, R., 258
Grass, G. A., 339
Grass, S. R., 339
Greemnwald, E., 207
Green, E. J., 159, 234
Green, T., 329
Greenberg, L. S., 78
Greenberg, N., 329
Greene, A., 219
Greene, J., 252
Greenstone, J. L., 163
Grief, 293–326. *See also* Bereavement;
      Mourners
  anger associated with, 300–301
  of children, 320–321
  cognitive-behavioral therapy for
      complicated, 318
  concept of, 303
  counseling, 293–294, 312–313
  cultural similarities and, 302
  delayed, 298–299, 302
  of depressed people, 301
  disenfranchised, 303–305
  dynamics of process of, 313
  family interventions and, 321
  feelings and process of, 297
  group support for, 319–320
  historical perspectives, 293–295
  interventions for, 312–321
  numbness and, 301
  overview, 293
  pain of, 298
  reactions, 293
  restoring life's meaning,
      313–317
  sibling, 307–308
  as subjective experience, 301, 318
  talking about death and, 320
  task model of process of, 298
  time and, 301

  understanding, 301–305
  yearning and, 300
Griffin, R. M., 171, 172
Grigsby, N., 163, 175, 178, 179
Groff, J. Y., 167
Grossman, F., 221
Grossman, L. S., 215
Gross v. Allen, 57
Groth, A. N., 196, 199, 213, 214, 215, 216,
      241
Group support
  for grief, 319–320
Group therapy, 208, 209
Gruber, M. J., 312
Guldin, M., 312
Gusman, F. D., 206
Guthrie. K. A., 336, 337
Guthrie, R., 337
Gutierrez, P. M., 338
Guze, S. B., 131

Haas, A., 89, 103
Haas, D. M., 332
Haj-Yahia, M. M., 169, 170
Hakkanen, H., 119, 121
Halifax, J., 325
Hallucinogens, 128
Halon, R., 221
Halpern, C. T., 173
Halpern, J., 335
Hamblen, J. L., 252
Hamdani S., 131
Han, B., 333, 334
Hankin, C., 332
Hann, N. E., 129
Hanson, R. F., 174
Harford, K. L., 221
Harm reduction
  substance use disorders, 150–151
Harper, F. D., 252
Harper, J. A., 252
Harrington, J. A., 90, 103, 106
Harris. J. I., 341
Hart, C. L., 129
Hart, Susan, 55
Hartig, Nadine, 324–325
Hartke, K. L., 112
Hartman, C. R., 201
*The Harvard Medical School Guide to Suicide
      Assessment and Intervention*, 91
Harvey, A. G., 206
Harvill, R., 208, 209
Hassouneh-Phillips, D., 173
Hatton, R., 122, 123
Haugaard, J. J., 222
Havel, V., 313
Havel, Vaclav, 313
Hawkins, S., 331, 333, 334
Hayden, S., 334, 338

Hays, D. G., 159, 160, 180
Headley, Jessica, 325–326
Health care, 50
Health care industry, 49–50. *See also*
   Health Insurance Portability and
   Accountability Act
Health care provider
   defined, 50
   IPV screening and, 174–175
Health Insurance Portability and
   Accountability Act of 1996 (HIPAA),
   47, 49–52
   crisis counseling and, 51–52
   described, 49–50
   FERPA and, interaction between, 55
   impact of, 50–51
   social media and, 51
Hearn, M. T., 79, 81
Hearst-Ikeda, D., 206
Heat waves, 258
Hebert, B. B., 252
Heckman, J. P., 211
Hedlund, J., 139
Held, T., 336
Hembree, E., 207
Hendin, H., 89, 103
Herbert, P. B., 58
Herlihy, B., 49, 50, 53, 54, 56, 57, 58, 59, 66
Herman, C. P. Z, 150
Herman, J. L., 261
Hermansen, L., 131
Hernandez, P., 41
Hernandez G., 131
Heroin, 127
Hester, R. K., 130, 131, 132, 133
Hettema, J. E., 143
Hetzel-Riggin, M. D., 234
Hewitt, S. K., 241
Hiebert-Murphy, D., 179
Higgins-Biddle, J. C., 139
Hill, Reuben, 3, 4, 6, 7, 10, 107
Hillbrand, M., 120
Hines, D. A., 169, 170, 171, 223
Hinman. J., 211
HIPAA. *See* Health Insurance Portability
   and Accountability Act of 1996
   (HIPAA)
Hispanics
   IPV prevalence, 167
Hissett, J., 334, 337
Hoffman, Rachel M., 46, 140
Hoge, C. W., 329, 332
Holland, J. M., 111, 122
Holmstrom, L. L., 201, 202
Holt, M. K., 174
Holtzworth-Munroe, A., 186, 189
Homicide, 310
   assessment, 112–113
   defined, 111

intervention, 110–125
   overview, 85
   referral and, 119
   risk factors, 112–113
   school, violence and, 113–115
   survivor needs, 122–124
   threat level assessment, 116–119
   treatment options, 119–122,
      123–124
   workplace, 115–116
Homish, D. L., 112
Honeymoon phase
   of cycle of violence theory, 160
Hooyman, N. R., 302
Hopper, J., 221
Horn, O., 329
Horne, C., 122
Horne, S., 167, 168
Horner, J., 49, 50, 51
Horowitz, M. J., 206
Horvath, A. O., 79
Horwitz, A. V., 312
Hoshmand, A., 327, 334, 338
Hoshmand, L. T., 327, 334, 338
Hostage situations, 261–263
   commercial, 263–264
   crisis stage of, 261, 262
   family, 264
   as responded to, 248–252
   stages of, 261, 262
Hotline workers, in crisis situations,
      22–23
Hotopf, M., 329
House, R., 330, 333, 334
Howard, D. E., 174
Howard , J. L., 329
Hoyert, D., 293
Hoyt, W. T., 312
Htchins, B. C., 121
Huebner, A. J., 339
Huguet, N., 332, 338
Hull, L., 329
Human resiliency
   in aftermath of Katrina, 17–18
Humphrey, K. M., 318
Humphreys, C., 161, 164, 179
Hunt, S., 220
Hunter, J., 114
Huprich, S. K., 59
Hurricane Floyd, 13
Hurricane Katrina, 1, 2, 11, 12, 17, 129,
      258
   human resiliency in the aftermath of,
      17–18
Hurricanes, 258
Huss, Magnus, 130
Hussein, E. M., 169
Hyman, R., 177
Hysteria, 5

IEDs. *See* Improvised explosive
   devices (IEDs)
Immigrants/refugees
   IPV prevalence and, 169–170
Improvised explosive devices (IEDs), 337
Inadequate pattern, of situational
   perpetrators, 239
Incapacitation, for sex offenders, 216
Infertility
   as ambiguous loss, 303–304
   as internal stressor, 7
   miscarriage and, 303–304
Information accuracy of death
   notification, 346–348
Informed consent, 62–63
In-home counseling, 35
Inman, A., 169
"In pairs" death notification, 346
"In person" death notification, 346
Insel, B., 311
Institute of Medicine (IOM), 328, 337
International Association for Suicide
   Prevention, 101
Interpersonal-psychological theory of
   suicide, 338
Intervention model
   substance abuse, 143–144
Interventions
   after act of terrorism, 252–255
   after disaster, 252–255
   family, 321
   for grief/loss, 312–321
   homicide, 110–125
   for PTSD with military personnel,
      335–336
   substance abuse, 145–149
   suicide, 86–110
Interviews
   suicide risk assessment, 99–101
Intimate partner violence (IPV),
      157–190
   anger management and, 188
   batterer intervention (*See* Batterer
      intervention)
   common crisis issues, 162–164
   cycle of violence theory, 159–160
   dating violence among adolescents and
      young adults, 173–174
   disability status, 172–173
   Duluth model, 161
   elder abuse, 173
   emotional consequences, 180–182
   examples, 168
   female-to-male violence, 170–171
   financial resources and, 188–189
   immediate safety, establishing, 163
   immigrant status and, 169–170
   learned helplessness theory, 161–162
   LGBT violence, 171–172

lifetime victimization rates, 166
in movies, 162
overview, 157–159
patriarchal family structure and, 169
physical and emotional abuse (case
    study), 158–159
physical injury, 163
police intervention, requirement of,
    163–164
race/ethnicity considerations, 165–170
religiosity and, 170
response to disclosure, 177
safety and harm reduction planning,
    178–179
screening for, 174–177
self-awareness assessment, 164
shelters, opportunities and challenges,
    179–180
socioeconomic status and, 169
in special populations, 165–174
underreporting of incidents, 187–188
IOM. See Institute of Medicine. (IOM)
IPV. See Intimate partner violence (IPV)
Iversen, A., 329
Ivey, A. E., 67, 68, 70, 72, 73, 76, 79, 81
Ivey, M. B., 67, 68, 70, 72, 73, 76, 79

Jackson, D. A., 302
Jackson-Cherry, L., 340, 341, 348
Jacobs, A. K., 205, 254
Jacobs, D. G., 92
Jacobs, E., 208, 209
Jacobs, T. O., 329
Jacobson, G. R., 137
Jacoby, A. M., 338
James, R. K., 2, 4, 5, 22, 74, 81, 111, 143,
    144, 249, 250, 277
Jasinski, J. L., 167
Jaycox, L., 206, 331, 334
Jaycox, L. H., 333, 334
Jellinek, E. M., 130, 131
Jensen, A. B., 312
Jensen, D. G., 49
Jensen, P. S., 332
Jobes, D. A., 91, 94, 100, 102, 103, 338
Johnson, K., 267
Johnson, K. R., 69
Johnson, L., 338
Johnson, P., 51
Johnson, R. E., 332, 333, 336
Johnson, R. J., 219
Johnson, T. C., 224
Johnston, S. M., 234
Joiner, T. E., 91, 97, 102, 338
Jones, D. P, 221
Jones, J., 257, 258
Jones, K. D., 57
Jongsma, A. E., 112, 120, 121
Joo, Y., 51

Jordan, J. R., 107
Joseph, S., 15
Juhnke, G. A., 139
Juhnke, Gerald, 95

Kabat-Zinn, J., 319
Kalafat, J., 97
Kaloupek, D. G., 206
Kanan, L. M., 114
Kane, D., 254
Kanter, G. K., 167
Kaplan, M., 332, 338
Kashani, J. H., 112
Kaukinen, C., 167
Keane, T. M., 206
Keeler, G., 130
Keene, S., 53
Keller, E. L., 159, 175
Kellogg, N. D., 224
Kennedy, J., 211
Kennedy, M. C., 332
Kent, M., 335
Kercher, G., 240
Kerr, M. M., 19, 267, 270, 271
Kessler, R. C., 312
Kia-Keating, M., 221
Kilpatrick, D. G., 129, 194, 206
Kinder, B., 221
Kishor, S., 169
Kissinger, D., 39
Kistenmacher, B. R., 189
Kleespies, P. M., 93
Kleinplatz, P. L., 195
Klott, J., 112, 120, 121
Knapp, S., 58
Knox, K. S., 274
Koffman, R. L., 329, 332
Kogas, S., 87
Kohlberg, L., 184, 185, 315
Kolodinsky, J. M., 183, 187
Koopmans, J. R., 131
Koss, M. P., 194
Kovac, S. H., 87
Kowalski, R. M., 113
Kozu, J., 167, 168, 170
Kramer, A., 163, 175
Kramer, J., 302
Kraus, J., 337
Kraus, R. F., 114
Kress, Victoria E., 29, 178
Kressin, N., 332
Krug, E. G., 219
Ksir, C., 129
Kubany, E. S., 206
Kubler-Ross, E., 295, 296, 297, 301
Kullgren, G., 121
Kulwicki, A., 169
Kung, H., 293
Kupper, L. L., 173, 332, 333, 336

Laajasalo, T., 119, 121
Laanan, F. S., 259
Lachs, M. S., 173
La Greca, A. M., 130
La Guardia, Amanda C., 98
Laidlaw, T. M., 336
Lambie, G. W., 39
Landau, J., 334, 337
Landis, L., 163, 164, 188
Landry-Meyer, L., 34, 110, 117, 119
Language of death notification, 348–349
Lanning, K., 223, 238, 239
Lara-Cinisomo, S., 333, 334
Largen, M. A., 193
Larkin, G. L., 170
Larson, D. R., 312
Larson, M., 183, 187
Laux, J. M., 110
Laws, D. R., 215
Lawson, G., 40, 48
Lawson, G. W., 129
Layne, C. M., 205, 254
Lazarus, R. S., 10, 15
Le, T. V., 341
Leadership roles
    in MCRTs, 247–248
Learned helplessness theory, of IPV,
    161–162
    alternatives to, 161–162
Leary, M. R., 113
Lee, R., 196
Lee, R. K., 168
Lee, S. M., 39
Lee, V. V., 113
Legal considerations. See Ethical and
    legal considerations
Lemberg, J., 167
Lesbian, gay, bisexual, and transgender
    (LGBT), 157, 158, 165
    violence, 171–172
Leung, W., 179
Levesque, D. A., 189
Leviton, S. C., 163
Lewellen, Cheryl, 118
Lewis, C. S., 298, 301
Lewis, J. A., 150
Lewis, N. K., 164
Lewis, S., 280
LGBT. See Lesbian, gay, bisexual, and
    transgender (LGBT)
Li, G., 129
Li, S., 219
Liang, B., 164
Licensed Professional Counselor (LPC), 17
Liebschutz, J. M., 175
Life-skills training, for sex offenders, 215
Lincoln, A., 330, 331, 333, 339, 340
Lindemann, Erich, 4, 295, 300
Lindhorst, T., 164, 175

Linley, P., 15
Lippman, J. T., 236
Lipsky, S., 167, 170
Listening
  asking open/closed questions and,
    72–76
  basic sequence of, 72–73
  summarizing and, 81–83
Litz, B., 311
Liu, F., 332
Living Works, 89
Local authorities
  safety and, 28–30
Loeb, T., 221
Loeber, R., 112
Longpre, R. E., 207
Lord, H., 343
Lord, J., 318
Lorenzon, D., 163, 175
Loss
  ambiguous, 303–305
  attachment and, 299–301
  feelings of, 293
  interventions for, 312–321
  of pets, 308–309
Lou, K., 338
Louis, D., 224
Lozano, R., 219
LPC. See Licensed Professional Counselor
    (LPC)
Lutenbacher, M., 175
Luthar, S. S., 16
Lyall, M., 110, 120, 121

MacDermid, S., 330–331
MacIan, P. S., 48
MacIntosh, H. B., 226
Macklin, M. L., 207
MacLachlan, C.Z, 183, 187
MacNeil, G. A., 39, 40, 43
Macy, R.J., 164, 175
MADD. See Mothers Against Drunk
    Driving (MADD)
Madrid, P. A., 258
Madsen, L. H., 179
Main, M., 223
Maisto, S. A., 136
Major Depressive Disorder, 311, 312
Male-coerced female perpetrators, 240
Male perpetrators
  of child sexual abuse, 238–240
  preferential perpetrators, 239–240
  situational perpetrators, 238–239
Malley-Morrison, K., 169, 170, 171
Malone, A., 51
Malpractice, 60
Mancini, A., 311
Mancini, J. A., 339
Mann, J. J., 89, 103

Mann, M. A., 336
Mannarino, A. P., 207, 233, 234, 236
Mansfield, A. K., 332
Marijuana, 127
Marino, D. C., 35
Marion-Jones, M., 87
Maris, R. W., 91, 92, 99
Marlatt, G., 150
Marlyere, K., 111
Marques, J. K., 216
Marriage, couple, and family counseling,
    246
Marriage and family counselors, 19
Marrington, P., 234
Marshall, W. L., 215
Martin, J., 338
Martin, J. A., 339
Martin, L., 331, 333, 334
Martin, S. L., 164, 173, 175, 177, 332, 333,
    336
Martis, B., 215
Martz, Erin, 63
Maryland State Police, 345
Mascari, J. B., 48
Maslow's hierarchy of needs, 4, 29
Masson, R., 208, 209
MAST. See Michigan Alcoholism
    Screening Test (MAST)
Masten, A. S., 16, 17
Mateer, C. A., 337
Mathews, R., 240
Matthews, J. K., 240
Mattson, S., 170
Mawdsley, R. D., 54
Mayo Clinic, 122
McCausland, M. P., 201
McClarren, G. M., 57
McCloskey, K., 163, 175, 178, 179
McCloskey, K. A., 238
McCollum, M., 123
McConnell, A., 28
McCorkle, D., 179
McCormick, J. S., 282
McCubbin, H. I., 6, 7, 9, 107
McDaniel, J., 271
McDavis, R. J., 153
McDonald, S. J., 55
McFarland, H., 332, 338
McFarlane, A., 335
McFarlane, J., 167
McFarlane, J. M., 167
McGlothlin, Jason, 24–25
McGoldrick, M., 306, 326
McGurk, D., 329, 332
McHugo, G. J., 152
McKee, J. E., 337
McKenry, P. C., 2, 6, 9, 10, 13, 15
Mckenzie, B., 42
McLaughlin, K. A., 312

McLeod, A. L., 160, 180
McNulty, P. A., 331, 333
McPherson, K., 219
MCRTs. See Multidisciplinary crisis
    response teams (MCRTs)
McWhirter, P. T., 167, 168
Mechanic, M. B., 168, 180
Mediators, for mourning process, 305–312
Meichenbaum, D. H., 208
Meisenhelder, J. B., 340
Melby, T., 57
Mental health
  military stigmatization and, 329–330
Mental health worker. See also
    Counselor(s)
  in forensic inpatient units, risks for, 35
  hotline workers, 22–23
  paraprofessionals, 21–22
  professional counselors, 19–20
  psychiatrists, 20
  psychologists, 21
  role of/collaboration during crisis of,
    19–23
  social workers, 21
Mental Measurements Yearbook, 100
Mental Status Exam (MSE), 136
Mercer, D., 343
Mercy, J. A., 219
Meredith, L., 334
Merikangas, K. R., 131
Messer, S. C., 329, 332
Messinger, A. M., 171
Messman-Moore, T. L., 236
Mettenburg, J., 219
Meyer, D., 42
Meyer, S., 186
MI. See Motivational interviewing (MI)
    approach
Michigan Alcoholism Screening Test
    (MAST), 138, 139
Microskills
  for crisis intervention, 67–68
  for following a disaster, 252
Mild traumatic brain injury (MTBI), 332
Military deployment and reintegration
    issues, 327–331, 327–341
  adaptation within military families,
    339–340
  anonymous responses, 341
  case study, 341
  counselor interventions, 334–340
  cultural differences, 328–329
  cycle of deployment, 330–331
  familial stress, 332–333
  mental health and military
    stigmatization, 329–330
  for military families, 332–334
  military families and TBI, 334
  for military personnel, 331–332

PTSD, interventions for, 335–337
relevance of military personnel and families to counselors, 327–328
relevance of military population to counselors, 328–331
reservists and national guard *vs.* career active duty military, 329
reunification, 333–334
risk assessment, 338
spirituality and religious needs, 340–341
supporting military families, 338–339
TBI, interventions for, 337–338
Military Leadership Diversity Commission, 327
Miller, D., 332
Miller, G. A., 139
Miller, J. M., 114
Miller, T., 114
Miller, W. R., 130, 131, 132, 133, 140, 143
Miller-Perrin, C. L., 215, 216, 224, 240, 241
Milliken, C. S., 329, 332
Milliken, N., 174, 175
Miscarriage, as ambiguous loss, 303–304
Mitchell, C. W., 223
Mitchell, J., 251, 252, 254
Mitchell, R., 60, 63, 64, 251, 252, 254
Mitzel, J., 175
Moate, Randall M., 317
Modzeleski, W., 289
Moe, J., 174, 175
Moline, M. E., 60, 62
Monson. C. M., 336, 337
Monteiro, M. G., 139
Montgomery, B. S., 234
Montgomery County Emergency Service, Inc., 106
Mood altering substances, 127
Moracco, K. E., 164, 175, 177
Moral development theory for batterer, 185–186
Morally indiscriminate pattern, of situational perpetrators, 239
Moral model substance abuse, 131
Morris, L. J., 336
Morse, R. M., 131
Moser, C., 195
Mothers Against Drunk Driving (MADD), 89
Motivational interviewing (MI) approach, 140–141
Moulds, M., 337
Mourners, tasks of, 295
Mourning
disordered, 300
mediators for process of, 305–312
process, 299–301
as transition, 300

Mourot, J. E., 171
MSE. *See* Mental Status Exam (MSE)
MTBI. *See* Mild traumatic brain injury (MTBI)
Mueller, G., 163, 175
Mueser, K. T., 152, 252
Muldoon, J. P., 185, 187
Mullen, P. C., 34
Muller, D., 319
Multicausal model substance abuse, 133
Multiculturalism
issues, 65–66
sexual assault and, 212
substance abuse and, 153–156
Multidisciplinary crisis response teams (MCRTs)
leadership roles in, 247–248
Munch, S., 35
Munfakh, J. L. H., 97
Muran, J. C., 206
Murch, R. L., 7, 15
Murdock, T., 335
Murphy, C., 186
Murphy, C. M., 162
Murphy, G., 88, 102, 105
Murphy, M., 170
Murphy, S. L., 293
Murray, C. E., 174
Murray-Swank, N., 341
Myers, J. E., 40

Nabe, C. M., 309
Nademin, E., 338
Nagy, L. M., 206
Narcotics Anonymous (NA), 152
Nason, S., 42
NASP. *See* National Association of School Psychologists (NASP)
National Alliance of Mental Illness, 152
National Association of School Psychologists (NASP), 283
National Center for the Analysis of Violent Crime ((NCAVC), 115, 117
National Center for Victims of Crimes, 205
National Center on Elder Abuse, 173
National Child Abuse and Neglect Data System (NCANDS), 219
National Child Traumatic Stress Network, 207, 253
National Coalition Against Sexual Assault (NCASA), 194
National Coalition of Anti-Violence Programs, 171
National Crime Victimization Survey, 194
National Domestic Violence Hotline, 177
National Education Association, 279, 285
National Guard/reservists
vs. regular service members, 329

National Incidence System (NIS), 219
National Institute on Drug Abuse (NIDA), 130
National Military Family Association, 328
National Organization for Victim Assistance (NOVA), 194
National Organization for Women (NOW), 194
National Suicide Prevention Lifeline, 23, 92, 97, 98, 102, 105
2009 National Survey on Drug Use and Health, 127
Natural disasters, 28
CCP for, 256
consequences of, 256
death from, 310
earthquakes as, 256–257
floods as, 257
heat waves as, 258
hurricanes as, 258
tornados as, 258–259
wildfires as, 259
winter storms as, 256
Naugle, A., 205
Naureckas, S., 163, 164, 188
NCANDS. *See* National Child Abuse and Neglect Data System (NCANDS)
NCASA. *See* National Coalition Against Sexual Assault (NCASA)
NCAVC. *See* National Center for the Analysis of Violent Crime (NCAVC)
NDCHealth, 129
Negative-interrogatives, 74
Negligence, 60
Neimeyer, R. A., 111, 122, 308, 319
Nelson, J. P., 339
Nelson, C., 216
Neria, Y., 311
Neumark-Sztainer, D., 174
Neurobiological models substance abuse, 131–132
Newell, J. M., 39, 40, 43
Newman, C., 104
Newsom, J., 332, 338
Newsome, D. W., 19, 113
Newton, S., 335
Nicotine, 128
NIDA. *See* National Institute on Drug Abuse (NIDA)
NIS. *See* National Incidence System (NIS)
Nixon, R. D. V., 337
Nonnormative stressors, 12
Nonprofessional referrals, 32
Nonsuicidal self-injury, treating, 98
Nordstrom, A., 121
Nordstrom, R. H., 321
Norlander, B., 189

Normative stressors, 7, 8
Norris, F. H., 252
Norris, H., 65
North, C. S., 129
NOVA. *See* National Organization for Victim Assistance (NOVA)
NOW. *See* National Organization for Women (NOW)
Nugent, F. A., 57
Nurcombe, B., 234
Nurius, P., 164, 175
Nuttall, J., 234

Oaksford, K., 237
Obradovic, J., 16, 17
O'Brien, J. A., 167
O'Connell, M. E., 337
O'Connor, M., 312
OEF. *See* Operation Enduring Freedom (OEF)
Office of Safe and Drug-Free Schools, 268
Office of the Deputy Under Secretary of Defense, 328
Office on Violence Against Women (OVW), 204
Ogle, N. T., 39
Ogrodniczuk, J. S., 123
OIF. *See* Operation Iraq Freedom (OIF)
Okie, S., 129
Oklahoma City bombing (1995), 129
O'Leary, D., 186
O'Leary, K. D., 174
Olsen, C. H., 332
On Death and Dying (Kübler-Ross), 295
Open questions, 72–74
    vs. closed questions, 75–76
Operation Enduring Freedom (OEF), 328, 331
Operation Iraq Freedom (OIF), 328, 331
Opiates, 128
Oppel, R.A., 111
Orr, J. J., 159
Orsi, R., 277
Oslak, S. G., 173
Oslin, D. W., 333
O'Toole, M. E., 113, 116, 117, 119
Outpatient management
    suicidal client, 104–106
OVW. *See* Office on Violence Against Women (OVW)

Pabian, Y. L., 59
Pain, of grief, 298
Paladino, D. A., 174
Palmer, Gina, 51
Panic attacks, 299
PANSI. *See* Positive and Negative Suicide Ideation Inventory (PANSI)

Panzer, P. G., 179
Paraphrasing, in Counseling, 76–78
Paraprofessionals, 21–22
Pardini, D., 112
Paredes, D. M., 139
Parents/guardians
    helping, during and after school crisis, 281–283
Parent Teacher Organization, 22
Pargament, K., 314
Park, C. L., 7, 15
Parker, B., 167
Parker, S., 314, 315, 316
Parkes, C. M., 298, 300
Parrila, R., 221
Pascual-Leone, A., 78
Pasley, K., 173
Pastoral counselors, 20
Patriarchal family structure
    IPV and, 169
Patterson, F. A., 337, 338
Patterson, J. M., 6, 7, 9
Paylo, Matthew J., 37
Payne, S., 114
Pazdernik, L. A., 332
Pearlin, L. I., 10
Pearlman, D. N., 167
Pearlman, L. A., 48
Pearson, D., 42
Pedersen, P. B., 153
Pedophilia, 195. *See also* Sexual assault
Peek, L., 66
Peer consultation
    ethical practices and, 48–49
Peled, E., 161, 162
Pepper spray, 34
Perpetrators. *See also* Sex offenders
    anger-motivated rape, 213–214
    of CSA, 238–240
    female perpetrators, 240
    male perpetrators, 238–240
    power-motivated rape, 213
    prevalence and characteristics of, 213
    sadistically motivated rape, 214
    of sexual assault, 213–214
Perrin, R. D., 215, 216, 224, 240, 241
Perry, K. J., 206
Peterman, L. M., 171, 172
Petersen, R., 164, 175, 177
Pets, loss of, 309
Petta, I., 219
Peugh, J., 236
PFA. *See* Psychological First Aid (PFA)
Pflanz, S. E., 338
Phelps, A., 335
PHI. *See* Protected health information (PHI)
Phillips, S., 113
Phillips, S. B., 254

Physical injury
    in IPV survivors, 163
Physical reactions, to sexual assault, 202
Physicians' Desk Reference lists, 128
Piasecki, M., 34
Pike, C. K., 189
Pillemer, K., 173
Pincus, S. H., 330, 333, 334
Piper, W. E., 123
Pitman, R. K., 207
Pizarro, J. M., 111
Place, N., 339
Planning summaries, 82
Plapinger, J., 255
Plionis, E., 254, 255
Poddar, Prosenjit, 56
Poire, R. E., 207
Poison Control Hotline, 23
Poland, S., 282
Polivy, J., 150
Pollack, S. J., 331
Pollock, Gregory, 124–125
Polusny, M. A., 330–331
Ponton, R., 42
Positive and Negative Suicide Ideation Inventory (PANSI), 100
Post-traumatic stress disorder (PTSD), 14, 180, 202, 251, 329
    AMT for, 207–208
    CBCT for, 336–337
    chronic, 14
    CPT for, 335–336
    diagnostic criteria for, 14
    exposure therapy for, 207
    family involvement in treatment of, 336–337
    interventions with military personnel, 335–336
    prevalence in military population, 332
    resilience related to, 335
    TF-CBT for, 335
Potoczniak, D. J., 171
Potoczniak, M. J., 171
Powell, M. B., 34
Power and control theory
    for batterer, 184–185
Power-motivated rape, 199
    perpetrators of, 213
Powers, M., 335
Powers, P., 201
PRACTICE, 207
Prealcoholic stage of alcoholism, 130
Predisposed female perpetrators, 240
Preferential perpetrators
    defined, 239
    diverse pattern of, 239–240
    introverted pattern of, 239
    patterns of, 239

sadistic pattern of, 240
seduction pattern of, 239
Preparedness
crisis, 27–28, 272
emergency, 245–291, 267–291
proactive approaches of, 28
standards for, 245–247
Presbury, J. H., 337
President's DNA Initiative Sexual Assault
Medical Forensic Examinations, 212
Preventive psychiatry, concept of, 4
Price, S. J., 2, 6, 9, 10, 13, 15
Prigerson, H. G., 298
Princeton Religious Research Center, 340
Privacy
protection of, 52
record keeping and, 61
Privacy Rule, 49, 50, 52
Private violence, 167
Problem-focused coping, 15
Prochaska, J. O., 139, 140
Prodromal stage of alcoholism, 130–131
Professional counselors, 19–20
Professional negligence, 60
Professional referrals, 32
Professional self-assessment, 37–43
burnout and compassion fatigue, 39–40
of counselor during crises, 38
countertransference, 38–39
self-care, 42–43
vicarious resiliency, 41
vicarious trauma, 40–41
Protected health information (PHI), 49–50
PsychAbstracts, 100
Psychiatrists, 20
Psychodynamic model
substance abuse, 132–133
Psychoeducation
for sex offenders, 215
for sexual assault survivors, 208
Psychological First Aid (PFA), 4, 205–206,
253–254
Psychological model
substance abuse, 132–133
Psychologists, 21
Psychotherapeutics, 128
Psychotherapy, for sex offenders, 215
PTSD. *See* Post-traumatic stress disorder
(PTSD)
Public education
suicide prevention and, 89–90
Pulchaski, C. M., 314
Pulchaski, Christine, 314
Puleo, S., 43
Purcell, R., 34
Putnam, F. W., 221, 224

Question-Persuade-Refer (QPR)
gatekeeper training curriculum, 89

Questions
closed, 74–76
open, 72–74, 75–76
Quinnett, P., 89
Quiroz, S. E., 34

Race
CSA and, 221
IPV intervention and, 165–170
RAINN. *See* Rape, Abuse and Incest
National Network (RAINN)
Raja, S., 180
Rajab, M. H., 91, 97, 102
Rajabi H., 131
Randall, W., 221
Range, L. M., 87
Rape, 167. *See also* Sexual assault
acquaintance, 196
anger-motivated, 199
defined, 195–196
myths about, 201
perpetrators of, 213–214 (*See also* sex
offenders)
power-motivated, 199
sadistic, 199–200
spousal, 198
statutory, 198–199, 223
types of, 199
Rape, Abuse and Incest National
Network (RAINN), 193,
194, 202
Rape Hotline, 23
Rape trauma syndrome
symptoms of, 201, 202
Raphael, Beverley, 4–5, 238
Raphael, D. N., 238
Rapists. *See also* Rape; Sex offenders
myths existing related to, 213
Rapport
development of, 67–68
Reaction(s)
from trauma, 14
Record keeping, 60–61
in schools, FERPA and, 53
Recovery
in schools after crisis, 279
Reel, S., 167
Referral(s)
homicide and, 119
mechanisms, 32
nonprofessional, 32
phone calls screening, 32
professional, 32
self-referred clients and, 32, 34
Reflecting skills, 76–83
paraphrasing, 76–78
reflecting feelings and emotions,
78–81
summarizing, 81–83

Regressed pattern, of situational
perpetrators, 239
Regular military personnel
vs. National Guard/reservists, 329
Reichenberg, L., 311
Reid, J. C., 112
Relapse
crisis and, SUD and, 149–150
"Relationship enhancers," 79
Relationships, interpersonal, 10
Relaxation techniques, 208
Religiosity, 313
IPV prevalence and, 170
needs of deployed military service
members, 340–341
Remley, T. P., 49, 50, 53, 54, 56, 57, 58,
59, 66
Rennison, C. M., 167
Renzenbrink, I., 323, 325
Renzetti, C. M., 172
Reporting, CSA, 231–233
past incidents of, 233
policies, 231
Resick, P. A., 180, 206, 336
Resilience, 16–17
defined, 16
related to PTSD, 335
religious and spirtual connections
and, 17
social groups and networks and, 17
Resiliency
vicarious, 41
Resnick, H., 129, 194
Resources
community/individual, 9
of fortified coping, 6–7
stressor events and, 9
Responses
cognitive, 14
to crises in higher education settings,
289–291
to crisis, 1
crisis counselors' effective, 245–264
disaster, 248–252
emotional, 14
hostage situations and, 248–252
in schools, 267–291
spiritual, 14
strategies for crisis, 12
terrorism, 248–252
to trauma, 14
Reunification, 333–334
Rich, J. M., 185
Richardson, A., 331, 333, 334
Richman, J. A., 129
Riger, S., 180
Riggs, D. S., 206, 335
Riley, P. L., 271
Riordan, K., 163, 164, 188

Risk(s)
  acute *vs.* chronic, for suicide, 93–96
  level, for suicide, 96–98
  of workplace violence, 116
Ristock, J., 179
Ritter, R. H., 63
Rivera, J., 35
Rivkin, I., 221
Roan, S., 332
Roberts, A. R., 274
Roberts, G., 234
Roberts, Tracy, 341
Rock, E., 113
Rock, J., 308
Rock, M., 308
Roe-Sepowitz, D., 112
Rogers, C. R., 67, 79, 313, 326
Rogers, R. E., 223
Rolling, E., 162
Rollnick, S., 140
Romano, E., 223
Roncone, R., 336
Rosen, C. S., 65
Rosenberg, M. S., 183, 189
Rosenblatt, P. C., 302
Rosenfeld, R., 112
Rosenkranz, M., 319
Rosie, J. S., 123
Rospenda, K. M., 129
Ross, J., 333
Rothbaum, B. O., 206, 207, 208, 335
Rothman, J., 339
Rothschild, B., 237
Rowe, C. L., 130
Rowe, L. P., 55
Rudd, M. D., 91, 97, 102, 145, 147, 148
Ruder, T., 333, 334
Ruiz, E., 170
Rural community
  crisis counseling in, 30
Russ, E., 252
Russell, P., 206
Russo, C. J., 54
Ruzek, J. L., 205, 254

Sackville, T., 206
Sadistic rape, 199–200
  perpetrators of, 214
SAFE. *See* sexual assault forensic exams (SAFE)
Safety
  batterer intervention, 183
  of counselors, 27–37
  in crisis situations, 27–46
  IPV survivors, 163
  local authorities and, 28–30
  physical, 31–37
  precautions, 27–37
  referrals and, 32

Safety plan/planning, 102, 103
  IPV and, 178–179
Salazar, L. F., 182
SAMHSA. *See* Substance Abuse and Mental Health Services Administration (SAMHSA)
Sammons, M. T., 331
Sampson, N. A., 312
Samson, L. F., 51
Sandin, E., 186
Sandoval, J., 280
Sandover, J. C., 240
Santorelli, S. F., 319
Santos, S. C., 179
SASSI-3. *See* Substance Abuse Subtle Screening Inventory-3 (SASSI-3)
Saunders, B. E., 129
Saunders, D. G., 189
Saunders, J. B., 138, 139
Savell, J. K., 221
Savic-Jabrow, P. C., 43
Sawyer, Alissa, 209
Sayers, S. L., 333
Saywitz, K. J., 233, 234
Schaffer, K., 337
Schimmel, C., 208, 209
Schmidt, F. E., 183, 187
Schmidt, M. C., 183, 187
Schneider, R. B., 59
Schnicke, M. K., 206
Schnurr, P. P., 336
School counseling, 246
School counselors, 20
Schooler, C., 10
School homicide, violence and, 113–115
School(s)
  case studies, 285–287
  crisis in, 267–284
  crisis planning for, 271, 276–279
  crisis preparation for, 272
  crisis team in, 271–272
  death/accident/event, notifying students of, 283–284
  debriefing, 280
  elementary, death notification in, 344
  emergency preparedness and response in, 267–291
  FEMA recommendations, 273, 274
  helping parents/guardians during and after crisis, 281–283
  helping students during and after crises, 280–281
  mitigation and prevention of crisis in, 268–670
  recovery in, 279
  responses to national crises, 284–285
  risk asessment in, 115
  shootings in, 310
  suicide, dealing with, 281

  written crisis plan implementation in, 272–276
School Survey on Crime and Safety, 271
Schuettler, D., 17, 174, 175, 341
Schuh, J. H., 259
Schulenberg, J. E., 139
Schulsinger, F., 131
Schulze, B., 119
Schumacher, J., 319
Screening
  substance use disorders, 134–136
Secondary traumatic stress, 40
Sedlak, A. J., 219
Segal, M. W., 339
Self-assessment
  of counselor during crises, 38
  professional (*See* Professional self-assessment)
Self-awareness assessment
  IPV survivors, 164
Self-care
  components, 43
  in crisis situations, 27–46
  professional self-assessment, 42–43
  working with suicidal clients and, 46
Self-confidence, 5
Self-esteem, 5
Self-referred clients, dangers of, 32, 34
Seligman, L., 311
Seligman, M. E., 161, 300, 301
Selye, Han, 12, 13
Selzer, M. L., 139
September 11 attack, 1, 13, 129
Sethi, S., 91
Sevin, E., 332
Sex offenders. *See also* Perpetrators
  behavior modification for, 215
  CBT for, 216
  chemotherapy for, 215
  incapacitation for, 216
  life-skills training for, 215
  psychotherapy for, 215
  treatment, 214–216
Sexual assault, 193–194. *See also* Rape
  cognitive/behavioral effects of, 203
  defined, 195–196
  drug-facilitated, 198
  emotional reaction to, 202–203
  ethical issues, 209–210
  FBI on, 193
  forcible, 195
  legal issues, 210
  multicultural issues and victims with special needs, 212
  perpetrators of, 213–214 (*See also* Sex offenders)
  phases of women's response to, 201, 202
  physical reactions to, 202
  prevalence of, 194
  psychological reaction to, 202–203

RAINN on, 193, 194
  spirituality and religious beliefs, 210–212
  survivors, interventions with, 203–205
  survivors, treatment of, 205–209
Sexual assault forensic exams (SAFE), 204
Sexual sadism, 195. *See also* Sexual assault
Shafranske, E., 314
Shalev, A. Y., 252
Shawky, G. A., 169
Shea, M. T., 332
Shea, S. C., 99, 101, 133
Shea, W. M., 133
Shear, M. K., 312
Shelters, IPV
  opportunities and challenges, 179–180
Shen, H., 337
Shen, J., 51
Shepard, M. F., 189
Sheridan, J. F., 319
Shizgal, P., 131
Shorteno-Fraser, M., 330, 331, 333, 339,
    340
Shuchman, M., 55
Sibley, A., 189
Siblings, death/grief of, 307–308
Signal summaries, 82
Signs
  of concern for clients in crisis, 33–34
Silence
  in counseling session, 71–82
Silovsky, J., 224
Silva, C., 167
Silverman, M. M., 91, 92
Silverman, P. R., 295, 297
Simon, R.I., 57, 90
Simons, A., 289
Simpson, Sherdene, 242–243
Sira, C. S., 337
SIT. *See* Stress inoculation training (SIT)
Situational perpetrators, 238–239
  defined, 238
  inadequate pattern of, 239
  morally indiscriminate pattern of, 239
  patterns of, 239
  regressed pattern of, 239
Skinner, K., 332
Skovholt, T. M., 39
Slaikeu, K. A., 2
Sleeper effects, 224
Slep, A. M. S., 174
Sleutel, M. R., 169
SMART, 152
Smile-Talk-Reach (STR), 89
Smith, D. W., 129
Smith, L., 113
Smultzer, N., 186
Snyder, C. M. J., 189
Sobsey, D., 221
Social learning model
  substance abuse, 132

Social media
  HIPAA and, 51
Social workers, 21
Society
  substance use and, 127–130
Sociocultural model
  substance abuse, 132
Socioeconomic status
  IPV and, 169
Soeken, K., 167
Sokoloff, N. J., 159
Sokolowski, I., 312
Sorsoli, L., 221
Southerland, J., 196
Speltz, K., 240
Spencer, P. C., 35
Sperry, L., 314
Spiritual biases, 65
Spirituality, 313, 314
  in counseling process, 314
  issues, 65–66
  needs of deployed military service
    members, 340–341
Spousal rape, 198
Spouse, death of, 308
Stalking, by clients, 34
Stanley, B., 102, 103
Stark, S., 335
Staton, A. R., 337, 338
Statutory rape, 198–199, 223
Stauffer, M. D., 131, 132, 138
Staves, P. J., 338
SteelFisher, G. K., 333, 336
Steer, R., 236
Steer, R. A., 312
Steigerwald, F., 277
Stein, K., 189
Steketee, G. S., 207
Stenehjem, J., 337
Sterner, W., 340, 341
Stevens, R., 337
Stevens, S. P., 336, 337
Stewart, A., 343
Stewart, J., 131
Stewart, L., 335
Stickney, D., 321
Stigmatization, military
  mental health and, 329–330
Stills, A. B., 252
Stimulants, 128
Stone, P. S., 35
Stone, Tori, 288
Storms, winter, 256
STR. *See* Smile-Talk-Reach (STR)
Strentz, T., 261
Stress
  contextual factors affecting, 10–11
  as defined, 12–13
  theory's elements, 7–9
Stress inoculation training (SIT), 208

Stressor(s)
  accumulated, 6–7
  acute, 8–9
  catastrophic, 8
  as categorized, 11
  duration/severity of, 8–9
  events as provoked, 7–9
  events' sources, 7
  external, 7, 8
  internal, 7–8
  meaning/perception of, 9
  nonnormative, 12
  normative, 7, 8, 12
  provoking, 6
  traumatic events as type of, 13
  types of crisis-inducing, 8
  unexpected, 8
  volitional, 8
Strosahl, K. D., 91, 102
Student affairs and college counseling,
    246–247
Substance abuse. *See also* Alcoholism
  biopsychosocial model, 133
  cognitive model, 132
  conditioning model, 133
  co-occurring disorders and, 152–153
  crisis issues and, 155–156
  defined, 129, 137
  disease (medical) model, 130–131
  etiology, 130–134
  general systems model, 132
  genetic models, 131
  harm reduction, 150–151
  intervention model, 143–144
  interventions, 145–149
  moral model, 131
  multicausal model, 133
  multicultural consideration, 153–156
  neurobiological models, 131–132
  psychodynamic model, 132–133
  psychological model, 132–133
  relapse and crisis, 149–150
  risk factors, 130–134
  social learning model, 132
  sociocultural model, 132
  support groups, 151–152
  traditional approaches, 143
  treatment and crisis, 142–153
Substance abuse/alcoholism hotlines, 23
Substance Abuse and Mental Health
    Services Administration
    (SAMHSA), 91, 127
Substance Abuse Subtle Screening
    Inventory-3 (SASSI-3), 138, 139
Substance dependence
  defined, 129
  etiology, 130–134
  risk factors, 130–134
Substance use
  crisis situations and, 129–130

Substance use (*continued*)
defined, 129
research on, 129–130
Substance use disorders (SUD), 127–156.
See also Substance abuse; Substance
dependence
assessment, 136–137
co-occurring disorders and, 152–153
diagnosis, 137–138
drugs and terminology, 128–129
harm reduction, 150–151
multicultural consideration, 153–156
relapse and crisis, 149–150
resistance to change, evaluation of,
139–141
screening, 134–136
screening/assessment measures,
138–139
society and, 127–130
support groups, 151–152
treatment admission and placement,
141–142
treatment and crisis, 142–153
SUD. *See* Substance use disorders (SUD)
Sue, D. W., 153
Suicide Prevention Hotlines, 23
Suicide Prevention Resource Center, 90
Suicide(s), 1, 31
acute *vs.* chronic risk, 93–96
assessment, 92–93
case studies, 107–109
cause of death ranking, 86, 87
client, 95
competency and attitudes, preventive
measures, 90–91
gatekeeper strategy, 89–90
incidence, 86
interpersonal-psychological theory
of, 338
intervention, 86–110
interviews, 99–101
level of risk, 96–98
multiple types of assessment,
101–102
outpatient management, 104–106
overview, 85
postvention, 106–110
prevalence, 86
prevention, 88–91
public education, 89–90
rate, 86, 87
resources and websites, 285
school-based prevention programs, 89
in schools, dealing with, 281
training, 91–106
treatment planning and care
management, 102–104
written instruments, 99–101
Sullivan, A. M., 35
Sullivan, L., 332

Summarizing, in Counseling, 81–83
Supervision, ethical practices and, 48–49
Support groups
substance use disorders, 151–152
Survivors
CSA, 233–234
sexual assault, 203–209
Survivors of Loved Ones' Suicides, Inc.,
106
Swenson, C. C., 233, 236
Swift, E., 330, 331, 333, 339, 340
Systemic theories of crisis, 5

Talbott, L. L., 103
Tallon, J., 223
Tanielian, T., 331, 333, 334
Tanigoshi, H., 138
Tarasoff, Tatiana, 56
*Tarasoff v. Regents of the University of
California*, 56–59, 111
crisis counseling and, 58–59
effect of, 57–58
Task model of grieving (Worden), 298
Taylor, B., 211
TBI. *See* Traumatic brain injury (TBI)
Teacher/lover female perpetrators, 240
Tedeschi, R. G., 7, 15
Tension-building phase
of cycle of violence theory, 160
Terminal illness, 309–310
Termination
in crisis intervention, 63–65
Terrorism
interventions after act of, 252–255
responses to, 248–252
Terry, K. J., 223
Texas Association of Hostage Negotiators,
96
TF-CBT. *See* Trauma-focused cognitive
behavioral therapy (TF-CBT)
Thiara, R. K., 161, 164, 179
Thienhaus, O. J., 34
Thoennes, N., 194
Thompson, V. L. S., 168
Threat level assessment
homicide, 116–119
Thrower, E., 43
Thuras, P., 341
Timeliness, of death notification,
346–348
Tishler, C. L., 34, 110, 117, 119
Tiwan, A., 179
Tjaden, P., 194
Tobacco, 127
Toll-free hotlines, 23
Toray, T., 298, 308, 309
Tornados, 258–259
Tower, L. E., 163, 174–175
Tower, M., 163, 174, 175
Towl, G. J., 120

Transcrisis, 35
Trauma
from acts of deliberate cruelty, 13
as defined, 13
function as impaired by reaction to, 14
reactions to events of, 14
responses to, 14
vicarious, 40–41
Trauma-focused cognitive behavioral
therapy (TF-CBT), 207
for PTSD, 335
Traumatic brain injury (TBI)
brief therapy for, 337–338
CBT for, 337
interventions with military personnel,
337–338
military families and, 334
prevalence in military population,
331–332
Tribbensee, N. E., 55
Trickett, P. K., 221
Tripp, T., 332
Trippany, R. L., 40
Trump, K. S., 272, 276
Trusty, J., 277
Tucciarone, P., 338
Tummala-Narra, P., 164
Turner, M. G., 196
Twemlow, S. W., 34

U. S. Department of Health and Human
Services, Administration on
Children, Youth and Families, 221
U. S. Department of Justice, 128, 193, 194,
195, 201
Uhlemann, M. R., 79, 81
Ullman, S., 220
Ulmer, W. F., 329
Unexpected stressors, 8
United Nations, 169–170
University of South Florida, 89, 269, 270,
278, 279
Uppal, S., 91
Uppercue, Tricia, 270
U.S. Department of Defense, 328, 334,
335
U.S. Department of Education, 54
U.S. Department of Education, National
Center for Educational Statistics,
271
U.S. Department of Education, Office of
Safe and Drug-Free Schools, 268,
285, 289
U.S. Department of Health and Human
Services (DHHS), 49, 51, 52, 53,
220, 221
U.S. Department of Justice, Bureau of
Justice Statistics, 111, 115, 195, 213
U.S. Department of Justice, Office for
Victims of Crimes, 123, 205

U.S. Department of Justice, Office of
   Violence Against Women, 194, 204
U.S. Secret Service, 113–114, 116
*Uses and Disclosures of Protected Health
   Information: General Rules,* 50

Vacc, N. A., 139
Vaillant, L. M., 68
VandeCreek, L., 58
Van den Bout, J., 318
Van den Hout, M. A., 318
Van der Hart, O., 237
Van der Kolk, B. A., 237
VandeWeerd, C., 189
Vandiver, D., 240
Van Ommeren, A., 216
Van Rooijen, L. J., 139
VAWA. *See* Violence Against Women Act
   (VAWA)
Vedsted, P., 312
Velicer, W. F., 189
Venart, B., 48
Verbal underlining, 70
Verhoek-Oftedahl, W., 167
Vernberg, E. M., 205, 254
Veterans Administration (VA) and
   Department of Defense (DoD)
   Clinical Practice Guideline
   Working Group, 335
Veterans Benefits, Healthcare, and
   Information Technology Act of
   2006, 328
Veteran's Health Administration,
   334, 335
Vicarious resiliency, 41
Vicarious trauma, 40–41
   guidelines for prevention, 40–41
Vick, Maegan, 45–46, 243, 344
Victims
   of CSA, intervention strategies, 224, 226
   primary, 87
   secondary, 87
   of sexual assault, 212
   with special needs, 212
Vieweg, B., 139
Villalba, J., 169
Villalobos, S., 59
Vincent, R., 129
Vinokur, A., 139
Vinson, D. C., 135
Violence. *See also* Homicide; Intimate
   partner violence (IPV); Sexual
   assault
   cessation, batterer intervention and, 183
   clients and, 34, 35
   female-to-male, 170–171
   LGBT, 171–172
   school homicide and, 113–115
   workplace, categories of, 115–116

Violence Against Women Act (VAWA),
   194
Virginia Youth Violence Project, 113
Vlahov, D., 129, 252
Vocal tone of counselor, 70–71
Volitional stressors, 8
Voyeurism, 195. *See also* Sexual assault
Vujaniovic, A. A., 332

Wade, D., 335
Wagner, Kami, 297
Wakefield, J. C., 312
Walfish, S., 111
Walker, L. E., 159, 160, 161, 163, 164,
   170, 180
Walsh, F., 306, 316, 321, 323, 326
Walsh, R. P., 302
Wang, C. C., 306, 313
Wang, M. Q., 174
Ware, W. B., 339
Warnke, M. A., 170
Warshaw, R., 194
Washington, E. L., 51
Watlington, C. G., 162
Watson, K., 167
Watson, P. J., 205, 254
Watts, R. E., 212
Way, A. A., 169
Weathers, F. W., 206
Weaver, T. L., 180
Webber, J. M., 48
Websites, 285
Weeks, K. M., 52, 53
Wefel, E., 59
Wei, E. H., 112
Weintraub, S., 164
Weiss, R. L., 189
Welfel, E. R., 37, 38, 111, 112
Wellesley Project, 4
Wellness strategies
   ethical practices and, 48
Werner-Wilson, R. J., 161, 162
West, C. M., 167
Westcott, H. L., 221
Westen, D., 252
Wester, K. L., 174
West-Olatunji, C., 30
Whalen, D., 161
Wheeler, M., 49, 50, 51
Whelan, T. A., 40
Wherry, J. N., 237
Whiffen, V. E., 226
White Kress, V. E., 40
White women
   IPV prevalence, 167
Whitfield, C. L., 224
Wiederanders, M., 216
Wilbourne, P. L., 143
Wilcox, R. M., 339

Wilcoxon, A. S., 40
Wildfires
   as natural disasters, 259
   types of, 259
Wiley, Cindy, 54
Williams, G. T., 60, 62
Williams, J., 221
Williams, O., 187
Williams, R., 135
Wilner, N. J., 206
Wilson, M., 179
Winokur, G., 131
Winstok, Z., 161, 162
Winter storms, 256
Wislar, J. S., 129
Withdrawal, 321–323
Wolf, P., 332
Wolfe, L. R., 172
WomensHealth.gov, 198
Wooding, S., 234
Worden, J. W., 298, 302, 311, 312, 313, 320,
   321, 324, 325, 326
Workplace, emergency preparedness and
   response in, 245–264
Workplace homicide, 115–116
Workplace violence
   categories of, 115–116
   risk of, 116
World Health Organization, 87, 138, 139
World Trade Center bombing (1993), 1
Wortman, C. B., 308
Wozny, D. A., 48
Written suicide assessment instruments,
   99–101
Wunsch-Hitzig, R., 255
Wyatt, G., 221

Xenakis, S., 332
Xu, J., 293

Yan, F., 174
Young, J., 210, 314
Young, J. P., 139
Young, K. A., 58
Young, M. E., 69, 70, 77, 78, 79, 82
Young, M. L., 173
Young, M. S., 221
Young-Xu, Y., 336
Youth Risk Behavior Survey, 173

Zalaquett, C., 65
Zappalla, Steve, 143
Zaslavsky, A. M., 333, 336
Zawitz, M. W., 159
Zielke, R., 111
Zierler, S., 167
Zimmerman, T. S., 161
Zoellner, L., 206, 207
Zwi, A. B., 219